Organizational Invention in Renaissance Florence

JOHN F. PADGETT

OXFORD
UNIVERSITY PRESS

OXFORD
UNIVERSITY PRESS

Oxford University Press is a department of the University of Oxford. It furthers the University's objective of excellence in research, scholarship, and education by publishing worldwide. Oxford is a registered trade mark of Oxford University Press in the UK and in certain other countries.

Published in the United States of America by Oxford University Press
198 Madison Avenue, New York, NY 10016, United States of America.

CIP data is on file at the Library of Congress.

ISBN 9780197789223

ISBN 9780197789216 (hbk.)

DOI: 10.1093/oso/9780197789216.001.0001

The manufacturer's authorized representative in the EU for product safety is Oxford University Press España S.A. of Parque Empresarial San Fernando de Henares, Avenida de Castilla, 2 – 28830 Madrid (www.oup.es/en or product.safety@oup.com). OUP España S.A. also acts as importer into Spain of products made by the manufacturer.

To Wendy

Organizational Invention in Renaissance Florence

NETWORK MECHANISMS SERIES

The study of social networks is rapidly expanding, and the *Social Network Mechanisms* series connects this burgeoning field with network science to produce interdisciplinary insights for scholars in both areas. The series features both quantitative and qualitative books on the mechanisms by which social networks form, shape behavior, give life to institutions, and so play their role in the flow of events. Diverse in style and data, books in the series introduce or establish evidence of mechanisms consequential for the emergence, stability, or consequences of location in network structure. The series was founded by Ronald S. Burt (University of Chicago) and Mario L. Small (Columbia University). For more details on the series and its diverse editorial board, please see: www.oxfordSNMseries.com.

Series Titles
Organizational Invention in Renaissance Florence, John F. Padgett
Strong Bridges: Trust beyond Structure, Ronald S. Burt and Sonja Opper
Ctrl+Alt+Doubt: Decoding the Language of Online Conspiracy, Hayagreeva Rao and Henrich Greve
Organization: Formal and Informal Networks, Giuseppe Soda

Contents

Acknowledgments

My biographical route to this study of Renaissance Florence was not linear, but it was helped and guided by many along its zigzag way.

As an undergraduate, I was an electrical engineer, working summers helping to design sonar systems in nuclear submarines. My worldview of networks descends from those circuits.

Interesting as that job was, Vietnam threw me off that career path toward social "do good" internships—Camden Legal Aid, Trenton Model Cities, and New Jersey Neuro-Psychiatric Institute—to which Princeton University generously gave course credit. I am thankful to all of those organizations for encouraging me to find my own way, even without a clear goal. The second of these internships led to an exciting job working for the mayor of Trenton. He guided me into Political Science. I wouldn't go as far as to say that Art Holland was like Cosimo de' Medici, but I learned much about indirect leadership from him.

At the University of Michigan, I devoted my engineering skill set to mathematically modeling organizations—specifically, federal budgetary processes. I got my PhD, in other words, without an historical bone in my body. But I did gain a deep methodological commitment to the assembly of large quantitative datasets, which spanned decades of political change. For that methodology, I thank Pat Crecine.

Mathematical modeling got me an assistant professor job at Harvard and then tenure at the University of Chicago. Harrison White at Harvard first got me interested in history through a joint course we taught together on "Organizations in Historical Context." In the wide variety of descriptive empirical texts that we explored, Harrison focused on inductively constructing one's own theory or interpretation. Creativity was his pedagogical goal, not classifying research into existing schools of thought. (This does not mean that I do not also believe in subsequent validation—the Michigan side of me.)

With an engineering and social-science background like this, how did I counterintuitively arrive at Renaissance Florence? The answer is the institution of tenure. Once I received tenure at the University of Chicago, I looked around for something new to do. I used my now autonomous Harvard course as a search engine to find new topics. Using the search filters of networks + quantitative + historical, I zoomed in on the topic of "historical political clientage" to explore in more depth. This led me to Dale Kent's impressive prosopographical book, *The Rise of the Medici*. Archives rich in systematic quantitative materials are exceedingly rare in the field of History, but Kent's book taught me that Florence was an exception to that rule. Given labor, Florence's archives proved more than sufficient to reproduce my Michigan "big data" methodology farther back in time.

It is one thing to learn about research potential, however, and quite another to develop the intimidating archival skills necessary to mine the pre-Guttenberg handwritten documents in Tuscan and Latin that the Florentine archives contain. At this vulnerable point, a number of historians in the Florentine research community unexpectedly showed deep generosity by reaching out to educate and to help a rank outsider like me, especially after I stubbornly continued to show up at the archives. Face time matters.

The first helping hand of encouragement I received was from Gene Brucker, who, in California shortly before his death, appreciated the early graphs I produced for my Robust Action article, based primarily on Dale Kent. The second important helping hand was David Herlihy. Paul McLean and I taught ourselves how to read difficult Florentine handwritten documents from microfilms that Herlihy had deposited at the Center for Research Libraries at Chicago. Based on transcribing and translating some of those microfilms (our Rosetta Stone), Paul and I decided to go to Florence to see the originals for themselves.

In the archive line to check out documents, I accidentally saw that the guy in front of me was none other than David Herlihy, by then president of the American Historical Society. I blabbered something sycophantic like "I worship the ground you walk on." He archly raised his eyebrow and was about to dismiss me before I luckily uttered the word "numbers," which appealed to the pioneering cliometrician in him. We had lunch together, after which he said, "But you don't know much, do you?" I replied, "I know, Professor Herlihy, that's why I want to learn from you." His response was beyond generosity: He devoted 30 minutes at the end of every of his valuable summer archive days to walk me through the *catasto* tax documents, in order to explain them to me and to convert me to his cause.

When I came home to Chicago, I would write letters to him, in those days before email, asking him about this source or that. More often than not, he would respond with a floppy disk. "Don't worry about tracking this down and coding it. Here are the data." I have always labeled David Herlihy in my mind "Saint David." From others I have since learned that he was like that with many: He believed in history as a collaborative, not a competitive, enterprise. He is the reason I decided to turn my amateur hobby into a professional career.

The final but most important Florentine historian to whom I acknowledge deep gratitude is Richard Goldthwaite. Had it not been for my family, I would have dedicated this book to him. The European University Institute and Harvard's Villa I Tatti for whatever reason decided to give grants to me and my family to spend a year in Florence. That year is when I most intensively dove into the archives, collecting and codifying my data. The relationship with Richard developed organically, simply by sitting at an archival desk next to him, day after day, month after month. Richard Goldthwaite was not the friendliest person in the world (not without grounds: he knew more than you), but we came to respect the sheer number of hours of each other's labor. He slowly took me under his wings and corrected my flaws, always on the basis of merit, never of ego. I have 60 pages of email correspondence with him about my AJS Organizational Invention article, the foundation of this book, where he would suggest a new source, and I would go check it out—sometimes confirming him, sometimes not. To say that "we became friends" is stretching it for someone as professional as him, but we spent much time together and came to appreciate each other. He (unfortunately now deceased) is my role model of the true scholar.

The last, but hardly least, acknowledgement that I will proffer is to my Italian research team: Francesco Bettarini, Claudia Tripodi, and especially to Katalin Prajda. Once I received research grants from the Santa Fe Institute, the Hewlett Foundation, the National Science Foundation's Program on Human and Social Dynamics, and the University of Chicago's Neubauer Foundation, I had the funds to hire these Italian History PhDs to man/woman the archives in my absence. To say that "I coded this data" is an egregious aggrandizement. They, plus Paul McLean (then University of Chicago graduate student) and myself, deserve the collective credit. See two Scientia articles (2018, 2021), on my University of Chicago webpage, for journalistic reports and pictures about this bountiful research team. I love all four of them, serious published scholars in their own rights, with numerous distinguished books among them.

Back at the University of Chicago, David Sallach had the mixed blessing of introducing me to relational databases, in my case Microsoft Access. Relational databases link multiple data sources into a single integrated computer system, through shared person (and company and family) IDs. This relational database structure is the secret to analyzing multiple networks: What are the economic partnership and credit networks of one's marriage in-laws? The "mixed blessing" part, about which Sallach failed to educate me, is that constructing and matching names and IDs across multiple datasets exponentially increases the labor. This procedure allowed me to aggregate about 100,000 people into about 2,000 father-son and father-daughter genealogies, with intermarriages—the key to tracing family descent through two centuries. This "deep social history" payoff was worth it, however tedious it seemed at the time. A multiple-network book like this cannot exist without relational databases to tame the archival profusion.

Upon publication of this Oxford book, this relational data will be posted online, following the path-breaking role model of "Saint David" Herlihy. I hope this repays the investment that he unexpectantly and unjustifiably placed in me, 40 years ago. Pass it down.

At the end of this zigzag journey, final notes of grateful thanks go to Ronald Burt, editor of this series, and to Ron Breiger and Mark Mizruchi, commentators on the book workshop that Ron Burt organized for my book proposal. An author cannot receive better, more intelligent advisors than these. James Cook, Sindhuja Padmanaban, and Elise Davies were my editors at Oxford University Press.

But of course, this book is dedicated to my family, Wendy, Ray, and Olivia, who patiently or not put up with this project for many decades. They liked living and going to school in Florence.

Research grants received were Hewlett Foundation #2002–7845: "Co-evolution of States and Markets" (2002); National Science Foundation program on Human and Social Dynamics #0433006: "Coevolution of State and Market" (2005); National Science Foundation program on Sociology #072613: "Co-development of Economic, Political, and Kinship Networks" (2015); and three University of Chicago Neubauer Collegium grants:

"The Changing Social and Rhetorical Foundations of Renaissance Republicanism" (2014); "Visualizing the Changing Spatial and Social Ecology of Renaissance Florence" (2016); and "Private Letters in Renaissance Florence" (2019).

1

Historical Introduction and Overview

Organizational Invention

Inventions of any sort are hard to understand. They seem to come out of the blue, a rupture with the past, yet close investigation always reveals historical roots. Individual geniuses sometimes create them, but is "genius" just our celebratory label for a process that worked, which we do not understand?

The terms "innovation" and "invention" have both been used in the literature to describe the process of generating novelty—a crucial component in any evolutionary process.[1] But semantic ambiguity surrounds the distinction between these concepts: Schumpeter, our preeminent economic theorist of innovation, prioritized the term innovation over invention, indeed sometimes conflated the two,[2] but according to the Oxford English and Merriam-Webster dictionaries,[3] contemporary English language more sharply distinguishes these two concepts by degree of originality. I lean more toward contemporary definitions than toward Schumpeter's usage, but there is no deductively correct right or wrong usage; the main thing is to be clear about what one means.

[1] Biological equivalents are "generation of variation" (~organizational innovation) and "speciation" (~organizational invention).

[2] See Ruttan (1959). Schumpeter's own definition of innovation (1939, 87) was as follows: "We will now define innovation more rigorously by means of the production function previously introduced. As we know, this function describes the way in which quantity of product varies if quantities of factors vary. If, instead of quantities of factors, we vary the form of the function, we have an innovation. But this not only limits us, at first blush at least, to the case in which the innovation consists in producing the same kind of product that had been produced before by the same kind of means of production that had been used before, . . . but also covers the case of a new commodity, as well as those of a new form of organization such as a merger, of the opening up of new markets, and so on."

[3] For example, (1) OED definition of innovation: "The act of innovating; the introduction of novelties; the alteration of what is established by the introduction of new elements or forms." (2) OED definition of invention: "The original contrivance of a new method or means of doing something, of an art, kind of instrument, etc. previously unknown." (3) The Merriam-Webster distinction is similar—focusing on the originality of invention. "*Innovation*, for its part, can refer to something new or to a change made to an existing product, idea, or field . . . One might say that the first telephone was an *invention*, the first cellular telephone either an *invention* or an *innovation*, and the first smartphone an *innovation*."

Organizational Invention in Renaissance Florence. John F. Padgett, Oxford University Press.
 DOI: 10.1093/oso/9780197789216.003.0001

To proffer our distinction, which we use in this book: innovations improve on existing ways (e.g., products and production procedures) of doing things, while inventions change the collective actors or organizational forms (e.g., roles and role sets) that do that production.[4] Under these definitions, "organizational innovation" refers to new products and procedures, patented or otherwise, something the field has studied heavily. But the less studied "organizational invention" refers to the invention or emergence of new types of organizations themselves.[5] The empirical chapters in this book on Renaissance Florence are all examples of the latter. Florence is interesting because there were many of these in the domains of economics, politics, and even kinship.

The central thesis of this book is that organizational invention was a process of spillover among and across underlying social networks, which were intertwined because people participated in many of them at once.

The key to classifying something not just as an invention but as a successful invention is the degree to which it reverberates out to alter the interacting system that reproduces it.[6] To some extent we understand micro-logics of combination and recombination into innovation (e.g., Barley 1990, March 1991, Powell et al. 1996, Fleming 2002, Burt 2004). Yet the invention puzzle is that some of these innovative recombinations cascade out to reconfigure entire interlinked ecologies of "ways of doing things," whereas most innovations do not. The poisedness of a system to reconfiguration by an invention is as much a part of the phenomenon to be explained as is the system's production of the invention itself. Invention "in the wild" cannot be understood through abstracting away from concrete social context because inventions are permutations of that context (Hutchins 1995, Latour 1988, Galison 1997). But to make progress in understanding discontinuous change, we need to embed our analysis of transformation into the routine dynamics of actively self-reproducing social contexts, where constitutive elements and relations are generated and reinforced.

Renaissance Florence is the empirical site for this study of an extended historical process of socially embedded invention. While the uniqueness of

[4] See Padgett and Powell (2012, 5).

[5] "Organizational invention" in this book is the same as "emergence" in the language of Padgett and Powell. Schumpeter himself never studied organizational invention or emergence.

[6] In the way I use these terms, incremental "innovation" often refers to a single organization although, in the Florentine cases analyzed here, many organizations simultaneously were hit with similar macro forces. The more major "inventions" often tip an ecology of organizations, as in the formation of a new industry.

the Italian Renaissance in world history is debatable, the creativity of that particular place and time is not. Inventions in literature (Dante, Boccaccio), in art (Giotto, Masaccio, Donatello, Michelangelo), in letters (Petrarch), in architecture (Brunelleschi, Alberti), in science (Leonardo, Galileo), in constitutional design (Bruni, Savonarola), in political theory (Machiavelli, Guicciardini) and in business (Datini) were produced in breathtaking numbers and speeds. Indeed, the most striking global feature about Renaissance Florence is the sheer multiplicity of domains in which inventions occurred: Inventions seemed to cascade from one domain to another. These developments did not occur in isolation from the rest of northern Italy (e.g., Witt 2003), but Florence was a particularly catalytic site in the northern Italian Renaissance web of invention.

This book will not focus on all of these domains of Florentine invention, particularly not on the famous cultural domains most associated with the word "Renaissance."[7] It will focus instead on lesser studied evolutions in Florentine social networks and organizations, which I argue were similarly innovative for their time and influential for the future. In particular, this book will focus on documenting and explaining evolutionary change over time during the late-medieval/early-Renaissance period in Florentine economic networks, in Florentine kinship networks, and in Florentine political networks, and on developmental interactions and spillovers among these three organizational domains. In particular, in Florentine economic networks, I will focus on the rise and collapse of the diversified partnership-system form of business organization. In Florentine kinship networks, I will focus on the formation of urban patrilineage and its diffusion from upper classes to middle classes. And in Florentine political networks, I will focus on the factional transformation of oligarchic elites. Causal interactions and spillovers among these three social networks, I will argue, shaped organizational evolution in each of these social networks, thereby creating a linked multiple-network architecture which coevolved through time.

This introductory chapter summarizes and provides an overview of the empirical chapters in this book: namely, a brief history of Florentine organizational invention. Chapter 2 develops the theoretical framework that I use to explain the emergence of these linked Florentine organizational inventions.

[7] However, the relationship between double-entry bookkeeping and linear perspective in art is discussed in my Cornell seminar presentation on YouTube: https://www.youtube.com/watch?v=NtegztKqBu4.

Causal Narrative of Florentine Organizational Inventions

Figure 1.1 shows how the chapters fit together causally into a narrative through time—in other words, how the organizational inventions described in this book fed into each other's development through coevolution. The

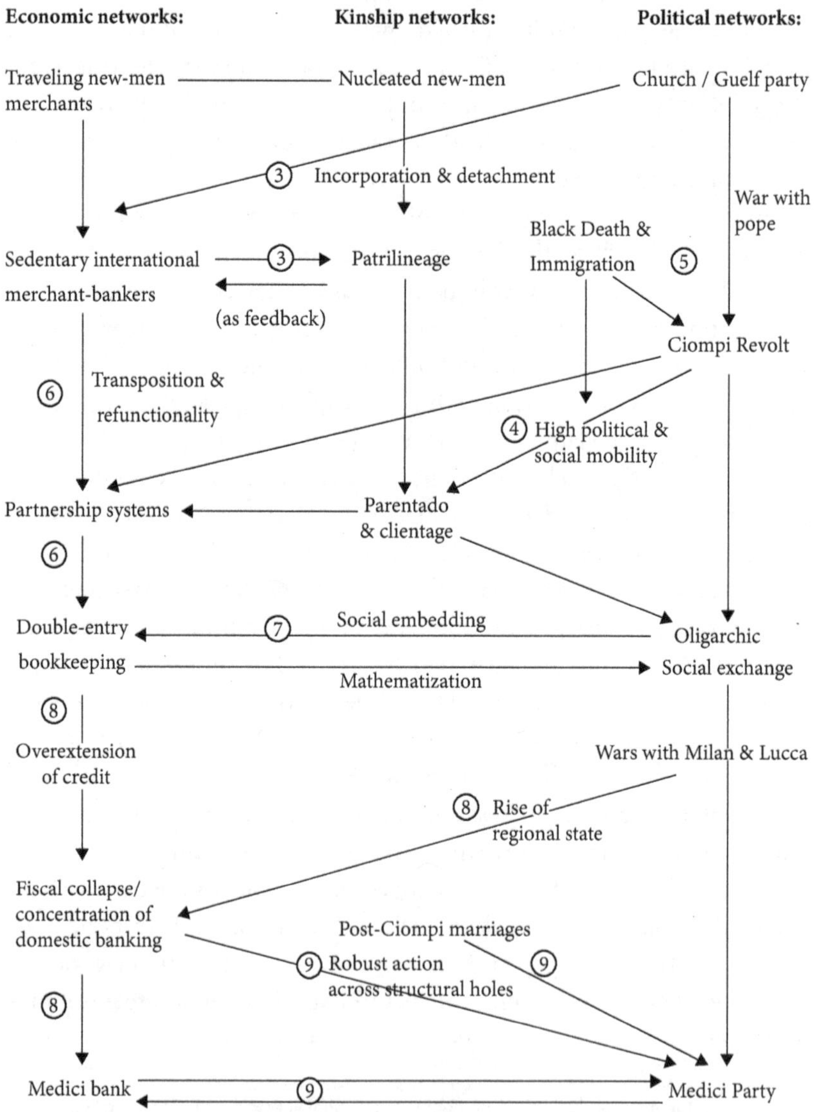

Figure 1.1 Causal Narrative of Florentine Organizational Inventions

columns in figure 1.1 are the three social networks out of which Florentine organizational inventions were composed: namely, economic networks, kinship networks, and political networks.

These were the underlying social raw materials or lattices upon which historical network mechanisms (yet to be described) operated to generate business, kinship, and political organizational inventions. Circles in figure 1.1 identify the chapters in this book that develop and prove the causal connections so identified in more detail.[8] Both chapters and circles are arrayed chronologically. Taken as an ensemble, figure 1.1 describes the coevolutionary argument in the book. The key is that organizational inventions are constructed out of the multiple underlying social networks that intersect through them. Changing the way that social networks are blended changes the organizations that are constructed thereby.

Going down the economic-network column on the left, the historical progression of organizational inventions (at the elite level of internationally oriented Florentine merchant-banks) was from traveling new-men merchants, to sedentary international merchant-bankers, to partnership systems (a corollary of which was double-entry bookkeeping), to fiscal collapse due to wars, to the domination of the Medici Bank. Going down the middle kinship column, the historical progression of organizational inventions was nucleated merchant families turning into urban patrilineages (which emphasized "vertical" father–son descent through multiple generations), to the diffusion of that family system down into the middle classes, to the strengthening of the "horizontal" dimension of oligarchic alliances of patrilineages via intermarriage through females. Going down the right-side political network column, the historical progression of organizational inventions in political factions went from Guelf party factions, titularly rooted in the Church, to Albizzi-Ricci factions, to the Ciompi Revolt, to the post-Ciompi oligarchy, to the Medici Party.

These developmental sequences do not imply homogeneity in organizational form in Florence at any one time. They instead describe the "leading edges" of new organizational forms that were invented at their times.

The word "coevolution" is central in this book because the causal/processual explanations that I discovered for these respective organizational inventions emphasize cross-network causal influences rather than simple vertical inheritance or "path dependence." I do not deny the existence of

[8] Needless to say, this is not a complete organizational history of Florence. It is based on the archival data that I have analyzed in this book. Therefore, I welcome follow-up research by other scholars to flesh out this narrative skeleton.

path dependence (since nothing emerges out of nowhere), but nonlinear change and evolution,[9] I observe, comes from cross-network spillover and hybridity. I stand firmly opposed to the historiographical segregation of Florentine (or any other) history into separate disciplinary bins, like "economic history," "political history," "social history," etc. Those categories define history the way that we categorize ourselves rather than in the multidimensional ways in which Florentines actually interacted. These disciplinary categories also tend to push researchers toward monocausal (sometimes even teleological) styles of explanation, which privilege their own tribe.

There are two types of cross-network causal arrows (or "spillovers") drawn in figure one: (1) "recombination" causal influences are arrows pointed diagonally down in time, from one vertical column to another, and (2) "catalysis" causal influences are arrows pointed horizontally at same time. The first "recombination" style represents the injection of hybridity from one network into the path-dependence inheritance of another. The second "catalysis" style represents a positive feedback between reproduction rates; this transforms initial tentative invention into long-lasting successful invention.

The overall topology of the causal narrative here is not a branching bush from a single ancestor, like in Darwin.[10] This is rather a cross-cutting mixture of numerous lines of development, which interpenetrate. One may well find elements in this Florentine mixture in common with other contemporary Italian city states, like Venice or Genoa. But the mixtures and blendings in each of these various cousin cases are unique. Humanist-oriented historians emphasize uniqueness and contingency. Social-science-oriented historians emphasize causal regularities and generalization. I believe there is no deep contraction between these two approaches—more a matter of which side one chooses to emphasize. This book represents one approach to try to combine them both, not in competition but in cooperation—namely, general principles like network coevolution, but always operating on unique, historically specific raw materials, often with nonlinear combinatorial results.

[9] Called "speciation" in the evolutionary biology literature. As in Darwin's "Origin of Species." See chapter 2 in Padgett and Powell (2012) for a comparison of the biology and the social-science versions of this concept.

[10] Even though Darwin's powerful metaphor of "The Origin of Species" is a core motivation for all of my research. It needs to be said, without criticism, that Darwin himself never did explain "the origin of species," only the natural selection of species variation, which emerged offstage. See Padgett and Powell (2012), chapter 2, for more information about the current evolutionary biology literature on speciation and the origin of life.

Synopses of Empirical Chapters

Chapter 3 is the most expansive of the empirical chapters, both geographically and in terms of the number of social networks that (are known to) have autocatalyzed each other. There are actually two organizational inventions in chapter 3: in economic networks, the emergence of sedentary merchant-bankers in the 1360s, and in kinship networks, the adoption soon thereafter of aristocratic patrilineage by urban merchants. As summarized in chapter 3, figure 3.1, the first mover (the "perturbation") in this sequence of inventions was the Pope, who mobilized transient Tuscan bankers in the Champaign fairs into becoming his financiers for his "Italian crusades" against a series of German emperors. To ensure repayment of their massive loans, those Tuscans became the Church's tax collectors, distributed in bishops' castles around Europe. (In Padgett and Powell, we called this "incorporation.") In their new administrative posts, the Tuscan financiers (Sienese as well as Florentine) absorbed the Church's more advanced organizational practices (a.k.a., "recombination")—in particular, writing letters/orders to their stationary agents spread around Europe rather than traveling with their own goods on mules to fairs.

Once the Italian crusades ended, these Tuscan financiers had no more papal business to sustain them, so they took their organizational invention across the channel to the King of England and set up an innovative customs service for him, to be repaid in sacks of wool collected thereby. (In Padgett and Powell, we called this "detachment.") This led Florentines to ship that English wool back home to Florence, to fuel a new, rapidly growing wool-manufacturing industry in Florence. It was that industry, more than elitist international banking, that led to an immigrant boom in the working-class population of Florence. In other words, to the emergence of Florence itself as a full-fledged city in the late 1200s.[11]

The innovation on the kinship side, urban patrilineage, came from Florentine merchant-bankers' attempts to raise their social status[12] to be equal to their new European aristocratic trading partners. I show in chapter 3, through a series of case studies, that Florentine surnames did not emerge through the sequence of "family-into-company," as virtually all previous literature presumed, but rather through the more counterintuitive sequence

[11] According to Wikipedia, in 1300, Florence was the fourth or sixth largest city in Europe, after Paris, Milan, and Granada (all around 150,000 population size), with Florence, Venice and Genoa at around 100,000 population size.

[12] In medieval times, merchants were distinctly lower in status than aristocrats. See Duby (1980).

of "company-into-family." The new business form of sedentary merchant-banking emerged first (through incorporation and detachment); then patri-lineage emerged second to catalyze the continued reproduction of sedentary merchant-banking.[13] Family surnames were formed from the names of the original senior partners of merchant-banks.

Chapter 4 documents, over a long period of two centuries (1282–1494), Florentine rates of social mobility (in household wealth and political power) and of cross-class marriage, all of which were astonishingly high, especially for a premodern time period. The ultimate causes are not so surprising—namely, commercial capitalism and political republicanism, both of which generated considerable population churning and turnover, both in markets and in politics. But my primary new finding here is on the side of catalysis. I document orthogonality—that is, zero correlation—between household rank orders of wealth, of political office holding, and of age of lineage. That means, on average, that any attempt at class closure through intentional endogamous marriage on one dimension generated unintentional cross-class exogamy in marriage on other dimensions. I use the metaphor of one hand on a door and the other hand on a window: Closing the door opens the window. Orthogonality of statuses was produced through periodic (generational) tumult in republican political revolt. That diminished under the late Medici and vanished after the end of republicanism in 1500. As the astonishing social mobility and churning that I document declined, Florence's impressive organizational inventiveness seems to have diminished as well, becoming more like a standard aristocracy (albeit a small one).[14]

Chapter 5 covers the Ciompi Revolt. I follow and extend Brucker (1962, 1968) in concluding that the 1378 Ciompi Revolt was generated not by a Marxist-style 60% of the Florentine population revolt, as an earlier literature had maintained, but by a social-class (not an economic-class) split within the ruling elite, caused by war with the Pope, Florence's prior Guelf ally. This elite split was between waves of immigration: the original founding generation of *popolani* and *magnati* families, analyzed in chapter 3, versus "the rise of the new men," who were upper-level immigrants from Tuscan towns after the 1348 Black Death.[15] The Ciompi Revolt reveals that recombination is

[13] An example of "the invention puzzle is that some of these innovative recombinations cascade out to reconfigure entire interlinked ecologies of 'ways of doing things.'"

[14] That is not to say that Florence lost its innovativeness in the intellectual domains of art, science, and political theory. On the economic front, silk remained a bright spot.

[15] The Black Death killed about 60% of the Florentine population in three months. Subsequent replacement immigration was recombinant flow of people on a massive scale.

not always a story of happy hybridity. Sometimes "recombination" is a matter of smashing network ties (a.k.a. "creative destruction"), not just a matter of forging new ones.

The contribution of chapter 5 to existing historiography is its documentation that, despite undoubted factionalism and even violence in political behavior at that time, political speech in advisory councils emphasized only unity. There was an intense contradiction, in other words, between speech and action. The desire/aspiration/norm was for all Florentine citizens to agree with the "General Will" as the dominant (coercive?) consensus defined it. Political factions were considered verboten, even traitorous.

When the final outcome of the Ciompi Revolt became a victory of political moderates, who defeated both the radical working-class guild on the left and the reactionary *Parte Guelfa* on the right, the stage was set for resumption of cross-class network ties, this time adding the invention of a new form of business organization, the partnership system, discussed at length in chapter 6. This chapter is a reprint of the 2006 AJS article by Padgett and McLean, where the recombination + catalysis theoretical framework discussed in chapter 2 made its first appearance in print.

The recombinant mechanism behind this novel organization was labeled "transposition and refunctionality" in that original AJS article and here. To rebuild international trade, which had been destroyed by war with the Pope, newly victorious political moderates sent politically reliable domestic *cambio* bankers to foreign capitals to take the place of elite *popolani* and *magnati* merchant-bankers. These domestic bankers brought their master-apprentice way of organizing business with them but inserted their old guild relational protocol into brand new international business settings. Here, "junior partner" no longer meant eager sixteen-year-olds but rather older and experienced (but not familial) Florentines residing in the foreign city.

"Catalysis" was the incorporation of this new economic partnership network into the augmented multiple-network elite structure of Florence, via the "open elite" marriage and political network mechanisms discussed in chapter 4. In this sense, the post-Ciompi invention of the economic partnership system built upon the open-elite marriage and political mechanisms was generated in the pre-Ciompi past.

One corollary of the partnership-system analysis in chapter 6 was my documentation of the Florentine adoption, from Venice, of double-entry bookkeeping—originally for the Florentine purpose of intra-system organizational management. Through an economy-wide measurement of inter-company credit registered in the 1427 catasto, chapter 7 shows how this accounting adoption diffused throughout the entire Florentine economy of commercial credit. Paul McLean and I documented both how widespread this adoption was, even down to artisan shoemakers,[16] and the high levels of leverage (total debt/credit divided by founding capital) it induced. It is an exaggeration to say that the Florentine economy domestically was cashless, but in the inter-company sphere, credit recorded and offset within account books among recurrent-transaction companies was the primary currency of the realm.

The primary empirical finding in chapter 7 is social embedding or social exchange. In other words, behind the apparently austere impersonality of account-book entries, Paul McLean and I show through both statistics and letters that Florentine businessmen in fact knew a great deal about each other and their networks: family, marriage, neighborhood, political alliance, and political office. This social embedding of economic networks in other social networks shaped to whom they gave credit. Weber notwithstanding, Florentine account books only appear to be impersonal because we do not know as much about their trading partners as they did. This "personality of markets" requires a more historically grounded theoretical framework than the "impersonality of markets" of neoclassical economics.

In addition to social embedding undergirding commercial credit, double-entry bookkeeping in turn made social exchange mathematically precise. "Social exchange" became more than just "trust" (Granovetter 1985). Accounting extended the mathematical perspective of the "merchant's eye" (Baxandall 1988) into social relations in general—what Goldthwaite (2015) has called "the culture of accounting."[17]

Chapter 8, however, reveals the downside of this explosive growth in intercompany credit. The Florentine 1427 catasto is rightly renowned in historiography for being one of the first, if not the first, modern taxation registration systems in European history. It was not an income tax as we know it, but a wealth tax, where "wealth" innovatively included liquid/moveable assets (in other words, business) and not just more visible real estate. Heads

[16] Almost 70% of Florentine male households were literate/numerate, as measured by their ability to fill out complex tax returns in their own hand (Black 2007, 35). This astonishing level of premodern literacy was produced primarily by vocational guild schools, established precisely in order to teach account books.

[17] See also my Cornell seminar on linear perspective in business, painting, politics, and social status (//www.youtube.com/watch?v=NtegztKqBu4).

of households had to fill out page after page of meticulous legally mandated financial reports (including lists of credits and debits), not unlike our own IRS filings.

Chapter 8, however, is not about the genesis of this astonishing fiscal invention, but about its consequences. We document, across the 1427, the 1433, and the 1458 catasti, that it was an economic disaster, especially in domestic and international banking industries. Who says that inventions only succeed?

The exogenous perturbation that triggered the creation of the catasto in the first place was "the rise of the regional state"—specifically, repeated wars between Florence and Milan (and later Lucca)—which demanded huge expenditures for mercenaries to maintain Florentine independence and expansion. Florence wanted a tax system that extracted money more effectively from a recalcitrant population, especially from businesses. In this, they succeeded all too well.

The problem was not just the magnitude of tax extraction (in gold) but also the highly developed, indeed over-leveraged, commercial credit system documented in chapter 7. In times of economic growth, this extended commercial credit system fueled more growth. But in times of fiscal stress, it created a credit bubble where one bankruptcy triggered others in chain reactions.

This is a case where recombinant innovation did not receive the catalytic cross-network support necessary to turn it into lasting successful invention.

Crucial for the next chapter, one unintended side effect of the economic collapse of the domestic banking industry was the widespread collapse of the partnership system, which typically had domestic banks as its center, its "home office" so to speak. The surviving Medici Bank rose from these cinders to dominance,[18] as its previously vibrant competition fell away.

Chapter 9, "Robust Action and the Rise of the Medici, 1400–1434," was the first article on Florence I published (with Christopher Ansell), in 1993. Written before I launched myself into the archives to do my own extensive primary research, this early article was based on coding and computerizing a rich prosopography by Dale Kent on the factional rise of Cosimo de' Medici. My contribution was to add social-network statistical precision,

[18] Molho (1971) has pointed to the Medici Bank's special position as state financiers of short-run, high-interest loans as one factor in this rise to dominance.

robust-action interpretation, and "deep history" macro context to historical themes first adumbrated by her.

A number of readers of this volume may be familiar with my robust action argument. For those who are not, I reproduce here the abstract of that article: "We analyze the centralization of political parties and elite networks that underlay the birth of the Renaissance state in Florence. Class revolt and fiscal crisis were the ultimate causes of elite consolidation, but Medicean political control was produced by means of network disjunctures within the elite, which the Medici alone spanned. Cosimo de' Medici's multivocal identity as sphinx harnessed the power available in these "structural holes"[19] and resolved the contradiction between judge and boss inherent in all organizations. Methodologically, we argue that, to understand state formation, one must penetrate beneath the veneer of formal institutions, groups, and goals down to the relational substrata of peoples' actual lives. Ambiguity and heterogeneity, not planning and self-interest, are the raw materials of which powerful states and persons are constructed." (Padgett and Ansell 1993, 1259).

This invention of the Medici Party highlights an innovation/invention theme not prominently displayed in other chapters, except for chapter 3—namely, "networks as layered temporalities." The short-term economic clientage half of the Cosimo de' Medici story has now received deeper analysis in chapter 8. But the long-term other half—namely, of marriage residues from the Ciompi Revolt—introduces long time lags into the causal story. The Medici Party was the coupling, through Cosimo himself, of short-term economic with long-term kinship network evolution dynamics. To succeed in overcoming these contradictions, all Cosimo had to do was be utterly opaque in his goals and objectives. At the micro level of "genius" leadership, multivocality, opportunism, and quick reaction dominated over strategy and forethought.

Next, after this historical introductory chapter, will come a theoretical chapter, which relates these empirical analyses both to evolutionary theory in general and to Padgett and Powell (2012) in specific. Then follows the chronologically ordered empirical chapters just summarized. Except for the

[19] This Ronald Burt theme perhaps was foreshadowed in this book by the "orthogonality of status dimensions," discussed in chapter 3. In both cases, it was systematic gaps in the social structure that channeled the formation of new ties: (a) blockage in endogamous marriage within the elite leading to "open elite" social-mobility marriages with new men; and (b) orthogonality between marriage and economic networks leading to both networks reaching out to each other through Cosimo as "robust action" broker.

last Robust Action chapter, these are all based on original coding (by me and my research team) from primary-source archival documents, handwritten in medieval Tuscan and Latin, of social networks among 100,000 Florentines over 200 years. These have then been computerized and assembled into an interlinked relational database, which will be released to the public upon publication of this book. An appendix describes these archival sources and computerized data.

2

Recombination and Catalysis in Multiple Networks

This theory chapter develops the micro-foundations of the causal-narrative overview of figure 1.1 in the last chapter. In particular, it identifies the cross-network social mechanisms that generated Florentine organizational inventions. As such, it overlaps with but also supplements and adds to the eight generative social mechanisms identified in the more broadly comparative Padgett and Powell (2012, 12–26).

In this chapter, I first describe the raw material out of which organizational inventions emerge—namely, the overlay architecture of multiple networks. Then I elaborate on the meaning of "recombination" and "catalysis," the core social-science concepts of evolution used in this book. In table 2.1, I apply those concepts to the empirical chapters 3–9 in order to highlight the generative social-network mechanisms contained therein. Finally, I describe some dynamical consequences for elite transformation of feedbacks among recombination and catalysis causal links.

Multiple Networks

The logic of multiple-network architecture in this book is illustrated in figure 2.1. Dots are not people, exactly, but "people in roles." A person is a vertical line that assembles roles into people. From a network perspective, for example, Cosimo de' Medici as person = Cosimo as businessman + Cosimo as father + Cosimo as politician. An "economic network" has three components: partnerships, which build companies; trading or exchange, which makes products and profit; and names of companies, which signal institutionalized legal status. A "kinship network" likewise has three components: father-son relations of patrilineal descent, which define genealogies; arranged marriages of daughters, which made *parentado* or in-law connections between patrilineal families; and surnames, which label

Organizational Invention in Renaissance Florence. John F. Padgett, Oxford University Press.
 DOI: 10.1093/oso/9780197789216.003.0002

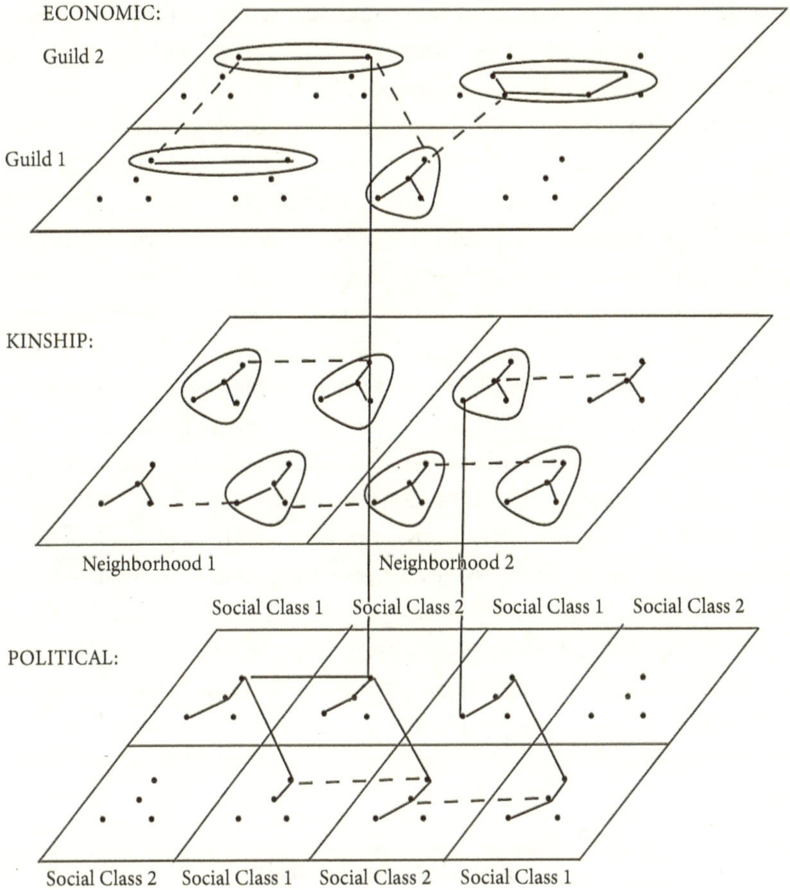

Figure 2.1 Multiple-Network Ensemble Renaissance Florence

Note: (a) Solid lines are constitutive ties. Dotted lines are relational social exchanges. Oblongs are formal organizations (families and firms.). (b) People in multiple roles are vertical lines connecting corresponding dots in the domains of activity in which people are active. (Only two are shown for illustration.)

legitimate lineages.[1] A "political network" in Florence usually had only two components—namely, long-term alliances and short-term deals—because acknowledged parties or factions were illegitimate, even traitorous.

"Coevolution" is movement of such a multiple-network ensemble through time, like in a movie. "Interaction and spillover" among networks occur because people participate in multiple roles—especially

[1] Lines of descent with no circles indicate illegitimacy.

Florentine elites, who were merchant-republicans. The multi-functionality of many Florentines established the architectural plumbing for Florence's observed high rate of network spillovers.

Not coincidentally, figure 2.1 also describes the core logic of the relational database on which all of the empirical chapters depend. Over three decades, my research team and I[2]—Paul McLean, Katalin Prajda, Francesco Bettarini, Claudia Tripodi, and John Padgett—have constructed, from primary-source handwritten documents[3] in archives, a large relational database containing both network and attribute information on 64,622 surnamed[4] Renaissance Florentines in 2,369 lineages,[5] who lived during the 1300–1500 period. This relational database, in Microsoft Access, is composed of 122 spreadsheets, which range across the multiple networks in figure 2.1 but also across attributes of the people involved: political office and guild memberships, wealth and neighborhood information from ten comprehensive tax censuses, and much else, all of these across two centuries of time. Each of these 122 component spreadsheets codes a distinct *Archivio di Stato di Firenze* source.[6] As with all relational databases, in order to enable assembly of heterogeneous information about people from disparate sources, linkage across files is achieved through assigning unique IDs to each person and applying those consistently across component files. That is the operational meaning of the vertical lines in figure 2.1.

Recombination and Catalysis

This book's theory of organizational invention as the coevolution of multiple networks is an adaptation and extension of the theoretical framework developed in a previous 2012 book coauthored with Woody Powell, entitled

[2] See Scientia article (September 5, 2018) for a description of the most recent Padgett archival research team of Padgett, Prajda, Bettarini, and Tripodi. Reprinted on my webpage: home.uchicago.edu/jpadgett.

[3] In both Latin and Tuscan or *volgare* (the predecessor of modern Italian).

[4] The database focuses on surnames because it is impossible to uniquely identify and therefore to link the numerous non-surnamed Giovanni di Piero's that exist in primary sources. Considerable information on such non-surnamed Florentines does exist in my database (comprising ~60% of the total, making well over 120,000 persons in the full dataset), but without linking IDs, I cannot do cross-domain statistical analysis. This is not a dataset of elites only, as "middle class" surnamed persons are also included. But it is harder to study the non-surnamed poor, even with substantial attributional data on poor individuals (but not on their networks).

[5] Different lineages with the same surnames were separated by tediously constructing genealogies.

[6] See the original articles on which these chapters are based for *Archivio di Stato di Firenze* and the appendix to this book for source citations.

The Emergence of Organizations and Markets. In that sense, this book is an empirically more tightly focused sequel to that book. The previous book covered a much broader range of empirical cases: not only Renaissance Florence but also early-modern Amsterdam, late nineteenth-century Germany, communist and post-communist Soviet Union and China, contemporary Silicon Valley, even the origins of life on earth. It sought to demonstrate the breadth of the theory's potential applications. The current, more empirically focused book adds greater temporal depth—path-dependent histories and interweaving causality over long periods of time—to the theoretical mix.

But the word "sequel" is misleading since most of the chapters in this book are adaptations or reproductions of articles published before that previous book appeared. In that sense, this book is more of a prequel than a sequel—the empirical soil out of which its later 2012 generalization sprang.

The theoretical centerpiece of the Padgett and Powell book was autocatalysis. Network autocatalysis is a set of nodes and transformations in which all nodes are reconstructed through transformations among nodes in the set (see Padgett and Powell, 2012, pp. 8ff.). As reviewed in chapter 2 in that earlier book, this concept originated in the chemistry origin-of-life literature as the simplest definition of life: a chemical-reaction network metabolism that reproduces itself (given energy), even in the face of constant turnover or "death" in its chemical parts. We extended that origin-of-life concept to our social-organizational domain in three ways: production autocatalysis to study the emergence of economic production, biographical autocatalysis to study the emergence of social roles and networks, and linguistic autocatalysis to study the emergence of language.[7] (These three subtypes are represented in figure 2.1 as dotted lines, solid lines, and circles, respectively. Each of these aspects of networks reproduce over time, not in literal topology but in stochastic distributions of types of nodes and relations.)

Network autocatalysis alone, however, does not produce novelty. Quite the opposite, it produces reproduction, resilience, and repair. However, newly established interaction and feedback between more than one autocatalytic network can tip either or both into modified autocatalytic networks, which inherit components from ancestors but recombine and rewire them

[7] Production and biographical autocatalysis were studied extensively in the Padgett & Powell book, but linguistic autocatalysis was not. For subsequent work on linguistic autocatalysis, however, see John F. Padgett, "Faulkner's Assembly of Memories into History: Narrative Networks in Multiple Times," *American Journal of Sociology*, 124 (2018): 406–78>. I consider Bill Sewell's (2005, chapter 3) "eventful temporality" to be a fellow traveler on the linguistic side, although certainly without the chemistry framing.

in new ways (Fontana and Buss 1994). In the Padgett and Powell approach, novelty emerges from autocatalysis tippings among multiple networks that interact.

The present book uses my earlier language of "recombination and catalysis" (Padgett and McLean 2011) more than does in Padgett and Powell's 2012 book, which extended that to "autocatalysis." These are really the same theory, just viewed from different levels of analysis. "Catalysis" is a local, triadic concept, in which an unchanged molecule or element affects the reaction rates (positively or negatively) of two other molecules or elements with which it is in contact. "Autocatalysis" is a global network concept, wherein multiple catalytic triads are strung together into grand positive feedback loops, in which each element in the network receives catalytic support. Metabolic "life" is autocatalysis, not catalysis. Since I am sampling on successful organizational inventions that have survived long enough to influence history,[8] I assume that autocatalysis exists in the background of all of my cases, to keep the full reproducing multiple-network system alive, even when I cannot see all of its parts. But the more local "catalysis" allows me to zoom in greater empirical detail on particular segments of the overwhelming complexity of the full autocatalysis picture.[9]

Go back to the opening distinction between "innovation" and "invention." Organizational innovation is the creation of new products and/or production procedures ("Production autocatalysis" in the language of Padgett and Powell.) Organizational invention is the creation of new organizational forms. ("Relational autocatalysis" in the language of Padgett and Powell.) Successful organizational invention is the reproduction of that invention in the social context in which it is embedded. Successful organizational invention requires both "recombination" and "catalysis." In the context of figure 1.1 in chapter 1, "organizational inventions" (dependent variables, or DVs) are the sequences of new organizational forms that developed and reproduced in Florence within the three social networks listed there: namely, (a) in economic networks, the evolutionary progression of merchants traveling to Champaign fairs to sedentary merchant-bankers, to partnership systems, to the collapse of partnership systems and dominance

[8] In Padgett and Powell, 2012, Powell's innovative chapter 14 avoided this "sampling on success bias" by comparing three American cities that succeeded in developing biotechnology ecosystems with three other plausible American cities that tried but failed.

[9] Chapter 3 in this volume presents a more global picture of full autocatalytic tipping—namely, the medieval emergence of Florence itself.

of Medici Bank; (b) in kinship networks, the evolutionary progression of the formation of patrilineage in the upper merchant classes to its diffusion to the middle classes through cross-class marriages and high social mobility, to *parentado* (in-laws) and clients; and (c) in political networks, the evolutionary progression of the pro-Pope Guelf party to the Ciompi Revolt, to the emergence of the Albizzi oligarchy, to the political rise of the Medici. These organizational changes go chronologically down the vertical lines in figure 1.1. Causal lines of multiple-network developmental influence cross-cut between those single-network evolutions, showing how the three network evolutions causally influenced each other through time. As in the Padgett and Powell (2012) book, I insist that to segregate history into insular subfields like "economic history," "political history," and "social history"[10] is to doom each of these histories to mere description, with no explanation (other than teleology) possible.[11]

What are those multiple-network causal cross-linkages? Recombination and catalysis.

Imagine people (or roles within people) as packages or carriers of production practices (or skills) for how to make things, of relational protocols for how to socially connect with others, and of cognitive categories for how to classify the world (including others). Recombination is changing the mixture of practices, protocols, and categories packaged together within a person or within an organization of persons—here, businesses, families, and factions. Catalysis is the reproduction of that new combination through social interaction with other persons and organizations in the innovating organization's ongoing networks.

Table 2.1 fleshes out this book's table of contents more analytically in terms of the specific network mechanisms of "recombination" and "catalysis" found in its various empirical chapters. In addition to relisting the organizational inventions (the DVs) already described, this overview table describes the macro contexts of the inventions in question and the recombination and catalysis network mechanisms which channeled those macro perturbations into Florentine organizational inventions.

[10] I would add "intellectual history" except that I do not analyze that here.

[11] "Explanation as teleology" I regard as failed causal explanation. On the other extreme, as much as I otherwise admire Schumpeter, unfortunately his monomaniacal emphasis on entrepreneurs as the drivers of innovation is too close to a "great man (or men) theory of history" for me to embrace. See March (2008) for a broad critique of business schools' typical worship of "leadership."

Before walking through table 2.1, chapter by chapter, to classify the book's empirical findings, it perhaps will be useful first to offer a few overview reflections about the recombination and catalysis mechanisms listed in this table.

Repeatedly, my empirical studies reveal some exogenous shock or perturbation to Florence in the background, which then triggered a series of unanticipated chain reactions that resulted in organizational innovation and invention. Sometimes those shocks were large, like wars and revolts; sometimes they were small, like interrupted international trade. The existence of initiating shocks at the beginning of causal chain reactions could create in the reader a simplistic linear interpretation of exogenous shock ➔ organizational invention. Not false exactly, but drastically misleading in terms of process. Shocks can induce a wide variety of system responses.

In a graduate-school class I took with Charles Tilly,[12] he offered a diamond-cutter metaphor that resonates with what I found: A diamond is strong. Sledgehammers can't break it. But a diamond cutter can put on an eye glass, look closely at that diamond, and then crack it apart with just a tap. The point is this: Does that tap go along the line of that diamond's internal cleavages? To turn a precious stone into a jewel, it is not the force of the perturbation that matters. It is the alignment of that perturbation with the internal structure of the diamond. To understand the response of any system to shock, it is important to understand the internal networks and cleavages that transmit and channel that shock. A war on Florence does not have the same effect on Florence as a war on Milan has on Milan.

Tilly's metaphor is not perfect, because it refers only to the breakage of ties, not to the formation of new ties or to the rewiring of previous ties. But it is enough to throw the spotlight on internal network cleavages as the key to understanding system response.

As for recombination, a general observation I would make about the mechanisms under that column reported in table 2.1 is that, in Florence, system perturbations at the macro level were channeled into recombinations of production practices, relational protocols, and cognitive categories at the micro level usually through reshaping people's biographies and careers.

[12] For Tilly himself, the context of his metaphor was the effect of war on state formation. Tilly (1975, 1992) famously argued that "states make war, and wars make states." But he was perfectly aware that wars can also make class revolutions (cf. Skocpol 1979), and that wars can cause economic and social collapse. Tilly [at least by the time he was teaching me] thought of his own argument as one possible developmental trajectory, not as a linear inevitability.

Table 2.1 Organizational Invention in Renaissance Florence

Chapters:	Macro Context:	Recombination: (= flow of people)	Organizational Invention:	Catalysis: (= social embedding)
3A. Medieval Corporations	Italian Crusades	cooptation into Church	sedentary merchants in unitary corporations	patrilineage
3B. Medieval Corporations	International Trade	business with European aristocrats	patrilineage	elections & offices
4. Open Elite	commercial capitalism + republicanism	high social mobility	cross-class marriage (with dowries)	orthogonal status hierarchies
5. Ciompi Revolt	war with Pope: contradictory mix of war and religion	immigration after Black Death → new men	denunciation and exclusion from office	Parte Guelfa (class conflict)
6. Partnership Systems	Ciompi Revolt	local bankers sent to other countries	partnership system	absorption into open elite (→ merchant republicans)
7. Economic Credit	Albizzi oligarchic regime	partnership system	commercial credit through double-entry account books	social embedding in family, politics, & neighborhood
8. Fiscal Innovation Gone Bad	regional-state wars: Milan and Lucca	massive tax extraction and banking collapse	Medici Bank as quasi-monopoly	state finance through short-term loans
9. Robust Action	war with Lucca	tax clientage	centralized Medici Party	brokerage across business and marriage structural holes

Big shocks like wars and little shocks, like reconstituting international trade routes, had their organizational innovation or invention effect by channeling different types of people (with their constitutive packages of practices, protocols, and categories) together into interaction. On a more routinized level, extraordinarily high social mobility and political republicanism, which turned over city councilors every two months, remixed packages of practices, protocols, and categories on a regular basis—again a distinctive Florentine feature.

As for catalysis, social embedding in Florence produced (at least) three general classes of cross-network reinforcement: (a) learning, (b) legitimacy, and (c) analogies. An exemplar of the first practice-oriented type of catalytic mechanism is when father-son relations in kinship taught youngsters how to do authority relations in business (chapter 3). Another example of behavioral learning is when commercial credit operated like social exchange (chapter 7).[13] An exemplar of the second legitimacy type of catalytic mechanism is when election to public office—which was a public recognition as "honorable" citizen—had the side effect of certifying "credit worthiness" for business credit (also see chapter 7). An exemplar of the third cognitively oriented type of catalysis is when patrilineage family gave an organization model (*società* "council of elders") for early international merchant banks to imitate (see chapter 3). A second example of cognitive catalysis is when civic humanism (Baron, Maxon) created a new "cultural capital" status ordering (Bourdieu), which motivated competitive elites to shine in advisory-council discussions and debates. Other examples of Florentine cross-network catalysis are listed in table 2.1.

Regimes and Elite Transformations: Networks as Layered Temporalities

Cross-network causal flows of catalysis imply relationships of adaptation or "fit" among social networks. In no way is this strong enough to imply identical network topology in each domain,[14] but each network was shaped in part by its interaction with its overlaying neighbors (as in figure 2.1). This causal interaction, loose as it may be, gives rise to the notion of a "network

[13] Florentine instrumental *amicizia* was "making friends to do business," as in our own "social capital." But Florentines also thought the reverse: "doing business to make friends," implying more than just economic profit as a goal.

[14] In "Robust Action" chapter 9, indeed, "fit" meant cross-cutting topologies between marriage and business, which formed the network infrastructure of Cosimo's first Medici party.

regime," where temporally contemporaneous networks are coupled together into mutual catalysis.[15] In other words, into autocatalysis. When empirical focus is directed toward organizational inventions—the leading edges of organizational evolution—the general notion of "network regime" drifts more specifically into "elite network regime." As organizations and networks change, elites built out of those components are transformed in global structure and inner logic.

Graphically, candidates for "elite network regimes" in this book appear as contemporaneous rows of the "causal narrative" figure 1.1 in the previous chapter. This graphical procedure suggests three empirical candidates for multi-network regimes in Renaissance Florence:

> Regime #1: first two rows of figure 1.1. Namely, patrilineage + sedentary international merchant-bankers + Guelf Party.
>
> Regime # 2: third and fourth rows of figure 1.1. Namely, partnership systems + *parentado* and clientage + oligarchy.
>
> Regime #3: last row of figure 1.1. Namely, Medici Bank + *parentado* and clientage + Medici Party.

These networks refer mostly to elites, although bear in mind that the word "elite" needs to be interpreted broadly as "open elite" (chapter 4), especially since 30% in 1351 and 50% in 1480 of Florentine families had surnames.

Lending at least prima facie plausibility to an assumption of autocatalytic "fit" among these three combinations is that all three networks of the three triples seem to share similar underlying relational models or protocols among themselves: (a) in regime #1, father-son is the core relationship, serving as relational prototype for all three; (b) in regime #2, lateral reciprocity and credit is the basic relational prototype; and (c) in regime #3, it is centralized clientage. Sharing similar underlying relational protocols for building organizations creates catalysis both through the behavioral mechanism of learning—knowing how to relate in one network helps one learn how to relate in overlapping networks—and through the cognitive mechanism of analogy. Certainly, there are many more relational protocols in the whole population of Florence than these,[16] since at all times all of these modalities

[15] How tight this coupling is must be demonstrated empirically.

[16] For example, guilds and neighborhoods. How these open-elite organizations fit with the guild and neighborhood organizations of lower-class people is a topic for another book.

are observed to some extent, but in different periods the primary relational building blocks that Florentines used to construct their organizational inventions and composite elites evolved.

In regime #1, family *palazzi* (essentially apartment buildings for lineages) and the males assembled within them were used to dominate their local neighborhoods and to house the types of organizations just described. In regime #2, intermarriages and patronage were used as social anchors and lattices upon which to construct political oligarchies and economic credit. In regime #3, intermarriages and patronage remained as core building blocks but in a more centralized topology dominated by the Medici at the hub.

A key macro event triggering transition from regime #1 to regime #2 was the Ciompi Revolt.[17] Key macro events triggering transition from regime #2 to regime #3 were wars with Milan and Lucca.[18]

The challenging regime transition question is how do these "punctuated equilibria" multiple-network shifts occur—not just in single organizational inventions, examined one at a time, but also in sets of interlinked organizational inventions, cascading from one to another?

Before addressing this challenging question, let me first provide some empirical evidence that there was a punctuated dynamic of large-scale change in Florence, at least in the political domain. Copied from my AJS Robust Action article, this particular figure 2.2 shows the number of new families first admitted to city council, by year. The data show three waves of explosive expansion in governing "political elite" and a much smaller wave associated with the takeover of the Medici. The first initiating wave—associated with the formation of the republic in 1282—defined a political cohort or social class of families called "popolani." The second wave of families—associated with the overthrow of an external "tyrant" in 1343, followed closely by the 1348 Black Death—I call "new men." The third wave or cohort of entering families I call in my work "new-new men." The much smaller fourth wave (and thereafter) of families, I call Mediceans. There were also two other social classes in Renaissance Florence, not diagrammed in figure 2.2—namely, magnates were families in power before 1282 but excluded from office by the popolani in 1393; and "never admitted" were

[17] The process was probably begun in the previous 1343 revolt, diagrammed in figure 2.2 below, but I have not studied that period.

[18] Bear in mind that transition through organizational invention does not imply that all previous organizational forms were eliminated. Organizational inventions were "leading edge" organizational forms which coexisted with older baselines, which continued to be feeders.

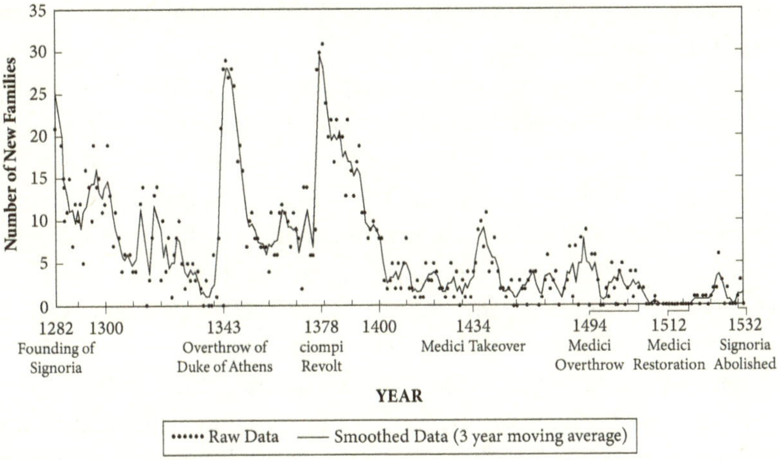

Figure 2.2 New Families Admitted to the Signoria, 1282–1532

Source: Najemy, pp. 320–22

surnamed families never admitted to the Signoria. Social classes were clearly defined in Renaissance Florence because of the punctuated character of these political cohorts.

The first two of these waves—the formation of the Florentine republic in 1282, and the overthrow of an external "tyrant" in 1343 (followed closely by the 1348 Black Death)—are not studied in this book, but the third and fourth waves were. In the third wave in particular, I clearly demonstrated invention spillover from political networks to business networks to kinship networks, just as the autocatalytic model of "regime" expects.[19]

The causes of the volatile waves of expansion and contraction shown in figure 2.2 are known: namely, economically successful new-men immigrants—mostly from upper echelons of surrounding Tuscan towns—continuously pushed for citizenship rights (including republican eligibility for elected public office) commensurate with their economic success. The existing political elite usually resisted these demands, which diluted their own power and control. If ever the united front of the old guard ruptured into elite factions, however, members of the more liberal elite faction often would support new-men demands, in order to gain leverage over their rivals. If the new cross-class alliance succeeded, then the waves of new entrants in

[19] The autocatalytic model certainly predicts spillover from one interlinked network to another. Discontinuous punctuated change, associated with large-scale regime changes such as these, however, is not a necessary corollary. Smooth, more gradual spillovers in time are also possible.

figure 2.2 resulted.[20] While details of course differ, all four of these Florentine waves fit this general pattern.

Tilly's diamond-cutter metaphor argued that the reaction of a system to an external shock (like Black Death or wars) depends upon how that perturbation aligns with internal cleavages in that system, which channel its chain-reaction effects. At the detailed level of specific organizational inventions, those cleavages are the social networks studied in this book. But at the more macro level of regime transition, I propose enduring social classes (laid down from previous waves) and emergent factions as the prominent system-level cleavages that transformed external shocks into the repeated waves of new entrants graphed in figure 2.2.[21] The social class structure in Florence was the historical residue or "memory" of the tumultuous Florentine history graphed in figure 2.2. These successive cyclical waves, institutionally grounded in republicanism, were the largest social mixing mechanism in Florence.

Interpreted through the theoretical lens of autocatalytic regime, this republican cycle of roughly generational revolt is a story of one newly emergent multi-network regime confronting previous multi-network regimes, each induced by the infusion of waves of (recombinant) new men, who were then coopted. This is the empirical basis of my interpretation of these elite regime transitions as "networks as layered temporality." Social networks patterns that reproduce over time can be interpreted as structural memories of the long-ago events that first created them, whether actors are aware of that descent or not. Through the causal chains of recombination, catalysis, and path dependence outlined in figure 1.1 of chapter 1, layers of the past in Florentine history reverberated down through overlapping network architectures into chain-reaction sequences of organizational inventions. The concept of autocatalysis then adds: which reproduce through positive feedback loops of cross-network catalysis.

To decompose this macro regime-transition account into dynamic sequences of network transformation, it is useful to note the different time frames upon which our three networks reproduced and adapted. Kinship networks are the slowest (but also longest lasting) to adapt because kinship ties last for life (except in the case of divorce, which did not exist then). Economic partnerships change on the order of the length of partnership

[20] The wave of new entrants dies down because the newly expanded regime now wants to close the door behind it to defend its own newly established control.

[21] Until, that is, the Medici put a stop to this "open elite" political-mobility dynamic through their disemboweling of Florentine republicanism (Rubinstein 1966).

contracts—about three years, although renewable. Economic credit turns over faster than that. Florentine political factions, since illegitimate, were usually episodic, although the Guelf Party and the Medici Party institutionalized them much longer than that.

These distinct time scales induce what physicists call a separation of time scales: namely, external shocks were transmitted into domestic network structure first through political and economic ties and more slowly and gradually (except during Black Death) through kinship ties. Kinship ties functioned as network "genes," not in the sense of blueprints for constructing everything else, but in the sense of encoding memory of the deep past into contemporary network and class structure.

This separation-of-time-scales observation implies that when our focus is on recombinant-driven genesis of organizational inventions, political and economic networks are likely to loom large in our causal interpretation. But when our focus is on the catalysis side of organizational reproduction, and even more so on autocatalysis-driven regime transition, the deeply important role of history-encoding kinship is likely to rise in our interpretation, at least in Florence.[22]

That said, one epoch-changing shift in mid-fourteenth century Florentine kinship networks was the gradual and long-lasting shift within patrilineage from the male-oriented father-son relational protocol to the marriage-oriented *parentado* (in-law) relational protocol.[23] That kinship realignment, plus the later fourteenth-century birth of the homologous partnership system, shifted Florentine elite structure from volatile intra-class alliances of solidaristic, neighborhood-based patrilines to a multiple-class citywide oligarchy, based primarily on intermarriage. This is not an example of one kinship system replacing another (as had occurred in the 1260s), but rather of different parts of the patrilineage family system being emphasized for different purposes,[24] with profound consequences for the structure and functioning of elites.

With that layout of my recombination-and-catalysis conceptual framework, I proceed now with the empirical cases from which it was derived.

[22] Needless to say, in other times and places, other networks can take the "elite network regime" role of encoding the past in the present. In contemporary America, one thinks of educational careers as a functionally equivalent candidate.

[23] Chabod (1995) showed that the Florentine female dowry eventually surpassed male inheritance in monetary value.

[24] See chapter 4 regarding refunctionalization of patrilineage from economic to political purposes.

3

The Emergence of Corporate Merchant-Banks in Dugento Tuscany

Introduction

The idea of the corporation in its modern sense of a joint-stock company with limited liability did not exist in the Middle Ages. At that time, there was no limited liability, no stock market, no Industrial Revolution with factory production. Still, economic historians do speak of a Commercial Revolution in the "long 1200s" of the late 1100s into the early 1300s.[1] Along with the formation of the internationally oriented Champagne fairs in France, the rise of the large unitary merchant-bank in Tuscany ranks among the most important features of this Commercial Revolution.[2] Instead of mobile merchants from many nations traveling with their wares to and from central markets in France, a network of Italian (mostly Tuscan) merchant-banks developed in the mid-1200s effecting international movements of both goods and currency through themselves. Such banks were constructed out of sedentary merchants arranged in geographically distributed *filiali* or branches, sending letters to each other. Despite its geographical dispersion, this medieval Tuscan company was unitary in two legal senses: (a) a single multi-year partnership contract, with different partners often heading different branches, and (b) a single master account book, located in the head office back home, in which all activities were tabulated and held accountable.

Chapter 5 in Padgett & Powell, *The Emergence of Organizations and Markets*, Princeton University Press, 2012: 121–167. Republished with permission.

[1] Gras 1939, Lopez 1976, Sapori 1970, de Roover 1963, Spufford 1988, Goldthwaite 2009.

[2] I will not analyze in this chapter the opening of trading routes to the Levant, which involved Genoa, Venice, and Pisa, even though these eastern trade routes provided part of the flow of trade underneath the Commercial Revolution. This flow from the east involved spices and other luxury goods. Florence, Siena, and Lucca were more centrally involved in the countervailing flow from the west, involving woolen textiles produced in Flanders, and later in Florence, and silk textiles produced in Lucca. During the height of the Champagne fairs, Genoese merchants participated in both sides of these trade flows. Geographically distributed Tuscan merchant-banks, however, gradually displaced the Champagne fairs in the late 1200s.

Organizational Invention in Renaissance Florence. John F. Padgett, Oxford University Press.
 DOI: 10.1093/oso/9780197789216.003.0003

An impressive list of early innovations in basic business technique followed this "rise of the sedentary merchant": regularized business correspondence, bills of exchange,[3] complex account books,[4] and the making of deposits into investments.[5]

Beneath these fundamental innovations in business technique achieved by the sedentary merchant-bankers of the 1200s (the so-called Dugento), I maintain, lay the organizational invention of the corporation—not in the modern sense of joint-stock ownership but in the medieval sense of corporate body. This medieval-style corporation grew up within the Roman-law framework of the partnership, but it developed a temporal permanence and a continuity transcending its partners. The English word *corporation* is descended from the Latin *corpus* or body. In the context of the Italian medieval company,[6] the *corpo* was the starting capital contributed by its founding partners (*compagnie* or *soci*). Operationally, *corpo* was used to initiate a joint financial account (*ragione sociale*) in which the economic transactions and financial obligations of all the partners were effected and registered. The *ragione sociale* implemented, in a practical way, two organizational ideas: (a) unlimited liability of all the partners, and (b) corporate economic and legal existence above and beyond that of its constitutive members. In medieval terms, the rise of the "corporation" meant a move from a temporary alliance of companions or *compagnie*, with fluid partners, to the corporate body of a *società*, with stationary branches or *filiali*.

[3] In the absence of much surviving internal business records from the 1200s, it is impossible to prove the causal relationship that led from corporate organizational form to innovations in business technique. Nonetheless, what little data there are point in this direction. Bills of exchange between cooperating banks are first mentioned explicitly in 1291 in two business letters by the Cerchi company, one of the Florentine merchant-banks of this study, operating in England. The language suggests that this technique was routine by this date. Usher (1943, 80) draws the causal connection between bills of exchange and organizational form: "These new types of financial transactions are closely related to developments in the form of business enterprise. They rest upon the establishment of more or less permanent branch houses and agencies." The *instrumentum ex causa cambia* was the method of choice before the bill of exchange emerged (de Roover 1963, 67). This notarized contract, used heavily by the Genoese, also transferred money between places and currencies but on a legal contractual basis through notaries rather than as a private relational understanding among bankers

[4] Similarly, advances in accounting are linked to the emergence of this new unitary and corporate form of banking. Fragments of a cash book from the large Salimbene company of Siena in 1277–1282 document, through references to missing books, the existence of a complex accounting system of at least a half-dozen interrelated account books (de Roover [1956] 1974, 127). Such an accounting system was very sophisticated, but it does not imply the existence of double-entry bookkeeping.

[5] Sapori [1939b] 1955.

[6] The word "company", in turn, descends from *compagnie* or companions. As I will explain later in this chapter, the organizational terms *compagnia* and *società* had elastic meanings in the Middle Ages, going well beyond the domains of economic production and exchange.

The Roman-law form of the founding partnership contract did not change,[7] but there was a new reality and a new sense of continuity through time—continuity through generational time—that had not existed before in business.

In medieval times, the words *company* (*compagnia*) and *corporation* (*societas*) did not refer exclusively to an economic enterprise. Guilds of educators could be corporations,[8] as could militia companies of soldiers,[9] as could protection alliances of noble families,[10] as could protection alliances of anti-noble families.[11] Whatever the activity, from the perspective of the Church, what was required to transform a voluntary contract among men into an organizational body that transcended those men was incorporation into the body of Christ (later called the body politic). Legally speaking, this amounted to a charter or a commission, either from the pope or from the king.[12] Medieval merchants were business partners (companions or *compagnie*) in principal–agent alliances before their transformation into corporations. But upon incorporation, the larger *compagnie* became something more—namely, collective enterprises with geographical spread, temporal depth, and corporate liability.

My thesis in this chapter will be that religious incorporation was more than a metaphor in the origins of the Dugento merchant-banks. Tuscan merchant companies or *compagnie* became merchant-banking corporations or *società* when they were mobilized by the pope into a crusade—to become the state-finance arm of the "body of Christ militant," if you will. Reproduction of this new organizational form beyond its origins in the crusades came through the refunctionality of these economic corporations first into

[7] "In general, the conceptions of a corporation held by civil and canon lawyers of the thirteenth century were lacking in precision. A corporation might be called a *corpus, universitas, communitas, collegium, societas*, or even . . . a *consortium* or *schola*." (Post, 1934, 29). Maitland (1900, xxii–xxiii), however, insists on the sharp distinction between *societas* and *universitas*. I am no Roman-law scholar, but I see a slippage between rigid legal language, which did not change much, and social realities, which were fluid.

[8] Post 1934, 27–60. The language used in this Parisian case was *universitas*. Organizationally, I do not think that the Tuscan merchant-banks and the Parisian university were the same, but there was a similar *corpo* sensibility behind both.

[9] Waley (1969, 165–66) discusses these *societas militum*. Cf. the Tolomei company below, which appears in the Papal Registers, both as an economic company and as a soldier company. This is not the mystery it appears to be to modern eyes: In the 1200s, Italian merchants could turn themselves into Guelf cavalry just by getting onto horses, especially if they were noble. Sapori (1970, 9–14) emphasizes the militarism of Italian merchants of this period.

[10] See Santini 1887 on *società della torre*.

[11] See Waley 1969, 183–86 on *societas populi*.

[12] The pope, kings, and Holy Roman Emperor contested political and legal supremacy in this period.

English customs and wool and then into the patrilineage kinship system of Tuscan city-state elites. As social context changed, Tuscan merchant-banks were released from their crusader origins in the Church and developed new social interactions and economic functions. But the organizational inflection point of economic development in international banking, I shall argue, was catalyzed by the Church—a fact that is not discussed in the economic-history literature.

Simple quantitative indicators of the organizational invention being discussed are the numbers of partners and employees. In the Champagne fairs of the early 1200s, merchants were organized into small partnerships of *compagnie* (often brothers or friends) that went to the fairs together, either as cloth merchants or as money changers. These numerous small companies were fluid both geographically and in partner composition.[13] The corporate merchant-banks of the second half of the 1200s and the first half of the 1300s, in contrast, were both large and organizationally stable. Exact numbers are very hard to come by in this era of sparse surviving business records, but indicators are good enough. During the early 1300s, after the period of this chapter, the largest three Florentine merchant-banks were the Bardi, the Peruzzi, and the Acciaiuoli. In 1310, the Bardi bank had 16 partners; in 1330, it had 11.[14] Over the time period of 1310 to 1345, the Bardi bank employed 346 factors.[15] During the period from 1300 to 1335, the number of partners in the Peruzzi bank ranged from 14 to 21.[16] Over the time period of 1331 to 1343, the Peruzzi bank employed 133 factors.[17] The Acciaiuoli employed 53 factors in 1341.[18] More data on 22 early fourteenth-century Florentine companies are provided in a 61-page memo on my website.[19]

Data as precise as this are difficult to obtain for the 1200s. But according to Kaeuper, the Ricciardi company of Lucca had 74 factors and partners active from 1256 to 1300.[20] According to data from the papal registers and the English Liberate rolls, recorded in the appendix to this chapter, the Bonsignori company of Siena had at least 66 factors and partners active from 1250 to 1267. Also recorded in the appendix, the Scali company of Florence

[13] The same can be said for the sea-voyage *commenda* of Venice and Genoa, although these lie beyond the land-oriented scope of this chapter. See Lopez and Raymond 1955.

[14] Sapori 1926, 243–249.

[15] Sapori 1955b, 730–754.

[16] Sapori 1955, 665–669.

[17] Sapori 1955, 718–729.

[18] de Roover 1963, 86.

[19] Padgett 2005a.

[20] Kaeuper 1973, 56–59.

had at least 35 factors and partners from 1229 to 1269. By the standards of the Middle Ages, these are all large numbers.

In contrast to these large merchant-banks of the mid-1200s to mid-1300s, the largest Florentine bank of the 1400s was the famous Medici bank. Organizationally, this was a partnership system not a unitary corporation.[21] In 1435, the Medici holding company (central office) had only four partners, with seven branch managers as collateral junior partners in their respective branches.[22] In 1469, the Medici bank had a total of 60 employees in all branches, including both clerks and factors.[23] The unitary corporate merchant-banks of the 1200s and early 1300s, in other words, were often larger than the largest bank of the 1400s. The Tuscan merchant-banks in late Dugento and early Trecento were the largest private economic enterprises in Europe in the late Middle Ages.

The organizational invention of the corporation in its medieval sense, I intend to show, was induced by mobilization of the market, in the form of the Champagne fairs, by the Catholic Church for purposes of state finance—namely, to fund its Italian crusades against the Holy Roman Emperor. War pulled the markets into the Church to create something new. Crucial business techniques were invented in the fluid merchant world of the Champagne fairs.[24] But the organizational drive toward sedentary *filiali* was imprinted on the market by the visible hand of the Church. The Church was not just an organizational model to imitate: It actively mobilized Tuscan bankers into becoming papal administrators. The contemporary but separate organizational techniques of Church and business thereby merged. This fusion quickly and directly transformed banks as organizational forms; it slowly and indirectly transformed banking practice.

On a practical level, the financial problem the Church faced was this: landed church assets were spread all over Europe, transcending the national boundaries of kingdoms. Asset dispersion in the "universal church" required comparable geographical dispersion among the Church's financial agents to mobilize those resources. On an ideological level, the fundamental Augustinian "two body" conception of human community—living simultaneously on earth and on the way to heaven—tried to impose an impersonal office

[21] See Padgett and McLean 2006 and chapter 6 in this volume for more details.
[22] de Roover 1966, 81, 377–79.
[23] de Roover 1963, 86.
[24] In particular the idea and methods of procurator or agent. See Face (1958) and Berlow (1971).

conception of organization onto the deeply personalistic world of European feudalism. The mechanism of ideological influence on economic organization was not prescriptive command. It was the dual functionality of private merchant and papal administrator—in other words, being embedded in two worlds at once.

I shall call this bridging mechanism of organizational invention "incorporation and detachment." From the perspective of the state, private merchants (*mercatores*) operating in the fairs and organized as partnerships of companions (*compagnie*) were administratively absorbed or incorporated into the pope's curia (*in nostra camera*) to run papal finance. After the pope's wars were over, these new corporations (*societas*) partially detached themselves and discovered new business for themselves—first with the king of England and then with wealthy aristocratic customers all over Italy, France, and England. From the perspective of the market, these new private unitary merchant-banks operated in and began to dominate international trade, so much so that the Champagne fairs that originally spawned them were eventually driven out of business in the late 1200s in wool-textile trade and in the early 1300s in money exchange.

In this chapter, I shall develop this thesis about the organizational invention of medieval banks in several stages. After this introduction, I present a brief literature review, just to place my thesis in historiographical context. Next I state my argument in "mechanisms of invention" terms compatible with the goals of this volume. Then I offer a macro-historical survey of the primary political and economic events of this period, including both the rise of the Champagne fairs on the economic front and the Italian crusades or wars between the pope and the Holy Roman Emperor on the political front. My coevolutionary narrative seeks to identify the intersection of these two streams of development, tracing consequences for both state and market. Next I offer an organizational analysis of the development of partnership structures among Italian merchant-bankers, as observed and coded from the papal registers of 1243 to 1268,[25] from the English Liberate rolls from 1228 to 1307, and from secondary sources.[26] In the penultimate

[25] These raw data—namely, 87 pages of extracts from these registers, in Latin—are posted on my web page: http://home.uchicago.edu/~jpadgett. For the English reader, Lunt (1934, 302–04, 306, 317–18, 330–31, 338–39) has translated a small sample of this material.

[26] This material—in the form of 123 pages of extracts from various secondary sources—is also posted on my web page: home.uchicago.edu/~jpadgett.

section, I derive some consequences of this organizational form for the evolution of the patrician family. Ultimately, the seed of corporate merchant-banks found fertile soil to reproduce in the *consorteria* social framework of Tuscan patrilineage. The mid-1200s social-network context of the Church was replaced by the late 1200s social-network context of noble patrilineage. The conclusion will offer a brief coda about the fourteenth-century extinction of this organizational form.

Previous Literature

There are quite a few specialist studies of particular companies and towns, mostly written in languages other than English. Curiously, much of the intensive work of this type was done early in the twentieth century, apparently now having gone out of favor, at least outside Italy. I shall utilize these valuable case studies in the section below on organizational evolution.

At the level of broad synthesis, there is not as much research; there are only a few authors who are cited by everyone else. Being economic historians, these synthetic authors explain the rise of merchant-banks through economic factors alone. Robert Lopez (1952, 1976) coined the term *Commercial Revolution.* The sweep of his vision is vast, but he emphasizes the traditional themes of trade opening to the east and the consequent rise of the Champagne fairs as well as the theme of improvement in agriculture. Genoa, Venice, and shipping loom large in his account. Raymond de Roover (1963), without exactly contradicting Lopez, emphasizes instead the "internal" development of superior business techniques. The Tuscan merchant-banks were the culmination of the Commercial Revolution according to de Roover, but the Church and war are not part of his discussion. Peter Spufford (1988) is a monetarist who emphasizes, in his work, the discovery, in the late 1100s, of large volumes of silver in Germany and, to a lesser extent in Italy, outside Siena. Spufford's monetarist focus was fresh when his book was published, but it applies to an earlier period than that with which we are dealing in this chapter. Without denying in any way their importance to macroeconomic takeoff, agriculture, trade, and silver are simply assumed as background in this chapter. My focus instead is on organizational form.

More than anyone else, Armando Sapori (1926, 1955b, 1955c, 1955d, 1970) studied the large, unitary merchant-banks that are the topic of this chapter. His work is the point of departure here. Sapori proposed that Italian unitary merchant-banks emerged through three stages of development.[27] First, companies were built on the basis of families. Second, family companies reached out to recruit outside partners in order to extend their start-up capital (*corpo*). Finally, family-plus-outsiders mobilized depositors to extend their working capital (even though that *sopracorpo* did not technically count as *corpo*). This simple developmental scheme, driven by growth in capital, will provide a null hypothesis against which my own alternative, a more political account, can be evaluated.

In my own papal register data on merchant-banks of the mid-1200s, which will be presented later in the chapter, I shall find empirical problems with Sapori's developmental scheme. It is not that I shall find no relationship between family and company. But I shall find the causality reversed. Instead of Sapori's "company emerging out of family," I shall find "family emerging out of company." The family-alliance (*consorteria*) hypothesis of Blomquist[28] I believe more accurately describes the initial structure of the mid-Dugento Tuscan merchant-banks that I see in the papal registers. From that beginning, family reproduction of partners within the banks, through generational time, transformed merchant nuclear families into magnate patrilineages. The relative dominance of a single "noble" family within the bank thereby grew. Challenging someone with the authority and depth of knowledge of Sapori is not to be done lightly, but I shall report my findings and leave it to future research to sort through the apparent contradictions.

To the best of my knowledge, this papal explanation for the birth of the Italian unitary merchant-bank is original in the historiographical literature. Researchers of the Bonsignori company have certainly understood the papal connection, but I try to generalize the insights of case-study specialists.

Mechanism of Organizational Invention: "Incorporation and Detachment"

Stated at an abstract level suitable for this comparative volume, the mechanism of organizational invention I find illustrated by this Dugento Italian case is "incorporation and detachment." Namely, small and fluid organizational forms of partnership, originally adapted to the Champagne-fair world of the market, were absorbed or incorporated into the new domain of state

27 Sapori 1970, 45–49.
28 Blomquist 1980, 1982.

finance, first by the pope in the 1260s and then by the English king in the 1270s. Organizational invention ensued: Fluid and temporary partnerships evolved into "corporations" (*società*), in the medieval sense of that word defined earlier in the chapter. To repeat the definition: (a) a unitary *corpo* and *ragione sociale* that outlived its contributing partners, with (b) sedentary and more or less permanent geographical branches or *filiali*. Legally, the partnership contract, with its implicit unlimited liability, was elastic enough[29] to absorb this fundamental change in organizational form without requiring any change in Roman law.[30]

In my previous research on Renaissance Florence, I discovered three other multiple-network mechanisms for inventing new forms of organization: namely, "transposition and refunctionality,"[31] "fusion and hybridity,"[32] and "multivocality and robust action."[33] All of these organizational-invention mechanisms involve recombining *different types* of preexisting networks in new ways. Multiple functionality—the participation of hybrid actors in more than one domain—is a common feature of these four mechanisms. "New ideas," coming out of nowhere, are not.[34]

Innovation does not by itself imply that "it worked." To survive beyond antiquarian curiosity, any organizational innovation must first fit into, and be reproduced by, the autocatalytic flows out of which it emerged. This is the meaning of "selection" in an autocatalytic network context.[35] If those flows themselves are altered, then the word (systemic) *invention* is warranted, above and beyond just the word (organizational) *innovation*. Innovation is a new form of organization or artifact. Invention is a system tip induced by that innovation—a change in the selection regime that reproduces that innovation.[36] When, as in this case, there are two flows being

[29] Indeed, as will be discussed below, "partnership" was an organizational concept that could be extended to other than economic purposes—for example, military militias (*societas militum*), family alliances (*consorterie*), and joint-ownership tower societies (*società delle torri*).

[30] For an analogous elastic expansion, in nineteenth-century America, of the legal template of "commercial contract" to cover the radically different meanings of merchant custom, "meeting of the wills," and standardized obligations, see Horwitz 1977.

[31] Padgett 2001, Padgett and McLean 2006), and chapter 6 this volume.

[32] Padgett 2006.

[33] Padgett and Ansell 1993.

[34] For this reason, I dismiss the concept of "genius" or "great man" as a scientific explanation, even if such a person exists. The use of such labels generally implies that the researcher has not understood social context deeply enough to uncover the exact sequence of moves that were made. Galison (2003) deconstructs even Einstein into the sequence of his intellectual moves, involving trains as well as physics.

[35] This definition of "selection" is essentially identical with biologists' conception of "fitness" as relative reproduction but not with economists' conception of "fitness" as relative performance.

[36] Padgett and McLean 2006, 1468–71.

combined—for example, international trade flows, centered on the Champagne fairs, and state finance flows, centered on popes and kings—then the dual-functionality innovation must be reproduced by two (not necessarily consistent) flows at once. Innovation in banks would become invention in banking[37] if the emergence of the new organizational form of bank transformed both the international-trade flows and the state-finance flows in which it participated, in some way that reproduced that organizational form.

Dugento Tuscan merchant-banks qualify as an invention because they altered international trade flows without interruption. The geographical dispersion of sedentary merchants in their interconnected *filiali* delivered luxury goods and textiles to (high-end) consumers more directly than did the traditional market of the Champagne fairs. The fairs gradually declined in the late 1200s and early 1300s, inversely with the rise of the sedentary merchants. This alteration in international trade flows did not occur suddenly. Merchant trade at the Champagne fairs declined in the late 1200s, but currency exchange continued; only in the early 1300s did currency exchange itself at the Champagne fairs decline, leading to the extinction of the fairs.

Dugento Tuscan merchant-banks also qualify as an invention because they too altered state finance without interruption. Individual Italian bankers (*campsores*), sometimes in syndicate, gave short-term loans to popes even before the rise of the large, unitary merchant-banks. With the help of the newly emergent merchant-banks, however, popes and later the English king could assemble money for their armies more quickly, taking loans from their Italian bankers in anticipation of extraordinary tax assessments, which were collected slowly and painfully. Merchant-bankers were repaid, often directly, from the state collections of substantial tax revenues that came in later. Because of this administrative arrangement of sharing tax collection, Italian merchant-banks became insinuated into, and indeed became partial authors of, the budding state-finance administrative machineries of their sponsors.

In the 1270s the English king Edward I introduced a wrinkle into this loans-against-future-taxes financial system, originally invented by the popes, which would have enormous consequences for the developing economy of Florence. Mercantilist English law prohibited the export of precious metal from the kingdom, so loans to the English king had to be repaid in raw

[37] I thank Walter Fontana for suggesting the useful distinction between banks and banking, a distinction upon which Goldthwaite (2009) also insists.

wool, coming largely from monasteries. The introduction of a new English customs system, with Italian merchant-bankers participating in its administration and design, was the innovative solution for achieving this repayment. Organizational innovation in papal banking redounded into organizational invention in English state fiscal administration, which supported the original banking innovation. The enormous consequence for the Florentine economy was the diversion of high-quality English wool exports from their original destination of Flanders to the newly developing textile industry of Florence. Florence thereby came to displace Flanders as the primary center for wool-textile production in Europe.

With this new macroeconomic link between wool textiles and state finance came high merchant profits to couple with enormous (but risky) banking profits. The large unitary merchant-banks entered a self-sustaining "takeoff" phase, with steady merchant business anchoring their highly volatile state-finance business.

A final autocatalytic flow involved people, not money or goods. Originally, Italian bankers were smallish money changers, sometimes but not always Jewish, tainted with the odor of usury. Participation in international trade could improve their social prestige from mere domestic money changers to international merchant-bankers—a considerable climb in social status, though still below the rank of nobility. In the fluid stage of the early 1200s, traveling Italian merchants clustered abroad in expatriate communities and neighborhoods called *nazioni*, with the permission of local potentates. Social bonds within *nazioni* could become close—the social foundation for economic cooperation among overseas nationals—but in the early period, local potentates did not grant permission to stay in their territory for more than three or four months at a time.

With the rise of the large, unitary merchant-banks in the mid-1200s, however, international merchant-bankers became associated with popes and kings. Such legitimation and protection attracted substantial deposits from lay and clerical aristocracies all over Europe. A multiplier effect on the growth of capital thus kicked in, a point that Sapori in particular has emphasized. My compatible point, from a social mobility perspective, is that such customers gave to successful leaders of large, unitary merchant-banks a plausible claim for noble status for themselves. This is my finding of "family coming out of company." Successful bankers in unitary banks became noble-mimicking patrilineages through bringing sons and relatives into the bank and through purchasing property in their native city and in its countryside.[38] This social consolidation contributed to the longevity and corporate character of the bank: Company *corpo* became family patrimony. It also integrated bankers into the ruling patriciate of their city.

Once these audacious claims by merchants to noble status were recognized by their feudal peers, a spillover occurred into Italian elite family structure. A subset of Italian feudal nobility became more mercantile than their French, English, and German counterparts. In the tumultuous politics of the 1200s, which will be described a bit later in the chapter, fragile Italian communal elites had every incentive to reach out for sympathetic allies, as long as the volume of such families was not too substantial. This process of gradual and highly restricted[39] social absorption reached a point in Florence such that merchant families like the Bardi and the Cerchi were declared magnates in 1293, along with other more truly feudal families.[40]

The sequence of organizational invention just described is presented visually in figure 3.1, which identifies by circled numbers the temporal stages of cross-network spillover in this simplified diagram of the European political economy.

To summarize, the Dugento mechanism of organizational invention was the pope reaching into the Champagne fairs to absorb the international merchant-bankers he found there. The unitary merchant-banks, thereby created, warrant the label "invention"—not just "innovation"—because of the systemic spillovers they induced, which reinforced the reproduction of these banks. These multiple-network systemic spillovers included the following: (a) the deflection of international trade from the Champagne fairs of the banks' origin into themselves; (b) the development of the capacity of state finance to anticipate slow revenues; (c) the creation of the English system of customs; (d) the growth of the Florentine textile manufacturing industry; and (e) the absorption of elite merchants into noble family systems of patrilineage. This autocatalytic ensemble of multiple-network flows made not just innovative banks but also a Commercial Revolution.

[38] Blomquist is particularly good at demonstrating these patrilineage spillovers for the companies and families of Lucca.

[39] Restricted because there were not that many large unitary merchant-banks.

[40] This observation speaks to a long-standing debate in Florentine political historiography; see Ottokar 1962, among others.

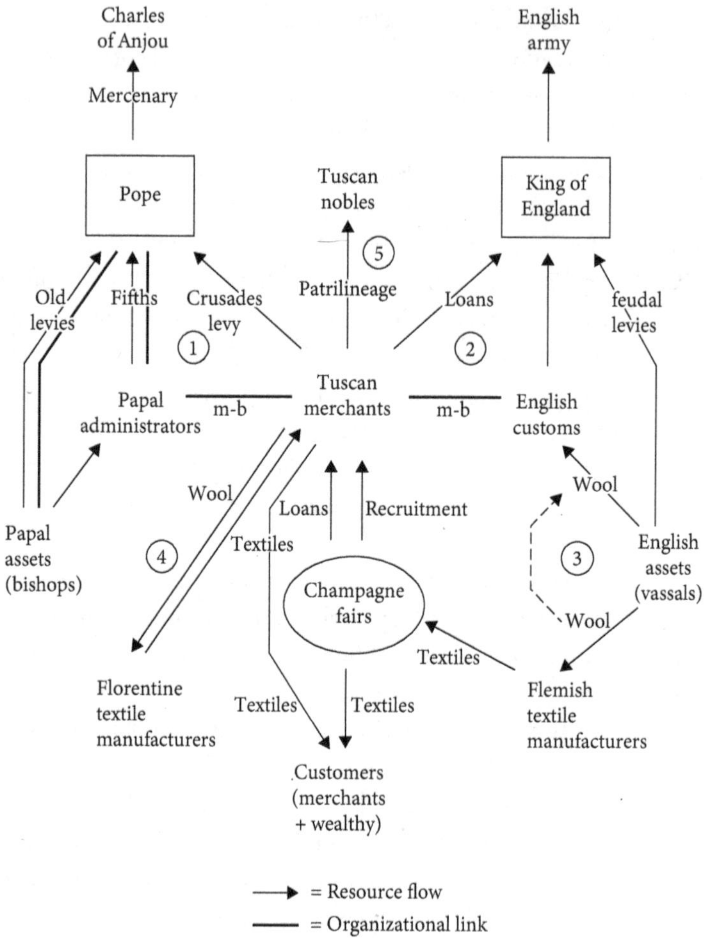

Figure 3.1 Sequence of Emergence of Dugento Tuscan Merchant-Banks

Macro-historical Overview

Such at least is my causal interpretation, based on considerable reading of primary and secondary sources.[41] Now what about evidence and proof? In this section I provide a macro-historical narrative of the wars and political context of the organizational development of the Tuscan unitary merchant-banks. I provide new evidence from the papal registers dating the main innovative incorporation intervention by Pope Urban IV to 1262.

[41] Again, see the lengthy extracts of primary and secondary sources, in various languages, that appear on my web page (Padgett 2009a, 2009b).

In the next section, using both papal registers and existing case studies, I trace the "dependent variable" that responded to this papal intervention, as best I can with imperfect data—namely, growth and transformation in the partnership and branch structures of Italian merchant-banks.

Champagne fairs

The economic seeds out of which the Tuscan unitary merchant-banks grew were the short-term partnerships and agency relations among the geographically fluid Italian merchants who participated in the Champagne fairs outside Paris and in *nazioni* expatriate communities in England, in Flanders, and in other parts of France. The first documented "caravan merchants" to the Champagne fairs, in the 1190s, were from Arras in Flanders and from Asti in the Italian Alps.[42] By 1253, the Genoese had moved to a position of dominance in this merchant trading and exchange business.[43] Italian merchants moving within the orbits of their *nazioni* and hometowns developed short-term agency or "power of attorney" relations[44] with each other in order to take care of each other's business in cities while they were absent. These delegation contracts were primarily between merchants from the same hometown. Longer-term partnerships, to the extent they existed, were often between brothers. The Genoese in particular, because of their sea trade, had the capacity to extend these agency or procurator relations east to the Levant as well as north to Champagne.[45]

The Champagne fairs sprung into existence, probably in the mid-1100s, as a result of the macroeconomic conjuncture of the development of trading routes to the Levant, the discovery of silver in Germany, and the emergence of textile production in Flanders. In its origins, the Champagne fairs had nothing to do with papal finance.

[42] Reynolds 1952.

[43] According to Face (1969, 76): "Using as my criterion their appearance as principals in a contract drawn on a fair of Champagne in the fourth volume of the unpublished cartulary of the Genoese notary Bartholomeus de Fornarion for the year 1253, I have identified 278 individuals as belonging to that group of merchants who dominated the trade between Genoa and Champagne in the middle of the thirteenth century . . . Of these 278 individuals, 146 or approximately 52% are Genoese; 50 or approximately 12% are Florentines; 21 are Sienese; 7 are from Lucca; 6 are from Parma; 4 are from Pistoia; and 3 are from Cremona. In contrast there remain only 6 Asti men. To my knowledge there are no longer any men from Arras in the group." Of course, the fact that the source for this information was a Genoese notary may inflate the estimated Genoese percentage somewhat.

[44] More specifically, delegation contracts of *procurator*, *nuncio*, or *misso*. See Face 1958.

[45] Face (1969) provides a colorful example.

Crusades

Local feudal fighting was of course a constant during this period. But the really big military actions were the crusades. The incorporation intervention that mattered for the invention of corporate banks was not the usual crusades directed toward Jerusalem but the unusual crusades directed back inward toward Italy itself—the so-called Italian crusades of the popes against the Holy Roman Empire starting in 1254 and recurring intermittently until 1302.[46]

Financing of the First Crusade (1096–99) was a decentralized affair of the crusaders themselves, mostly feudal lords but also poor pilgrims who mobilized their own troops and funds.[47] In the Second, Third, and Fourth Crusades (1147–49, 1187–92, 1202–04), kings started to exert more centralized control, starting in the Third Crusade, through levying special taxes mostly on the towns and on the church properties in their reigns.[48] The Fourth Crusade demonstrated the weakness of secular control from the perspective of the Church: The crusaders and their Venetian shippers struck a private deal to capture Constantinople instead of continuing on to conquer the Holy Land.

In the Fifth Crusade (1217–21), Popes Innocent III and Honorius III started to develop the fiscal administrative machinery necessary to exercise centralized papal control. More or less standardized taxes on dispersed church properties were collected by appointed papal nuncios and bureaucrats rather than by local bishops alone.[49] The Knights Templar, as early papal "bankers,"[50] were used to move precious metals collected from local churches and monasteries all over Europe to the East, there to be distributed by papal legates, like Pelagius. Such centralized fiscal distribution blurred the line between crusaders and mercenaries.

Many strides in papal fiscal administration thus were made, including within the pope's central office or *camera* (literally "bedroom"). Without these, the later Italian merchant-banks would have had no one on the papal

[46] The narrative in this subsection draws heavily from Grossman 1965 and Housley 1982.

[47] Or else scavenged them en route.

[48] The first general tax levy was called the Saladin Tithe, a precursor to national taxation. Nobles usually escaped these levies because they (a) directly participated in the military; (b) paid someone to take their place; or (c) simply refused, when the king did not have enough power to coerce them.

[49] Lunt 1934, 1939.

[50] Bankers is in quotes because this refers to physical transport only; no loans were involved.

administration side to work with. But the dramatic failure[51] of the Seventh Crusade (1248–54), led by an alliance between Pope Innocent IV and King/Saint Louis IX of France, illustrated the weakness of even this improved system: Neither slowly assembled monies (i.e., precious metals) nor troops could be delivered fast enough in emergency situations.

Italian Crusades

Enter the Holy Roman Emperors—first the dashing Frederick II (1194–1250), then his tough sons, legitimate Conrad IV (1228–54) and illegitimate Manfred (1232–66), then his adolescent grandson Conradin (1252–68). From their inherited and wealthy base in Sicily, as well as from their disorderly homeland in Germany, all of these emperors aspired to making their grandiose but chimeral titles into reality. All that was necessary was to take over the popes' heartland of Italy using a military squeeze play.

This was not an unattainable goal because all of Italy was militarily fractious at the time—too busy fighting their neighbors to come together to defend "themselves," whatever that meant.[52] Upon Frederick II's revival of the pope-versus-emperor wars,[53] all these local feudal bands of Italian nobles clustered themselves into Guelf and Ghibelline factions. Technically, the labels meant "pro-pope" and "pro-emperor," respectively, but these military bands were concerned primarily about their hostile neighbors. Hence their titular "leaders" could not always rely on them.[54] What this meant for Frederick and for his opponent popes Gregory IX and Innocent IV was that whenever any of them blew a whistle, they could assemble a hodgepodge of unpredictable Italian noble militia to supplement whatever core troops they had. All this made for a very combustible military situation in Italy throughout the 1200s.

Wars in Italy broke out repeatedly: between Frederick and Pope Gregory in 1237–41, between Frederick and Pope Innocent in 1246–48, and between Manfred and Pope Innocent in 1254. With the Tuscan Ghibelline victory in

[51] Including the Muslim capture and ransom of the French king for an amount equivalent to an entire year's tax revenue in France.

[52] Waley 1969 is an especially good survey account of the politics and domestic warfare of the Italian communes during this period. Jones 1997 is a learned but less readable version.

[53] The Investiture Controversy had been in 1075.

[54] Famous theater line: "enter stage right, Guelfs and Ghibellines fighting."

1260 in support of Manfred at Montaperti (outside of Siena), the emperors' dream of control over Italy seemed finally within reach. Since 1232 the popes no longer even had a stable home in Rome: they fled from one mountaintop to another, in search of security and friends, all the while frantically issuing papal bulls that made it seem like their bureaucracy still functioned.[55] The popes were in very grave danger indeed, in spite of their administrative reforms.

Overall, then, the Dugento presents to modern eyes a contradiction: on the economic side, a budding "modernity" of trade, contracts, and markets; on the military side, a bewildering morass of feudal fighting at multiple scales, always with armies of questionable loyalty. These were the raw social-network materials out of which the new Tuscan merchant-banks were built.

Pope Urban IV

Figure 3.2 presents data on the total number of papal bulls or commands issued per year, from 1243 to 1268, as recorded in the papal registries of four consecutive mid-Dugento popes (see entries in the bibliography). Figure 3.3 presents data on the subset of these papal bulls that mentioned Italian bankers.[56] Figure 3.2 demonstrates a heavy papal workload, whose temporal rhythms were tied to their successive wars with the Holy Roman Emperor. Figure 3.3 shows that, while the first connections between popes and Italian bankers certainly preceded Urban IV,[57] it was only under his reign that Italian bankers suddenly became actively organized into these strenuous war efforts. One effect of this mobilization appears to be that the efficiency of bull-issuing behavior by Urban IV skyrocketed: he issued nearly two thousand bulls in 1264, in preparation for his upcoming war with Manfred.[58] Even this unprecedented effort underestimates that year's amazing bull-production rate, since pope Urban died on September 11,

[55] Reading the bureaucratic formality of the papal registers while noticing the skittish movements of the popes who issued these "commands" makes for a somewhat poignant experience. These popes quite literally were running for their lives, barely escaping a number of military traps.

[56] The complete list of these bulls, with verbatim extracts from each, is presented in Padgett (2009a).

[57] A fact to which I shall return later.

[58] "The character of the new pope [Urban IV] was well described by a Sienese merchant, who wrote of him that 'he does what he wishes and no one dares contradict him; he acts more like a temporal lord than a pope and he wants to make the land submit to him as much as he can; no pope since Alexander III has been so constant in his deeds and words.'" Waley (1961, 165).

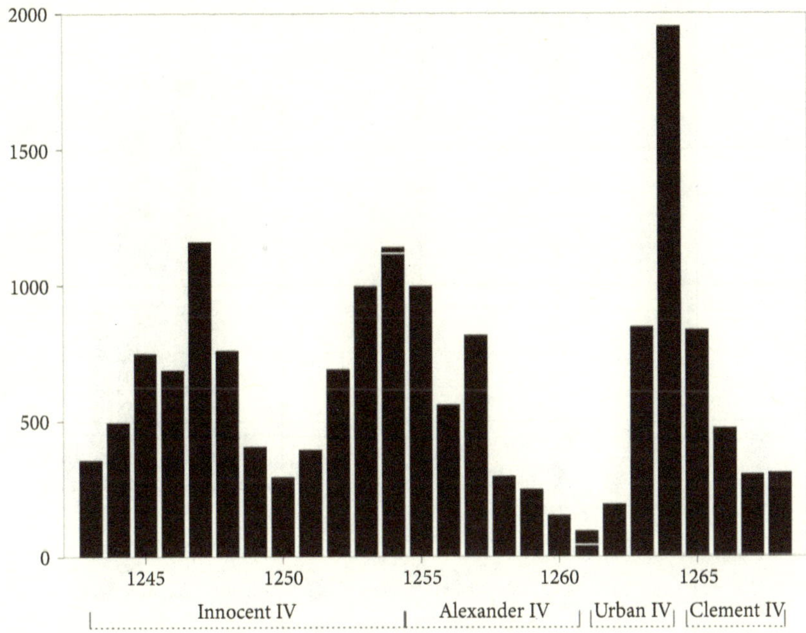

Figure 3.2 Total Number of Papal Bulls, 1243–1268

1264, thereby depriving the time series of over three months of otherwise observable behavior.[59]

What led Urban IV to strenuously mobilize Italian bankers into his war-making fiscal machinery? The problems that Italian merchant-bankers could solve, which the Knights Templar could not, have already been mentioned: (a) transfer of money using *cambium* contracts through their dispersed network of agents (rather than lugging precious metal around on horses) and, most important of all, (b) loans, using capital raised at the Champagne fairs. Italian bankers could solve the fiscal speed and hence the military coordination problems that plagued tax extraction at that time.

Obviously these economic-efficiency advantages were fundamental for lock-in and selection. They represented a major innovation in state finance. But this statement of fiscal consequences is not enough to explain Urban's act of innovation. Given the fairs of Champagne, other popes before Urban could have done the same thing. Both motive and opportunity were there.

[59] Did Pope Urban IV die of overwork?

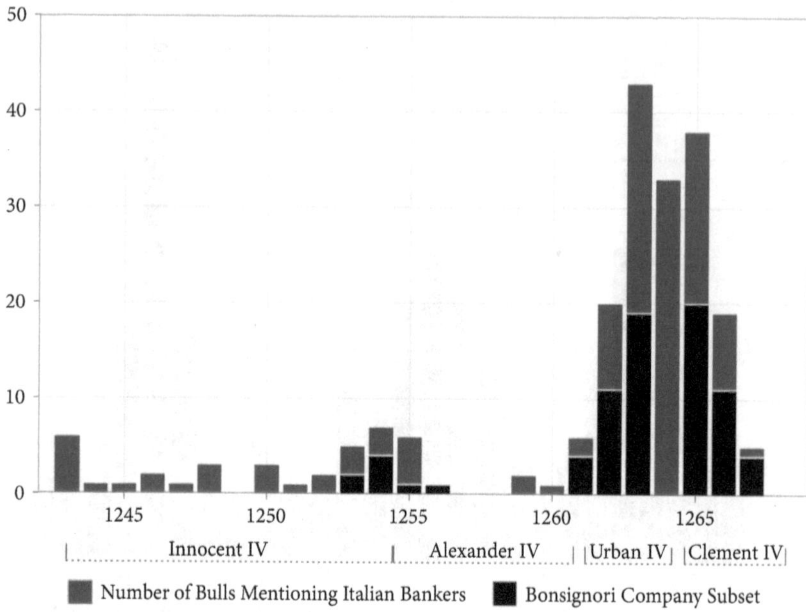

Figure 3.3 Number of Bulls Mentioning Italian Bankers

But only Urban did it. Functionalist explanations of consequence, however helpful for understanding selection, are not causal explanations of genesis.

Urban IV's predecessor, Pope Alexander IV, had the major strategic idea, but not the organizational skills or knowledge to pull it off—namely, to preach "crusade" against the "Anti-Christ" in Italy. The Jerusalem experience of generalized tax levies on church properties (e.g., the *decima*) thereby came on line, and Italian Guelf militias were catalyzed. Some complained that this was a perversion of the crusader ideal.[60] But for the popes of the time, this was a life-or-death matter.

Alexander's specific and quite plausible idea was to preach this crusade in England, where English King Henry III had previously expressed his interest to Innocent IV in commuting Henry's earlier "true" crusader pledge into a "Sicilian Venture" that allowed his second son, Edmund, to invade and to take over Sicily instead of going off himself to the Holy Land. In spite of Innocent's intense struggle with Frederick, this pious pope said to Henry, in effect: "No thanks, go off to the Holy Land." Which Henry never did.

[60] Housley 1982, 37.

Pope Alexander, on the other hand, decided to take up Henry on his offer after all. Taxes on English church properties were raised for the venture, but tax collection was so slow and English resistance so high[61] that enough money never could be assembled quickly enough. The incomplete tax revenues ended up in who-knows-whose pockets. Eventually, this "illegitimate" tax extraction led to the Barons' Revolt in 1258, to the military defeat of King Henry, and to the temporary loss of Henry's power.[62]

Pope Urban took this failed English idea of Alexander and made it French. Urban himself was French, from Troyes in Champagne, not Italian like his predecessors. His previous job had been Patriarch of Jerusalem, in which capacity he was intimately familiar with (normal) crusade finance. One result was that Charles of Anjou, brother of King/Saint Louis IX, was chosen to be the pope's champion instead of Edmund of England. "Crusade" against the Holy Roman Anti-Christ was launched, using church properties in France as the tax base, and the Champagne fairs as liquidity. Charles of Anjou himself was to contribute nothing except himself and his troops. A prince and future king in name but a mercenary, in fact.

Presumably Urban became familiar with the merchant-banking techniques of the Genoese while in his previous job. So then, why did he choose the Tuscans and not the Genoese to be his Italian merchant-bankers? Because his Tuscan merchant-bankers were politically Guelf, and the Genoese were not.[63]

As crusade finances were preached and Tuscans chosen to administer them, unsuccessful Alexander and successful Urban attached these cameral merchants,[64] as they were now called, to the existing papal collection system for its normal levies. First the Bonsignori company of Siena, and later others, were declared *campsores domini papae*, or official bankers to the pope.[65] On the one hand, this involved giving large loans to the pope. On the other hand, this involved transferring papal tax monies from papal nuncios, bishops, and

[61] Gasquet 1905, 347–74.

[62] This interlude of king Henry as only a figurehead led to the creation of Parliament. In 1265, his son Edward I defeated the barons and restored full monarchy, taming but not eliminating the Parliament. The Barons' Revolt of 1258, of course, built upon the more famous Magna Carta revolt of 1215.

[63] The intimate intertwining of Tuscan finance and Tuscan politics will be examined later in the chapter.

[64] Lunt 1934, 51–56; 1939, 599–603.

[65] Jordan 1909, 9–44. In his bulls addressed to third parties, Urban IV himself referred to his chosen bankers not with this official language but with the more personal language of *nostri et ecclesie Romane devoti* (nos. 171–72, 426, 508, 518–21, 536, 542, 562, 2245).

abbots to the pope. By 1277, this also involved being the depositories for papal tax revenues collected overseas.

For such new papal tax-collection activities to be acceptable to local kings—the king of England under Alexander's failed Sicilian venture and the king of France under Urban's successful Angevin venture—there had to be authorizing commissions for the Tuscans from the pope, acceptable to the kings. Such commissions granted permanent residency to the Tuscan cameral merchants, quite an extension from the transient three-month authorizations previously granted to visiting Italian merchants, organized in their *nazioni* communities. Permanent residency of merchants, a prerequisite for permanent organizational branches, grew within this legal umbrella.

Transferring and holding papal tax revenues gave the Italian bankers an enormous float that they could invest for their own profits, through their own international trade. Private merchant activity and papal banking activity were therefore simpatico: Merchants made huge money without popes paying much. With papal (and soon regal) business providing the stable and more or less legally secure foundation, wealthy prelates and barons started making large deposits in Tuscan merchant-banks, as Sapori has emphasized. The earliest such deposits indeed were for the purpose of paying taxes. Later more voluntary investments had ecclesiastical courts to back them up. As Lunt (1934, 56) puts it, "The prominent position held by the Italian bankers in European financial affairs must be attributed in no small degree to the business and protection of the papacy."

Such was the sequence of moves that led to Urban's administrative innovation. Urban himself had a foot in both worlds—the Champagne fairs and the Church, especially the "Church militant" of the crusades. His French biography made mobilization of the market for the church a natural, especially given his Italian predecessor's creative perversion of the idea of the crusade.

However created, Urban's innovation of using Tuscan merchant-bankers as papal fiscal agents locked in because it worked decisively on the military battleground. Urban never lived to see the culmination of his extraordinary efforts. But unlike the previous war failures of Innocent and Alexander, the subsequent (also French) Pope Clement IV and his champion, Charles of Anjou, won a decisive battle in 1266 at Benevento over the fearsome Manfred, killing him directly on the battlefield and seizing his treasure. Another decisive battle over the grandson Conradin in 1268 at Tagliacozzo eliminated him as well. Major emergency loans by Tuscan merchant-bankers, against future tax collections, were essential in these mercenary victories. The Hohenstaufen dynasty of the Holy Roman Empire thereby came to a permanent end, even though other papal wars of various sorts continued, eventually even against Charles of Anjou.

As a subplot in these Italian crusades, Florence temporarily swung Ghibelline in 1260 after Montaperti, with many Florentine Guelf noble families becoming exiles, but then swung back to Guelf in 1266 after Benevento, with many Florentine Ghibelline noble families exiled. Civil war raged, and much of the city and its tower houses were physically destroyed. Similar domestic upheaval occurred in Siena. Reverberations across levels of analysis are common in this period.

The English Customs Service

The next chapter in this political-economic narrative of banking invention is the creation of the English customs service in 1275, which taxed the flow of English wool to Flanders. This new service enabled new English king Edward I, Henry's first son, to copy Pope Urban IV's fiscal innovation and to transplant it to England. Italian merchant-bankers were repaid in wool because precious metals could not legally be taken out of the country by private citizens. Figure 3.4 documents the simultaneity of this creation of the English wool customs and the intense involvement of the Ricciardi company of Lucca at the outset of the long reign of Edward I.

The diffusion of the basic idea to Edward also involved the crusades, a great mixer and shaker in this period. While still a prince, Edward led the failed Ninth "true" Crusade (1271–72) to the Holy Land, belatedly fulfilling his father's pledge. During his slow return, he dawdled for a year in Gascony, then under his own inheritance. Luke Natale of Lucca, acting in the traditional role of transient banker/money changer for the crusades, traveled with Edward during his perambulations and became close friends with him. Luke already had been part of the networked Luchese *nazione* in England, out of which the huge Ricciardi company of Lucca was soon to spring.[66] I have no "smoking gun" quote to prove this, but I presume that Luke educated Edward about the virtues of Urban IV's recent innovations. Siena and

[66] More details on this will follow.

Figure 3.4 Italian Bankers in Extracts from the Liberate Rolls of the King of England

Florence, after all, were not distant from Lucca, and Tuscans mingled in their *nazioni*. For implementation in England, the only hitch was that there needed to be a way to repay loans by the Italian merchant-bankers (like Luke himself). Since Lucca as a city was economically founded on silk manufacturing and trading, the solution lay close at hand. The Luchese *nazione* in England already moved around textiles as a business, and was quite prepared to diversify its mercantile trade from silk to wool, as were the Sienese and Florentine *nazioni*. Thus Urban IV's innovation diffused to England through the self-interested intermediation of the Tuscan merchant-bankers themselves. They then implemented their own advice by inserting their respective *nazioni* into the king's fiscal administration.

The English creation of the wool customs in 1275 was an enormous step toward centralized monarchy. A new and centralized flow of tax revenues was made available to the king, independent of Magna Carta-type fiscal constraints, upon which the Barons' Revolt had recently insisted. The serious financial-cum-political problems that Henry the father had experienced were solved by Edward the son—with help from Italians, who had implemented an originally French idea. Patent-law assumptions about private property notwithstanding, ownership of "inventions" becomes distributed when systems tip.

Overall, my contention is that organizational invention in the "visible hand" of the market was rooted in state finance—or more precisely, in the simpatico linkage between international trade and state finance.

Organizational Evolution

In appendices A–D I present four case studies in tabular form of the organizational development and transactional activity of the largest banks from this period. The case studies are the Bonsignori company of Siena, the Scali company of Florence, the Tolomei company of Siena, and the Ricciardi company of Lucca. These tables array by year the transactional references that I have found to these companies in multiple secondary sources and in two primary sources: (a) the papal registers of Popes Innocent IV, Alexander IV, Urban IV, and Clement IV; and (b) extracts from the Liberate Rolls of the king of England, assembled by Bond (1840). The case-study tables document both the origins and the explosive growth in the 1260s of the Bonsignori, Scali, and Tolomei companies under the sponsorship of the popes (although, in the Tolomei case, this growth was aborted). They also document the origins and the rapid growth in the 1270s of the Ricciardi company under the sponsorship of King Edward I of England.

In appendix E, I provide a comprehensive snapshot of the 20 banks that were absolved from excommunication by Pope Urban IV in 1263 (plus four more in 1265) at the height of his most intensive mobilization of Tuscan merchant-bankers into supporting his Italian crusade against Manfred, both economically and politically.

Origins of Case-Study Companies

As far as my sources enable us to see them, most of the early partners in these four large case-study banks were drawn from the transient Italian merchant communities or *nazioni* in Champagne and in England. They were then mobilized into cross-*nazioni* corporations by the popes or, in the Ricciardi case, by the English king.

The largest early Tuscan bank was the Bonsignori company of Siena. One is tempted to say that numerous famous later Florentine banks (e.g., Frescobaldi, Bardi, Peruzzi) were modeled on this early template, except for the fact that numerous such banks were born at almost the same time.[67] The Bonsignori were the largest, the most favored, and the most successful of the first-generation corporate banks.

The brothers Bonifacio di Bonsignore and Orlando di Bonsignore[68] were bankers (*campsores*) who operated in Genoa and Champagne.[69] In 1252 Bonifacio first appears to have been appointed official banker to the pope (*campsor domini papae*).[70] Bonifacio's first loans to the Church were not corporate in character, by which I mean that they were offered by temporary syndicates of merchants, who reshuffled across transactions through time.

In 1255 or 1256, however, this "di Bonsignore" partnership of brothers was reorganized—throwing out leader Bonifacio and incorporating outsiders instead, the most important of which was Bonaventura di Bernardino. The apparent reason for this becomes clearer through the English Liberate Rolls. Bonaventura's father, Bernardino di Prosperino, had been active in loaning money to the king of England, for expenses and the like, along with other Sienese residents in England. These loans were also not really corporate in character but were offered by syndicates of *nazione* merchants, who reshuffled among themselves.[71] The new nonfamily partnership between Orlando di Bonsignore and Bonaventura di Bernardino (and others), in other words, was a partnership connection between Champagne and England. We shall see similar cross-geographical links develop at the same time in the Scali company.

Why the timing of this? This is the period of the failed English Sicilian venture. Pope Alexander IV gave to King Henry III of England permission to

[67] See appendix E for a quasi-census.

[68] In this context "di" means "son of." Such a name ("John son of Paul"), with no surname, connotes a non-patrician status. Indeed the relative lack of wealth of the early Bonsignori was verified by Chiaudano (1935, 113–14) using early Sienese tax censuses.

[69] See Chiaudano (1935) on Genoa.

[70] English (1988, 12n8) thinks that Bonifacio's appointment by Innocent IV was due to his past link to the previous *campsor domini papae* of Pope Gregory IX, Angelerio Solaficu from Siena. This is quite plausible, but I could not verify that and hence do not record Angelerio in the Bonsignori table.

[71] Indeed, the appendix shows that temporary syndicate partners in England of Bernardino di Prosperi later became regular partners in the Scali and Tolomei companies.

label as a "crusade" Henry's desire to send his second son, Edmund, to invade Sicily, thereby attacking the Holy Roman Emperor. Alexander authorized the collection of crusade tithes on English church property. As discussed above, ultimately this failed, leading to the Barons' Revolt in England. The point here is that this first triggering of the sedentary Bonsignori "corporation" was due to Alexander's early drive toward Italian-crusade papal finance.

In addition to internal English political constraints, a second reason for the failure of this particular war mobilization effort was Alexander's passivity in directing this tax-collection effort (as indicated in figure 3.2). Alexander delegated the collection of taxes on English church property to his hated[72] legates. In sharp contrast, Pope Urban IV directed his own frantic tax-collection drive himself, sending out orders all over France and Italy, but mainly France, in a much more centralized style.

While the details of the early formation of the Scali company are of course different, the broad contour is similar. Contra the general argument of Sapori, the core of the Scali company was not really the della Scala family at all. Rather it was a clique of four Florentine merchants resident in England—Amieri Cosa, Spigliato di Cambio, Rocco di Cambio, and Mainetto Spini. These merchants had been importing cloth into England since 1229, the beginning of Italian *nazioni* communities in England. These merchants also offered a variety of loans to the king from 1245 to 1254 in the reshuffling syndicate manner typical of the time, one deal of which involved Jacobo della Scala.[73]

The alliance between this clique and the della Scala family took place from 1255 through 1257. In 1255, a large loan was given in Gascony to King Henry III's first son, Prince Edward (later King Edward I), in order to raise some troops.[74] In 1256, a substantial partnership in England crystallized to service the Sicilian venture. In 1257, Jacobo's son Cavalcante

[72] The chronicle of Matthew Paris reflects contemporary English attitudes toward this tax collection and toward Italian bankers in general: "The usurers called Chorsins, who went under the name Christians, found a place of refuge and peace in England. First tolerated, and then afterwards openly protected by the pope, they unblushingly called themselves merchants or money-changers of the pope. Prelates were suspended from the collation to benefices until the pope's avarice on behalf of his unworthy barbarians [i.e., mercenaries], who never appeared in England." (Vaughan [1247–1250] 1986, 275; see also pp. 98, 103, 165).

[73] The family surname "della Scala" indicates a higher social status than the others.

[74] Borsari 1994, 19.

joined this new company on a permanent basis, thereby contributing the company's name.[75]

Syndicate loans directly to the English crown continued in 1258 and 1259, but in 1261 we see the massive entry of a greatly enlarged "Scali" company into the pope's own service. This was the year that the Scali company was appointed *campsores domini papae*, joining the Bonsignori company in this role.[76] The appointment of this second "favored banking company" was made by Pope Alexander IV at the very end of his life, probably in order to strengthen his (failed) financial connection to England. The Bonsignori had restructured themselves to strengthen their own English connection, but their economic roots remained primarily in France. The "Scali," however, had been in England from the Italian *nazioni* beginning.

The Tolomei company comes closest to fitting the Sapori model of "family plus outsiders" because of the extensive involvement of the patrician Tolomei family, mostly in small loans to the city government. But even these various Tolomei family members combined and recombined in their transactions in a fluid manner.

The Tolomei case is complicated by the fact that when the pope first mobilized them into papal finance, during the failed Sicilian venture, he actually mobilized two companies of them. The first was the earlier family-dominated business. This set of partners moved for a few years into papal finance but then dropped out and went back to wool trading. The second apparently new company, the Scotti-Tolomei company, was an alliance between three of the Tolomei with numerous other Sienese, including four of the Scotti. This second company was appointed official *campsores domini papae* by Alexander late in his life. This second company also did not stay long in papal finance. Urban launched an investigation into its unsatisfactory financial performance.[77] The first Tolomei company was called in to broker a compromise between Pope Urban and the Scotti-Tolomei. While the first Tolomei company escaped blame in the matter, neither company figured as major papal bankers again.

[75] I hypothesize that the Scali name was chosen for the firm, in spite of its leadership by others, because of the superior social status of that name. An alternative hypothesis is that the name was chosen because of the greater capital contribution of della Scala. But no partnership contracts, which would list capital contributions, of any of these companies survive. Later the less prestigious Cambii family spun out of the Scali company to form their own company. When they did so, they took on a new, more noble family name for themselves: the de Mozzi.

[76] Jordan 1909, 11.

[77] Jordan 1909, 15; Lunt 1939, 602–3; Mucciarelli 1995, 105–6.

I do not have much partnership data over time on the Scotti-Tolomei, probably because they did not last long. But the fact that the regular Tolomei, when they dropped back to normal wool merchants, also dropped back to shifting partnership patterns is the exception that proves the rule.

My fourth and final case study of the Ricciardi company shows how the popes' financial innovation worked when it was transposed 10 years later to England by the finally new[78] king Edward I. King Edward made an extension to this state-finance system of enormous consequence for the wool industry in Florence: the introduction of a wool customs to pay back Tuscan bankers' loans to the English king.

The first page of the Ricciardi table in the appendix, which takes us through 1266, demonstrates that originally there were two almost completely distinct sets of Lucchese merchants who later combined into the unified Ricciardi company: one set operating in Lucca, the other set operating in England. The Lucchese merchants in Lucca were manufacturing fine silk cloth. The Lucchese merchants in England were selling that silk cloth to wealthy clients, including to King Henry III himself. The Ricciardi name descended from the Lucca half of this cooperation—in particular, from one Ricciardo di Graziano di Ricciardo, a silk dyer or *tintor*. Each of these two geographically distinct subsets of merchants demonstrated considerable fluidity in their partnerships—namely, partnerships formed and re-formed among merchants within these two locations over time. The "almost" part of the first sentence in this paragraph refers to the one exception of Peregrino Sesmundi, who in 1241 apparently moved from Lucca to England, thereby creating the only partnership bridge in these early data between these two subsets of merchants.

Based on these data, historians have assumed that an integrated Ricciardi company existed in the 1240s and 1250s, with one branch making silk and the other branch selling silk. In my opinion, this reads history backward: inferring early structure from what followed. No doubt there were cooperative exchange relations between these two complementary halves of the supply chain. But I don't see the evidence, such as it is,[79] as demonstrating anything more than regularized cooperation.

The Ricciardi company exploded in partnership size, however, in the 1270s, with geographical branches appearing not only in England but also

[78] King Henry III's reign lasted 56 years. King Edward I's own reign lasted 35 years.

[79] To repeat footnote 75, no founding contract of any partnership has survived from this period, so this disagreement in interpretation of the data is not capable of definitive resolution.

in Ireland and Paris. The original Lucca silk-manufacturing branch recedes from sight in the sources, but an extensive partnership list in 1286 leads to the presumption that the silk-manufacturing "home office" was still there, in the misty background. The Lucca branch itself was overshadowed by the transformation of the Ricciardi company into the primary bankers of the English king. As a consequence, the most important partner of the company was no longer one of the Ricciardi family but rather Lucasio Natale (Luke of Luka in English sources), the personal banker and friend of King Edward I.

Judging from timing, the triggering event in this transformation of the Ricciardi company appears to be loans[80] given to the still prince Edward in Genoa in 1272 during his leisurely return to England from his failed Ninth Crusade. Lucasio Natale had accompanied Edward throughout his crusade, such travels building upon the earlier social and business ties established between his compatriots and King Henry III in their previous roles as silk salesmen to the king.[81] It seems plausible to assume from their speed of implementation, immediately after Edward's November 1272 accession to the throne, that the financial innovations by Edward—namely, to appoint the Ricciardi company as favored state financiers, and to make wool customs the mechanism of repayment—were rooted in these travel conversations and these loans between Lucasio and Prince Edward. Through *nazioni* linkages with other Tuscan bankers abroad, Lucasio would have been well-informed about the contemporary financial innovations made by his Sienese and Florentine colleagues. If this is correct, then Tuscan bankers were not only the beneficiaries but also the (self-interested) authors of innovation in English state finance.

Tuscan bankers in general, and the Ricciardi company in particular, benefited greatly in trade from their increased control over the flow of English wool exports in repayment for their loans to the English king. In 1273, 24.4% of all licensed wool exports from England were in the hands of Tuscan companies. The distribution of wool export trade in that year was as follows:[82]

[80] Kaueper 1973, 81; Del Punta 2004, 163. In 1255, Edward had received large loans in Gascony from the Scali, so he was directly familiar with Tuscan bankers. That previous event had triggering consequences for the Scali company as well.

[81] As is well-known, by Weber (2003) among others, state financial administration and the "king's wardrobe" blended in medieval government. Indeed the literal translation of the papal *camera* is the pope's "bedroom." Orlando Bonsignori, Pope Innocent IV's favorite banker, slept in the pope's bedroom, though I assume not in the pope's bed.

[82] Schaube 1908, 68, 183, reproduced in Kaeuper 1973, 43–44.

Scotti of Piacenza	2140 sacks
Riccardi of Lucca	1080 sacks
Frescobaldi of Florence	880 sacks
Bardi of Florence	700 sacks
Nicholas Testa of Lucca	700 sacks
Macci of Florence	640 sacks
Falconieri of Florence	620 sacks
Cerchi of Florence	400 sacks

Twenty years later in 1294, a crisis year, the wool exports in the hands of Tuscan companies that were seized by the king were as follows:[83]

Riccardi of Lucca	412 sacks
Frescobaldi of Florence	360 sacks
Cerchi Neri of Florence	350 sacks
Cerchi Bianchi of Florence	301 sacks
Mozzi of Florence	261 sacks
Pulci of Florence	257.5 sacks
Frescobaldi Neri of Florence	154 sacks
Spini of Florence	153.5 sacks
Bardi of Florence	99 sacks
Bettori of Lucca	35 sacks

These English wool-export lists give a hint of the growth in numbers of Tuscan unitary merchant-banks during the second half of the Dugento, after the initiating events analyzed here.[84]

Pope Urban IV and the Corporate Organizational Form

Before he was elected pope in 1261, Urban IV was Jacques Pantaléon of Troyes. Troyes was the largest of the four towns that comprised the Champagne fairs. Urban IV, in other words, was from the Champagne fairs. Speaking a bit metaphorically, Urban IV was himself the incorporation of the fairs into the papacy. Speaking less metaphorically, he knew how they

[83] Kaeuper 1994, 44.

[84] A longer list of 16 Tuscan firms active in England, from 1283, is provided in Lunt (1939), appendix VI, 641–65. Blomquist (1971, 173–78) provides a valuable comprehensive list of export-oriented companies in Lucca in 1284, which includes more than companies involved in English trade.

worked. This knowledge was used and polished through his appointment in 1255 as Patriarch of Jerusalem, shortly after the disaster of the failed Seventh Crusade.[85] Rather than being an insular man of Rome,[86] Urban IV was a man comfortable in the extended trading and military networks of medieval Europe.[87]

In figure 3.2, we have already seen evidence of Urban IV's capacity for hard work, most of which involved financing Charles of Anjou's army for war against Manfred. Urban IV did not delegate like Alexander IV; he took charge personally. Looking a bit more into the details of figure 3.3 reveals an interesting wrinkle in Urban's mobilization of Italian bankers. At first, Pope Urban IV relied heavily on the Bonsignori company, which he had inherited from his predecessors. The switch from projected English troops to projected French troops, after all, actually played to Bonsignori strengths. In 1264, at the very peak of Urban IV's frenzy, however, he dropped the Bonsignori company entirely, relying instead on a diversified range of other banks. One long-term consequence of this shift in centralized papal strategy was to propel the diffusion of the corporate organizational form beyond a few papal favorites out into the market at large.

What lay behind Urban's sudden shift toward diversification? I suggest that Urban IV's tactical approach in 1264 was not inconsistent with the Champagne fair experience of Jacques Pantaléon—except that the companies involved now emerged at a vastly larger scale and scope than before, with permanent branches instead of fluid partnerships. Urban IV from Champagne was using the market logic of Champagne to mobilize for war.[88]

Reasonable as this cognitively predisposing factor may be, Edward English has discovered that Urban had more on his mind than efficient market logic when he chose his bankers. The Guelfs and the Ghibellines of Siena and Florence had just had their battle of Montaperti in 1260, resulting in Ghibelline victory and in the installation of pro-emperor regimes in both Siena and Florence. This was the battle that led to the nadir of the popes' fortunes in Italy. Urban was basically surrounded by his enemies. His strategy for counterattack was to excommunicate both Ghibelline cities but then

[85] This was the crusade where the army of King/Saint Louis IX was defeated in Egypt. He was captured and ransomed for about one year's revenues of the entire kingdom of France.

[86] Indeed as I mentioned above, he was too much on the run ever to reside in Rome.

[87] See footnote 58 above.

[88] Padgett and McLean (2006) refer to such examples of "old tool for new purpose" as the organizational-invention mechanism of "transposition and refunctionality."

to target with absolution particular lists of Guelf allies and potential allies.[89] Foremost among these absolution lists were companies of merchants and companies of soldiers.[90] These lists are the source of the 1263 quasi-census of internationally oriented Florentine and Sienese companies presented in the appendix. It is worth noting that most of the new companies in this 1263 list are Florentine, not Sienese. Not all of the companies absolved in 1263 were ultimately used for papal finance in 1264 (at least in the data I coded), but many of them were. This may be the first intimation of a gradual takeover of papal business by the Florentines. If so, it places the politics of Guelf versus Ghibelline at the center of the explanation of the economic victory of Florence over Siena in the late Dugento.[91]

There was a political logic involved in the diversification of banks, in other words, as well as a market logic. Not only the original Bonsignori and Scali companies but also most of the Guelf-inclined international bankers in Siena and Florence were mobilized into Urban's crusade against Manfred—this in opposition to the regimes of their own cities.[92] Papal oil was thrown on the fires of Tuscan civil wars. When Charles of Anjou finally defeated Manfred in 1266, previously exiled Sienese and Florentine Guelfs triumphantly returned to their cities, exiled ruling Ghibellines in their turn, and destroyed their tower houses. Powerful noble Ghibelline families[93] fled to the hills and to friendlier cities, bitterly plotting their revenge and giving Dante much to write about.

[89] English 1988, 21. See Urban IV bulls vol. 1, nos. 71, 161; vol. 2, nos. 175, 362–4, 410–11, 428–30, 447, 463, 465, 501, 532, 557, 570, 701; vol. 3, nos. 86, 124, 143.

[90] For companies of nobles, see Urban IV bulls nos. 175, 274. (January 5, 1263; March 6, 1263.) For companies of merchants, see Urban IV bulls nos. 161, 362–24, 410–11, 428–30, 447, 463, 465, 501, 511, 532, 557, 570, 701–03. (Dates range from July 5, 1263 to August 3, 1264.) The two bulls absolving nobles contained long lists of companies of *nobiles viri*; whereas the bulls absolving merchant companies were on a case-by-case basis. Note that nobles were absolved before merchants; this supports English's interpretation of a political motivation to Urban's technique of mobilizing Tuscany for crusade—namely to excommunicate *en masse* Siena and Florence but then to absolve Guelf factions that supported him within the cities. Nobles and merchants were just different wings of the church militant, in Urban's eyes.

[91] I do not deny the additional crucial importance of the new Florentine wool industry in this economic victory.

[92] This contested civil-war context led sometimes to strange contradictions. Orlando Bonsignori, for example, the "lead" partner of the Bonsignori banking company of the pope, actually aligned himself with the Ghibelline regime of Siena—so much so that he fought in the Sienese Ghibelline army at Montaperti against his papal employer's allies the Guelfs. This is someone who chose city over company, suffering exile as a consequence. Needless to say, Orlando laid low in the papal registers after this political choice, with Bonaventura emerging instead as the economic leader. But Orlando still functioned officially as one of the four directors of the firm. Pope Urban IV's effort to splinter the politics of Tuscan cities, in other words, sometimes splintered the politics of his companies instead. Perhaps this was one triggering stimulus that led Urban to drop the Bonsignori as primary bankers in 1264.

[93] Listed in Libro di Montaperti.

The aspect of this story that interests us here is the organizational consequence of this successful mobilization, both political and economic, of Tuscan bankers for the Italian crusade. Corporate organizational form, in the medieval sense of that term, is evident in the four case studies in the appendix in the following ways:

1. Home-office (director) partner roles and branch-office (nondirector) partner roles are distinguished linguistically in the papal bull documents.[94] In the appendix, this linguistic differentiation of roles is indicated by underlining the bull number of the home-office partner, where such language appears.
2. Branches are indicated by the geographical clustering of different nondirector partners (*soci* in the documents) into specialized transaction locations.[95]
3. In contrast, director-partners are characterized by geographical diversity, as they write "home office" letters to all of their branches.
4. Under the reign of Urban IV, the highly corporate language of *societas*[96]—as in *Societas Ricciardorum*—first appears in the papal registers, although it is not yet common.[97] Language such as in footnote 94 was more commonly used instead. Lack of standardization in language is yet another indicator of how new this emergent organizational form was.

I have emphasized the temporal simultaneity of the emergence of the corporate organizational form in Tuscan banking and of financial mobilization by the popes for their Italian crusades. It seems clear that papal finance

[94] An example would be "Andree Jacobi, Facio Juncte et Bonsignori Raynerii, sociis delectorum filiorum Rolandi Bonsignoris, Bonaventura Bernardini et Raynerii Jacobi, civium et mercatorum Senensium, campsorum camere nostre. . ." (Registres d'Urbain IV, 2, n. 9.) Here Andrea di Jacopo, Facio di Giunte and Bonsignore di Raineri were carrying out in France a financial order issued by Urban IV, in the name of their company directors Orlandino di Bonsignore, Bonaventura di Bernardino, and Raineri di Jacopo. Lunt (1934, 306) translates a similar example as ". . . take care to assign that money in our name to the beloved sons Andrew Jacobi and James Gregorii, colleagues of the beloved sons, Bonaventura Bernardini and Rayner Jacobi, citizens and merchants of Siena." (Registres d'Urbain IV, 2, n. 154.)

[95] This criterion alone is not decisive, because it could also indicate only *nazioni*, as mentioned above. Indeed, members of branch offices of unitary firms were still members of *nazioni* communities, just like their more fluid colleagues. But this criterion, even by itself, does rule out "caravan merchants" (Reynolds 1952).

[96] This contrasts with the previous language of *soci* or partners.

[97] Urban IV: bull number 159 (July 5, 1263). Under Clement IV, the language becomes somewhat more frequent: bull numbers 86, 124, 731, 803. But still not as common as it becomes later, when language is more standard.

linked the Champagne fairs to war. For where, after all, did the Tuscan bankers get their original monies for loans to the pope, and later to the English king, in the first place? From the fairs.

I want to close this section by speculating about "why" the corporate organizational form in particular. Different aspects of this form were connected to different aspects of bankers' connection with the pope. "Large" seems induced by the magnitude of the extraordinary crusade taxes on Church properties, under the constraint that only a few favored banks were selected for the job. "Geographically dispersed" seems induced by the geographical dispersion of those Church assets. Loan money could be raised centrally in Champagne, but repayment was scattered all over Europe. Tuscan bankers had to be stably attached to papal administrators all over Europe for them to be repaid. The official church office of the *campsores domini papae* was the legal method to achieve this most securely. These practical aspects lead us toward, but not quite all the way, to the concept of "corporate."

Corporate in the medieval sense meant body, in particular collective body, as in "body of Christ."[98] This conception implied the continuity of the organization beyond the participatory contributions of its members—as in procession, it was hoped, all the way to heaven.[99] I see no evidence whatsoever of Tuscan merchant-bankers thinking in terms of religious theology. But the pope certainly treated them as part of the "body of Christ militant," along with other more overtly military arms of that "procession" called crusade. They became absorbed—officially with titles, bulls, and commissions—into the papal cameral administration of taxes. This was not just one aspect of their business (although it was that); this was the legal and economic foundation for most of their subsequent "private" business. The central organizational consequence of this absorption or incorporation, in my view, was continuity—residential continuity, regularized business-flow continuity, long-term loans, legal-liability continuity across partners, and finally social-attributional continuity, both by bankers of themselves and by others of them. The practical innovations in business technique discussed at the beginning of this chapter—namely, regularized business correspondence, bills of exchange, complex account books, and long-term investment—presuppose organization continuities of these sorts. In the next section, I evaluate how Tuscan bankers turned this organizational

[98] Cf. Kantorowicz 1957.

[99] Duby (1980) provides a rich discussion of "body of Christ," "procession," and "crusade" ideology in practical political use within the highly conflictual context of twelfth-century France.

continuity into social reality through passing their business down through the generations of their newly constructed patrilineages.

One quotidian way in which corporate business technique was imparted to Tuscan merchants by their Church absorption should not escape mention just because it is obvious. Where might Tuscan merchants have gotten their revolutionary idea of a home office sending regular correspondence to sedentary *filiali*? To whose letters, after all, were they themselves responding? Long before merchants adapted bulls to private business, volume upon volume of papal registers bear silent testimony to the sophistication of medieval church organization.[100] Even though I have never seen this suggestion in the literature, it does not seem so outlandish to suggest that Tuscan unitary bankers absorbed a secular version of church organization into themselves when they became agents of—indeed when they became part of—the papal *camera*.

The "origin of banking" framing of most economic historiography on unitary merchant-banks and otherwise is modernist in that it looks to explain economic consequences by economic causes.[101] I too am interested in explaining organizational genesis. But I insist that the multiple social-network contexts of inventions be taken seriously, for these are the raw materials being recombined into invention. Multi-functionality and spillover are rife in social invention processes, not only in part because of objective turmoil but also in part because other times and places may not parse "the economic," "the political," and "the social" as we do. Scientific explanation requires historical sensitivity to context, to mentalité, and to feedback.[102]

Family Out of Company

Church documents in the 1200s were in Latin. Hence, second names ending in "i" usually implied the ablative "of"—for example, "Franciscus Guidi" meant "Francis son of Guido." Because of this medieval method of

[100] Chandler (1977) is not making so different an argument when he points to military antecedents of the revolutionary nineteenth-century industrial organization of the railroad.

[101] Recent efforts by economic historians to be multidisciplinary, such as Greif 2006, do so only by translating politics and kinship into their economic aspects rather than by taking alternative logics on their own historical terms.

[102] It would take me too far afield to develop this point, but I am arguing here for a processual or "mechanism" (Hedstrom 2005) view of science, rather than an input-output "covering law" view of science. This processual view makes go away much of the usually assumed contradiction between history and science.

naming, kinship relations can be inferred from names. With two names strung together to make a person, one can infer the nuclear-family kinship relations of brother and father[103] but not that of cousin. With three names strung together in ablative form, first cousins can be identified. As ablatives evolved into surnames,[104] more distant "clan" relations can be inferred from a common surname. Patricians or nobles in the Dugento often added a "de" to their last names. Hence both kinship and social status can be inferred directly from names—a fact, of course, that was no accident to the people involved.

According to the documents that I examined, when Sapori referred to the first stage of unitary company development as "family," he must have been referring to nuclear family. Non-noble persons, with only ablative names, overwhelmingly predominated in the Dugento partnership lists, even though noble family names do occasionally appear. Interestingly, however, the overall company name, once it developed, frequently referred to the noble member of the partnership, even though that member may not have been the true economic leader.[105] An example discussed above is the Scali company—named after Jacobus de Scala, even though that company was founded and led primarily by a clique of four non-patrician merchants in the Florentine *nazione* in England. Using the family name of the company to infer the "family foundation" of the company, therefore, is a surprisingly precarious enterprise, at least for the mid-Dugento.

In this section I shall measure kinship connections among partners directly. I shall find that Blomquist's *consorteria* hypothesis fits the cross-sectional partnership data of the mid-Dugento better than does Sapori's more famous "core family plus outsiders" hypothesis. Viewed over time, Sapori's "company out of family" portrait is not wrong as long as the word "family" refers to alliances of mostly non-noble nuclear families. This caveat is not commonly observed in the literature, wherein the family name of the company is usually what is referenced. When the word "family" means

[103] Although not without some chance of error in cases where two unrelated persons had fathers with the same first name.

[104] Three names strung together implies self-consciousness of lineage, at least at the common grandfather level. As such self-consciousness of lineage develops, grandchildren and beyond can turn their ablative ancestor name "of Guido" into a new surname for themselves of "Guidi."

[105] "Leader" in this sentence is defined in terms of the transactional behavior documented in the appendix. As I have said numerous times, no partnership contracts survive from this period; these would have listed the start-up capital investment of the various partners. It is possible, indeed likely, that noble families contributed more than their fair share of the *corpo*, even if they were passive investors.

patrilineage, I find that the image of "family out of company" fits the data much better, with merchant nuclear families growing into patrician patrilineages if the unitary company succeeded.

Summary statistics about kinship relations among the partners of the companies whose excommunication pope Urban IV had absolved in 1263–64, and pope Clement IV absolved in 1265, are as follows:[106]

proportion partners in largest-family (nuclear or otherwise) subset of partners

$$= (\Sigma_i \text{ \# largest family subset}_i)/(\Sigma_i \text{ \# partners}_i)$$

$$= 71/197 = .360$$

proportion partners in any-family (nuclear or otherwise) subset of partners

$$= (\Sigma_i \text{ \# partners with any kin as partners}_i)/(\Sigma_i \text{ \# partners}_i)$$

$$= 124/197 = .629.$$

Small companies with four or fewer partners do not really fit my unitary-bank definition. If these are excluded, then the kinship proportions shrink to .297 and .600,[107] respectively.

The connection between kinship and unitary merchant-banks, therefore, was high. But this connection was not just a single core family per company. Within these companies there were about as many partners in kinship relations outside the largest kin group as there were partners within the largest kinship group. If Dugento companies are to be described as "family plus outsiders," then it must be understood that "outsiders" had many family relations among themselves. Indeed, simple inspection of the lists shows that Dugento unitary companies were alliances of families—not alliances of noble patrilineal families, like the military tower societies,[108] but alliances of merchant nuclear families.

Blomquist (1980, 18) has noticed this already, with regard to the Ricciardi company:

> Despite its legal status as a simple partnership, the Ricciardi enterprise appears to have been similar functionally to the consortial organizations

[106] Readers are free of course to look in the appendix at the particular companies comprising these aggregate statistics. I included all absolved companies, including the Bonsignori, Scali, and Tolomei, in the statistics.

[107] The exact ratios are (52 / 175), and (105 / 175).

[108] Santini 1887; Waley 1969, 170–78.

> into which the families of the Lucchese urban elite commonly banded together. I am suggesting here that the large-scale international *societas* differed from a consortium (in Lucca called *consortatus*) only in that its purpose was to engage in commerce and finance rather than to provide political and [military] refuge for its members.

One further documentary example confirms directly Blomquist's hypothesis of a Dugento parallel between *societas* and *consorteria*. The absolution for the (regular) Tolomei company of Siena appeared in a long list[109] of other Sienese "companies," most of whom were composed of *socii nobelium*—a term that did not appear otherwise in my extract of papal bulls about Italian merchant-banks. Comparison with another bull[110] to the exiled Guelf militia of Siena in 1263 confirms the impression that the first list was a list of soldier companies, not of merchant companies. The Tolomei company was apparently both a merchant company and a soldier company at the same time,[111] probably because the family in question was noble.

Medieval Italian documents from the 1200s refer to *societas militum*,[112] which were noble families or alliances of noble families organized into cavalry bands.

City militias were alliances of such bands.[113] The Tuscan civil wars of the 1260s between Guelfs and Ghibellines were carried out by *societates* of noble soldiers from Florence and Siena. The Tuscan financial mobilization of the 1260s by Urban IV, as we have seen, was carried out by *societates* of mostly non-noble merchants from Florence and Siena. Urban's purpose in absolving the merchant companies from his excommunication of their fellow citizens was to mobilize them[114] for war—specifically for his "religious" crusade against Manfred—which he successfully did. This

[109] *Registre d'Urbain IV*, 2, n. 175 (5 January 1263).
[110] *Registre d'Urbain IV*, 2, n. 274 (6 March 1263).
[111] See the registration of *Registre d'Urbain IV*, 2, n. 175 in the 1263 column of Appendix C. Orlando Bonsignori is another prominent Sienese example of a merchant who was also a soldier. The linguistic and social ambiguity of the Tolomei persisted in the deliberations of the Siena city council in 1293: "Cum societas et nobilis viri de societate filiorum ser Jacobi de Talomeis" (cited in Mucciarelli 1995, 19).
[112] Waley 1969, 166, 183.
[113] Waley (1969, 83): "Joint inheritance might cause the obligation to fall on a number of co-heirs, particularly at a time when there had been no recent review of cavalry service: those owing it would then have to provide a cavalryman between them. This must considerably have complicated the task of organizing the militia, for nearly two-thirds of the Florentine horses recorded in the *Libro di Montaperti* (1260) were owed jointly by *consortes*." Waley (1969, 135): "The approximate numbers of Florentine cavalrymen engaged in the four great battles of 1260 to 1325 are as follows: 1260 (Montaperti) 1,400."
[114] "Them" here means both noble soldiers and non-noble merchants.

intertwining of military with economic with religious organization, all in the name of crusade, can't get much more intimate than this. With crusade the pope spanned deep social-class divisions within Tuscan cities[115] and united pro-pope but fractious social segments in Florence, Siena, and Lucca into "Guelf."

Blomquist's observation about *societas* as *consorteria* adds an important subtlety to our point about papal absorption. Yes, incorporation imparted continuity ideologically through the "body of Christ militant" and practically through papal administration. But the modular units being so incorporated were medieval at their core: *societas militum* and the like. Odd as it may seem to us, unitary merchant-banking companies in Tuscany were, in their origins, the economic wing of a holy army that the pope built for his Italian crusade. The family-alliance or *consorteria* nature of the internal partnership structure of unitary banks reflected the way that Dugento Italy normally organized itself into militia. Diversification of one favored merchant company, the Bonsignori, into a state-finance "market" of economic companies paralleled the assembly of noble military companies into a feudal army.

Once released from their papal origins, international merchant-banking companies preserved their organizational imprinting as modular *consorterie*, reinforced in the late 1200s not by war but by kinship.

As discussed earlier, "corporate" in the medieval sense implied collective continuity through time. One hypothesized implication for economic organization of continuity is that partners of corporate companies should recruit their sons to replace them, to carry on their successful business after they died. To test this hypothesis, one needs lists of partners over generational time. In my 1260s case, this means lists of the partners into at least the 1280s. With only three case studies that do this, my conclusions about this hypothesis can only be suggestive. Nonetheless, for what they are worth: (1) five of the twenty-three partners in the Bonsignori company of 1289 were descendants of Bonsignori company partners in the previous generation;[116] (2) eight of the sixteen partners of the Scali company of 1282 and 1284 were

[115] I have not the space to go deeply into these social-class cleavages, but they were deep. In 1250, for example, the Florentine non-noble *Popolo* rose up militarily, on their organizational foundation of guilds, to make a 10-year interlude of republican government. This lasted until the Ghibelline victory at the battle of Montaperti in 1260. The emergence of this non-noble (even anti-noble) *societas populi* roughly in the same period as the merchant-bank *societas* may not be causally connected, but together they imply a partial diffusion of noble forms of social organization, like *societas* and *consorteria*, downward.

[116] Four were the same people and hence do not count in the denominator.

descendants of Scali company partners in the previous generation;[117] and (3) five of the seventeen partners of the Ricciardi company of 1286 were descendants of Ricciardi partners in the previous generation.[118] Are these numbers high? I have no baseline model against which to statistically evaluate these numbers. But they at least are not inconsistent with the "sons replace fathers" continuity hypothesis. As telling as anything is the obvious fact that these three companies (and quite a few others) reproduced their organizational survival over decades in the first place. The fluid partnerships and syndicates of the Italian merchants in overseas *nazioni* before the 1260s did not do this. The "Scali" as a company, for example, survived over generations; the partners comprising it biologically reproduced partners as well. In the future, I hope to continue my coding of the papal registers in order to increase the number of merchant-banks with which to evaluate further this hypothesis.

Blomquist provides evidence about yet a third kinship aspect of "corporate" on which I have no data. In my relational dataset on Trecento and Quattrocento Florence, I have rich quantitative information on the marriage, economic, and political networks of Florentines.[119] I have no such network-contextual information on Dugento Florence. But in his archivally rich case study[120] of the Ricciardi and the Guidiccioni families of Lucca, who allied to make the Ricciardi company, Blomquist unearthed considerable information about the marriages, property purchases, and neighbors of members of these two families. Those data demonstrate something that I cannot—namely, that many of even the "non-kinship outsiders" partners in the company were linked to the dominant two families by marriage or by other means.

> The evidence at hand seems sufficient to warrant the conclusion that the Ricciardi Company was in fact a long term alliance for commercial ends between families descending from the early partners in the enterprise, an alliance that was augmented by recruiting new members from other families which were through blood, marriage, consortial or neighborhood ties already linked to the group. I would assume that admission to partnership status of an individual lacking these ties must have been rare.
>
> (Blomquist 1980, 18)

[117] One was the same person and hence does not count in the denominator.
[118] Six were the same people and hence do not count in the denominator.
[119] Padgett and Ansell 1993; Padgett and McLean 2006; 2011.
[120] Blomquist 1980, 1982.

Much of the analysis in this section extends and confirms this superb, but unfortunately obscure,[121] case study by Blomquist.

All these pieces about kinship add up to my section conclusion: Successful leadership of unitary merchant-banks transformed merchant nuclear families into noble patrilineages—that is, "family out of company." This unitary-bank channel of social mobility was very restricted compared to the republican channels of the Renaissance. But the consequence when it happened was the same: the diffusion of corporate versions of "the family," from the nobility down to mimicking merchants, in the form of patrilineage. Again, Blomquist's rich case study of the Ricciardi and the Guidiccioni of Lucca provides details that my study cannot—namely, the purchase and construction of large blocks of real estate, both in the heart of the city (tower houses) and in the areas of the countryside or *contado* from which the family had migrated. Profits from the bank provided the money for these real estate purchases. But other Florentine banking families apparently made the same social-mobility journey—namely, descendants of Spigliatus and Rustichellus Cambii turned into the Mozzi, descendants of Manetto Spine turned into the Spini, descendants of Bonaguide Bardi turned into the Bardi, descendants of Circulus Oliverii Circuli turned into the Cerchi, and descendants of Lambertus Fruscobaldi turned into the Frescobaldi. These family names are prominent as companies in the English wool-export lists reported above. But they are also prominent on the 1293 list of Florentine magnates declared to be legally excluded from ever holding public office in the future.[122] This magnate category was created by a "populist" revolt against patricians.[123] How quickly successful unitary-bank families of the 1260s took on a noble behavior that made them hated in populist eyes![124]

To close this section, I want to emphasize the common consortial logic of many forms of Dugento social organization—in the domain of economics, in the domain of military, in the domain of real estate, and in the domain of family. To try too hard to distinguish whether a family name referred to a patrilineage or to a unitary company ignores the consortial logic of both.

[121] According to the Web of Science, in the 30 years since their publication, each of Blomquist's excellent *Actum Luce* articles has been cited exactly once.

[122] Lansing 1991.

[123] "Populist" is in quotes because many of the revolters were patricians themselves in alliance with middle-class guilds.

[124] This point about nobility through unitary banks helps make sense of a puzzle in the political history of Florence: how merchants could have gotten onto a list of feudal magnates in the eyes of contemporary *popolani*. See Ottokar 1962.

Family was property, at least in the patrilineage sense of family. And property was family, at least in the patrimony sense of *corpo*. We are very far away from modern kinship concepts like romance.

Multifunctionality was everywhere in the organizations of the 1200s. This is a social science way of saying that the linked concepts of *societas* and *consorteria*[125] were plastic social-organizational tools of the Dugento, capable of mobilization for a variety of purposes. All sorts of micromotivations underlay the construction of particular such organizations—profit, war, social mobility. But both actively and passively, the Church stood behind them all, sending these motivations down particular organizational trajectories. Dugento organizational inventions were secular recombinations of social relations and concepts in a religious tool kit of practices.[126]

Conclusion

If the Tuscan corporate merchant-banks were born because of the pope, they survived because of the king of England. Repayment through the customs service turned wool into simultaneously a commodity in international trade and a commodity in state finance. Wool had to be manufactured into textiles both for merchants to make their profit and for the king to make his soldiers. As sedentary merchant-banks expanded, the Florence wool-textile industry grew and the Champagne fairs declined. Tuscan (now mostly Florentine) merchant-banking houses simultaneously funded international trade in wool textiles and funded kings in state finance. The textile business often depended on the state-finance business for its authorization.

This autocatalytic feedback lasted until the famous bankruptcies of the Bardi and Peruzzi companies in Florence in 1342. But in truth, this trading system had been in decline since the turn of the century: The Bonsignori company went bankrupt in 1298; the Ricciardi company went bankrupt in 1300; the Scali company went bankrupt in 1326; and the Frescobaldi company went bankrupt in 1313.

[125] Here I am using the term *consorteria* both in its sense of family alliance and in its sense of patrilineage. Kent (1977) has emphasized that in the Renaissance the word *consorteria* came to be more restricted to mean "patrilineage" itself. The earlier Dugento meaning of "family alliance" had faded away, along with the reality of that form of social organization. Most likely one reason for this fade was the emergence of the republic, which undercut the military function of patrilineage.

[126] The tool-kit metaphor and idea is borrowed from Swidler (1986).

My own data from the Florentine banking guild's annual registration of banks[127] also trace a grim picture of steady decline in total numbers of registered bankers in the guild from 1299 onward: 355 partners in 1299; 313 partners in 1300; 277 partners in 1301; 238 partners in 1314; 146 partners in 1320; 116 partners in 1323; 100 partners in 1329. The bankers in these guild registration lists were extremely heterogeneous in nature, ranging from humble local money changers to grand international merchant-bankers. But even if we restrict our attention to the larger banks in these lists—those with more than five partners—the same story of early fourteenth-century decline appears:[128]

Bonciani company (7) last observed in 1300,
Abbati company (8) last observed in 1300,
Tedaldi company (7) last observed in 1300,
Canigiani company (12) last observed in 1301,
Marini company (9) last observed in 1301,
Guadagni company (6) last observed in 1314,
Macci company (14) last observed in 1314,
[no family name] company (8) last observed in 1314,
Pazzi company (17) last observed in 1314,
Sassetti company (10) last observed in 1314,
dell'Antella company (7) last observed in 1329,
Peruzzi company (21) bankrupt in 1342.

These declines were due to a series of wars between the king of England and the king of France. Secular wars between France and England were not as profitable for Tuscan merchant-banks as were the "holy" crusades in the peninsula of Italy. The reason for this difference is directly related to the flow of wool, which passed through France. The Italian crusades and the fiscal reforms of Edward I had fueled that flow, but subsequent wars with France by Edward II and Edward III had disrupted it. The king of France never adopted the innovative state-finance methods of pope Urban IV. King Philip the Fair of France attacked England in part by jailing Italian merchants resident in France and confiscating their goods on the charge of usury. The kings

[127] Archivio di Stato di Firenze, Arte del Cambio 11.
[128] In parentheses, I list the largest number of registered partners of the named company during 1299–1329.

of England in their turn, with their smooth state finance failing, shortsightedly also jailed their own bankers and confiscated their goods.[129] In spite of the English king's questionable credit rating, for a while one Tuscan banker replaced another in the king's service: The Ricciardi company was followed by the Frescobaldi company, which was followed by the Bardi company. Eventually profits in the wool trade were not sufficient to offset their shabby royal treatment. At the end, Edward III owed the Bardi company the equivalent of an entire year's English production in wool. Edward wouldn't pay it, and the organizational invention whose birth has been analyzed in this chapter became extinct. Busts following booms have been with us in history for a long time.

Ultimate extinction notwithstanding, the Tuscan unitary merchant-bank was an amazing organizational invention, especially for its time. Bills of exchange and account books changed banking forever, and the Commercial Revolution moved Europe out of its economic backwater. Dare I utter that historiographically out-of-fashion sentiment that the Middle Ages ended? If so, then this chapter has argued that the Middle Ages ended through the recombination of organizational elements that were, by themselves, deeply medieval. The "rise of capitalism" was real, but that does not mean that one coherent logic called "traditionalism" was displaced with another called "modernism." Traditionalism and modernity are two influential (and egocentric) concepts that I regard as without either historical or scientific precision.

For us as social scientists, the lessons of this venture into history are "incorporation and detachment" as one multiple-network folding mechanism for organizational genesis, with catalytic spillover into neighboring networks to reproduce and grow that genesis. Medieval invention in banking was not inevitable, but "historical contingency" does not have to mean something as intellectually flabby as a great idea, a great man, or even an accident. Multiple systems can feed back into each other occasionally to produce unpredictable tipping effects when such interacting systems are poised. Properly understood to exclude teleology and Social Darwinism, nonlinear path dependence is as characteristic of invention in social evolution as it is of speciation in biological evolution.

[129] This perhaps being one benefit of outsourcing state finance.

Appendices: Transactions from Papal Registers and English Liberate Rolls

A. Bonsignori company (Siena): 1250–1289
B. Scali company (Florence): 1229–1284
C. Tolomei company (Siena): 1223–1279
D. Ricciardi company (Lucca): 122?–1286
E. 1263–64 companies absolved from excommunication

Bonsignori company 1203:	**1250:**	**1251:**	**1252:**	**1253:**	**1254:**	**1255:**	**1256:**
Bonsignore di Bernardo salt							
Bonifacius Bonsignoris	4815		5608,6777[a]	**L/6264,6386,*6381***, 6861,6878	7342,7406,**7489**, *7980,8034*	*XXVIII*	
Orlandius Bonsignoris	4815		5608	**L/6264,6386,6446**, 6861	**7197**,7406	Ch[b] (dir.)	**1148**
Orlando Bartolomei Malavolti		**L/5469**		***6381***		Ch	
Aldebrandinus Bartholomei				***6381***			
Hugolinus Belmontis[c]		**L/5469**		**L/6264,6386**	**7197,7489**	165	**1148**
Capitino Buctin/ Capucino Bucci[d]						165	**1148**
Bartholomeo Guidii Ciabacte						165	**1148**
Andrea Iacobi						Ch	
Facius Juncte				**L/6264**			
Bartholomeo Christophori				6861,6878			
Theobaldum Thebalducii		**L/5469**					
Rainerium Tetii		**L/5469**					
Albizo Deuteaute					7342		
Bernardino Prosperini Cendonazi				*XXIII,XXV,XXIV*	*8034*		
Bonaventure Bernardini				**6381,6446**	*7980*	Ch,165,*XXVIII*	**1148**
Aldebrando Aldebrandini				*XXIII,XXV*		*XXVII,XXVIII*	
Ruskitello Cambii[e]				*XXIII*			
Amanatto Spinetti[f]				*XXIII*			

Bonsignori company	1261:	1262:	1263:
Orlandi Bonsignoris	9,L/44,48,51,L186	53,209	157, 220,277,491
Raynerii Jacobi	9,L/44,48,L186	L/40,73,121,L/179,180,182,209	491
Bonaventura Bernardini (continued)	9,L/44,48,51,L186	L/40,53,73,L/179,182,209	157,159,161,166, 172,173,174,175,176,177, 178,220,277,370,480,491,426
Francisci Guidonis		73,121,L/179,180,182	159,161,166,172,173,176,177,277,370,480,426
Hugolinus Bellimontis			172,426
Facius(Bonifacius) Juncte	9	72,76	172,426
Jacobo Gregorii		L/40,73,180,182	163
Andree Jacobi	9	L/40,72,76,180,182,209	157,159,163, 220,370,480,491
Tholomeo Manenti			157,159,163,166,172, 220,370,480,426
Bonsignori Raynerii	9	73,180,182,209	157,159,163,166,172,220,370,480,491,426
Manno Ildebrandini		73,209	163,491
Jacobo Gilli		73	157,220
Raynerio Bonaccursi	48,51,L186	53,L147	159,163,166,173,220
Deutavivae Guidi	L/44,48,51,L186	53,L147	
Ildebrando Ildebrandini			173
Jacopo Ildebrandini			177
Castraleone Hugolini			177
Jacopo Romei			177,277
Gregorio dicto Gonnella			177
Martinello Rubei			177
Rostorius Juncte			163
Bonadota Capud Nigri			163
Corrado Jacobo	(87)		
Jacobus Curradi			161
Vivolo Salvanelli	(87)	121,L/179	161,176
Venturae Cambii	(87)	121	161,176
Ventura Benedicti		L/179	161
Lottus Ugolini			161

Bonsignori company (Siena)	1265:
Orlandi Bonsignoris	1427,731,**1428**
Bonaventura Bernardini	1427,726,728,729,730,731,735,738,739,746,**747,753,754,*755***,756,1428,***1464***,***1465***,***1480***,***1482***
Raynerii Jacobi	1427,728,729,730,746,**747,753**,755,756,**1428**,1465
Francisci Guidonis	1427,726,728,729,730,731,735,738,739,746,**747,748,753**,***755***,756,**1428**,***1464***,***1465***,***1469***
Facius(Bonifacius) Juncte	1427,728,746,**747,753**,1428,***1464***
Restauro Juncte	***1464,1480***
Andree Jacobi	
Bonsignori Raynerii	1427
Raynerio Bonaccursi	
Tholomeo Manenti	1427
Manno Ildebrandini	1427
Blandum Aldebrandi	1427
Jacobo Gilii	1427,746,**753**,***1480,1482***
Hugoni Jacobi	1427,728,746,**747,753,1428**,***1464,1480,1482***
Jacobo Egidi	728,**747**,***1464***
Lotto Hugolini	1427,728,746,**753**,1428,***1464***
Gascum Trapillicini	1427,***1464,1480,1482***
Bindum Aldebrandini	1427
Aldebrandum Aldebrandini	1427,729,730,***755***,756
Paltonem Deutesalvi	1427,729,730,***755***,756
Facium Berignonis	1427,***755***,756
Gregorio Peruti	731
Jacobo Gregorii	738,739
Vivolum Salvanelli	1427
Gregorium Rigoli	1427
Deutaiuvam Guidi	1427
Bindum Falconis	1427
Bonfilium Contadini	1427
Incontratum Philippi	1427
Jacobum Skermi	1427

continued

continued

Bonsignori company (Siena)	**1265:**
Conradum Jacobi	1427
Bettum Ferrantis	1427
Tholomeum Jacobi	1427
Thomam Viviani	1427
Leonardum Jannis	1427
Facium Ranerii	1427
Pacchinam Ranerii	1427
Meum Monaldetti	1427

Sources:
Arabic numbers are papal bull #s, hence connected to papal curia.
Latin numbers are Liberate Roll #s, hence connected to king of England.
"Ch" refers to info from Chiaudano; "L" refers to info from Lunt; "E" refers to info from English.

Bold = France (anywhere else);
Italic = England;
Bold Italic = Montpelier;
Bold with doted line = Champagne;
Italic with doted line = Spain;
Bold Italic with dash line = Charles of Anjou

___ codes if leadership language (i.e., not in transaction, but referenced). ( ) means not Bonsignori company.

[a]First mention as campsor domini papae (actually campsoris nostri).
[b]This reorganization (initiation?) of company connected to Sicilian venture. (See Chiaudano 1935, p. 114.) Scali also mobilized as *campsors papae* at this time.
[c]In June 1255, part of Tolomei company (English, p. 15).
[d]In June 1255, part of Tolomei company (English, p. 15).
[e]Part of Scali company (though not really consolidated yet).
[f]Part of Scali company (though not really consolidated yet).

Bonsignori company	**1266:**	**1267:**
Orlandi Bonsignoris	*761*,789	798,
Bonaventura Bernardini	*761*,*779*,**783**,*784*,794,**1483**,**1484**	797,798,
Raynerii Jacobi	*761*,*779*, **L173**	
Francisci Guidonis	*779*,780,781,**783**,*784*,788,**1483**,**1484**	
Facius(Bonifacius) Juncte	*779*,*784*,**1483**,**1484**, **L173**	
Guidoni Juncte	**1483**,**1484**	**803**,804
Restauro Juncte	**1483**,**1484**	804
Hugoni Jacobi	**783**,**1483**,**1484**	**803**,804
Raynerio Jacobi	**783**,**1483**	
Andree Jacobi	*761*	
Bonsignori Raynerii	*761*	
Manno Ildebrandini	*761*	
Raynerio Bonaccursi		
Tholomeo Manenti		
Jacobo Gilii		
Jacobo Egidi	**1483**,**1484**	
Lotto Hugolini	*779*,*784*,**1483**,**1484**	798
Aldebrando Aldebrandini		
Jacobo Aldobrandini		797
Paltono Deutesalvi		
Gregorio Peruti		
Jacobo Gregorii	794	
Pultrono Frederici	794	
Facio Berignonis		
Gasconi Trapillicino	**1483**,**1484**	
Bartholomeo Henrici	**1484**	**803**
Gregorio Gonnelle		798

Mario Chiaudono (1935), p. 134–35:

Soci e capitani della Compagnia dei figli di Bonsignore (Societas filioum Bonsignoris) nel 1289:

Figli di Orlando Bonsignore:	
1. Fatius eques	
2. Ugo	
3. Guilelmus	
4. Bonsignore	
Figlio di Bonifazio Bonsignore:	
5. Nicolaus eques	
Soci estranei alla famiglia Bonsignori e loro capitali:	
6. Bonaventura Bernardini	6800 lib.
7. Rainerius Iacobi	5200 lib.
8. Pagnus Giliocti	3000 lib.
9. Fatius Berignonis	3000 lib.
10. Conradus Berignonis	2500 lib.
11. Manfredus Ranucii de Balzis	3000 lib.
12. Gerius Montanini	3000 lib.
13. Mevius domini Orlandi de Malavoltis	2500 lib.
14. Bindus Aldobrandi	2500 lib.
15. Tura Bartholomei	2500 lib.
16. Claritus Iohannis	2500 lib.
17. Thalomeus Manentis	2100 lib.
18. Ventura o Tura Bonamici	1500 lib.
19. Arbor Bernardini	1200 lib.
20. Bartholomeus Henrici	—
21. Vannes Henrici	—
22.Mattheus Albizi	—
23. Angelus Benvenuti	—
Total capital	40,800 lib.

Scali company (Florence)	1229:	1233:	1235:	1245:	1249:	1250:	1253:	1254:	1255:	1256:	1257:	1258:	1259:
Mainetto Robertin				*XV*									
Bonaccorso Inglesk		*B:Eng.*											
Amieri Cose	*B:Engl.*	*B:Eng.*	*B:Eng.*	*XV*						*B:Eng.*	*B:Eng.*		
Spigliato Cambii[g]	*B:England*		*B:Eng.*	*XV*					**B:Gasc.**	*B:Eng.*[h]			
Rocco(Rustichello)			*B:Eng.*				*XXIII*	*XXVI*	**B:Gasc.**	*B:Eng.*	*B:Eng.*	*XXXIII*	
Cambii[i]									*XXXV,XXXVII*				
Manetto Spini(Spineti)			*B:Eng.*		*B:Eng.*	*XXI*	*XXIII*	*XXVI*	**B:Gasc.**	*B:Eng.*	*B:Eng.*		
Pietro Benincase[j]									**B:Gasc.**	*B:Eng.*			
Ranieri Abbati										*B:Eng.*			
Hugoni(dicto Mazze)						*XXI*				*B:Eng.*			
Simonetti													
Deuteayuto Guillelmi										*B:Eng.*			
Jacopo della Scala					*B:Eng.(+others)*			**7529**	**B:Gascony**				
Cavalcante(Cante) de Scala											*B:Eng.*		
Jacobi Giberti[k]							7069	**7529**,7227					
Hugoni Gilberti						*XXI*							
Benvenuto Will'i						*XXI*							
Gerardo Ricobaldi						*XXI*							
Bernardo Persperin[l]							*XXIII*						

continued

continued

Scali company (Florence)	**1229:**	**1233:**	**1235:**	**1245:**	**1249:**	**1250:**	**1253:**	**1254:**	**1255:**	**1256:**	**1257:**	**1258:**	**1259:**
Aldebrando Aldebrandini[m]							*XXIII*					*XXXIII*	*XXXV*
Jacobo Dananzaci												*XXXIII*	*XXXV*
Berardo Ricobaldi												*XXXIII*	*XXXV*
Petro de Sabaudia													*XXXVII*
Luterio Bonycase													*XXXVII*

Sources:
Arabic numbers are papal bull #s, hence connected to papal curia.
Latin numbers are Liberate Roll #s, hence connected to king of England.
"B:" info from Borsari.

Bold = France (anywhere else);
Italic = England;
Bold Italic with dash line = Gascony.

___ codes if leadership language (i.e., not in transaction, but referenced).

[a]First mention as campsor domini papae (actually campsoris nostri).
[b]This reorganization (initiation?) of company connected to Sicilian venture. (See Chiaudano, 1935, p. 114.) Scali also mobilized as *campsors papae* at this time.
[c]In June 1255, part of Tolomei company (English, p. 15).
[d]In June 1255, part of Tolomei company (English, p. 15).
[e]Part of Scali company (though not really consolidated yet).
[f]Part of Scali company (though not really consolidated yet).
[g]Due to strange English spellings, I assume Spigliato Cambi = Spinello Campano.
[h]These loans part of Sicilian venture: a papal-English taxation joint venture. But also some of them straight to king. Jordan, p.11, says Scali made campsor papae.
[i]Rocco Cambi = Rustichello Cambi, according to both Borsari and Kay. [See article by Richard Kay in Studi Danteschi on his suicide.]
[j]Due to strange English spellings, I assume Pietro Benincase = Petro Bonacaso.
[k]As of 1262, he is in Bellindotti company.
[l]As of 1255, his son, Benvenuto Bernardini, is part of Bonsignori company of Siena.
[m]As of 1255, this Sienese is part of Bonsignori company.

Scali company (Florence)	1261:	1262:	1263:	1264:	1265:	1268:	1269:
England:							
Jacobum Cambii				1012			
Diritta(Dricta) Cambii			A,363	519			
Rucco(Rustichello) Cambii[a]	XXXVIII	B:p/E,L/125	A,363,479,327	519			
Manetto(Maynetto) Spine	XXXVIII	B:p/E,L/125	A,363,479	519	1469		
Lotherio Benincase		B:p/E	A,363,479	519,1012			
Ranieri Abbati		B:p/E,L/125	A,363,479,327	519		XLI	XLIII,XLIV,XLV
Hugonetto(Mace) Simonetti							XLIII,XLIV,XLV
Florence and elsewhere:							
Amieri Cose	B:p		A,363	519,1012			
Jacobus(Lapus) Amierii Cose	B:p		A,363,212	519,1012			
Jacopo de Scala	B:p	B:p/E,L/125	A,363,327	519,1012	726		
Cavalcante(Cante) Jacobi de Scala	B:p,22		A,363,212	519,1012			
Spina Jacobi de Scala	B:p		A,363,212	519,1012			
Teghia Jacobi de Scala			A,363,212	519	1469		
Thomasio(Maso) Spiliati	B:p,22		A,363,212	519	1469		
Pietro Benincase	B:p	B:p/E,L/125	A,363	519,1012			

continued

continued

Scali company (Florence)	1261:	1262:	1263:	1264:	1265:	1268:	1269:
Dino Perini	B:p	B:p/E,L/125					
Jacobo Lecca	B:p		A,363,212	519	726		
Campana Francisci	B:p		A,363,212	519,1012			
Hugo(Ugo) Spine	B:p		A,363	519			
Teghia Amadoris	B:p		A,363,212	519			
Gerardinus Beliotti	B:p		212				
Rustichello Tedaldi	B:p						

Sources: numbers are papal bull #s; hence connected to papal curia. "p" means pope.
Latin numbers are Liberate Roll #s; hence connected to king of England. "p/E" means pope/England relations.
"B:" info from Borsari; "L" info from Lunt; "A" info from Arias: "Sottomissione dei Banchieri Fiorentini alla Chiesa."

[a]Cambii family later becomes the magnate family of de Mozzi. Therefore, Mozzi (also Spini) banks spins out of Scali bank.

Scali company [from Edouard Jordan]	**1282 & 1284:**
Cieffus Bonisegne	Martini IV die 13 septembris 1282 et die 13 augusti 1284 datis
Maynettus Hugonis	Martini IV die 13 septembris 1282 et die 13 augusti 1284 datis
Lapus de Scala	Martini IV die 13 septembris 1282 et die 13 augusti 1284 datis
Jacobus Aymerii Cosae	Martini IV die 13 septembris 1282 et die 13 augusti 1284 datis
Johannes Aymerii Cosae	Martini IV die 13 septembris 1282 et die 13 augusti 1284 datis
Albertus Aymerii Cosae	Martini IV die 13 septembris 1282 et die 13 augusti 1284 datis
Folia Aymerii Cosae	Martini IV die 13 septembris 1282 et die 13 augusti 1284 datis
Alamannus Aymerii Cosae	Martini IV die 13 septembris 1282 et die 13 augusti 1284 datis
Castellanus Lapi	Martini IV die 13 septembris 1282 et die 13 augusti 1284 datis
Lippus Petri Benincasae	Martini IV die 13 septembris 1282 et die 13 augusti 1284 datis
Riccasrdus Petri Benincasae	Martini IV die 13 septembris 1282 et die 13 augusti 1284 datis
Tegla Amadoris	Martini IV die 13 septembris 1282 et die 13 augusti 1284 datis
Bonacosa Cosa Fulchi	Martini IV die 13 septembris 1282 et die 13 augusti 1284 datis
Ugolinus de Vichio	Martini IV die 13 septembris 1282 et die 13 augusti 1284 datis
Lotherius Bonaguide	Martini IV die 13 septembris 1282 et die 13 augusti 1284 datis
Bonapresa Importuni	Martini IV die 13 septembris 1282 et die 13 augusti 1284 datis

Tolomei company (Siena)	1223:	1226:	1227:	1230:	1243:	1248:	1251–3:	1253:	1254:	1255:	1255:	1255:	1257:	1260:
Ranierio Raulii			M:lc											
Catalano di Alfano		M:lc												
Bartolomeo di Guazzolino		M:lc												
Manente d'Uguccione	EM:cl.	M:lc												
Tolomeo di Tolomeo della Piazza	EM:cl.	M:lc	M:lc	M:lc										
Tavena di Tolomeo Tolomei				M:lc			M:lc[a]			453				
Lotterengo di Tolomeo Tolomei				M:lc			M:lc							
Pelacane di Tolomeo Tolomei				M:lc			M:lc							
Jacopo della Piazza														
Tolomeo di Jacobo Tolomei							M:lc			453	M:p[b]	ME:p		
Cristoforo di Tolomeo Tolomei						M:lc							E:Ch	
Jacobo di Tolomeo Tolomei							M:lc						E:Ch.	
Rinaldo di Jacobo Tolomei							M:lc			453	M:p	ME:p	E:Ch.	
Cristoforo di Jacopo Tolomei							M:lc							
Andrea di Cristoforo Tolomei								6468			M:p	ME:p,28,29		
Lotterengo d'Uguccione Tolomei							M:lc					E:p		E:Eng.
Bartolomeo di Pietro Tolomei												ME:p,28,29		
Orlando Bonasera					347		M:lc				M:p			
Deutaviva di Guido								6468			M:p	ME:p,28,29		
Turchio di Ranieri								6468			M:p			
Leo di Teodorico											M:p			
Ofriduccio di Rustibello											M:p			
Dietisalve di Benintende											M:p			
Accarigi di Ranuccio											M:p			
Petrus Montanarius												29		
Johannes Cesarii												29		

	1223:	1226:	1227:	1230:	1243:	1248:	1251–3:	1253:	1254:	1255:[c]	1255:	1255:	1257:	1260:
Raynaldus Renerii								6468	7981					
Jacobi Theci								6468						
Luca Ricovarii								6468						
Montanino Deutesalve					347			6468						
Bartholomeo Comitis					347									
Henrico Deuteaiut					347									
Jacobo Rustikino					347									
Hugolino Gentili					347									
Albizo Deuteaiut					347									
Capitano di Bucce[d]											ME:p			
Ugolino di Belimonte[e]											ME:p			

"cl." = cloth; "lc" = loan to city; "p" = pope; "v" = vescovo; "Ch." = Champagne; "Eng." = England; "Fl." = Flanders.

[a]The loans below are from various combinations of these Tolomei, over this period of time. Not clearly integrated into unified block of soci yet.
[b]This, on the other hand, is a single loan to pope. (Mucciarelli, 1995, pp. 99–100)
[c]This, on the other hand, is a single loan to pope. (Mucciarelli, 1995, pp. 99–100)
[d]Also partner in Bonsignori company.
[e]Also partner in Bonsignori company.

Tolomei company (Siena)	1262:	1263:	1264:	1265:	1269:	1279:
Orlando di Baldistricca Tolomei	E:Siena					
Tolomeo di Jacobo Tolomei	E:Siena				E:exile	
Pietro di Cristoforo Tolomei	E:Siena	175		745		
Andrea di Cristoforo Tolomei	E:Ch.	175	521?	745,E:Ch.	E:Ch.	
Minus di Cristoforo Tolomei		175				
Guillelmus et		175				
Meus Raynaldi, eorum nepotes		175				
Tholomei Reginaldi				745		
Christofori Tholomei				745		
Lotheringi Uguicionis				745		
Federigo Doni	E:Fl.	175		745,E:Eng.	E:Fl.	
Tebaldus Alteville		175				
Barthol omeus et Aringherius Jacobi			521?			
Tolomeo di Rinaldo Tolomei						E:Siena
Luca di Bonsignore						E:Ch.
Tofano di Bonsignore						E:Ch.
Cino di Pietro						E:Ch.

[Apart from the heavy and repeated business of the Tolomei family, this not really solidly consistent. Still a fluid partnership structure, even with noble family participation. The pope mobilized by creating the combined Scotti-Tolomei company (even if short-lived), not by using this existing Tolomei one very consistently.]

Scotti and Tolomei company (Siena)	1255:	1256:	1258:	1262:[a]
Petrus Scotti Dominici	J	M:p	J	46
Rinaldus Tolomei	J		J	
Tholomeo Raynaldi				46
Reinaldum Rainerii[b]		M:p		
Gregorius Bernardini			J	46
Lotteringus Corradi			J	46
Jacobus Raynaldi			J	46
Christoforus Tolomei		M:p	J	46
Raynucius(Raynerius) de Vallestricte			J	46
Aldebrandinus Tholomei			J	46
Petrus Christophori			J	46
Raynucius(Raynalducio) Johannis			J	46
Bonuncuntrus Scotti Dominici			J	46
Scotto Dominici				46
Jacobus Romei			J	46
Rubeus Consilii			J	46
Raynerius Citadini			J	46
Paulus Albertini			J	46
Jacobus Balioni			J	
Ventura Martini			J	
Bonrestorus Scotti			J	
Jacobus Ugolini			J	
Bonagratia Ardimanni			J	
Bencivenne Consilii			J	
Ventura Fornari			M:Eng.	
Raniero Barbotti			M:Eng.	
Ermino Erminii			M:Eng.	
Giacomo Teci			M:Eng.	

[a]This actually was a "trial" of Scotti-Tolomei bank by pope Urban IV. Alexander IV had appointed this company as *campsores papae*, but for some reason Urban IV was unhappy with them.

[b]This guy shows up a lot in early papal refs, connected to other partners. Track these down & staple together (in 1256 only?)

Ricciardi company (Lucca)	122?:	1227:	1231:	1234:	1241:	1245:	1247:	1251:	1253:	1254–5:	1256:	1263:	1266:
Paganino Guidiccioni				P:Luc.									
Aldibrandino Guidiccioni							BP:Luc.						
Bandino del Lucano Bugianensis							BP:Luc.						
Opizi(Opitone) Malisardi							BP:Luc.						
Ricciardo di Graziano di Ricciardo, tintor	P:Luc.	P:Luc.	BP:Luc.	P:Luc.	BP:Luc.		BP:Luc.						
Perfetto di Graziano di Ricciardo			BP:Luc.			BP:Luc.							
Gottifredo di Conetto [uncle?]			BP:Luc.										
Orlandino del Antelmino Minusvetti													
Alamanno (monete contraffatte)	P:Lucca												
Rosselmo del Mainetto Minusvetti	P:Lucca												
Mainetto Minusvetti	P:Lucca												
maestro Giovanni	P:Genoa												
Orlandino Arnolfi					BP:Luc.								
Guglielmo Rosciompelli					BP:Luc.								

Peregrino Sesmundi	BP:Luc.	K:England	RK:Eng.	K:Eng.	RKP:Eng.			
Reynero detto Senaci Guidiccioni(?)		K:England	R:Eng.		RKP:Eng.			
Henrico Saraceni			RK:Eng.	K:Eng.	RKP:Eng.			
Bartholomeo Bendini					RKP:Eng.			
Luco(Luke) Natali					RKP:Eng.	K:Eng.	K:Eng.	
Reiner Magiari							K:Eng.	
Baroncinus di Gu(W)alterius de Vulturna						(K:Eng.)	(K:Eng.)	
Richardo Guidechonis								(K:Cham)
Theobaldino Maniumac								(K:Cham)
Guido Panichi: procurator only							(P:Genoa)	

( ) = not yet part of comp

Ricciardi company (Lucca)	1272:	1273:	1276–83:	1283:	1284:	1286:
dominus Andree Parentii Ricciardi						A:Luc.
Philippi domini Raynerii Ricciardi						A:Luc.
Ricciardus domini Raynerii Ricciardi						A:Luc.
Pagani/uccio Guidi Guidiccionis					B:Luc.	A:Luc
Guidiccione Paganini Guidiccionis					B:Luc.	A:Luc.
Raynerii Bandini						A:Luc.
Philipucii Talgardi						A:Luc.
Saraceni Macchi	P:G[a]					A:Luc.
Iohannis Gambardi						A
Lucasio Natale[b] (Luke de Luka)	P:G	KP:Eng.	KP:Eng.	L:Eng.		(d.1279)
Bandino del Lucano		P:Eng.				
Uguccione Maghiari		P:Eng.				
Ranieri(Raynerius) Maghiarii[c]		K:Eng.	RKPL:Eng	L:Eng.		A
Orlandino di Pogio[d] (Podio)			RKP:Eng.	L:Eng.		[why no A?]
Henricus de Podio			K:Eng.	L:Eng.		K:Gascony
Bartolotto del Buggianese Bandini			P:Eng.,Paris	L:Eng.	B	
Matteo Rosciompelli			RKP:Eng.	L:Eng.		
Adiuti Rosciompili			K:Eng.			A
Vannes Rosciompeli					B	A
Abbate Talgardi			K:Eng.	L:Eng.		A
Giovanni Simonetti Sismondi	P:G		KP:Eng.	L:Eng.		A
Riccardo Paganini Guidiccionis[e]	P:G		KP:Eng.	L:Eng.	B:Luc.	[why no A?]
Tommasinus Paganini Guidi Guidiccionis		K:Eng.	KP:Eng.	L:Eng.	B:Luc.	A

Aldebrandino Guidiccioni			K:Eng.			
Federigi Venture			K:Eng.			A
Riccardo Bonifacii[f]						K:Eng.
Baroncino Gualteri[g] (in Eng 23 yrs before)			RK:Eng.	L:Eng.		K:left comp
Brunetto Baroncini Gualteri						K:left comp
Riccardo Baroncini Gualteri						K:left comp
Opizzo(Opiso) Malisardi (inlaw of Gualteri)	P:G		K:Eng.			K:left comp
Hugolino Rosciompelli		R:Ire.	K:Ireland			
Percival Gerarducci			K:Ireland			
Bendino Panichi(Peruchi)	P:G		KP:Ireland			A:Ireland
Ghirardo Chimbardi						K:Ireland
Francesco Malisardi						KP:Ireland
Riccardo Rosciompelli			K:Gascony			
Francesco Maneumach			K:Paris			
Lotto Aldebrandini			K:Paris			
Bindo di Giovanni Simonetti			P:Paris?			
Barchetta Barche			P:Paris?		B	
Ricciardinus domini Bonfatii Gottori					B	
Labro Volpelli		K:Eng.	KP:curia			KP:curia
Dino Tadolini			P:curia			

continued

continued

Ricciardi company (Lucca)	**1272:**	**1273:**	**1276–83:**	**1283:**	**1284:**	**1286:**
Frederigus Sarracini Incallocchiati						A:Ravenna
Nicolucius Bonacursii Mignosii						A:Ravenna
Guido Panichi, procurator only[h]		(P:Genoa)				
Bandino de Fondora, procurator only		(P:Genoa)				

[*Sources:* R = Re; K = Kaeuper; B = Blomquist; P = Del Punto; L = Lunt; A = Arias]

[a]P:G refers to one-shot loan in 1272 at Genoa to Prince Edward (future Edward I), coming back from crusades. See Del Punta, p. 163.
[b]Liberate Roll #s: In 1273: 48, 49, 49b, 50. In 1274: 52, 53, 56, 57, 58. In 1275: 61, 64, 65. In 1276: 68, 71.
[c]Liberate Roll #s: In 1278: 76, 78. In 1279: 79, 82. In 1280: 83,
[d]Liberate Roll #s: In 1277: 72, 73. In 1278: 74, 75, 76, 77. In 1280: 80, 80b, 84. In 1296: 95.
[e]Liberate Roll #s: In 1281: 86. In 1289: 89. In 1290: 90, 93. In 1292: 94.
[f]Liberate Roll #s: In 1290: 90, 93.
[g]Liberate Roll #s: In 1281: 85, 86. In 1282: 87. In 1285: 88.
[h]The exception that proves rule? Genoa uses agents, not filiali.

Ricciardi company (Lucca)	1286:	Pope Martin IV
dominus Andree Parentii Ricciardi	A:Luc.	
Philippi domini Raynerii Ricciardi	A:Luc.	
Ricciardus domini Raynerii Ricciardi	A:Luc.	
Pagani/uccio Guidi Guidiccionis	A:Luc	J
Guidiccione Paganini Guidiccionis	A:Luc.	
Franciscus Guiditionis		J
Raynerii Bandini	A:Luc.	J
Philipucii Talgardi	A:Luc.	
Saraceni Macchi	A:Luc.	J
Iohannis Gambardi	A	
Ranieri(Raynerius) Maghiarii	A	J
Orlandino di Pogio[a] (Podio)	[why no A?]	J
Henricus de Podio	K:Gascony	
Riccardus Pogii		J
Bartolotto del Buggianese Bandini		J
Adiuti(Adjustus) Rosciompili	A	J
Vannes Rosciompeli	A	
Abbate Talgardi	A	
Giovanni Simonetti Sismondi	A	J
Riccardo Paganini Guidiccionis[b]	[why no A?]	J
Tommasinus Paganini Guidi Guidiccionis	A	J
Aldebrandino Guidiccioni		
Lotto Aldebrandini		J
Federigi Venture	A	
Riccardo Bonifacii[c]	K:Eng.	
Bendino Panichi(Peruchi)	A:Ireland	
Ghirardo Chimbardi	K:Ireland	
Francesco Malisardi	KP:Ireland	
Labro Volpelli	KP:curia	J
Dino Tadolini		J
Vantes Honestis		J
Ricciardinus domini Bonfatii Gottori		J
Paganellus seu Nellus Gualandi		J
Ghinus Christophori		J
Bonaventura Romanioli		J
Nicolutius Liene		J
Banus Pili Rictii		J

[*Sources:* A = Arias: J = Jordan]

[a]Liberate Roll #s: In 1296: 95.

[b]Liberate Roll #s: In 1289: 89. In 1290: 90, 93. In 1292: 94.

[c]Liberate Roll #s: In 1290: 90, 93.

1263–64 companies absolved from excommunication[130,131,132]
[Bull numbers from *Registres d'Urbain IV*, vol. 2.]

1) **de Burgo company** of Florence [n. 362: 5 August 1263]

Dulcis de Burgo
Boldus de Burgo
Hugo Monaldi
Moczius de Burgo
Gualterus de Burgo
Gerus de Burgo
Castra Gualfredi
Hugettus Symonetti
Spinellus Symonetti
Donatellus Octaviani
Dulcis Octaviani
Johannes Bonaviti
Rubeus Bacharelli
Lapus Stibaldi
Johannutius Bajamontis
Ranutius Ardingi

2) **Rimbertini company** of Florence [n. 364: 27 August 1263]

Philippus Radulphi
Frankettus Rembertini
Maynettus Rembertini
Jacobus Rembertini
Franciscus Rembertini
Frankettus Bencivenni

[130] This procedure makes these lists of partners complete, unlike the usual case with papal transactions.

[131] The Bonsignori, Scali, and Tolomei companies are not listed here, because they were coded elsewhere in the appendix. Their Urban IV bull numbers and dates of absolution were the following, respectively: n. 161, 5 July 1263; n. 363: 27 August 1263; and n. 175, 5 January 1263.

[132] *Discipuli* or non-partner employees were also included in the registers, but these are not reproduced here.

Raynaldus Uberti
Dosius Uberti
Ubertus Raynaldi
Pucius Raynaldi
Guelfus Raynaldi
Scolarius Radulphi
Rota Amannati
Michael Amannati
Bucca Amannati
Matheus Bonfilioli
Cantius Symonetti
Bonvicinus Nicolai

3) **Bardi company** of Florence [n. 410: 27 September 1263]

Gianni Bonaguide Bardi
Matheus Bonaguide Bardi
Lapus Bonaguide Bardi
Coltus Bonaguide Bardi
Riccus Beltrami
Guarnerius Mathei
Antoninus, filius Gerii

4) **Bellicozi company** of Florence [n. 411: 26 September 1263]

Cambius Manerii Bellicozi
Persus Manerii Bellicozi
Perus Manerii Bellicozi
Giannianus Tebaldi
Zione Tebaldi

5) **Bellincioni company** of Florence [n. 428: 23 October 1263]

Ildebrandinus Bellincionis
Bellincione(Cione) Ildebrandinus Bellincionis
Cambiutius Ildebrandinus Bellincionis
Caccia (notarius) Bonciani
Cenni Bonciani

6) **Benvenuti del Bene company** of Florence [n. 429: 27 October 1263]

Ildebrandinus Benvenuti del Bene
Franciscum Benvenuti del Bene
Phylippus Benvenuti del Bene
Ugolinus Benvenuti del Bene

7) **Acquerelli 'company'** of Florence [n. 430: 2 November 1263]

Ildebrandinus (judex) Gerardi de Acquerellis
Giacottus Gerardi de Acquerellis
Peroctus Gerardi de Acquerellis
Roggerus (patruus suus) quondam Ildebrandini de Acquerellis
Dinus Joseppi
Cervellinus(Cinus) Dini Joseppi
[but word 'socii' not used in this 'company']

8) **de Bella company** of Florence [n. 447: 10 November 1263]

Comparinus Tedaldi de Bella
Janus Tedaldi de Bella
Hugo Melioris de Bella
Gabriel Donati Bucetunde
Dessus Donati Bucetunde

9) **Puccii et Dosii Albizi** of Florence [n. 463: 5 December 1263]

Dosius quondam Albizi
Pepus(Puccius) quondam Albizi

10) **Vinciguerre company** of Florence [n. 465: 23 December 1263]

Duccius Rogeri Vinciguerre
Nerus Rogeri Vinciguerre
Rusticus Rogeri Vinciguerre

11) **Phylippi company** of Florence [n. 501: 5 February 1264]

Cambius Phylippi
Raynerius Phylippi

Capiardinus Guillelmi Danielis
Lapus Bizochi Marci
Marcutius Bizochi Marci

12) **Rossi company** of Florence [n. 557: 29 April 1264]

Johannes Rossi
Catellus Rossi
Marus Rossi
Rossus Conradi(Cafagii)

13) **Abbati 'company'** of Florence [n. 570: 14 May 1264]

Lambertus(Tuctius) Abbatis
Jacobus (clericus et procurator) Abbatis
[but word 'socii' not used in this 'company']

14) **Cerchi** founder in Florence (not company) [n. 574: 28 May 1264]

Circulum Olivieri

15) **Frescobaldi company** of Florence [n. 701: 3 August 1264]

Bardus Lamberti Frascobaldi
Jacobus Lamberti Frascobaldi
Coppus Joseppi
Corbolinus Bencii

16) **Donosdei company** of Pistoia [n. 702: 3 August 1264]

Egidius Donosdei
Melior Pelegrini
Accursis Lesii
Bonadies Bonadiei
Henrigetti Bonadiei
Pecora Novanterii
Stancollus(Collus) Raynuzini
Meo (domini) Raynuzini
Matheus Thomasini
Bindus Armaleonis

17) **Ammannati company** of Pistoia [n. 703: 30 July 1264]

Bandinus Ammannati
Bartholomeus Ammannati
Framericus Baldeti
Fuccius Soffredi
Forese Jacobi
Corradutius Jacobi
Sarracenus Jacobi
Conte Montancolli

1265 companies absolved from excommunication
[Bull numbers from *Registres de Clement IV*]

18) **Cerchi "societate"** of Florence (again) [Clement IV n. 86: 2 juin 1265]

Circuli Oliverii Circuli
Bindus Galligaii de Mactis
Teglarius Tedaldi
Ubertus Cambii
Manfridus Oderici
Naddus Boniczi
Taldus Raynerii
Guiducius Oderici
Naddus Boniczi
Taldus Raynerii
Guiducius Cavalcanti
Bonsignore Bonaiuti

19) **Frescobaldi company** of Florence (again) [Clement IV n. 87: 3 June 1265]

Jacobus Riccomandi
Albertinus Rote
Ghinus Fruscobaldi
Barduccius Lamberti Fruscobaldi
Jacobus Lamberti Fruscobaldi
Hugolinus Benivieni

Coppus Joseppi
Rainerius Joseppi
Corbolinus Benivi
Meliorellus Allioni
Puccinus Amatoris
Restorinus Spiliati

20) **Rubei et Arditionis company** of Florence [Clement IV n. 143: 13 July 1265]

Fuctius Rubei
Cinus Jacobi Arditionis
Ricchus Jacobi
Julianus Ricchi
Clarus Oliverii
Riccus Bonaguide
Nerus Fornarii
Angelerius Bonelle
Petrus Corbizi
Ricchus Salvaterre

21) **Rimbottus Bonaiuti** of Siena [Clement IV n. 158: 23 October 1265]

Rimbottus Bonaiuti
Tucius et Acherisius, filii ejus

4
Open Elite? Social Mobility, Marriage, and Family in Florence, 1282–1494

Introduction

Lawrence Stone asked the "open elite?" question for early-modern England and answered it largely in the negative. Richard Goldthwaite in a series of works has asked this question for Renaissance Florence and has answered it in the affirmative. Anthony Molho asked this question for Florence but answered it in the negative.[1] In this article, I answer this same question for Florence largely in the affirmative. The contradictions among these answers are not as sharp as they first seem because cross-currents in any society are more complex than can be captured by binary answers. "Social mobility" is a multivalent concept, and much depends upon exactly what is measured. The solution to the research problem of conceptual ambiguity is not less but more precision. At the level of orienting theory, one needs to abandon global stereotypes, and to understand internal tensions and processes. At the level of measurement, one needs to collect data from a variety of sources, and to examine how possibly inconsistent data interrelate. In these two respects, the interrogation strategies of the sciences and the humanities are not as distinct as both sides presume.

Despite the wealth of quantifiable material in the Florentine archives, historians have not in large numbers followed the path-breaking lead of Herlihy and Klapisch-Zuber in analyzing these archival materials from a statistical point of view. Exceptions include Cohn, Weissman, Molho, Litchfield, Barbagli, Padgett, McLean, Emigh, and Botticini.[2] Statistical tools remain

Renaissance Quarterly 63 (Summer 2010): 357–411. Republished with permission.

[1] Stone and Fawtier-Stone 1984; Goldthwaite 1968, 1993, 2009; Molho 1994.

[2] Herlihy and Klapisch-Zuber 1978, 1985; Cohn 1980, 1988, 1992, 1996, 1999, 2002; Weissman 1982; Molho 1968b, 1994, 2000; Morrison, Kirshner, and Molho 1985; Litchfield 1986; Barbagli 1984; Padgett and Ansell 1993; McLean and Padgett 1997; Padgett and McLean 2006; McLean 1998, 2007; Emigh 1997a, 1997b, 2000, 2003; Botticini 1999, 2000, 2003. Outside of Florence, prominent examples of historical studies using quantitative methods include Tilly 1964, 1995; Laslett 1965,

Organizational Invention in Renaissance Florence. John F. Padgett, Oxford University Press.
 DOI: 10.1093/oso/9780197789216.003.0004

invaluable, however, for answering a variety of historiographical questions, including the social-history ones in which Herlihy was interested. What were family structures in Renaissance Florence for different categories of people? What were intermarriage patterns among these families? How much social mobility was there in Renaissance Florence? Did any of this change during the Trecento and Quattrocento? Statistical methods are not the only approach to questions such as these, but they provide a useful perspective, especially on aggregate patterns and trends.

Herlihy and Klapisch-Zuber, along with the follow-up by Barbagli, posed their questions about Renaissance family structure at the level of the household. In contrast, this article poses its similar questions at the level of the lineage. The best current point of departure for this level of analysis is the study of Florentine marriage by Molho.[3] In addition to providing a statistical overview of Florentine marriage patterns, Molho's study usefully linked the two related topics of lineage intermarriage and political elite structure. Molho argued that stability both in Florentine lineages and in Florentine "ruling class" composition were caused by endogamous intermarriage, which recycled substantial dowries among a relatively closed set of elite lineages, thereby buffering them against the high elite-family extinction rates common in other countries in Europe.

The statistical results herein will support Molho's conclusion about the importance of marriage for sustaining the resilience of Florentine lineages over perilous demographic time. But they will not support Molho's conclusion about elite stability and closure, at least for the two-century time period of this study. I shall document high rates of relative social mobility among lineages on the dimensions of wealth and political office, and less high but still substantial rates of social mobility on the dimension of marriage, especially during the Albizzi regime.

The resolution of this apparent paradox between lineage stability and elite fluidity will come from my statistical finding that there were in Renaissance Florence three distinct dimensions of status stratification among lineages—wealth, ruling political faction, and lineage size. Marriage endogamy and elitist exclusion were evident on each of these three dimensions. That is, wealthy lineages disproportionately married each other, politically powerful

1972; Stone 1965; Stone and Fawtier-Stone 1984; Sewell 1985; Markoff 1996; Hoffman, Postel-Vinay, and Rosenthal 2000; Clark 2007. Due ultimately to the richness of its sources, the depth and diversity of the quantitative data in the Padgett relational database is unusual even by these high standards.

[3] Molho 1994. See also Fabbri 1991.

lineages disproportionately married each other, and large lineages disproportionately married each other. But a surprising fact about Renaissance Florence, documented in this article, is that these three status dimensions were statistically almost independent of each other. Wealthy lineages were not the same on average as powerful lineages, and they were not the same on average as large lineages. Powerful lineages in turn were not the same on average as large lineages. These multiple, inconsistent stratification logics made it very hard demographically to find someone to marry who was similar to you on all three dimensions at once. By marrying intentionally into a family that was similar on one status dimension, one usually married unintentionally into a family that was dissimilar on other dimensions. The counterintuitive consequence of exclusive and elitist marriage behavior by upper strata, therefore, became the widespread recruitment of middle-strata families into upper-strata patrilineage families. Florentine elites, like elites everywhere, tried to close social-mobility doors behind them. But their inability to converge on a single dominant criterion of status twisted their inconsistent closed-elite intentions into open-elite mobility for others. This created political turmoil, but it also renewed Renaissance Florentine elites.

One other consequence of elites marrying non-elites was the diffusion of patrilineage family ideals downward into the middle strata of Florentine society. This downward diffusion occurred at the same time as patrilineage declined among its original exemplars—namely, among large magnate[4] clans. Trecento and Quattrocento Florentines intensely imitated a family model that was itself decaying. This is how I resolve the Goldthwaite-Kent debate[5] in the 1970s about the decline of the Renaissance Florentine lineage: In the older-family core, it declined; but in the broader society it diffused.

My overall answer to the "open elite?" question for Renaissance Florence therefore largely will be yes, in spite of Florentine elitist intentions to the contrary. This answer suggests a reconceptualization of the concept of "elite"—more as a fluidly reproduced aspiration and ideal than as a stable demographic reality.

I develop my statistical evidence for these conclusions in the following sequence. The next section will describe the data and its sources. The third section will present basic demographic information on family population

[4] Magnate families in Florence were old quasi-feudal lineages that the Ordinances of Justice in 1292 legally prohibited from holding high political office because of their proclivity to violence.

[5] Goldthwaite 1968, 1983; Kent, 1977.

and on birth and death rates of lineages over time. A fourth section will document the mobility of Florentine families, relative to each other in wealth, in political office, and in intermarriage. A fifth section will document the lack of correlation among various dimensions of "elite." A sixth section will analyze statistically the social, economic, and political causes of intermarriage among Florentine families. A seventh section will analyze statistically the social, economic, and political causes of growth and decline in lineage size. A penultimate eighth section will examine changes in the internal structure and cohesion of these lineages. A conclusion will discuss how all of these trends in mobility, marriage, and lineage were contingent upon the institutional context of Florentine republicanism. Republicanism, I shall argue, induced statistical independence among status dimensions in the first place. For this reason, I do not expect to see the same degree of elite fluidity in non-republican political contexts, such as in Florence after the Quattrocento.[6]

Data and Sources

The overall quantitative dataset from which material for this article was drawn has been assembled from multiple archival and secondary sources and compiled and computerized over a 20-year period. Over one hundred archival sources have been computerized and linked into the overall "Padgett relational dataset."[7] Following the scholarly practice of Herlihy, and also of the sciences, I shall make this data publicly available over the internet in due course. This dataset contains economic, political, and kinship information on 42,763 Florentine males (37,128 with identifiable

[6] Cf. Litchfield, 1986.

[7] A relational database is a set of individual data files that have been linked or interconnected through case IDs. These case IDs allow the computer, upon command, to extract and to compile customized combinations of data from multiple computerized archival sources. Mostly these IDs refer to people, but linkages through family IDs and company IDs were implemented as well. Excel spreadsheets are well-known examples of individual data files. Microsoft-Access is a well-known relational database program; it was the program used here. Oracle and MySQL are other commonly used relational database programs. In the archives, I transcribed primary-source documents into Excel format. At home, I linked through Access newly coded Excel files with previous Excel files by assigning case IDs. The practical complexities involved in assigning IDs to 55,683 people were considerable (e.g., multiple languages and spellings, different people with the same names, truncated names, nicknames, distinct lineages with the same last name, etc.) However, cross-reference through IDs gives the computer its ability to answer multiple-source data questions like these: Who was the wife of this banker? What business was this city councilor in? Who lived near this faction leader? In the future, this data set will be useful for many research projects.

family memberships) and 12,875 Florentine females (11,714 with identifiable family memberships), who lived during the 200-year time period of 1282 to 1500. Archival, primary, and secondary sources for the subset of this information analyzed statistically in this article are listed in the bibliography.

Based on all sources, 1,697 distinct Florentine families have been identified over this 200-year period, using the criterion of common last name (taking care to split similar last names into separate families if they were not related). Of these 1,697 last-name families, 1,177 could be further classified as patrilineages, using the additional criterion of my being able to trace genealogical descent at least from grandfather to father to son. Out of all persons in common-last-name families, 76.1% of them, males and females, were successfully linked to fathers also present in the dataset.

A comprehensive listing of these last-name and lineage families, along with information about their social status and sizes, is provided in a 35-page appendix to the online version of this article. For the 1352–1480 period spanned by the tax censuses, this list is essentially a complete enumeration of Florentine common-last-name families.[8]

Of most direct relevance to this article are three sets of data: tax censuses, political offices, and marriages. Six tax censuses have been coded and incorporated into the relational database. The tax censuses in question, selected to be approximately 25 years apart, are the 1352 *estimo*, the 1379 *prestanze*, the 1403 *prestanze*, the 1427 *catasto*, the 1458 *catasto*, and the 1480 *catasto*.[9] These tax censuses will be the basis for estimating social-mobility rates in wealth as well as for measuring neighborhood (*gonfalone*) residence. Archival sources for these tax records are provided in the bibliography. I discuss below the standardization procedures used for making comparable the disparate assessments underlying these various tax censuses.

[8] One measure of the completeness of any dataset's enumeration is the percentage of persons in newly coded sources who have already appeared in the preexisting dataset. Recently Katalin Prajda, employed as my research assistant, coded all speakers in the *Consulte e Pratiche* advisory councils, from 1348 to 1500. She has found that 97% of the speakers in her coding were already in my dataset.

[9] David Herlihy and Christiane Klapisch-Zuber (1978, 1985) originally coded the 1427 *catasto*. This is now available online (//cds.library.brown.edu/projects/catasto). Anthony Molho (1994) and Julius Kirshner originally coded the 1480 *catasto*. These data were generously donated to Padgett by Molho. Padgett and Katalin Prajda coded the 1352 *estimo* and the 1379 *prestanze* coded in their entirety, partly on the basis of microfilmed copies of these two tax censuses generously donated to Padgett by Sam Cohn. Nicoletta Baldini, employed as Padgett's research assistant, coded a large portion (51.9%) of the 1403 *prestanze*. Padgett coded a large portion (56.3%) of the 1458 *catasto*. The latter two tax censuses were coded under the following restriction: "code all households with last names and all households with tax assessment above 1 florin." My research team is currently in the process of completing the coding of all households in these latter two tax censuses. For 1403 and 1458, I have counted the total numbers of households in each tax census—information required for figure 4.1 below.

In addition to taxes, I coded all members of the Florentine city council or Priorate, from its origin in 1282 until 1500 from the Priorista volume in the Newberry Library in Chicago. These lists of city-council members will be the basis for measuring social-mobility rates in political office. Subsequent to my coding, office-holding data from the post-1383 *Tratte* have been made available online through the efforts of Herlihy, Litchfield, Barducci, and Molho.[10] From this and supplementary archival sources, office holding in the *Buonuomini* and *Gonfalonieri* advisory colleges, and membership in the *Calimala*, *Cambio*, *Lana* and *Por Santa Maria* guilds have also been incorporated into the relational database, dating back to the origins of these institutions.

Finally, 11,107 Florentine marriages over 200 years have been coded (10,306 with identifiable last-name family memberships), with exact dates when recorded[11] in sources or with estimated[12] dates when not recorded. Two clusters of sources form the basis of this marriage dataset: (a) the *carte dell'Ancisa*,[13] located in the *Archivio di Stato di Firenze*, and (b) published genealogies, the most numerous and thorough of which were compiled by Luigi Passerini in the nineteenth century. In all, the marriages of 416 families were directly coded, 378 families from the *carte dell'Ancisa* and 59 families from published sources. By virtue of someone's interest in their compilation, coded families tended to be the larger and the more well-established families in Florence.[14] It is important to note that I coded all the reported marriages of these 416 families, even to other Florentine families not in the directly coded subset. Including families indirectly coded through their intermarriage with the directly coded families, at least some of the marriages of 1,253 last-name

[10] //cds.library.brown.edu/projects/tratte.

[11] The *carte dell'Ancisa* sometimes recorded the same marriage multiple times, due to the multiple primary sources consulted by Pier Antonio dell'Ancisa. In such cases, the earliest recorded dell'Ancisa date was taken to be the marriage date, as long as this was consistent with other temporal data about the couple.

[12] Estimation of marriage dates, when necessary, was performed through triangulation against other secure dates in the computer records of offspring—especially, birth dates of children—and in the target person's own computer records—for example, birth dates, guild matriculation dates, political office dates, etc. Birthdates were coded from the *Libri d'età* (A.S.F., *Tratte* 77, 79).

[13] Pier Antonio di Filippo dell'Ancisa spent much of his seventeenth-century life compiling 14 thick volumes of lists of Florentine marriages from a variety of archival sources. The wide variety of sources consulted by Ancisa, most prominently dowry contracts, are listed in A.S.F. index volume N/187, p. 153. Most of the original sources consulted in the mid-1600s by Ancisa—especially his most important source, dowry contracts—have unfortunately now been lost. For an amusing and appreciative comment about the character of Pier Antonio, see the remarks by his near contemporary Gamurrini 1671, 415.

[14] Sample bias against small obscure families is much less severe for the extensive *carte dell'Ancisa* than it is for published sources.

families are represented in the dataset. What are missing from my sample, by virtue of omission in the sources, are marriages among small, usually obscure Florentine families. Marriages between nuclear families without last names at all—the *popolo minuto*—are not included in this dataset.

In spite of its constraints, data coverage for marriage is substantial. I estimated the percentage of all Florentine marriages contained in my dataset through the following procedure: For each tax census, I calculated the percentages of fathers[15] for whom I had a record of their marriage. This estimation procedure revealed that from 39% to 62% of all marriages[16] among Florentine last-named families appear in my dataset.

Demography of Florentine Families

The simplest level at which to begin the data analysis is basic demography: first the population of Florentine households within lineages and then the birth and death rates of Florentine lineages over time. Basic demography can settle certain overarching issues about trends that have sometimes been contested within the literature.

What percentage of the Florentine population was contained within social families? Here the word "family" refers not to biology or to households but to social identification: namely, what percentage of the Florentine households in tax censuses had last names? And what percentage of Florentine households in tax censuses were members of patrilineages? Especially within the artisanal *popolo minuto*, most Florentines had names like "John, son of Francis, blacksmith," not names like "John Francis Smith." Identifying oneself as a member of a corporate descent group through a public last name, and being so recognized by others, was one sign of having attained social stature in the city. Especially in an erratically growing city like Florence, with many immigrants, the attainment of a recognized family name was the result

[15] Namely, male household heads with known children. I ignore the quantitatively minor issue of illegitimate children (so-called *naturali*) in this estimation procedure. Had I been able to identify and exclude them consistently, estimated sample rates would have been higher than reported, because the (now legitimate) father denominator would have been decreased.

[16] Specifically, the estimated sample coverage rates were these: (a) for 1352, the estimated percentage of all marriages among my identified 1,697 families that was coded was 47.2%; (b) for 1379, it was 39.3%; (c) for 1403, it was 39.6%; (d) for 1427, it was 41.2%; (e) for 1458, it was 53.3%; and (f) for 1480, it was 61.9%. These sample rates are very high for such a distant past. They are a testament both to the richness of the original archives and to the assiduousness of the many researchers over the centuries whose labors have been assembled and computerized here.

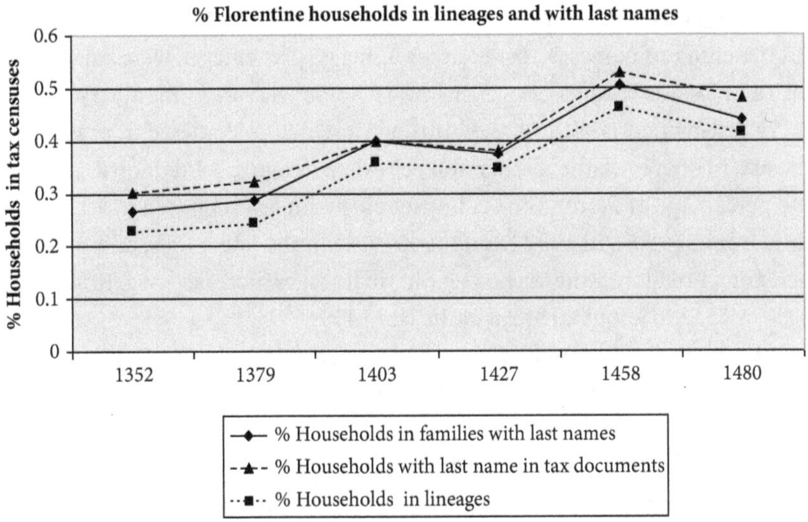

Figure 4.1 Percentage of Tax-Census Households in Lineages and with Last Names

Archival sources: *Estimo* 306 (for 1352), *Prestanze* 367–69 (for 1379), *Estimo* 268 (for 1379), *Prestanze* 1989–2020 (for 1403), *Catasto* 64–85 (for 1427), *Prestanze* 834–37 (for 1458), Molho and Kirshner (for 1480)

of a dynamic process of becoming accepted as contributing members of the community and citizens in the republic.[17] Attaining a last name, in other words, was itself one measure of social mobility. Goldthwaite in 1968 argued that the lineage had declined as a mode of organizing families in Renaissance Florence. Kent in 1977 forcefully denied that claim. Molho (1994) provided an overview of the literature relating to this debate.[18]

Figure 4.1 presents data, over time across the six tax censuses, on the percentages of Florentine tax households with reported last names and in patrilineages. Last-name percentages were measured in two ways: (a) percentages of household heads with last names, as these appeared in the tax documents,[19] and (b) percentages of household heads who were members of the 1,697 families with last names, confirmed across multiple sources.

[17] For example, children of Piero, identified by *di Piero*, might evolve into the *Pieri* family. (In Latin, *Pieri* can mean either a last name or an ablative.) The same logic often held for place names, e.g., *da Vinci*.

[18] Molho 1994, 3–6. See also Jacks and Caferro 2001, 7–9.

[19] "As they appear in the documents" means either (a) I recognized the family name (often with the assistance of either *de'* or *da* prefix), or (b) three consecutive names were listed, the third name of which might be ambiguous (especially in Latin) about whether it referred to a last name or to a grandfather.

These two measurements closely agree in their results because of successful matching of names across sources. Lineage percentages were calculated on the basis of various tax-census households who were members of the 1,177 last-named families linked through verified male descent, at least to the extent of grandfather-father-son. The data in figure 4.1 demonstrate that the percentage of Florentine tax households with last names increased over time from 27–30% in 1352 to about 45–50% in the late-1400s, and that the percentage of Florentine tax households in lineages increased over time from 23% in 1352 to about 40–45% in the late 1400s.[20]

If Goldthwaite's original claim is interpreted to apply to trends in the global population of Florentine families, then it was not correct. On the other hand, Kent's cautious counterclaim, that lineage did not decline during the Renaissance, was too cautious. Actually, the utilization of last names and lineage in the overall Florentine population almost doubled from 1352 to 1480.

There is not much practical difference between the categories of last-named family and of lineage, because most of the last-named families that were not lineages were tiny and inconsequential.[21] The trend upward in all measurements is roughly linear, but slight accelerations are noticeable after changes in political regime—for example, after the post-Ciompi (or Albizzi) regime that commenced in 1382, and after the Medici regime that commenced in 1434.

For more precision, figure 4.2 subdivides last-named families into various social strata, in order to display different trends in family size, measured as average number of households per last-named family. "Social strata" are defined by political age of families—that is, by the dates at which their ancestors first entered the Priorate. In particular, "popolani" were those families whose ancestors were first elected to the Priorate between 1282, the year of the Priorate's origin, and 1342. "New men" were those families whose

[20] These percentages are consistent with the estimates for 1427 and 1480, reported in Molho 2000, 240. But for 1342, Molho reported the percentage of households with surname to be only 12.8%, much lower than my own estimates for 1352. The reason for Molho's low number is his very conservative coding rule, for 1342 only, of counting a third name as a surname only if the partitive *de'* was included in the document.

[21] Explicit listings of these various categories are provided in an online appendix. Many of the non-lineage last-named families are either (a) nuclear families, with no grandfather, or (b) place names of immigrants from the same town, who were not directly related, or (c) unrelated descendants of ancestors with coincidentally the same first name (e.g., del Ricco). Moreover, 57.3% of non-lineage, last-named families were in the lowest "not admitted" social strata (see below), compared to 23.9% of the lineage families.

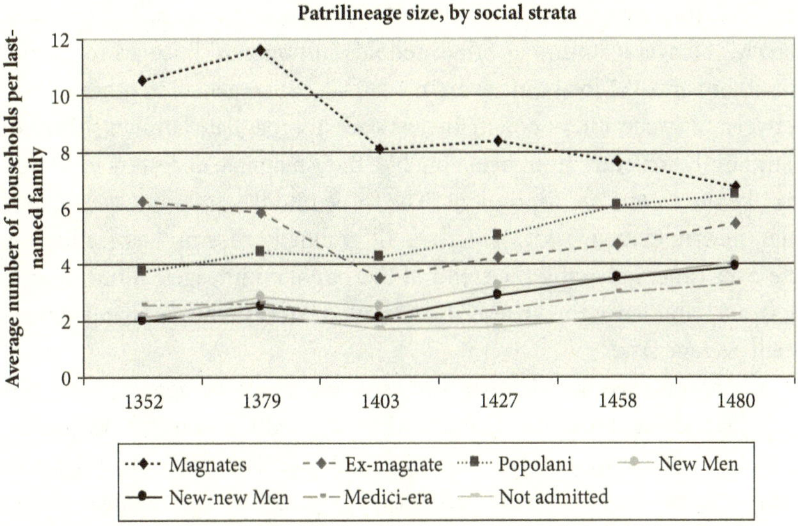

Figure 4.2 Average Family Size (i.e., Number of Households in Families), by Social Strata

Source: Padgett relational database, using archival sources listed in note to figure 4.1. Social strata classifications based on date of first Prior information contained in Newberry Library, *Priorista descritto a Tratte riscontro con quello delle riformagioni e con altre scritture publiche*

ancestors were first elected to the Priorate between 1343 and 1377.[22] "New-new men" I define as those families whose ancestors were first elected to the Priorate between 1378 and 1433. "Medici era" I define as those families whose ancestors were first elected to the Priorate between 1434 and 1493. And "not admitted" I define as those families which never had a member in the Priorate before 1494. "Magnates" were those families legally prohibited from holding high political office by the Ordinances of Justice in 1393. Magnate families were reclassified as "ex-magnates" at the date at which their legal banishment was repealed, if it ever was.[23]

The data on family size in figure 4.2 reveal sharp distinctions in family structure across social classes, which gradually became muted as the Renaissance proceeded. The average number of households in magnate lineages

[22] Cf. Brucker 1962, 21.

[23] For insightful discussions of the conflictual politics among social strata, see Brucker, 1962, 1977, Cohn, 1980, 1999, and Najemy, 1982, 2006. For new men, see Becker and Brucker, 1956, and Becker, 1962. For magnates, see Becker, 1965, and Lansing, 1991, 239–40. For ex-magnates, see Klapisch-Zuber, 2006, 453–57. The entire category of magnate was abolished in 1434 by the early Medici regime, but I continue to label magnate families as such after this date, in order to determine how their social treatment in marriage was affected by their altered legal status.

declined gradually from about ten in 1352 to about seven in 1480.[24] Conversely, the average number of households in popolani lineages rose from about four in 1352 to about seven in 1480—a convergence, in other words, between magnate and popolani lineage sizes. Ex-magnate families shifted in their family structure from behaving like their magnate ancestors to behaving like their popolani aspirations. The three middle-strata lineages of new men, new-new men, and Medici era all gradually rose in average lineage size over time, following the trend of the popolani lineages. Alone among all strata, families in the lowest "not admitted" stratum never changed their small average size.

This social-class breakdown shines a more subtle light on the old Goldthwaite–Kent debate. Goldthwaite was right about the magnates. Evidence in table 4.5, moreover, will reveal that it was not just magnates but also large clans in general that decayed during the Renaissance, unless explicit resources were recruited into these families to resist their decay. Binary debates about lineage going up or down in importance are too crude. There was rather a rearrangement of family structure across social classes. Family-size trends in the magnate, ex-magnate, and not admitted strata suggest that membership in political office was one factor in this family restructuring: Families active in the republican state expanded in size, and families not politically active declined in size. This suggestion will be tested and refined in section seven, below.

The survival rates or longevity of lineage are one of the few statistics for which it is possible to compare Florence with other early-modern European polities.[25] All of the comparison studies refer to nobility and gentry rooted

[24] For a case study of one magnate family's decline, see Bizzochi, 1982. Numerical itemization of the decline of various magnate families is provided in Klapisch-Zuber, 2006, 464.

[25] For Forez in south-central France, Perroy 1962, 31, has shown French noble *lignages* to have survived at the rates of 46.3% for 1300–1400 and 44.9% for 1400–1500. For Bayeux in Normandy, Wood 1977, 7, has shown French noble *lignages* to have survived at the rate of 46.6% for 1463–1598. This extrapolates to a 100-year estimated rate of 51.5% for 1463–1562. For two regions in South Hesse, Gensicke 1965, 129–30, has shown that German noble families survived at the rate of 48.9% for 1430–1555. According to Van Nierop 1993, 51, Holland's noble families first had the very high survival rate of 72.4% for 1555–1650 but then experienced the rapidly declining survival rates of 48.0% in 1600–1700 and 28.6% in 1650–1750. On the other side of the English Channel, Stone 1965, 169, has calculated that English peerage families survived in their male lines at the rate of 58.7% for 1559–1659. For an earlier period, McFarlane 1973, 172–73, has shown English "baron" families to have survived at the low rates of 34.6% for 1300–1400, and 34.0% for 1400–1500. However, McFarlane used the primogeniture criterion of continuous, unbroken male descent, appropriate for dynastic families, rather than the criterion of "any male descendant" used here and in the previously mentioned studies. Grant (1985, 225–231) also used the primogeniture method of defining extinction for the Scottish nobility. I used his data to calculate 100-year Scottish noble-family survival rates of 48.8% for 1325–1424 and of 62.9% for 1400–1500.

Table 4.1 Survival Rates of Lineages by Social Strata

Number of lineages:	1352	1379	1403	1427	1458	1480
Magnates	77	76	75	73	64	60
Popolani	249	239	220	212	182	164
New men	119	175	166	154	141	129
New-new men	94	146	206	226	199	181
Medici-era	41	67	92	112	127	127
Never admitted	93	155	188	224	211	172
Total	673	858	947	1001	924	833

100-year survival rates:
Magnates: 1352–1458 = 64/77 = 83.1%
Popolani: 1352–1458 = 182/249 = 73.1%
New men: 1379–1480 = 129/175 = 73.1%

in landed estates. One might think that such an economic foundation would lead to greater family stability than would the volatile commercialism of the Florentine urban economy. But Molho has forcefully emphasized the counterintuitive durability of Florentine lineages.[26]

In table 4.1, I present data on the survival of lineages, by social strata across time. Because lowest-strata families only gradually came into existence in the period under study, 100-year survival rates could be computed only for the upper strata of magnates, popolani, and new men. For magnates, popolani, and new men, these lineage survival rates were 83.1%, 73.1%, and 73.7%, respectively. These numbers are consistent with the findings of Molho. Florentine lineages exhibited remarkable resilience over time, more so than did their counterparts in northern Europe. In table 4.5 below, I examine statistically the reasons for their demographic success.

To complement the survival/death statistics in table 4.1, I present in table 4.2 data on the frequency of birth of new lineages over time. These data show a huge wave of new-lineage formation in the generation after

[26] Molho 1994, 365–410, identified 471 fifteenth-century lineages, which he labeled the "Florentine ruling class." Of these 417 lineages, 68.3% appeared also on the list by Litchfield 1986, 362–382, of 714 "patrician" Florentine families in the sixteenth through eighteenth centuries.

Table 4.2 Birth of New Lineages by Social Strata

Number of lineages:	1352–1379	1379–1403	1403–1427	1427–1458	1458–1480
Magnates					
Popolani					
New men	55				
New-new men	49	50	24		
Medici-era	29	23	19	15	4
Never admitted	65	45	48	16	3
Total	198	118	91	31	7

the Black Death, as might be expected in a city recovering from a mortality of ~60%, mostly through new immigrants. The Albizzi regime of 1382–1433 continued to exhibit a high volume of new-lineage formation, after the Ciompi Revolt. The Medici regime of 1434–1493, in contrast with that of the Albizzi, exhibited a much-reduced rate of new-lineage formation.[27]

The demographic story of new-lineage formation in Florence, therefore, is that of a huge tidal wave after the Black Death, which gradually subsided. The political story of absorbing new lineages into the Florentine polity is not so simple. Figure 4.3 plots the number of Florentine families who were elected for the first time to the city council or Priorate. Sharp surges of new families into government are evident even before the Black Death during the major political crises of 1282, 1343, and 1378. The sharpness of these surges explains the distinctiveness of social strata in Florence. As every political historian of Florence knows, the Florentine republic incorporated new families into its higher elected bodies in a crisis-filled manner.[28] Among its other effects, this recurrent political turmoil, I shall argue, induced and sustained inconsistency in Florentine status principles.

[27] The last number in table 4.2 of seven new lineages formed in the period between 1458 and 1480 might be artificially suppressed because of truncation effects. That is, new lineages in that late period might not have had enough time to witness the formation of grandfather-father-son genealogies by 1480, even if they were in the process of doing so. The true 1480 number, therefore, is probably higher than the seven reported in table 4.2 but also probably lower than the 31 new lineages accurately reported for 1458.

[28] Brucker 1962, 1977 and Najemy 2006 present the best and most comprehensive overviews.

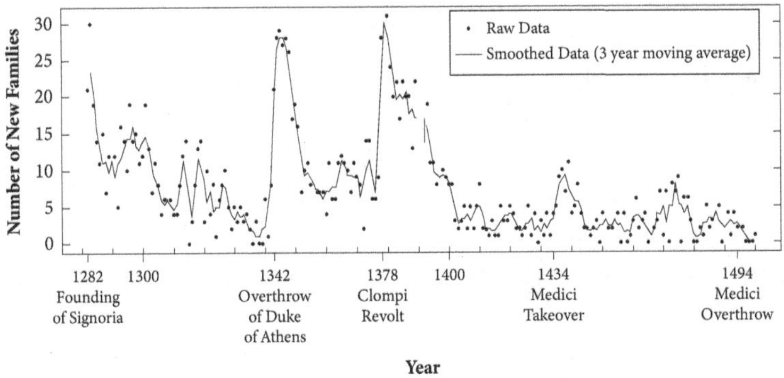

Figure 4.3 Total Numbers of New Families Admitted to the Florentine Priorate, 1282–1532

Data source: Najemy, 1982, 320–23

Social Mobility of Florentine Families

I now shift from demography to social mobility. Given the families described in aggregate in the previous section, how much relative mobility was there among these families? Over almost two centuries, how much did they change rank, on various measures of social stratification—wealth, political office, and marriage hierarchy? Molho 1994, has emphasized the closed-elite character of Florentine "ruling class" families, but I shall respectfully differ. I find that rates of mobility among Florentine families in relative wealth were very high, and that rates of mobility in political office were almost as high.[29] Rates of mobility in marriage were usually low, consistent with Molho, but that they were higher during the Albizzi regime after the Ciompi Revolt. There was thus considerable churning in the rank ordering of Florentine families on various status dimensions, not always in consistent directions.

Figure 4.4 presents data on social mobility in relative wealth, for families in the six tax censuses. The 1427 *catasto* measured and reported net wealth from all revenue streams by household.[30] The 1480 *catasto* measured and reported real-estate wealth by household.[31] The other *estimi* and *prestanze* levied and reported tax assessments, not wealth.[32] Currency units were in lire for 1352 and in florins thereafter. Genealogies and last names enabled

[29] Molho 1968b also found high mobility in political office.
[30] Herlihy and Klapisch-Zuber 1985, 10–20.
[31] Molho 1994, 361–64.
[32] Barbadoro 1933, 615–23; Conti 1984, 119–49, 247–61, 281–87.

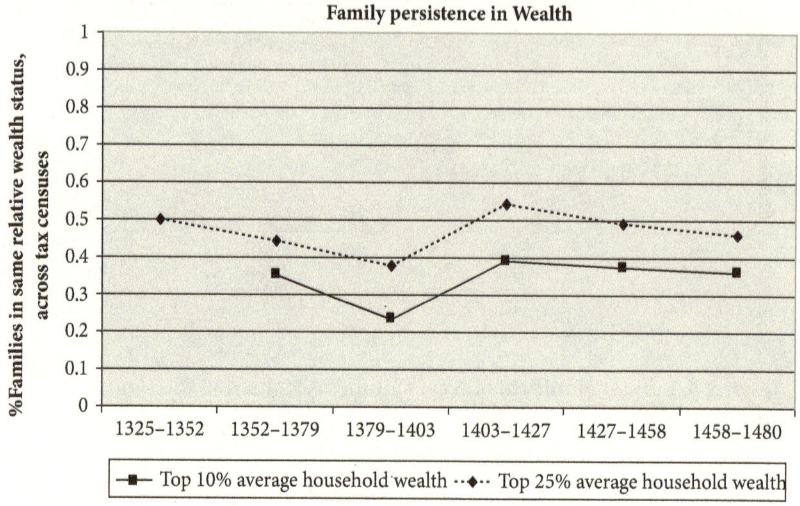

Figure 4.4 Family Stability in Wealth

Sources: A.S.F., Manoscritto 496 (for 1325) plus archival sources listed in note to figure 4.1

the tracking of lineages through these tax censuses, despite their changing composition of households. Changing Florentine tax-assessment procedures creates a challenge for the researcher seeking to establish comparable units of wealth over time and required to measure economic mobility.

The approach taken here to these measurement challenges was not to try to measure "true" absolute wealth, a task that is impossible with heterogeneous tax registers, but rather to focus on *relative* tax assessment or wealth, with families only ranked ordinally with respect to each other. Mobility then is change in relative rankings. Specifically, I first calculated "average wealth per household" or "average tax assessment per household," depending on the census, for each last-named family by dividing the total sum of the wealth (or tax assessments) for all the tax households in each last-named family by the number of households in that family.[33] Secondly, I simplified these family-average statistics into ordinal rankings of relative wealth, in order to

[33] Per capita standardization is crucial to any economic comparison across families, otherwise lineages could be deemed "wealthy" only on the basis of their larger demographic size. The same point applies to political comparisons. Across many authors, the Florentine historiography paints a portrait of economic and political concentration in part because of its failure to apply per-capita standardization. Molho (1968b, 409) is a praiseworthy exception. A different way to put the same point is that economic and political concentration can be produced by patrilineal family dynamics as well as by economic and political dynamics. For clear interpretation, these various causal dynamics need to be teased apart.

abstract away from problems of varying monetary units.[34] Thirdly, I aggregated these rankings into coarse categories—namely, into the categories of top 10% of families[35] in average-per-household wealth, 10–25% in wealth, 25–50% in wealth, 50–75% in wealth, and lowest 25% in wealth. Aggregation into relative strata dampens the effect of measurement error.

Figure 4.4 tracks the movement of Florentine families across these average-household-wealth strata across time, as families rose and declined relative to each other. The data exhibit high rates of relative economic mobility among Florentine families during the Renaissance. During the 1352 to 1480 era of these tax censuses, only about 25% to 40% of Florentine families persisted in the wealthiest top 10% relative-wealth bracket from one 25-year census to the next. Over the 1325 to 1480 period,[36] only about 40–55% of Florentine families persisted even in the top 25% relative-wealth bracket from one tax census to the next. Stability in relative wealth, in other words, was unusual rather than common among families in fourteenth- and fifteenth-century Florence. Stability in family wealth was especially low during the post-Ciompi transition from the 1379 tax census to the 1403 tax census. Turnover rates like these, every 25 years or so, made it difficult for Florentine families to maintain themselves in the upper brackets of relative wealth over long periods of time.[37]

Next I turn to family mobility in politics. Figure 4.5 reports stability of Florentine last-named families in their membership in the Priorate or city council, from 1318 until 1493.[38] Two strata of political participation rates in

[34] This procedure also eliminates the need to correct for inflation.

[35] Given wide dispersion in number of households per family, "top 10%" refers to the top 10% of numbers of households contained in the wealthiest families, not the top 10% of the wealthiest families. The latter approach could have produced far more than 10% of households. Note that this procedure ranks relative wealth only within the population of Florentine families. *Popolo minuto* like "John, son of Francis, blacksmith" are excluded in these calculations, because the goal is to measure social mobility of families.

[36] This is the only time in this paper that computerized data from the 1325 estimo are used because the records from only one *sesto* or large neighborhood have survived. Data are too scanty in 1325 to support serious statistical analysis. Data on "top 10%" for 1325 are not reported in figure 4.2, for example, because there were only 13 such families—far too small for ratios to be statistically reliable.

[37] The percentage of top 10% relative-wealth and top 25% relative-wealth families in 1352 who survived as such to 1480 was 14.9% and 18.3%, respectively. The percentage of top 10% and top 25% families in 1379 who survived as such to 1480 was 11.5% and 23.8%, respectively.

[38] The Priorate was founded in 1282. I have data on Priorate memberships dating back to this origin but, absent tax censuses from that far back, I have no data on family sizes (i.e., numbers of tax households per family) with which to standardize these Priorate participation rates. Even standardizing the 1318–1348 political period with family-size data from the 1352 estimo is pushing it. Normally Priorate participation was standardized by the average of family sizes reported in the two tax censuses that bracketed the period. For example, standardized family participation rates were calculated by dividing the number of times that a family appeared in the Priorate during 1348–1378 by the average household size of that family, as reported in the 1352 and 1379 tax censuses.

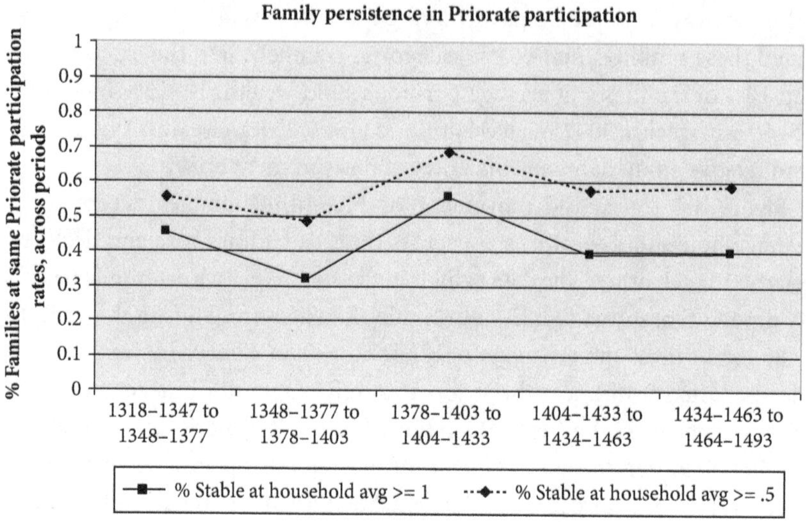

Figure 4.5 Family Stability in Priorate Participation

Sources: Newberry Library *priorista* plus archival sources listed in note to figure 4.1

this so-called *reggimento* were defined for purposes of measuring movement across these thresholds: (a) a family average of one or more Priorate seats per household, within each 30-year period, and (b) a family average of only 1/2 or more Priorate seats per household, within each 30-year period. Figure 4.3 reports the percentages of families who maintained themselves within the Priorate across time at these two different participation-rate thresholds.

At the higher participation rate of one or more Priorate seats per household every 30 years, only 30–55% of Florentine families maintained this level of political participation from one 30-year period to the next. At the lower participation rate of only 1/2 or more Priorate seats per household every 30 years, 50–70% of Florentine families maintained their participation from one period to the next. Some political stability is observed here, but clearly family turnover in Florentine politics was high. Figure 4.3 also reported this in a different way. Consistent with the temporal patterns in economic mobility documented in figure 4.4, the highest rate of political turnover in Renaissance Florence occurred between the *reggimento* of 1348–1377 and the *reggimento* of 1378–1403. Both in wealth and in political office, the highest levels of family mobility are observed in the Albizzi regime after the Ciompi Revolt.

Najemy has made the cogent point that political office was not the same thing as political power, especially in a world as dense in patron–client relationships as was Florence.[39] My research assistant Katalin Prajda is currently in the process of coding speakers to the advisory body, the *Consulte e Pratiche*. This coding will eventually permit an explicit measurement of turnover in this more hidden face of political power. However that measurement turns out, it was the public face of elected political office that was central to the status concerns of rising new men.[40]

Finally I have calculated social mobility in marriage. It is not straightforward to measure the "prestige" or the "value" of a lineage in the Florentine marriage market,[41] and hence its change over time. But social-network methods can be used to assess the degree to which a last-named family was in the core or on the periphery of the Florentine intermarriage network. In particular, the statistical concept of "structural cohesion"[42] measures the minimum number of links, anywhere in the network, that must be severed in order to disconnect any particular node (perhaps including its neighbors) from the rest of the network. For example, a family having structural-cohesion level of one means that only one (well-chosen) marriage has to be eliminated in order to detach that family from the rest of the Florentine marriage network. "Periphery" can be defined as the set of nodes in such fragile network positions. But to take another example, a family having structural-cohesion level of four means that a minimum of four (perfectly chosen) marriages must be deleted in order to detach that family, perhaps along with its in-laws, from the rest of the Florentine marriage network. "Core" can be defined as the set of nodes in such deeply integrated and hard-to-remove network positions. Algorithms were constructed to calculate Florentine families' structural cohesion levels (from zero to eight), over time, from the marriage data described above.[43] Social mobility in this marriage context means movement of a family, through its pattern of marriages with other families, into or out of the core of the city's marriage network.

Using the same 30-year periodization as in previous figures,[44] figure 4.6 reports the rates of movement of families into or out of the Florentine

[39] Najemy 1982, 263–300. See also Brucker 1962, 109–127.

[40] Brucker 1962, 125.

[41] Dowries would have been valuable data to use for this purpose, but I do not have data on dowries. For other researchers' samples, see Cohn 1980, 54–56; 1998, 189; Lansing 1991, 130; Fabbri 1991, 213; Molho 1994, 310; Chabod 1995, 103; and Botticini and Siow 2003, 1392.

[42] Moody and White 2003.

[43] I thank Peter McMahan, 2007, for his labors constructing a structural cohesion algorithm in the PC-oriented R programming language to do these analyses. This algorithm is publicly available on my website. James Moody originally implemented the algorithms in mainframe-oriented SAS.

[44] For example, to prepare marriage networks for analysis, a "1348–1377 marriage network" among Florentine families was assembled out of my global dataset from all marriages with dates in this range. And likewise for all other 30-year time periods.

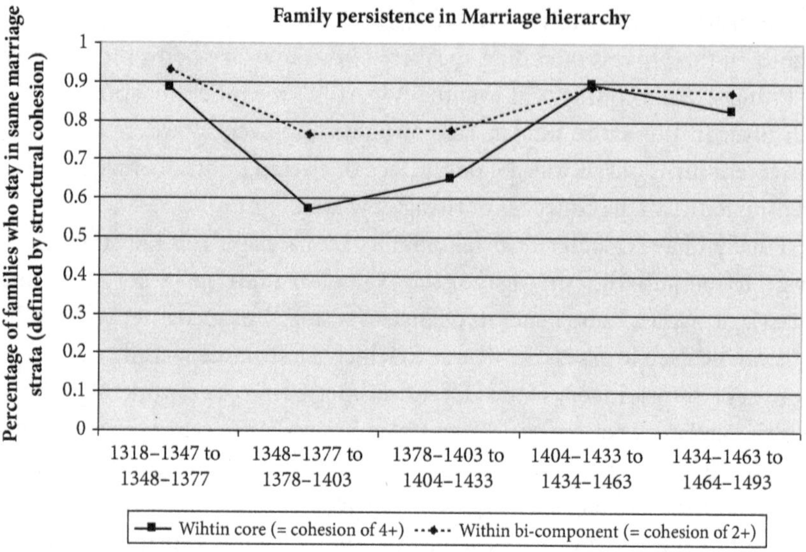

Figure 4.6 Family Stability in Marriage Hierarchy

Sources: A.S.F., *Manoscritti Carte dell'Ancisa* 348–61 plus genealogies in secondary sources listed in bibliography

marriage-network core over time. Two levels of structural-cohesion were used as thresholds for measuring movement: (a) "core" is operationally defined in that figure as a structural-cohesion level of four or more; (b) "bi-component" is defined there as the weaker structural-cohesion level of only two or more. Movement into or out of the core can be interpreted as movement of families into or out of the Florentine "marriage elite." Movement into or out of the bi-component can be interpreted as movement of families into or out of the Florentine marriage market itself.

Here, data are somewhat at variance with the generally high-mobility story told in figures 4.4 and 4.5. As a bi-component whole, the Florentine marriage market was very stable over time: 80–90% of Florentine families persisted at the low structural-cohesion level of two or more. Since this low structural-cohesion level measures only the persistence of Florentine families in the marriage market, this is not so surprising. However, for three out of the five transitions between periods measured, Florentine elites also were very stable in their global marriage-network patterns, even at the high structural-cohesion level of four or more. In particular, for the transition surrounding the Black Death (namely, from 1318–1347 to 1348–1377) and for the two Medici-era transitions (namely, from 1404–1433 to 1434–1463, and from 1434–1463 to 1464–1493), about 80 to 90% of Florentine families in the Florentine marriage-network core succeeded in preserving their core marriage status into the next 30-year period, in spite of the high levels of economic and political turnover documented above. Consistent with the interpretation of Molho 1994, this is clear evidence for conservatism in Florentine intermarriage: Elite marriage acted as a barrier (successful or not) against strong currents of economic and political mobility.

This elite conservatism in marriage, however, weakened significantly during the Albizzi regime, following the Ciompi Revolt (in other words, from 1344–1377 to 1378–1403 and from 1378–1403 to 1404–1433). In those decades, rates of successful persistence of families within the Florentine marriage core dropped sharply to only 55–65%. In the subsequent Medici regime, the marriage core rebounded to its pre-Ciompi high rate of endogamy. The family composition of this reconstituted marriage "elite" under the Medici, however, had changed because of the intervening, more socially open period. All three measures of social mobility—economic, political, and marriage—agree that the greatest period of fluidity in Florentine families' relative status occurred after the Ciompi Revolt. However "oligarchic" the Albizzi regime was in its politics and policies, it was not so in its degree of social mobility.

Multiple Dimensions of Florentine "Elite"

Despite demonstrable resistance in marriage to social fluidity (except during the Albizzi regime), high rates of Florentine social mobility in wealth, in political office, and in last names are evident. The consequences of such high rates of mobility for elite structure, however, depend upon how these various dimensions of mobility were interrelated. If stratification dimensions were strongly correlated, then Florentine families could move up or down the various dimensions roughly in tandem—perhaps led by success or failure in wealth, which eventually translated into other domains. Such consistency among stratification dimensions would produce temporal succession of families—the displacement of one cohort of families by another—within an elite structure that remained well-defined taken together. On the other hand, if the stratification dimensions were empirically not correlated, then Florentine elite coherence itself becomes very much an issue. In that case, the data would point not to an "elite" or to a "ruling class" but rather to the existence of multiple contending Florentine "elites," each standing at the head of a different status hierarchy. Not only our interpretation of Florentine social mobility but also our interpretation of Florentine politics depends upon how the multiple dimensions of Florentine stratification fit together—to induce either coherence or incoherence in Florentine elite structure.

Table 4.3 presents empirical correlations among four dimensions of Florentine stratification—social status, wealth, political office, and family size—at different points in time. The table documents generally low correlations

Table 4.3 Intercorrelations of Social Class, Wealth, Political Office, and Family Size

Correlation (i.e., r) between:	1348–1377	1378–1403	1404–1433	1434–1463	1464–1493
Popolani and Family Size	.1206	.1497	.2026	.2121	.2481
Popolani and Political Office	.1577	.0707	.1558	.0435	−.0237
Popolani and Wealth	.0342	−.0017	.0022	.0781	.0892
Wealth and Political Office	.1009	.0515	.0833	.1715	.1944
Wealth and Family Size	.0333	.0091	.0238	.1498	.1733
Political Office and Family Size	−.0737	−.1014	−.0261	−.0305	−.0396

N.B.: (a) "Popolani" is a 0/1 dummy variable, depending upon whether family's ancestor was first admitted to Priorate, during period from 1282 to 1342, and was not declared to be magnate in 1293. Popolani were the most prestigious social stratum in Florence.
(b) Per capita "wealth" is defined here as normalized average wealth (for 1427, 1480) or tax assessment (for 1352, 1378, 1403, and 1458) per household in each patrilineage. "Normalized" means that, for each census, each family's average household wealth or tax assessment was divided by the mean overall wealth or tax assessment in my coded data, in order to make otherwise diverse monetary scales comparable across censuses. "Average" is defined both over all households in each last-named family and over available tax censuses [i.e., the tax censuses of 1352, 1379, 1403, 1427, 1458, and 1480] at beginning and end of period.
(c) Per capita "political office" is defined here as number of Priorate offices held per household in each last-named family during the period listed. "Per household" means dividing total number of Priorate offices held by a family by that family's average number of tax households.
(d) "Family size" is defined here as average number of tax households in each last-named family. "Average" here and throughout was defined over available tax censuses at beginning and end of period.

among these various dimensions, and therefore incoherence within the structure of the Florentine "elite."[45]

"Social status" is measured in this table by *popolani*, previously defined as that set of families whose ancestors first were elected to the Priorate between 1282 and 1342. This *popolani* social stratum embodied the republican conception of honor—namely, "service to the state," even to the extent of "creators of the [republican] state." On average, this large stratum of families dominated the culture and politics of Florence during this period more than did any other, even though their political fluctuations were considerable.[46]

Political stratification is measured in table 4.3, like in figure 4.5, by the average per-capita number of Priorate offices held by a family during various 30-year periods of examination. The Priorate was a city council of nine members, which turned over every two months. Hence, potentially a large number of families could (and increasingly did) participate in Florentine governance over time.[47] In order to control for the tautology of larger families having more chances to be elected, each family's total number of Priorate offices in each period was standardized, like in the previous section, by dividing by family size, as measured by the average number of that family's households in adjacent tax censuses.

Economic stratification is measured in this table by each family's normalized average tax assessment per household. "Normalization" means dividing the average wealth/tax assessment per household by the average tax assessment (or wealth declaration, as the case may be) in each census, across all Florentine families' households. This procedure induces standardization in a more continuous way than the discrete strata approach in figure 4.4. Average (normalized) household wealth was then calculated for each family, pooling the two tax censuses before and after the period under study.[48]

[45] Of course self-conception could have been a different story (cf. Baron 1966). If Baron is right about the success of Albizzi-regime elites in constructing a coherent "civic humanist" conception of themselves, the fact that this did not have a clear demographic foundation affects one's interpretation and appreciation of that cultural achievement.

[46] Brucker 1977, 254–55, and Najemy 1982, 263–317, both made the cogent point that power was concentrated among families in this stratum after the Ciompi revolt, even though participation diffused. Padgett and McLean 2006, 1526, traced the economic fortunes of this stratum, which also rose after the Ciompi revolt. Below I resolve the tensions between these observations and the elite-fluidity findings in this article by emphasizing the mimetic more than the dictatorial power of this group.

[47] Molho 1968b, 409; Witt 1976, 247–51; Brucker 1977, 254; Najemy 1982, 150, 199, 201, 293–95.

[48] For example, "average household (normalized) wealth for the period 1343 to 1377" was calculated using the tax censuses of both 1352 and 1379.

Pooling was done in order to smooth out statistical noise due to potentially small numbers of households in any one lineage.

Demographic stratification is measured in this table by family size—that is, by the number of households listed in each tax census for each family. Again, family averages were calculated over the two tax censuses at the beginning and end of each study period, in order to smooth out the statistical noise in small numbers.

Table 4.3 presents the simple correlations among these alternative dimensions of elite status. The main message contained in the table is the low values of these correlations. With the exception of *popolani* and family size, no pair of stratification measures is correlated at a level greater than the correlation level of .2.

Within these generally low correlations, details are consistent with well-known facts in Florentine political history:

(a) The correlation between *popolani* and family size increased over time, eventually to the correlation level of .25, because the average number of households within *popolani* families rose over this period from 3.7 taxed households per family in 1352 to 6.5 households in 1480, as was shown in figure 4.2. Conversely, the average size of magnate families fell from 9.6 households in 1352 to 6.8 households in 1480.

(b) *Popolani* disproportionately were elected to city council in 1343–1377 and in the Albizzi regime of 1403–1433, but they lost power during the Ciompi Revolt and during the Medici regime.[49] What is mildly surprising is that the correlation between *popolani* status and political office was not higher than it was in these two periods.

(c) There is a small but consistently negative correlation between political office and family size because of the operation of the *divieto*, a law which limited the number of times any one family could serve on the city council.[50]

What is most remarkable in these generally low numbers is the absence of correlation between wealth and everything else—except during the Medici regime, when the correlations between wealth and political office and

[49] Brucker 1962, 1977; Cohn 1980, 1999; Padgett and Ansell 1993; Najemy 2006.
[50] Brucker 1962, 67–68.

between wealth and family size increased somewhat. Even granted that any vibrant commercial economy induces volatility in wealth, it is surprising to find a strongly commercial society where wealth is not the foundation of dominance on other dimensions. But in Florence, politics and family age contended with wealth as alternative markers of elite status.

As unusual as these low correlations may be comparatively,[51] the statistical evidence about elite incoherence in table 4.3 is consistent with the lively contemporary contestation and debate in Renaissance Florence about the meaning of fundamental hierarchical words like "nobility" and "honor."[52]

Marriage Among Florentine Families

So far, the evidence presented in this article has supported interpretations of Renaissance Florentine history that emphasize social fluidity among lineages: (1) Despite considerable resistance in marriage, social mobility in wealth, in politics, in last names, and even in marriage itself during the Albizzi regime was substantial. This mobility induced considerable turnover and churning in the stratification of Florentine families. (2) So much so that Florentine elites were cross-cutting and inconsistent in their multiple status orderings. (3) Yet the lineage units underneath this collective churning were remarkably stable, compared to northern European noble families. What mechanisms produced this apparent paradox of lineage stability and high rates of relative family mobility? In the rest of this article, I shall look underneath aggregate trends to search for answers to this question—first by examining statistical determinants of marriage in this section, and then by examining statistical determinants of growth in lineage size in the next section.

To anticipate the findings to be presented in this section, Florentine lineages tended to marry each other when they (a) were both large lineages, (b) lived near each other, (c) were both magnates or were both new men, (d) were similar in wealth, and (e) participated in the same political faction. On the other hand, (f) common political-office participation and (g) common *popolani* status did *not* increase likelihood

[51] Unfortunately the comparative part of this statement cannot be made more precise in the absence of statistical studies similar to this one for other countries. I hope that such studies will appear in the future.

[52] Rabil 1991, 16–23; McLean 2007, 59–89.

of intermarriage. These factors channeled lineages together into cross-cutting marriage alliances, with important consequences for Florentine elite structure.

More broadly, the findings in table 4.4 will identify the not-always-consistent historical cross-currents underlying Florentine marriage networks. On the dimensions of political office (*reggimento*) and *popolani*, Florentine elites were surprisingly open to the incorporation of newcomers through marriage. On the dimensions of wealth and political factionalism, however, victorious elites tried to "close the door behind them" through endogamous intermarriage, attempting to cut off in-mobility. These elite-closure efforts ultimately failed, since history kept moving on, creating yet another rising wealthy cohort, yet another factional cleavage. As a result of political turmoil, the Florentine marriage network tended to lurch, over 30-year-regime units of time, from one endogamous core to another, subjecting the elite system as a whole to repeated shocks. Patrilineage itself was the main stabilizing force fighting against episodic churning. For older families, large Florentine patrilineages supported each other in marriage, not always successfully, whenever tumultuous forces beset them. For new families, the attainment of a recognized last name was perhaps the only mobility victory that was permanent.

Table 4.4 presents the results of my statistical analysis of Florentine marriages, over a two-century time span. The dependent variable being explained by the variables reported in the rows of table 4.4 is the number of marriages taking place between two families, during the time period identified in the columns. The unit of analysis is family-pairs, that is, the two-family couplet who could have married (or not). Zero-inflated Poisson regression[53] is the correct variant of multiple-regression analysis to use, given the count structure of this dyadic data. What all this means is this: (a) that for each time period under study,[54] the set of all families with at least one observed marriage was assembled, (b) that all pairings of such families were constructed, and (c) that a count was made of how many

[53] Poisson regression is appropriate for count data. "Zero-inflated" is a two-stage logit-regression correction used for datasets, like this one, in which the vast majority of family pairs had an observed count of zero (Long 1997, 242–47).

[54] Aggregating intermarriage data into 30-year study periods mitigates errors that may exist in dates of marriage. Both observed and estimated marriage dates could easily be off by a few years, but they are very unlikely to be off by 30 years, or even by 15. Thus, given the data, macro trends over centuries can be studied reliably, whereas estimating year-by-year fluctuations has measurement errors (as do all data).

Table 4.4 Zero-Inflated Poisson Regressions on Inter-Family Marriages[a]

	1282–1317	1318–1347	1348–1377	1378–1403	1404–1433	1434–1463	1464–1493
Controls:							
Expected baseline[b]	6.9468***	3.9616***	1.2964***	3.1385***	2.9784***	5.5228***	4.6914***
Male family seen	.0140	.0923	.3645***	.1131	.1480	.1773*	.1703**
Female family seen	–.0258	.1117	.1688*	.0184	.0671	.0969	.1200(*)
Large Lineages[c]							
Households≥5			.1205	**.2166****	**.2318****	.0885	**.1493****
Neighborhood:							
same quarter (ngonf)	**.4176****	**.3716*****	**.3556*****	**.1470***	**.1422***	**.1563****	.0281
same gonfaloni[d]	**.8896*****	**.6324*****	**.5614*****	**.5581*****	**.4988*****	**.5362*****	**.2046***
Social strata:							
Magnate-magnate	–.0010	.2348	**.5880*****	**.6974*****	**.5978****	**.4390***	**.4483***
Magnate-exmagnate[e]			.1222	–.1804	–.3143	.0489	.1730
exmagnate-exmagnate			–11.080	.1047	.3194	.6601	.5342
magnate-popolani	–.0455	–.1211	–.0258	.0537	.0534	.0868	.1277
exmagnate-popolani			–.1352	.1159	–.1167	–.1119	.0193
popolani-popolani	.0027	.1885	–.0235	–.0130	–.0905	–.0245	.0568
popolani-new men[f]	–.3662	–.0819	.0456	–.1459	–.0492	–.0028	.0400
New men-newmen	1.1615	**.8756***	.0209	**.3322***	.0102	–.0494	–.0465
Exmagnate-newmen			–.2031	–.7210*	–.1229	–.2945	–.1883

continued

Table 4.4 *continued*

	1282–1317	1318–1347	1348–1377	1378–1403	1404–1433	1434–1463	1464–1493
Magnate-newmen	−.3420	−.3337	**−.4190****	**−.3272***	−.2457	−.1114	−.0550
Wealth: tax assessment averages[g]							
male & female: top 10% of wealth			**.4062****	**.3625****	**.4707*****	**.2654***	**.3995*****
male & female: top 10–25% of wealth			**.2256****	**.2099***	**.1622**$^{(*)}$	**.1570***	.0941
male top 25%—female bottom 50%			−.1292	**−.2597****	**−.3224****	**−.3330*****	**−.1680***
male bottom 50%—female top 25%			**−.2079***	**−.2128***	**−.2602****	**−.2593****	**−.1645***
male & female: bottom 50%			.1102	−.0202	.1919	.1341	.0378
Guild: matriculation[h]							
Calimala (trading)		.2151	.2851	.0746	**.2014***	**.1759**$^{(*)}$	**.1874***
Cambio (banking)		−.1394	.1360	.0318	**.1712***	.0315	−.0118
Lana (wool)[i]		−.3674	.1179	.1254	**.1665***		
Por S. Maria (silk)				−3.358	−.1410	.1101	−.2778
Company partnerships:[j]							
Int'l merchant-bank				1.0382	−.0787	−.1053	
Domestic banking	−2.5547	−.1714	.0257	.0169	**.5469***	.0881	**.0711****
Wool manufacturing					.3880	.1819	
Silk manufacturing					**1.1257****	.45349	

Political office:							
Cumulative Priorate[k]							
male & fem. top 25%	−.2517	−.3482	.2525	.1013	**.2650***	−.2101	.0059
Political office: Priorate[l]							
male & female ≥3	−.0576	−.1536	−.1134	.0561	−.1653	.0676	.0977
male & female 1–2	.0444	−.0437	.1792	−.0676	−.1058	−.1147	−.1859
Political office: Mercanzia							
male & female ≥1	.1425	.0489	.1222	.1535	.0953	.0987	.1141$^{(*)}$
Political factions:							
Black guelfs (1301)	**.3995***	**.4802*****	**.4577*****	**.2480***			
White guelfs (1301)	−.4561	.3194	.1824	.2181			
Albizzi partisans	.0950	.1843	.0963	.0900			
Ricci partisans	.5190	−.1990	.2688	.2957			
anti-ciompi (1378)	−.0454	.0258	**.3418*****	**.5562*****	**.2418***	.1780$^{(*)}$	.0483
pro-ciompi (1378)	.3288	**.48947*****	.0739	**.2534***	.2283	.1493	.0656
Oligarchs[m] (1433)					.2354$^{(*)}$	.0468	.0604
Mediceans (1433)					.1544	.0942	**.2134****
Mediceans (1449)					.0883	.1303	**.2278***
anti-Mediceans[n] (1466)					.1603	**.2792****	−.0650
Poisson constant	−3.798***	−3.837***	−3.742***	−4.198***	−4.078***	−3.989***	−3.987***
Inflated zeros:							
Expected baseline	−393.52***	−377.84***	−218.41***	−602.34***	−443.49***	−344.13***	−362.62***
zeros constant	4.178***	4.157***	3.830***	3.959***	3.827***	3.679***	3.698***
# dyads	40,000	116,964	425,104	416,025	372,100	501,264	497,025
# non-zero dyads	244	589	1561	1262	1258	1888	2183

Log likelihood	−1136.79	−2836.28	−8091.84	−6787.32	−6622.74	−9884.76	−11041.36
LR chi^2	101.25	279.53	629.65	543.49	466.47	552.82	675.28

*** = ($p < .001$); ** = ($p < .01$); * = ($p < .05$); (*) = ($p < .06$)

[a] Families were included in these dyad-based Poisson regressions only if at least one marriage (son or daughter) by them was observed in the period in question.

[b] "Expected baseline" was calculated from marriage marginals (i.e., total numbers of brides and grooms) in chi-square manner. This calculation controls for the tautological aspect of family size—namely, the fact that size is statistically important simply because large families produce more children to marry.

[c] "Family size" was calculated as the lineage's average number of households, as measured by tax censuses at beginning and end of reported periods [i.e., the 1352, 1379, 1403, 1427, 1458, and 1480 tax censuses]. "Large lineages" is a binary variable defined as 1 if both lineages had greater than or equal to five households in average family size, and zero otherwise. Because of the inclusion of "expected baseline" as control, the statistical effect of this variable is above and beyond the tautological aspect of family size.

[d] For this purpose, "modal gonfaloni" was measured in tax census at end of respective period. For the first 1282–1317 period, gonfaloni data from the first available 1352 tax census was projected backward.

[e] Klapisch-Zuber (2006) provides valuable information on when some magnate families' legal status was repealed. All magnates' legal status was repealed in 1434, but in the last two regressions I maintain the 1433 status of magnate families to see if there was a residual effect on marriage even after legal repeal.

[f] Because of similar coefficients between new men and new-new men, in this table I aggregated new men and new-new men into the combined stratum of "new men"—namely, "ancestor admitted to priorate 1343–1433."

[g] Tax assessment "averages" in two senses: (a) tax census at beginning and at end of period, and (b) household average within each patrilineage. In order to average them, tax censuses first were made comparable through normalization at mean of respective tax assessments of households in my dataset.

[h] "Families in same guild" defined as both lineages having had at least two members matriculate in the guild during the period in question.

[i] I have not yet finished coding the matriculation records of *Arte della Lana* for 1441–1500.

[j] "Company partnerships" defined in units of partner-years. That is, the independent variable here is the total number of times a company partnership is observed between the two patrilineages' members, over the years of observation of companies available to me. Because of the varying numbers of years available to my observation, company-partnership coefficients are not comparable in magnitude across periods, as they are for all other variables

[k] "Cumulative Priorate" was measured by total number of priorate offices held by families since 1282. Dummy-variable measure equaled 1 when both male and female families were in set of top families collectively having held 25% of seats, and it equaled 0 otherwise.

[l] "Priorate" was measured by number of priorate offices held by families during period in question. Dummy-variable measure equaled 1 when both male and female families were in set of families with ≥ 3 offices (or as indicated), and it equaled 0 otherwise.

[m] The coefficient for "oligarchs" was significant for 1404–1433 until the anti-ciompi variable was included. This indicates that marriage *was* an important organizational component of that faction, but that this inherited component was a residue of the Ciompi Revolt, as discussed in Padgett and Ansell (1993).

[n] Families of the top 125 signatories of the anti-Medicean petition reported and discussed in Pampaloni (1964). "Top 125" chosen as cutoff to make comparable with sizes of Kent's 1433 lists.

marriages occurred between each pair of families during the examination period—zero, one, two, three, etc. Care was taken to distinguish the gendered directionality of marriage—namely, the number of marriages between a groom's family and a bride's family was distinguished from the number of marriages between the same two families with bride and groom roles reversed.

Details of how independent variables, likewise dyadic in nature, were constructed and are presented in the footnotes of table 4.4. A positive coefficient in table 4.4 usually means endogamy—namely, families similar on that independent-variable dimension tended to marry each other. A negative coefficient in the table usually means exogamy—namely, families similar on that dimension tended to avoid marrying each other. When these independent variables' values ranged from zero to one (the case with most variables), the numerical values of their coefficients are comparable, but otherwise they are not. More important than magnitude are the significance levels reported in table 4.4, denoted by asterisks.[55] Sometimes numerical values of estimated regression coefficients can be high without achieving statistical significance. This usually means that the number of observed cases underlying that coefficient was too low for reliable inference. Readers should pay attention mainly to reported coefficients with statistical significance.

Passing over the three variables listed first in the table, which statistically control for potentially confounding issues of family-size tautology[56] and sample bias,[57] the first finding of interest is the effect of family size itself on the likelihood of intermarriage. Above and beyond the tautological fact that large families were more likely to marry each other simply because they had more children, large Florentine lineages were more likely to marry each other. This result points to a patrilineage logic in marriage above and beyond wealth, status, politics and all the other variables in the regressions. While not statistically true in every period, it was true in four out of six observed periods.

[55] The more the asterisks, the higher the level of statistical significance, as explained at end of table 4.4.

[56] Namely, large families are more likely to marry each other simply because they have more sons and daughters. Including this variable as a control eliminates this issue from confounding other effects.

[57] Namely, as explained above, families who have been directly coded from *carte dell'Ancisa* and other sources are more likely to have reported marriages than families who were indirectly coded. Including these two binary variables explicitly as controls eliminates this issue from confounding other effects.

This non-tautological effect of family size, coupled with the tautological effect of family size, implies that large patrilineages formed a dense cluster of intermarrying families at the center of the Florentine marriage network. One reason for not discarding the concept of "elite" altogether, in spite of its incoherence problems, is the patrilineage itself. Patrilineage family structure within Florence was perhaps the most essential mechanism that concentrated and channeled Florentine intermarriage into a dense marriage-network core in the first place. Patrilineage was the social glue that held the Florentine marriage network together at its core, in the face of strong centrifugal forces of economic and political mobility threatening to tear it apart.[58]

The second set of significant findings concerns the effect of neighborhood on the likelihood of intermarriage. Measured either at the fine-grained (sixteen-unit) level of *gonfaloni* or at the coarser-grained (four-unit) level of quarter, the effect of neighborhood propinquity on intermarriage was consistently significant. Families that lived near to each other married each other. This finding will hardly come as a surprise to Florentine historians.[59] More surprising is the fact that the magnitude of this effect steadily declined over the two-century period under study. In the first two periods of our study, 1282–1317 and 1318–1347, neighborhood was the strongest effect of all in those regressions.[60] As the Renaissance proceeded, this geographical grounding to Florentine marriages gradually dissolved, until it became barely detectable in the time of Lorenzo de' Medici.[61]

The third set of significant findings concerns the effects of social class—namely, of magnates, ex-magnates, new men, and *popolani*.

(a) In their legal beginning from 1293 to 1343, when magnate families were still strong and threatening, they did not tightly marry each other. Rather they continued to intermarry with their titular

[58] Cf. Adams 2005.

[59] Cf. Kent and Kent 1982; Kent 1987.

[60] The statistical power of these early neighborhood coefficients is especially notable because in these two early periods, family "neighborhood" was measured from the 1352 tax census and then projected backward. Before 1343, the administrative map of Florence was divided into six (*sesti*) instead of into sixteen (*gonfaloni*) and four (quarters). Thus it is impossible to measure *gonfaloni* residence from contemporary documents before 1343. Neighborhood measurement based on 1352, with the heroic assumption of no residential mobility, is the best that one can do for earlier years. The fact that neighborhood coefficients are so strong in table 4.4, in spite of this shaky assumption, implies (a) that geographical mobility really was quite low, especially for patrilineages with large medieval houses-cum-towers, and (b) that the true effect of neighborhood propinquity on Florentine marriage was even higher than reported in table 4.4.

[61] Cf. Cohn 1980, 52–59; Padgett and Ansell, 1993, 1288, 1299.

enemies, the *popolani.*[62] After their final defeat in 1343, however, magnates turned in on themselves through endogamous marriage. In defeat, Florentine magnates were like a deposed and dying aristocracy, which history had passed by, but whose proud but archaic collective memory of their own history remained strong. Magnate endogamy remained strong even after the Medici eliminated their legal status in 1434 and after the magnates declined demographically (see figure 4.2 above).

(b) Once ex-magnate lineage branches splintered off from their magnate roots,[63] the marriage behavior of these ex-magnates changed. They did not switch toward endogamy with some other social-class group. Instead ex-magnates became almost[64] social-class blind in their intermarriage behavior, like the *popolani* whom they aspired to be.

(c) "New men," defined in this particular table as the union of new men and new-new men,[65] were also endogamous in the periods 1318–1347 and 1378–1403. Very pronounced was the marriage antipathy between them and the magnates (including even the ex-magnates). This social-class aversion reached levels of statistical significance in the two periods 1348–1403, but a milder form of it is detectable throughout the two centuries under study, via the negative-coefficient signs in the regressions.

(d) The most surprising finding among these social-strata coefficients is a counterintuitive finding of non-significance. The highest social stratum, namely the *popolani*, never exhibited at any time any social-strata preference in their marriage behavior, either endogamy among themselves or exogamy regarding anyone else. Amazingly enough, the *popolani* were social-class blind in their marriages, on average, after accounting statistically for wealth, family size, and other endogamy factors. According to republican standards, *popolani*

[62] For the early period 1285–1294, Ottokar 1962, 47–89 documents many close ties between magnates and popolani, including marriages. For the post-1350 period, see Klapisch-Zuber 2006, 383–408.

[63] The splintering of ex-magnate lineages from their magnate roots usually entailed adopting a new last name. Klapisch-Zuber, 2006, 209–19, 453–59, provides a valuable tabulation of these lineage descents.

[64] The "almost" is due to (c).

[65] These two social-class categories were combined in this regression analysis to achieve better precision, once it became clear that the marriage patterns of new men and new-new men were very similar, statistically speaking.

> families were the highest prestige group in Florence, having founded the republic, yet in their marriages, *popolani* families never enacted the dimension that put them on top. Lack of marriage closure within this most prestigious stratum is one of the reasons behind the open-elite structure of Florence.

This demographic group of *popolani* exemplifies a recurrent puzzle in this article: The purported "ruling class" had little social-stratification cohesion. The marriage data suggest that "social class" was a status dimension kept alive not by the most prestigious *popolani* themselves, but rather by strong antipathy between the magnates and the new men. In marriage networks, the high prestige *popolani* stood not above but in between the magnates and the new men, bridging the polarized class differences beneath them. This network integration function of *popolani* families in marriage may help to explain how they could have credibly positioned themselves not as a self-interested oligarchy but rather as public-spirited "citizens of Florence," at least during some periods in their history.[66] Conversely, as the antipathy between magnates and new men faded under the Medici, so also did the saliency of *popolani* as a demographic category, though not necessarily as a fondly remembered ideal.

The fourth set of significant findings concerns the effect of wealth on intermarriage. The results are easy to state. Namely, in all periods of possible observation, from the 1352 to the 1480 tax censuses, Florentine families were sharply endogamous on the dimension of wealth. Wealthy families married other wealthy families. Furthermore, the wealthier the family the more intense was the marriage endogamy according to wealth. These conclusions are based on the following coefficients in table 4.4: (a) consistently significant endogamy coefficients for families both in the top 10% of wealth and in the top 10–25% of wealth; (b) higher magnitude and significance coefficients for families in the top 10% of wealth than for families in the top 10–25% of wealth; (c) strong and significant negative/aversive coefficients for intermarriage between families in the top 25% of wealth and families in the bottom 50% of wealth. Molho combined a number of criteria in his composite definition of "ruling class," but the most important criteria he used was wealth, as measured in the 1427, the 1458, and the 1480 *catasti*.[67] To the extent that wealth was the dimension driving Molho's statistical results, his

[66] Cf. Baron 1966, 443–62; Cohn 1980, 59–60.
[67] Molho 1994, 204–05.

study and mine agree that the Florentine "elite" practiced endogamy in marriage.[68]

Continuing in the economic vein, another battery of variables in table 4.4 investigates the relationship between marriage and economic industrial structure—in particular, the effect of business partnerships on marriage between partners' families. Strong empirical correlations between business partnership and intermarriage between the families of partners are found across multiple industries only for the period of 1403–1433. This finding is consistent with Padgett and McLean's explanation for the invention of the partnership system.[69] This Albizzi-regime correlation between marriage and partnership systems both reinforced the economic reproduction of that new mode of making companies, and it blended an economic logic into marriage, making it natural to use dowries as start-up capital for firms.[70] It was during the Albizzi regime that commerce and marriage fused most seamlessly into a merchant-republican "elite."

The final set of significant findings in table 4.4 concerns the effect of politics on intermarriage. Two separate sets of political variables are investigated in table 4.4: the effect of political office-holding on the likelihood of intermarriage and the effect of political factions on intermarriage.

For all four of the political-office variables listed in table 4.4, the consistent finding is *no* marriage endogamy within the *reggimento*. This statistical non-finding for *reggimento* parallels the equally surprising non-finding for *popolani*. Two aspects of the top office of Priorate or city council were investigated—namely, that of family office-holding during the interval of the regression (contemporary "power") and that of cumulative number of offices held by the family since the 1282 creation of the Priorate (historic "state service"). Office-holding in the Mercanzia or commercial court is also investigated in table 4.4. Only one out of the 28 political-office coefficients was statistically significant, which is negligible. It will perhaps surprise political historians of Florence, as much as it did me, that a statistical relationship between marriage and political office-holding did not exist in republican Florence after controlling for other variables. Impressions to the contrary are

[68] Molho was perhaps too quick to extend this sound conclusion about Florentine marriage endogamy in wealth to conclusions about Florentine "ruling class" marriage endogamy in general. Combining multiple (inconsistent) measures of "elite" into a composite index, as in Molho 1994, 205–07, was a mistake, in my humble opinion. I do not wish to imply thereby that I am myself without mistakes.

[69] Padgett and McLean, 2006, 1468–74.

[70] Cf. Dati diary in Brucker 1967, 110, 114, 121.

created by spurious correlations of both marriage and political office with other factors that affect both.

Political factions, on the other hand, did affect marriage, and dramatically so—especially victorious political factions. Victorious political factions continued to affect marriages for astonishingly long periods of time after the crisis events that created them had passed. For example, the victorious alliance[71] of families that crushed the Ciompi Revolt was statistically endogamous during the periods 1348–1377, 1378–1403, 1404–1433, and even a bit[72] into 1434–1463. In other words, the tumultuous events of the Ciompi Revolt in 1378 continued to affect Florentine marriage networks for 100 years after that searing event.

A similarly long-lasting shadow was inscribed into Florentine marriage networks by the Guelf struggle in 1301 between Blacks and Whites. Institutionally reinforced by the *Parte Guelfa*, the victorious Black Guelf families[73] of 1301 were endogamous in marriage during the periods 1282–1317, 1318–1347, 1348–1377, and 1378–1403. Again the marriage data reveal behavioral evidence of about a 100-year memory of searing political events of the past among the victors.

In contrast to the Ciompi Revolt and to the equally bitter struggle between Blacks and Whites, the political contest between the Albizzi and the Ricci factions[74] in 1348–1377 was not severe enough to leave observable traces in marriage.

Finally, during the post-1433 Medici regime, Medicean partisans[75] underwent an intriguing evolution in their marriage behavior. Under Cosimo de' Medici, Medicean partisans were not endogamous in marriage. This finding is consistent with the unusually centralized political-party structure of Cosimo, analyzed in Padgett and Ansell.[76] But they became endogamous under Lorenzo de' Medici, partly under Lorenzo's own brokerage.[77] Medici partisans were originally open in marriage to outsiders, but then they closed into themselves, perhaps in response to the Pazzi conspiracy. According to the robust-action analysis of Padgett and Ansell, such increased marriage

[71] As identified in the chronicle of Stefani 1903, 308, 317–18, 321–22, 328, 338–40, 343, 347–48, 350–51, 359, 363–66, 370–71, 393–94.

[72] That is, $p < .06$, which means almost significant.

[73] As identified in Compagni 1986, 24–27 and in Raveggi et al. 1978, 324–26.

[74] Partisans coded from narrative of Brucker 1962.

[75] As identified in Kent 1978, 352–54, Rubinstein 1966, 236–43, Sapori 1955 419–21, and Pampaloni 1964, 234–35 (first 125 signers only of latter petition were used).

[76] Padgett and Ansell 1993, 1274–80, 1286–305.

[77] Cohn 1980, 53–56; Bruscoli 1997.

closure should have weakened the political control of Lorenzo, as compared to that of Cosimo, by constraining its reach.

Viewed cross-sectionally, all these effects on marriage are variables in a statistical analysis. Viewed temporally, however, these statistical effects are layers of history superimposed on each other.[78] These two perspectives are not as incompatible as they might seem. The former can be a method for uncovering the latter, just as the latter can be an interpretive tool for understanding the results of the former. Florentine marriage networks registered the collective memory of contemporary Florentines on many scales of temporality at once—conscious, institutional, and ultimately even biological.

Growth and Decline of Florentine Families

What difference did these mobility and marriage dynamics make for the demographic success or failure of Florentine families? Table 4.5 reports the results of a statistical analysis of family growth or decline, between the various tax censuses at my disposal. "Family growth/decline" is simply the difference in numbers of tax households registered for each family in the successive tax censuses. Since these differences ranged from −13 to +15, normally distributed around zero, ordinary least-squares regression was the statistical method employed. Details of independent-variable construction are reported in the footnotes to table 4.5.

The overall picture is that three factors drove the demographic growth or decline of Florentine families during the Renaissance: (a) wealth, (b) political factional success, and (c) being within the marriage-network core.[79] Political participation, in the sense of Priorate membership, and social identity of wife, above and beyond her family's being in the marriage-network core, were irrelevant to a family's demographic success.

The conjunction of the effect of marriage-core on family growth in table 4.5 and the effect of family size on marriage endogamy in table 4.4 implies that there was a positive feedback of demographic success at the

[78] Cf. Braudel [1949] 1972.

[79] The definition of "being in the marriage-network core" is the same as above—namely, families with a structural cohesion level of four or more, within the Florentine marriage network of the time period.

Table 4.5 OLS Regressions on Growth or Decline in Family Size

"Family size growth/decline" = (Number of family's tax households in later tax census) – (Number of family's tax households in early tax census)

	1352–1379	1379–1403	1403–1427	1427–1458	1458–1480
Constant	.5279	**1.4478*****	.3365	**2.0277*****	.4105
Family size	**–.1003*****	**–.3515*****	**–.1190*****	**–.2594*****	**–.0924*****
Magnate	.4686	**–1.0371***	–.0235	–.7143	–.6317
Ex-magnate	–.6975	–.3343	.4260	–.9027*	.1442
Popolani	–.0382	.1969	.2027	–.2686	–.0856
New men	**.7510***	.0709	**.4932(*)**	–.3717	.2259
New-new men	**.6602***	.3240	**.8087****	–.2323	–.2555
Medici-era	.5988	.1362	.2968	.3338	.1440
Avg. Hshd. Wealth	**.1547***	**.2654*****	**.1583****	**.3083*****	–.0810
Avg. Priorate partic.	–.0997	.0426	–.1194	.0154	.1381
Marriage core	**.7121***	**.8160****	**1.2561*****	**.8253*****	**.5258***
% Popolani Wives	.2995	–.1134	.3328	.1593	–.1338
% Wealth wives	–.5752	.1989	–.3310	.3701	.2246
% Priorate wives	.2960	.5232	.1346	–.4346	.7552(*)
Black guelfs (13101)	**1.3349****	.2972			
White guelfs (1301)	.4053	.3576			
Albizzi faction	**1.4738****	**1.1573****			
Ricci faction	.4577	**1.1063****			

Anti-ciompi (1378)	.4376	−.0726	**.9081****	**1.0136****	.6385
Pro-ciompi (1378)	**.8682****	**−.4731***	.0432	−.0014	**−.6454***
Oligarchs (1434)			**1.5758*****	.0149	−.4297
Mediceans (1434)			.0969	.1987	.4641
Mediceans (1449)			**1.5153*****	**1.6840*****	**1.0442****
Anti-mediceans (1466)			**.6682***	**.9036****	−.0318
# observations	724	817	861	877	812
Prob > F	.0000	.0000	.0000	.0000	.0000
R^2	.1092	.4238	.1621	.2920	.0808

*** = ($p < .001$); ** = ($p < .01$); * = ($p < .05$); (*) = ($p < .06$)

Notes to table 4.5:

(1) "Family size" is each last-named family's number of households in the tax census at beginning of period.

(2) "Average Household Wealth" is ordinal clustering of average household wealth of families into quartiles: 1 = top 10%, 2 = 10–25%, 3 = 25–50%, 4 = 50–75%, 5 = 75–100%, at beginning of period. [In the table, I reverse signs from computer output to be more intuitive because "richest" is the lowest number in these ordinal codings.]

(3) "Average Priorate participation" is ordinal clustering of average household Priorate p articipation into 1 = ($x \geq 1$), 2 = ($1 > x \geq .5$), 3 = ($.5 > x > 0$), and 4 = ($x=0$), during the period. [In the table, I reverse signs from computer output to be more intuitive because "most powerful" is the lowest number in these ordinal codings.]

(4) "Marriage core" is the set of families in the inner core of the marriage network of that period. "Core" is defined as those families with structural cohesion of 4 or more.

(5) "% Popolani wives" is the percentage of male marriages into female families who were popolani in social class, during the time period in question.

(6) "% Wealthy wives" is the percentage of male marriages into female families in the top 25% of average per-household wealth, during the time period in question.

(7) "% Priorate wives" is the percentage of the male family's wives whose families were in top ordinal class of Priorate participation that period.

(8) All political faction variables are simple binary (0/1) indicator variables, identifying whether one or more member of the family was an active member of the faction in question.

heart of the Florentine kinship system—large patrilineages intermarrying, breeding growing patrilineages, who intermarried, etc. To the extent that there were any stable elite at all in the face of widespread economic and political turnover, it was this inner motor of patrilineage that generated it.

In addition to marriage-core, a family's average household wealth at the beginning of each period mattered for the subsequent demographic fortune of that family at the end of each period. Simple material ability to support larger numbers of children is perhaps sufficient to account for this statistical effect.[80] But probably more subtle mechanisms of dowry and of marriage attractiveness were also involved. Whatever the detailed mechanisms, a positive feedback of wealth thus also existed alongside patrilineage—namely, wealthy families intermarrying and breeding growing families, who intermarried, etc. Whereas the patrilineage feedback on average was a force for stabilizing old families within the core, the wealth feedback on average was a force for injecting new and growing families into the core, even though its "intent" was wealthy families closing ranks. Patrilineage and wealth were both forces for social closure (on different dimensions), but not being correlated, they worked at cross-purposes.

Political factional success also resulted in growing families—examples are the Black Guelfs even as late as 1352–1378; the Albizzi faction in 1352–1378 and in 1378–1403; the Ricci faction in 1378–1403; the anti-Ciompi in 1403–1427 and even as late as 1427–1458; the pro-Ciompi in 1352–1378; the Albizzi oligarchs in 1403–1427; and the Mediceans in 1403–1427, 1427–1458, and 1458–1480. Political exiles are well documented in Florentine historiography,[81] but from a broad demographic perspective, the consequences of political success on family growth are more evident in table 4.5 than are the consequences of political failure on family decline.[82] Since these political-faction results are also matched in the marriage results in table 4.4, their conjunction points to yet a third positive feedback in Florentine kinship—namely, political victors intermarrying and breeding growing families, who intermarried, etc. The main difference between this third feedback logic and the other two was that the patrilineage and wealth logics operated consistently throughout the time period under study, whereas the definition of "political victors" lurched in composition from one political crisis to the next. Even though "political victor" was always a salient

[80] Herlihy and Klapisch-Zuber, 1985, 241–46; Clark, 2007, 88.
[81] For example, Baxendale 1991 and Shaw 2000.
[82] Cf. Morelli's *ricordi* in Branca 1986, 61, 71–74.

dimension of stratification among Florentine lineages, the content of this kept shifting through periodic political crises. Of all the political crises, the Black–White Guelf, the Ciompi Revolt, and the Medici ascendance were the most consequential crises for Florentine intermarriage and lineage growth.[83]

Other than these three drivers of family growth, the results in table 4.5 imply large-family-size decline: (a) having a large family size, absent renewal from one of the three feedback logics, led to a decline in that family's size, and (b) magnate (and to lesser extent ex-magnate) families declined. These "entropy" trends were also evident in figure 4.2, which plotted average family sizes over time, broken down by social class. In figure 4.2 it was evident that the largest medieval-era magnate families suffered dramatic shrinkage in size, through splintering and other mechanisms, during the period under study,[84] whereas all other social classes grew in their average family sizes. Figure 4.2 attributes this shrinkage in very large family sizes specifically to magnates, but table 4.5 reveals that the phenomenon also involved others, even if magnates epitomized the large-family demographic problem. Demographically successful Florentine families could not passively rest on their past laurels if they wanted to survive.[85] They needed to participate actively in one or more of the three positive-feedback logics of patrilineage-plus-marriage-core, of wealth, or of victorious political faction in order to maintain their demographic strength in the face of entropy.

Absent inherited membership in the marriage core, two routes were available for new families to grow—wealth and political faction. Social mobility and demographic growth were two of the incentives for new men to enter politics, in spite of the subordinate clientage position in which this entry placed them at first. Figure 4.5 reveals that, indeed on average, these social-mobility mechanisms led to demographic success for newcomers. By 1500, *popolani*, new-men, new-new-men, and Medici-era families had grown in their average household sizes to almost eliminate the dramatic social-class differentiation in family sizes that had existed in 1352 and before.

All these trends together (see also figure 4.1) point to the diffusion of previously upper-class patrilineage ideals down from older medieval *consorterie* into the middle-class ranks of Florentine society. The irony is that

[83] Perhaps the protracted 1282–1293 struggle between magnates and popolani deserve inclusion on this list, but I cannot measure lineage growth and decline before the 1352 tax estimo.

[84] Bizzocchi 1982; Klapisch-Zuber 2006, 209–19, 453–59.

[85] Alberti 1971, 27–34, presents one famous description of what such decline felt like to participants.

the demographic reality of these same ideals was disintegrating within those older medieval-era families that had first created it.[86] To conceptualize diffusion and growth with a collapse at the center, the metaphor of a volcano comes to mind: Patrilineage aspiration was the lava pushing up many nouveaux families to congeal, even as it induced the true model to which they were aspiring to collapse. In my assessment, Goldthwaite and Kent essentially were both correct in their debate about the decline of patrilineage in Florence: The decline was due to the coexistence of these apparently contradictory trends of patrilineage diffusion and collapse.

Internal Structure of Florentine Families

So far in this article, lineages and last-named families have been treated as unitary entities, in order to maintain a *longue durée* focus on macroscopic dynamics and trends. This is a simplification for analytical purposes. I turn now to looking inside of lineage to see if there was any change in the internal structure and function of Florentine lineages over this time period.

The point of departure for this assessment of internal change within lineages is again the debate between Goldthwaite and Kent. On the basis mostly of economic evidence, Goldthwaite 1968, provocatively argued that Florentine patrilineages progressively disintegrated into nuclear families over the course of the Renaissance. On the basis mostly of non-economic evidence, Kent 1977, forcefully denied that claim. Both sides of this extended debate focused on fine-grained examinations of small numbers of "representative" families.[87] In this section, I reassess both sides of this argument, based on a larger number of families.

A broad statistical approach like that in this article and in Herlihy and Klapisch-Zuber cannot hope to match the level of detail possible in case studies. But some light can be cast by aggregate statistics on the evolution of internal family structure, even if only at a coarse-grained level of resolution. In exchange for loss of detail and texture, what is gained is global information on trends in the population as a whole. I look first at how spatially concentrated were lineages, next at how important families were in

[86] When families like Pucci (già "di Puccio"), Gucci (già "di Guccio"), Serristori (già "di ser Ristoro"), and Ginori (già "di ser Gino") became the new "aristocracy" of Medici Florence, the bones of the Adimari, the Buondelmonti, and the Vicedomini must have turned over in their ancient graves.

[87] Other studies of particular Florentine families include Klapisch-Zuber 1985, 68–93; Foster 1985; Kuehn 1991, 129–175; Ciappelli 1995; Crabb 2000; Jacks and Caferro 2001; Plebani 2002.

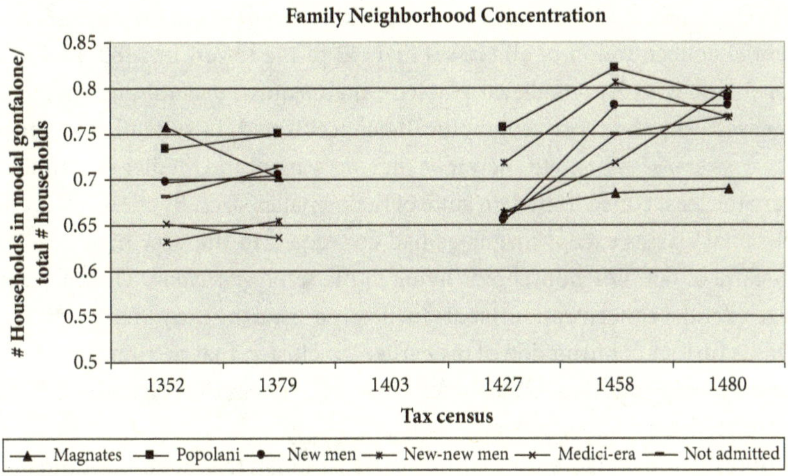

Figure 4.7 Residential Concentration, by Social Strata

Sources: Padgett relational database, using tax censuses listed in note to figure 4.1

Florentine businesses, next at wealth inequality in lineages, and finally at political-office inequality in lineages—all of these indicators were measured over time. The diverse results I report do not add up as crudely as increase or decrease in internal cohesion of lineage over time. Instead, they point to a change in the relative function of lineage: less important in economics, more important in politics. Thinking through inconsistencies in data is more revealing than tallying points for one or the other side of an argument.

"Family solidarity" is a complex concept with many aspects. But one indicator that is measurable with the statistics at my disposal is how densely the various households in a lineage lived together. Figure 4.7 presents data over time, subdivided by social strata, on the percentage of lineages' households that lived in the same modal *gonfalone* neighborhood. *Gonfaloni* were the 16 administrative wards into which the city was subdivided.[88] These are the smallest geographical units itemized in the tax censuses. (The exception was the 1403 *prestanza*, which reported residence only at the quarter level of aggregation; hence the gap in figure 4.7.)

Consistent with the argument of Kent, Florentine families generally increased in their residential concentration during the Renaissance. The exception, as always, was the magnates, whose demographic disintegration is

[88] Before 1343, the city was divided into six *sesti* instead. I have also estimated pre-1343 *gonfaloni* residence even before such existed (see footnote in table 4.4), but that is not relevant for figure 4.6.

reflected in their residential deconcentration as well—from the highest residential concentration of all classes in 1352 to the lowest in 1480. In 1352, consistent with late-medieval patterns, high-status *popolani* and magnate lineages were the most geographically concentrated, in spite of their large sizes; whereas lower-status new men, new-new men, and Medici-era families were the least concentrated, in spite of their smaller sizes. By 1480, however, all social classes except magnates had converged to the very high level of 75–80% of families' households living in the same *gonfalone*. This increase in residential concentration occurred mostly during the early Medici regime. This is further confirmation of my earlier conclusion that patrilineage ideals were diffusing out into Renaissance Florence, even as the original sponsors of those ideals were collapsing.

Information on Florentine family participation in the functional domains of economics and politics is provided in figures 4.8a, 4.8b, 4.9, and 4.10. Figures 4.8a and 4.8b present data on the connection between family and business—namely, what percentages of Florentine business partnerships were formed between patrilineal kin. Figure 4.8a presents annual-census data on partnerships among domestic bankers, originally collected by the *Arte del Cambio* or banking guild. Figure 4.8b presents sketchy, but available, data on other industries—international merchant traders, wool manufacturers, and silk manufacturers—collected from a variety of ad hoc sources listed in the bibliography.

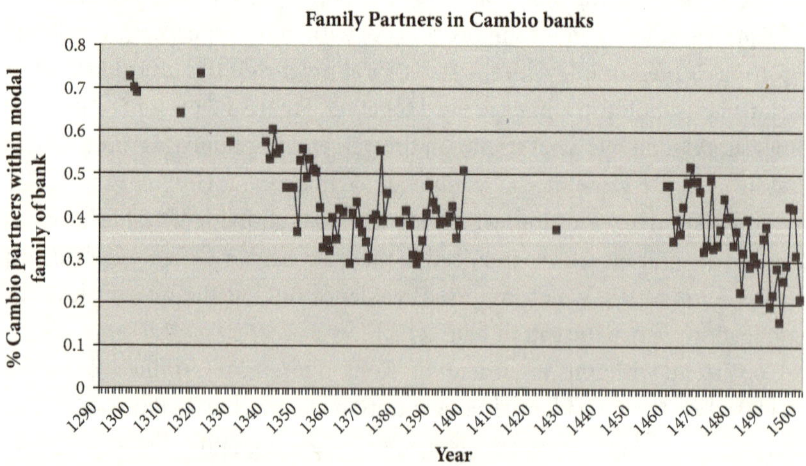

Figure 4.8a Family Basis of Economic Partnerships

Sources: A.S.F., *Arte del Cambio* 11, 14, 15, 16

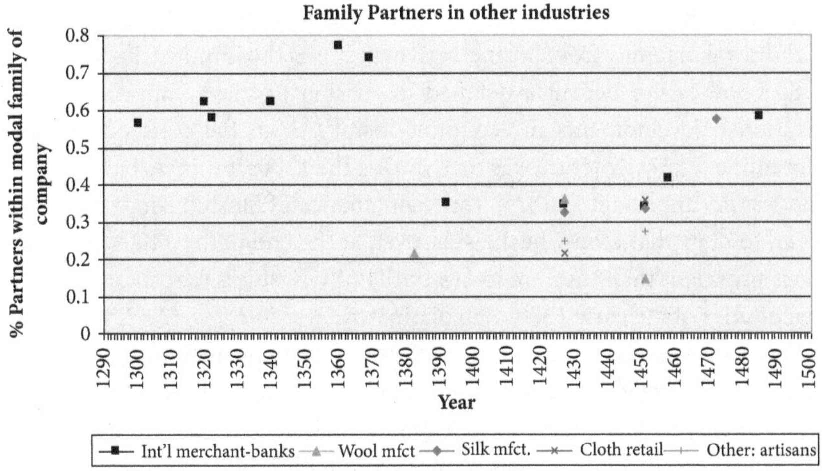

Figure 4.8b 000Family Basis of Economic Partnerships

Sources: A.S.F., *Arte della Lana* 46 (for 1382), *Carte Strozziane V* 22 (for ~1485); Dei 1984 (p. 126 for 1472), Melis 1962 (tavole 27, 28, 31, 32, 35, 36, 39 and 40 for ~1395), Molho 1970 (for 1451), Padgett 2005a (for 1300–1380), 2005b (for 1427), Silva 1908 (pp. 679–83 for 1369), Strozzi account book (for ~1485)

Consistent with the argument of Goldthwaite, both figures 4.8a and 4.8b show the withdrawal of Florentine families-qua-families from the constitution of business partnerships. Around 1300, an astonishingly high 70–75% of cambio-banking partnerships were constructed out of paternal kin—fathers, sons, brothers, uncles, or cousins of varying degree. Over the first half of the 1300s, this percentage dropped gradually to about 40%, at which level it remained until 1460, after which it declined further to 20–30%. As shown in figure 4.8b, the international merchant-banking industry, located for the most part in the *Arte della Calimala*, shows an even more dramatic drop: about 60–80% of partners in international merchant-banking companies were paternal kin until the Ciompi Revolt in 1378, after which suddenly only 35–40% were. This sharp organizational change was due to the invention of the partnership system, analyzed in Padgett and McLean 2006. Unfortunately, no data prior to 1382 exist to document partnership structures in the wool- and silk-manufacturing industries from their beginnings.[89]

[89] Silk manufacturing was essentially nonexistent in Florence before the 1380s, but wool manufacturing was strong in Florence from the early 1300s onward. For wool-textile production statistics, see Hoshino 1980, 203, 207, 227, 229, 283; Franceschi 1993a, 9, 13.

But data from that date forward are consistent with the fourteenth-century withdrawal of family from business partnership in those industries as well.[90]

Space does not permit a detailed discussion of these important organizational developments in economic history.[91] But the consequence for Florentine family structure was that, during the 1300s, business became less and less an important factor in the maintenance of kinship solidarity. This is not to deny that family businesses, even at the end of the 1400s, were far more prevalent than they are today. But family-business percentages of the magnitudes of the early 1300s had dissipated.

One consequence of this family withdrawal from business was increased inequality in wealth among the households within families. When many family members were in business together, their economic fortunes tended to rise and fall together. But as economic activities diverged among different households within the family, so did their economic fortunes. Figure 4.9 plots Herfindahl indices[92] for wealth concentration, averaged across families of various social strata. Low values indicate relatively egalitarian distributions of household wealth within lineages; high values indicate relatively unequal distributions of household wealth within lineages.[93] Except for magnates, always the exception, inequality in household wealth increased within lineages in all social strata in Florence—particularly in the 1352–1378 period.[94]

Rising inequality of wealth was not an indicator of rising "individualism" in family households,[95] because other evidence shows that wealthy branches of the family often helped their poorer cousins financially.[96] But regardless of intra-lineage financial assistance, the gap between wealthy and poorer branches of patrilineages increased during the Renaissance.

[90] At the very end of the time-series, around 1480, family participation jumps back up in both silk-manufacturing and international merchant trading. I have no explanation for this anomaly, which goes directly contrary to the more solidly documented trend in cambio-banking at that same time.

[91] See references and analysis in Padgett and McLean 2006.

[92] In economic industries, the Herfindahl index is the sum over firms of their squared market shares. Here, the Herfindahl index is the sum over households of their shares of their family's total wealth. (Normalized to make varying household-sized families comparable.) See http://en.wikipedia.org/wiki/Herfindahl_index.

[93] Varying monetary scales in different tax censuses are not a problem because the Herfindahl index standardizes those away.

[94] A slight decline in wealth inequality is evident in 1480, but this may be because the 1480 catasto measured "wealth" only in terms of real estate.

[95] Burckhardt [1860] 1954, 100–27.

[96] For example, Brucker 1967, 140.

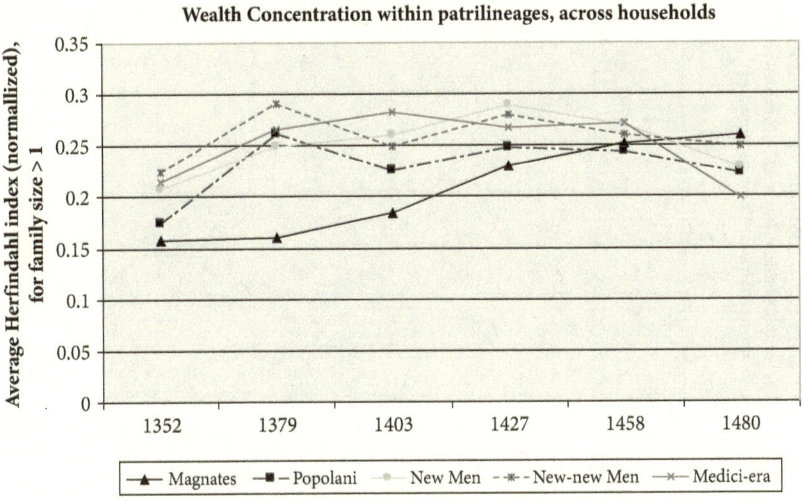

Figure 4.9 Wealth Inequality within Florentine Families, by Social Strata
Sources: Padgett relational database, using tax censuses listed in note to figure 4.1

Finally, Herfindahl indices for inequality in political office, specifically in Priorate office-holding, are presented in figure 4.10. Here, inequality means that one or a few heads-of-household monopolized the Priorate seats of the entire lineage in the time period (assuming that there was more than one seat). Equality in contrast means that the family's Priorate seats in the period were widely distributed across its household heads.

The data in figure 4.10 shows exactly the opposite trend in political office-holding as was seen in wealth in figure 4.9. Namely, intra-family inequality in political office-holding suddenly decreased after the 1378 Ciompi Revolt and stayed that way. This temporal trend could have been caused by institutional reasons, by cultural ones, or by a combination of the two. Whatever the mechanism, fifteenth-century Florentine lineages, more than fourteenth-century Florentine lineages, exhibited a careful balance in their distribution of offices within themselves.[97]

Collectively, figures 4.7 through 4.10 suggest a change in the economic and political function of lineage within Florentine society—less important in economics but more important in politics. The Goldthwaite-Kent debate

[97] I have coded the scrutiny voting of the 1382, 1393, 1411, and 1433 elections. The voting mechanism that produced dispersion of office within families will be investigated in a future paper.

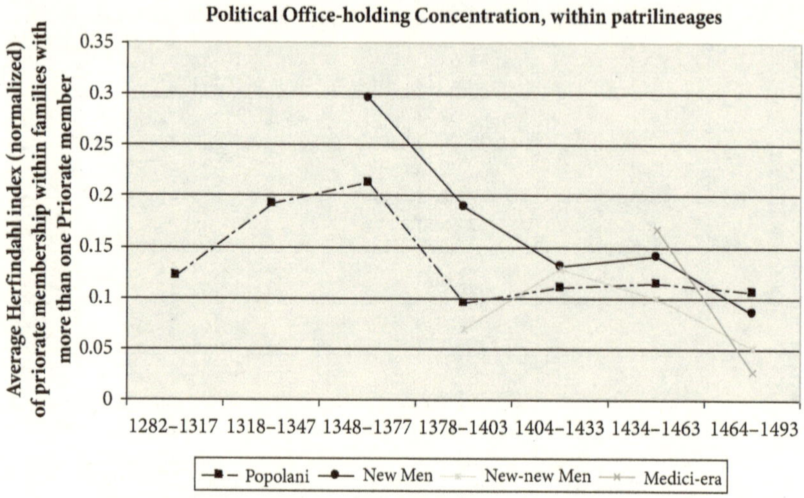

Figure 4.10 Political-Office Inequality within Florentine Families, by Social Strata

Sources: Newberry Library *priorista*, plus tax censuses itemized in note to figure 4.1

can be usefully reframed from the issue of lineage "decline" to the issue of changing lineage function.

Conclusion

The specific empirical findings in this article follow:

(1) The percentage of the Florentine population in lineages almost doubled from 1352 to 1480. (See Figure 4.1.)
(2) Magnates decreased in average family size over this period, but all the other social classes increased. (See figure 4.2.)
(3) Political incorporation of new families into the Florentine republic was erratic and episodic but, in the end, extensive. (See figure 4.3.)
(4) Florentine lineages had very high relative mobility in wealth. (See figure 4.4.)
(5) Florentine lineages had almost as high relative mobility in republican political office. (See figure 4.5.)

(6) The relative mobility of Florentine lineages in marriage was much lower than in wealth and in political office, but it was nonetheless considerable during the Albizzi regime. (See figure 4.6.)

(7) Florentine lineages had very high survival rates, compared to northern Europe. (See table 4.1.)

(8) The intercorrelation of various status orderings in Florence—wealth, political office, family size, and popolani social class—was very low. (See table 4.3.)

(9) Intermarriage among Florentine lineages was affected by lineage size, neighborhood, social status (magnate and new men, but not *popolani*), wealth, and victorious political faction. Political office did not affect likelihood of intermarriage. The political struggles of the Black versus White Guelfs and the Ciompi Revolt were inscribed into Florentine marriage patterns for 100 years after those searing events. (See table 4.4.)

(10) Lineage size grew or shrank depending upon wealth, being in the elite core, and membership in victorious political factions. But absent renewed resources of these three sorts, Florentine lineages experienced entropic decline in their numbers of component households. (See table 4.5.)

(11) Florentine lineages increased in their residential concentration in urban space, especially during the early Medici regime. (See figure 4.7.)

(12) Florentine business partnerships were less and less comprised of families. (See figures 4.8a and 4.8b.)

(13) Florentine lineages increased in the wealth inequality among their component households, especially in the generation after the Black Death. (See figure 4.9.)

(14) Florentine lineages decreased in the political-office inequality among their component households, especially after the Ciompi Revolt. (See figure 4.10.)

In summary, social mobility in relative rankings among lineages in Renaissance Florence was high—especially in wealth and in political office but also in marriage hierarchy during the Albizzi regime. A vibrant commercial economy and a turbulent political history lay at the base of this social mobility, but these economic and political histories were translated into family history through inconsistency among three contending status-stratification principles: wealth, winning political faction, and patrilineage size. Norms of marriage endogamy applied to each of these three status dimensions, but because these dimensions were empirically uncorrelated, endogamy on one dimension implied exogamy on the other dimensions, on average. Efforts to consolidate their own family positions forced "elites" (defined on any of the three dimensions) to reach down to marry middle-tier families, recruiting them as in-laws. These cross-strata marriages, in turn, became one factor feeding back to keep economic and political histories dynamic, at least for the duration of republicanism.

How can this open-elite conclusion square with the dominant portrait of elitism and oligarchy prevalent in Florentine historiography today? In brief, my answer is through mimesis: "di Puccio," "di ser Ristoro," and "di ser Gino" became Pucci, Serristori, and Ginori, respectively. New men tried hard to become patricians and buried or reinvented their actual pasts to that end.

While I disagreed with Molho on some particulars, I agreed with his fundamental point that it was through marriage that patrician Florentine lineages, old or new, successfully preserved their demographic existence through perilous times. But "endogamy" did not produce a self-enclosed group. There were three independent causal feedbacks linking marriage and demographic success—marrying for money, marrying for power, and marrying for lineage size. Florentine lineages had to maneuver among these inconsistent cross-currents in order to achieve upward-mobility success. Or, more to the point, they had to so maneuver in order to avoid otherwise almost inevitable downward mobility and extinction.[98] Apparently unlike their northern European counterparts, Florentine citizens were usually adept enough in their balancing of heterogeneous marriages to preserve their lineages over long lengths of time.

With regard to middle-strata citizens, Najemy has made the cogent argument[99] that electoral reforms—episodically throughout the Trecento, but particularly after the Ciompi Revolt—expanded the franchise, thereby co-opting complaisant new men into patrician-dominated republican power structures. I am making a similar argument in the domain of social history. Through exogamous marriage, the patrilineage family ideal of patricians diffused downward into the Florentine population, thereby reinforcing the

[98] The strong negative-growth coefficient on family size in table 4.5 supported Herlihy's contention that large, upper-strata houses faced strong social-mobility pressure downward due to high birth rates in the absence of aversive action to the contrary. Herlihy 1973, 632, 641.

[99] Najemy 1982, 299–300, presents an especially striking formulation of his view.

cultural dominance of patrician ideals. I add that this diffusion pressure was so strong that it dissolved the marriage-network content of the "ruling class" categories of *popolani* and *reggimento*. It was not so much the *popolani* class that dominated, as it was the *popolani* ideal that dominated. Through co-optation in both elections and marriage, new men adopted the family ideals of their *popolani* status superiors, becoming like them.

The focus of this article has not been on the position of women in Florence, about which there is an active historiography.[100] But to the extent that patriarchal values were associated with patrilineage family systems,[101] then the analysis in this article sheds some indirect light on why Joan Kelly answered no to her famous question, "Did Women have a Renaissance?"[102] Namely, the patrilineage model diffused to wider segments of the Florentine population during the Renaissance. This diffusion of patriarchy was not only the reactionary reassertion of sexism. It was also a corollary of high social-status fluidity in the male society.

Finally, there are two ways in which the findings in this article depend upon the institutional framework of republicanism—cognitive comparability and political factionalism. At the household level of analysis, Herlihy argued that medieval households throughout Europe gradually became comparable across social strata, through the spread of peasant agriculture and through the Church's homogeneous policies on incest and marriage.[103] A similar point at the level of lineage can be made about republican elections.[104] As more and more males became eligible for citizenship and election, more and more families adopted the family organizational form of the archetypal citizens. Political and social co-optation mechanisms worked hand in hand. As adaptation of Florentine lineages to republican electoral reforms proceeded, the function or "purpose" of lineage, while always mixed, appears to have shifted from predominantly military[105] to predominantly economic to predominantly political.

[100] For a survey of the social-history historiography on women in Renaissance Italy, see Cohn 1996, 1–15.

[101] For complex and multi-vocal evidence on this connection, see Alberti [1433] 1971 and Strozzi 1997.

[102] Kelly-Gadol 1977. See Herlihy 1985b, for one reply.

[103] Herlihy 1985a, 59–62.

[104] Molho 2000, 244–50 makes the related point that the Florentine state had an increased interest in registering and classifying its population, for both electoral and tax reasons. While Molho emphasizes state registration, and I emphasize co-optation, the two points are not incompatible. Two sides, perhaps, of a "dialogue of power." Cf. Najemy 1991.

[105] The military functioning of upper-class Florentine patrilineages or *consorterie* mostly preceded the time period examined here. See Waley 1969, 164–82.

Political turmoil was crucial not only for the definition of winning political faction but also for the maintenance of low correlation among Florence's three status dimensions. With political stability, one can expect that the dimensions of economic wealth and political power will become more aligned. In the case of republican Florence, however, periodic political crises induced sharp lurches in the composition of winning political factions, and thereby in the marriage-network core. Such crises were not entirely the exogenous shocks they appear to be, because these political crises may have been induced in part by social fluidity in the first place.[106]

The lurch from the Black Guelf "oligarchy" to the anti-Ciompi "oligarchy" after the Ciompi Revolt of 1378 was responsible for the greatest volume of elite fluidity observed in the two-century time period of this study.[107] The regime instituted by Cosimo de' Medici in 1434 consolidated mimetic new men through political absorption, and it initiated the protracted process of imposing factional stability. While political turmoil continued for three decades beyond the end of my data, thus began the gradual extinction of the "Renaissance" social-mobility processes documented here.[108]

[106] Cf. Brucker 1962, 27–56.

[107] I leave the tracing of the complex feedbacks between the social processes analyzed here and the intellectual revolution described by Baron 1966 to someone more qualified than me. Hankins 2000, 12, while severely critical of Baron, nonetheless agrees that "Civic humanism was in origin a discourse that changed the self-understanding of Florentine elites by helping them see their polity, not as a congeries of self-ruling corporations set within the larger medieval juridical order, but as a sovereign secular state led by an aristocracy of virtue." My data cannot speak to the debate about the content and origins of civic humanist ideas. But they do speak to the character of the elites to which civic humanism appealed.

[108] Note again the uptick during the fifteenth-century Medici regime in the correlations between wealth and everything else, reported in table 4.3. This foreshadowed the end of family mobility: The percentage of households with last names failed to continue its Trecento and Quattrocento rise, documented in figure 4.1, into the 1500s and 1600s (Molho 2000, 240). See Litchfield 1986, 24–51, for a valuable discussion of these later closed-elite developments.

5

Conflict and Revolt in the Name of Unity

Florentine Factions in the *Consulte e Pratiche* on the Cusp of the Ciompi Revolt

Introduction: Speech and Action

What is the relationship between speech and action? Out-and-out prevarication notwithstanding, we moderns tend to assume the relationship to be fairly unproblematic. The basic, modernist, and methodologically individualist assumption is that we think, then we speak, then we do. We have no conceptual problem imagining the reverse—namely, rationalization: act first and then speak. But either way, we presume consistency between speech and action.

In our empirical case of the Florentine *Consulte e Pratiche* in 1376–1378, right before the Ciompi Revolt, however, we claim to see a sharp disjuncture between speech and action—namely, strong rhetorical emphasis on consensus and agreement within this public-policy room of elite debate, simultaneously with intense conflict in action outside the room, among those same speakers, who tried to exile each other from Florentine citizenship. It is not as if policy differences didn't sometimes emerge in *Consulte e Pratiche* speeches, but they did so obliquely and mutedly, often in the guise of agreement.

Historians of early-modern republicanism, including James Madison, will recognize this as a deep-seated, early-modern worry about and disavowal of faction, which had destroyed so many Italian republican experiments in the not-so-distant past. We do not challenge this insight as much as we are overwhelmed by it. What sort of split-minded *mentalitée* is required to say one thing in public debate and then do the opposite outside the room? One hypothesis is simple lying and hypocrisy. We cannot disprove this hypothesis, but, Machiavelli notwithstanding, we have too much respect

Poetics 78 (February 2020): 101386, with Katalin Prajda, Benjamin Rohr, and Jonathan Schoots. Republished with permission.

Organizational Invention in Renaissance Florence. John F. Padgett, Oxford University Press.
 DOI: 10.1093/oso/9780197789216.003.0005

for the sophisticated Florentines to give it top priority. If everybody is lying, there is no point in a conversation to give policy advice. A second more credible hypothesis is wishful thinking: Florentines really, really wanted unity, in spite of the obvious evidence against it. Factional policy differences are discernible in *Consulte e Pratiche* speech, but what impresses us even more is the degree to which Florentines went, in speech and in the ritual of speech, to enact publicly the obvious falsehood about their agreement. A third hypothesis is editorial hand: Namely, Coluccio Salutati, the notary-Chancellor who transcribed these speeches, cooked the books by imposing a transcribed consensus on what was not there in reality. We dismiss this otherwise possible hypothesis on the basis of our finding in our first article—namely, no trace of Salutati humanist rhetoric is detectable in these dry notarial summaries of speeches, which Coluccio wrote in a flash in order to meet the deadline of next day's Signoria meeting. A second reason for dismissing the editorial-hand hypothesis is that we do occasionally, even if rarely, see policy disagreement in Coluccio's records. In reading his *Consulte e Pratiche* transcriptions, we observe Coluccio Salutati to be acting in his "day job" of notary, not in his more famous chancellor role of exalted humanist, composing beautiful foreign-policy letters from the Florentine government to other potentates.

In terms of Florentine historiography, a broader way of framing this puzzle is this: Was Florentine republicanism a beacon of the future, as its civic-humanist champions, like Baron (1966) and Pocock (1975) have proclaimed? Was it a valiant failure, as Najemy (1982; 1991; 2000) implies? Or was it hypocrisy and propaganda, masking elite domination, as critics like Hankins (1995) have argued? Our primary conclusion will be that pre-Ciompi republicanism was a valiant failure, albeit for a different reason than Najemy pointed to.

In the context of this special issue of *Poetics* on socio-semantic networks, what is unusual about this case is that the mapping between the social networks of faction and the semantic networks of elite discussion is orthogonal, not homologous. The reason for the disjuncture—a boundary condition, if you will, in the study of socio-semantic networks—is institutional context, in our case republicanism.[1]

We develop this theme of Florentine tension between conflict and consensus in five sections: First, we describe the escalating conflict outside

[1] Gibson (2012) provides a beautiful micro-level case study of another interplay between discussion/debate and institutional context in his conversational analysis of the Cuban Missile Crisis.

of the *Consulte e Pratiche* room, which exploded into the Ciompi Revolt. Second, we reiterate the institutional barriers against exactly that sort of factional conflict, which were built in to Florentine republicanism. Third, we statistically analyze *Consulte e Pratiche* speeches in 1376–1378, searching for evidence both of factions and of consensus. Fourth, we give qualitative examples of the rhetoric/façade of Florentine unity, namely, the special case of Parte Guelfa leader Lapo da Castiglionchio, and various semantic usages of the keyword *union*... in *Consulte e Pratiche* discussions. We conclude with broad Braudelian observations about "how institutions think" in history.

Conflict and Revolt: The Action Side

The topics and content of discussion in the *Consulte e Pratiche* during our period have already been analyzed in the first of this complementary pair of articles (Padgett et al. 2020). The "action side" of escalating domestic conflict is presented in table 5.1. This is the explosive backdrop of the *Consulte e Pratiche* speeches analyzed both in our first article on narrative networks

Table 5.1 Escalation of Exclusions

Date:	Pope & Parte Guelfa:	Civic:
Autumn 1371		[breakup of Albizzi & Ricci factions]
1376–78		Italian league & war with Pope confiscation of clergy wealth
March 1376	interdict & excommunication	
March 1377	P.G. rumblings in background	peak of calls for unity in CP anti-magnate petitions
Oct 1377		outlawing interdict (i.e., forced attendance at mass)
Oct 1377–May 1378	P.G. anti-Ghibelline campaign	
Mar 30, 1378	[death of Gregory XI]	
June 25, 1378	impending P.G. coup	
June 22, 1378		Ciompi Revolt stage 1: minor guilds
June 25, 1378		1378 Balìa punishes and exiles P.G.
July 20, 1378		Ciompi Revolt stage 2: Ciompi more houses burned; worker state

and in this second article on the tension between faction and consensus. This run-up to the Ciompi Revolt has been thoroughly described in Brucker (1962). In table 5.1, all we do is summarize, in an extremely abbreviated manner, his account.

The *Longue Durée*

Before recapitulating this three-year run-up to Ciompi, however, first it will be useful to place the Ciompi Revolt into its *longue durée* context. Figure 5.1 presents, the number of new families elected, over time, into the Signoria or city council for the first time. Entrance into the Signoria was important for Florentine lineages for long-term social-class and status reasons, even more than for short-term political influence. To be admitted to the Signoria was public recognition, by and signal to the society, of that family having "made it" since status recognition of lineage subsequently was inherited through the generations.[2]

The figure reveals that admission to Signoria historically was a highly punctuated affair: one political explosion of "new men," followed by a

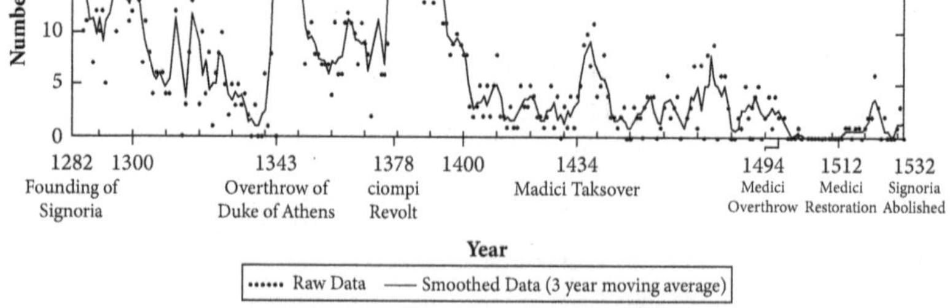

Figure 5.1 Conflict and Revolt over the Longue Durée

[2] Such election to city council frequently altered family structure itself—for example, by family members now assuming a last name as assertion of self-importance (Padgett 2010). Part of the motivation for families collecting family libraries was to document significant family-history events like this. In turn, part of the richness of today's Florentine archives stems from the volume of such family libraries having been deposited in the now centralized archives.

gradual "oligarchic" tightening up, followed by another political explosion, followed by another gradual tightening up, etc. The Ciompi Revolt, seen in this light, was merely the third explosion documented in the repetitive early history of the Florentine republic. The first peak, in 1282, was the establishment of the Florentine republic itself—namely the creation of an elected city council. The families in this first foundational political generation were called the *popolani* social class. The previously powerful families, whom the *popolani* overthrew in 1282 and then legally proscribed in 1293 from holding republican office,[3] were called *magnati* or magnates. The next political generation was the 1343 explosion, associated with the brief external dictatorship of the Duke of Athens.[4] This wave of new entrants were referred to as *gente nuova* or "new men" by Ciompi contemporaries. The third, immediately post-Ciompi, wave of new entrants, which established the 1378–82 minor-guild regime, has been called "new-new men" by Padgett (2010), not having a better label. This was the consequence of events itemized in table 5.1.

Thus, even though a family's social status theoretically was measured as the continuous "date of first entrance into the city council/Signoria," because of the episodic political history documented in figure 5.1, in fact social status was discretely divided into social classes: namely, the social classes of magnate, *popolani*, new men, new-new men, and not yet admitted.[5] The tumultuous republican history of late-medieval Florence thereby was

[3] Except for Parte Guelfa and the legislative Council of the Commune. The first of these exceptions will loom large below.

[4] Becker (1967) talks the most about this.

[5] This non-modernist Florentine definition of "social class" can be further justified by Brucker: "Historically, Florence's social structure had always been flexible, characterized by a constant shifting in the composition of its various classes."... [See Padgett and McLean (2011) for statistical proof of this statement, which makes modernist definitions of stable "economic class" unviable in the Florentine context. Florentine "bankers," for example, actively practiced that occupation on average only seven years of their lives (*Arte del Cambio libro delle compagnie* data). The popular phrase "Renaissance man" accurately points to the fluidity of Florentine biographies. . . . "To construct a valid and useful picture of the social structure, one must employ several criteria for distinguishing between classes. These criteria may be listed as wealth, occupation, family antiquity, marriage connections, behavior patterns, and attitudes. Applying these standards, Florentine society after 1350 may be divided into four groups: 1) the patriciate; 2) the *gente nuova*, the newly enriched mercantile element; 3) the petty bourgeois artisan-shopkeeper class; and 4) the unorganized and propertyless laborers. . . The patriciate, in turn, was subdivided between magnates and *popolani* not on the basis of social criteria but on the basis of legal exclusion from high political office. . . One of the most significant indications of high social status for *popolani* families was the incidence of membership in the Signoria. There are numerous copies in Florentine libraries and archives of elaborate prior lists or *prioriste*, describing the details of each family's representation in the Signoria between 1282 and 1530. . . Florentines who compiled *ricordanze* (family histories) invariably made reference to the *antichità* of their house, and the imposing role their ancestors had played in the life of the city" (Brucker 1962, 27–28).

inscribed into the political demography of contemporaries in 1376–1378 Florence. Each of these social classes jostled and contended with each other in a competition for republican offices, status, and power.

The reason this historical background is important to our story is the intense social tension generated by these successive demographic waves of new entrants. Each wave was deeply resentful of subsequent waves, who diluted their previous dominance. This resentment always was successful in tamping down recent inflow, but never was successful in abolishing previous waves altogether. The net effect of these swirling cross-pressures was the most formally open and participatory political republic in the Italy of that time (see footnote 22).

Status as Hieratic Authority

The status side of this tense contestation among Florentine social classes can be modeled as hieratic authority (Dumont 1970; Obert and Padgett 2012). Hieratic authority is the exemplification of a totality by one of its parts. The archetype of hieratic authority is patriarchal cultural domination: the male gender (a.k.a., man) more purely exemplifies the totality of humanity (a.k.a., MAN), to which the other gender, woman, gains access through subordination to (even sublimation in) the "more pure" exemplar or role model. Many religions work like this: Catholic laity, for example, gain access to the Body of Christ (i.e., humanity's trans-historical procession to salvation) through means of subordination to priests and bishops, who more perfectly exemplify the Church (Dix 1946). Hieratic authority can be considered to be a formal representation of Weber's charisma: Ancient Israelites became the "chosen people" by virtue of listening to their Old Testament prophets, out of whose mouths God spoke (Weber [1917–19] 1952). Another example is when the defeated and demoralized Germany becomes GERMANY again, by listening to Hitler, who recalled Germans to their historic (and Aryan) destiny. In all of these examples, the reason that the subordinate buys into this status "trick" is that there is a threatening and demonized nonhuman identity lurking in the background, into whose clutches the subordinate might fall. For example, in the above examples: sexless untouchable in patriarchy, hell and the devil in the Catholic Church, Egyptian slavery for Ancient Israelites, and Jews for Germany, respectively.

In this nested conceptualization of status, demonization is the flip side of purity (see also Douglas 1966).

In the case of Florence, social classes competed on the dimension of status to the extent that there was contestation about "Who was (the more perfect exemplar of) Florence?" The founding generation, the *popolani*, had the clearest claim to be the most perfect exemplars of Florence, and thus superior in status, if Florence was defined as the Republic itself—with "true Florentines" being citizens = guildsmen, as the 1282 republican constitution had provided. But ousted magnates could reclaim their lost superior status position if the definition of "Florentine citizen" reverted to what it had been earlier in the 1200s, namely, the Guelfs. New men did not have the strongest claim in history, but if attention was focused on the recent past, they could make a plausible claim to be the "true Florence," in the sense that they were essential in rebuilding the Florentine economy after the devastating Black Death of 1348, which killed 60% of the Florentine population. Without massive immigration after the Black Death, Florence would have been a mere shadow of its previous economically dynamic and proud self—an historical fact about parvenus that magnates and *popolani* conveniently tended to ignore.

The nesting of these contending claims is diagrammed in figure 5.2. Any of these concentric circles could make status claims to being the "true Florence," thereby drawing the boundaries of FLORENCE (i.e., citizenship) in either narrower or more expansive ways.

Associated with each of these competing claims to superior social status as "true" Florentine was an associated "demonized other," just as the hieratic-authority model expects. The demonized other for *popolani* were the magnates, who represented the violent feudal past, not the economically precocious and forward-looking future.[6] The demonized other for pro-pope Guelfs, including magnates, was Ghibelline, the hated pro-emperor nemesis of multiple civil wars in the 1200s. The demonized other for new men were non-guildsmen, like the Ciompi, who did not partake in guild-based citizenship. The demonized other for all patriotic Florentines were foreigners, which made the status of recent immigrants precarious, before they became assimilated into guilds.

[6] Not that one side of the *mentalitée* of *popolani* did not also yearn for a little medieval manly glory. But they preferred the safer route of titles to that glory, not the magnates' riskier route of performance in combat.

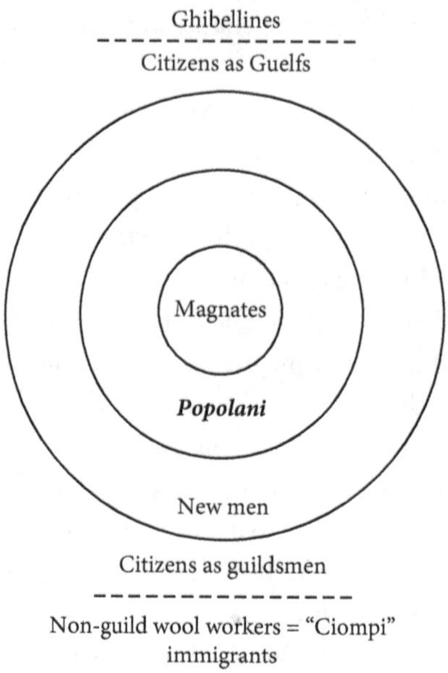

Citizen social classes = {magnates, *popolani*, new men}
Non-citizens = {Ghibellines, non-guild workers, immigrants}
Factional dynamics: Parte Guelfa trying to exile opponents as "Ghibellines"
Civic trying to exile opponents as "magnates"

Figure 5.2 Hieratic Authority of Social Classes: Who is Florence?

Hieratic authority has not to do with the institutional structure of republicanism; it has to do with the social tensions flowing through Florentine republicanism. These were rooted in the tumultuous political history of the previous century. The reason this concept is so important to the explanation of the Ciompi revolt is that, in the realm of action more than that of speech, it explains why Florentine political conflict so readily and easily veered into an escalatory politics of denunciation and exile. In the hieratic model, the key to victory in status competition is to elevate the saliency of one's preferred demon: namely, to stigmatize one's opponents, not as people with whom one disagrees, but as traitors—either of the magnate or of the Ghibelline or of the foreigner/immigrant varieties. This was the volcano building outside the door of the *Consulte e Pratiche*, whose speakers pretended on the contrary that everything was consensus and unity. In the hieratic model, everything also is conceptualized as "unity" (as in the superordinate identities MAN/FLORENCE), but status conflict and denunciation ensues when the exemplar of that unity becomes up for grabs. The War of the Eight Saints with the pope blew new wind into the old Guelf sails, at least for an anti-war conservative minority of the population.

The Run-Up to the Ciompi Revolt

Now back to table 5.1: In Autumn 1371, the stage for elite factional realignment was set by the breakup of the Albizzi and Ricci factions, which had dominated Florentine elite politics from 1350.[7] The factional realignment that ensued, once the War of the Eight Saints began, is described in figure 5.3. The contending Albizzi and Ricci factions had been traditional elite-faction alliances, organizationally grounded in marriage and business networks, which competed to get their members elected to republican offices (Brucker 1962, 124–26). "No Faction" republicans were, for the most part, new men who were deeply opposed to both of these more elite *popolani* factions.

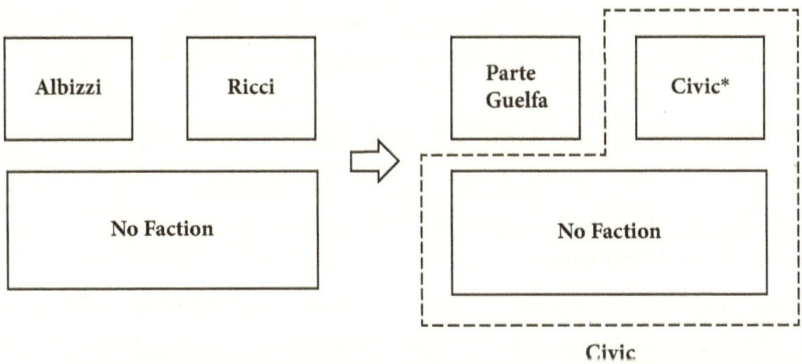

1350-1371
Traditional elite factions

Membership in Albizzi and Ricci faction given in Brucker (1962).

1375–1378
Hieratic "patriotic" factions

*Civic measured as 1378 (A.S.F. Balia, vol. 16)
Parte Guelfa measured as lists, in Zeras's appendix IA (1987: 231–237), of parte Guelfa leaders in 1377–78.

Figure 5.3 Factional Realignment, Due to War of Eight Saints

[7] The reason for the breakup of previous factional alignment was simple corruption: Patriarchs of the Ricci family accepted bribes from leading members of the Albizzi faction when the Ricci family experienced financial difficulties (Brucker 1962, 248–49).

The War of the Eight Saints injected the searing foreign-policy conflict described in our first article into the remnants of these older domestic factions: The old Albizzi faction evolved into a new anti-war Parte Guelfa "faction," and the old Ricci faction evolved into a new pro-war Civic "faction." One important difference between the old factional alignment and the new was that new factions no longer were symmetric organizationally. The new anti-war Parte Guelfa "faction" was hunkered down and headquartered, not in loose and sprawling elite networks, but rather in the old magnate-dominated Parte Guelfa palace or club, left over from the 1200s. The Parte Guelfa had a history of functioning almost like the "city council" of the state, before any republican elected city council existed. The Parte Guelfa, in other words, was essentially the old 1200s government surviving within the newer 1300s republican state.

Conversely, the pro-war Civic "faction" had the patriotic upper hand, as long as the pope was the foreign-policy enemy. We operationally measured leadership of the Civic "faction" retrospectively by the 1378 balìa, formed after the first stage of the Ciompi Revolt in order to punish Parte Guelfa "traitors." As such, the Civic "faction" itself had a hieratic-authority structure: Namely, the 1378 balìa can be considered to be the higher-status representatives or exemplars of the No Faction patriotic mass of the citizenry.[8] Factional realignment in 1375–78 was not just a reshuffling of memberships; it also was a shift in organizational forms—hardly true "political parties" in the modern sense, but one organizational step in that direction.

The issues behind this partisan realignment from Albizzi/Ricci to Parte Guelfa/Civic were the narrative-network sequence of foreign and domestic topics and events associated with the War of the Eight Saints, analyzed in our first article. We will not repeat that complex issue-realignment explanation here.

Instead we will just highlight the culmination of that polarization. Namely, the newly revived Parte Guelfa launched a McCarthyite denunciation campaign to denounce Civic opponents and others as alleged "Ghibellines," thereby excluding them from citizenship altogether.[9] The October 1377

[8] The "Civic faction" defined in this 1378 balìa sense can be considered equivalent to the faction that Brucker called the pro-war "Liberal faction." We substitute our "Civic" label for Brucker's "Liberal" label, because "Liberal" sounds anachronistic to us.

[9] In a previous version of this paper, we presented statistical analyses of these Ghibelline denunciations, which appeared in two archival sources: court records (in particular *Esecutore degli Ordinamenti Giustizia*) and a chronicle by Marchionne di Coppo Stefani. At the suggestion of a referee, we have decided to delete that analysis here, in order to save space and to focus more on

timing of the initiation of this anti-Ghibelline campaign coincides exactly with chapter 4's *cleric*... keyword, identified in the narrative-network analysis of our first article as the topical hinge which internalized *Consulte e Pratiche*'s foreign-policy discussion into domestic discord.

We reproduce in figure 5.4 the scale and temporal time-series of those denunciations. Orchestrated by the Parte Guelfa, from October 1377 to May 1378, 672 denunciations of people accused of being Ghibellines appeared in the *tambura* docket of the *Esecutore degli Ordinamenti Giustizia* court.[10] We do not know how many of these accusations were finally convicted, but our main interest is in tracing the magnitude of the anti-Ghibelline denunciation and exclusion campaign itself. This is exactly the sort of vicious factionalism, edging to civil war, that republicanism as an institution was designed to combat.

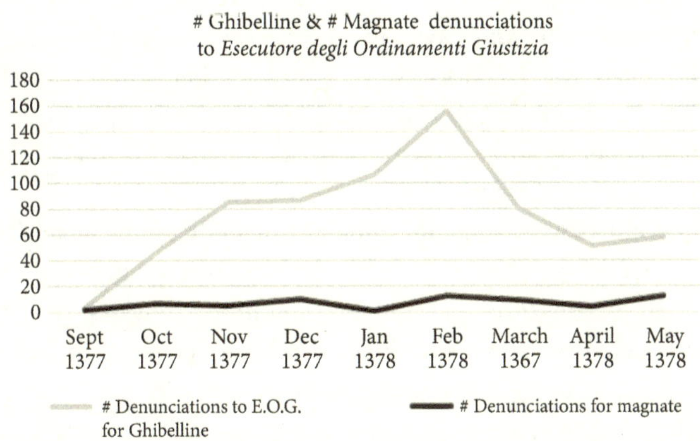

Figure 5.4 Parte Guelfa's Anti-Ghibelline Denunciation Campaign

speech (in line with the objectives of this special issue). A future article by Padgett, Claudia Tripodi, and Patrick Bergemann will explore those data in more depth.

[10] Out of these 672 anti-Ghibelline denunciations, 17 of these denunciations were of Florentine magnates, 150 were of *popolani*, 137 were of new men, 34 were of new-new men, 66 were of Florentines not yet admitted to the Signoria, and 268 were denunciations of immigrants who were not yet Florentines at all. The three last groups (54.8% of the total) cannot be explained for factional-politics reasons because those folks did yet participate in republican office. We speculate that in these cases the Parte Guelfa was trying to wall off future inflow into the Florentine citizenry. To see how drastically they failed, reconsult the third peak in figure 5.1. That wave illustrates just how many families were waiting just outside the gates for admission into Florentine politics. In other words, in the context of the high social mobility of Renaissance Florence (Padgett 2010), the reactionary worries of the Parte Guelfa were hardly paranoia.

From this anti-Ghibelline denunciation campaign by the Parte Guelfa, the steps to Ciompi Revolt were few: (1) The Parte Guelfa planned a *coup d'état* for June 25, San Giovanni day (the patron saint of Florence), when many troops could easily be snuck into the city. (2) Alerted to this, Salvestro de' Medici of the Civic faction proactively mobilized on June 22 a counter-coup by minor guildsmen, who marched off and burned numerous houses of Parte Guelfa leaders. (3) A balìa or extra-constitutional emergency convention—what we call the 1378 balìa—was established to ratify the Civic faction's violence and to massively purge and exile enemy Parte Guelfa leaders. (4) On July 21, 1378, the Ciompi wool workers themselves took to the street to riot, to burn more houses, and to demand their own guild and thereby representation in the state. This escalation by previously excluded non-guild workers was not planned by the Civic faction; indeed it represented a loss of control. (5) A Ciompi workers' state was declared, which forcibly expelled large numbers of *popolani* and magnate elites from the city, both Parte Guelfa and Civic. (6) After six weeks in July and August, this Ciompi state was in turn crushed on September 1, when an alliance of wool guild and minor guilds defeated the Ciompi in open street combat. (7) Subsequently, from September 1378 through 1382, there reigned a so-called "minor guild regime."[11]

Brief and cursory though this summary of the Ciompi Revolt is, it is sufficient to establish the action half of a drastic mismatch between republican emphasis on consensus and unity in *Consulte e Pratiche* speech, within the room of elite discussion, and the contradictory emphasis on factionalism, denunciation, and violence apparent in action in the courts and in the streets outside that room. The speech-action puzzle is that, up until the final populist explosion in June and July, the elite actors involved in both these activities were largely the same.

Republicanism: The Institutional Side

In figure 5.1 of our first article (Padgett et al. 2020), we provided a summary "organization chart" of Florentine republicanism. The nine-member

[11] We intend to analyze the *Consulte e Pratiche* discussions in this minor-guild regime, which Katalin Prajda has already transcribed, in a future "part III" sequel paper. Eventually there will be a *longue durée* book, by Padgett and Prajda, on the institutional evolution of the *Consulte e Pratiche* and republicanism.

Florentine city council was called either the Signoria or the Priorate. The original republican advisory councils, dating from the early 1300s, were the 12-member *Buonuomini* ("good men") and the 16-member *Gonfalonieri* ("neighborhood standard-bearers"). Collectively, these three "executive branch" councils were called *Tre Maggiori* perhaps because their rotating[12] memberships were drawn randomly from the same scrutiny bags. Together the *Buonuomini* and *Gonfalonieri* advisory councils were called the Colleges. The function of these advisory councils was to vet and to vote on proposed legislation, before the city council approved them.

After proposed legislation emerged from this "executive branch," final legal approval was in the hands of the two "legislative branches": namely, the Council of the *Commune* and the Council of the *Popolo*. From 1348 on, these large bodies did not discuss the executive-branch proposals, but simply voted them up or down.[13] A positive 2/3 vote was required for approval, in these and in all republican councils.[14]

The electoral system of selecting rotating membership in the *Tre Maggiori* governing councils was as follows: (1) In a first step, the so-called scrutiny, an electoral body[15] voted on lists of nominees, one by one, to become eligible for the three governing councils if they received 2/3 of the votes. These scrutiny elections took place once every three years, or sometimes after a crisis. Successful name tickets were then placed in three bags[16] for future random selection. In 1382, the closest year for which scrutiny lists survive, there

[12] Membership in the Signoria turned over every two months. Membership in the *Buonuomini* turned over every three months. Membership in the *Gonfalonieri* turned over every four months.

[13] Before the Black Death, discussion and debate (sometimes elaborate: see Gherardi 1896) did occur in front of these legislative councils. Those earlier discussions are recorded in volumes called *Libri Fabarum*. For the most part, these *Libri Fabarum* discussions were radically truncated around the time of the creation of the *Consulte e Pratiche*. *Consulte e Pratiche* executive-branch discussions, in other words, seem essentially to have substituted for *Libri Fabarum* legislative-branch discussions. (Although there were also jurisdictional differences: *Libri Fabarum* discussions were more domestic-policy oriented, whereas *Consulte e Pratiche* discussions were more foreign-policy oriented.) Social-class composition of speakers does not appear to have been altered by this institutional change shortly after the Black Death.

[14] However, if rejected, the executive branch had the right to demand a revote. Hotly contested legislation often went through numerous rounds of "1/3 opposed" rejection, before the executive branch, by hook or by crook, jammed the legislation through. Resistance from these republican legislative councils later induced the Medici to undermine republicanism altogether, by establishing more pliable, because appointed, Medici councils.

[15] In this time period, the voting body was composed of current members of the Signoria, the Colleges, various ex-officio groups, and 80 members chosen by the Signoria and the Colleges (Brucker 1962, 66).

[16] In addition to his substantive feedback, we thank John Najemy for catching an error at this point in a previous draft, plus for correcting other small glitches.

were 5,069 nominees and 869 elected to the *Tre Maggiori* scrutiny bag.[17] (2) In a second step, which was repeated every time a new council needed to be filled, friars randomly drew name tickets from the scrutiny bags. Before seating these names, a series of checks were made, having to do with whether relatives too recently had been in office (*divieto*), whether taxes were paid up (*specchio*), and whether the person was a resident in Florence.[18]

This odd (to modern eyes), rapidly rotating, and random membership system of the *Tre Maggiori* was set up explicitly to combat factionalism. The core idea was that no faction could gain a lock on the central institutions of governance when turnover was so high. Another consequence of rapid turnover in membership in governing councils, intended or not, was a huge rate of citizen participation in governance. There were no professional politicians: This really was citizens (mostly merchants and major guildsmen) governing themselves.

One downside of this rapid rotation system was that city councilors often were not experts in the matters they were deciding upon and often did not know what to do. The *Consulte e Pratiche* was established in 1349, right after the Black Death, in order to solve this expertise problem. These were ad hoc assemblies, called into being at the discretion of the city council to give it advice on any upcoming issue of its choice but mostly on foreign-policy matters.

In practice, membership in these ad hoc *Consulte e Pratiche* assemblies was selected by the "chairman of the board" of the Signoria: the *Gonfaloniere di Giustizia*. By tradition, representatives of the earlier advisory councils, the *Buonuomini* and the *Gonfalonieri*, were almost always included in *Consulte e Pratiche*, usually as the two lead speakers in those assemblies. In this sense, the *Consulte e Pratiche* advisory system was a historical descendant of the earlier one. The difference was that now membership could be expanded, at will, to include others (*richiesti*) either for reasons of expertise or for reasons of informal influence and power. When only office-holders were included in

[17] Ildefonso di San Luigi (ed.). 1770–89. These numbers refer to only the 14 out of 16 neighborhoods whose records survive. Multiplying the above numbers by 16/14 yields a citywide estimate of 5,793 nominees and 993 elected. An accurate enumeration of the total number of citizen heads-of-households in the city is contained in the 1378 estimo or tax census (A.S.F. *Tratte* 355). Counting males only, 12,429 male heads of household existed in that tax census. According to this seat-of-the-pants estimation procedure, 47% of the eligible Florentine population was nominated to the three highest governing councils in the city, and 8% was elected. These are extraordinarily high numbers for this 1300s time period. See also Molho (1968b), Witt (1976), and Najemy (1982, 270).

[18] Name tickets drawn were called *veduti* (seen). Names which passed all tests, to become actual members of the council they were selected for, were called *seduti* (seated).

membership, *Consulte e Pratiche* meetings were called *ristretto*. These were small (2–5 person) assemblies dealing with routine administrative matters. When influential non-office *richiesti* were added, *Consulte e Pratiche* meetings were called *allargato*. *Allargato* meetings were where really important issues were discussed.

While Padgett and Prajda (2015) have shown that the *Consulte e Pratiche*, in principle, was unrestricted in membership criteria, in reality it almost always[19] was selected from the pool of previously elected *Tre Maggiori* office-holders, which were called the *reggimento* or "ruling class." In this sense, the *Consulte e Pratiche* represented samples of the "General Will" of the ruling elite, who rotated through various offices within the Florentine republican system. The network graph linking *Consulte e Pratiche* speakers through previous co-membership in some *Tre Maggiori* council, was so dense that we could not visualize it.[20] The number of speakers in the *Consulte e Pratiche* collectively was not small,[21] but their previous experience with, and hence knowledge of each other, as well as each other's parents, was as high as it would be in the proverbial small town. Republican search for a "General Will" is not as ridiculous in a participatory political system like this as it would be in a larger, more heterogeneous society.

Underneath these institutional procedures lay what Brucker called a "political ideology": (1) "Although the Florentines did not write formal treatises on politics, they did possess common convictions which underlay their political behavior. In contemporary writings there frequently occur expressions of devoted allegiance to the communal government, an attitude which Paolo da Certaldo reflects in his book of proverbs: 'Never engage in any trade that your commune forbids . . . Cherish the honor and the good and the welfare of your city . . . and to this devote your property and person, and never support any other party but that of your Commune.' If not all Florentines followed these maxims to the letter, they were united in their determination to maintain the city's independence." (Brucker 1962, 72–73) An extraordinary version of this patriotism was expressed in a private letter from the young Coluccio Salutati, nine years before we observe him as

[19] After 1355, the percentage of *Consulte e Pratiche* who were members of the *reggimento* (that is, previous *Tre Maggiori* office-holders) was always above 80%. After 1390, it was always above 90%.

[20] That is, our network of "previous co-membership in *Tre Maggiori* offices" among *C e P* speakers looked like an uninterpretable "black hairball," regardless of layout algorithm.

[21] The annual number of distinct speakers and speeches was reported in our first article: 100–250 distinct speakers per year throughout the period 1348–1435, and 400 to 1200 speeches during the same period (Padgett and Prajda 2015).

chancellor: "If it would serve to defend or extend the homeland, we should not consider it a distasteful or hard task to thrust an axe into one's father's head, mangle our brothers, or deliver the unborn child from one's wife's womb with a sword." (Witt 1983, 73).[22]

And (2) "Deeply engrained in the Florentine political mentality was a fundamental precept of republicanism: the formulation of policy through group consultation. The right of free and untrammeled discussion was considered one of the bulwarks of independence, and it was thus stated in the preamble to one provision: 'For the conservation of liberty and welfare and for the direction of public affairs, nothing appears to be more advantageous than a free spirit in discussion.' . . . Rarely, if ever, did the priors flout the consensus of opinion expressed in the consultative assemblies."

To these core precepts, (3) we add below a demonstration of the Florentine commitment to unity in speech: "consensus," "general will," "cordiality," "school of fish," whatever you want to call it. Once a direction of sentiment appeared to congeal in *Consulte e Pratiche* discussion, most subsequent speakers rushed to join it. This is most evident in the high frequency of speeches that are recorded as saying *idem*, meaning "the same as"—either "the same as" some previous speaker (identified either by a name or by an office) or just *idem* without any reference, which we interpret to mean "same as the current sense of the meeting." 24% of the 1,330 speeches in our 1376–78 dataset contain *idem*, in one or another of these forms. We provide further evidence below about just how strong this norm of unity or consensus (feigned or otherwise) really was.

This republican emphasis on unity, in the face of divisive factions, no doubt intensified during wartime, when "rally round the flag" patriotism kicked in to strengthen it.

Consulte e Pratiche: The Speech Side

Quantitative Analyses

In this section, we present three types of statistical analysis of *Consulte e Pratiche* speech and, in the next section, two types of qualitative analysis of

[22] Below we trace the personal relationship between Coluccio Salutati and Lapo da Castiglionchio, leader of Parte Guelfa, which evolved from intimate to alienated over their two parallel lives.

such speech. In our first article (Padgett et al. 2020), we zoomed in on correlations, at the meeting level of analysis, among 15 core keywords, in order to trace the evolution of changing topics of discussion. The *Consulte e Pratiche* in that paper was treated not as rhetoric but rather as a measuring instrument for observing the flow of "objective" history outside the room, as perceived by speakers inside the room. In this complementary second paper, we focus more on how speakers inside the room treated each other. For this different purpose, the 15-keyword core skeleton of changing topics is insufficient. We are interested instead in variation around those core topics—in other words, in the republicanism theme of faction versus consensus, described in the introduction. All nouns (and in the OLS regression analysis, all nouns and all adjectives), at or above a threshold frequency of 10 (over our entire time period), will be the object of study. Correlations between frequencies of words will be measured in this second article at the fine-grained speech level of analysis, not at the coarser-grained meeting level of analysis, as in the first article. The lemmatized dataset for this more refined level of analysis was described in an online appendix to our first article.

First, we present a simple bivariate scatterplot of word frequencies, designed to highlight global differences in the "bag of words" of how different factions spoke. The main message will be how similarly, in the sense of word frequencies, the factions spoke. We also measure, with R^2, variation across time in this similarity between factions' speech. Almost shockingly, the Parte Guelfa and Civic factions increasingly spoke most similarly in chapter 5, at the very cusp of the Ciompi revolt.

Second, we present Wordfish, which is a word-scaling technique[23] designed to array factions, through their speech, on a one-dimensional pseudo left–right "ideology" scale. We place no credence on the Wordfish inventors' label of their statistical dimension as "ideology," even though that was their motivation. It turned out that, despite considerable effort, we could not discover interpretable meaning within either the "left" or the "right" clusters of words that Wordfish generated. We therefore simply use the technique minimally for the sole purpose of identifying whether any factional differences in speech can be detected through a technique specifically designed to find such differences. Low and behold, we do indeed find evidence of factional differences using this technique, especially between Parte Guelfa and everything else—exactly in the form predicted in figure 5.3.

[23] This technique was helpfully suggested by one of our reviewers.

Third, we present our primary statistical analysis: namely, OLS regressions on speech-similarity dyads (over tens of thousands of such speech-by-speech comparisons), into which various independent variables, including Parte Guelfa and Civic factions but also Same Meeting and Same Person, are introduced. This oldy-but-goody statistical technique proved to be the most synthetic and powerful of them all. The 15 topic keywords, analyzed in more depth in our first article, in effect are captured through the "Same Meeting" variable in these regressions. The consensus findings of Scatterplot are reproduced, in part, through the high constants observed in these regressions. The factional-differences findings of Wordfish are captured through the faction variables, especially when the institutional control of speaking role (Office versus No Office) is introduced. In addition, a new insight is added by OLS regression: namely, the "Same Person" variable reveals statistical significance but surprisingly modest coefficient size. In other words, while we can indeed statistically detect differences among speakers,[24] those individual differences are quite weak. We interpret this last finding as republican pressure for conformity. Since meeting topics themselves change over time, pressure for conformity within a meeting is equivalent to repeat speakers being chameleons over time.

In a subsequent section, we shall illustrate this qualitatively by the special case of Lapo da Castiglionchio, the uber-conservative *arciguelfo* leader of Parte Guelfa, who led their anti-Ghibelline denunciation campaign. In action, this factional leader had his house burned by Ciompi mobs and then suffered exile by the 1378 balìa. We demonstrate that, extremism in action notwithstanding, factional leader Lapo usually appeared within the *Consulte e Pratiche* room to be the epitome of good citizenship and loyalty: the ultimate chameleon.

Scatterplot[25]

In figures 5.5a and 5.5b, we present two examples of bivariate scatterplot comparisons of the word frequencies[26] of all nouns used by Parte Guelfa and the members of the 1378 balìa: our operational indicator of "Civic faction."

[24] Thereby decisively disproving the "editorial hand" counter-hypothesis.

[25] We were inspired to do this by Kessler (2017). But actually we did not employ any of Kessler's Scattertext software. Yuanhao Liu, a new member of our team who joined us this year, wrote his own program in R using ggplot2 (Silge and Robinson 2016) to produce these results. We appreciate the simple and easily interpretable character of this low-tech content analysis.

[26] These word frequencies have been normalized into percentages of words spoken by each faction in order to control away possible differences in the number of speeches given by different factions at different times.

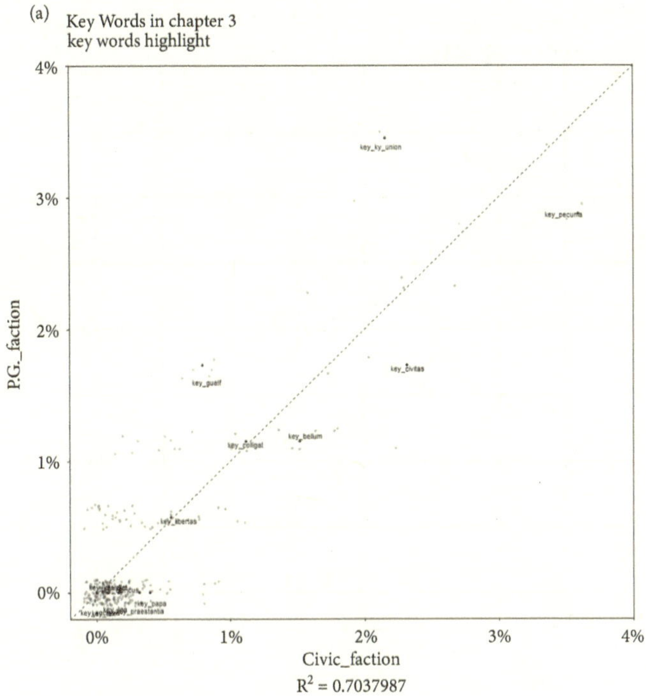

Figure 5.5a Scatterplot: Parte Guelfa vs Civic, chapter 3

Words had to have been spoken a minimum of 10 times, by anyone over the entire period, in order to be included in these scatterplots. The fifteen keywords upon which we concentrated in our first article are highlighted in red. Underneath each scatterplot, we report a measure of how tightly the scatterplot clusters around the 45 degree line—namely, the R^2 of a simple regression run through these points.[27]

Figure 5.6 plots the summary R^2's for all of our faction comparisons, not just the two example comparisons in figures 5.5a and 5.5b. Two findings are evident: (a) The highest correlations between word frequencies, ranging consistently in magnitude of R^2's between .7 and .8, are between Civic and No Faction. This is completely consistent with the hieratic structure predicted in figure 5.3. More surprisingly, (b) the word-frequency correlations between the two opposing factions of Parte Guelfa and Civic, and also between Parte Guelfa and No Faction, actually increase, from .5 to .8,

[27] Technically, the regression coefficient need not be the 45 degree line—in other words Y = (1.0) X—but practically speaking, it always is.

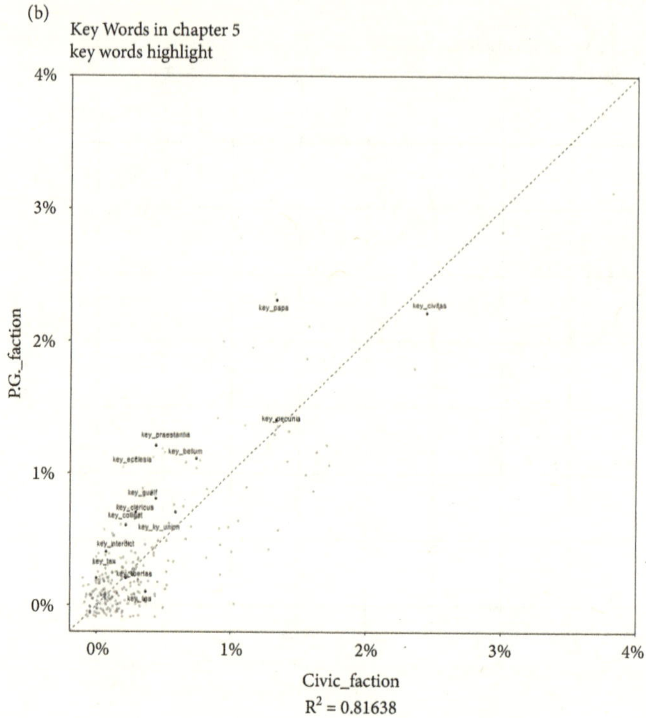

Figure 5.5b Scatterplot: Parte Guelfa vs Civic, chapter 5

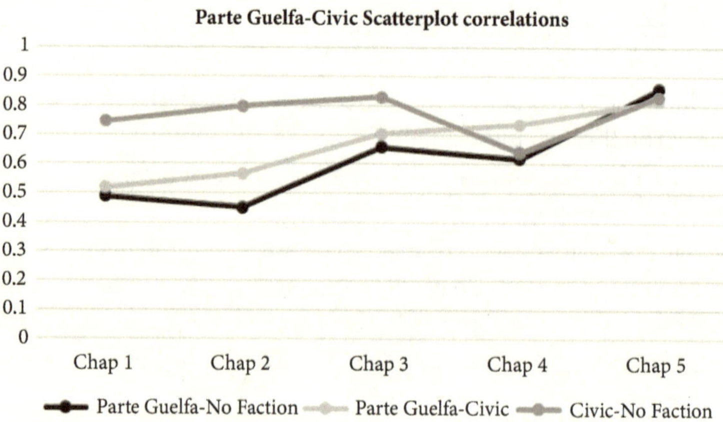

Figure 5.6 Scatterplot R^2's

over time! This is the central puzzle of this paper: Namely, at the very same time that the Parte Guelfa and the Civic factions were moving aggressively towards open civil war in the realm of action, the content of their public-policy speeches became more difficult to distinguish in the elite debates of the *Consulte e Pratiche*.[28]

To put these Florentine R^2's into some sort of comparative context, we obtained the modern speech data analyzed in Kessler (2017), which are the Democratic and Republican nominating speeches for president in their 2012 national conventions. These speeches eventuated in the nominations of Obama and Romney, respectively. To make R^2's statistically comparable, in spite of their wildly different cultural contexts, we applied our own data-processing normalization procedures to Kessler's data—namely, (a) we thresholded only words that appeared 10 or more times in the entire corpus, and then (b) we normalized word frequencies into word percentages, by dividing word frequencies by the total number of words spoken by each party. These are the same data-processing procedures that we applied to our own data.

The resulting R^2 of similarity between Democratic and Republican nomination speeches in 2012 is .048. Compare this with the (.5–.8) range of R^2's that appear in figure 5.6. It is nice to see statistics confirm what we know already—namely, that there is a vast cultural difference between politicians in Renaissance Florence and politicians in contemporary America. Contemporary American political parties are trying to differentiate themselves in speech from each other. Renaissance Florentine factions were trying to deny in speech the (dangerous) differences that they knew existed in action.

Wordfish

Next, Wordfish: Figures 5.7(a)–5.7(e) present the one-dimensional scaling output produced by applying the Wordfish word-scaling algorithm to each of our five chapters, within which each faction's speeches have been pooled into individual "documents" and then scaled relative to each other. As we said above, the Wordfish inventors (Slapin and Proksch 2008) used the label "ideology" to refer to their one-dimensional scale because this tool was

[28] This is not to say, of course, that one cannot find exceptions to this generalization—for example, the December 26, 1377 meeting where "For the first time, the oligarchy abandoned its protective mantle of silence and spoke its mind." (Brucker 1962, 333) But that was the exception, not the rule.

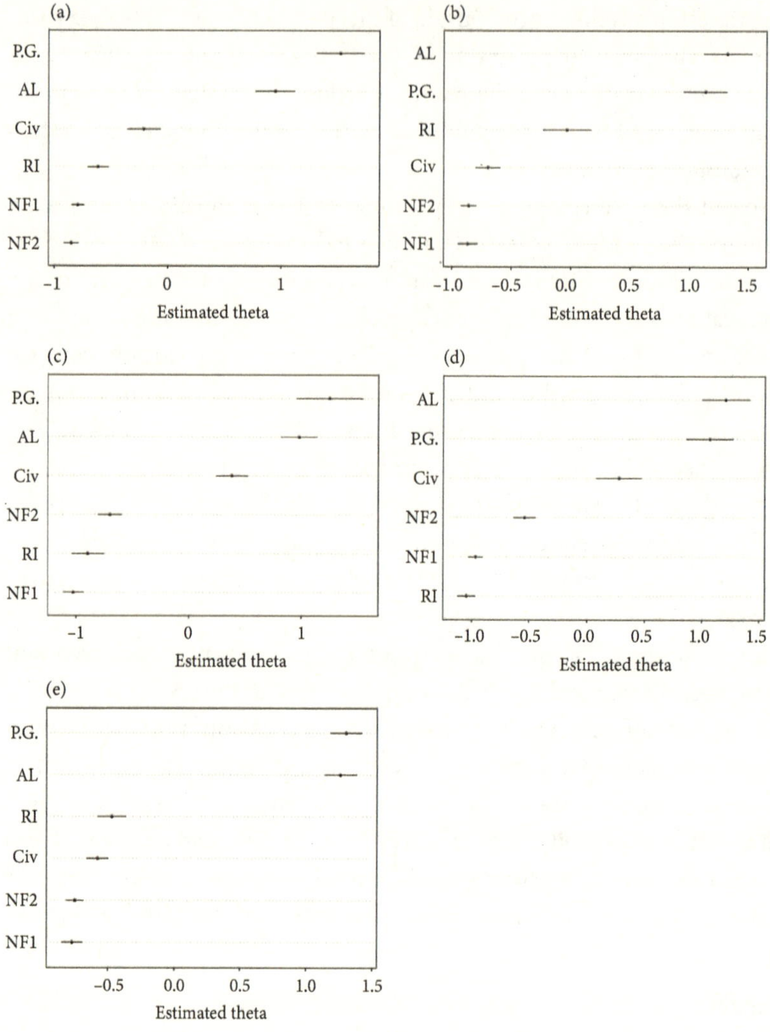

Figures 5.7a–5.7e Wordfish Scaling of Factions

designed to infer "left" versus "right" from political speeches. But we prefer Grimmer and Stewart's (2013) more cautious interpretation.[29] Hence we

[29] "But the lack of supervision and the use of an IRT model implies that the model will seize upon the primary variation in language across actors. This might be ideological. Or, the differences across actors may be about their focus on policy or pork, the style in which the essays were written, or the tone of the statements. Because the model does not include supervision explicitly, it is difficult to guarantee that the output of the model will reliably identify the revealed ideological locations of political actors. It is worth emphasizing that this is not a shortcoming of wordfish. In fact, we will show below that non-ideological locations that wordfish identifies are quite useful. But this does

will refrain from imposing misleading semantic, and modernist, labels onto what is only an inferential statistical-search algorithm.

Even though Wordfish's "estimated theta" dimension has no substantive meaning that we can detect, this algorithm does an astonishingly good job of finding and distinguishing factional speech, even though *Consulte e Pratiche* speakers were trying to hide that. A simple and neutral way of thinking about this Wordfish scale is that it is looking to find the orthogonal axis in the Scatterplots. Namely, instead of Scatterplot's emphasis on the 45-degree (NE/SW) line of similarity in word-frequency usage, Wordfish is looking to find the off-diagonal 135-degree (NW/SE) line of dissimilarity in word-frequency usage. We are impressed by how well it does this, in ways consistent with summary descriptions by expert historians like Brucker (1962), even though we cannot interpret semantically what the scale actually means.[30]

At this faction level of analysis, the Wordfish findings are these: (1) Parte Guelfa and the earlier Albizzi factions, which are highly overlapping in memberships, are consistently on the "right," maximally separated from all other groups. Conversely, (2) the two "No Faction" groups (one defined as relative to the old Albizzi and Ricci factions[31] and the other defined with respect to the new Parte Guelfa and Civic factions) consistently are on the far "left" in the Wordfish scale's placement. This scaling separation in speech between these two extremes is consistent with the sharp social-class divisions that underlie these two sides: Albizzi and Parte Guelfa are both referred to in the literature as "oligarchic factions." Whereas No Faction is more heavily composed of new men and artisans who desired an end to the sometimes violent factional feuding of their social superiors.

The surprise finding in these Wordfish results is the temporal wandering of the "swing vote" factions, Ricci and Civic, respectively, between these

suggest that one should not assume that wordfish output measures an ideological location without careful validation" (Grimmer and Stewart (2013, 293).

[30] Our Chicago Latinist, Brendan Small, spent much time trying to interpret the word vectors that Wordfish produced, by looking closely at clusters of "extreme" words that appeared at each end of the scale. His conclusion: "While the underlying scale certainly identifies statistical differences between factions, we were unable to discern a coherent pattern to the words underneath of that scale. Moreover, extremum word clusters tended to be unstable in composition across chapters, and words like *Ghibelline* that did act consistently were used too infrequently (only four times throughout all five chapters). Therefore we cannot interpret the semantic meaning of this scale with any confidence." (Unpublished memo from Small to Padgett.)

[31] The old Albizzi and Ricci factions had dissolved by this point, but their members still existed. Therefore, Wordfish analyses of those factions treat speakers as if they were still members of their previous alignments.

two extremes. In chapters 1, 2 and 5, the Civic faction—operationalized as 1378 balìa—is much closer to the No Faction end of the scale, consistent with the diagram in figure 5.3. But in the middle chapters 3 and 4, Civic moves closer to the oligarchic end of the scale, thereby becoming almost indistinguishable from it. But in chapter 5, Civic sharply lurches back to its original alignment with No Faction, leaving Parte Guelfa not only extremely located on one side, but now isolatedly so. This last Wordfish finding of cleavage between Parte Guelfa and Civic in chapter 5 directly contradicts Scatterplot's opposite finding, based on R^2's. We will leave it to OLS regression to adjudicate this disagreement.

Figure 5.8 presents the Wordfish scaling results at the speaker, not at the pooled faction, level of analysis. This means that here all speeches by a single speaker within each chapter are pooled into numerous quite small "documents," one for each speaker x chapter. The numbers along the y-axis of

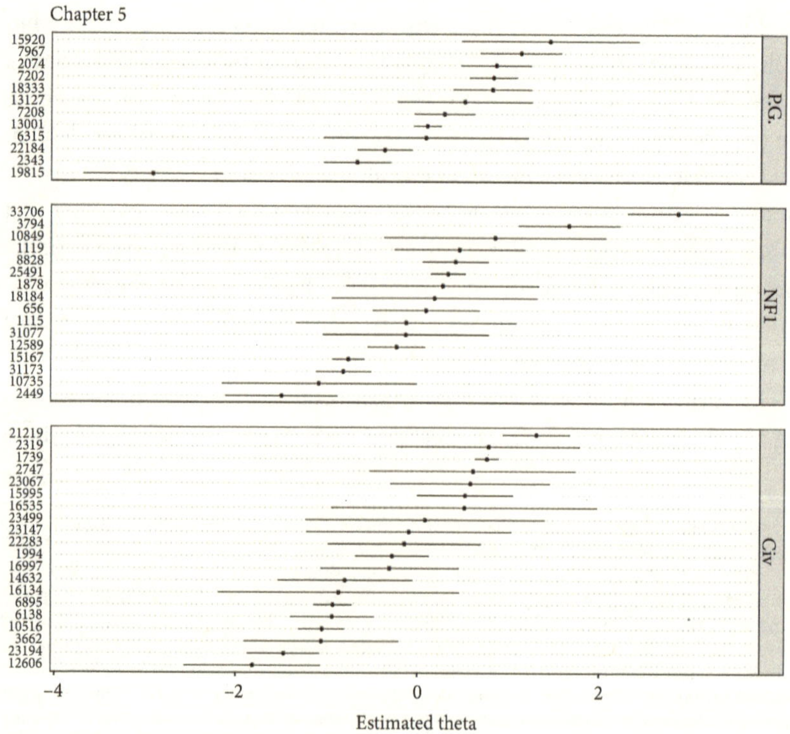

Figure 5.8 Wordfish Scaling: Individual Speakers, chapter five

figure 5.8 refer to the ID codes of the individual speakers within each faction. Confidence intervals are much wider in figure 5.8 than in figures 5.7 because the number of words in each Wordfish analysis is so much lower in figure 5.8 than in figures 5.7. To save space, only the chapter 5 results are reproduced in figure 5.8 because the global pattern of high overlap of individuals' scales across factions is the same in chapters 1–4.

The obvious finding here is the huge overlap in words that members of the various factions spoke. This is consistent with the high similarity or "consensus" finding of Scatterplot, as measured by R^2 (figure 5.6). Figures 5.7, in contrast, showed sharp and consistent differences between factions. The apparent contradiction is resolved just by appreciating how much larger are the "bags of words" in figures 5.7, as compared to figure 5.8. This is analogous to a regression finding of "statistically significant, but not large in magnitude." Visually one can clearly see, even at this finer-grained speaker level of analysis, the identity of Civic and No Faction in chapter 5. And one can see a slight, but very slight, leaning of Parte Guelfa to the "right." Wordfish is powerful enough to distinguish between the speeches of Florentine factions by pooling, but that does not mean that factional speech differences were clearly apparent at the level of an individual speaker.

Speech-Similarity Regressions

Finally on the statistical side, we come to our *pièce de la résistance*: OLS regressions on speech similarity. The dependent variable here, "speech similarity," was constructed first by filtering our full corpus of lemmatized and thresholded Latin words into "all nouns and adjectives," and then by constructing vectors of word frequencies for every speech. Speech "similarity" was computed by correlating each pair of speech vectors, for speeches that occurred within the same chapter.

Our independent variables are as follows:

(a) Same Meeting, which hypothesizes that speeches are similar to each other because they were dealing with the same topics within the same meetings. This, of course, is what we analyzed through keywords in our first article.

(b) Same Person, which hypothesizes that speeches are similar to each other when they were uttered by the same speaker. Presumably this would be either because of consistent policy preferences or because of consistent speaking styles.

(c) Same Faction, which hypothesizes that speeches are similar because they are spoken by speakers in the same faction, where "factions" are defined as Parte Guelfa versus Civic. The baseline against which "faction effect" is measured is the omitted category of No Faction.

(d) In order to assess the effectiveness of institutional control, Same Faction was interacted with "role of speaker"—namely, speaking on behalf of (or representing) an Office and speaking on behalf of No Office (that is, speaking on behalf of self). For example, we divided speech pairs into Parte Guelfa speeches when both speakers spoke freely in No Office, and Parte Guelfa speeches when either speech was restricted by the Office role of speaker. "Office" here means any office mentioned, which immediately followed the speaker's name in the protocols.

At the end of our table 5.2 results, we add a visualization of the magnitudes of the coefficients reported in the table, in order to see more quickly and easily changing patterns of regression coefficients over time.[32] (Consult table 5.2 itself to see significance levels.)

The findings are as follows:

(a) Same Meeting is the independent variable consistently with the strongest effect on speech similarity. This is not surprising: speeches were most similar when they talked about the same topics. The content of what meetings talked about changed over time, as was analyzed in the narrative networks of our first article.

(b) Above and beyond Same Meeting/similar topic and anything else, the second highest effect was the Constant terms in these regressions. We interpret this as a pervasive background norm of agreement (or perhaps of mimicry), above and beyond the topic of discussion.[33] The magnitudes of Same Meeting and Constant do not vary over time, nor would we expect them to.

[32] There is not the usual "standardized vs unstandardized" complication in comparing regression coefficients because all independent variables are binary in character.

[33] "Norm" might sound vague, but a consultation of the translated transcript provided in appendix to part I will make it clear enough what we mean. Not only did speakers talk about the same topics, they often did so in similar sequences and formats.

Table 5.2 Speech-Similarity OLS Regressions: All Nouns and Adjectives Parte Guelfa vs. Civic, with Office vs. No Office Interactions

	Dependent variable: sim_corr_all				
	Chapter 1	**Chapter 2**	**Chapter 3**	**Chapter 4**	**Chapter 5**
constant	0.065** (0.001)	0.060** (0.001)	0.082** (0.001)	0.076** (0.001)	0.090** (0.001)
Same Meeting	0.177** (0.004)	0.137** (0.005)	0.161** (0.005)	0.180*8 (0.005)	0.158** (0.005)
Same Person	0.013** (0.003)	0.017** (0.003)	−0.005 (0.004)	0.022** (0.004)	0.022** (0.003)
both Parte Guelfa: both no office	0.054** (0.018)		0.120 (0.063)	0.087** (0.018)	0.058** (0.018)
both parte Guelfa: Either office	0.012** (0.002)	−0.003 (0.003)	0.0013** (0.005)	−0.0004 (0.003)	−0.010** (0.002)
both 1378 Balìa: both of office	0.172** (0.029)	−0.022 (0.023)	0.114** (0.034)	−0.074 (0.043)	−0.097* (0.045)
both 1378 Balìa: Either office	−0.011** (0.003)	−0.001 (0.002)	0.022** (0.003)	−0.025** (0.009)	−0.001 (0.002)
Observations	27,028	23,436	18,145	20,503	36,585
R^2	0.076	0.039	0.051	0.073	0.027
Adjusted R^2	0.076	0.038	0.051	0.073	0.027
Residual Std. Error	0.093	0.088	0.107	0.105	0.110
Degrees of freedom	27,021	23,430	18,138	20,496	33,578
F Statistic	369.377**	188.652**	164.091**	268.633**	168.802**

* p < .05
** p < .01

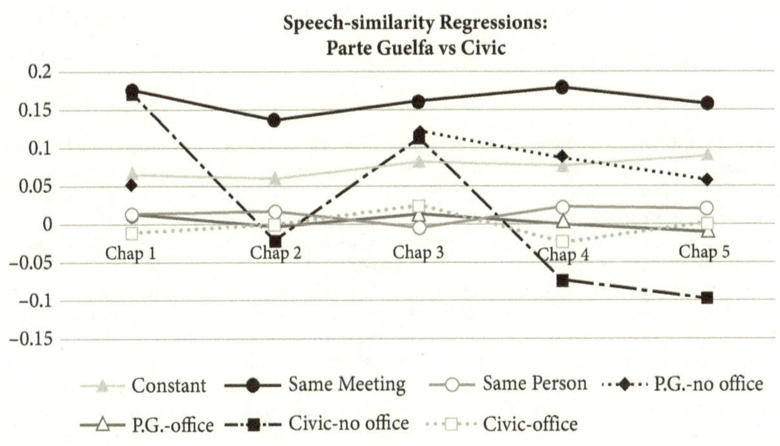

(c) Same Person is consistently statistically significant. In that sense, it is encouraging that our regression technique, crude as it is, can indeed pick up "personality" differences between people. No one thinks that Renaissance Florentines were privately the same. Yet the time-series visualization at the end of table 5.2 consistently reveals the magnitude of Same Person coefficient to be modest indeed[34]—statistically significant, in other words, but not substantively important. Florentine republicans did not want to stand out from the crowd; they wanted to blend in.

(d) Same Factions are the variables whose effect show variation over time. Among unconstrained No Office speakers, where we most expect factions' existence to be manifest in speech, we find:

Parte Guelfa speeches are similar to each other, both in statistical significance and in coefficient magnitude, in chapters 1, 4, and 5. In chapters 2 and 3, at the peak of the war, Parte Guelfa coefficients in the No Office condition disappear perhaps because of a "rally round the flag" effect. Wordfish, in contrast, showed consistent Parte Guelfa effects, regardless of chapter.[35]

Civic speeches stand out, compared to their No Faction speeches omitted-category baseline, in chapters 1 and 3.[36] In chapters 2, 4, and 5, in contrast, "Civic," as measured by 1378 balìa, blended in with No Faction, just as in our "hieratic" diagram of them in figure 5.3. The "Civic Faction," in other words, really was just the leadership of all republicans who disliked faction. They were a "faction" only in the asymmetric sense that they defended themselves against the assault of the increasingly aggressive anti-war Parte Guelfa, who more accurately deserve the slanderous (to Florentines) label of "faction."

[34] These Same-Person coefficients do not change if faction variables are dropped. In a baseline model that includes only the variables of Same Meeting and Same Person, the five-chapter vector of Same-Person coefficients is (.016***, .016***, .007*, .019***, .021***). Like in the full regression, these coefficients are statistically significant but small in magnitude. Standard modernist political-science concepts like "policy preferences" for individuals, we believe, are misleading for Renaissance Florentines, at least in the domain of their public speech.

[35] We criticized Wordfish for inability to produce interpretable clusters of words to help interpret its scale. (See Monroe et al. 2008 to see that this is a general problem, not specific to this paper.) For equity, it is worth saying that speech-similarity regressions are no more capable than is Wordfish of giving linguistic content to its coefficients. This limitation of both methods is why quantitative analyses must be complemented with qualitative analyses for a full understanding to emerge.

[36] This is consistent with Wordfish, except that Wordfish showed Civic to stand out from No Faction in chapter 4.

(e) Institutional control conceptualized as type of role was very effective indeed. As expected, when *Consulte e Pratiche* speakers spoke on behalf of an Office, faction effects for both Parte Guelfa and Civic disappear. In addition to the pervasive normative effects of republicanism, which we believe to be revealed in regression constants, factional speech was regulated by office-holding in republican offices. After all, in such roles speakers were conveying background consultations in the councils from which they came.

Collectively these regression findings reveal not that republicanism had collapsed on the cusp of the Ciompi Revolt. On the contrary, the *Consulte e Pratiche* remained a republican bastion against increasingly violent factionalism raging outside its door. Hence our summary judgment of it, mentioned in the introduction, as a "Valiant Failure."[37]

Qualitative Analyses

What do these global statistical patterns of *Consulte e Pratiche* speech look like on the ground in particular speeches and sentences? We cannot, of course, reproduce here the 1,427 speeches from late 1375 to mid-1378 that we have transcribed.[38] But we will provide two examples that illustrate what we are talking about: the special case of Lapo da Castiglionchio and the rhetorical use, in argument, of the *union* . . . keyword.

Lapo da Castiglionchio

Lapo da Castiglionchio[39] was widely recognized by contemporaries as the leader of the Parte Guelfa faction, one of the central instigators in fact of that faction's *ammonizione* anti-Ghibelline denunciation campaign (Brucker 1962, 339). He was "rewarded" for his aggressive behavior by being the

[37] In this, Brucker (1962, 360) concurs: "The legislation resulting from these four weeks of intensive deliberation was a feeble compromise . . . Remaining intact were both the *ammonizione* machinery and the procedure for designating magnates. In its moderate tone and its aversion to radical reform, this legislation epitomized the regime's political philosophy. Yet, by its failure to grapple with fundamental issues, these laws emphasized one of its most serious weaknesses. However cautious and limited in scope was this 'reform', it did reflect the strong sentiment in favor of political moderation."

[38] Some of these transcriptions were of meetings before our January 1, 1376 starting date for analysis.

[39] We are grateful to Brendan Small, PhD graduate student in Renaissance Florentine History, who provided translations of a selection of Prajda's Latin transcriptions into English—namely, all of Lapo's speeches, plus the *Consulte e Pratiche* meetings of March 5–7, 1377.

first to have his house burned by the Ciompi "mob." (Stefani [1380] 2008, 319; Brucker 1962, 368; Zervas 1987, 233) This populist judgment was ratified officially by Lapo's formal exile from Florence to Rome by the 1378 balìa, which emerged soon after those fires.[40] Lapo da Castiglionchio was the epitome of an extremist in action. Brucker repeatedly characterizes Lapo as *arciguelfo*, Guelf extremist, oligarchic, and the like.

At the same time, earlier in his youth, Lapo had been a leading member of a learned Florentine circle of early humanists, which had received and welcomed visits from Petrarch in 1350 (Witt 1983, 57). From 1363–64 onward, Coluccio Salutati also was an active member of that humanist circle (59). Lapo da Castiglionchio and Coluccio Salutati, in other words, knew each other very well, from their youthful days as fellow students and discussants of ancient Latin texts. Witt speculates (122) that Lapo and his humanist circle may have been central in the appointment of Coluccio to the prestigious office of chancellor in 1375.[41] The relationship between Lapo and Coluccio was so close, in fact, that Coluccio composed the epitaph for Lapo's tombstone. At the same time, Coluccio was bitterly disappointed at his close friend's "betrayal" of Florence, as Coluccio saw it, later in Lapo's life.[42]

But does this mean that Lapo da Castiglionchio, so extremist in action, was extremist in his speeches within the *Consulte e Pratiche*? Not at all.

Of the seventeen speeches that Lapo da Castiglionchio gave during our five-chapter period, only Lapo's speech on December 26, 1377 contains

[40] He died there in 1380.

[41] That sponsorship notwithstanding, however: "If Salutati had conspired with the Guelf party leadership, he seems to have become independent of it very quickly. While factionalism dominated the life of medieval Italian communes, men in these centuries had an abhorrence for parties and looked on divisions in the citizen body as unnatural and the work of evil men. From his first writings, Salutati dwelt on the necessity of putting the interests of one's country before personal concerns or those of a party." (Witt 1983, 123)

[42] "[After the Ciompi Revolt,] Salutati soon learned that he personally had nothing to fear. He was saved both by his reputation for fair administration of his office and by his identification with the war against the Church, a cause vigorously opposed by the Guelf party. His political propaganda was not merely a product of his professional duty as chancellor: Salutati really believed in the justice of Florence's cause and became something of a war hero. True, he liked the company of men from old and wealthy families and his preferred political class was one heavily weighted with patrician elements. But the leadership of the Guelf party was clearly on a ruinous course. Secure in the knowledge that he had reached the height of his expectations with the chancellorship and fearing adverse change, Salutati could only be critical of the extreme stands the Guelf leaders adopted in 1378 that pushed the Republic toward civil war. While he willingly composed the epitaph for the tomb of Lapo Castiglionchio, who died in exile in Rome in 1381, Salutati considered the Guelf partisan unwise 'to have bent his mind to the swollen desires of ambition'" (Witt 1976, 136–37).

obvious[43] objections to the war against the pope.[44] In contrast, we count seven of Lapo's speeches as overtly supporting the war against the pope and urging its "manly" (*viriliter*) prosecution. The way that Brucker (1962, 333) describes this seeming prevarication is this: On December 26, "For the first time [in the debates recorded in the protocols], the oligarchy abandoned it protective mantle of silence and spoke its mind."[45] It is notable that this unusual open opposition to the war was spoken only when an obviously pre-arranged phalanx of six anti-war speakers had been assembled to speak in unison, throwing down a gauntlet, so to speak.[46] Meanwhile the Parte Guelfa's anti-Ghibelline purges had been surging since October 1377. (See figure 5.4.)

In light of this context, it is notable that out of the eight times that Lapo explicitly agreed[47] with previous speakers in our data, three of those agreed-with speakers were with fellow Parte Guelfa partisans, but five of them were with the opposing Civic "faction." Especially striking, in the searing first half of 1378, at the very cusp of civil war, the speaking behavior of Lapo was two times to agree with previous speakers of his own Parte Guelfa allegiance, and four times to agree with previous speakers of the opposite Civic persuasion. With the exception only of that meeting on December 26, 1377, Lapo da Castiglionchio consistently spoke evenhandedly, with balance, as if he were "No Faction."

In a previous draft of this article, we reported regressions on *idem* Agreed-With dyads, such as those just described for Lapo.[48] Those regressions discovered that office—in particular the office of *Gonfaloniere*, which usually spoke first—was the primary predictor of Agreed-With relations, which we therefore interpret not as policy agreement but rather as "deference to office."

[43] The ID of Lapo in figure 5.9 is 7967. Maybe if you squint hard enough, you can talk yourself into believing that Wordfish sees something more than we humans can.

[44] Brucker (1962, 334) translated the first of these as "The city of Florence is in grave danger, since it is engaged in a struggle with an invincible enemy, who, even though it has been dislodged from Italy, still possesses much [power] *in facto et in iure* . . ."

[45] Brucker (1962, 306–07) elaborates: "Perhaps fearing that any vocal opposition would only provoke further reprisals, the minority of loyal Guelfs who regarded the war as a calamity remained discretely silent during the early stages of the conflict. No word of criticism against the commune's foreign policy was inscribed in *Consulte e Pratiche* protocols; these records would suggest that the war was universally popular in the city. . . Pro-war statements by such *arciguelfi* as Lapo da Castiglionchio and Filippo Corsini must be interpreted as prudent genuflections to majority opinion, not as manifestations of their true sentiments."

[46] The December 26 coalition of anti-war speakers was Antonio Ridolfi, Lapo da Castiglionchio, Donato Barbadori, Pazzino Strozzi, Carlo Strozzi, and Filippo Corsini—all leaders of Parte Guelfa.

[47] In the sense of *idem*—namely, speaker said "the same as" some previous speaker.

[48] At the suggestion of a referee, we eliminated that in this draft, to save space.

In other words, the reason that Lapo agreed so much with his erstwhile enemies was not that he liked them or their policies, but rather that he, like everyone else, respected and deferred to republican office, no matter who sat in that seat.

Obviously everyone, including the Ciompi mobs, knew exactly what *arciguelfo* Lapo da Catiglionchio was doing outside the room—in particular what he was doing in his other Parte Guelfa room. Hence it is impossible *not* to believe that Lapo's evenhanded speaking style and deference behavior within the *Consulte e Pratiche* was a charade—or more politely a ritual—in which Lapo and his audience were all complicit.[49] Lapo da Castiglionchio was a chameleon, like many Florentines were (cf. Weissman 1989, Padgett and Ansell 1993). "Chameleon" in this case of the Florentine *Consulte e Pratiche*, however, seems not to be so much a personality trait as an institutional consequence of conformity to public ritual, the ritual of republican debate, in a context where the content of debate oscillated considerably over time. We do not mean to offend the sophisticated Florentines by this metaphor, but Florentine collective decision-making in the *Consulte e Pratiche* was a bit like a school of fish, with everyone super-attentive to and mimicking speech by other speakers.

The Rhetoric of Unity

Before addressing the way in which unity itself was discussed within the *Consulte e Pratiche*, it is important to make an observation about words NOT spoken in the *Consulte e Pratiche*. Already mentioned is that, except for one meeting, opposition to the War of the Eight Saints against the pope was not expressed inside the *Consulte e Pratiche*, even though this was the primary foreign-policy advising body in the Florentine Republic. Not only were anti-war arguments not present, but indeed most "hot button" high-conflict words were avoided, in order to maintain the façade of republican agreement and consensus. Divisive social-class words like magnate (*grandi* or *magnati*) and new men (*gente nuova*) were rarely mentioned, even though (or more likely because) that was the most profound underlying conflict in the city. This linguistic avoidance of social class took place at the same time as anti-Ghibelline *ammonizione* denunciations by Parte Guelfa and their magnate supporters were raging against the latter group plus new

[49] Nicholas Baker (2014) makes a similar argument about the ritual dimension of *Consulte e Pratiche* speech, for a later period in time.

immigrants who had not yet been admitted to citizenship.[50] A third example of conflictual words not spoken is *ammonizione* itself. "Not a whisper of protest against *ammonizione* appears in the protocols; indeed the colleges actually commended the Parte for rooting out subversives from the electorate." (Brucker 1962, 357) The associated word Ghibelline likewise was rarely mentioned. Basically anything that brought serious factional conflict into the room was avoided. All in the name of desired (and proclaimed) unity.

We mentioned in our first article that the word "worker" (*operar*) was not mentioned in the protocols. In this case, that may not have been a matter of suppressing divisive elite conflict so much as of simple inattention, due to the upper-class skew in *Consulte e Pratiche* speakers. A related word not spoken in the *Consulte* of our period is "guild" (*ars, arte, artes, artem*), even though that word explodes into discussion in the next period, after the Ciompi Revolt had occurred.[51]

It is easy to interpret this avoidance of conflictual words as out-and-out hypocrisy, a simple denial, for whatever reason, of obvious reality.[52] But close examination of the sentences surrounding the repeated calls for citizen unity—to the point of banality[53]—reveal them to be more than empty talk or hot air. Almost always there were procedural recommendations attached to such calls: usually advice to the Signora to assemble a very small ad hoc council of 6–8 office-holders to work out a solution. It's just that

[50] Look again at the post-Ciompi hump in figure 5.1, however, to remind yourself just how many new immigrants were waiting just outside of the door of citizenship at that time.

[51] The four listed Latin versions of "guild" were spoken zero times in volume 14 (December 14, 1375 to March 31, 1377) and only three times in volume 15 (April 1, 1377 to June 27, 1378), two of those on June 21, 1378 at the very tail end of our period in this chapter. In the next period, beyond the timeframe of our articles, however, number of mentions of guild rise to 38 in volume 16 (July 2, 1378 to May 7, 1379) and nine in volume 17 (May 11, 1379 to August 31, 1379). This is consistent with the observation of Najemy (2006, 162)

[52] Brucker (1962, 307–08) comes close to accusing Coluccio Salutati, our notary scribe, of such hypocrisy: "To a friend who cited internal discord as a source of Florentine weakness, Salutati had replied stoutly: 'I, who attend the secret council sessions every day, have always witnessed the most perfect concord, and you should believe me, when one fights for liberty, all civic discord will cease, and you will see this most numerous people, as one body, turn over its substance for the expenses [of war] and hurl its spirit against perils.'... This passage can be interpreted in two ways: either Salutati was sincere and unperceptive, or he was engaged in his familiar role as propagandist, employing humanist rhetoric and hyperbole on behalf of his employers." For once, we beg to differ with Brucker in his interpretation. If Coluccio was deluding himself on this point, so was everyone else in the room. They all said such things publicly, whatever they thought privately.

[53] Brucker calls this "a theme that appears with monotonous regularity in later protocols: *unitas civium*. 'All citizens should be led back to unity,' intoned Ser Domenico da Certaldo, and his sentiments were echoed by his colleagues, none of whom publicly favored the pastime of quarreling with neighbors—a pastime in which nearly all of them engaged" (1962, 129).

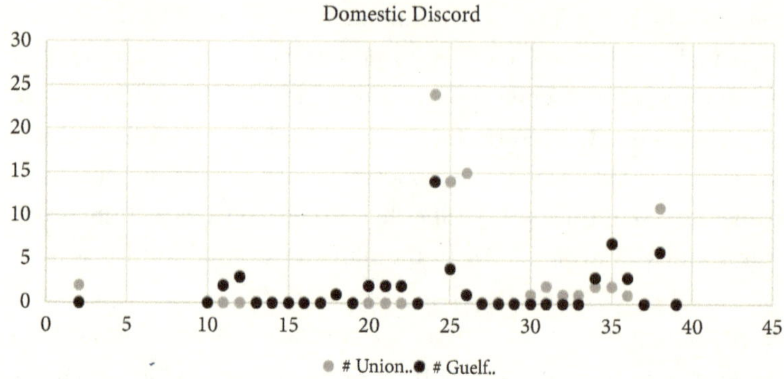

Figure 5.9 Time Frequency, by Month, of Domestic Discord Keywords

there is no evidence, at least within the *Consulte e Pratiche* itself, of such back-room procedures ever working, perhaps because this idea is not so radically different from the *Consulte e Pratiche* itself.

Figure 5.9 presents the frequency of usage, by month, of the two keywords we identified in our first article to indicate "domestic discord"—namely, *union* . . . and *guelf* . . . (excluding the word Parte Guelfa itself). The first and largest peak is in March 1377. The second peak is in February 1378 and in May 1378, right before the Ciompi Revolt. These dates correlate with our narrative-network diagrams A3 and A5 in the appendix to our first article. If the reader reconsults those diagrams, he or she will know already much of what he or she needs to know about the "rhetoric of unity"—which really has to do not with the keywords themselves, but rather with changing other keywords with which they were associated in *Consulte e Pratiche* speech.

To review those previous findings: In chapter three (first half of 1377), the "domestic discord" keywords *union* . . . and *guelf* . . . were strongly associated with foreign-policy keywords. But in the first half of 1378), those same keywords became much more tightly coupled with domestic-policy keywords, like *cleric* . . . (local priests) and taxation. This was the refraction of foreign conflict into domestic conflict in the realm of action, as observed in our *Consulte e Pratiche* "observational instrument" of topical speech. We discuss in this second article three important meetings in finer-grained detail than was possible in the aggregate narrative networks of the previous article—namely, March 5–7, 1377, December 26, 1377, and May 15, 1378.

The foreign-policy usage of *union* . . . and *guelf* . . . was most voluminously and densely evident in the large, extended *allargato* meeting of March 5–7,

1377. There, *union* . . . was used in two distinct ways: *civium unionem*, the "unity of citizens," and *guelforum unionem*, "the unity of Guelfs." The first usage occurred 14 times. The second usage occurred eight times. (Unity was mentioned with no qualifier five times.) Civic and No Faction speakers overwhelmingly emphasized the former usage.[54] Parte Guelfa speakers more emphasized the second usage.[55] Everyone agreed on "unity," in other words, but unity of whom was subtly contested.

Regardless of linguistic inflection, however, the recommendations of both sides to the Signoria were the same: for the city council to form a small ad-hoc committee of either Priors and Parte Guelfa captains (in nine speeches), or a *pratica* of Priors, Colleges, Parte Guelfa captains, the Eight of War, and the Ten of Liberty (in 11 speeches), in order to "look after the unity of the citizens." Parte Guelfa speakers (in their five speeches) always recommended the former, more restrictive procedural solution. Whereas, for the most part, Civic speakers (in six out of eight of their speeches) recommended the latter, more expansive solution, as did No Faction speakers (also in six out of eight of their speeches).

It was rare in the protocols to have any explicit reference to exactly what was the problem to which all these pleas for unity were responding. But there were a few exceptions: Tommaso Strozzi, one of the Eight of War, on March 5 recommended that "Regarding the unity of the citizens, they should look that citizens do not speak against the undertakings of the Commune by speaking against the Commune in the streets." On March 7, Marchionne Stefani, a Civic partisan, said: "And they foresee to stop bad speeches that are in the city and punish contradictors." Similarly on March 5, Bartolomeo Peruzzi, a No Faction member, said: "The priors, in conjunction with the Parte captains, should procure the unity of the citizenry, so that Guelfs speak in concord and are guided by one hand." A few days later, on March 14, Bonaccorso Lapi, a Civic partisan, added: "The priors should complain to the captains concerning the news which they have heard, pointing out to them the commune's desperate need for unity, and informing them that scandal and discord between themselves and Guelfs is abhorrent."

In other words, in March 1377, Guelf dissatisfaction with the War of Eight Saints outside of the room of *Consulte e Pratiche* finally was starting to become noticed inside the room. The recommended solution was for

[54] Civic and No Faction together used *civium unionem* (or equivalents) 12 times, *guelforum unionem* (or equivalents) 4 times, and *unionem* (or equivalents) with no qualifier 2 times.

[55] Parte Guelfa speakers used *guelforem unionem* (or equivalents) 4 times, *civium unionem* (or equivalents) 2 times, and *unionem* (or equivalents) with no qualifier 2 times.

Parte Guelfa leaders inside the room to crack the whip and bring their dissatisfied followers back into patriotic line in support of the war. "Unity of citizens" in effect meant coercion of Parte Guelfa members by co-opted Parte Guelfa leaders, such as Lapo da Castiglionchio himself. This was the cross-pressured political position underneath Lapo's behavior as chameleon: he was playing a double game—factional leader of Parte Guelfa and patriotic contributor to *Consulte e Pratiche*.[56] In March 1377, *Consulte e Pratiche* speakers still optimistically believed that the latter republican role would trump the former illegitimate one.

As has already been mentioned, December 26, 1377 was the date of the meeting when Parte Guelfa leaders finally came out into the open with their own coordinated opposition to the war. Not surprisingly, in light of this shock, there were only two forlorn pleas for unity, by the probably stunned Civic faction. Instead, in rhetoric we find something completely unanticipated: simultaneously with Parte Guelfa leaders openly opposing the war, Parte Guelfa speakers went on an aggressive attack against "unknown" Florentine citizens traitorously writing secret letters to the pope, which revealed Florentine foreign-policy secrets. The surprise is that those unknown traitors that Parte Guelfa leaders were attacking were in all likelihood themselves. Lapo da Castiglionchio, for example, on December 26 said: "The Priors should direct the Eight to collect letters of some citizens which are against the honor of the Commune, so that they can remove the suspect and punish them, to be an example for everyone." The chorus continued: Piero Baldovinetti: "That they are upset by hearing that the Eight say that it is known that some citizens write [privately] to the Curia. The priors should take care that the Eight punish them . . . publicly." Antonio Ridolfi: "The Eight should search for those revealing and writing the secrets of the Commune, so that they punish them in a way that shall be an example for all." In all, nine Parte Guelfa speakers,[57] and only two additional No Faction speakers, lined up to denounce and to insist on punishing the traitorous leaking of secrets to the pope, whom they supported.

The obvious interpretation is that Parte Guelfa leaders were struggling rhetorically to escape from the "traitor" label, which they knew others in the

[56] The details are different, but the structural brokerage position of Lapo and his fellow Parte Guelfa leaders is similar to the "robust action" of Cosimo de' Medici (Padgett and Ansell 1993).

[57] These were, in speaking order, Antonio Ridolfi, Lapo da Castiglionchio, Pazino Strozzi, Carlo Strozzi, Filippo Corsini, Piero Canigiani, Priore Baldovinetti, Filippo Corsini (again), and Bartolo Siminetti.

room mentally applied to their now open and unpatriotic opposition to the war.[58] This strikes us as a transparent ploy, which we doubt fooled anyone. But it is striking nonetheless how fervid was the Parte Guelfa pitch, and how absent was any countervailing challenge in public by the Civic group. This surely is "unity" stretched very thin indeed, but it was a veneer still painted, perhaps not to foreclose future options.

Finally, we examine *Consulte e Pratiche* meetings in the six months immediately preceding the Ciompi Revolt in June 1378. As can be seen in figure 5.9, there were two sequences of 1378 meetings where *union* . . . was discussed: one in February and one in May.

The February *C e P* meetings,[59] which took place at the very peak of the Parte Guelfa's anti-Ghibelline denunciation campaign, for the first time addressed the *ammonizione* issue directly. But not to denounce it! Parte Guelfa speakers, as expected, mentioned "unity," not at all in the sense of "unity of citizens," but rather in the sense of "unity of Guelfs" twice, "Guelf" twice, and even "Ghibelline" twice—emphasizing the need to remove them from office. What is more surprising is to find the Civic group essentially agreeing with them: They mentioned "unity of citizens" twice, "unity of Guelfs" twice, "Guelfs" once, and "Ghibelline" once. There was no difference in *ammonizione* rhetoric between sides.

On May 15 and a few follow-up meetings later, this matching profile was repeated with a twist: now petitions by the Civic side to turn Parte Guelfa supporters into magnates were also added to the agenda. One month before the Ciompi Revolt, in other words, hot-button conflictual issues, like anti-Ghibelline *ammonizione* and anti-magnate petitions, finally took the floor of the *Consulte e Pratiche*. These February and May 1378 meetings were the only times in the protocols that the words *ammonizione* and Ghibelline appeared.

The *C e P* discussion of these hot-button issues, however, was curious indeed. The need for unity of course was mentioned across the board (12 times). Anti-magnate petitions were discussed in conjunction with *ammonizione* in five speeches. Anti-magnate petitions were discussed by themselves in eight speeches. But *ammonizione* by itself was discussed in

[58] Referring to earlier in the year, Brucker essentially agrees with this interpretation: "Opposition to the war increased in the winter and spring of 1376–1377. It is difficult to trace this development, since critics of the war did not voice their opposition publicly. Vocal dissent would have been considered tantamount to treason" (1962, 319).

[59] We would not call these "intensive discussions," as does Brucker (1962, 360)—more like *en passant* remarks spread over six meetings.

zero speeches! As Brucker also noted (see above), the Civic group within *Consulte e Pratiche* showed no more agitation about the searing *ammonizione* issue than did Parte Guelfa speakers themselves. Anti-Ghibelline denunciations were blandly mentioned by both sides as the legitimate pursuit of "unity of the Guelfs."

This relative emphasis in *C e P* discussion on anti-magnate petitions, as compared to anti-Ghibelline denunciations, should be compared to the reality of the numbers of actual *Esecutore degli Ordinamenti Giustizia* court cases, as graphed in figure 5.4. From September 1377 through May 1387, there were 62 cases of anti-magnate denunciations that appeared in the docket (or *tambura*) of the *E.O.G.* court, as compared to 672 cases of anti-Ghibelline denunciations that appeared in that same docket. *Consulte e Pratiche* discussion, in other words, focused more on the molehill than on the mountain.

Why then does Brucker (1962, 339) call the Parte Guelfa anti-Ghibelline campaign "political madness"? The answer comes from a small subset of those accused. As mentioned earlier in "The Action Side" section, most *Esecutore degli Ordinamenti Giustizia* anti-Ghibelline denunciations were of recent immigrants. This, apparently, bothered no one, regardless of faction. What Brucker emphasized instead, however, were those far fewer cases where the Parte Guelfa targeted really powerful people—including even one of the Eight Saints![60]

In his own words: "This purge differed from earlier ones in certain important respects. First, the Parte inaugurated the practice of screening those men whose names were drawn from the *borse* to fill the priorate and the colleges . . . Nor did the Parte flinch from striking men while they held office . . . But the Parte achieved a high point of reckless bravado when it placed the Ghibelline stigma upon one of the Eight Saints, the druggist, Giovanni Dini.

> These provocative actions were matched by the proscription of several distinguished citizens of the highest social rank, men who combined active business careers with prominent roles in the communal government. Such were three bankers, Niccolò Rimbaldesi, Nofri dell'Antella, and Giovanni

[60] The pope had been strongly urging exactly that, to the point of declaring all of the Eight-Saints leaders of war against him to be heretics. Brucker has no smoking gun of explicit coordination between the pope and the Parte Guelfa (but cf. those "secrets" in private letters to the Curia mentioned on December 26), but coordination through signaling at the very least seems clear.

> de' Mozzi, Bettino Covoni, and Lapo Tolosini; and one of Florence's richest citizens, the international trader and financier, Francesco Rinuccini. (Brucker 1962, 341)

Targeting immigrants and non-powerful new men bothered no one. But attacking a few very powerful people, including some inside the *Consulte e Pratiche* room itself, was prelude to revolution—or at least *coup de état.* The asymmetry between modest response to persecution of the masses and super-sensitive response to persecution of themselves points to the social-class compositional skew of the *Consulte e Pratiche.*[61] The *Consulte e Pratiche* was unquestionably an elite institution. As much as politically it was divided against itself, the *Consulte e Pratiche*, and the republican elite it represented, socially unified in the face of lower-class agitation and even in the face of potential immigration. Like many social climbers throughout history, Florentines of all social classes wanted to get into the door themselves, but then to close that door behind them to subsequent generations.

In all, these qualitative analyses reveal multiple meanings of "unity": citizens versus Guelfs, pro-war patriots versus anti-war traitors, elite versus immigrant. These various binary semantic categories, however, were anything but mutually exclusive on the grounds of demography and action. Most citizens were also Guelfs. Patriot versus traitor could be an attribution of motives more than a clear-cut deed. Even the deeply conservative Florentine cultural *mentalitée* of "elite" versus "mass" hid a reality of widespread social mobility, where objective boundaries between social classes were far from clear, either in social networks or in family demography (Padgett 2010).

"Unity" was one of those multivocal words, in other words, which could mean many different things, depending upon the context. Republican "unity" in *Consulte e Pratiche* discussion was achieved by keeping all these multiple linguistic meanings in play, without insisting on clarification—which could only have a polarizing effect.[62]

[61] The percentages of *Consulte e Pratiche* speeches given by *popolani* speakers during our period were these: chapter 1: 75%, chapter 2: 70%, chapter 3: 65%, chapter 4: 75%, and chapter 5: 90%. In comparison, the percentages of *popolani* on the Signoria during our period were as follows: chapter 1: 44%, chapter 2: 48%, chapter 3: 60%, chapter 4: 60%, and chapter 5: 60%.

[62] Compare the concept of "quasi-resolution of conflict" in Cyert and March (1963).

Conclusion: The Dark Side of Unity

What is the relationship between speech and action? In this Renaissance Florentine case of the *Consulte e Pratiche*, obviously there was a glaring contradiction between these two sides: namely, unity in the rhetorical domain of participatory republican speech, but violence and exile in the factional domain of exclusionary action. Machiavelli, astute observer as he was, unsurprisingly noticed this contradiction: In his *Discourses on Livy* ([1531] 1996, 98), he alluded to a popular Florentine proverb from his day, "these men have one mind in the piazza and another in the palazzo."[63]

Granted this contradiction, the question next arises about whether there is any causal relationship at all between these two sides. We contend that there is, which we label "The Dark Side of Unity." The Florentine republican system—which was designed originally to counter the revolutionary dangers of factionalism, and which was performed in contemporaneous time in self-conscious awareness of those dangers—delegitimized opposition, once "consensus" had been achieved. To be a loyal Florentine meant to fall in line behind the elected (and rotating) leadership, once the Florentine republican "General Will" had been discovered.

The dark side of this was that continued espousal of policies that already had been discussed and rejected risked attribution by observers of "not being a loyal (and hence true) Florentine." Hence, (a) it was very rare for opposition to be espoused in public speech, and (b) rumblings to the contrary nearly always provoked the procedural solution of trying to clarify "consensus" or "General Will" by assembling small committees of republican leaders. Most important in this time period was the inclusion, or cooptation, into these small committees of Parte Guelfa captains, who were supposed to crack the whip against their disgruntled Parte Guelfa membership.[64]

These observations, on the speech side, imply that discussions in the Florentine *Consulte e Pratiche* were more than debates about public policy. This is not to say that they were not debates about public policy, but in addition to that, there was a ritual side, wherein *Consulte e Pratiche* speeches were also about demonstrating speakers' commitment to the values of the institution

[63] We thank Brendan Small for this reference.

[64] Obviously this did not work, once Parte Guelfa leaders decided, on December 26, 1377, to behave more like Parte Guelfa than like *Consulte e Pratiche*.

and about signaling that commitment to others in the room.[65] This ritual side of discussion shows up in the mechanics of speech format in the protocols: (a) the large number of speeches recorded as *idem*—namely, "the same as" some previous speaker, most frequently the Gonfaloniere who initiated and set the agenda for the meeting; and (b) the format of longer speeches, which frequently followed the same topic sequence as the opening speaker. This "latent function" of ritual was not useless for the "manifest function" of formulating public policy, because the next day the Signoria could see from the protocols who supported the recommended policy (less so, however, who opposed the policy). From that point of view, contentless *idems* were not without information.

This ritual side of *Consulte e Pratiche* speech also showed up in our statistics: (a) the effectiveness of Office representation for suppressing factional coefficients; and (b) the low and unimpressive "Same Person" coefficients, which revealed how difficult (but not impossible) it was for consistency of individual voice to shine through. Florentine speakers wanted to blend in, not to stand out.

From a modern point of view, this "excessive" emphasis on consensus and unity raises the question about how decisions actually were made, to which speakers so readily agreed. Part of the answer is obvious: Many speakers were "Office speakers." Namely, they were reporting the opinions not of themselves but of the councils they represented. Obviously, therefore, there had been background discussions about the topics at hand, before their final airing in the *Consulte e Pratiche*. What is not so obvious is how these multiple previous background discussions were coordinated into "consensus" before the *Consulte e Pratiche* meeting itself. But somehow they clearly were so coordinated, most probably through informal networks.[66]

The "Dark Side of Unity," however, is deeper than just attribution of disloyalty to oppositional deviants, who had been coerced into apparent agreement. The norm of "unity" could tip differently in the discussion forum of the *Consulte e Pratiche* than in the discussion forum of the Signoria or,

[65] Robert Merton (1968) would have called the former the "manifest function" of the *Consulte e Pratiche* and the latter the "latent function" of the *Consulte e Pratiche*.

[66] Rapidly rotating memberships in republican councils meant that most council members had served together in the past with members of other councils, most probably in yet other councils. As already mentioned, we tried at one point to visualize the network of previous council co-memberships, but we gave up because of the "hairball problem"—namely, the network in question was too dense. This was the political-network *reggimento* foundation behind the Florentine "General Will."

most importantly of all in this period, in the discussion forum of the Parte Guelfa. These republican councils were all "schools of fish," with speakers in each forum ritualistically mimicking each other in order to signal membership and commitment. Whenever background coordinating informal networks weakened, these "schools of fish" were in danger of tipping in different directions, thereby threatening a constitutional crisis if the issues and conflicts were serious enough. In our opinion, republican councils were not the ultimate cause of underlying factionalism, but they might channel factionalism into constitutional crisis if self-sorting of private opinions overwhelmed cross-cutting elite networks.

On the action side, even deeper "Dark Side of Unity" social-class dynamics coursed through the veins of these republican institutional channels. These were the status tensions of competing hieratic authorities, which we discussed in the "Action Side" section of this paper. The social-class problem underlying the "unity of Florence" was this: Who was Florence? The *popolani*, as the founding generation of the Florentine republic (in 1282), considered themselves to be the exemplars of Florence, having established the principle of "citizen" in the first place. The rhetoric of "unity of citizens" served their interests by placing them at the top of a hieratic-authority status order of citizenship. New Men, who entered the state in the 1343 wave and thereafter, enthusiastically supported this *popolani* citizenship definition of "Florence" because that definition placed them definitively in, although in deferential second place. Magnates had been excluded from citizenship in 1293. Hence they preferred the alternative operationalization of the "true" Florence to be old "Guelf" because that definition harkened back to the pro-papal 1200s, when they (together with older Albizzi-faction *popolani* families) had ruled Florence. "Oligarchic" Albizzi-faction *popolani* came out on top under either definition; hence they were comfortable either with "unity of citizens" or with "unity of Guelfs." They preferred not to stress any contradiction between the two.

The dark side of hieratic authority is exclusion. "Not to be Florentine" meant not to be eligible for republican office or even for citizenship. The Parte Guelf used the anachronistic denunciation of Ghibelline to exclude their opponents from public office (and/or from future public office). And the Civic group less aggressively counter-used the legal category of magnate to ban their opponents from public office. The reason that public-policy disagreement over the war with the pope was refracted not into debate but into escalation of competing exclusions cannot be explained solely by republican norms of unity. Those republican norms of unity became so dangerous because there were deep-seated status tensions in the background about "Who is Florence?" fueling the foreign-policy fire. Because this was a war not against Milan, but against the pope, the old Guelf label was revived to a white-hot pitch of passion—but still within the "patriotic" rhetorical rubric of multivocal "unity." The war with the pope pushed latent contestation over "Who was (the exemplar of) Florence?" to the foreground—not of speech but of action. After denunciations and escalating exclusions within Florentine republican elites, there were not many steps left to intentional attempted *coup d'états* and then to unintentional spillovers into the streets of mob violence.

Hence we see the feedback between speech and action, under the norm and rhetoric of unity, to be the following: Republican norms of unity in speech within the *Consulte e Pratiche* and other interlinked republican councils—the Signoria, the Colleges, the Eight, and the Ten—pushed suppressed opposition to the War of the Eight Saints into the "reactionary" forum of the Parte Guelfa, where "consensus" tipped in a different direction. For a while, co-opted Parte captains may indeed have argued against aggressive assault. But by October 1377, Parte captains had shifted roles and allegiances from *Consulte e Pratiche* to Parte Guelfa. Escalation into competing exclusions resulted from the available *ammonizione* institutionalized option for public action, fueled by deep private motivations for social-class revenge.

Thus the run-up to the Ciompi Revolt was crystallization of "unity of citizens" in the room of the *Consulte e Pratiche* and crystallization of "unity of Guelfs" in the room of the Parte Guelfa, with lack of recognition in the multivocal speech of the former of the obvious contradiction in action triggered by the latter. In our opinion, the tragedy of "the valiant failure of republicanism" in Florence was that intense wishful yearning for unity in speech induced, under the background of social-status conditions of competing hieratic authorities, an intensification in action of the very revolutionary forces that it most desperately wanted to suppress.

We close by picking up the institutional-channeling thread in the above story. Namely, how superposed "Braudelian" ([1949] 1972) layers of historical times reverberated through the sediments of political demography and institutions laid down by past generations.

This is a version of Mary Douglas's (1986) *How Institutions Think*. The concept of role is perhaps more powerful in this Renaissance institutional context than is the modernist concept of person. For sure, we did detect statistical significance in the "Same Person" variable in our speech-similarity regressions, so we are not saying that distinct voices cannot be discovered in these speeches, summary and cryptic though they are. But the quantitative magnitude of differences among individual voices was modest indeed. Florentines like Lapo da Castiglionchio were chameleons, seemingly unconcerned with conceptual consistency or with feeling guilty about its violation. Nor did we ever find comments by observers to the effect, "But Lapo, yesterday you said . . . " External circumstances and political roles were always changing, especially in this rapidly rotating Florentine republican system.

History in Florence, in other words, played out through roles (both as actors and as speakers) not through coherent and self-consistent people. This is the part that moderns like us have trouble comprehending.

Both Florence's institutional republican system of offices and its social-class demography of families were deposits in the present of previous generations of multiple Florentine histories. Current conflict was always interpreted through the office and the family lenses of Florentines' pasts. But "which Florentine past is relevant to the present?" This actually is the same thing as "Who is (the epitome of) Florence?" Vicious conflicts of exclusion and insistent institutional emphasis on unity both were hardwired, as flip sides, into the hieratic-authority *mentalitée* of status in which Florentines conceptualized these questions.

More generally, history and identity are flip sides of the same collective assembly of memories—history is memory viewed from the outside, and identity is memory viewed from the inside (Padgett 2018). Identity answers to deeply ambiguous questions like "Who is Florence?" were not decisions or even debates. Competing political identities and actions crystallized out of superposed layers of political demography and institutions in reverberation, in amplifying or dampening response to contemporaneous perturbations (Padgett and Powell 2012). Speech and action interacted with each other, to produce identities through conversational tipping, but only in loosely coupled, roundabout feedbacks, mediated through institutional structures inherited from the past. Roles, not persons, were the agentic vehicles of these feedbacks.

6

Transposition and Refunctionality

The Birth of Partnership Systems in Renaissance Florence

Introduction

Inventions of any sort are hard to understand.[1] They seem to come out of the blue, a rupture with the past, yet close investigation always reveals historical roots. Individual geniuses sometimes create them, but is "genius" just our celebratory label for a process that worked, which we do not understand? To proffer a tentative distinction: innovations improve on existing ways (i.e., activities, conceptions, and purposes) of doing things, while inventions change the ways things are done. Under this definition, the key to classifying something as an invention is the degree to which it reverberates out to alter the interacting system of which it is a part. To some extent we understand micro-logics of combination and recombination (e.g., Barley 1990, March 1991, Powell et al. 1996, Fleming 2002, Burt 2004). Yet the invention puzzle is that some of these innovative recombinations cascade out to reconfigure entire interlinked ecologies of "ways of doing things," whereas most innovations do not. The poisedness of a system to reconfiguration by an invention is as much a part of the phenomenon to be explained as is the system's production of the invention itself. Invention "in the wild" cannot be understood through abstracting away from concrete social context, because inventions are permutations of that context (Hutchins 1995, Latour 1988, Galison 1997). But to make progress in understanding discontinuous change we need to embed our analysis of transformation in the routine dynamics of

Chapter 6 in Padgett & Powell, *The Emergence of Organizations and Markets*, Princeton University Press, 2012: 168–207. Republished with permission.

[1] This chapter is an abridged version (30% cut) of John F. Padgett and Paul D. McLean, "Organizational Invention and Elite Formation: The Birth of Partnership Systems in Renaissance Florence," *American Journal of Sociology* 111 (2006), 1463–1568.

Organizational Invention in Renaissance Florence. John F. Padgett, Oxford University Press.
 DOI: 10.1093/oso/9780197789216.003.0006

actively self-reproducing social contexts, where constitutive elements and relations are generated and reinforced.

Biological evolution stands as one exemplar that theoretical analysis (without prediction) is possible even in open-ended, endlessly generative systems of self-reproducing recombination and feedback. Imitation of biological science by the social sciences should never be slavish: Social systems have no genes, and social systems have no consciousness. But from biology comes the fundamental insight that organic entities, structures, and artifacts are not static "objects"; they are vortexes of cross-entity chemical flows that reproduce themselves (Maturana and Varela 1980, Nicolis and Prigogine 1989, Fontana and Buss 1994, Padgett, Lee, and Collier 2003). Among other things, social systems are one form of "life" (Luhmann 1995). As such, uncovering social analogues to cross-entity chemical flows, which transform and reproduce actors through interaction, is a prerequisite for systematically analyzing punctuated tippings or inventions in the reproductive dynamics of any human entity, be that a body, an organization, a market or a city.

Renaissance Florence is the empirical site for this study of the historical process of socially embedded invention. While the uniqueness of the Italian Renaissance in world history may be debatable, the creativity of that particular place and time is not. Inventions in literature (Dante, Boccaccio), in art (Giotto, Masaccio, Donatello, Michelangelo), in letters (Petrarch), in architecture (Brunelleschi, Alberti), in science (Leonardo, Galileo), in constitutional design (Bruni, Savonarola), in political theory (Machiavelli, Guicciardini) and in business (Datini) were produced in breathtaking numbers and speeds. Indeed, the most striking global feature about Renaissance Florence is the sheer multiplicity of domains in which inventions occurred: Inventions seemed to cascade from one domain to another. These developments did not occur in isolation from the rest of northern Italy (e.g., Witt 2003), but Florence was a particularly catalytic site in the northern Italian Renaissance web of invention.

While there is no gainsaying these facts about inventiveness, recent historians have challenged the "renaissance" interpretation of late medieval Florence, preferring instead to emphasize the traditional and conservative character of the place (Kent 1977, Kelly-Gadol 1977, Molho 1994). The historiographical puzzle this revisionism poses is not which competing interpretation is correct. The puzzle is how both can be correct. How did such a traditional and conservative place, not at all motivated to innovate per se, nonetheless invent so prolifically? Large macro-historical issues about the "rise of the West" are linked to the answer to this question (Lopez 1976, Abu-Lughod 1989).

The particular Florentine economic invention whose emergence we will trace in this article is the discovery, in the late 1300s, of a new organizational form that Melis (1962) called the "business system" (*sistema di aziende*). We find his label to be imprecise, but what Melis (1962, 130) meant was not imprecise: a set of legally autonomous companies linked through one person or through a small set of controlling partners. In Melis' definition, "legally autonomous companies" meant either ownership by a single person (*individuale*) or ownership by a partnership of persons (*collettiva*). If at least one of the companies linked into *sistema di aziende* is a partnership, then we will translate Melis' term as "partnership system." The partnership system was an innovation in company ownership in which a single controlling partner (or a small number of partners), if he did not manage the branch himself, made a set of legally separate partnership contracts with branch managers in different locations and/or industries. This new "network-star" ownership structure largely displaced earlier legally unitary companies, often built collectively by patrilineage families, which were common in the late 1200s and early 1300s (Sapori 1926, Renouard 1941, Padgett and McLean 2006). Viewed formally, this splintering of a unitary company into overlapping parts was decentralization because it allowed various branches and business markets to be managed separately, through legally independent account books. Viewed operationally, this devolution was centralization because it dissolved unitary committees of numerous owner-directors and substituted dominant ownership by just one or, at most, a few persons (de Roover 1966, 78). Melis (1962) himself studied the extraordinarily well documented case of Francesco Datini, the famous "merchant of Prato" whose system lasted from 1382 to 1410 (see also Origo [1957] 1992). The Datini system was among the first, if not the first, example of this new organizational form. de Roover (1966) studied the slightly later case of the Medici bank.

This new organizational form is important in the history of financial capitalism because it protected owners (to some extent) against the unlimited-liability risk of complete financial ruin and because it easily allowed diversification into multiple product markets. The earlier unitary companies often had been generalist in character, doing whatever type of merchant or banking business made sense to it at the moment. The new partnership system was also generalist in ensemble, but each component company was more specialized than before. Component specialization required a more abstracted system of articulation among branches than before. This, in our account, was the organizational driver for the rapid diffusion of double-entry bookkeeping in Florence in the late 1300s.

A stock market did not yet exist in the Renaissance, but apart from this major difference in ownership structure, the invention of the partnership system in Renaissance Florentine banking is similar managerially to the shift in American manufacturing from the functional to the multidivisional form discussed by Chandler (1962). In economic *mentalité*, Florentine partnership systems are early exemplars of the "financial conception of control" discussed by Fligstein (1990). Partnership systems are also members of the class of organizations that Powell (1990) called "network organizations"; indeed, historically they may have been the first member of this class. Each of these modernist classifications is accurate, depending upon which aspect of the new organizational form one chooses to emphasize. Viewed in the context of its time, however, partnership systems were sui generis although deeply embedded in the local Florentine and Tuscan context.

A companion article to this one, "Economic Credit in Renaissance Florence" (Padgett and McLean 2011), examines economic invention not at the level of organizational structure but at the level of organizational practice—namely, the operation and dramatic growth of economic credit in Renaissance Florence in the late 1300s and early 1400s. Formally, ongoing relations of business credit were recorded primarily in the bookkeeping device of current accounts, tabulated in bilateral format. Extensive and deep credit relations among Florentine merchant-bankers were the primary reason for the century-long dominance of international finance in Europe by Florence. In that companion article, we demonstrate the historical connection between the rise of inter-company credit and the invention and spread of partnership systems as new nodes of exchange in that credit.

Theoretical Framework

Dynamic Multiple Networks

Inspired by biochemistry, our theoretical approach to the topic of organizational invention is to situate invention in the dynamics of reproduction of multiple networks—specifically, in the cross-network processes of transposition, refunctionality, and catalysis. Recombinant innovation in organizations is produced, this case study shows, when one or more social relations are transposed from one domain to another, mixing in use with relations already there. This transposition-induced hybridity is the raw material for invention, but that is only the first step. Refunctionality is when transposition not only improves existing uses but also, more radically, leads to new uses, that is, to new potential objects for interaction and transformation. Catalysis is when these new interactions feed back to alter the way existing relations reproduce. The entire multiple-network ensemble may tip into true invention when catalytic feedback loops are modified in the autocatalytic transformational process of network reproduction (Maturana and Valera 1980, Kauffman 1993, Fontana and Buss 1994, Padgett et al. 2003), either by adding new positive feedback loops or by subtracting old negative feedback loops.

To draw out the operational meaning of this perspective for Florence, see figure 6.1. We represent "social context" by multiple-network architectures. Actors are clusters of relational ties. In the activity plane of economics, for example, collective actors called companies are composed of partnership ties. These companies trade with each other. In the domain of kinship, for another example, collective actors called patrilineages are composed of genealogy ties. These patrilineages marry each other. And in the domain of politics, collective actors called factions are composed of clientage ties. These factions do political deals with each other. We label the strong-tie relations that constitute collective actors "constitutive ties," and we label recurrent weak-tie relations through which actors deliver resources to each other "relational ties." Within each domain, relational ties "feed" constitutive ties. Reproduction is when constitutive ties, using input resources, make new constitutive ties.

All important for a multiple-network setup, people are also conceived as constitutive ties: Namely, they are cross-domain composites of roles. Purposes are domain-specific features of roles within individuals; they are not features of individuals per se. In figure 6.1, people are represented as vertical lines, linking roles across planes. Not all people participate in all networks at all levels, but many do, inducing patterns of multiple-network overlay or "social embeddedness" (Granovetter 1985). Cross-domain connections, through people, regulate the reproductive formation of constitutive and relational ties. Conversely, network reproduction generates people as social actors by shaping and composing the roles that act though them.

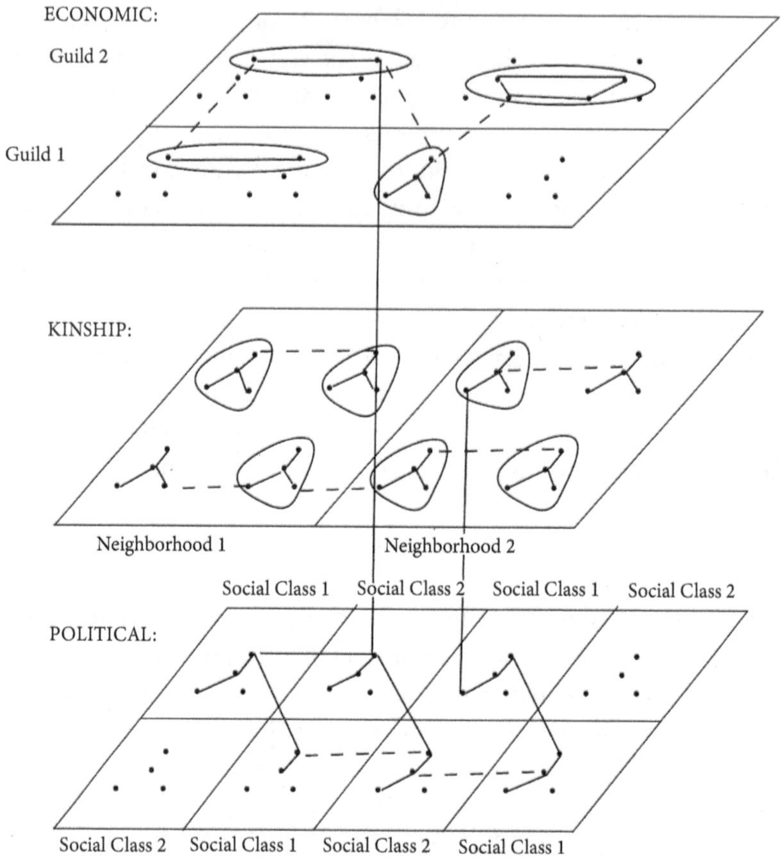

Figure 6.1 Multiple-Network Ensemble Renaissance Florence

Note: (a) Solid lines are constitutive ties. Dotted lines are relational social exchanges. Oblongs are formal organizations (families and firms.). (b) People in multiple roles are vertical lines connecting corresponding dots in the domains of activity in which people are active. (Only two are shown for illustration.)

Patterns of social embeddedness are important for us not only because of "trust" but also because they regulate the dynamic reproduction of constitutive ties in each domain through the aligning and sequencing of multiple roles.

Multiple-network overlays frame and regulate the flows and processes that generate and reproduce the social relations that construct social actors, making them "alive." Uncovering generative flows is the prerequisite for empirically investigating qualitative tips in the dynamics of relational reproduction. Such system tips are how we conceptualize organizational invention.

If organizations are the units of analysis—firms, families, and factions—then one obvious flow through them, bringing them to life, is people. "In organizations, biological or social, rules of action and patterns of interaction persist and reproduce even in the face of constant turnover in component parts, be these molecules or people. In the constant flow of components through organizations, the collectivity typically is not renegotiated anew. Rather, within constraints, component parts are transformed and molded into the ongoing flow of action" (Padgett 1997, 200). Attending to the flow of people, and to the action rules they bring with them, leads to an analytic focus on careers and biographies as these wend their way across organizations and domains. Organizations reproduce through people and other resources flowing through them. The structure of biographical flow among organizations, both within and across domains, channels constitutive-tie transpositions of previously acquired network ties and learned rules of action and interaction. Organizational structure is the blending, transformation and reproduction, on site, of networks and interaction rules transported by people into the site from numerous sources (Padgett 2001). People, conversely, are the hybridized residues of past networks and rules acquired through interaction at their previous organizational sites (cf. Breiger 1974). In other words, both organizations and people are shaped, through network coevolution, by the history of each flowing through the other.

Florentine Transposition of Economic Networks into Politics (and Back Again)

In this article, the general theoretical framework above will play out in Florentine history as follows: After the Ciompi Revolt of 1378, as part of a political reconsolidation-repression to be discussed below, domestic or cambio bankers were mobilized into core political offices within the republican state. Before this political mobilization, cambio bankers operated for the most part domestically within the city, changing money and also doing deposit banking for their Florentine customers. They participated in state offices through the medium of their guild. International trading (mostly of woolen cloth), on the other hand, was the province of socially high-status merchants often organized into large unitary family firms. This international versus domestic division of labor was reinforced administratively by the guild structure—*Arte della Calimala* for international traders of finished cloth and *Arte del Cambio* for domestic bankers. With aggressive political mobilization of them by elite moderates after the Ciompi Revolt, however, cambio bankers systematically were pulled up into the "jet stream" of international trading, thereby injecting domestic banking organizational forms and accounting practices into international trading. We show below that a majority of the new partnership systems were constructed by cambio bankers reaching overseas to construct new trading branches abroad. This engagement in international trade had been inhibited, though not prohibited, by the guild system before the Ciompi Revolt. Making bankers into city councilors is our example of transposition of roles across domains, through collectively restructuring political biographies.

As cambio bankers were transported into new settings, both economic and political, they brought with them their old master–apprentice logics of contracts and careers. They then adapted these to the new international-trading setting, blending with the patrilineage family logics already there. The result was a modularized hybrid—short-term contracts with both family and nonfamily branch managers—in other words, the partnership system. Refunctionality was when this new organizational form led Florentine businessmen to new ways for companies to relate to each other in the market, through current accounts, credit, and double-entry bookkeeping. Together transposition and refunctionality created the potential for revolutionizing international finance via modularity and liquidity, depending upon how the rest of the multiple-network system of Florence responded to these innovations.

The catalysis that catapulted this organizational innovation into systemic invention, which restructured both banking and elites, was the social embedding of this partnership system into marriage and clientage. In politics, the Ciompi Revolt triggered the formation of a "republican oligarchy" to succeed "guild corporatism" (Najemy 1982), in two stages. After 1393, a more conservative political regime succeeded the major-guild moderate innovators of 1382–92. Higher-status popolani and magnates demographically took over the partnership systems which had been developed, for the most part, by cambio bankers. This second stage of biographical transposition brought economic partnerships into tighter correlation with elite marriages. And this in turn established sinews for the percolation of partnership-system economic techniques, like current accounts, out into the broader network structure of the ruling social elite at large, making that elite itself more mercantile in its thinking. For markets, this new correlation of partnership with marriage provided social foundations for *fiducia* (trust) within the merchant community to make the credit system function. The final product, on the one hand, was a vibrant financial system that dominated European international finance for a century. On the other hand, it was an intensely status conscious but politically permeable merchant elite that created generalists ("Renaissance men") for whom economics, politics, family, art, and philosophy were all refractions of each other.

In sum, the economic invention in late-medieval Florence of the partnership system was one corollary (not the only corollary) of elite transformation. As the social-network constituents of the Florentine elite shifted from patrilineage and guild into marriage and clientage, new business forms were invented, new political mobilization techniques were developed, and kinship was incrementally rewired to emphasize marriage. Each of these organizational changes spilled over to support the other, to create a multiple-network ensemble that we might label the Renaissance oligarchic-republican regime.

The "rise of financial capitalism" here is not a grand teleological process of inevitable modernization. It was rooted instead in particular places and histories, which refashioned their own multiple networks in crucial punctuated-equilibrium moments. Florence was unusually creative in part because of its tumultuous political history, which repeatedly transposed and refunctionalized its underlying social networks. Florentine elites did not invent because they wanted to but because they had to in order to conservatively preserve their threatened positions. Naturally there is more to explaining invention than political turmoil, but in the case of Renaissance Florence, that was the core mechanism that recomposed its economic, political, and kinship networks into tipping (cf. Stinchcombe 1965). Other case studies no doubt will add to the list of annealing mechanisms that induce transposition, refunctionality, and catalysis in social networks in such ways that evolution, not collapse, is the result.[2]

This chapter will develop this argument in the following stages: After reviewing prior historical research on Florentine partnership systems, I pinpoint the exact timing of this invention to be 1383. Most of the partnership system builders of this period will be identified to be cambio bankers, who politically were mobilized into government at increased rates after the Ciompi Revolt. After identifying the innovators, I then describe the politics

[2] See Powell et al., (chapter 13, 2012) for another example of transposition and refunctionality.

of the Ciompi Revolt and its repression in some detail, and show how political mobilization created a post-Ciompi republican oligarchy, absorbing cambio bankers and other businessmen into this newly augmented elite through marriage. This social embeddedness of banking in marriage catalyzed the reproduction of partnership systems in economics, and helped to transform the new oligarchy politically into mercantile republicans. *Tutti insieme*, post-revolt Renaissance Florence is a dramatic case example of the punctuated coevolution of economic markets and political elites.

Documenting the Emergence of Florentine Partnership Systems

Existing Literature

The previous literature on the Florentine partnership system, both overviews and detailed case studies, was reviewed extensively in the article out of which this abridgement is drawn (Padgett and McLean 2006). That review will not be repeated here, except to note that the two most important works that precede this study are the study of the Datini system by Melis (1962) and the study of the Medici system by de Roover (1966).

As documented in these and other studies, the complete set of organizational features that Datini and the Medici employed to construct and to manage their businesses were:

(a) legally distinct partnerships with branch managers (or the owner) in each location;
(b) separate sets of account books for each branch;
(c) diversification of companies into multiple industries;
(d) a "holding company" arrangement, in which Datini's Florentine partnership owned parts of other partnerships (Melis [1965] 1991, 169);
(e) centralized oversight of branches through vast numbers of business letters between Datini and his branch partners and through regular meetings between Datini and his branch partners;
(f) double-entry bookkeeping in bilateral format; and
(g) current accounts both among partnership-system companies and with major trading partners (de Roover [1956] 1974, 144–49).

The first element in this list narrowly defines the partnership system, but the historical significance of the partnership system comes from this whole package of organizational correlates, working together.

Quantitative Documentation of Growth and Diffusion

The full article out of which this abridgement was drawn went to considerable length to document the precise timing of the invention and diffusion of this new organizational form. The reason for temporal precision was to narrow down causality. The previous literature had documented the form and operation of the partnership system, but not the exacting timing of its invention and diffusion. Based on primary sources, this documentation was presented in a 13-page appendix (Padgett and McLean 2006, 1548–60) and in an online 61-page memo (Padgett 2005a).

To summarize, the primary findings about timing of emergence were:

(a) Francesco di Marco Datini, the famous and well documented "Merchant of Prato" (Origo [1957] 1992), was indeed one of the original founders of the partnership system, who first developed his new organizational form in 1383 (Melis 1962, 130).

(b) But four other partnership systems, none documented like Datini with surviving internal business records, were founded that same year: Vieri di Cambio de' Medici, Davanzato and Manetto di Giovanni Davanzati, Francesco di Neri Ardinghelli, and Ardingo di Corso Ricci and Gualtieri di Sandro Portinari. What had appeared to previous scholarship as the invention of a single business genius (Datini) was actually a simultaneous invention by a cluster of interrelated Florentine and Pratese businessmen.

(c) All of the original inventors, except for Datini himself, were Florentine cambio bankers, who had been in business under more traditional organizational forms prior to their simultaneous adoption.

(d) Given its first appearance in 1383, the new organizational form diffused very rapidly through the upper reaches of the Florentine, and then the Tuscan, economies. The original article documents 48 such systems in Florence before 1400, and it discusses other examples in Lucca and in Pisa during the post-1390 period.

(e) The size distribution of number of partners in cambio banks (information contained in annual guild registers) underwent a sudden phase shift exactly at 1382, as the organizational role of many of them shifted to being headquarters for partnership systems.

Composition of Post-Ciompi Partnership Systems

So much for timing, now what about agency? That is, other than Francesco Datini, Vieri di Cambio de' Medici and the others already mentioned, who exactly were the Florentines who collectively invented the partnership system?

Table 6.1 tabulates the industrial composition and the centralization frequencies of the newly emergent partnership systems listed in the appendix of Padgett and McLean (2006). While some of the new partnership systems, like Datini himself, emerged out of international trading, the bulk of them, like Vieri de' Medici, emerged through a fusion of cambio banking with international trading. The role of wool-manufacturing companies in the emergence of partnership systems was minor. Among the 24 cambio-plus-international-fusion partnership systems, 19 were formed sequentially by cambio bankers entering into international trading or merchant banking. Only five (including Datini) were formed in the reverse order, by international traders entering into cambio banking. In other words, Florentine partnership systems primarily emerged in the industry domains of domestic banking and international trading, fusing them together, with cambio bankers taking the lead in organizing this fusion.

Table 6.2 presents statistical information on who the post-Ciompi partnership-system innovators were, in comparison to time periods both

Table 6.1 Industrial Composition of 1385–99 Partnership Systems

# partnership systems	Int'l trading ± cambio bnk	Int'l trading only	Int'l trading ± wool mfct	Cambio bank ± wool mfct
3+ partnerships	13 (11)	7 (4)	1 (0)	0 (0)
2 partnerships	11 (10)	9 (3)	3 (0)	3 (2)
Total	24 (21)	16 (7)	4 (0)	3 (2)

( ) indicates the number of centralized partnership systems.
Source: appendix A.

Table 6.2 Social and Political Embedding of Businessmen in Multiple Companies

Poisson regression coefficients over time:	**Number of Industries**		**Number of Partnerships**	
	Alberti int'l. 1348–58 + Cambio 1348–58 + Wool 1353	**Pisa 1369 + Cambio 1369 + Wool 1382**	**Datini 1385–99 + Cambio 1385–99 + Wool 1382**	**Catasto 1427 (all industries except "other")**
Social Class:				
Popolani	1.110	1.003	.342	**.688****
Magnate	[collinear]	[collinear]	.608	**1.030****
New Man	.718	1.465	.110	.007
Social Class of Wife:				
Popolani	.736	.541	**.673****	**.766*****
Magnate	.559	.147	.365	**.713***
New Man	1.722	.815	.497	−.079
Political Office:				
Priorate	−2.144	.054	−.288	.160
Calimala Consul	[-∞]	1.299	**.985***	−.307
Cambio Consul	**1.572***	**2.691*****	.198	−.341
Lana Consul	.907	**2.389*****	−.744*	.322
Mercanzia	1.909	−.993	−.345	−.470
Balia 1378			.408	
Balia 1393			−.234	
Reggimento 1382			−.574	

continued

Table 6.2 *continued*

Poisson regression coefficients over time:

	Number of Industries		Number of Partnerships	
	Alberti int'l. 1348–58 + Cambio 1348–58 + Wool 1353	**Pisa 1369 + Cambio 1369 + Wool 1382**	**Datini 1385–99 + Cambio 1385–99 + Wool 1382**	**Catasto 1427 (all industries except "other")**
Balia 1384			**.746***	
Balia 1393			−.200	
Reggimento 1393			**.995****	
Political Factions:				
Albizzi	[-∞]	.523	.726	
Ricci	.602	**1.178***	−.333	
Anti-ciompi			.331	
Pro-ciompi			−8.18	
Albizzeans				.095
Mediceans				**1.371*****
Quarter:				
Santa Croce	1.187	.068	−.217	.057
Santa M. Novella	.126	.520	−.345	−.169
San Giovanni	−.022	−.183	.042	.260
Log likelihood	−54.4	−79.2	−311.0	−287.1
# obs. (persons)	850	502	829	533

L.R chi^2	17.31	88.6	79.3	93.9
Prob > chi^2	.185	.000	.000	.000
Pseudo R^2	.137	.359	.113	.141

*** = (p < .001); ** = (p < .01); * = (p < .05); (*) = (p < .06)

Notes:

(1) Given that businessmen participated as partners in at least one company or industry (see table 6.1), the dependent variable is number (minus one, to fit Poisson format) of partnerships, or industries in the first two periods, that Florentine businessmen owned or participated in. "Number of Industries" is used as proxy for number of companies in the 1348–58 and 1369 periods because organizational systems, where companies were legally split into multiple partnerships, did not exist then. Nonetheless single unitary firms sometimes participated in multiple markets in these earlier times, at the low rates shown in table 6.1.

(2) On the independent variable side, only those marriages and political offices with dates prior to the last date of the logit regressions (i.e., 1358, 1369, 1399, 1427, respectively) are included in these estimations. Negative binomial regressions performed slightly better than Poisson regressions for the latter two periods, though the differences in estimated coefficients are quite minor. Nonetheless, Poisson regression were used throughout table 6.3 in order to preserve comparability across all four regressions. The first two regressions would not converge using negative binomial, due to the absence of fat tails (see table 6.1).

Sources:

1. *Numbers of industries and partnerships*: see table 6.1 for list of sources.
2. *Social class*:
   (a) Magnates: Lansing (1991: 239–42) records original patrilineage membership in 1293 and 1295. See Klapisch-Zuber (1988) for important qualifications about changing membership in this group over time.
   (b) Popolani, new men, and new-new men: defined by the date that an ancestor from patrilineage first entered Priorate, as recorded in A.S.F., *Manoscritto Carte dell'Ancisa*, 248–52. "Popolani" are defined by first date in priorate between 1282 and 1342; "new men" are defined by first date in priorate between 1343 and 1377; "new-new men" are defined by first date in priorate between 1378 and 1433. See Padgett and Ansell (1993: 1261) for a time-series plot of rates of new entry of families into the priorate, which makes obvious the discreteness of the political cohorts of families defined by these particular dates.

3. *Marriages*: recorded from multiple sources, but primarily A.S.F., *Manoscritti Carte dell'Ancisa* 348–61.
4. *Political offices*:
   (a) Priorate: Newberry library copy of A.S.F., *Manoscritti Carte dell'Ancisa*, 248–52.
   (b) Mercanzia: A.S.F., *Mercanzia* 129.
   (c) Merchant guild consuls: cds.library.brown.edu/projects/tratte.
   (d) Banking guild consuls: A.S.F., *Arte del Cambio* 12.
   (e) Wool guild consuls: www.stg.brown.edu/projects/tratte.
   (f) 1378 balìa: Gherardi ([1389] 1876): 505.
   (g) 1382 balìa: Stefani ([1385] 1903, 394–96); later additions or *arroti* in A.S.F., *Balìa* 17: 22.
   (h) 1384 balìa: A.S.F., *Arte della Lana* 46: 154–66.
   (i) 1393 balìa: A.S.F., *Balìa* 17: 80–86, 105–107.
   (j) Reggimento 1382: Ildefonso di San Luigi (1770–89): 125–260.
   (k) Reggimento 1393: A.S.F., *Tratte* 357: 7–20.
5. *Political factions*:
   (a) Albizzi and Ricci: Brucker (1962): no specific pages, narrative references throughout book.
   (b) Pro-Ciompi and anti-Ciompi: Stefani ([1385] 1903):
   (c) Albizzeans and Mediceans: Kent (1978: 1352–57).
6. *Neighborhood, both gonfalone and quarter*:
   (a) 1351: A.S.F., *Estimo* 306.
   (b) 1378: A.S.F., *Prestanze* 367–369, *Estimo* 268.
   (c) 1427: A.S.F. *Catasto* 64–85.

earlier and later. Poisson regressions were performed to discover the social and political features of those active Florentine businessmen who organized the most companies. The dependent variable in these regressions is the number of legally distinct companies in which a businessman is a partner. Businessmen involved in many companies were the organizers and central commanders of partnership systems. Archival sources for the data in these regressions are listed in the notes to the table.

Before the 1378 Ciompi Revolt, the only businessmen who participated in multiple industries in statistically significant numbers, few in absolute numbers as these were, were guild consuls—that is, elected political leaders of the banking, the wool, and to a lesser extent the international trading guilds. The pre-Ciompi regressions in table 6.2 reflect the fact that business careers were specialized within the guild until guildsmen reached the pinnacle of success, at which point they might branch out into other economic activities, using their originally more specialized company as a base.

With the onset of partnership systems, the sociopolitical backgrounds of businessmen engaged in multiple companies changed. In 1385–99, immediately after the Ciompi Revolt, businessmen participating in two or more partnerships were distinguishable socio-politically in two ways from businessmen involved in only one company: (a) politically they were mobilized into the 1384 *balìa* and the 1393 *reggimento*, and (b) socially they married upper-class popolani wives. Why did these particular political and social factors correlate with the economic activity of founding partnership systems?

Balìe were special ad hoc committees set up in order to reform the Florentine political constitution, sometimes in minor, sometimes in major ways (Molho 1968a). The 1384 *balìa* was set up to reform the wool manufacturers' industry and guild (A.S.F., *Arte della Lana* 46), a central locus of *ciompi* agitation. The *reggimento* was the set of Florentines successfully elected to be eligible for the Priorate or city council (Kent 1975), through an election procedure called the scrutiny (Najemy 1982). As such, it was Florence's political ruling class. To say that partnership-system businessmen were disproportionately members of these two groups is to say that, for those years at least, they were members of the political elite.

It is not surprising that the 1378 *balìa* coefficient, during the height of the Ciompi Revolt itself, is not statistically significant. But it is interesting that in 1382, a year associated with repression of the Ciompi Revolt, the political membership variables of 1382 *balìa* and 1382 *reggimento* were *not* statistically significant predictors of partnership-system builders. This temporal pattern of coefficients helps us to interpret direction of causality: It was the new 1382 post-Ciompi political elite that subsequently recruited and co-opted businessmen (about to become partnership-system businessmen) into the political elite, rather than these businessmen who created the new political elite in the first place.

The other statistically significant effect in table 6.2, for 1385–99, is for marriage to popolani wives. In the republican conception of status in Renaissance Florentines, social class was defined as the political age of one's patrilineal family—namely, the year in which one's male ancestors first were elected to city council. The highest prestige *popolani* were the politically founding generation of those Florentine families who first entered the Priorate during 1282–1342—namely, that era between the constitutional founding of the republic and its first major political convulsion in 1343. To say that partnership-system businessmen disproportionately married popolani wives is to say that they were being absorbed into the social elite, whether or not they were born into it.

The natal social-class coefficients reveal that the 1385–99 partnership-system businessmen (unlike their 1427 successors) were not themselves necessarily born into the social elite. Instead they were socially quite heterogeneous in class background—some high prestige like Vieri de' Medici, and some low prestige like Francesco Datini. Either way, they wound up marrying popolani wives, indicating a systematic process of social, as well as political, co-optation. Even outsider Datini from Prato took a popolani Florentine wife.

The vector of 1427 coefficients shows how these partnership-system businessmen settled into the social structure of Florence over time. Businessmen's marriages to popolani wives (and now also to magnate wives) became an even more powerful predictor of their capacity to build partnership systems than was the case in 1385–99. The big change from the late 1300s to 1427 was that partnership-system businessmen themselves became more homogeneously elitist in social-class background. By 1427, natal birth into the popolani and magnate social classes had become strongly associated with leadership of partnership systems. Indeed by 1427, the social distinction between popolani and magnates had been largely effaced: These two upper social classes fused in the economic domain, as they gradually took over the partnership systems that others had created. It is facts like these that lend credence to the "oligarchic" interpretation of the Albizzean regime (Schevill [1936] 1963, Martines 1979, Cohn 1980).

The statistically significant 1427 coefficient for the Medici faction is consistent with existing historiography. The Medici bank was a crucial component in the new Medici political party (Padgett and Ansell 1993). To put this point more generally, ultimately economic organizational invention, in the form of new partnership networks, became incorporated into the organizational structure of political parties, thereby changing the dynamic of state formation in Florence. After a number of intervening decades, economic invention eventually cascaded back into political invention.

I have not yet coded from the archives *balìa* and *reggimento* data for 1427, so my interpretation for that period needs to be provisional. But there is no evidence in table 6.2 to suggest that political mobilization, in the form of political office holding, played an important role in the ongoing maintenance of the Florentine partnership system, after its birth. Political mobilization was clearly related to economic partnership-system building in the 1383–99 phase of its genesis. But 40 years later, during the phase of its ongoing reproduction, natal social class had taken over as the dominant social embedding for partnership systems. Marriage to popolani wives remained the network that dynamically bridged the transition between these two phases, guiding the partnership system from its political genesis to its social-class institutionalization.

Explaining the Emergence of Florentine Partnership Systems

Given these newly discovered facts about the Florentine invention of the partnership system in the 1380s, my causal explanation of these facts will be developed in the following stages: First, summarizing the extensive secondary literature on this topic, I briefly describe the Ciompi Revolt and the stages of its repression. Second, I examine the roles of both cambio bankers and international merchants in the political reconstructions of the state and of the elite after the Ciompi Revolt. Demobilization of guilds and politicization of marriage and clientage were central features in these reconstructions. Next I show how the social logics of cambio-banking and international-merchant partnerships, viewed separately as individual spokes of the partnership system, changed through this elite reconsolidation process, enabling those components organizationally to fit together and socially to be reproduced. In the final section of this chapter, I adumbrate the economic consequences of these organizational transformations for bookkeeping, liquidity, and credit in the Florentine banking system.

The Ciompi Revolt and Its Repression

The Ciompi Revolt was the only (temporarily) successful workers revolution in European pre-industrial history (Rodolico 1905; Cohn 1980; Stella 1993; Trexler 1998). Some prominent Florentine historians do not accept this economic-class characterization (Brucker 1968; 1977; Najemy 1981, 1982), even though direct involvement of wool workers and other *popolo minuto* or "little people" (collectively called *ciompi* or "comrades" by contemporaries) in violently overthrowing the state and in evicting large numbers of popolani and magnates from Florence was indeed the most striking feature of this dramatic event in 1378. The major reason for their rejection is because the objectives of the *popolo minuto* emphasized guild-corporatist demands for inclusion and citizenship rather than overthrow of the means of production. Seen in the light of contemporaries, however, the political "reforms" proposed and forcibly implemented for a short time by the *ciompi* were radical indeed (Cohn 1980). Here we shall narrate these searing events with an emphasis on the role of and the impact on international merchants and domestic bankers, who collectively invented the partnership system.

The Ciompi Revolt emerged out of the War of the Eight Saints (1375–78) with the papacy. Intense political struggle between two elite factions had been building up for two decades before this climatic war, with a "conservative" side (the Albizzi faction in alliance with the *Parte Guelfa*) consistently pushing for restriction of the republican franchise to patrician families and with a "liberal" side (the Ricci faction in alliance with artisan guilds) consistently pushing to open the franchise to new men who had recently established themselves in the city economy (Brucker 1962). Three traumatic events in the 1340s—namely, the 1342 bankruptcies of the large Bardi and Peruzzi banks, the 1343 political convulsion which that economic crash triggered, and the 1348 Black Death which killed about two-thirds of the Florentine population (Herlihy and Klapisch-Zuber 1985, 69)—had opened up both the economy and the political regime to an infusion of new men (*gente nuova*). This post-1343 infusion generated deep resentment on the part of the older patricians who had founded the republic in 1282. Political struggle between patricians and new men had been a consistent trope in late medieval Florence—even more so than in other Italian city-states—because of high rates of economic and social mobility. Contradictorily, each generation of elites between 1200 and 1500 sponsored mobility in the economic domain but resisted it in the political domain. The political expression of this underlying social-mobility contradiction, however, changed substantially through time.

In the 1343–1378 generation, political struggle was manifest in an escalating series of McCarthyite purges (*ammonizione*) by both factions—the Albizzi-faction-cum-*Parte Guelfa* side purging selected liberals by denouncing them as Ghibellines, and the Ricci-faction-cum-guild side purging targeted conservatives by denouncing them as magnates (Brucker 1962). The 1375–78 war with the pope, then resident in Avignon, was perhaps inevitable given the two territorial consolidations by Florence in Tuscany and by the pope in central Italy, which collided. Internationally, the pope through his spiritual interdict of Florence organized a largely (though not completely) successful boycott of European trade with Florentine businessmen, temporarily crushing the Florentine economy (Trexler 1974). Domestically, war with the pope desecrated deep and long-standing Guelf loyalties in many Florentines, especially among traditionalist patricians. Ultimately the rejection of city-state loyalty to the pope set the stage for the birth of civic-humanist republicanism (Baron 1966). But in the short run, this intersection of domestic with international politics fueled Florentine factional struggle to the boiling point. Each side, but in particular the Guelf side, progressively denounced and purged the other to the point where eventually Salvestro d'Alamanno de' Medici led liberal guild forces in the burning of conservative houses and the forcible eviction from Florence of many *Parte Guelfa* leaders on June 18, 1378.

This violence within the citizenry opened the door to the potentially revolutionary entrance of previously disenfranchised *ciompi* onto the public stage. On July 21 and then again on August 31, waves of wool workers, organized as a "mob," surged into the streets and public squares of Florence, forcibly dissolving the existing government with plunder and arson and demanding reorganization of the state in order to incorporate themselves as three new guilds. These new guilds provided the organizational core of the temporarily victorious *ciompi* state: an expanded guild-corporatist alliance between previously non-guild workers and minor-guild artisans, which lasted only six weeks. Throughout these tumultuous events, conservative popolani and magnates left Florence in droves in fear of their lives, and all export-oriented economic activity, already damaged by the pope's interdict, ceased.

It is not the purpose of this article to explain the Ciompi Revolt itself, but historians have pointed to a (contested) combination of three factors as causes: (a) chronic dissatisfaction of wool workers with political disenfranchisement, due to their economic subordination within the guild system; (b) the self-immolation of elites in factional struggle, the liberal side of which had systematically raised enfranchisement expectations; and (c) a wool-industry economic slump, due both to short-run pressures from the papal war and to long-term pressures from the growth of a competitive English textile industry (Carus-Wilson 1963, 1967), which constricted the import of high-quality English wool to Florentine, thereby generating unemployment (Hoshino 1980, Franceschi 1993a). In future research, I hope to "endogenize" the Ciompi Revolt by explaining it as the consequence of chronic contradiction in fourteenth-century Florence between the two organizing principles of patrilineage and guild, which the above short-term pressures intensified.

More important in this chapter is the reaction of various exiled and non-exiled groups to this searing political event. Florentine reaction developed in three stages, each stage involving progressively more elitist actors. The first stage was not really an elite reaction at all; it was the counter-mobilization on September 1, 1378 of minor-guild artisans to take back "their" guild-corporatist state from six-week control by non-guild *ciompi*. Minor guildsmen, led by liberal popolani like Salvestro Medici, Tommaso Strozzi, Giorgio Scali, Benedetto Alberti, and Uguccione Ricci confronted radical wool workers in the streets and defeated them in combat. The largest and most radical of the new *ciompi* guilds was disbanded, and a relatively democratic guild-corporatist state was established, which lasted from 1378 to 1382.

The second stage of reaction, in January 1382, was essentially a coup d'état by "cloth manufacturers and bands of aristocrats, who had armed their servants and retainers, and the peasants from their country estates" (Brucker 1977, 60). The constitutional *balìa* produced by this coup abolished the remaining two minor guilds set up by the *ciompi*, burned the 1378 regime's scrutiny bags, and forcibly tilted office-holding away from artisans back toward the major guilds, like international traders, cambio bankers, and wool cloth manufacturers (*lanaiuoli*), who had been in charge before the revolution. Rather than purely reactionary in character, this second-stage counterrevolution was led by factional "moderates"—that is, wealthy major-guildsmen in the political center, who opposed factional extremes both on the left and on the right. Their guiding policy was elite "consensus" (Najemy 1982), in the pursuit of which, ominously, deeply reactionary exiles and magnates were invited to return to Florence. This elitist but relatively moderate regime of 1382–93 was the "favorable business climate" that induced Francesco Datini to return to Tuscany in 1383, thereby initiating the construction of his partnership system.

The third and final stage of counterrevolution occurred in 1393, with the accession to power of Maso degli Albizzi and his "oligarchic" allies. Reinforced by an international context of dangerous wars with Milan, returning conservatives resumed their purging ways, first in 1387 and then in 1393, this time more selectively targeting the most powerful remaining leaders of the liberal popolani—namely, the Alberti family of international merchant bankers. With the Alberti and their close popolani allies sent into exile, the Albizzi-led regime destroyed remaining guild-consul scrutiny bags and held new elections to restructure the political *reggimento* by fusing elite moderates with elite conservatives.

There has been a lively debate in the historiographical literature about the character of this post-Ciompi Albizzean regime. The traditional interpretation shared by chroniclers and historians alike (e.g., Machiavelli [1525] 1988, Guicciardini [1512] 1994) is that the Albizzean regime was an oligarchy, politically dominated by a fairly well-defined set of conservative families, mostly popolani but also including new-men and magnate sympathizers. But Hans Baron's (1966) famous book on civic humanism emphasized the forward looking philosophical and patriotic vision of republicanism forged by this "oligarchy" in its wars with Milan. In support of this revisionist interpretation, careful empirical analyses by Molho (1968b), by Witt (1976) and by Najemy (1982) have shown the high degree of election of new individuals in the 1382 and 1393 scrutinies, well beyond any purported closed circle of elite families. Najemy (1982, 276–300) resolved this contradiction to some degree by showing that openness in election was offset by tight institutional controls (e.g., *accoppiatori* and *borsellini*) on the translation of election into real political power. But still this dual vision of oligarchy versus republicanism remains to confound clear understanding of the period.

Following Najemy (1982), our position on this puzzle will be that the entire 1282–1382 century in Florence can be understood as a long-term contradiction between the patrilineage and the guild modes of organizing social, economic, and political mobility. The original *Popolo* pattern in the 1250s was older elites organized into patrilineages confronting rising groups organized into guilds. But the dynamic of political development came from organizational crossover in the late 1200s and early 1300s—namely, popolani dominating markets and the state through major guilds, and new men mimicking patrilineages in their family structure (Padgett, Chapters 3 and 4, this volume). Najemy focused on the formal institutional and electoral sides of this organizational contradiction. The complementary focus here is to trace this deep contradiction through the evolution of social networks. Padgett (2010) traces mobility patterns through marriage networks over 200 years, demonstrating the contesting principles at work. Civic-humanist republicanism was the early fifteenth-century ideological face of this underlying social-network reorganization of mobility channels into the reconstituted Florentine elite.

Biographical Transposition: the Political Co-optation of Cambio Bankers

To repeat, for editorial clarity: "transposition" was the political co-optation of guild-based cambio bankers into high political office. "Refunctionality" was the conversion of these co-opted domestic bankers into international system builders. And "catalysis" was the absorption of partnership systems into socially elite marriage networks.

During the reaction to the Ciompi Revolt, domestic cambio bankers, more so than international merchants, were mobilized strongly into the republican institutions of the state. Table 6.3 documents this point. In the post-Ciompi period of 1380–1399, 26–36% of cambio bankers and 51–59% of cambio-banking companies were represented at some time in the city council or Priorate of the city, up from pre-Ciompi representation rates of 15–25% and 35–38%, respectively. In the more economically focused Mercanzia or commercial court, political mobilization of cambio bankers was even more dramatic: from 4–6% of cambio bankers and 6–11% of cambio-banking partnerships in the Mercanzia before the revolt, to 23–24% and 44–48% after the revolt, respectively. These high cambio-banker representation rates compare with the much lower representation rates of 13–17% for international merchants and 17–26% for international merchant-banking companies during 1380–1399. Temporally refined *balìe*

Table 6.3 Political Mobilization of Cambio Bankers and International Merchants

A. *Cambio Banking*:

	% Bankers in:					% Partnerships in:				
	1348–1362	**1363–1376**	**1380–1389**	**1390–1399**	**1427**	**1348–1362**	**1363–1376**	**1380–1389**	**1390–1399**	**1427**
Governing offices of the state:										
Priorate	.254	0.147	**.262**	**.356**	.272	.353	.376	**.514**	**.587**	.405
Mercanzia	.063	.043	**.235**	**.244**	.087	.057	.113	**.436**	**.482**	.108
Balìe:										
1378 Balìa			.027					.069		
1382 Balìa			.040					.073		
1384 Balìa			**.154**					**.362**		
1393 Balìa				**.106**					**.255**	
Reggimenti:										
1382 Scrutiny			**.248**					**.512**		
1393 Scrutiny				**.313**					**.605**	

continued

Table 6.3 *continued*

B. ***International Trading*:**

	% Merchants in:				% Partnerships in:	
	1348–1358	**1369**	**1385–1399**	**1427**	**1385–1399**	**1427**
Governing offices of the state:						
Priorate	.297	.479	.167	.100	0.263	.149
Mercanzia	.122	.028	.131	.100	.175	.108
Balìe:						
1378 Balìa			.012		.035	
1382 Balìa			.024		.018	
1384 Balìa			.083		.088	
1393 Balìa			.048		.105	
Reggimenti:						
1382 Scrutiny			.107		.105	
1393 Scrutiny			.167		.228	

N.B.: On the left, these are percentages of businessmen on the identified political bodies. On the right, these are percentages of partnerships with at least one partner on the identified political bodies. For priorate and Mercanzia, time periods refer, for example, to "bankers active in 1348–62 who were ever on Priorate before 1362."

representation rates reveal the post-Ciompi mobilization inflection point exactly to be 1384, a date that makes perfect sense in light of the Ciompi-revolt narrative above: Cambio bankers did not initiate the second-stage 1382 major-guild regime that quickly mobilized them, but by 1393 they were fully integrated into the Albizzean "oligarchic" or "civic humanist" regime.

This differential political mobilization of cambio bankers, compared to international merchants, is surprising in light of the strictly economic history of the period. The pope emerged victorious in his 1375–78 war with Florence not because of the military power of his weak mercenary armies but because of the economic power of his spiritual interdict of Florentine merchants—namely, his ordering other cities' merchants not to trade with Florentines, under the sanction of withholding sacraments. Florentine international merchants, not everywhere but in many places (Trexler 1974), were decimated economically by this interdict, as foreign merchants seized their goods and exiled them back to Florence. From the perspective of rebuilding the damaged Florentine economy, it was the international merchant-bankers, not the domestic cambio bankers, that most needed political support.

To probe this and other aspects of the political mobilization of cambio bankers, I present tables 6.4 and 6.5. Within the context of a sampling universe of tax censuses of the entire male head-of-household population of Florence, these two tables present various social and political predictors of active participation in cambio banking (table 6.4) and in international trading (table 6.5), at various points in late medieval time. Numerous findings in these logit regressions are of interest, to which I shall return, but the answer to the current puzzle about the greater political mobilization of cambio bankers than international merchants is to be found in the political-faction section of those logit-regression tables. Both before and during the Ciompi Revolt, cambio bankers and international merchants were politicized into the various factional struggles of the time, as was the entire city. But in the struggle between Albizzi and Ricci factions, cambio bankers were neutral, and in the Ciompi struggle itself cambio bankers were politicized into both sides equally. In contrast, international merchants by 1369 had swung predominantly to the guild side (Brucker 1962, 124–27). The political redoubt of the leading Alberti family, later to be exiled by conservatives in 1387 and in 1393, was the most internationally oriented guild of them all—the *Arte della Calimala*, home of international traders and import cloth finishers.

Leaders of the moderate regime of 1382–93 were *lanaiuoli* and other domestically based major guildsmen—socially and economically "elite" but politically opposed to both factional extremes. They had experienced decades of violent political and street warfare among fractious elite families, which had opened the door to revolution from below. These moderate major

Table 6.4 Political and Social Embedding of Cambio Bankers

Logit coefficients:	**1348–62**	**1363–76**	**1380–89**	**1390–99**	**1427**
Patrilineage:					
Cambio patrilineages	**1.624*****	**3.229*****	**2.199*****	**2.534*****	**2.196*****
Social Class:					
Popolani	.267	−.765**	−.008	−.388	.098
Magnate	.210	−.130	.347	−.138	**.732***
New man	**.815***	.106	.541	0.483	−.003
Social Class of Wife:					
Popolani	**.961*****	**1.258*****	**.689***	**.660****	**1.836*****
Magnate	.022	−.550	.180	.008	**1.113**
New man	**1.595****	**1.799****	**1.437****	.164	**1.343***
Political Offices:					
Priorate	**1.091*****	−0.60	**.339**	**.319**	**1.211*****
Mercanzia	**1.021***	.835	**1.486*****	**1.219*****	.296
Balia 1378		.198	.185	.524	
Balia 1382		.081	−.394	.005	
Reggimento 1382		**.669***	.231	−.625	
Balia 1384		**2.658*****	**1.622*****	**1.283****	
Balia 1393			−.756	−.354	
Reggimento 1393			**1.192*****	**1.694*****	
Political Factions:					
Albizzi	.234	−.548	−0.131	−0.158	
Ricci	.997(*)	.122	−1.526	−1.23	
Anti-ciompi		**1.289***	.503	**.721**	
Pro-ciompi		**1.089***	−.474	−.517	
Albizzeans					.564
Mediceans					**1.405****
Quarter:					
Santa Croce	.074	−.198	.331	.070	.372
Santa Maria Novella	.467	**.796****	**.712****	**.606***	−.177
San Giovanni	.384	.313	**.771****	**.597***	.477
Log likelihood	−576.7	−467.7	−574.2	−594.2	−416.1
# observations (persons)	5005	7129	7129	7129	8376

Logit coefficients:	1348–62	1363–76	1380–89	1390–99	1427
L.R. chi^2	138.2	250.1	299.1	342.9	180.8
prob > chi^2	.000	.000	.000	.000	.000
pseudo R^2	.107	.211	.207	.224	.179

*** = (p < .001); ** = (p < .01); * = (p < .05); (*) = (p < .06)
Notes:

(1) In each logit regression, the universe of persons to whom these cambio bankers were compared was the time-appropriate tax census (that is, 1351 *Estimo*, 1378 *Prestanze* or 1427 *Catasto*) of household heads, plus those household heads' fathers.
(2) Only those marriages and political offices with dates prior to the last date of the logit regressions (i.e., 1362, 1376, 1389, 1399, 1427, respectively) were included in estimations.
(3) "Cambio patrilineages" were patrilineages with three or more members in the cambio-banking industry, during the time period in question.

Sources: See citations in table 6.2.

Table 6.5 Political and Social Embedding of Merchant-Bankers

Logit coefficients:	Alberti 1348–58 (Intl+Pisa +Florence)	Pisa 1369 (Intl+Pisa + Florence)	Datini 1385–99 (Int'l+Pisa)	Catasto 1427 (Int'l+Pisa)
Patrilineage:				
Int'l m-b patrilineages	**2.287*****	**2.964*****	**2.937*****	**2.098*****
Social Class:				
Popolani	−.665	−.375	.048	−.089
Magnate	−1.367**	−1.413	−.352	−.060
New man	.392	−.113	.320	−1.492*
Social Class of Wife:				
Popolani	**1.368*****	.781	**.821****	**2.333*****
Magnate	**1.492*****	**1.243***	−.431	**1.579****
New man	1.173	**1.755***	.550	1.364
Political Offices:				
Priorate	**.977****	**2.385*****	−.985(*)	−.865
Mercanzia	**1.581****	−1.657	.730	**1.675****
Balia 1378		**1.260*****	−.557	
Balia 1382		.128	.436	
Reggimento 1382		**1.038****	−.010	
Balia 1384		**1.598****	**1.510****	

continued

Table 6.5 *continued*

Logit coefficients:	Alberti 1348–58 (Intl+Pisa +Florence)	Pisa 1369 (Intl+Pisa + Florence)	Datini 1385–99 (Int'l+Pisa)	Catasto 1427 (Int'l+Pisa)
Balia 1393			−649	
Reggimento 1393			**1.376****	
Political Factions:				
Albizzi	**1.431***	.983	−1.150	
Ricci	**1.863****	**1.550***	.057	
Anti-Ciompi		.529	.746	
Pro-Ciompi		**1.907*****	.028	
Albizzeans				**1.425****
Mediceans				**2.202*****
Quarter:				
Santa Croce	.396	.529	−.509	−.247
Santa Maria Novella	.487	.616	−.189	−.653
San Giovanni	**.771***	.081	−.519	−.174
Log likelihood	−313.9	−257.9	−389.0	−321.6
# observations (persons)	5005	7129	7129	8376
L.R. chi^2	142.8	279.9	135.1	166
prob > chi^2	.000	.000	.000	.000
pseudo R^2	.185	.352	.148	.205

*** = (p < .001); ** = (p < .01); * = (p < .05); (*) = (p < .06)

Notes:

(1) In each logit regression, the universe of persons to whom these international merchant-bankers were compared was the time-appropriate tax census (that is, 1351 *Estimo*, 1378 *Prestanze* or 1427 *Catasto*) of household heads, plus those household heads' fathers.

(2) Only those marriages and political offices with dates prior to the last date of the logit regressions (i.e., 1362, 1376, 1389, 1399, 1427, respectively) were included in estimations.

(3) "International merchant-banking patrilineages" were patrilineages with three or more members in the international merchant-banking industry, during the time period in question.

(4) The first two of these regressions include merchant bankers whose companies were resident in Florence, as well as those whose companies were resident elsewhere (i.e., international + Pisa), because the primary data in these two periods did not differentiate residence well. Because of this, some of the overlap across industries—in these two periods only—is tautological.

Sources: See citations in table 6.2.

guildsmen desperately wanted to reestablish peace and control both for their own sanity and in order to rebuild the manufacturing and export economy, so damaged by war with the pope, upon which their livelihoods depended. Instead of crushing opposition, they sought to achieve the difficult objective of annealing conflicting forces back into economic and political synergy. Statistical support for this "leading reform role of the moderates" interpretation is given by the disappearance of all significant political-faction coefficients in tables 6.5–6.9 after 1382. Because of the sequentiality of annealing, the crushing of pro-Ciompi revolutionary forces in 1382 did not automatically imply that reactionary forces took over.

The political problem faced by the 1382 moderate-elite regime trying to restore order was the following: Repression of the radical *ciompi* obviously was the sine qua non, but that had already been accomplished by the previous 1378 regime of minor guilds and liberal popolani. The next step was to solve the structural problem of the guild-corporatist constitutional order, which had served major guildsmen so well in earlier generations, but which had badly malfunctioned. The *ciompi* had hijacked this institutional order to mobilize revolution, and minor guildsmen with their liberal popolani allies had used it to seize control from major guilds, both immediately before and immediately after the Ciompi Revolt. Najemy (1981) has shown how the economic-class tension associated with the Ciompi Revolt shredded political cohesion within the guild of wool-manufacturers, and presumably within other major guilds as well, thereby enabling these defeats.

Whatever the reasoning, the 1382–93 regime moved quickly to dismantle the autonomy of those very guilds, both major and minor, which had previously been the institutional foundation of their own economic and political power. In 1382, all elected guild consuls became subject to the approval of the Mercanzia; in 1383 and in 1390 the Mercanzia exercised this review power to alter the results of the election of consuls in the cloth retail and silk guild; and finally in 1393 the *balìa* burned all guilds' scrutiny bags, containing the results of previous consul elections, and requested that the Mercanzia appoint guild consuls directly "by hand" (Najemy 1972, 582–601; Franceschi 1993b, 886–89). In addition, in 1384 a special-purpose *balìa* of major guildsmen, including both cambio bankers and international merchants, was appointed to reform the wool-manufacturers' guild (A.S.F., *Arte della Lana* 46, 164–66). The previous constitutional system of federated economic and political self-governments by guilds was dismantled, in other words, in favor of more direct "oligarchic" oversight by those in control of the central institutions of the republican state (namely, the priorate, the *balìe*, and the Mercanzia).

Previous histories have not always clearly differentiated between moderate and conservative elements in the post-Ciompi oligarchic-cum-republican regimes. Nor have they precisely identified the differing roles of various major guildsmen, such as wool manufacturers, cambio bankers and international merchants, in this constitutional reconstruction. The data show clearly, however, that 1382 reformers actively reached out to cambio bankers for allies in their institutional reforms. But they did not reach out similarly to international merchants, apparently because they were often not politically reliable. This mobilization collectively lifted cambio bankers to political heights not previously attainable.

This co-optation strategy by political moderates fits neatly with the findings of Molho (1968b), Witt (1976) and Najemy (1982), who demonstrated the high degree of openness by the post-1382 "oligarchic" regime to the (highly selective) election of newcomers. Cambio bankers were not the only ones being co-opted. In pursuit of their annealing objectives, elite-but-moderate reformers reached out for support in all sympathetic directions, as long as they, not the guilds, controlled the routes of access. But whereas many were mobilized as clients, cambio bankers were mobilized into the very core of the regime.

Without sharply distinguishing between moderates and conservatives, Najemy puts the same point eloquently, if somewhat cynically, like this:

> In short, as the number of participants reached new heights, real power in the system underwent an unprecedented process of centralization. The thousands of individual Florentine citizens who willingly entered the lists of the electoral lottery, each nourishing his private hope of elevation to the priorate, gave the republican regime a stability it had not previously known. They played the game as faithful creatures of the regime, hardly aware that their own acquiescence in the illusion of political equality, their very willingness to play by rules they no longer shared in defining, and their acceptance of participation without actual power were the bedrock of consensus on which the stable and elitist polity of fifteenth-century Florence was built. Even less were they aware of having created the conditions that shaped the new republican ideology of civic humanism. (Najemy 1982, 299–300)

Organizational Refunctionality: Domestic Bankers into International System Builders

From the perspective of our theoretical framework for analyzing organizational invention, co-optation of bankers into politics was biographical transposition. This lead to organizational refunctionality—namely, the perception of new purposes for old practices and tools. The old practices and tools were those of the domestic cambio bankers; the new perceptions and purposes were those of international trade.

Twenty-five to thirty percent of cambio bankers were elevated into the central institutions of the state—the priorate, the *balìe*, and the Mercanzia—where government policy was made. Coming from previous experience in domestic deposit banking, this political promotion introduced them to international contacts and to an internationalist perspective from which they had previously been, if not excluded, then inhibited by the specialized guild system. Before the Ciompi Revolt, a few cambio bankers had sometimes engaged in international trading on the side, but that was hardly their primary activity. International trading instead had been dominated by merchants in the Calimala guild, not by bankers in the Cambio guild. Now however, the state had an urgent need to rebuild its war-damaged, export-oriented wool-manufacturing and international trading economies. Cambio bankers were recruited into this economy-rebuilding effort, and they became a core part of the very state that was recruiting them.

As shown in tables 6.4 and 6.5, the 1384 special-purpose *balìa* on the wool industry (A.S.F., *Arte della Lana* 46, 164–166) was one prong in this rebuilding effort in which cambio bankers were centrally involved. This *balìa* reformed the terms of trade and the administration of disputes, fines, and fees among various members of the wool industry (manufacturers, dyers, laborers, etc.), in an apparent effort to simultaneously restructure this recently politically explosive guild and revive this crucial but declining economic sector in Florence. Apart from this important industry-specific *balìa*, I am aware of no other special governmental commission that was set up to propose other economic reforms. Rather there was "just" the strong encouragement and backing of the state for those who wished to fill the international-trading vacuum. In future research into the records of these governmental bodies, I hope to elaborate the precise form which this encouragement took.

Whatever the particular inducements, some experienced cambio bankers—men like Vieri di Cambio de' Medici and Manetto di Giovanni Davanzati, but also some international merchant-bankers like Francesco Datini and Tommaso di Guccio Soderini—responded to the new opportunities to expand their business by opening new branches in overseas cities. In addition, a new generation of cambio bankers—men like Giovanni di Bicci de' Medici, Francesco di Simone Tornabuoni and Giovanni di Jacopo Orlandini, descended from the earlier generation of cambio bankers—broadened their domestic base into international merchant-banking. A few newcomers, like Niccolò da Uzzano, did the reverse and extended their international trading origins into cambio banking. The specific issue is how did this flow of domestic banking into international trading trigger the invention of the partnership system, which organizationally fused these two industries?

My answer is in two parts: careers and practices. Before the Ciompi Revolt, the guild system had channeled economic careers into industrial specialization, which also became one important basis for political representation. After the Ciompi Revolt, the guild system was effectively dismantled, and a more centralized system of elite monitoring of the activities of businessmen was imposed through the Mercanzia. This breakdown of effective intermediation through corporatist organizations "individualized" the biographical flows of businessmen through the state, inducing political and eventually social stratification. Selected businessmen from various industries were placed onto the same political career tracks, through the priorate, the *balìe*, the mercanzia, and other republican offices of the state. Thereby it became easier, through dialogue and shared position within leading formal and informal (*consulte e pratiche*) councils of the state, and without the constraint of corporate representation, for each major guild's businessmen to see the world more easily from the perspective of the other major guilds. This is similar to the social-network concept of structural equivalence (White, Boorman and Breiger 1976), except here we have parallel career flows instead of highly correlated network profiles. The cognitive implication of career-flow equivalence, I hypothesize, was to replace the specialized perspective of industry and guild with the generalized perspectives of "Florence" and "business."

The precise micro-mechanism that translated this new career-flow equivalence into partnership systems was the transposition of cambio bankers' existing master–apprentice way of making domestic partnerships (Padgett 2001, 227) onto the international stage. In their domestic companies, cambio bankers were used to short-term (often three year) renewable partnership contracts between cambio masters and a series of ex-apprentice younger junior partners, who fully expected to split from their master's company upon financial success to form their own firms. For compensation, the junior partner received a share of the profit higher than his share of the capital contribution, as reward and incentive for hard labor. These were exactly the typical terms of formal contracts between founders and branch managers in partnership systems, except that in partnership systems there were simultaneously many such contracts with multiple branch managers, often spanning more than one industry. This cambio-banking, guild-partnering logic—previously constrained to be sequential because of its domestic and specialized-industry guild setting—was unleashed to become modular, cross-cutting multiple geographical settings and industries. Thereby it supplanted the older unitary patrilineage form of international merchant-banking, which after the 1340s was very much on the ropes in any event.

There were macroeconomic forces moving this industrially diversified partnering logic down the tracks of geographical diversification as well. The War of the Eight Saints with the pope had altered the landscape of European trading outlets. Before this war, Florentine long-distance international trade, mostly in woolen cloth, traveled primarily along an almost straight line, running from London and England in the north, down through Flanders, Paris, and Avignon in France; to Genoa, Milan, and Pisa in northern Italy; and continuing on to Rome and Naples in southern Italy (e.g., Goldthwaite et al. 1995, xlv–lxxx). Venice (Mueller 1997a, 255–75) and other smaller Italian cities also were in Florence's international trading network, off this primary geographical axis. The spiritual interdict of the pope, with its mixed success in host cities of organizing boycotts and exiles of resident Florentine businessmen, helped to diversify this economic geography. To simplify a complex topography: after the war, England and Avignon went down, and Spain and Venice went up, as relative Florentine trading partners, in immediate response to their respective national profiles of cooperating, or not, with the pope (Trexler 1974, 44–108).

To be sure, the various political responses of host countries to anti-Florentine pressure from the pope reflected their own economic interests. That is, they reflected ongoing economic trends. The fact remains that after the war, the King of England expelled Italians for decades, in his successful import-substitution effort to develop domestic wool production. Exports of high-quality raw English wool to Florence plummeted (Carus-Wilson and Coleman 1963), with deleterious consequences for the Florentine wool manufacturing industry (Franceschi 1993a). Trading connections with Catalonia and Mediterranean Spain, on the other hand, centered around silk and raw wool, blossomed (Lopez 1952, 347). And Venice, also in response to its War of Chioggia with Genoa, liberalized its free-trade policy, thereby currying the favor of Florentine merchants (Mueller 1997a, 266).

Thus when Florentine international trading revived after the Ciompi Revolt, Florentine companies, using their new organizational tool of partnership systems, faced a more dispersed economic geography than before, centered as much around the western Mediterranean as around the old French route to London. This was the "demand side" facing the "supply side" of new partnership systems. Modularity had a wide variety of geographical sockets to plug into.

To summarize, our contention about organizational refunctionality is that when cambio bankers flowed through newly centralized political institutions, these institutions transposed existing ways of doing economic business into new purposes. Politically moderate elite leaders of the new regime were just trying conservatively to reestablish control and to rebuild their decimated economy. But the unintended consequence of them co-opting cambio bankers and select international businessmen into their electoral system was to catalyze cambio bankers and their international partners into reshaping themselves. Sequential cambio partnerships became transformed into modularized simultaneous partnerships, which spanned industries. This new organizational form permitted the ready exploration of geographically dispersed markets, which had been produced through the war with the pope.

Multiple-Network Catalysis: The Embedding of Partnership Systems in Elite Marriage

Political co-optation in response to revolt explains the transposition and refunctionality mechanisms of organizational genesis. But for novel innovation to become transformative invention, there must be something more. Innovation must reverberate out into collateral ways of doing business, thereby reshaping the interactive system in which the invention is embedded. This is the difference between the incremental evolution of banks, which is variation within species, and the punctuated evolution of banking, which is emergence of new species. The same post-Ciompi political process in Florence that induced organizational innovation, however, also rewired the social embedding of partnership into surrounding networks, thereby altering the contextual feedbacks which reproduced that invention. The Florentine partnership system was not just the incremental diffusion of a good organizational idea; it was part of a larger punctuated-equilibrium reconstitution of the Florentine elite, which resituated the Florentine business community within its surrounding social and political contexts. Some call this a shift from medieval to Renaissance.

To demonstrate this changing social embedding of economic partnership in late medieval Florence, I present tables 6.6 and 6.7, which disaggregate partnership systems into their constitutive parts—namely, cambio partnerships and international merchant-banking partnerships, viewed separately. Tables 6.6 and 6.7 present logit regressions on partnership dyads in these two industries over time. These logit-regression tables report the effects of many contextual social and political variables on economic partnership.

The strongest time-series message in these tables is marriage, but before I discuss those results I shall discuss three other statistically significant findings in tables 6.6 and 6.7, as interesting preliminaries. The first is essentially a reconfirmation of the discussion in the section about biographical transposition: Political mobilization of cambio bankers, through the 1380–99 priorate, the 1384 *balìa*, the 1393 *balìa*, and the 1393 *reggimento*, had a significant effect on the formation of cambio-banking partnerships. Table 6.5 showed that cambio bankers were mobilized politically after the suppression of the Ciompi Revolt. Table 6.6 shows that this mobilization had an impact on cambio bankers' partnership behavior—namely, mobilized bankers were significantly more likely to form partnerships. Table 6.7 shows the same *not* to be true for international merchant bankers. While international merchants were also mobilized into the 1384 *balìa* and the 1393 *reggimento*, this lesser mobilization had no detectable effect on their partnering behavior. Political mobilization not only affected cambio businessmen but it also affected their banks.

Secondly, examination of the coefficients for natal (not in-law) family in table 6.6 reveals the following trend: The causal importance of family—both at the level of the nuclear-family and at the level of the patrilineage—for predicting the likelihood of forming cambio-banking partnerships declined smoothly in magnitude over the 1348 to 1427 period. But it remained statistically significant throughout. The same trends are revealed in table 6.7 for international merchant-banking partnerships over

Table 6.6 Political and Social Embedding of Cambio-Banking Partnerships

Logit coefficients:	1348–62	1363–76	1380–89	1390–99	1427
Patrilineage:					
Nuclear family	**8.273*****	**7.998*****	**6.296*****	**5.830*****	**4.006*****
Patrilineage (excl. nucl.)	**3.720*****	**2.435*****	**3.245*****	**2.966*****	**2.487*****
Marriage:					
Nuclear in-law partners	.851	1.055	**2.888*****	**1.102****	**1.379****
Patrilineage inter-marriage	**.684***	–.602	**1.566*****	**.382(*)**	**.915*****
to Popolani	**.182***	**.300****	**.455*****	.115	.014
to Magnates	–.215	–.184	–.331	–.626***	–.024
to New men	**.433****	**.680*****	.036	–.594***	–.579
Neighborhood:					
Same Gonfalone	**1.268*****	**.956*****	**.483*****	**.614*****	**1.129*****
Same Quarter (excl. gonf.)	**.384*****	–.034	**.270****	**.457*****	.327
Social Class:					
Both Popolani	–.168	.018	–.099	–.028	**.883****
Both Magnates	–2.515***	**.235**	.315	–1.092***	**1.240***
Between Pop. & Magnates	–.317*	.113	–1.377***	**.703*****	**1.006****
Between Pop. & New men	–1.409***	–.446**	–.545***	–.600***	.288
Both New men	–1.293***	–.176	–.695***	**.422****	**2.343*****
Both New-new men			–.256	.211	.577
Political Offices:					
Priorate	–.100	**.388****	**.340*****	.124	–.138
Cambio Consuls	**.414*****	–.388***	–.348***	.008	.068
Mercanzia	–.528**	–.722***	–.146	–.068	.025
Balia 1378		.004	.152	.014	
Balia 1382		.353	–.198	.213	
Reggimento 1382		.181	.136	.016	
Balia 1384		.128	**.181***	.087	
Balia 1393			**.384*****	**.286****	
Reggimento 1393			**.369*****	**.200***	
Political Factions:					
Albizzi	–.435*	**.762*****	–.116	–.964**	
Ricci	.145	**.874*****	–.841**	–.552*	
Anti-Ciompi		.113	–.327*	.152	
Pro-Ciompi		.074	–.049	–.181	

Logit coefficients:	1348–62	1363–76	1380–89	1390–99	1427
Albizzeans					−.037
Mediceans					−.161
Log likelihood	−3837.6	−2340.1	−3546.9	−4332.2	−628.3
# observations (dyad-year)	81,535	36,688	75,288	97,060	12,430
L.R. chi^2	3044.4	1306.1	1605.3	2173.6	349.0
prob > chi^2	.000	.000	.000	.000	.000
pseudo R^2	.284	.218	.185	.201	.217

*** = (p < .001); ** = (p < .01); * = (p < .05); (*) = (p < .06)

Notes:

(1) The (0/1) logit dependent variable equaled one if the dyadic partnership actually formed sometime in the time period in question, and it equaled zero if the dyadic partnership was possible but never formed in the time period in question. The universe of "possible partnerships" was constructed by dyadically crossing all cambio bankers who were observed to have been active as partners in the industry, solo or with somebody, during the time period in question.

(2) Only those marriages and political offices with dates prior to the last date of the logit regressions (i.e., 1362, 1376, 1399, 1427, respectively) were included in estimations.

(3) "Patrilineage intermarriage" was calculated on basis of existence of at least one intermarriage between patrilineages (excluding a direct nuclear in-law) in the 30 years prior to last date of regressions.

(4) Political offices, factions, and marriages with social class were coded as (0/1/2), depending on the number of partners in the category in question.

Sources: See citations in table 6.2.

the shorter observable time period of 1385–99 to 1427. These results confirm the gradual decline of natal family as an organizing principle of economic partnership throughout the early Renaissance, just as Goldthwaite (1968) has argued. On the other hand, these results also confirm the historical continuity of patrilineage in early Renaissance Florence, as Kent (1977) has counter-argued. Both historians were correct in their assessments; they just emphasized different sides of the late-medieval kinship transition. "Family" did not go away in importance in Renaissance Florence; rather its economic role changed. The medieval dominance of the patrilineal father–son relation became supplemented, to some degree supplanted, by early Renaissance economic relationships among in-laws. More specifically in the kinship history of Florentine elite families, the *consorteria* horizontal solidarity of medieval families, rooted primarily in factional feuds, land, and the military (Lansing 1991), evolved into more internally differentiated Renaissance patrilineages, with sharp wealth distinctions between senior and cadet

Table 6.7 Political and Social Embedding of Merchant-Banker Partnerships

Logit coefficients:	**Alberti 1348–58**	**Pisa 1369**	**Datini 1385–99**	**Catasto 1427**
Patrilineage:				
Nuclear family			**5.138*****	**3.865*****
Patrilineage (excl. nuclear)			**3.591*****	**2.058*****
Marriage:				
In-law partners			[−∞]	**2.395***
Patrilineage inter-marriages			[−∞]	**.682****
to Popolani			.056	−.152
to Magnate			−.229	−.327
to New Men			−.753	−.391
Neighborhood:				
Same Gonfalone			**.970(*)**	−.264
Same Quarter (excl. gonfalone)			.193	**.619****
Social Class:				
Both Popolani			.118	−.080
Both Magnates			.226	−.670
Between Pop. & Mag.			−1.337	.319
Between Pop. & New men			[−∞]	[−∞]
Both New men			.417	[no cases]
Both New-new men			[−∞]	1.485
Political Offices:				
Priorate			.347	−.161
Calimala Consuls			−0.699	**1.006***
Mercanzia			−.997	−.205
Balia 1378			[collinear]	
Balia 1382			.426	
Reggimento 1382			−.183	
Balia 1384			.073	
Balia 1393			−.595	
Reggimento 1393			.534	
Political Factions:				
Albizzi			.836	
Ricci			2.621	
Anti-Ciompi			1.127	
Pro-Ciompi			−1.478	
Albizzeans				.130
Mediceans				.268
Log likelihood	[insufficient	[insufficient	−275.1	−623.2
# observations (dyads)	data]	data]	13,366	7,260

Logit coefficients:	Alberti 1348–58	Pisa 1369	Datini 1385–99	Catasto 1427
L.R. chi^2			185.7	199
prob > chi^2			.000	.000
pseudo R^2			.252	.138

*** = (p < .001); ** = (p < .01); * = (p < .05); (*) = (p < .06)

Notes:

(1) The (0/1) logit dependent variable equaled one if the dyadic partnership actually formed sometime in the time period in question, and it equaled zero if the dyadic partnership was possible but never formed in the time period in question. The universe of "possible partnerships" was constructed by dyadically crossing all international merchant-bankers who were observed to have been active as partners in the industry, solo or with somebody, during the time period in question.

(2) Only those marriages and political offices with dates prior to the last date of the logit regressions (i.e., 1362, 1376, 1399, 1427, respectively) were included in estimations.

(3) "Patrilineage intermarriage" was calculated on basis of existence of at least one intermarriage between patrilineages (excluding a direct nuclear in-law) in the 30 years prior to last date of regressions.

(4) Political offices, factions, and marriages with social class were coded as (0/1/2), depending on the number of partners in the category in question.

(5) [−∞] means "independent variable = 1 predicts partnership = 0 perfectly," so variable dropped from logit regression.

Sources: See citations in table 6.2.

branches and with diffuse and negotiable membership boundaries (Herlihy 1985b, Fabbri 1991, Molho 1994). Economic evolution and kinship evolution were linked.

Thirdly, examination of the coefficients for neighborhood in table 6.6 reveals the following temporal pattern: Statistically significant effects of residence-in-same *gonfalone* on cambio partnerships declined and then rose in magnitude over time. These results are consistent with Kent and Kent (1981) and Kent (1987), who argued for the general importance of neighborhood in structuring sociality of all kinds in Renaissance Florence, at the level of the 16 *gonfaloni* or administrative wards in the city. But they also are more specifically consistent with the overall thesis of the dissolution of guild, rooted in neighborhood, and then the consolidation of clientage, also rooted in neighborhood but in a different way. Like family, neighborhood never went away in its structuring impact in Renaissance Florence; rather its specific catalytic relationship with economic networks was reconfigured. Before the Ciompi Revolt, guild brought cross-class neighbors together in banking partnership through the social model of master and apprentice.

After Ciompi, clientage brought cross-class neighbors together somewhat in banking partnership, but even more so in credit (Padgett and McLean 2011), through the social model of patron and client.

On the core issue of the increasing social embeddedness of economic partnership in marriage, there are two modalities of marriage embeddedness presented in each of these tables: (a) the intermarriage of the partners themselves, either at the level of their nuclear families or at the level of their patrilineage families, and (b) the marriages of partners into various social classes, elite or otherwise. The logic of the first modality is multiplexity: namely, intermarriage with one's partner meant that economic and in-law kinship roles were mixed, with normative framing consequences for each of those roles. The logic of the second modality is access: namely, marriage to popolani meant that businessmen and their companies had kinship access into socially elite and usually politically powerful families, whether or not they themselves were elite.

The simplest message about marriage in these tables is that both forms of partnership embeddedness in marriage increased after the Ciompi Revolt. But there was a difference in the fate of these two marriage influences after the 1380–89 period of partnership-system invention. Direct multiplexity mattered in all periods from 1380 onward. For this reason, the economic logic of partnership, and the social logic of marriage between, became intertwined in how partners viewed each other.

But on the second dimension of marriage, access into the popolani social elite, that was crucial during the 1380–89 period of invention, faded from statistical significance thereafter. During the invention period of 1380–89, cambio-banker founders were diverse in social-class backgrounds, consistent with their roots in the guilds. It did not matter whether cambio bankers were themselves popolani; what mattered was whether they had married into the popolani elite. After the founding generation had passed, however, bankers of more prestigious popolani social-class backgrounds took over these new central economic roles. New-men cambio bankers involved in innovative partnership systems were either absorbed through marriage into the newly reconfigured elite or they were pushed aside (Padgett 2010).

All of these marriage results are far more muted for international merchants. Only in 1427 do the two direct intermarriage coefficients in table 6.7 for international merchant partnerships achieve statistical significance. And never is *parentado* marriage into the popolani important for international merchants forming partnerships among themselves.

Consistently, the pattern here is of deeply socially embedded cambio bankers linking up with relatively unembedded international merchants to form partnership systems. Cambio bankers, being physically resident in Florence, were more connected into (and presumably more constrained by) their social and political contexts than were Florentine international merchants, who lived much of their active business lives abroad. To put this another way, in the period after the Ciompi Revolt, residentially domestic bankers, newly connected to international merchants through partnership systems, helped to broker those sometimes new merchants into the dense social-network structure of their own Florence back home.

This increased correlation between partnership and marriage has the testable corollary that the economic value of marriage should increase. Chabod (1995, 103) provides information on average Florentine dowry prices over time, among families established enough to write surviving *ricordanzi* or private diaries. Consistent with the time series that we expect, the average price of the Florentine dowry reported by Chabod rose from 592 florins (n = 18) in 1314–1349, to 845 florins (n = 24) in 1350–1399, to 925 florins (n = 54) in 1400–1449, to 954 florins (n = 35) in 1450–1499. This rise in the value of dowries eventually became so strong that money circulating among elite families through daughters came to be central in the maintenance of patrilineage economic position within the elite (Molho 1994).

The post-Ciompi fusion of cambio bankers into the popolani elite therefore had two consequences for the changing the Renaissance meaning of banking partnership. In the first transposition-plus-refunctionality stage, political mobilization brought master–apprentice logic out of the guild world into the international domain to produce partnership systems, as has already been discussed. But in the second network-catalysis stage, social incorporation of cambio bankers into the popolani elite brought the logic of marriage, and hence dowry, out of the world of popolani kinship into banking, reinforcing and rewiring the social embedding of banking partnerships into the elite. Dowries became used as start-up capital (Brucker 1968, 114, 121). And marriage logic applied to partnership reinforced industrial diversification: One's son-in-law was often in a different occupation from oneself. Once economic partnership became correlated with and symbolically framed as marriage, it took on the normative overtones and the catalytic reproductive support of the older popolani and magnate elites who embraced it.

This second causal stage of catalysis-through-embedding-in-marriage also fits neatly into the temporal history of the oligarchic reaction to the Ciompi Revolt, just as did the first causal stage of transposition-and-refunctionality-through-co-optation. In 1382, consensus-oriented major-guildsmen moderates reached out to their "right" of patrician exiles by inviting everyone home, and also to their "left" of new men through relatively open electoral access, as well as to the "center" of cambio bankers through direct mobilization. It was primarily rapprochement with conservatives, culminating in the rise of Maso degli Albizzi in 1393, that lead to the renewed "oligarchic" political dominance of the popolani. Consistent with what Baron (1966), Molho (1968b), Witt (1976) and Najemy (1982) have argued, however, this popolani oligarchic dominance was not achieved through methods of exclusion. It was achieved through methods of political, economic, and kinship co-optation. This turned non-popolani families mentally and behaviorally into popolani "wannabes."

Whether the leaders of the 1382 regime were as foresighted and strategic as our narrative makes them appear is doubtful. Unlike Cosimo de' Medici in 1434, a couple of generations later (Padgett and Ansell 1993), the almost forgotten 1382 moderates are not among the most famous and celebrated names in Florentine history. Just because they achieved lasting success does not imply that they were unusually clever. More plausible than rational choice as micro-decisional foundation is learning—in which intelligent but adaptive agents are channeled by events into adopting a new perspective that redefines their own rationality (March 1999). Cosimo de' Medici appears both to us and to contemporaries like a genius because the same historical forces that produced him also constructed a glorified political position or stage for him far above that of other men (Brown 1961). The 1382 moderates in contrast are forgotten because they knit together a "consensual" republican regime in which many citizens had at least the illusion of access and influence. Both Cosimo de' Medici and the 1382 moderates were equally inventors—products of their time who changed their time. That they did so was not because they were superior in cognitive abilities, intelligent though no doubt they were. What they shared in common instead was the more profound perspicacity to observe the ways that others were moving tumultuously around them well enough to blend those others' biographies into reproducing sequences that can be called careers (chapter 4, this volume). New self-reproducing biographical sequences, in turn, induce new perspectives and goals in those shaped by them.

No greater testament to the achievement of the 1382 elite moderates can be made than to point to the speeds of the ideological demise of deeply entrenched medieval loyalty to the pope and of the subsequent rise of civic-humanist republicanism to take its place (Baron 1966). The 1382 moderates did not themselves make the intellectual revolution of the Renaissance. But they altered the social-network feedbacks in Florentine history enough to make that intellectual cascade appear to be almost inevitable in hindsight.

Economic Consequences: The Evolution of Banking

Most banks today are shining lobbies and offices, temples to modernism and the capitalist spirit. Renaissance banks did not look like this of course. They too had their *palazzi* (Goldthwaite 1972), from which modern bank lobbies are descended, but they were smaller and more intimate in physical and manpower size. In spite of this difference, however, Renaissance banks also epitomized, indeed they were central in inventing, financial capitalism—namely, partnership systems, limited liability, double-entry bookkeeping and current accounts. The historiographical puzzle is the one that opened this article: How could such a traditionalist time and place, not motivated to innovate, nonetheless have invented so prolifically? In particular, how did it invent financial capitalism? The political context of the Ciompi Revolt and the post-Ciompi homology between partnership and marriage have taken us a considerable way toward understanding the changing Renaissance meaning of the partnership company. Now I show how this change in partnership logic transformed the banks internally.

Melis (1962) and de Roover (1966) have already documented at length these organizational changes, of course. In this section I extend their strictly economic inquiry by analyzing this economic transformation more explicitly in its social context. I examine banks not as disaggregated sets of businessmen dyads, as in the logit regressions of the previous section, but rather holistically as coherent collective actors. In particular, I demonstrate transformation in the role of the lead banker from guild entrepreneur to partnership-system financier. Closely connected with the partnership system were important changes at the level of transactional practice—namely, widespread adoption of double-entry bookkeeping, current accounts, and economic credit. Together these organizational changes in partnership and credit transformed international banking and finance. But that subsequent diffusion is a story for another time.

Bookkeeping

At the level of bookkeeping, *conti correnti* or current accounts registered repeat relational trading based on credit. These spread rapidly among Florentine bankers after 1380. *Conti di esercizio*, which emerged at about this same time (Melis [1972] 1987, Dini 2001), were a similar bookkeeping device for registering credit between bankers and manufacturers. Double-entry bookkeeping as an algorithm, which for the first time permitted an integrated calculation of assets, debts, and profit, was invented decades earlier, perhaps in Genoa, perhaps in Tuscany. But in Florence this technique diffused widely only after 1380 (de Roover [1956] 1974, xxx). Bilateral or *contrapposto* format was a visualization of current accounts in Florentine bankers' account books: namely, a client's (person or company) debits (*dare*) were listed neatly on the left-side page (*verso*) of the company's account book and the client's credits (*avere*) were listed on the right-side facing page (*recto*) of the same account book. With bilateral format, businessmen could see easily the state of each of their various economic relationships at a glance, laid out for them neatly on the pages. This is in contrast with earlier chronological listings of transactions, with complex cross-referencing to how these were cleared. And it is in contrast with the earlier clustering of debits in the first half of an account book and credits in the second half, again with complex transactional cross-referencing to how these were cleared (de Roover [1956] 1974). Bilateral format categorized transactions into economic relations, whereas earlier methods (including notarized contracts) coded transactions just as transactions. This conceptual transformation in business practice from transactional to relational accounting, I argue, was in Florence one corollary of the partnership system.

Piera Morlacchi and Ethel Santacroce have examined 77 Florentine account books located in the Archivio di stato in Florence from the period 1259–1427, in order to trace the emergence of the bilateral format in Florence over time. This sample of account books was drawn from two exhaustive inventories of extant account books compiled by Richard Goldthwaite, namely, Goldthwaite, Settesoldi, and Spallanzani (1995: cxxvii-cxxxii), which covers the years 1211 to 1355, and Goldthwaite (private communication), which covers the years 1363 to 1427. Fifty-one of these account books were *libri di debitori e creditori* (and equivalents like *libri del dare e dell'avere*) company account books from merchant banking, cambio banking, and the wool and silk industries. For comparability, they coded only these books. The full coded dataset, with citations to all qualifying account books, is provided in Morlacchi (2005).

Not double-counting multiple account books in single companies, and the results of this survey were as follows: (a) during 1259–1299, 0/10 = 0% of the companies kept their books in bilateral format or *contrapposto*; (b) during 1300–1349, 0/7 = 0% of the companies were *contrapposto*; (c) during 1350–1377, 0/3 = 0% were *contrapposto*; (d) during 1382–1399, 5/5 = 100% were *contrapposto*; (e) during 1400–1427, 12½/14 = 89% were *contrapposto*. There was a sharp and unambiguous transition to bilateral format in Florentine company account books, exactly around 1382, the date that the partnership system was born.

To verify this apparently causal connection between partnership system and bilateral format more closely, we examined carefully the first Florentine cases of bilateral format that survive: Paliano di Falco and Francesco Datini. Ethel Santacroce transcribed the *ricordi* of Paliano di Falco, the first known Florentine to adopt bilateral format on October 12, 1382. Paliano di Falco was a cambio banker who enrolled in the *Arte del Cambio* in 1369, soon afterward running his own small bank as a solo *cambiatore* in 1370 and in 1371. Paliano next appears in our records, through his *ricordi*, as a Perugia-resident partner within the Florentine partnership system of Giovanni Portinari and Ardingo Ricci, who themselves were Florentine cambio bankers, starting their company in Florence in 1372. The home-office account books of Portinari and Ricci have been lost, but the fact that Paliano initiated bilateral format on exactly the same day on which the partnership in Perugia between Paliano and Ardingo Ricci was formed (A.S.F., *Carte Strozziane*, serie II, 7, p. 4) suggests a linkage between these two adoption events, even though Paliano's *ricordi* was actually a personal, not a company, account book. Paliano does not say so explicitly, but we presume that Paliano's bookkeeping practice conformed with that of his new senior partners. Very telling is the notation *scriverollo alla viniziana* at the outset of Paliano's account book, suggesting that he knew that he was adopting an accounting technique borrowed from the Venetians.

To confirm even further this connection between partnership systems and bilateral-format bookkeeping, Piera Morlacchi consulted many of the account books of Francesco Datini, preserved in the Archivio di Stato in Prato (and hence not part of the previous sample). As hypothesized, Datini's adoption of bilateral format in his bookkeeping procedures coincided perfectly in date with his adoption of the partnership system. Datini did not use bilateral format early in his career, when he ran his unitary trading company in Avignon. Indeed, even after Francesco left that city, his original company of Avignon lagged behind in adopting *contrapposto*, not switching to bilateral format until 1398. Rather, Datini's first adoption of bilateral format and double-entry bookkeeping was in his new Pisa branch in 1383, where Datini initiated his partnership system. Subsequent branches adopted bilateral format as they were founded: in Florence in 1386, in Genoa in 1391, and in Barcelona in 1393.

The final example of the micro-connection between partnership system and bilateral double-entry bookkeeping is Averardo di Francesco de' Medici. A 90-page fragment of Averardo's account book has survived from 1395, two years after Averardo in Florence formed a partnership system with his father Francesco in Genoa. This account book was in bilateral-format double-entry bookkeeping (Ceccherelli 1913).

Therefore, if the account-book survey and the first three known examples of usage are any guides, in Florence the adoption of the partnership system and the adoption of *contrapposto*-format bookkeeping were two sides of the same organizational invention. Florence did not itself invent bilateral-format bookkeeping, but it perceived this accounting technique as facilitating the management of its new partnership system.

My interpretation of the causal linkage is as follows: Bilateral format and double-entry bookkeeping were useful in centrally managing the heterogeneous companies that the partnership system created because bilateral format lumped dense and recurrent flows with clients into easily visible current accounts. Cross-branch, within-system transfers were the densest flows that required such inspection and central approval.

Heavily used current accounts among inside partners and employees existed in older unitary companies and were called *conti interni*. In older Florentine companies, *conti externi* with outside clients were transactionally specific, with little recurrent use (Goldthwaite et al. 1995: cxiii, cxvi). Partnership systems almost tautologically took *conti interni* and turned them into *conti externi*. As such, the logics governing internal transfers became externalized into the domain of inter-company relations, especially as external business relations became more correlated with the enforceable "trust" inherent in Florentine elite structure. Intra-system transfer of credits among branches was the transitional step toward inter-company transfer of credits across systems. As the partnership system diffused, credit protocols, such as current accounts and bilateral format, were standardized and spread rapidly.

Economic Credit

Rather than bookkeeping evolution being an expression of some impersonal and teleological "spirit of capitalism" that left traditionalism behind, à la Weber, current accounts, bilateral formats, and double-entry bookkeeping were the formalization and measurement of deeply personalistic and multivocal relationships, which transcended economics. It is within these relationships themselves, and not in the formal accounting of them, that the secrets of Florentine financial capitalism—namely, merchant trust or *fiducia*, organizational flexibility, and credit liquidity—are to be found.

In Padgett and McLean (2011), which analyzes commercial credits among 406 export-oriented companies in the 1427 *catasto*, we document these claims. Among international merchant-banks, large domestic merchant-banks, and wool and silk manufacturing companies, there developed extensive, deep, and recurrent commercial credit relations, all managed through current accounts in bilateral accounting format. Total credit-to-asset leverage ratios rose to industry averages of 5:1 in the banking sectors. Export-oriented companies routinely extended each other commercial credit, in the course of their repeated business with each other, even without having paid off previous debts. Statistical analysis showed that repeat-business commercial credit relations between companies were highly correlated with personal and political relations between businessmen in different companies. Personal embedding of cross-company commercial ties included relations of kinship and neighborhood, which linked partners in different companies. Political embedding of cross-company commercial ties included participation of businessmen in the elected political office of Priorate or city council. Election to city council, indeed, was like a public certification of one's honor. (The Italian word *onore* means political offices as well as personal honor). This had implications for the credit-worthiness of one's company as well as for the marriage-worthiness of one's daughter.

Sophisticated account books may look to insufficiently knowledgeable observers as the epitome of an impersonal mathematical measurement that abolishes personal favoritism. The Florentines knew better. Underneath their dry account-book entries was a rich social-network world full of dense knowledge about each other (McLean 1998, 2007). Clients were not strangers or automatons to whom businessmen were "objectively" loaning money and goods. Florentine businessmen knew tons about each other, beyond what was written in their books. This personalism behind the account books was not a marginal aspect, on the edges of impersonal markets. The densest and most high-volume flows of Florentine commercial credit and business coursed through personal and political ties, precisely measured and documented in bilateral current accounts.

From Entrepreneur to Financier

For the remainder of this chapter, I focus on data from the annual census of cambio-bank partnerships, administered by the Florentine banking guild (A.S.F., *Arte del Cambio* 11, 14), as a regulatory check on usury. The full registration of such banks is heterogeneous in nature—ranging from individual money changers, to domestic deposit banks, to international merchant-banks, to headquarters of partnership systems. But this was the soil out of which partnership systems first emerged. With these data I can demonstrate, with a temporal precision not possible for other industries, changing organizational form at the level of individual component companies, not just of ensembles of companies. In particular in this section, I document organizational change in the role of senior partner from entrepreneur to financier, before and after the Ciompi Revolt. In the next section, I show how guild and family principles fused into a mixed-kinship form of cambio banks after Ciompi.

Figure 6.2 sets the stage. Immediately after the suppression of the Ciompi Revolt, there was a dramatic growth in the demographic representation in cambio banking of partners with popolani social-class backgrounds. Other social classes were not purged, but popolani families captured almost all of the successful post-Ciompi economic rebound in banking after the war with the pope. All of this was achieved through partnership systems. The disproportionate social-class character of this rise is consistent with the political-mobilization and social-incorporation mechanisms already

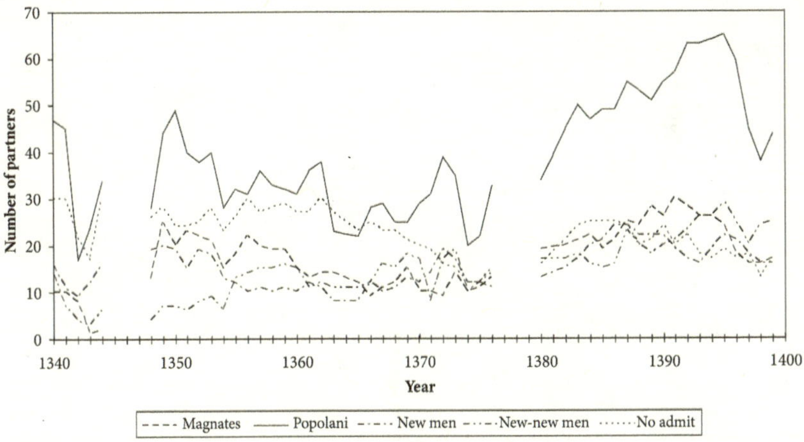

Figure 6.2 Number of Cambio Bankers, by Social Class, in the Fourteenth Century

identified. These popolani bankers were men like Vieri di Cambio de' Medici—located physically in Florence, deeply involved in politics, simultaneously building internationally oriented partnership systems and transforming their cambio banks into the headquarters of those partnership systems. In the original transposition-and-refunctionality stage of organizational innovation, the inventors of partnership systems were not all popolani, but in the catalysis stage of organizational reproduction, cambio bankers with popolani social-class backgrounds took over.

Table 6.8 presents a cross-tabulation of these 1348–1399 cambio-bankers, arranged into partners and subdivided by social class, where the partnership dyad is ordered by relative experience in banking. That is, the rows contain the more senior partner, as defined by years of active experience in the industry, and the columns contain the more junior partner, defined the same way. Only nonfamily partnerships (including nonfamily components of mixed-kinship companies) are sensible to cross-tabulate in this manner because partners within families are, by definition, within the same social class. A simple graphical device is presented on the right-hand side of the cross-tabulation to help the reader quickly see the asymmetries in this table.

Before the Ciompi Revolt nonfamily cambio-banking partnerships were organized according to the master–apprentice guild logic. In the context of this table, this means that relative experience and relative social prestige were, in the aggregate, highly correlated. A junior partner of lower social class would "apprentice" himself with no status difficulty to a senior partner

Table 6.8 Relative Experience of Nonfamily Cambio-Banking Partners (Including Nonfamily Subset of Mixed Companies)

1348–1376:

	Less Experience in Cambio Banking:						**%MExp.>**		**Less Experience:**					
More	**P**	**NM**	**NNM**	**M**	**ND**	**Total**	**LExp.**	**More**	**P**	**NM**	**NNM**	**M**	**ND**	**Total**
Experience:								Experience:						
Popolani	191	49	56	78	157	531	+.424	Popolani	0	+	+	++	++	+++
New Men	36	13	17	45	52	163	+.716	New Men	–	0	+	+	+	++
N.N. Men	38	4	52	22	40	156	+.083	N.N. Men	–	–	0	+	+	+
Magnates	27	6	12	26	60	131	–.388	Magnates	– –	–	–	0	+	– –
No Date	81	23	7	43	100	254	–.379	No Date	– –	–	–	–	0	– – –
Total	373	95	144	214	409	1235		Total	– – –	– –	–	++	+++	

1380–1399:

	Less Experience in Cambio Banking:						%MExp.>		Less Experience:					
More	M	NM	ND	NNM	Pop.	Total	LExp.	More	M	NM	ND	NNM	Pop.	Total
Experience:								Experience:						
Magnates	13	17	29	18	131	208	+.518	Magnates	0	0	0	0	++	++
New Men	8	16	25	55	65	169	+.174	New Men	0	0	0	+	0	+
No Date	30	22	36	6	99	193	–.045	No Date	0	0	0	0	0	0
N.N. Men	17	27	15	24	82	165	–.098	N.N. Men	0	–	0	0	0	–
Popolani	69	62	97	80	240	548	–.110	Popolani	– –	0	0	0	0	– –
Total	137	144	202	183	616	1283		Total	– –	–	0	+	++	

N.B.:
"+" ≡ [(i,j) – (j,i)] ≥ 10; "++" ≡ [(i,j) – (j,i)] ≥ 50
"–" ≡ [(i,j) – (j,i)] ≤ –10; "– –" ≡ [(i,j) – (j,i)] ≤ –50
Source: A.S.F. *Arte del Cambio* 14.

of higher social class. But junior partners of higher social class never violated (in the aggregate) the Florentine status hierarchy by "apprenticing" themselves to senior partners of lower social status than themselves. Just because banking was based on guild did not mean that bankers were not deeply conscious of status and social class distinctions among themselves. The only exception to this pre-Ciompi "rule" of occupational authority mimicking social-class status was the peculiar position of magnates—high social status within feudal patrilineage logic, but low social status in guild corporatist thinking. All in all, guilds were internally socially stratified, as was all of Florence, but these cross-class partnerships acted as a powerful engine of economic mobility for lower social classes.

After the Ciompi Revolt, in sharp contrast to this guild-based equation of vertical occupational experience with vertical social class, two complementary horizontal layers of class-endogamous "alliances" developed: (a) popolani and magnates were more likely to form banking partnerships with each other than with the middle and the lower social classes, and (b) new men and new-new men were likewise more likely to form cambio-banking partnerships with each other than with upper classes, presumably in response to fewer opportunities extended to them by the upper classes. A two-tiered segmentation of companies within the domestic-banking industry therefore developed—an upper-class tier of popolani and magnates, which integrated international merchant and domestic banking businesses into partnership systems and a middle-class tier of new men and new-new men, which carried on the traditional domestic banking.

The most striking information contained in this table is the inversion of the occupational experience ordering of the popolani, before and after the Ciompi Revolt. In the pre-Ciompi guild logic, high-status popolani were also more occupationally experienced, on average. These were entrepreneurs, founding, owning, and running their own companies. In sharp contrast, after the Ciompi Revolt, popolani actually descended to the bottom of the occupational experience hierarchy. This did not necessarily mean that popolani had fewer years of experience in the industry. But it did mean that, whatever their own experience levels, popolani tended to partner with others of even more experience in the industry than themselves. No more reaching down to youngsters, except perhaps their own kin, in-laws, or clients. Instead they searched out and hired branch-manager partners who really knew the business, and then turned over daily management of that business to them—with close supervision, of course.

This is evidence not just for the evolution of organizational forms but also for the evolution of authority roles. Instead of senior partners doing the daily work themselves they delegated that to branch partners, assuming for themselves the role of investor–supervisor—something roughly akin to the actively monitoring of venture capitalists today (cf. Gompers and Lerner 1999). In addition to measuring clients, account books helped senior partners to keep tabs on their branch managers and to evaluate their relative performances from afar.

In the previous section, I did not mention the negative finding in Padgett and McLean (2011) that social-class was <u>not</u> a statistically significant determinant of commercial credit among companies in 1427. This is in contrast to the strong social-class basis of cambio-bank partnerships, just demonstrated. Putting these two findings together, economic relations across social classes were transposed from guild partnership before the Ciompi Revolt to commercial credit after the Ciompi Revolt. This bears an eerie resemblance to contemporary social-network developments in politics. Especially after the third conservative stage of 1393, victorious political elites closed in on themselves within oligarchic-republican institutions like *balìe*, *mercanzia*, and *consulte e pratiche*, even as they absorbed lower-class supporters into the Priorate through clientage and marriage. In economics, they did something similar—social closure through partnership but social openness through commercial credit. In both the economic and the political domains, elite control was increasingly exercised not directly, but from behind the stage of active daily decision-making by others.

Popolani Mixed-Kinship Banks

How did these mostly popolani cambio bankers reconstruct their Florentine domestic banks to link into and indeed to become central nodes within their partnership systems? Table 6.9 gives over-time data on the differential kinship character of those cambio banks that participated in partnership systems with both international and domestic activities, versus those cambio banks that did not. "Not" means those traditional domestic bankers who maintained their guild roles as deposit bankers and money changers—in the parlance of the day, called *banchieri*, *cambiatori*, or *tavolieri* (LaSoursa 1904, Usher 1943, de la Roncière 1973, Goldthwaite 1985). The first half of table 6.9 subdivides cambio banks (actually partner-years of cambio banks)

Table 6.9 Family Types of Cambio-Banking Partnerships

A. Aggregate percentage distribution:

	Solo	**Family**	**Mixed**	**Nonfamily**	**Total**
1357–1366	.265	.159	.177	.399	1.00
1367–1376	.325	.171	.173	.332	1.00
1380–1389	.275	.153	.190	.382	1.00
1390–1399	.254	.173	.217	.357	1.00
1427	.152	.161	.312	.375	1.00

B. Percentage also in other merchant-banking activities or partnerships:

	Solo	Family	Mixed	Nonfamily	Total
1357–1366	.078	.239	.266	.107	.149
1367–1376	.094	.130	.264	.134	.143
1380–1389	.090	.095	.350	.123	.153
1390–1399	.096	.125	.316	.268	.210
1427	.118	.333	.400	.190	.269

Notes:

1. Unit of analysis is partner-year.
2. "Solo" defined as company with only one owner. "Family" defined as company with all partners in the same nuclear or patrilineage (="same last name") families. "Nonfamily" defined as company with all partners in different families. "Mixed" defined as company with some partners in same family, but also with some other partners from different families.
3. For overlaps of cambio banking with other industries/companies, 1357–66 and 1367–76 periods use "merchant banker" to be 1369 Pisa list—hence the word "activities" in the title. 1380–89 and 1390–99 periods use Melis' Datini list of partnerships. 1427 uses industry = 1,2,3 in catasto. Starting date of 1357 chosen to make 1357–76 period comparable (20 years) to 1380–99 period.

Source: Annual cambio bank censuses, plus 1427 catasto.

into (a) whether the partners all came from the same family (nuclear or patrilineage), (b) whether they all came from different families, (c) whether they came from a mixture of same family and nonfamily backgrounds, or (d) whether the bank had only a single owner. The second half of the table records whether this kinship modality of cambio banks affected participation in international trading, above and beyond normal domestic deposit-bank business.

The message in table 6.9 is the growth in importance, after the Ciompi Revolt, of the mixed-kinship or hybrid type of cambio bank. In raw numbers, the percentage of partner-years involved in the mixed type of cambio bank rose from 17% before Ciompi to 31% in 1427. More important to us, the likelihood of partners in such mixed-form banks engaging in international trading rose from 26% before Ciompi to 40% in 1427. The mixed form was always more likely to engage in international trading than family or nonfamily cambio banks, but this differential grew after Ciompi. The key point is this: At the nodal center of the new partnership systems lay cambio banks that had been restructured, through blending family (patrilineage) and nonfamily (guild) logics, into hybridized economic headquarters.

These internal organizational developments can be illustrated perfectly with the Medici banks. As can be seen in more detail in Padgett and McLean (2006, 1549–50), the original Medici bank of Vieri di Cambio de' Medici started out as a domestic cambio bank, which had been founded in 1349. Before 1380, that successful cambio bank had been built entirely on the basis of nonfamily partnerships with many social classes, in classic guild manner. In 1382 or 1384 for the first time, however, Vieri di Cambio built his partnership system by using his distant nephew (and past apprentice) Francesco di Bicci de' Medici both to diversify internationally into Genoa and to make his domestic bank into mixed-family form. Francesco's brother Giovanni di Bicci soon followed as partner-cum-branch-manager of Vieri's new Rome branch in 1385. After 1382, even the meaning of "nonfamily" partner changed: for example, one of Vieri's domestic banking partners, Niccolò di Riccardo Fagni, married the now late Vieri's sister Cilia in 1399 after her first husband had died.

The timing of these economic system-building moves was not accidental: Vieri was very active in Ciompi and post-Ciompi politics. Like the classic guildsman that he was, Vieri participated heavily in his own *Arte del Cambio* guild, serving as consul seven times before the Ciompi Revolt. Despite his long years of guild service, however, Vieri never attained the exalted levels of the Mercanzia or the Priorate until after the Ciompi Revolt—in 1383 and in 1392, respectively. This institutional elevation was status recognition of Vieri's very active Ciompi and post-Ciompi involvement in the political reconstruction of the republic: Vieri was a member of every one of the reforming *balìe* in our dataset (1378, 1382, 1384, and 1393). Leading up to the Ciompi Revolt, Vieri di Cambio de' Medici had been a conservative leader of the *Parte Guelfa*, clearly aligned with the Albizzi faction and personally involved in anti-Ghibelline persecutions (Brucker 1962, 204, 340, 343n). In spite of his undoubted personal conservatism, Vieri served on the revolutionary 1378 *balía* under the leadership of his firebrand cousin Salvestro d'Alamanno de' Medici (Gherardi [1389] 1876, 505). In reward for this service, the Ciompi regime knighted him in 1378 (Stefani [1385] 1903, 324). Even as late as 1393, artisans in street battles appealed futilely to Vieri, and to his cousin Michele de' Medici, for leadership (Brucker 1977, 141n). This contradictory political behavior by Vieri can only be understood in the context of the cross-cutting social-network position of the Medici family itself (Brucker 1957, Padgett and Ansell 1993). To call Vieri a "political moderate" is too simple, but he clearly operated on both sides of the fence, whatever his own conservative views. His cross-cutting network position pushed Vieri late in life into a position of inventive leadership, both within the republican state and within economic partnership systems.

These points could be illustrated at even greater length by the more famous Medici bank of Giovanni di Bicci and Cosimo di Giovanni, which descended from Vieri di Cambio, but de Roover (1966) has already done that job. The only aspect of that later famous Medici bank, which I would like to highlight here, is their increased reliance on a higher social class of general and branch managers. In the early Medici bank of Vieri di Cambio, only 30% of the nonfamily partners had been either popolani or magnates. In the later Medici bank of Giovanni di Bicci and Cosimo di Giovanni, 64% of the nonfamily partners before 1427 (de Roover 1966, 377–78) were popolani or magnates. In 1413, Cosimo himself married into the Bardi family of his bank's general managers. These changing personnel policies of the two Medici banks were quite consistent with overall trends in Florentine banking during the Albizzean republican era.

This popolani economic behavior of constructing mixed kinship forms of cambio banks at the peak of one's career was consistent, I suggest, with the social behavior of any popolani patriarch—supporting through patronage and generosity one's own kin, in-laws, friends, and neighbors (Klapisch-Zuber 1985, 68–93), in the pursuit of the honor and glory of the patrilineage one leads. This generalized *padrone* role came to be gradually well known within Florentine elite circles during the Renaissance (Alberti [1433] 1971). What was new in this role, right after the Ciompi Revolt, was the combination of this behavior from the kinship domain with behavior in the economic domain, thereby displacing the previously dominant role of guild master. First, the cross-network relationship between banking and politics was rewired, and then the cross-network relationship between banking and kinship was rewired, locking in the first so tightly that it operated almost automatically. To be a calculating merchant and to be a generous patriarch-patron were no longer so distinct: A merchant was a patron, and a patron was a merchant.

Open Elite?

Throughout this study and throughout the historiography on the Florentine Renaissance, there has lurked the recurrent interpretative dilemma of oligarchy versus republicanism. On the one hand, there is plenty of evidence to support the oligarchic interpretation: After the Ciompi Revolt, popolani elites took over back-stage political institutions, even as they opened up elections to city council. Clientage was the new method of elite control over the Priorate. And economically, socially elite popolani families moved into a position of dominance over newly created partnership systems, even though those systems distributed commercial credit widely. It is easy to see the force of Najemy's resolution of this interpretative dilemma: namely, that republican "consensus" was a sham to legitimate reconsolidated elite domination. My economic data on partnership, indeed, support Najemy's (and Molho's) views.

On the other hand, on balance I lean more toward the republican interpretation. How can that possibly be? Padgett (2010) presented extensive data to show not only that, across two centuries, popolani families married very widely across social classes but also that their social openness in marriage was at its peak in the supposedly oligarchic period under discussion. Therefore to say that economic and political elites were reorganizing themselves around high-social-status popolani marriage (a true statement) is not to say that these elites were exclusionary in the core networks that constituted themselves. Political and social co-optation was not a sham. It reorganized the very elites doing the co-opting. The openness of Florentine elite families to organizational and social-network change was the secret to their resilience across tumultuous history. Out of conservative motivations, they adjusted their networks, thereby unintentionally reconstituting themselves.

Padgett (2010) also presented data on the consequences of political and economic co-optation for Florentine kinship. Over two centuries, generations of Florentine middle-class *parvenu* mimicked and absorbed the patrilineage kinship model of their social superiors, thereby extending the social reach of this patriarchal ideal. During the same time, however, the magnate citadel of this patrilineage model of kinship collapsed. The Florentine middle classes, in other words, increasingly imitated an upper-class kinship ideal that no longer existed in fact. It was not so much the popolani elite that emerged victorious, it was the popolani ideal that emerged victorious, widely shared by many who aspired to it.

"Republicanism" is open; "oligarchy" is closed. The Renaissance Florentine resolution to this conceptual contradiction, I suggest, was a politically and socially open elite that conceptualized itself as purer and higher than the rest of humanity. It was not only the older popolani elite that found this vision of merchant-plus-citizen-plus-patron (the cultured and generalist "Renaissance man") attractive to walk toward.

All of this system building and political reorganization added up to great wealth for Florentine bankers. Padgett and McLean (2006, 1536) document a progressive increase in the wealth of domestic bankers, relative to upper levels of the population as a whole, from 1351 to 1378 to 1403 to 1427, especially among the upper reaches of bankers, before its decline in 1460 after the period of our study. Coupled with the transformation in multiple social identities which produced this wealth, great wealth for Florentine bankers as individuals also translated into wealth for all those artists and clients whom they now sponsored. Perhaps we need not belabor the point that the artistic inventions traditionally associated with the onset of the Renaissance—e.g., the new linear perspective of Brunelleschi, Masaccio, and Donatello—are dated around 1400, the terminus of the 20-year banking and political consolidation that is analyzed here. The creation of great wealth and social-network patronage are the links between the well-known artistic story of the Renaissance and our own economic–political account (cf. Kent 2000).

Conclusion

Despite the fact that Renaissance Florentines invented financial capitalism and much else that we associate with modernity, we agree with contemporary historians who stress the traditionalist *mentalité* of the era. Florentines were too drenched in concerns with family, marriage, status, and clientage—not to mention the ever looming threat of early mortality (Cohn 2002)—to appear cognitively to be very much like us, even though they frequently did things that were like what we do. Social science efforts to impose modernist models of ourselves on the past do violence to our comprehension of that past. More importantly, they lead us to miss the opportunity to learn what the ancients have to teach us about social science, among other things. Listening to, not testing preconceived ideas about, the past is how to learn.

Vasari ([1550] 1991) and Burckhardt ([1878] 1990) created the concepts of individual genius and Renaissance to explain the remarkable achievements of late medieval Florence. But if we try to listen to the Florentines of the past through systematic sifting of their voluminous records, then we can learn about those achievements' institutional and social-network dimensions, which do not speak straightforwardly to us in words. What those aggregated thousands of archival voices have told us—albeit in our own descriptive language, not in theirs—is transposition, refunctionality, and catalysis. Organizational inventions (as opposed to innovations) are transpositions of relational logics from one domain to another, which attain new purposes in the new domain, whose reproduction is positively reinforced to the point that it alters interactions among others in the new domain. Florentine inventions were more than good ideas. They were discontinuous system tippings, rooted in reproductive feedbacks among dynamic multiple social networks. This process explains how genesis and path-dependence historically go hand-in-hand.

Transposition, refunctionality, and catalysis are "network folding" mechanisms that collectively produce organizational inventions. Important as Renaissance Florence is in its own right, the discovery of these mechanisms is a theoretical contribution beyond even this paradigmatic case because it opens the black boxes of "stochastic process" and "genius," the usual two non-explanations of invention. In biology, life is the self-organization and reproduction of two forms of chemical flow: metabolic flow of food among species within generations, and genetic flow of DNA within species across generations. Speciation is the reorganization and reproduction of these chemical transformations. This article has proposed an analogous perspective on the emergence of actors out of intersections of social-relational flows, within a multiple-network architecture. "Metabolic flow" was operationalized as biographies. Biographies wend through organizations and transform the people flowing through them, usually into reproducing the roles and interests contained within those organizations. Not often but occasionally when catalyzed to do so, biographies and the people flowing along mobility paths tip their own self-regulation and transform themselves. "Genetic flow" was operationalized as organizational reproduction of relational logics. Selection in the multiple domains of markets, politics, and kinship lock in sets of relational logics that catalyze each other, not always optimally, through coevolution. Interdependent "ways of doing things" usually require predictability in inputs and outputs, collectively, to function. But occasionally, the rewiring of old logics into new purposes opens a new trajectory for path-dependent system transition. We look to transformational feedback between interlinked biographies, on the one hand, and the reproduction of relational logics, on the other, to analyze the poisedness of a multiple-network system either to equilibrial lock-in or to organizational tipping and invention.

Specifically, the Florentine invention of the partnership system was a hybridization of the two relational logics of patrilineage and guild through the means of political republicanism. Rechanneling the political biographies of guildsmen, after the guild system had been politically defanged, broke down the previous segregation of patrilineal logic in international business and guild logic in domestic business. And it blended modular guild partnership methods from domestic cambio banking into the patrilineal world of international trade. A decisive system-tipping move into politics (not entirely by choice) was to dramatically increase the number of Florentines eligible for and nominated to political office at the same time as selection procedures for those offices were centralized. The more-or-less direct effect in politics was an explosion of patron-client relations. Organizational change in economics was an indirect effect as the *padrone* role emerged in Florence to influence the partnership and credit logics of the upper tier of business as well. Internal, continued pressure on the patrilineage to differentiate may have been a third consequence, although that was also a long-term trend. All of these interlinked organizational changes were aspects of the emergence of a new style of elite—part businessman, part politician, part patriarch, part intellectual esthete—that we have come to call the Renaissance man. In network terms, we interpret this emergence as an expression of an underlying transformation in the core relational logics of the society from patrilineage and guild to marriage and clientage.

This chapter has focused more on mechanism than on structural preconditions. More research into the earlier period (cf. Brucker 1962, Najemy 1982) is required to uncover the exact topology of the patrilineage-guild ensemble that tipped into the Ciompi Revolt. But even at our current level of understanding, it is clear why Florence had a different evolutionary trajectory than did Vence and Genoa, the two most obvious comparative cases. Namely, even though the relational logic of patrilineage was similar in all three of these cities, the relational logic of guild was strong only in Florence.

Venice and Genoa had their own forms of economic invention, to be sure, but not in international finance or partnership systems. Patrilineage was pervasive everywhere within the elites of northern Italy (Waley 1969), but guild corporatism was politically weak in the comparison cities, depriving those cities of the guild half of the Florentine fusion. Perhaps related to this historical fact, neither city experienced the degree of social mobility-driven political turmoil that Florence did. Venice exhibited great stability in its legally closed aristocracy; hence it was known as the *serenissima* or most serene republic. The corollary in Venetian banking of this almost caste-like political stability was a strict segregation between domestic deposit banking, in which the small number of specialized Rialto bankers excelled, and international banking, which was delegated to the Florentines (Mueller 1997a, 3–32, 255–87). Rich Venetian merchants were shippers and traders (Lane 1967), not mixed-mode merchant-bankers like the Florentines. And Genoa, like Florence before the Black Death, had deep and persistent factional feuds and civil wars based on patrilineage (Hughes 1975a, 1975b, 1977, Epstein 1996). The corollary in Genoese banking of this intra-elite turmoil and distrust was a strong transactionalist focus, with economic actors on both the domestic and the international levels spreading around short-term economic partnerships, investments and accounts among many alters, to cushion risk (Heers 1983, 77–80, 136–141). In coarse-grained contrast to Venice on the one side and to Genoa on the other, post-Ciompi Florence appears to be relational and oligarchic, with porous (because of co-optation) elite boundaries.

Besides the deep interconnection between organizations and elite networks, one final matter about which the Florentines can teach us is the perspectival construction of identity. As developed by Brunelleschi and Masaccio and explained by Alberti ([1435] 1991), visual perception of objects operate through linear perspective, in which the two-dimensional spatial arrangement of objects in a painting are artfully arranged to create the illusion of a third dimension—a line in the painting stretching from a focal-point location on the horizon toward the viewer, which invites the viewer to move into the painting. I believe that the partnership system, with its array of account books at its base, had a similar effect on the perceptions of Florentine businessmen. In a modularized partnership system, the senior owner is both inside (entrepreneur) and above (financier) his array of companies at the same time. The multiplicity of heterogeneous account books that he is forced to manage—keeping track of complex cross-flows of goods, finance, and credit—necessitated systematization and abstraction analogous to the arrangement of space in a linear-perspective painting (cf. Baxandall [1972] 1988). Current accounts, which really were reified people and customers, were arrayed mathematically, with double-entry bookkeeping used to calculate the financial flows and the businessman's own line of movement, called profit. Businessmen always want to make money, in some loose sense, as well as do other things. But the precision involved in "maximization of profits" over multiple streams of transactions is inconceivable without the array of cross-connected account books that lies at the base of the partnership system. In the sense of perception, the account books themselves induced the Florentine businessman to walk into this line of movement. More generally, I conclude that goals are our cognitive perspectives on the trajectories of flows, financial and biographical, to which organizational networks subject us in their processes of reproduction (cf. chapter four, this volume).

I end on this note of appreciation: innovation in the sense of getting someone to try something new is relatively easy. Invention in the sense of getting an entire system to tip into a new trajectory of evolution is extremely hard. Because of this, I salute both the *ciompi* and the forgotten 1382 moderates for the Florentine Renaissance.

7
Economic Credit in Renaissance Florence

Introduction

> It has been rarely remarked how seldom a competitive spirit comes into play in the relations among these [Renaissance Florentine] merchants.[1] The vast correspondence of Datini and of the Medici themselves (the largest collections of business letters to survive before the sixteenth century) yields hardly a hint of competition... However individualistic the Florentine world appears in contrast with the tight corporate structures elsewhere—the Venetian senate, the Hanseatic league, the south-German cartels, the London regulated companies—it was still permeated with something of the spirit of medieval corporatism. This is what the *fiducia* Florentine business historians make so much of really comes down to—that sense of trust in one another that in a way also kept everyone in line.[2]

What were the social and institutional factors that led to, and reinforced, the precocious emergence of Florentine commercial capitalism, especially in the domain of international merchant-banking?[3] The dominant stream of answers, emphasized by economic historians and by economists, focuses

Journal of Modern History 83 (March 2011): 1–47, with Paul McLean. Republished with permission

[1] We would like to acknowledge and thank those who have directly contributed invaluable research labor to this project over the years: Christopher Ansell, Nicoletta Baldini, Skye Bendor-deMoll, Nick Collier, Matteo Columbi, Sasha Goodman, Michael Heaney, Doowan Lee, Peter McMahan, Piera Morlacchi, Pip Pattison, Katalin Prajda, David Sallach, Ethel Santacroce, Douglas White, and Xing Zhong. Paul D. McLean also appreciates the valuable comments of Chip Clarke, Frank Dobbin, Neha Gondal, Ann Mische, and Tom Rudel. John F. Padgett acknowledges the generous financial support of this project from the Santa Fe Institute, the Hewlett foundation, and the National Science Foundation's program on Human and Social Dynamics.

[2] Richard A. Goldthwaite, "The Medici Bank and the World of Florentine Capitalism," *Past and Present* 114 (1987): 3–31, 23–24.

[3] For an overview, see Raymond de Roover, "The Organization of Trade," in *The Cambridge Economic History of Europe*, vol. 3. *Organization and Policies in the Middle Ages* (Cambridge, UK, 1963), 42–118. See also Richard A. Goldthwaite, *The Economy of Renaissance Florence* (Baltimore, 2009).

Organizational Invention in Renaissance Florence. John F. Padgett, Oxford University Press.
 DOI: 10.1093/oso/9780197789216.003.0007

on the invention in late-medieval and Renaissance Italy of a variety of innovative business techniques, such as bills of exchange, double-entry bookkeeping, partnership contracts, and commercial courts. If these impressive organizational inventions are interpreted as facets of a broader rise of efficient impersonal markets, then a tension emerges in Florentine, and indeed in European, historiography between economic historians and the research of social and political historians, who emphasize the deeply personalistic—mainly familial and clientelist—character of social relationships of the period. Were impressive early capitalist business techniques really the signs of a teleological breakthrough of the market from its traditional social shackles, as the master narrative of modernization would have it? Or, instead, were economic relations in the market embedded in, and hence reflective of, trends in the surrounding social and political networks of the time, as anthropologically oriented economic historians have argued?[4] If evidence can be found in support of both propositions, then how are we to reconcile these seemingly contradictory interpretations?

In this article, we address these historical questions through both a statistical analysis of Florentine commercial credit in the early Quattrocento and a documentary study of business correspondence from the same time. Our conclusion will be that commercial credits among Florentine companies were indeed highly correlated with a wide range of noneconomic, social relationships among the partners of these companies. Correlations between economic and social relations were highest in the merchant-banking pinnacle of the Florentine economy—precisely in the industries where reliance upon advanced capitalist business techniques was greatest. New capitalist business techniques did not displace the oligarchic social networks of the time, we argue; rather, they built on and formalized these relationships into markets. In particular, family and neighborhood provided strong traditional foundations to Renaissance Florentine credit markets. In addition, Florentine republicanism—especially through its elected city council—provided the political scaffolding that allowed personalistic social networks, and the economic credit networks built upon them, to "open out" topologically toward expansive liquidity and growth instead of closing inward into cliques and corruption. We identify two mechanisms through which republicanism

[4] See for example, Karl Polanyi, "The Economy as an Instituted Process," in *Trade and Markets in the Early Empires*, ed. Karl Polanyi, Conrad M. Arensberg, and Harry W. Pearson (Glencoe, IL, 1957), 243–69. See also Mark Granovetter, "Economic Action and Social Structure: The Problem of Embeddedness," *American Journal of Sociology* 91 (1985): 481–510.

influenced the emergence of economic credit markets: public certification of reputation (*onore*) through co-optative elections, and the incorporation of carefully filtered newcomers into expansive economic-cum-political networks of exchange.

Causality, however, did not run from social and political networks to economic credit markets only. The logic of accounting and credit infused social and political relations of the time, transforming categorical social distinctions into negotiable gradients of status. The Ciompi Revolt in 1378 fused economic, social, and political networks into a new socially open oligarchic-republican elite that remade not only commercial markets but also political factions and kinship.[5]

Because of these correlations between social and economic ties, Florentine economic credit was built on the social models of friendship and gift-giving reciprocity, and it formalized these in mathematically sophisticated ways. Reputations cleared markets as much as did prices.

We develop this thesis about the structure and operation of the Renaissance Florentine economy through the following steps. After describing our comprehensive quantitative data on commercial credit from the 1427 tax census (*catasto*), we first document the magnitude of reliance on commercial credit among Renaissance Florentine companies in various industries and markets. Next, we analyze these commercial credits statistically in order to measure correlations between business credits and various social and political relations among the partners of paired companies. Finally, we examine a sample of business letters from the period in order to illustrate the cultural *mentalité* through which these statistical effects were produced. Florentine businessmen's frequent use of the language of friendship (*amicizia*) and of honor (*onore*), in their letters to each other, illustrates both how deeply the language of social obligation infused their economic relations and how business credit expanded the range of application of such personalistic mental models well beyond their family and neighborhood origins. We conclude with brief comparisons of Florence to Venice and Genoa and with some implications of this historical research for contemporary economic theory.

[5] John F. Padgett and Paul D. McLean, "Organizational Invention and Elite Transformation: The Birth of the Partnership System in Renaissance Florence," *American Journal of Sociology* 111 (2006): 1463–1568; John F. Padgett and Christopher K. Ansell, "Robust Action and the Rise of the Medici, 1400–1434," *American Journal of Sociology* 98 (1993): 1259–1319; John F. Padgett, "Open Elite? Social Mobility, Marriage and Family in Renaissance Florence, 1282–1494," *Renaissance Quarterly* (Summer 2010): 357–411.

The Industrial Structure of Florentine Commercial Credit

The statistical part of this study is possible because of the 1427 *catasto* or tax census, described at length in the path-breaking book of David Herlihy and Christiane Klapisch-Zuber.[6] Herlihy and Klapisch computerized large portions of this rich archival source and analyzed their data primarily from a demographic and family-history perspective. In addition to the data those authors coded, however, the *catasto* also contains extensive lists of debtors and creditors, with amounts owed, for each household tax return, which McLean has coded.[7] Business *debitori* and *creditori* were included within the household tax return of the lead partner in the company—an indicator of the incomplete separation of personal and business domains in the Florentine world. Such lists of debts existed in the *catasto* because this very innovative taxation procedure systematically assessed taxes on the basis of net wealth—that is, assets minus liabilities. Debts, in other words, were tax deductible. Florentine law required the itemization of outstanding credits as well as debts in order to give tax officials the ability to disallow deductions, if one person's declared debit did not equal the other person's declared credit.

This remarkable breakthrough in public finance was possible only because of the highly commercialized character of Florence's underlying economy. Florentine merchants filled out the business parts of their 1427 tax returns by copying summaries of their account books into their tax declaration, as those account books existed as of the date of the tax submission. Later *catasti* in Florence became notoriously unreliable, but this first *catasto* seems to have been fairly accurate in the financial data it contained.[8] Hence

[6] David Herlihy and Christiane Klapisch-Zuber, *Tuscans and their Families: A Study of the Florentine Catasto of 1427* (New Haven, CT, 1985). The Herlihy-Klapisch dataset is publicly available online at cds.library.brown.edu/projects/catasto/overview.

[7] Archivio di Stato di Firenze (hereafter ASF), *Catasto* 64–85 contain scribal summaries (*campioni*) of all Florentine households' tax declarations in 1427. ASF, *Catasto* 15–63 contain the original tax submissions (*portate*) of the Florentine households. The latter set of documents was consulted whenever the first set of documents did not itemize the entire list of debtors and creditors for any given business.

[8] Historians have often found examples of cheating on Renaissance Florentine tax returns. Most of these refer to *catasti* after the original one in 1427, e.g., Raymond de Roover, *The Rise and Decline of the Medici Bank, 1397–1494* (New York, 1966), 25, 30, 73–74, 99, 236, 312–13; William Caferro, "The Silk Business of Tommaso Spinelli, Fifteenth-Century Florentine Merchant and Papal Banker," *Renaissance Studies* 10 (1996): 421–22. A study that finds truthful reporting in 1427 is Rebecca Emigh, "Loans and Livestock: Comparing Landlords' and Tenants' Declarations from the Catasto of 1427," *The Journal of European Economic History* 25 (1996): 705–23. To sidestep this difficult issue of lying, we analyze below the existence versus nonexistence of a credit, not the reported value of the

the 1427 *catasto* provides a high-resolution snapshot of the credits and debits of the entire Florentine economy at one specific, fleeting moment in time. Virtually all of the account books, out of which this information originally was drawn, subsequently have been lost.[9] This Florentine source therefore is remarkable: No other comparably comprehensive dataset about economic transactions exists for such an early time.[10]

The details of our coding of these *creditori* lists were reported in a previous publication; hence that description will not be repeated here.[11] Both business and personal debts were coded, even though only business debits and credits will be analyzed in this article. The main coding rules relevant to this article were these: Only debts of value greater than or equal to 10 florins were coded, and only debts to other Florentines were coded. An effect of the first coding rule is mostly to exclude artisans from our dataset. An effect of the second coding rule is that trading among Florentines (even when they were resident abroad) is the focus of the dataset, rather than trading between Florentines and foreigners. The joint effect of both constraints is that the data describe, with great richness, the structure of the core export-oriented segment of the Florentine economy as of 1427, including both merchant-bankers and cloth manufacturers.[12]

Within these constraints, coverage is thorough. Numerous passes through the *catasto* were performed in order to code a high percentage of companies'

credit. In addition to the administrative procedure of comparing creditor's and debtor's declarations, tax officials could also request to see legally liable business account books in the case of disputes. While hardly foolproof, these two procedures at least inhibited massive cheating in 1427.

[9] Richard Goldthwaite has brought to our attention three surviving account books, which overlap with our *catasto* summaries of them: those of Andrea Banchi, silk manufacturer; Alamanno di Jacopo Salviati, wool manufacturer; and Lorenzo di Palla Strozzi, merchant-banker.

[10] The only other published study of premodern credit on this scale. One is Philip T. Hoffman, Gilles Postel-Vinay, and Jean-Laurent Rosenthal, *Priceless Markets: The Political Economy of Credit in Paris, 1660–1870* (Chicago, 2000). That study of Parisian bankers covers a period two centuries after ours. Comparison is limited because that is a study of brokered personal lending rather than commercial credit. The most comparable other research, albeit without the equivalent social and political contextual data of ours is a quantitative study of medieval Genoese contracts: Quentin Van Doosselaere, *Commercial Agreements and Social Dynamics in Medieval Genoa* (Cambridge, 2009).

[11] Paul D. McLean and John F. Padgett, "Was Florence a Perfectly Competitive Market? Transactional Evidence from the Renaissance," *Theory and Society* 26 (1997): 209–244. Our full dataset, including both personal and business debts, contains 15,317 debts; the company subset analyzed here contains 4,992 debts.

[12] The export sector was comprised of the following industries: (a) Florentine international merchant-banks resident in non-Tuscan locations; (b) merchant trading companies in Pisa; (c) domestic banks and merchant-banks in Florence; (d) silk manufacturers (*setaiuoli*); (e) wool manufacturers (*lanaiuoli*) in San Martino district (high-quality cloth); (f) wool manufacturers (*lanaiuoli*), other districts (lower-quality cloth); (g) cloth retailers (*ritagliatori*); and (h) cloth dyers (*tintori*). Companies were coded into industries on the basis of their self-identification, their location, and or their primary transactional content.

accounts or *bilanci*. Ultimately, 65.4% of the *bilanci* of active companies in our core industries were coded. Comprehensive coding was least successful for international merchant companies located abroad, for small low-quality wool companies whose accounts were hardest to distinguish the credits from the debits of the household, and for a number of companies who were connected to the export-oriented sector but were not formally located within any of the key industries we targeted.[13] For Florence- and Pisa-based banks, merchants, merchant-banks, silk manufacturing, high-quality wool manufacturing, and cloth-retail companies, the *bilanci* coding rate approached 80%. Debts were coded not among a predefined list of all companies (such a list did not exist until this study) but rather among all companies and people meeting the above standards. As a result of our procedure of coding credits to Florentine companies outside of previously coded *bilanci*, however, even the debits of companies whose accounts were not coded directly often were found indirectly in the credit accounts of coded companies. Because of such cross-referencing, we were able to compile, for the first time, a complete census of companies active in the year 1427. A tabulation of this census, industry by industry, is presented in table 7.1. The detailed list of the companies underlying table 7.1 is publicly available on Padgett's web page (http://home.uchicago.edu/~jpadgett).

We estimate, through procedures explained in an earlier version of this article[14] that 33.4% of the total number of all debits and credits of companies participating in the export-oriented industries of the Florentine economy were finally included in our dataset. Likewise, we estimate that 62.3% of the total monetary value of all debits and credits are included in our dataset.[15]

The first stage in our analysis is descriptive: How important was commercial credit to the Renaissance Florentine economy? In what types of markets and exchanges was credit most used? And what was the ratio of transactional to (multi-transactional) relational credit in various markets?

[13] The compliance of these firms with *catasto* requirements evidently was handled with some flexibility, perhaps due to the special difficulties they faced in preparing and submitting their books for examination in Florence.

[14] John F. Padgett and Paul D. McLean, "Economic and Social Exchange in Renaissance Florence," Santa Fe Institute working paper 02-07-032 (Santa Fe, 2002), 45–46.

[15] Two types of transactions present in our complete dataset are systematically excluded from analysis in this article: credits and debts with artisans and firms working outside the export-oriented economy, and credits and debts with individuals rather than with companies. Had it been possible to calculate the more complete denominator of "all debts and credits among companies in export-oriented industries," percentage coverage would have been higher than the conservative numbers reported here.

Table 7.1 Census of 1427 Companies/Partnerships in Major Industries

	High Certainty Companies			Low Certainty Companies		
	Florence	Overseas	Old	Florence	Overseas	Old
International merchant banks	0	45	7	0	10	2
Pisa merchant trading companies	0	20	1	0	1	0
Domestic banks and merchant banks	53	0	10	12	0	4
Cloth retail	32	3	5	4	1	2
Silk production	38	8	4	11	1	1
Wool production:						
San Martino	36	5	10	2	0	0
Via Maggio	27	0	2	1	0	0
San Pancrazio	8	0	0	0	0	0
San Pier Scheraggio	9	0	1	0	0	0
Unclear location	34	4	9	21	4	4
All wool firms	114	9	22	24	4	4
Cloth dyers	18	0	3	7	0	2
Other industries (partial)						
Fur	6	0	0	4	0	0
Gold	3	0	0	5	0	0
Linaioli	6	0	0	10	1	0
Merciai	6	1	0	5	1	1
Rigattieri	6	2	0	4	0	1
Speziali	11	0	2	1	0	0
Miscellaneous	7	1	5	6	0	1
Unknown industry	9	9	10	110	20	15
Totals	309	98	69	203	39	33

One common way in finance of measuring the magnitude of credit is leverage: the ratio of outstanding debt to assets. The higher the ratio, the more important is credit in the operation of the company. Higher leverage can generate higher profits, but at greater economic risk. "Assets" in the Florentine context primarily means the start-up capital specified in the partnership contract, called *corpo*. Table 7.2 reports leverage so defined, and it

Table 7.2 Capital Structure of 1427 Catasto Companies

	n	corpo1 = *corpo* only	corpo2 = corpo1 + reinv. profit + *sopraccorpo*	corpo3 = corpo2 + inventory
		Average Capital/*Corpo* Size of Companies, in florins:		
Merchant Banks (Int'l. + Pisa)	23	5080	5751	6973
Domestic Banks	24	6375	9941	10119
Cloth Retail	21	4305	5348	7102
Silk Manufacturing	25	3568	3928	4851
Wool Manufacturing (San Martino)	30	3239	3654	4373
Wool Manufacturing (other)	24	2030	2233	2517
Cloth Dyeing	8	1095	1195	1595
		Average Leverage = Σ_i (Total Debt)/Σ_i (Capital):		
Merchant Banks (Int'l. + Pisa)	12	5.42	4.98	3.62
Domestic Banks	14	4.93	3.29	3.20
Cloth Retail	14	2.20	1.66	1.15
Silk Manufacturing	19	0.94	0.86	0.66
Wool Manufacturing (San Martino)	23	1.17	1.04	0.84
Wool Manufacturing (other)	16	0.54	0.48	0.41
Cloth Dyeing	7	2.27	2.03	1.44

also provides two more liberal definitions of assets, which progressively add to *corpo* the partners' reinvestments of past profit and company inventory.[16]

Using the strict definition of leverage, our findings are that Florentine merchant-banks were leveraged on average at 5:1 of their *corpo*, that Florentine cloth retail and dyeing companies were leveraged at a little over 2:1 of their *corpo*, and that Florentine cloth production companies, wool and silk, were leveraged at about 1:1 of their *corpo*. These leverage ratios are not really comparable to modern figures, because modern firms borrow for the most

[16] Fixed-cost assets in this setting were low. Cloth manufacturing occurred in the home through the putting-out system and hence required low assets. Warehouses or *fondaci* were more valuable assets, but even these were not so large as to require depreciation (cost-accounting being an invention of the future).

part from specialized banks, whereas these companies borrowed for the most part from their trading and exchange partners. Nonetheless, the ordering of these ratios is consistent with the known facts that merchant-banks were generally more profitable as personal investments, but also riskier, than were wool and silk production companies.[17] In general, it is fair to say that virtually all Florentine companies, but especially merchant-banks, were highly leveraged and that most of their business was conducted on credit.

On average, larger and wealthier companies operated on higher leverage than did smaller companies. The most extreme example in our dataset was Cosimo de' Medici's bank branch in Rome, which had the highest outstanding debt of any company in Florence, yet its start-up capital was zero, generating a leverage ratio of infinity.[18] Such an extreme case makes it clear that name, reputation, and connections were more central in the generation of commercial credit in fifteenth-century Florence than were economic assets, narrowly defined as security. Without other firms being willing to extend credit to a given firm, that firm could not really be in business at all.[19] Credit, based on reputation, was the mechanism that "kept everyone in line."

Figure A1, available in the appendix of the online version of our *Journal of Modern History* article, presents a computerized visualization of our commercial credit data, using a network visualization program called Pajek. Figure 7.1 visualizes these company-credit data differently, as Leontief input-output flows of credit between and within industries. In particular, figure 7.1 shows observed deviations of credit flows from randomly expected credit flows, the latter calculated on the basis of aggregate volumes of industry credit alone.

Four specific trading patterns are worth highlighting in this global macroeconomic picture of inter-industry credit flow:

a) Credit flow among merchant-banks of all three sorts (Florentine merchant-banks located in foreign countries, Florentine merchant

[17] Federigo Melis, *Aspetti della vita economica medievale: Studi nell'Archivio Datini di Prato* (Siena: 1962), table 69. de Roover, *Rise and Decline of the Medici Bank*, 47, 55, 69. Richard A. Goldthwaite, *Private Wealth in Renaissance Florence* (Princeton, NJ, 1968), 48. Tommaso Spinelli in the second half of the fifteenth century earned profit rates in silk comparable to those among merchant bankers: Philip Jacks and William Caferro, *The Spinelli of Florence: Fortunes of a Renaissance Merchant Family* (University Park, PA, 2001), 78–79.

[18] The rather astonishing total debt figure for this one branch was 158,238 florins. The corresponding total credit figure was 147,987 florins. Cosimo's companies, like others but even more so, relied on massive volumes of two-way turnover and credit flow, organized through a partnership system.

[19] A dramatic example of this will be discussed in quotations below from the diary of Gregorio Dati, one of the successful silk manufacturers in our dataset.

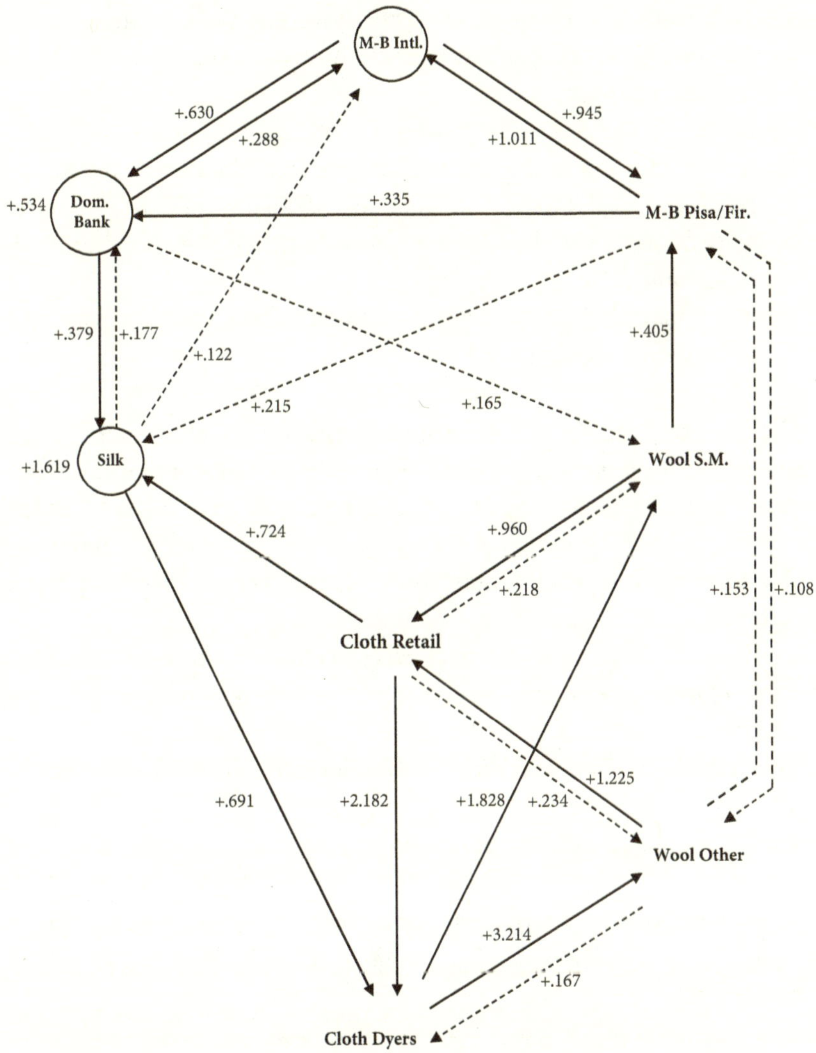

Figure 7.1 Input-Output Volume of Credits Between Industries: Shown if [(Observed Credits – Expected Credits) / (Expected Credits)] > .10

N.B.: [(O–E)/E] controls for raw volume of credit effects. Dotted lines show weaker ratios.

trading companies located in Pisa, and Florentine domestic banks or *tavole*) was enormous. Metaphorically speaking, the merchant-banking sector was a whirlwind of products, bills of exchange, and credits cycling around. This high liquidity was one secret to Florence's economic success.

b) Woolen-cloth consignments, from woolen-cloth manufacturers (*lanaiuoli*), flowed more to local cloth retailers (*ritagliatori*) than to merchant bankers.[20]

c) Silk-cloth consignments, from silk-cloth manufacturers (*setaiuoli*), flowed more to merchant bankers than to local cloth retailers.[21] Reciprocally, *setaiuoli* received a higher flow of credits (including raw silk) from domestic merchant banks, relative to statistical expectation, than did *lanaiuoli*.[22]

d) Silk firms exchanged with and gave credit to each other, whereas wool firms for the most part did not.

Credit pattern *a* in Figure 7.1 documents statistically Goldthwaite's observation in the opening epigraph that Florentine merchant-banks were not an industry of independent firms in competition. They were instead a cooperative banking and trading network *system*, with "competing" merchant-bankers providing much liquidity and business to each other. This is the central economic fact that we seek to understand.[23]

Credit/trade patterns *b–d* reflect recent trends in the early fifteenth-century Florentine economy. The core of the Florentine economy in the fourteenth century had been the finishing, production, and export of woolen cloth. In the late 1200s and early 1300s, Florentine merchant-bankers in

[20] This statement remains true even when recalculated on basis of total florin value, instead of the basis of total numbers of debts. The total monetary value of Wool, San Martino credits to all merchant-banks combined (that is, international merchant-bank plus Pisa merchant plus domestic bank) was 40,592 florins, compared to credits of 58,392 florins to *ritagliatori*. And the total value of Wool, Other credits to all merchant-banks combined was 18,247 florins, compared to credits of 32,260 florins to *ritagliatori*. However, credits sent to international merchant-bankers tended to be larger than those sent to *ritagliatori*.

[21] Merchant-bankers still received roughly twice as much in volume of their cloth input from wool manufacturers as from silk manufacturers. Even though wool was on the decline, and silk on the rise, the older wool industry was still much larger in 1427 than the newer silk industry.

[22] Again, to measure this in terms of monetary value, rather than in terms of numbers of debts, domestic banks gave 33,662 florins of credits to *setaiuoli* in our dataset, whereas they gave 27,080 florins to Wool San Martino *lanaiuoli* and 15,682 florins to Wool Other *lanaiuoli*. As baseline comparison, there were over two-and-a-half times more *lanaiuoli* companies than *setaiuoli* companies in 1427 (see table 7.1).

[23] These data imply economically healthy banking and merchant-banking industries in 1427. This is not inconsistent, however, with a soon-to-come recession in 1430–33 induced by the fiscal crisis caused by war with Lucca. See Raymond de Roover, *Rise and Decline of the Medici Bank*, 230; Anthony Molho, *Florentine Public Finances in the Early Renaissance, 1400–1433* (Cambridge, MA, 1971), 153–63; Elio Conti, *L'imposta diretta a Firenze nel Quattrocento, 1427–1494* (Roma, 1984), 34. The high leverage rates documented in table 7.2 help to explain the vulnerability, of an otherwise healthy economy in 1427, to recession in 1430–33, since exorbitant tax extractions needed to be paid in cash, not in credits.

the *Calimala* guild imported unfinished cloth from Flanders and exported finished and dyed woolen cloth. By the mid-1300s, Florentines were importing raw wool and exporting completely manufactured woolen cloth. Florentine wool production, however, suffered serious and protracted contraction between 1373 and 1437, due primarily to aggressive expansion of woolen-cloth production in England.[24] The raw-material flow of prized English wool, upon which the high-end San Martino segment of woolen cloth production in Florence had depended, diminished, forcing a higher percentage of production of lower-quality woolen cloth, called *garbo*. The San Martino woolen cloth still left was sold both to merchant-bankers—especially those with warehouses in Pisa—and to *ritagliatori*, whereas *garbo* woolen cloth in this period was sold overwhelmingly to *ritagliatori*.[25]

The Florentine merchant community and government, under the political control of the Albizzi oligarchy at the time, responded to this economic crisis by trying aggressively to develop silk-cloth production.[26] The mechanism of this sponsorship was liberal credit and investment from upper-class merchant bankers to new-men silk manufacturers.[27] Woolen-cloth production still exceeded the newer silk-cloth production in total volume and also in total employment, but our data show that this centrally encouraged industrial transformation from wool to silk was well underway in 1427. The credit

[24] Franco Franceschi, *Oltre il "Tumulto": I lavoratori fiorentini dell'Arte della Lana fra Tre e Quattrocento* (Florence, 1993), 13; Hidetoshi Hoshino, *L'Arte della Lana in Firenze nel basso medioevo* (Florence, 1980), 227–31; Sergio Tognetti, *Un'industria di lusso al servizio del grande commercio: il mercato dei drappi serici e della seta nella Firenze del Quattrocento* (Florence, 2002), 16. Debates continue about the causes of this decline, but the argument in the literature that seems the most compelling to us is the rapid growth of English woolen-cloth production in this same period. This deprived Florence of much of its primary input—namely, high-quality English raw wool. Hoshino *L'Arte della Lana*, 233; E. M. Carus-Wilson and Olive Coleman, *England's Export Trade*, 1275–1547 (Oxford, 1963), 122,138.

[25] Eventually when the Ottomans conquered Byzantium, Florentine *garbo* woolen cloth found favor in international trade with the Levant, prompting a recovery in the low end of the wool industry in the second half of the fifteenth century. Hoshino *L'Arte della Lana*, 239–44, 268–75.

[26] Bruno Dini, "L'industria serica in Italia. Secc. XIII–XV," in *La seta in Europa*, Secc. XIII-XX, ed. S. Cavaciocchi (Florence, 1993), 91–123; Franco Franceschi, "Florence and Silk in the Fifteenth Century: The Origins of a Long and Felicitous Union," *Italian History and Culture* 1 (1995), 3–22; Sergio Tognetti, *Un'industria di lusso al servizio del grade commercio*, 11–42.

[27] In 1427, 66.4% of merchant bankers of all types (international, Pisa, and domestic) were upper-class *popolani* or magnates: see Padgett and McLean, "Economic and Social Exchange in Renaissance Florence," 48. Conversely 64.6% of *setaiuoli* were middle and lower class in social background (i.e., new men, new-new men, and never admitted to Priorate). Hence the economic sponsorship of silk manufacturing by merchant-bankers through liberal credit had the social-class overtones of patron–client relations. For comparison, 48.8% of wool manufacturers in 1427 were *popolani* or magnates. For cloth retailers, it was 39.7%, and for cloth dyers it was 14.8%. See also Tognetti, *Un'industria di lusso al servizio del grande commercio*.

mechanisms analyzed in this article help to explain how the Florentine economy successfully adapted to its challenging international situation.[28]

Table 7.3 provides information about the specific goods funded through credits, broken down by aggregated industrial clusters and by transactional versus relational credits, to be explained shortly. Unfortunately, only 11% of our credits had their content or purpose listed in the *catasto*. No doubt all of these purposes were described in detail in the original account books, but there was no tax reason for businessmen or their accountants to copy this text into their summary tax returns. Nonetheless, an 11% sample gives an adequate picture, as long as one is content with coarse-grained resolution.

The modal activities reported in table 7.3 are what any knowledgeable historian would expect. Namely, among merchant-banks, the modal type of credit was the current account (*conto corrente*). In these cases, a single recorded "credit" in the tax returns summarized many underlying business transactions.[29] As per their monikers, merchant-banks engaged in both merchant and banking activity, hence the content of these transactions was diverse. But the primary international banking transaction was the bill of exchange.[30] As such, bills of exchange were transactions, and *conti correnti* were the formalized economic relations containing these and other transactions. Between merchant-banks and other companies, the primary credit activity was trading raw material for cloth on consignment. Banking services also were provided on credit by merchant-bankers to textile producers.

[28] There is a long and contentious literature about whether or not there was a "depression in the Renaissance." One end of the debate was anchored by Robert S. Lopez and H. A. Miskimin, "The Economic Depression of the Renaissance," *Economic History Review* 14 (1962): 408–26. They pointed to the decline of the wool industry, among other things. The other end of the debate was anchored by Carlo M. Cipolla, "Economic Depression of the Renaissance," *Economic History Review* 14 (1962): 519–24, and by Richard A. Goldthwaite, *Wealth and the Demand for Art in Italy, 1300–1600* (Baltimore, MD, 1993), 13–39. They pointed to the rise of the silk industry, among other things. Judicious overviews of this debate are provided by Judith C. Brown, "Prosperity or Hard Times in Renaissance Italy?" *Renaissance Quarterly* 42 (1989): 761–80, and by Franco Franceschi, "The Economy: Work and Wealth," in *Italy in the Age of the Renaissance*, ed. John M. Najemy (Oxford, 2004), 124–44. No study based on a one-year cross-section like this one can resolve a debate about economic trends, but after this article was published, Bettarini and Padgett published a second article in *Journal of Modern History* (2025), reprinted here as chapter 8. We regard the fifteenth-century adaptation of the Florentine economy as a success story in the narrow sense that the silk industry was developed to offset decline in the wool industry. Whether the successful development of silk was quantitatively enough to offset the sharp contraction of wool is a topic we leave to others to decide.

[29] Because of this fact, our statistical summary underrepresents the significance of recurrent transactions funded through credit. When single unreciprocated credits (coded here as "transactional") were current accounts, then "relational" would have been a better linguistic description of that. We could have cleaned up this source of measurement error in our data if content information had been recorded for more than 11% of the credits.

[30] de Roover, *Rise and Decline of the Medici Bank*, 108–141.

Table 7.3 Substantive content of credits (when known)

Relational Credits (1)	Transactional Credits (2)	Specialization of Credits (when two contents known) (3)
A. *Among Merchant Banks and Banks:*		
70 Accounts	17 Accounts	51 Different categories
17 Banking activities	16 Banking activities	21 Similar: Accounts
19 Merchandise	6 Merchandise	45 Similar: Other categories
19 Cloth	6 Cloth	
16 Raw materials	3 Raw materials	
5 Other	4 Other	
B. *Between Merchant Banks and Others:*		
17 Accounts	10 Accounts	5 Different categories
8 Banking activities	27 Banking activities	7 Similar: Accounts
3 Merchandise	4 Merchandise	19 Similar: Other categories
45 Cloth	38 Cloth	
28 Raw materials	52 Raw materials	
0 Other	3 Other	
C. *Among Others:*		
0 Accounts	2 Accounts	0 Different categories
3 Banking activities	4 Banking activities	0 Similar: Accounts
0 Merchandise	1 Merchandise	2 Similar: Other categories
15 Cloth	34 Cloth	
1 Raw materials	14 Raw materials	
0 Other	4 Other	

Note: Merchant banks: Florentine merchant banks resident abroad, Florentine merchant trading companies resident in Pisa, and domestic *cambio* banks resident in Florence. Others: cloth retailers, silk producers, wool producers (San Martino), wool producers (other *conventi*), and cloth dyers. Specialization: contents in similar or different categories, when two contents are known.

Accounts called *conti di esercizio* orchestrated recurrent trade among such trading partners.[31] *Conti di esercizio* between merchant-bankers and textile manufacturers were not as common as were *conti correnti* between merchant-bankers. Among other cloth-producing companies, the modal credit activity was lending raw materials and cloth to each other on a transactional basis.

"Current accounts" and "accounts of use" were the formalized accounting vessels that contained and measured strong economic credit relationships among Florentine companies. Double-entry bookkeeping slowly percolated

[31] Federigo Melis, "La grande conquista trecentesca del 'credito di esercizio' e la tipologia dei suoi strumenti sino al XVI secolo," in *La Banca pisana e le origini della banca moderna*, ed. M. Spallanzani (Firenze, [1972] 1987), 307–24.

throughout northern Italy during the first half of the fourteenth century, but it became widespread in Florence only in the late fourteenth century.[32] Bilateral format in Florentine merchant account books was the physical layout of the account-book pages, debits to a person on one page, credits to the same person on the facing page. It was often associated with double-entry bookkeeping,[33] but the two correlated innovations became widespread in Florence only in the 1380s, precisely in conjunction with the invention and rapid diffusion of the partnership system.[34]

From the point of view of credit, the most significant aspect of bilateral format is its instantiation of the current account, which visually was displayed so neatly in bilateral-format pages.[35] Simplifying a bit, to open up an account book in bilateral format was to place into clear sight the history of writer's own economic relationship with a single person or company.[36] Credits (both monetary amounts and descriptions of content) between the writer and that person or company were listed on one side of the open account book, and debts of the writer with that same person or company on the facing page. Such accounts usually were initiated with an opening deposit or a credit of some sort, but after that initiation a whole series of transactions ensued, with accounting money (not necessarily physical money) flowing both in and out, all registered neatly and precisely in parallel columns.

Earlier more primitive single-entry account books, in contrast, were registers of the writer's transactions, ordered by date irrespective of trading partner, each described in paragraphs with complicated systems of

[32] Raymond de Roover, "The Development of Accounting prior to Luca Pacioli according to the Account Books of Medieval Merchants," in *Business, Banking, and Economic Thought in Late Medieval and Early Modern Europe*, ed. Julius Kirshner (Chicago, [1956] 1974), 143–46.

[33] Double-entry bookkeeping could be done without bilateral format, through an elaborate system of cross-references, but it was more cumbersome to do it that way. de Roover, "The Development of Accounting," 132n2.

[34] For documentation of the timing and rate of bilateral-format accounting diffusion, see Padgett and McLean, "Organizational Invention and Elite Transformation," 1539–42. For example, a fragment of Averardo de' Medici's 1395 account books explicitly states they were being kept "a partita doppia" (A.S.F., *Mediceo avanti il Principato* [hereafter *M.A.P.*] 133). And a fragment of the main ledger of the partnership of Francesco and Niccolò di Simone Tornabuoni from 1425 (A.S.F., *M.A.P.* 84, p. 9) clearly indicates that company's adoption of an accounts-centered organization of their books.

[35] In today's Italian Civil Code (chapter 26, articles 1823–24) *il conto corrente* refers to a contract between two private parties in which no money is exchanged but rather in which reciprocal credits are recorded. We thank Alessandro Lomi for bringing this modern descendent to our attention.

[36] The complication is that there could be more than one account linking the same pair of persons, if multiple start-up deposits or credits were made for whatever reasons.

cross-reference to help figure out whether the credit was ever repaid.[37] To put this accounting development simply: the foundational organizing unit of single-entry bookkeeping was the transaction, while the organizing unit of bilateral double-entry bookkeeping was the economic relationship.[38]

As relational accounts grew to manage business between companies, reliance on transaction-specific contracts declined. *Conti correnti* between merchant-bankers and *conti di esercizio* between merchants and manufacturers were the most advanced technical means in Florence through which economic credits were managed.[39] Essentially, paired companies began to maintain complementary and quasi-permanent "bins" within each other into which their credits and debts could be transferred at will on an ongoing basis. Such networks of open-ended credit involved both partnership systems, with legally separate branches linked through common partners, and separately owned companies who did frequent business with each other, so-called *corrispondenti*. In our section on business letters, we shall have occasion to see *corrispondenti* relations more closely in action.

Anticipating the statistical results of the next section about social embeddedness, we point out here that paired current accounts are not inconsistent in form from reciprocity in anthropological social exchange.[40] Both in primitive social exchange and in the technically sophisticated *conti correnti*, one party offers a "gift" to the other, thereby "making" or constructing that person (or his business), and is repaid not by cash but by reciprocal gifts, which thereby "make" in turn the initiating person (or his business). A credit or loan, in this social-exchange understanding, is just a non-reciprocated

[37] de Roover, *Business, Banking, and Economic Thought*, 121–25.

[38] There was a third transitional form of accounting in which credits were collected in the first half of the account book and debts in the second half, with elaborate cross-referencing between the two halves (de Roover 1974, 132–34). This form permitted double-entry profit calculations without making current accounts the fundamental unit of the system. A good example of this intermediate form is found in the Alberti *libri mastri* of 1348–58, published and analyzed by Richard A. Goldthwaite, Enzo Settesoldi, and Marco Spallanzani eds., *Due libri mastri degli Alberti: una grande compagnia di Calimala, 1348–1358* (Florence, 1995). In particular, "Accounts with other firms or outside persons were opened, for the most part, for single transactions. If later a client presented himself another time, the accountant of the Alberti preferred to open new accounts" (113). Truly ongoing current accounts did exist in the 1348–58 Alberti *libri mastri*, but only for Alberti family members and for company employees (so-called *conti interni*).

[39] At the international level, where different currencies were involved, current accounts could become quite complex, internally differentiating into four separate financial components: *nostro* (our) and *vostro* (your) accounts for each merchant-banking side of the ongoing economic relation.

[40] Marcel Mauss, *The Gift: Forms and Functions of Exchange in Archaic Societies* (New York, [1925] 1967); Alvin Gouldner, "The Norm of Reciprocity," *American Sociological Review* 25 (1960): 161–78. Andrew Strathern, *The Rope of Moka: Big-Men and Ceremonial Exchange in Mount Hagen, New Guinea* (Cambridge, 1971).

gift. Much recurrent business was conducted by Florentine companies in this open-ended gift-exchange manner of reciprocity, without requiring cash, even though of course serious risks of bad debts and cheating were incurred thereby.[41] These economic accounts formalized personal relations, we find, rather than making them impersonal. Economic and social relationships had a strong tendency to bleed into each other in Renaissance Florentine markets.[42]

An important subsidiary message in table 7.3 about exchange content is its diversity. Table 7.3, column 3, tabulates the dispersion of multiple credits across content categories, between specific exchange partners, in those pairs of companies where we were lucky enough to have more than one instance of content reported. With the exception of trading among cloth producers and *ritagliatori*, which was fairly specialized in character, the goods and services exchanged among merchant-banks and between merchant-banks and other companies were remarkably wide ranging in content. In recurrent exchange relationships between Florentine companies, merchant activities, banking activities, and account activities (which really could cover anything: merchandise, bills of exchange, even daughters' dowries) were all mixed up. While distinct in terms of guild membership, upper-tier Florentine companies were not sharply specialized in terms of actual exchange behavior. On the margins, Florentine industries blended into one another, with a single company quite capable of morphing its business into another industry.[43] Such company plasticity, we believe, was a

[41] Hence, "a French satirist, in the fifteenth century, marveled at the ability of the Italians to do business without money. In dealing with them, he said, one never sees or touches any money; all they need to do business is paper, pen, and ink" (de Roover, "Early Accounting Problems of Foreign Exchange," 381). Goldthwaite, *The Economy of Renaissance Florence*, chapter 6 discusses the use of "offset" among private Florentine individuals, as a form of "banking" outside of banks, without making any reference to anthropological social exchange. We thank Richard Goldthwaite for prepublication access to this impressively broad and deeply researched work, the capstone of a brilliant career. We would add that "offset" (or as we would say "relational credit") behavior was characteristic of the core of Florentine merchant banking as well as of Florentines as private citizens. That the same lending behavior was characteristic both of businesses in markets and of private people in their friendships reinforces our point about the homology between capitalist business *corrispondenti* and social exchange.

[42] The converse of economic logic bleeding into the social domain is evident in the famous Florentine family diaries or *ricordanze*, which often tell the narrative history of a family within the format of that family's account books. These *ricordanze* described personal events, and sometimes even feelings, mixed together with money matters.

[43] Three well documented examples of company plasticity are these:

(a) On the subject of domestic banks, Sergio Tognetti usefully has corrected one of Raymond de Roover's few mistakes. Sergio Tognetti, "L'attività di banca locale di una grande compagnia fiorentina del XV secolo," *Archivio Storico Italiano* 155 (1997): 595–648. de Roover

macro-industrial-structure consequence of the generalist social exchange instantiated (and precisely measured) within *conti correnti* and *conti di esercizio*.

Motivated by our knowledge of current accounts, in table 7.4 we move on to disaggregate overall credit flows into transactional and relational credits. "Relational credits" we define as credits between companies who had more than one cross-sectionally observed credit between them. "Transactional credits," in complement, are those credits between companies who had only one observed credit between them.[44] Relational credits in turn

(1966, 14–15) had argued, very influentially, that Florentine banks were sharply divided into three distinct and unrelated types: *banchi di pegno* (pawnshops), *banchi a minuto* (small domestic banks), and *banchi grossi* (large international banks). de Roover himself studied only the latter. Based on a careful study of the extensive account books of the Cambini bank, Tognetti instead argued that overlap of the latter two types was substantial: International banks frequently had domestic bank branches, and domestic banks frequently were involved in lucrative international business. Our *catasto* data, based on 100% of the banks extant in 1427, strongly supports the position of Tognetti. On the other hand, Goldthwaite's study of the small Cerchi *banco a minuto* in the 1450s reinforces de Roover's original description. Richard A. Goldthwaite, "Local Banking in Renaissance Florence," *The Journal of European Economic History* 14 (1985): 5–55. The resolution of this confusion is simple: there were two types of "domestic banks," one of which was involved intimately in international business, and one of which was not. Our data on credits to and from the domestic bank industry are dominated by the former type of bank, because those banks were much bigger and more central in the Florentine economy than were the *banchi a minuto*—in 1427, at least.

(b) The fifteenth-century business and career of Andrea Banchi, thoroughly studied by Florence Edler de Roover, is a clear example of this industrial fluidity of Florentine firms: see Florence Edler de Roover, "Andrea Banchi, Florentine Silk Manufacturer and Merchant in the Fifteenth Century," *Studies in Medieval and Renaissance History* 3 (1966): 223–85. Banchi, without any doubt, was a silk manufacturer (*setaiuolo*). Nonetheless, as Banchi went around all over Europe searching for silk-cocoon raw materials to buy and silk cloth to sell, he sometimes was paid in wool or other commodities, of which then he had to dispose (271). Banchi also acted like a banker, giving loans at interest to other *setaiuoli* "competitors" and to merchant-bankers (227).

(c) The Maringhi correspondence (Gertrude Richards (ed.), *Florentine Merchants in the Age of the Medici: Letters and Documents from the Selfridge Collection of Medici Manuscripts* (Cambridge, MA), 1932) similarly has numerous examples of how the core woolen-cloth-for-raw-silk exchange was augmented with all sorts of other goods flowing between the parties: various types of cloth, ribbons, cotton, rugs, pepper, rhubarb, drugs, fox pelts, horses, cheese, sausage, even caviar (the latter four items seeming very close to personal gifts). Indeed, in the Maringhi correspondence, it seems clear that the stronger the personal relationship between the traders, the wider the range of commodities exchanged.

[44] Having only one outstanding debt at a time, of course, does not preclude that debt being part of an iterated sequence of debts, which we cannot measure with cross-sectional data. We can offer one piece of anecdotal evidence from the *catasto* records to support our strong sense that many of our so-called transactional credits were iterated. Parigi di Tommaso Corbinelli's *bilanci* stand out for reporting the dates on which credits were initiated. One entry, a credit he had with the firm of Zanobi di Gherardo Corigiani & Co. for 53 florins, is crossed out and marked *pagato* on May 20. Subsequently, he records a credit with the same firm dated November 14. It is certain, therefore, that these reported relational-credit figures underestimate the true rate, were it possible to include repeat business in our operational definition of relational exchange.

Table 7.4 Volume of Credits: Relations vs. Transactions

(a) *Reciprocal Credits:*

creditor companies:	debtor companies: Banks	All Other Companies	Total
Banks	427/953 = .448	117/749 = .156	544/1702 = .320
All Other Companies	115/662 = .174	232/1959 = .118	347/2621 = .132
Total	542/1615 = .336	349/2708 = .129	891/4323 = .206

(b) *Multiple Credits:*

creditor companies:	debtor companies: Banks	All Other Companies	Total
Banks	474/953 = .497	169/749 = .226	643/1702 = .378
All Other Companies	160/662 = .242	400/1959 = .204	560/2621 = .214
Total	634/1615 = .393	569/2708 = .210	1203/4323 = .278

(c) *Relational Credits:*

creditor companies:	debtor companies: Banks	All Other Companies	Total
Banks	601/953 = .631	234/749 = .312	835/1702 = .491
All Other Companies	230/662 = .347	562/1959 = .287	792/2621 = .302
Total	831/1615 = .514	796/2708 = .294	1627/4323 = .376

N.B.: (c) is the union of (a) and (b).
"Banks" equals {Int'l. merchant-banks, Pisa/Flor. m-b, and Domestic Banks}.
"All Other Companies" equals {Cloth Retail, Silk Producers, Wool producers: both San Martino and other conventi, and Cloth Dyers}.

are of two types: (a) reciprocal credits, where credits flowed in both directions, and (b) multiple credits, where more than one outstanding credit existed in a single direction. Reciprocal credits are our observable proxies for *corrispondenti* relationships.[45]

It is not correct to interpret relational credits as "personal" and transactional credits as "impersonal," because any credit at all implies that the creditor knew the debtor at least well enough to judge him creditworthy.

[45] This is a conservative indicator in the sense that stochastically it could happen that *corrispondenti* had only one *conto corrente* outstanding between them at a given moment in time. Reciprocity would have been observed had the observation time been longer.

But relational credits go beyond mere knowledge of creditworthiness to connote a social relationship of trust. "Multiple credits" either means extending to someone a second (or more) credit even before they have paid off their first debt, or it means maintaining multiple accounts with the other. Some sort of trust in the debtor by the creditor seems virtually a prerequisite for this intense a level of repeated and risky lending behavior. It is notable in the Florentine case that such credits flowed back and forth (for example, two credits one way and three credits the other way), without them being aggregated into a net balance (for example, into one net credit owed). Each credit account ultimately had to be cleared separately, even if not necessarily in cash.

Within the high-volume merchant-banking sector, table 7.4 shows that 45% of the credits in our data were reciprocal credits, that 50% were multiple credits, and that 63% were relational credits of either version. Relational exchange, in other words, was fundamental to the operation of Florentine merchant banks.

Between banks and other companies, and among other companies, the proportion of total credits in relational form was not as high as it was among merchant-banks themselves, but it was still substantial. In our data, 33% of the credits between banks and other companies were relational credits, and 29% of the credits among nonbank companies were relational in character.

By these measures, credits within merchant-banking industries were on average more "personal," both in relational-credit style and in embedding in noneconomic social networks (see below), than were credits involving the textile-manufacturing and cloth-retail industries. Relational credit was the nonspecialized social-exchange logic through which the highest volume of Florentine commercial credit flowed, precisely recorded in account books through *conti correnti* and *conti di esercizio*. Regardless of whether credit was relational or transactional, however, commercial credit was crucial to the operation of all advanced sectors of the Renaissance Florentine economy.

Statistical Analysis of Florentine Commercial Credit

Florentine businessmen were not just businessmen. They were also fathers, brothers, neighbors, in-laws, republican officeholders, faction fighters, humanists, and patrons of the arts. The colloquialism "Renaissance man" reflects the Florentine social reality that the intellectual, economic, and political activities of its elite merchant-republicans were remarkably diverse.[46] Among their many activities, the pursuit of business did not necessarily assume first place in their career ambitions or in their biographies. The average number of years that a Florentine banker was actually doing banking was only 8.2 years.[47] Success in business often was a stepping stone toward other elite activities, like becoming a city councilor, an ambassador, a *rentier*, or even an art patron or humanist scholar.[48] Cosimo de' Medici was not unique in this regard. In such a social context, it should come as no surprise that "there is scant reason to expect that Renaissance economic exchanges, occurring within dense and multi-textured social networks, to lack broader cultural meanings shared by other Renaissance exchange systems: gift giving, hospitality, the exchange of greetings, or the exchange of women."[49] The strategic implication of this dense social-network overlap is that "single actions [such as the granting of business credit] are moves in many games at once."[50]

Renaissance Florence was not a large city by modern standards—in 1427, only 37,246 residents.[51] Thus most Florentine businessmen knew much about each other, both in business and outside of business, if only through reputation. Even were a Florentine businessman to desire to withdraw from the inquiring eyes of the social networks around him,[52] reputation and the subsequent flow of business credit and business opportunities would compel him not to, or else he would fail in his business. In this section, we analyze more specifically exactly which social networks were important for which commercial credit behaviors in which industries.

In statistical analyses to follow, the commercial credits already described will become the dependent variables. For social-context independent

[46] Vespasiano da Bisticci, *Renaissance Princes, Popes and Prelates. The Vespasiano Memoirs: Lives of Illustrious Men of the XVth Century* (New York, [ca. 1495] 1963); Jacob Burckhardt, *The Civilization of the Renaissance in Italy* (New York, [1860] 1990).

[47] Data compiled from the annual guild censuses of banks from 1340 to 1399 contained in Archivio di Stato di Firenze [hereafter A.S.F.], *Arte del Cambio* 11, 14.

[48] Lauro Martines, *The Social World of the Florentine Humanists, 1390–1460* (Princeton, NJ, 1963); Goldthwaite, *Private Wealth in Renaissance Florence*; Francis William Kent, *Household and Lineage in Renaissance Florence* (Princeton, NJ, 1977). Gene Brucker, *The Civic World of Early Renaissance Florence* (Princeton, NJ, 1977). Michael Baxandall, *Painting and Experience in Fifteenth-Century Italy* (Oxford, 1988); Padgett and Ansell, "Robust Action"; Jacks and Caferro, *Spinelli of Florence.*

[49] Ronald E. Weissman, *Ritual Brotherhood in Renaissance Florence* (New York, 1982), 35.

[50] Padgett and Ansell, "Robust Action and the Rise of the Medici," 1263.

[51] Herlihy and Klapisch-Zuber, *Tuscans and Their Families*, 56.

[52] As arguably Francesco Datini, the "merchant of Prato," would have liked to have done. Iris Origo, *The Merchant of Prato: Daily Life in a Medieval Italian City* (New York, 1957), 82–83. Richard C. Trexler, *Public Life in Renaissance Florence* (Ithaca, NY, 1980), 134.

variables, Padgett and his assistants have collected and computerized a wide variety of primary- and secondary-source data about the attributes and networks of these businessmen and others:[53] namely, patrilineage,[54] marriage,[55] neighborhood,[56] personal wealth,[57] political office holding,[58]

[53] These data, collected from primary sources over 40 years, were coded for purposes of Padgett's larger research project, which is documenting and studying the coevolution of political, economic, and kinship networks in Florence over two centuries, from 1300 to 1500. Currently in 2025 there are 68,960 Florentines (with last names, necessary to link people across their multiple archival records) in Padgett's ACCESS social-network relational database: 54,728 males and 14,232 females. Padgett gives special thanks to the people cited in the acknowledgments for helping him with this very large task.

[54] Parent-child relations were inferred (a) from last and middle names, since Florentine males took the name of their father as their own middle name: as in Giovanni di Francesco, and (b) from numerous collateral sources of dating information, to resolve ambiguities. This task was complicated by the fact that names are often not consistent across archival sources. Currently in there are 2,369 genealogically linked families in the dataset, each visually displayable into computerized family trees by the network-drawing program Pajek.

[55] Dated marriages were coded from numerous sources, the most important being the 14 volumes of the *Carta dell'Ancisa,* located in the Archivio di Stato in Florence. Pierantonio dell'Ancisa was a seventeenth-century antiquarian who devoted his life to extracting and recording Florentine marriages out of extant dowry contracts. Most of the original dowry contracts, from which dell'Ancisa worked, have now been lost. There are 11,039 marriages in the current Padgett dataset, estimated to comprise about 40–50% of all marriages between 1350 and 1500 of Florentines with last names. See Padgett (2010), "Open Elite?", for data details and statistical analysis of these marriages over time.

[56] Florence was divided administratively into four quarters—Santo Spirito, Santa Croce, Santa Maria Novella, and San Giovanni. Each quarter in turn was subdivided into four *gonfaloni* or wards, making 16 *gonfaloni* in all. Unfortunately, parish information was registered too sporadically in the *catasto* to be useful, there being no official tax reason to do so.

[57] Information on both neighborhood and taxable personal wealth is contained in the 1427 *catasto* itself and is publicly available online at www.cds.library.brown.edu/projects/catasto. In addition to integrating this online dataset into his relational dataset, Padgett and his team have coded and computerized other Florentine tax censuses as well: namely, the 1351 *estimo*, the 1378 *prestanza* (really *estimo*), the 1403 *prestanza*, the 1433 *catasto*, the 1458 *catasto*, the 1480 *catasto*, and the 1495 *decima.* Padgett thanks Sam Cohn for providing him microfilm copies of the 1351 *estimo* and the 1378 *prestanza.* He also thanks Anthony Molho who generously provided the 1480 *catasto* dataset coded by him and Julius Kirshner.

[58] All members of the Priorate or city council from 1282 to 1500 (11,312 members in all) were coded by Padgett from an early eighteenth-century copy of the *Priorista Mariani* (A.S.F., *Manoscritti* 248–252) located at the Newberry Library in Chicago—namely, *Priorista descritto a Tratte riscontro con quello delle riformagioni e con alter scritture publiche.* All members of the Mercanzia or commercial court from 1310 to 1500 (3,316 members in all) were coded by Astorri, McLean, Padgett, and Prajda from the *Fondo della Mercanzia* located in the Archivio di Stato in Florence. Subsequent to our independent coding efforts, the *Tratte* office-holding data coded by David Herlihy before he died became available on the web, thanks to the labors of R. Burr Litchfield and his assistants: www.cds.library.brown.edu/projects/tratte. From these online resources, Xing Zhong has integrated the political offices of *Buonuomini, Gonfalonieri,* and various guild consuls into the Padgett relational dataset. With coding help from Ethel Santacroce and Michael Heaney, the scrutiny votes in the elections of 1382, 1393, and 1411 also have been coded, computerized, and integrated, although these data are not used in this article. All 59,314 speeches from 1349 to 1480 in the *Consulte e Pratiche* advisory council have been itemized and computerized by Katalin Prajda. Analyzing those *Consulte e Pratiche* data will be Padgett's next publication.

voting,[59] social-class membership,[60] and factional affiliation.[61] These data will be used to reconstruct the "dense and multitextured social network" context within which Florentine commercial credit operated.

In an appendix table, available in the online version of this article in the *Journal of Modern History* under Supplemental Materials, we present our full logit-regression statistical analyses of commercial credits among our companies active in 1427, using various social attributes and social networks of the Florentine partners who owned them as independent variables.[62] This analysis was conducted for each market—for example, for the set of all pairings between domestic banks and silk manufacturers or among international merchant banks—and within markets, first for all commercial credits and then subsequently for credits divided into reciprocal-credit and asymmetric-credit subsets. To simplify the presentation, we extract only salient statistically significant coefficients from the more complete appendix table to present in table 7.5. Asterisks in the table refer to degrees of statistical significance.[63] Details on variable construction are presented in the online appendix.

For those readers who do not consult the full logit results in the appendix table, it is important to note that more variables were included in the

[59] Scrutiny votes in 1433, secret to citizens at the time, were recorded in A.S.F., *Tratte* 359 for *Tre Maggiore* public offices.

[60] Social-class background, in the Florentine context, refers to the date of first entry of a patrilineal ancestor to the Priorate, and hence can be reconstructed from Priorate office-holding data, together with family genealogies. Popolani were Florentine patrilineages who first were elected to the Priorate from 1282 to 1342; new men were Florentine patrilineages who first entered the Priorate from 1343 to 1377; new-new men (our label, not theirs) were Florentine patrilineages who first entered the Priorate from 1378 to 1433. Magnates were old "feudal" families specifically prohibited from holding Priorate office in 1292. Carol Lansing, *The Florentine Magnates: Lineage and Faction in a Medieval Commune* (Princeton, NJ, 1991), 239–40. Subsequently, some of the branches of these families were rehabilitated through specific legislation. Christiane Klapisch-Zuber, *Retour à la cité: Les magnats de Florence, 1340–1400* (Paris, 2006), 453–57. The subcategory of "ex-magnates" was created to cope with such rehabilitations. Any Florentine patrilineage not included in the above categories is here labeled "families never admitted to Priorate" (by 1433).

[61] Membership in the 1433–34 Medici and Albizzi political factions, previously analyzed in Padgett and Ansell, "Robust Action and the Rise of the Medici," were originally reconstructed and reported in Dale Kent, *The Rise of the Medici: Faction in Florence, 1426–1434* (Oxford, 1978), 352–57.

[62] A logit regression is a statistical procedure for measuring the effect of a set of independent or "predictor" variables on whether an outcome will occur—in our case, the presence or absence of a credit tie between any given pair of companies. Within this procedure, we controlled for heterogeneity. That means that we used company ID as a fine-grained categorical variable, to control for potentially important missing factors for which we do not have data. The conservative technique makes it more difficult to detect statistical significance, by correcting observed coefficients' estimated standard errors.

[63] In particular, * = ($p \leq .05$); ** = ($p \leq .01$); *** = ($p \leq .001$). The more the asterisks, the greater the statistical certainty.

Table 7.5 Extract of Significant Coefficients from Logit Regressions on Company Credit

Market	Between Partnership Systems	Partnership Systems	Nuclear Family	Patrilineage Family	*Parentado* Family	Gonfalone	Priorate	Scrutiny (1433)	Political Factions
All credits (dichotomous):									
International m-b/silk				3.128**				.00225**	M: 5.943***
International m-b/wool			5.534***						A: 2.905***
International m-b		6.496***	3.662**	2.721***					
Domestic bank/Intl. m-b		6.945**			1.822*	1.374***	2.118***		M: 2.305***
Domestic bank		5.291*	4.268*	1.974**		1.486***	1.471***		
Domestic bank/wool						.635*		.00165**	
Domestic bank/silk						1.071***			
Silk			5.571**						
Wool		13.726***	3.288*						
Ritagliatori/wool									
Ritagliatori		15.455**							
Ritagliatori/silk									
Reciprocal credits:									
International merchant/silk				8.064**	2.559**				M: 6.380*
International merchant/wool			22.105***	14.774***	5.633**			.00817***	
International merchant bank		7.322***	5.937***	3.526**				.00494**	A: 2.276*
Domestic bank/Intl. m-b		6.881***	3.202**		2.542*	1.426**	2.547*		M: 3.793***
Domestic bank	1.110***	10.831**				1.801**			
Domestic bank/wool		12.763**			3.739*	2.266***	2.684**		M: 4.351***

continued

Table 7.5 *continued*

Market	Between Partnership Systems	Partnership Systems	Nuclear Family	Patrilineage Family	*Parentado* Family	Gonfalone	Priorate	Scrutiny (1433)	Political Factions
Domestic bank/silk			13.902**			2.303***	2.969***		
Silk									
Wool									
Ritagliatori/wool			8.542**					.00357*	
Ritagliatori									
Ritagliatori/silk									
Nonreciprocal credits:									
International merchant/silk		9.182*	18.013*					.00213*	M: 6.084***
International merchant/wool						1.080**			A: 3.169***
International merchant bank									
Domestic bank/Intl. m-b						1.232**	1.796**		
Domestic bank			5.182**	2.148**		1.075**	1.861***		
Domestic bank/wool								.00166**	
Domestic bank/silk									A: 4.010*
Silk			5.942**						
Wool		14.484***	3.707*						
Ritagliatori/wool									
Ritagliatori									
Ritagliatori/silk									

Note: Subset of data from appendix available in online version of our article in *Journal of Modern History*. M = Medici party; A = Albizzi party.

full logit regressions than are presented in table 7.5. Five variables were added as statistical controls: (*a*) baseline null expectations of numbers of credits between companies, based on the sizes of the companies alone,[64] (*b*) two binary dummy variables for whether company accounts were coded directly from the *catasto* or were inferred indirectly from trading partners' accounts,[65] and (*c*) the total taxable personal wealth of all partners in creditor companies and in debtor companies, as reported in the *catasto*. Not surprisingly the first three of these control variables were almost always statistically significant.

Eight other substantive variables apart from those listed in table 7.5, were also analyzed, but we not find them to be significant: namely, (*a*) neighborhood at the coarse-grained level of quarter (above and beyond the more fine-grained *gonfaloni*), (*b*) three social-class endogamy variables (percentage "upper class" *popolani* and magnate partners, percentage "middle class" new-men and new-new-men partners, and percentage "lower class" families-never-admitted-to-Priorate partners), and (*c*) four political offices other than Priorate or city council—namely, the *Buonuomini*, the *Gonfalonieri*, the guild consuls, and members of the *Mercanzia* or commercial court. It is therefore a substantive finding, albeit a negative one, that quarter, social class,[66] and political offices other than Priorate did *not* consistently affect commercial credit in 1427. A ninth variable not included in table 7.5—namely, direct in-law marriage among partners in different companies—was frequently statistically significant, but that is not highlighted because the number of documented partners across different companies who were direct in-laws, at the nuclear family level, was quite small.

To facilitate later comparison with business letters, the findings in table 7.5 will be discussed within categories that our Florentines would understand—namely, *famiglia*, *amicizia*, *onore*, and, finally, partnership systems. We close this statistical section by supplementing our

[64] This computed like an expected count in a contingency table—namely, (total number of dichotomized credits of giving company) * (total number of dichotomized debits of receiving company)/(total number of dichotomized credits in the market in which they conduct their joint business). This is the expected number of between-company credits, if all that is known is the credit volume (sizes) of the respective companies in that market.

[65] Use of these binary variables is important to control for sample bias: namely, the fact that directly observed company tax records are more likely to produce credits for our dataset than are companies only indirectly observed.

[66] In Padgett and McLean, "Organizational Invention and Elite Transformation," 1513, we reported that social-class endogamy was statistically significant for domestic-banking partnerships, for all three social classes. Social class, in other words, influenced partnership (how banks were formed), but not commercial credit (what those banks did).

discussion of statistical significance of these social-embeddedness variables with discussion about the relative volumes of credits they explain.

Famiglia

Instead of taking an essentialist position on the historiographically sensitive question of what was the Florentine family,[67] we chose to measure "family" four ways and let the data decide. Two companies were measured to have a "nuclear family" relation with each other by the percentage that partners in the two different companies were members of the same nuclear family (that is, father and sons or brothers). Two companies were measured to have a "patrilineage family" relation by the percentage that partners in the two companies were members of the same patrilineage, above and beyond nuclear family (that is, cousins or uncles with same last name). Two companies were measured to have an "in-law" relation by the percentage that one set of partners married into the nuclear families of the other set. And two companies were measured to have a "*parentado* family" relation by the percentage that one set of partners had the same last names as the other set of partners' wives.

Not surprisingly, family relations among partners in different companies, when they were present, exerted frequent and strong effects on those companies' credit behavior toward one other. And these effects were ranked in the intuitive way—namely, nuclear family (14 significant coefficients) > patrilineage family (7 significant coefficients) > *parentado* family (5 significant coefficients).[68] All versions of Florentine "family," in other words, affected Florentine commercial behavior.

These statistical effects are not surprising because when family relations interpenetrated commercial relations, credit exchanges between companies became as much social obligations as economic investments. "Social obligations enforcing economic investments" or "economic investments enacting social obligations": either way of interpreting the empirical correlation is consistent with our data. Thus, insisting on the causal priority of one side

[67] We are referring to the debate between Goldthwaite, *Private Wealth in Renaissance Florence*, and F. W. Kent, *Household and Lineage in Renaissance Florence*, on the salience within Renaissance Florence of nuclear family versus patrilineage.

[68] Nuclear in-law relations were statistically significant six times, but we do not report this in table 7.5 because the number of examples of marrying the sister of another company's partner was small.

over the other is probably a mistake. We shall see in our business letters that even nonkin sometimes evoked fictional-kinship language with each other, which strengthened the obligatory connotations of economic exchange. In all domains, not excluding the economic, kinship was central in Renaissance Florentine thinking and behavior.

While true in almost all Florentine markets, there is a remarkable density of nine significant family coefficients in the four reciprocal-credit markets involving international merchant-bankers.[69] Reciprocal credits are our observable proxies for *corrispondenti* relations, often implemented through paired *conti correnti*. When Florentine businessmen were resident outside of their native soil, they relied even more than they did otherwise on family as the social ligaments upon which they constructed their *corrispondenti*. Apparently in their most risky business climates, Florentines tended to close ranks within intimate social relations for their deepest credit connections. Since Florentine families in international business were spread geographically all over Europe, some of the heaviest early fifteenth-century flow of international finance throughout Europe coursed through upper-class[70] Florentine families' veins, making them very wealthy indeed.[71]

Amicizia

Our imperfect proxy for friends is neighbors. We acknowledge the imperfection of the match, but neighbors are measurable in our data, whereas friends are not. The social intimacy of Florentine neighborhoods has been documented extensively in the literature, so the assumption is well grounded that neighborhood was highly correlated with social-interaction frequency, even though close interaction could lead to hostility as well to friendship within neighborhoods.[72]

[69] Family was almost always insignificant in all markets involving *ritagliatori*. Indeed, almost none of our social-context variables are significant in these relatively "impersonal" markets.

[70] See social-class data in footnote 27.

[71] Padgett and McLean ("Organizational Invention and Elite Transformation," 1536) document that Florentine domestic merchant bankers were wealthiest in 1427, compared to 1351, 1378, 1403 1458, and 1480. These analyses show that Florentine merchant-bankers reached their peak of relative wealth in 1427, compared to 1351, 1378, 1403, 1458, and 1480.

[72] Samuel K. Cohn, *The Laboring Classes in Renaissance Florence* (New York, 1980); D. V. Kent and F. W. Kent. *Neighbours and Neighbourhood in Renaissance Florence: The District of the Red Lion in the Fifteenth Century* (Locust Valley, NY, 1982); Christiane Klapisch-Zuber, "Kin, Friends and Neighbors: The Urban Territory of a Merchant Family in 1400," in *Women, Family, and Ritual in Renaissance Italy* (Chicago, 1985), 68–93; Francis William Kent, "Ties of Neighborhood and

Gonfaloni were the 16 administrative districts or wards into which Florence was divided geographically. We measured a "same *gonfalone*" relationship between companies as the percentage of times that the partners in two different companies lived in the same *gonfalone*. "Same quarter" (excluding same *gonfalone*) relations were measured similarly.

The statistical findings regarding same *gonfalone* are remarkably sharp: at very high significance levels, markets involving domestic merchant-banks resident in Florence almost always relied on neighborhood relations to structure their commercial credit relations. Put simply, Florentine banks and merchant banks resident in Florence disproportionately extended commercial credit to those wool-manufacturing companies, silk-manufacturing companies, international merchant banks, and other domestic banks and merchant banks, whose partners lived in the same *gonfaloni* as partners of the focal company. Whereas Florentine international merchant-banking business was organized substantially through family relations, Florentine domestic-banking business was organized substantially through neighbors and friends. As was the case with the association between family and international *corrispondenti*, moreover, domestic merchant-bankers and their recurrent exchange partners frequently referred to each other in business letters as friends, whether or not they really were. Causality went as much from business to friends as it did from friends to business.[73]

In another article, Padgett has demonstrated that the effect of neighborhood on marriage, while always statistically significant, declined in absolute importance from 1300 to 1500.[74] Whether a similar temporal decline in Florence was true for economic credit cannot be assessed with data on 1427.

Onore

The Italian word *onore* means both "honor" and "political office," reflecting the historical reality in Italian republics that to be elected to a public office was conceived to be an honor, bespeaking respect from one's fellow citizens.

Patronage in Renaissance Florence," in *Patronage, Art, and Society in Renaissance Italy*, eds. Francia William Kent and Patricia Simons (Oxford, 1987); Nicholas A. Eckstein, *The District of the Green Dragon: Neighborhood Life and Social Change in Renaissance Florence* (Florence, 1995); Gene A. Brucker, *Florentine Politics and Society, 1343–1378* (Princeton, NJ, 1962), 126, 131. Dale Kent, *Rise of the Medici*, 68, 178.

[73] Compare Herlihy and Klapisch-Zuber, *Tuscans and Their Families*, 89.

[74] Padgett, "Open Elite?" 18–19.

Office-holding in the Florentine republic was not a matter for professional politicians. Many normal "amateur," but respected and articulate, citizens were elected to serve short stints in Florentine public office, taking temporary and unpaid time out from their normal business or other pursuits.[75] It is surprising to modern eyes to see how anxious and honored Florentine republican citizens were to be elected by their social superiors and peers to high political office, with no overt reward or payment other than prestige.[76]

As mentioned above, no political office other than the top office—namely, the Priorate or city council—had consistent statistical effects on commercial-credit behavior among Florentine companies. But republican service in this very top office of Priorate, measured as percentage of both companies' partners serving in the Priorate prior to 1427, had frequent and strong consequences for commercial credit in all markets involving domestic merchant-banks.[77] This was especially true for reciprocal credits, but it was true also for all credits and for asymmetric credits. In this regard the variable "Priorate" behaved statistically just like "same *gonfaloni*." In addition to *amicizia*, the social logic of *onore*, conceptualized as personal honor but manifest as republican office-holding, was at the core of commercial credit among companies dealing with merchant-banks resident in Florence.

The concentration of strong statistical Priorate effects on commercial credit especially in markets related to domestic banking and to domestic merchant-banking makes sense. Florentine international merchant-bankers were scattered all over Europe, far away from Priorate service back home. And the density of social ties observing and calibrating *onore*, measured in scrutiny voting, was higher at home in Florence than it was abroad. Public reputation could not really be ignored anywhere, but it was especially salient and observable at home.

[75] For the nine-person Priorate or city council, elected tours of duty were for two months, during which time councilors physically moved into the *Palazzo Vecchio* or city hall, leaving their business to be run by trusted others. After electing a large number of eligibles through an oligarchic voting procedure called the scrutiny, successful name tags were placed into a monastically controlled bag, from which actual officeholders were selected randomly. Candidates did not know that they had been selected for city council until their name was drawn. The random component of this two-staged voting procedure was self-consciously designed to minimize self-reproducing control of the state by small factions. For the evolution of Florentine voting procedures, see John M. Najemy, *Corporatism and Consensus in Florentine Electoral Politics, 1280–1400* (Chapel Hill, NC, 1982); and Nicolai Rubinstein, *The Government of Florence under the Medici, 1434 to 1494* (Oxford, 1966).

[76] Gene Brucker, ed., *Two Memoirs of Renaissance Florence: The Diaries of Buonaccorso Pitti and Gregorio Dati* (New York, 1967), 125–6; Najemy, *Corporatism and Consensus*, 299–300, 302.

[77] In his *ricordanze* or diary, Gregorio Dati noted: "I was in debt for over 3,000 florins. That same year 1412, my name was drawn to be Standard-bearer of Justice [i.e., chairman of city council], and I served in that office. This was the beginning of my recovery" Brucker, *Two Memoirs of Renaissance Florence*, 139–140.

It has been shown elsewhere that political office-holding had effects on business and wealth, via state finance, at the very highest echelons of the elite.[78] However, this is the first demonstration of a pervasive office-holding effect on business throughout wide segments of Florentine society. Perhaps this widespread causal effect is related to the fact that eligibility for the Priorate had increased substantially from 1343 to 1427.[79]

In table 7.5, we also report statistical results for scrutiny voting and for political factions. Scrutiny voting in 1433, measured as the votes received by the sum of the highest vote receivers in each company, had numerous statistical effects on commercial credit in 1427, but these effects were scattered among international and domestic merchant-banking markets. Likewise, factional membership in the Medici and Albizzi parties of 1433 had numerous statistical effects on commercial credit in 1427, but these also were scattered among merchant-banking markets. These independent variables from 1433 were included to predict dependent-variable outcomes in 1427 under the presumption of stability in political attitudes over time. Perhaps the lack of clear market patterning may be related to the six-year gap between the two sets of data.

At the very least, we can conclude that politics mattered in economic credit markets in 1427. It is even clearer that economics mattered in the early 1430s construction of the Medici political party or faction.[80] Florentine commercial behavior, especially in merchant-banking, was no more segregated from political partisanship than it was from kinship or friendship.

Partnership Systems

The partnership system was a new organizational form in the history of financial capitalism, invented in Renaissance Florence.[81] Partnership systems were sets of legally autonomous companies, with their own account

[78] L. F. Marks, "The Financial Oligarchy in Florence under Lorenzo," in *Italian Renaissance Studies*, ed. E. F. Jacob (London: 1960), 123–47; Molho, *Florentine Public Finances*, 166–182.

[79] Anthony Molho, "Politics and the Ruling Class in Early Renaissance Florence," *Nuova Rivista Storica* 52 (1968): 401–20; Ronald G. Witt, "Florentine Politics and the Ruling Class, 1382–1407," *Journal of Medieval and Renaissance Studies* 6 (1976): 243–67; Najemy, *Corporatism and Consensus in Florentine Electoral Politics*, 263–76; Padgett and Ansell, "Robust Action and the Rise of the Medici," 1261; Padgett, "Open Elite?" 9, 47.

[80] Molho, *Florentine Public Finances in the Early Renaissance*, 166–182; Anthony Molho, "Cosimo de' Medici: Pater Patriae or Padrino?" *Stanford Italian Review* 1 (1979): 5–33; Padgett and Ansell, "Robust Action and the Rise of the Medici," 1276–77, 1305–06.

[81] See Padgett and McLean, "Organizational Invention and Elite Transformation," and the references therein.

books, linked in ownership through single persons or through a holding company of controlling partners. Usually, though not necessarily, the linked companies in question were diversified across industries, with international merchant-banks and domestic banks dominating in number, and with domestic banks serving as the managerial headquarters. Padgett and McLean (2006) documented the rapid diffusion of this organizational form, after its Ciompi Revolt-induced birth in 1383.[82]

Table 7.5 reveals strong credit interconnections in 1427 among companies linked in partnership systems throughout the merchant-banking sector and occasionally in other sectors as well. This is not surprising, for companies linked through common owners presumably were ordered to cooperate, even though they were legally autonomous.[83] More impressive, however, within the domestic banking industry is the extent to which partnership systems themselves cooperated strongly and significantly among each other through reciprocal credits. This demonstrates coordination among titular "competitors" at the very apex of the Florentine economy. Senior-partner leaders of these partnership systems became captains of finance in Florence, monitoring and managing large credit flows across multiple markets through their visible hands.

Such concentration of ownership of multiple companies into fewer hands is inadequately understood without placing it into its political context, namely, the consolidation of a citywide oligarchy among elite Florentine merchant republicans in response to the Ciompi Revolt in 1378.[84] Economic market restructuring through partnership systems was one aspect of a broader political and social transformation in elite structure. Through this elite-transformation process, economic partnership systems took their place among the social-network constituents of that elite, transforming merchants on the one side and republicans on the other even more deeply into multifaceted merchant-republicans.

Volume of Social-Context Effects

Statistical significance is a necessary but not sufficient criterion for assessing the volume of any factor's impact. "Nuclear family," for example, frequently

[82] Padgett and McLean, "Organizational Invention and Elite Transformation," 1474–85, 1548–60.

[83] The voluminous correspondence of the Milan branch of the Datini system offers copious evidence of this coordinated cooperation. See Luciana Frangioni, ed., *Milano fine trecento: il carteggio Milanese dell'Archivio Datini di Prato* (Firenze, 1994).

[84] Padgett and McLean, "Organizational Invention and Elite Transformation," 1494–522.

exerted a significant impact on companies' commercial credit to each other, when such close family relations linked those companies. But there were not really enough brothers to go around to organize an entire credit market. Table 7.6, therefore, reports the percentage of commercial credits affected by the significant social-context variables reported in table 7.5. We report volume only for markets involving merchant-banks, because retail *ritagliatori* markets were shown in table 7.5 mostly to have operated "impersonally," that is, independently of our social-context variables.

Table 7.6, column 5, reinforces our interpretation of reciprocal credits as social exchange. In merchant-banking markets (except for "International M-B/Silk"), from 42% to 96% of reciprocal commercial credits were rooted in dense and multi-textured social networks. Reciprocal credits were the inner skeleton of merchant-banking markets in Renaissance Florence, and these were constructed largely out of social-network materials.

Nonreciprocal or asymmetric credits were on the whole not as socially embedded as were reciprocal credits. But in two out of three markets internal to the merchant-banking sector, they were just as socially embedded: 76% and 89% of the non-reciprocated commercial credits in the "Domestic Bank/International M-B" market and in the "among Domestic Banks" market could be correlated with measurable social contexts, respectively.

Putting both the reciprocal and the nonreciprocal sides together, the global economic-network portrait that emerges is roughly one of concentric circles: (a) within the Florentine export-oriented economy as a whole, the merchant-banking sector was the credit core (see figure 7.1), (b) within the merchant-banking sector itself, reciprocal credits, often instantiated in *corrispondenti* relations, were the credit core (see tables 7.4 and 7.6), and (c) reciprocal credits, in turn, were built upon social-network foundations (see table 7.5). Conversely, as one moved away from the merchant-banking inner core of the Florentine economy, out toward its *ritagliatori* periphery, commercial credit relations became more nonreciprocal and impersonal, in the sense of not having correlations with observable other social networks. In general, the Florentine economy was socially embedded. But more specifically Florentine merchant-banks—in their commercial relations both with each other and with other companies—were embedded in, and regulated by, the social networks of a socially open republican oligarchy.

Even in 1427, Florentine commercial credit markets stood very firmly on the late-medieval social foundations of family and neighborhood. Yet two Renaissance institutional innovations—partnership systems and republican

Table 7.6 Volume of "Personal" Credits for all Merchant-Banking Markets, by Clusters of Coefficients

	Partnership-System Transfers (1)	**Family Embedding** (2)	**Neighborhood Embedding** (3)	**Political Embedding** (4)	**All** (5)
All credits:					
Domestic banking	3/260 = .012	29/260 = .112	79/260 = .304	232/260 = .892	239/260 = .919
Domestic bank/international merchant banking	55/339 = .162	39/339 = .115	147/339 = .434	261/339 = .770	287/339 = .847
Domestic banking/wool	0/336 = .000	0/336 = .000	80/336 = .238	0/336 = .000	80/336 = .238
Domestic banking/silk	0/258 = .000	3/258 = .012	53/258 = .205	0/258 = .000	55/258 = .213
International merchant banking	35/294 = .119	91/294 = .310	0/294 = .000	0/294 = .000	110/294 = .374
Intl. merchant banking/wool	0/359 = .000	27/359 = .075	0/359 = .000	10/359 = .028	36/359 = .100
Intl. merchant banking/silk	0/166 = .000	9/166 = .054	0/166 = .000	13/166 = .078	19/166 = .114
Reciprocal credits:					
Domestic banking	63/107 = .589	2/107 = .019	33/107 = .308	0/107 = .000	72/107 = .673
Domestic bank/international merchant banking	49/158 = .310	39/158 = .247	95/158 = .601	130/158 = .823	143/158 = .905
Domestic banking/wool	15/52 = .288	2/52 = .038	27/52 = .519	50/52 = .962	50/52 = .962
Domestic banking/silk	0/60 = .000	2/60 = .033	19/60 = .317	52/60 = .867	56/60 = .933

continued

Table 7.6 *continued*

	Partnership-System Transfers (1)	Family Embedding (2)	Neighborhood Embedding (3)	Political Embedding (4)	All (5)
International merchant banking	32/134 = .239	56/134 = .418	0/134 = .000	23/134 = .172	73/134 = .545
Intl. merchant banking/wool	0/41 = .000	17/41 = .415	0/41 = .000	0/41 = .000	17/41 = .415
Intl. merchant banking/silk	0/30 = .000	2/30 = .067	0/30 = .000	2/30 = .067	2/30 = .067
Nonreciprocal credits:					
Domestic banking	0/153 = .000	16/153 = .105	46/153 = .301	132/153 = .863	137/153 = .895
Domestic bank/international merchant banking	0/181 = .000	0/181 = .000	52/181 = .287	118/181 = .652	137/181 = .757
Domestic banking/wool	0/284 = .000	0/284 = .000	0/284 = .000	0/284 = .000	0/284 = .000
Domestic banking/silk	0/198 = .000	3/198 = .015	0/198 = .000	6/198 = .030	9/198 = .045
International merchant banking	0/160 = .000	0/160 = .000	0/160 = .000	0/160 = .000	0/160 = .000
Intl. merchant banking/wool	0/318 = .000	0/318 = .000	68/318 = .214	10/318 = .031	76/318 = .239
Intl. merchant banking/silk	4/136 = .029	1/136 = .007	0/136 = .000	11/136 = .081	15/136 = .110

electoral reforms—pushed families and neighborhoods into greater network intercalation with each other, at least within the political *reggimento*, thereby spanning previous deep cleavages and divides.[85] The complementary consequences of this increased social-network connectivity were greater liquidity in credit markets[86] and greater elite consolidation in politics.[87]

At the elite pinnacle of the economy, diversified partnership systems bridged not families but industries. This new post-1383 type of Florentine economic network emerged out of political reaction to the Ciompi Revolt, and it breached the previously sharp segregation of business partnerships into distinct guilds.[88] Senior partners in partnership systems evolved from being industry-specific entrepreneurs into being cross-industry financiers.[89]

Republicanism did not affect the organization of Florentine credit markets as directly as did partnership systems. But ex-members of the city council provided a pool of highly respected citizens, certified to have honor (*onore*).[90] Such persons were a filtered subset of citizens whose past behavior was judged to be exemplary not just as citizens but also (as we shall see in the Dati example below) as businessmen. They were elected in the first place because they were deeply enmeshed in Florentine networks and institutions—hardly the types to cut and run. Arguably such electoral filtering became stronger on the individualistic and elite-defined grounds of "character" after the post-Ciompi electoral reforms than before, when voting had been based more on group membership.[91] Of course, being a good citizen was not necessarily the same thing as being a reliable businessman, but the distinction between generalist "honor" and economically specialized

[85] Cohn, *Laboring Classes in Renaissance Florence*, 52, 118–23 has shown that greater rates of intermarriage across neighborhoods at the level of the elite was offset by decreased rates of intermarriage across neighborhoods at the level of working classes.

[86] The effect is similar to percolation models in physics and biology, which exhibit sudden phase transitions in both aggregate flow and in autocatalytic self-organization once the density of ties in random networks reaches a threshold critical value. "Giant component" connectivity suddenly emerges. See, for example, Stuart A. Kauffman, *The Origins of Order: Self-Organization and Selection in Evolution* (New York, 1993), 308.

[87] Cohn, *Laboring Classes in Renaissance Florence*; Najemy, *Corporatism and Consensus*.

[88] Padgett and McLean, "Organizational Invention and Elite Transformation," 1474–85.

[89] Ibid., 1535–39.

[90] The public certification aspect of office-holding is clear from fact that Priorate memberships were statistically significant, even with the simultaneous inclusion of scrutiny votes in the regressions. Scrutiny votes could be considered a more precise measure of reputation, but because they were secret they did not broadcast *onore* until office-holding was actually selected.

[91] Marvin B. Becker, "The Renaissance Territorial State and Civic Perspective," in *Florence in Transition*, Vol. 2 (Baltimore: 1968, 201–50); Najemy, *Corporatism and Consensus*, 262–300.

"credit worthiness" was not one that the Florentines shared. For them, a person was worthy of credit, economic or social, because he was honorable.[92]

In addition to its public certification function, republican election into the *reggimento* provided direct-access benefits to budding businessmen: (a) participation in verbally oriented political councils increased the level of direct observation that merchant-republicans had of one another, and (b) indirect introductions, recommendations, and gossip about reputation functioned far more efficiently within the republican elite than outside it. Thus, although the direct material rewards for businessmen joining the Priorate were nonexistent, the indirect payoffs of access and reputation were substantial for anyone trying to operate in commercial credit markets.

A dramatic example of this Florentine link between economic credit and republican election is provided in the diary of Gregorio Dati. Dati was one of the successful new-man silk merchants in our 1427 dataset, but earlier in 1408, after 24 years of partnerships in the silk business, he suffered this fate:

> As a result of the adversity which overtook us in Barcelona, and of the lawsuits which followed it, and of the suspicions concerning [my brother's] ventures and the calumnies that were spread around, we were very short of credit. So we were forced to withdraw from business and collect whatever we could to pay our creditors, borrowing from friends and using all our ingenuity, suffering losses, high interest, and expenses in order to avoid bankruptcy and shame. Although my partner was in favor of going bankrupt so as to avoid some losses and expenditures, I was resolved to face ruin rather than loss of honor.[93]

After four years of financial hardship but also of demonstrable integrity,

> I was in debt for over 3,000 florins. That same year 1412, my name was drawn to be Standard-bearer of Justice, and I served in that office. That was the beginning of my recovery.[94]

[92] In the words of an anonymous fourteenth-century businessman: "One should not be ambitious or aspire to fame only in order to show off, but only because he leads a judicious life. A good name is always derived when one leads a moderate life, for it is a precious and praiseworthy thing. This kind of life often aids and defends a man in circumstances in which ordinarily he would not be appreciated. Man does not have a clearer or dearer friend than his good name. For, whoever enjoys a good reputation cannot help but be good, just, and upright. All the things on this earth under the sky are here for whoever enjoys this condition of life." Molho (1969, 54–55)

[93] Brucker, *Two Memoirs of Renaissance Florence*, 130.

[94] Ibid., 139–140.

This financial recovery through revived commercial credit was healthy enough to allow Dati to report a taxable wealth of 3,368 florins in the 1427 *catasto.*[95] This placed him among the wealthiest 7% of Florentine households at that time.

Table 7.6 shows that, out of all of our various social-context effects, political embedding, and in particular past Priorate membership, had the largest volume of impact on commercial credit. Family and neighborhood provided strong traditionalist foundations, upon which Florentine commercial credit could grow. Partnership systems coordinated the cross-industry apex of the commercial-credit system. But previous election to city council induced the broadest reach and connectivity in Florentine credit markets.

One common criticism of personalistic markets is that they are inherently self-limiting in extensibility and scale, compared to impersonal markets. This criticism has less force when discussing topologically open-ended social networks, like porous elites, than it does when discussing topologically closed and fragmented social networks, like families. Florentine merchant-banking credit markets were very personalistic. Yet they geographically radiated all over Europe and brokered much of Europe's international trade, without reliable judicial support. The organizational secret of the Florentines in their markets was their blending of multiple personalistic social networks into dense but socially open merchant-republican elites, who reciprocally offered commercial credit to each other, not as competitors but as honorable Renaissance men. Using gossip, ostracism, and reputation to discipline their wide extension of credit to each other, such men "kept everyone in line" through the same dense and multi-textured social networks that had created them in the first place.

Business Letters and the Mentalité of Credit

We close this article with a textual analysis of business letters from the general time period, in order to illustrate the discursive framings and the cognitive *mentalité* of the Florentine businessmen who produced the commercial-credit behavior documented above. Statistical and textual evidence provide complementary perspectives on the phenomenon of commercial credit, we believe, as long as care is taken to align them. Textual

[95] A.S.F., *Catasto* 66, fol. 421ff.

evidence provides insight into the psychology of businessmen from a distant culture, at the risk of a tiny and perhaps unrepresentative sample. Statistical evidence measures the behaviors of the entire population of Florentine businessmen, at the loss of detail about individuals. Even with perfect data, there is no guarantee that these two perspectives will yield the same answers. Not all talk translates into action, and not all actions are self-conscious. Consistent answers or not, we believe that juxtaposing diverse evidentiary perspectives deepens our understanding of Florentine commercial credit.

Because of the importance of relational credits in our statistical analysis, we focus on letters between *corrispondenti*—that is, between legally autonomous companies that had extensive and recurrent two-way business with each other.[96] Primarily, we examine published business letters to and from the Francesco Datini company in Milan and unpublished business letters to and from the Andrea de' Bardi company in Florence.[97] Other relevant sources are occasionally mentioned as well. Within this small sample of business letters, we highlight Florentine businessmen's use of the language of friendship (*amicizia*) and of honor (*onore*) in discussing deals with each other.

An important theoretical point in our discussion will be the two-way causal relationship between language and behavior. On the one hand, linguistic expressions reference "real" social relationships and obligations in the writers' past experience. On the other hand, Florentine linguistic tropes and learned cognitive models, like "family" (*famiglia*) and "friends" (*amici*), were extended far beyond their objective references, as businessmen sought to frame and interpret each other's market actions in such terms. This loose coupling or ambiguity between Florentine language and behavior enabled both the creative construction of new social relationships and the creative construction of lies.[98] On the whole, the benefits of the former apparently

[96] Because of this focus on reciprocal *corrispondenti*, the extensive economic-theory literature on asymmetric principals and agents is not really relevant. That literature is more relevant to employers and employees or to home-office partners and overseas branch managers.

[97] On Datini, see Luciana Frangioni ed., *Milano fine trecento: il carteggio Milanese dell'Archivio Datini di Prato*. On Bardi, see A.S.F., *M.A.P.* 84, 87, 94. Andrea Bardi, like Goro Dati, was still actively in business in our 1427 dataset.

[98] For Florentine examples, see Padgett and Ansell, "Robust Action and the Rise of the Medici," on the "robust action" of Cosimo de' Medici; Paul D. McLean, *The Art of the Network* (Durham, NC: 2007), especially pp. 1–34; and Ronald Weissman, "The Importance of Being Ambiguous: Social Relations, Individualism, and Identity in Renaissance Florence," in *Urban Life in the Renaissance*, eds. Susan Zimmerman and Ronald Weissman (Dover, DE: 1989), 269–80. Ronald Weissman (*Ritual Brotherhood in Renaissance Florence*, 1–42), on "Judas the Florentine," cogently discusses the

outweighed the correlated costs of the latter.[99] Linguistic ambiguity was the medium through which economic and social relational logics bled into each other.

Here are two examples of *corrispondenti* relations between companies, in Florentine businessmen's own words:

> Of the affairs you still have to complete here, point yourself still towards Pisa with my company there, and also write often to me in Bruges, because I am going to live there, and in three days I am leaving here to go there. With the grace of God I will stay there a little while, and if there is anything I can do for you, write to me of it and I will do it, for you and for your whole company, as if it were for myself alone.[100]

> Anything that comes to you for us, you may commit to Paris or London, if it be to your own [company] there, to ours in Barcelona, in Lucca to Bartolomeo Belbani & co, and in Venice to the Medici: continue in this way if no one instructs you otherwise. We do not wish you to lend [*credere*] our money, nor the money of our company to any Venetian or Lombard, nor to Antonio Quarti & co, nor to Niccolaio Tonghi, nor to Filippo Rapondi or others that might bring business to you from Dino Rapondi of Paris. Follow these instructions, and with the others [with whom you correspond] do as you wish and as if it were for yourself, having always due regard to lending well and, again, not to get yourself too indebted with anyone, and especially with Diamante degli Alberti & co.[101]

unavoidable dark side of the credit behavior analyzed here. Lying and cheating, while no doubt existing (and documented here), were not common enough to destroy the system.

[99] For a formal model that demonstrates analytically the possible coexistence of self-reproducing "life" with many "parasites," see John F. Padgett, Doowan Lee, and Nick Collier, "Economic Production as Chemistry," *Industrial and Corporate Change* 12 (2003): 843–78. That model even demonstrates that tolerance and volume of parasites are correlated with complexity in evolution.

[100] Frangioni, *Milano fine trecento*, letter 657: Manno di ser Iacomo & Co. in Milan to the Datini company in Barcelona, March 24, 1397. This and subsequent translations are by McLean.

[101] A.S.F., *M.A.P.* 87, fol. 341r: Andrea Bardi to the Orlandini in Bruges, April 6, 1405. It is notable here that prohibited trade is specified more in terms of people than in terms of types of transactions. See also Andrea Bardi's letter to Domenico and Poldeo Pazzi in Paris, March 27, 1405 (ibid., fol. 352r), where he instructs them to honor bills of exchange for any amount with the Tornabuoni of Bruges, the Medici of Venice, and the Bardi companies of Barcelona and Florence, but imposes limits of 500 or 1,000 florins on exchanges involving certain other companies: the Sacchi, Antonio Grisolfi, Zanobi di Taddeo Gaddi of Venice, Guglielmo del Pontico of Lucca, and so on. Instructions written in 1441 for Gerozzo de' Pilli, the Medici's partner in London (A.S.F., *M.A.P.* 94, fol. 214ff.) are more detailed and include a longer list of *corrispondenti*, but otherwise remain substantially the same as those written around 1400. These instructions are described in detail in de Roover, *The Rise and Decline of the Medici Bank*, 91.

Within very explicitly stated constraints, partners in *corrispondenti* relationships each offered to do whatever the other requested and were authorized to take discretionary action on behalf of the other, taking advantage of local opportunities. The accounting methods for keeping tabs on these discretionary actions were the paired *conti correnti* and *conti di esercizio* discussed above. To spell out the mechanics of this: correspondent A would take discretionary action on behalf of correspondent B, charging B's current account in A's book and recording therein A's actions taken and B's financial commitments.[102] This was really A giving credit to B, since this was B's account money, but A's disposable cash being used. Typically B would do likewise for A, thereby paying back the "loan" not with cash but with reciprocated discretionary actions. If all went well, which it did not always, each side actively made money for the other.

The word "to lend" in these and other Renaissance business letters is *credere*, which normally means "to believe" or "to believe in."[103] The language of medieval and Renaissance Italian expresses the idea that to offer someone credit typically meant having confidence in them, not only financially but also morally. "To give credit" and "to believe in someone" were essentially the same idea. Having credit was a sign that others trusted you to record your debts accurately, regard them seriously, and pay them promptly. It was also a sign that you were a person of character and honor, in more domains than just the economic.

Amicizia

While fifteenth-century Florentine business letters overwhelmingly focus on the day-to-day details of transactions, spelling them out monotonously and repetitiously, it is also true that they are inflected sufficiently often with the rhetorics of friendship and fictive kinship to see these framings as constitutive of commercial interaction. This is how Andrea Bardi could directly link the terms *mercantivolemente* (in a merchant-like way) and *amichevolmente*

[102] The expression "pay it and post it to our account" (*pagate e ponete a nostro conto*) became a common feature of business correspondence in the 1390s. The earliest example we found in Datini's Milan correspondence appears in late 1383 (Frangioni, *Milano fine trecento*, letter 334). A variant of the expression appears in a letter of March 1387 from Lemo and Ghiselo and partners of Milan to the Datini company in Pisa (ibid., letter 137), the first occasion we find between companies not tied by a shared partner.

[103] Florence Edler, *A Glossary of Medieval Terms of Business* (Cambridge, MA, 1934), 34.

(in a friendly way) in a letter concerning the resolution of a *differenza* to the Orlandini company in Bruges on March 26, 1405.[104] Consider the following additional examples:

> Your offer we accept like dear friends [*chari amici*], and we see that by your Tommaso you have written concerning our condition and company: this he did as a worthy [*valente*] person and out of courtesy . . . And although you have many friends here who serve you, nonetheless we offer ourselves to all of your pleasures and, wanting advice concerning one thing or another, tell us and I will do it willingly [*faròllo volentieri*].[105]

> As much as you offer to do with love in this matter, all of it we have observed, and we thank you for it, and we are certain you would do even more; and if anything occurs in Avignon or here that needs to be done, we will commit ourselves to you loyally [*con fidanza*], advising you of it first . . . As for us, you may do with us as you would with your own, and we will do all we can. Thus we have told your Tommaso and prayed him to have such confidence in us as one could with you.[106]

> I will take confidence with you as I believe I may, and I would like that this confidence remain between us.[107]

In part, the language in these passages may reflect important concerns of the theologians who elaborated the Church's usury doctrine and whose ideas appeared in the confessional guidebooks consulted by the laity.[108] Here we have in mind specifically the idea that the economy was constituted by

[104] A.S.F., *M.A.P.* 87, fol. 339r.

[105] Frangioni, *Milano fine trecento*, letter 751: Giovanni Borromei to Datini and his company in Barcelona, April 1400.

[106] Ibid., letter 606: Manno di ser Iacomo & co in Milan to the Datini company in Barcelona, December 16, 1396.

[107] A.S.F., *M.A.P.* 87, fol. 353r: Francesco Bardi to Francesco Mannini in Bruges, June 5, 1405.

[108] For recent scholarship on the topic of usury, see for example Odd Langholm, *The Legacy of Scholasticism in Economic Thought: Antecedents of Choice and Power* (Cambridge, 1998); Joel Kaye, *Economy and Nature in the Fourteenth Century: Money, Market Exchange, and the Emergence of Scientific Thought* (Cambridge, 1998); Giacomo Todeschini, *I mercanti e il tempo: La società cristiana e il circolo virtuoso della ricchezza fra Medioevo ed età moderna* (Bologna, 2002); Giovanni Ceccarelli, *Il gioco e il peccato: economia e rischio nel tardo Medioevo* (Bologna, 2003); Lawrin D. Armstrong, *Usury and Public Debt in Early Renaissance Florence: Lorenzo Ridolfi on the Monte Commune* (Toronto, 2003); Giacomo Todeschini, "La riflessione etica sulle attività economiche," in *Economie urbane ed etica economia nell'Italia medievale*, eds. Roberto Greci, Giuliano Pinto, and Giacomo Todeschini (Laterza, 2005); and Diego Quaglioni, Giacomo Todeschini, and Gian Maria Varanini, *Credito e usura fra teologia, diritto e amministrazione* (Rome, 2005). On guidance pamphlets, see Langholm, *The Legacy of Scholasticism in Economic Thought*, 10 and Todeschini,

a community of the faithful linked together in love and the theologians' emphasis on the importance of a completely, unconditionally free will for an economic transaction to be considered legitimate.[109] But the language here also recalls the language of patronage letters. The final sentence of the Borromei letter is a common concluding element of much correspondence, but appears with particular regularity in patronage-related letters, where writers assure recipients of their loyalty to each other.[110] *Amicizia* was not a word that had a single, clear-cut meaning: It could be understood in religious, in political, in economic, or even in humanistic inflections, depending on the context.[111]

Florentines saw no contradiction between friendship and making money. Theirs was an instrumental conception of friendship.[112] One purpose of helping each other was to make money, but also one purpose of making money was to make friends, through generosity with gifts.[113] Profit and friendship were paired concepts in the Florentine understanding, both facets of the same social-exchange mentality of constructing each other through reciprocity.

Leon Battista Alberti put this idea this way, through the mouth of his businessman character Giannozzo:

> I should be glad to remain here with you as long as you like, but I see my friend whom I must help at the Palace. We made an appointment early this morning, and it will soon be time to appear there. I do not wish to fail my

"La riflessione etica sulle attività economiche," 184. While religious considerations are quite helpful for understanding the *mentalité* of Florentine businessmen, they are not as useful for explaining the evolution of Florentine business practices per se.

[109] See Todeschini, "La riflessione etica sulle attività economiche," 185; Langholm, *The Legacy of Scholasticism in Economic Thought*, 61ff. We also find other similar sorts of language, such as when Andrea Bardi insisted that a transaction be undertaken *liberamente* or that settlements be agreed to with *gran volontà* (A.S.F., *M.A.P.* 87, fol. 335r). Also, perhaps the idea that all parties be "happy and in agreement" (*contenti e d'accordo*) about the way a deal got settled (A.S.F., *M.A.P.* 87, fol. 342v). Recently scholars, such as Ceccarelli and Todeschini have taken to using the terms "lexicons" and "languages" to explore the ways in which theological debates informed economic practice and vice versa.

[110] See McLean, *The Art of the Network*, esp. chapter 4.

[111] Leon Battista Alberti wrote an extended debate on the various contemporary meanings of the idea of *amicitia*: see *The Albertis of Florence: Leon Battista Alberti's Della Familia*, ed. and trans. Guido A. Guarino (Lewisburg, PA [ca. 1433] 1971), book 4.

[112] As Weissman, *Ritual Brotherhood in Renaissance Florence*, 40 puts it: "It is useful to remember that although personal relations in the Renaissance were often accompanied by demonstrations of strong affection, it was the perception of moral obligation, not the modern criterion of psychological intimacy, that distinguished relations between friends from relations between strangers. And Florentines could be cold and calculating in their acquisition of personal relations."

[113] Alberti, *Albertis of Florence*, 263–73. Weissman, *Ritual Brotherhood in Renaissance Florence*, 36–41, gives many quotations to support this.

> friend, for I have always liked helping others rather than asking for help myself, and I have always preferred having others under obligation to me rather than the opposite. I like doing him a favor, helping him as much as possible with words and deeds, not so much because I know he loves me, but because I know he is a good and just man. You must always regard good people as friends and you must always love and help the just even though you may not know them.[114]

An actual businessman from a later period phrased the idea as follows:

> With regard to Galilei and company, I see that there is no more need of blandishments for in truth they do things like gentlemen. The letter which I have from them now is so full, so much to the point, and so agreeable that I feel under a permanent bond of obligation to them ... Maintain close relations with them and we over here will always perform our part duly as we do every day; of this you and they will be the judge.[115]

Interpreting business relations as friends occurred not only when business was going well but also when business went bad, even very bad:

> We want only what is owed to us. May it please you also to want to do thus, and truly, for in good faith not a little have we discussed this dispute between us. May you or yours also wish to settle it as is done between friends. And so let it please you that not having sent these letters [i.e., business correspondence germane to the dispute] to [your office in] Florence, to send them without further delay.[116]

> I am advised by many letters that Basciano [da Pessina] is not there. You will have spoken with him about these blessed accounts that, by his shortcomings, are not settled, and truly it is a great wrong; this is not the friendship [*amicizia*] and brotherhood [*fratelanza*] that I had with him, and he has

[114] Ibid., 253.

[115] Richards, *Florentine Merchants in the Age of the Medici*, 85: Giovanni Maringhi to ser Niccolo Michelozzi, May 4, 1501.

[116] A.S.F., *M.A.P.* 87, fol. 339r: Andrea de' Bardi to the Orlandini company in Bruges, March 26, 1405). In practically identical terms, Bardi also wrote to the Baldesi company in Bruges that "we have wanted, and still want, to settle this dispute as one must do between friends" (ibid., fol. 346r: July 6, 1405). And several times in the same letter he claimed to have acted toward them "with love and faith, as one must do between friends." According to another letter he wrote the same day to the Orlandini (ibid., fol. 347v), he believed that between friends "one may be more forthright in speech," and remarked that "we hold it dear that you have spoken from your heart at length."

> not done well in clamming up with me [*pigliare gozzo*], and I don't know why . . . And I must observe that when he made accounts with me in Avignon, that amounted to 40,000 pounds or so, there was not even a penny missing, we had such a great relationship, so that one could go so far as to say that if I owed him 1000 florins, I would approach him and say to him how I considered him more than a brother, and I still do. And despite what he has done to me, I will never forget the love and brotherhood that was between him and me.[117]

The ambiguous meanings of *amizicia*, or even of *amore*, were in no way precise enough to imply what exactly to do in markets. The invocation of *amicizia* in business was instead an attempt to negotiate empathetic understanding of one another's interests. Words by themselves could not enforce reliable economic behavior. For that, the social anchoring of language in actual families and in actual neighborhoods, with third-party observers and enforcers, was helpful. But ambiguities in shared language were essential for the creative relational extension and groping of Renaissance businessmen beyond the limits of their social inheritance. The language of *amicizia* was an important first step in this Florentine relational extension from family and neighborhood into markets. By itself, however, that dyadic trope was not sufficient for scaling up into large, far-reaching and highly connected credit networks.

Onore

Like *amicizia*, the word *onore* did not have a single unambiguous meaning in Renaissance Florence. As was evident in our statistics, the republican conception of *onore* as public office or service to the state was alive and well in the Florence of 1427. But medieval conceptions of *onore* as ancient lineage or as martial glory had hardly vanished, especially among magnates. And sober guildsmen conceptions of *onore* as thrift, discipline, and hard work maintained their appeal, especially among new men. Newer conceptions of *onore* as patronage, in the senses of liberality and *magnificenza*, so prominent in the Medici regime soon to come, were starting to gain traction. These alternative meanings of *onore* and nobility were put into debate with each

[117] Frangioni, *Milano fine trecento*, appendix, letter 8: Francesco Datini to Tieri di Benci in Avignon, August 4, 1392.

other in the humanist dialogues of the time.[118] To the extent that the inflection was on the republican conception of *onore*, service to the community was highlighted, with commercial credit flowing in recognition of that.

Regardless of precise inflection, business-letter discussions of honor came up most often in times of economic trouble. Thus, for example, in a dispute concerning 1,000 florins missing because of the actions of a certain Michele, Andrea de' Bardi wrote to both Antonio di Sandro Cittadini and Domenico Pazzi in May of 1405 that they should take action "for the honor of said Michele."[119] And in a letter of March 31, 1404, Bardi wrote to Alberto Aldobrandini in Paris urging him to settle a particular deal because it redounded to both his honor (*onore*) and his advantage (*utile*).[120] In the same letter quoted above about the deadbeat Basciano, Datini went on to assert that "I would come back a thousand miles to do my duty towards him and every other good affair; and it concerns his honor not to do likewise to me, even if I did not merit it."[121]

In this context, complimenting people about their honor might gain overtones of a veiled threat about loss of that honor:

> Dearest friend, . . . When I was there I spoke to you many times about the money that you owe to the heirs of your partner Antonio di Tuccio Manetti. And now Andrea di Buonaventura has arrived there, who comes there for this reason and for other business of his, and he has begged me that I write to you concerning this matter, and that I pray of you that you should wish to act towards him as the worthy man that you are. And I am quite certain it need not be said to you, that you will pay your debt to him in this matter, both out of duty, and also to lighten the burden on your heart. And I pray of you that you should wish to do this for them like the worthy man that you are.[122]

Indeed the question of honor was always tied, overtly or covertly, to the issue of reputation (*fama*). *Fama* typically refers to other merchants'

[118] See Alberti, *Albertis of Florence*; McLean, *Art of the Network*, chapter 3; and Albert Rabil, *Knowledge, Goodness and Power: The Debate over Nobility among Quattrocento Italian Humanists* (Binghamton, NY, 1991).

[119] A.S.F., *M.A.P.* 87, fols. 343r and 343v. Honor, he noted elsewhere, required that *corrispondenti* look out for each other's salvation (*salvezza*) as well as their own. (A.S.F., *M.A.P.* 87, fol. 345v).

[120] Ibid., fol. 335v.

[121] Frangioni, *Milano fine trecento*, appendix, letter 8: Francesco Datini to Tieri di Benci in Avignon, August 4, 1392.

[122] Ibid., appendix, letter 18: Tommaso di ser Giovanni to Lorenzo di Tingo, May 28, 1400.

collective evaluation of one's interior character or soul. Gossip—either orally or through letters—was the mechanism through which such collective evaluations were made. Such gossip could help you:

> I, Andrea, have received letters from Ciandrello. I have told him so much about you, and that you have done him such honor, that if something pertained to you alone it would suffice [to obtain his help]. And if it were not already the case that I were obligated [*obrighato*] to you in every respect, now I am [obligated to you] that much more, and I thank you.[123]

Or such gossip could hurt you:

> We have heard via letters from Montpelier that this Guglielmo Pigniolo has lost the confidence [of others: *avea perduto la fede*]. We do not know if this is true. These times are too dangerous. Tell us what you hear of it, and similarly how the affairs of the Bocci are proceeding, having seen these fail and how many evils have come this year to merchants.[124]

Tommaso Spinelli provides a clear example of the link between merchant gossip and personal anxiety about honor. In his letter to his friend Gherardo Maffei about the setbacks he received as a papal banker, Spinelli referred to his honor—as Jacks and Caferro put it, the banker's most precious commodity—half a dozen times in this letter, sometimes in salvific terms. He wrote that the Pope "has found out the truth and has recognized that I did my duty, and he has endorsed me as a faithful man and a good merchant, and it is clear that I have done the greatest service to the Church of God for a long time, and thus he absolves me and imposes silence on whosoever would speak to the contrary." The last part of the absolution pleased him the most, as it would clear his name "in the presence of merchants, and I greatly desire this strictly for honor's sake . . . I will have lost my [goods], but I will at least have conserved my honor." All of this was driven by Tommaso's strong

[123] A.S.F., *M.A.P.* 87, fol. 337r: letter of October 1, 1404 from Andrea de' Bardi to Orlandini company in Bruges. Honor typically communicated both an obligatory, internalized commitment and an expectation of assistance by others—a duality succinctly expressed by Bardi in a letter to Simone and Iacopo Covoni in the fall of 1404 (ibid., fol. 337v). Here he both expressed his obligation to them (*in su quello vi si scrisse esserne voi obrighato*), and urged them to honor their obligation to him: "as long as we both shall live I am certain you will do your duty" (*che quando viveremo sono certo farete il dovere*).

[124] Ibid., fol. 340r: Andrea de' Bardi to Lorenzo di Dinozzo & co in Avignon, April 4, 1405.

desire to leave the Pope's employ with a good reputation for himself [*ch'io lassi buona fama di me*].[125]

The establishment and measurement of honor through gossip among businessmen was important to the discipline of Florentine markets. But in social exchange there is also the deeper idea of making each other through gifts. "For Paolo da Certaldo, 'a man without a friend is like a body without a soul' and 'a man who loses his friends is worse than dead.'"[126] This was no mere metaphor in Renaissance Florentine markets. Because credit was the lifeblood of Florentine business, fellow businessmen made you by extending credit and business to you, and they could destroy you by withdrawing that from you. Social exchange, friends, and reputation were not peripheral to markets; they were the discipline that made personalistic markets work.

Republican elections to Priorate did not substitute for this process of intense gossip among merchants about one another's honor. Rather they built upon it by measuring and certifying gossip about character into a public status observable by all. Election to Priorate was not an automatic guarantee of one's economic creditworthiness. But it was an institutionalized signal that even someone not known directly by you might be worth taking a business chance on. Thereby, cliquish personal networks based on private *amicizia* opened out into elitist personal networks based on public *onore*.

Our emphasis on the blending of economic, social, and political logics in commercial credit is reinforced by the widespread presence of the same language of *raccomandazione* in both business and patronage letters.[127] By *raccomandazione*, Florentines did not simply mean being recommended to others, and certainly not only being recommended to others for specific tasks or opportunities. *Raccomandazione* was equally, but more profoundly, a plea for recognition. To recommend oneself to another, as Florentines so formulaically did in the conclusions of their letters, was to ask *to be remembered* by another, to respect and be respected by another. To be in a circle of *raccomandazione* yielded material benefits, but it also signified one's membership in a community of people who promised to act responsibly and supportively toward each other, in a manner similar to obligational claims to honor. To deny the need for *raccomandazione* was not to deny its value,

[125] See Jacks and Caferro, *Spinelli of Florence*, 75–76, 303–04. On the notion of *fama* in general, see Thelma Fenster and Daniel Lord Smail, eds., *"Fama": The Politics of Talk and Reputation in Medieval Europe* (Ithaca, NY, 2003).

[126] Weissman, *Ritual Brotherhood in Renaissance Florence*, 28.

[127] See McLean, *Art of the Network*, chapter 6.

but to uphold the certainty of its being offered. This is the cultural meaning behind Bartolomeo Rustichi's assertion to the Datini company in Genoa that "We do not recommend to you very much our own affairs: it does not seem to us necessary, but we consider you will undertake them employing such diligence as were they your own; and this we remind you, and pray of you and we will do the same for you."[128]

Businessmen in markets and politicians in state offices did not do the same things in Renaissance Florence, but they communicated in similar ways. This is not altogether surprising since there was so much dual-role overlap between these two sets of actors. Despite the potential for divergence across the two sets of evidence, in fact our statistical and textual analyses came to similar conclusions.

Conclusion

Here, first, we briefly compare Florentine commercial credit with financial activities in Venice and Genoa in order to situate Florence in a broader understanding of the late medieval and early Renaissance economy. Second, we outline what we consider to be crucial elements of a theory of personalistic markets, in order to guide future research in this area.

No quantitative study of Venetian credit exists, but the following observation of Reinhold C. Mueller about Rialto domestic banks (*banchi di scritta*) is pertinent: "Payment in bank money was a legitimate means of extinguishing a debt . . . . Bankers kept a cash reserve for only a fraction of their liabilities, and one banker kept current accounts with the other bankers."[129] These *giro* accounts acted like checking accounts, facilitating the clearance of debt across accounts and across multiple parties while also providing opportunities for overdrafts at crucial times. In these respects, Venetian *banchi di scritta* resemble the smaller Florentine *cambio* deposit banks and arguably predate them.[130] But commercial credit in Venice differs from that in Florence in crucial ways. The *banchi di scritta* were always very few in number—typically no more than four or so at a time. They were not international, with branch offices all over Europe, and they did not engage

[128] Federigo Melis, ed., *Documenti per la storia economia dei secoli XII–XVI* (Firenze, 1972), document 10: October 1395.

[129] Reinhold C. Mueller, *The Venetian Money Market: Banks, Panics, and the Public Debt, 1200–1500* (Baltimore, 1997), 16 and more generally chapter 1. See also Reinhold C. Mueller, "The Role of Bank Money in Venice, 1300–1500," *Studi Veneziani* 3 (1979): 47–96.

[130] Tognetti, "L'attivita di banca locale di una grande compagnia Fiorentina del XV secolo."

in merchant activity.[131] Florentine banking, in contrast, was less a specialized industry than it was a widespread system of extending credit among diverse companies.

Venetian international merchants, a group quite distinct from Venetian bankers, kept their accounts in venture accounting, that is, a separate account for each voyage.[132] Venture accounting of ship voyages is inconsistent with current accounts for persons and companies.

Florentine commercial credit was more like Genoa than Venice in its decentralized diffusion throughout the economy, but still, there were significant differences. On the basis of his quantitative analysis of the famous notarial records of medieval Genoa, Van Doosselaere has reported extensive credit contracts among Genoese merchants over two centuries.[133] These were technically sophisticated for their time. Van Doosselaere did not distinguish transactional from relational credits, but most of his credits appear to be transactional in character.[134] Genoese sea loans, overland and maritime exchange (*cambium*), and promissory notes were transaction-specific contracts, not account books.

In a study covering a time more contemporaneous with our own, Jacques Heers reports that Quattrocento Genoese companies were formed by capitalist investors fluidly pooling their money: Each investor often had investments in many companies, workmen in the industry were not included in investor partnerships, and investors easily switched from investment to investment.[135] This stands in contrast to Florentine systems, which were composed of more stable partnerships between a dominant investor and his industry-specialized branch managers. While data on Genoese commercial

[131] Indeed, the Florentines took care of Venetian international banking needs (Mueller, *Venetian Money Market*, 255–56).

[132] Frederic C. Lane, *Andrea Barbarigo: Merchant of Venice, 1418–1448* (Baltimore, 1944), 163–71, and "Venture Accounting in Medieval Business Management," *Bulletin of the Business Historical Society* 19 (1945): 164–73; de Roover, "The Development of Accounting," 161–64.

[133] Van Doosselaere, *Commercial Agreements and Social Dynamics in Medieval Genoa*, esp. chapter 4. While the volume of credit relations is roughly comparable between our studies, his data on notarial contracts thinly cover a long span of time, 1154–1406, whereas our data from the *catasto* thickly cover one year. Van Doosselaere explicitly challenges the "individualistic" stereotype of medieval Genoa modeled by Avner Greif, *Institutions and the Path to the Modern Economy* (Cambridge, 2006).

[134] Robert J. Reynolds, "Genoese Trade in the Late Twelfth Century," *Journal of Economic and Business History* 3 (1931): 362–81; R. D. Face, "Techniques of Business in the Trade between the Fairs of Champagne and the South of Europe in the Twelfth and Thirteenth Centuries," *Economic History Review*, 2nd ser., 10 (1958): 427–38; Rosalind Kent Berlow, "The Development of Business Techniques Used at the Fairs of Champagne," *Studies in Medieval and Renaissance History* 8 (1971): 3–31.

[135] "I found no fewer than forty-nine credit agreements tying him to forty-four different people" (Van Doosselaere, *Commercial Agreements and Social Dynamics in Medieval Genoa*, 144).

credit from this period do not exist because of the paucity of account books, it is unlikely that long-term relational credit on the Florentine scale could have developed on such a fluid capital foundation.[136]

Undoubtedly, the organization of financial markets varies a great deal across cases and across spatial, temporal, and cultural contexts. Neoclassical economic theory eviscerates this variation. The neoclassical approach, influential in economic history, is constructed on the assumption of impersonal markets—choices are made on the basis of goods and their prices, not on the basis of the identities of the persons transacting. Renaissance Florentine markets did not operate like this, especially in the most technically advanced sectors of the Florentine economy. Rather than simply dispute the core assumptions of neoclassical economics, however, we feel there is value in specifying positively the important elements that any alternative theory of personalistic markets should incorporate.

This multidisciplinary task has only begun, but the case of Florence suggests the following components:[137]

(a) Social exchange and reciprocity are the micro-mechanisms of economic exchange, with credit being the currency. Capitalist inventions like double-entry accounting and partnership systems formalized and perfected personal exchange; they did not displace it.
(b) Gossip about reputation provides discipline to the market, as much as do prices.
(c) Economic exchange in the market grows on the lattice of other social networks that provide its context. Socially embedded economic networks can be cliquish and incestuous, or they can be open and expansive, depending upon how multiple networks are arrayed. Porous elites with social mobility are helpful to sustain open and expansive personalistic markets.
(d) Political institutions are important for the development of markets not only because of the rule of law. Republican political institutions

[136] Jacques Heers, *Genoa nel '400: Civiltà mediterranea, grande capitalismo e capitalismo popolare* (Milan, 1983), 135–41.

[137] For useful but incomplete steps in this direction, see Neil J. Smelser and Richard Swedberg eds., *The Handbook of Economic Sociology* (New York, 1994, 2005), James E. Rauch and Alessandra Casella eds., *Networks and Markets* (New York, 2001), and the many works cited therein.

may add public transparency and efficiency to the operation of private gossip, and they can induce the overlay of multiple social roles, such as merchant and politician.

(e) Linguistic and network ambiguity induces creative exploration and innovation in social relationships, even as it enables free riding and lies.[138] Policing the latter should not be so strict as to squelch the former.[139]

How these findings generalize to other historical and comparative settings remains to be explored in depth, but we suspect their widespread applicability.

[138] McLean, *Art of the Network*, chapter 1.

[139] John F. Padgett, Doowan Lee, and Nick Collier, "Economic Production as Chemistry," *Industrial and Corporate Change* 12 (2003): 843–77, esp. 854–55 and 863–64.

8

Fiscal Innovation Gone Bad

Comprehensive Business Censuses from the Florentine 1427, 1433, and 1458 *Catasti*

Francesco Bettarini and John F. Padgett

The first descriptive purpose of this article is to document changes in the industrial composition of Renaissance Florence, through business censuses that we have extracted from household-wealth declarations in the 1427, 1433, and 1458 Florentine *catasti* or tax censuses. The finances of all Florentine businesses, both export oriented and domestically oriented, were comprehensively self-reported in these tax censuses, as an innovative new element in the fiscal calculation of gross and taxable household wealth. These consecutive censuses reveal decline in the number of businesses in many but not all of the industries in Florence over this 30-year period. The second purpose of this article is to explain this economic decline. We find, through both quantitative and qualitative evidence, that the innovative tax *catasti* themselves were to blame, through all too effectively extracting enormous levels of taxes from the wealthy Florentine population, in order to fund mercenary wars related to the emergence of Italian Renaissance regional or "territorial" states. The economic decline was due not only to the direct effect of heavy taxes but also to the indirect effect of default contagion among highly leveraged companies doing business with each other on credit. In a previous *JMH* article,[1] John Padgett and Paul McLean demonstrated that high business leverage was rooted in the social embeddedness of Florentine businessmen in dense underlying social and political

Journal of Modern History (March 2025): 1-43, with Francesco Bettarini. Republished with permission.

[1] John F. Padgett and Paul D. McLean, "Economic Credit in Renaissance Florence," *Journal of Modern History* 83 (2011): 1–47.

Organizational Invention in Renaissance Florence. John F. Padgett, Oxford University Press. © Oxford University Press (2026). DOI: 10.1093/oso/9780197789216.003.0008

networks. Hence, "credit bubbles" occurred even in early-modern economies operating through personalistic social exchange. This case study contradicts the rosy portrait in the social science literature of a positive relationship between state formation and economic growth. We show that newly emergent Italian Renaissance regional states did not always produce positive economic gains for the capital cities that constructed them. This raises questions about economic self-interest explanations of that expansion. An important corollary for Florentine political history is our finding that this economic slump contributed structurally to the political rise of Cosimo de' Medici, and hence to the birth of the long-lasting Medici regime, through drastic contraction and concentration in the domestic banking industry. This tax-induced contraction in the domestic banking industry left the Medici Bank and its associated partnership system towering above its previously vibrant competition, which mostly fell away. "Coevolution" to us means that politics and economics in Florence causally shaped each other's development.[2]

Introduction: The Italian Renaissance State

A number of disciplines have attempted to explain the Italian Renaissance style of state-building, which was the consolidation of feuding medieval city-states into a set of conflicting "territorial" regional states—such as Milan/Lombardy, Venice/Veneto, Florence/Tuscany, Rome/Papal States, and Naples/Southern Italy. Sociologists who follow Charles Tilly have classified leading cities in Northern Italy as the "capital-intensive route to [European] state formation," thereby emphasizing the urbanized and economically advanced social fabric of that area.[3] Except for Greif on Genoa,[4] economists

[2] For further development of this point, extended over two centuries of coevolution, see the present volume John F. Padgett, *Organizational Invention in Renaissance Florence* (Oxford, 2026).

[3] Charles Tilly, *Coercion, Capital, and European States, AD 990–1992* (Oxford, 1992). Charles Tilly, "War Making and State Making as Organized Crime," in *Bringing the State Back In*, ed. Peter Evans, Dietrich Rueschmeyer, and Theda Skocpol (Cambridge UK, 1985), 169–87. See also Sidney Tarrow, "From Comparative Historical Analysis to 'Local Theory': The Italian City-State Route to the Modern State," *Theory and Society* 33 (2004): 443–71; Richard Lachmann, *Capitalists in Spite of Themselves: Elite Conflict and Economic Transitions in Early Modern Europe* (Oxford, 2000); and Lars Bo Kaspersen and Jeppe Strandsbjerg, *Does War Make States? Investigations of Charles Tilly's Historical Sociology* (Cambridge, 2017).

[4] Avner Greif, "Cultural Beliefs and the Organization of Society: A Historical and Theoretical Reflection on Collectivist and Individualist Societies," *The Journal of Political Economy* 102 (1994): 912–50.

have not paid much attention to Italy, perhaps because Italy does not fit the standard transalpine institutional template of king versus parliament.[5] But in broad comparative work, economists and political scientists have emphasized the alleged historical (and cross-sectional) correlation between strong states, on the one hand, and strong markets and economic growth, on the other.[6] "Strong" in this social-science literature usually means rule of law and/or fiscal capacity to raise revenues.

Among historians, the groundwork for investigating state building and economic growth in Renaissance Italy brilliantly has been laid by a previous generation of historians who focused on specific Italian cities.[7] But the current generation of historians, following the lead of Georgio Chittolini,[8] has turned toward the study of Italian regional states, built by large cities around themselves in 1300–1500. This historiography has recently been surveyed and reviewed in a comprehensive edited book by

[5] Douglass North, *Structure and Change in Economic History* (New York, 1981). Douglass North and Barry Weingast, "Constitutions and Commitment: The Evolution of Institutions Governing Public Choice in Seventeenth-Century England," *Journal of Economic History* 49 (1989): 803–32. D. Acemulo, "Politics and Economics in Weak and Strong States," *Journal of Monetary Economics* 52 (2005): 1199–226.

[6] Mark Dincecco, "Fiscal Centralization, Limited Government, and Public Revenues in Europe, 1650–1913," *Journal of Economic History* 69 (2009): 48–103. Mark Dincecco, *Political Transformations and Public Finances: Europe, 1650–1913* (Cambridge UK, 2011). Political scientists trained as economists, like Dincecco, recently have taken a very aggregate comparative approach, with large-n statistical research relating country-level fiscal indicators (such as "fiscal capacity" = state revenues or government-bond interest rates) to types of regimes and types of external conflict, over long blocks of time. Using similar methodology for a large sample of European city-states, David Stasavage, *States of Credit: Size, Power, and the Development of European Polities* (Princeton, NJ, 2011) has demonstrated historical feedback between political "autonomy" and economic growth, proxied as population growth. "Was Weber Right? The Role of Urban Autonomy in Europe's Rise," *American Political Science Review* (2014) 108: 337–54.

[7] Touchstones for us in the Florentine literature include: (a) for Florentine fiscal history: Marvin Becker, *Florence in Transition*, volume two (Baltimore, 1968); (b) for Florentine political history: Gene A. Brucker, *Florentine Politics and Society, 1343–1378* (Princeton, 1962), Gene A. Brucker, *The Civic World of Early Renaissance Florence* (Princeton, 1977), and John M. Najemy, *Corporatism and Consensus in Florentine Electoral Politics, 1280–1400* (Chapel Hill, 1982); (c) for Florentine economic history: Richard A. Goldthwaite, *The Economy of Renaissance Florence* (Baltimore, 2009); and (d) for Florentine social history, David Herlihy and Christiane Klapisch-Zuber, *Tuscans and Their Families: A Study of the Florentine Catasto of 1427* (New Haven, 1985). Many of these distinguished historians lamented the lack of close integration between their specialized subfields, even when studying the same city. Of these, Brucker was the best at synthesis. Among this earlier generation of Florentine historians, the primary points of departure for this particular paper will be Goldthwaite, *The Economy of Renaissance Florence*; Anthony Molho, *Florentine Public Finances in the Early Renaissance, 1400–1433*, (Cambridge, MA, 1971); and Elio Conti, *L'imposta diretta a Firenze nel Quattrocento, 1427–1494* (Roma, 1984).

[8] Giorgio Chittolini, *La formazione dello Stato regionale e le istituzioni del contado: secoli XIV e XV* (Torino, 1979). Giorgio Chittolini, "Cities, 'city states,' and regional states in north-central Italy," *Theory and Society* 18 (1989): 689–706.

Gamberini and Lazzarini.[9] Compared to the Weberian centralized bureaucratic stereotype of "state" often adopted by social scientists, current historians have emphasized the cobbled-together and negotiated character of Italian Renaissance regional states.[10] Among this current generation of historians of Italian Renaissance states, our points of departure will be the economic historians: Stephan Epstein, Paolo Malanima, Franco Franceschi, William Caferro, Guido Alfani, and Luciano Pezzolo.[11]

Epstein was the trailblazer in this latter group. He focused directly on the implications of Italian Renaissance state formation for economic growth. Basically, Epstein argued that "market integration" was the best formula for economic growth in premodern Italy—namely, the removal of barriers to trade among otherwise feuding city-states. Renaissance regional states could achieve this to the extent that they imposed standardized economic policies throughout their heterogeneous territories. Sicily and Milan were the cases that Epstein used to exemplify this path of high regional growth, because those two states had centralized political sovereignties. Florence was the case Epstein highlighted that did not, because its merchant-republican polity split satellite Tuscan cities from each other, through idiosyncratic hub-and-spoke economic and political policies designed to maintain economic domination by the central city.[12,13]

[9] Andrea Gamberini and Isabella Lazzarini (eds.), *The Italian Renaissance State* (Cambridge UK, 2012). See also William J. Connell and Andrea Zorzi (eds.), *Florentine Tuscany: Structures and Practices of Power* (Cambridge UK, 2000).

[10] Historians often resist the teleology latent in continuous-variable classification principles like "strong versus weak" states. In social-science parlance, however, Italian regional states were "strong" in terms of fiscal capacity, but "weak" in terms of organizational coherence, thereby violating the economists' alleged correlation.

[11] S. R. Epstein, *Freedom and Growth: The Rise of States and Markets in Europe, 1300–1750* (London, 2000). Paolo Malanima, "La formazione di una regione economica," *Società e Storia* 6 (1983): 229–69. Franco Franceschi and Luca Molà, "Regional states and economic development," in *The Italian Renaissance State*, eds. Gamberini and Lazzarini, 444–66. William Caferro, *Mercenary Companies and the Decline of Siena* (Baltimore, 1998). William P. Caferro, "Warfare and Economy in Renaissance Italy, 1350–1450," *Journal of Interdisciplinary History* 39 (2008): 167–209. Guido Alfani, *Calamities and the Economy in Renaissance Italy: The Grand Tour of the Horsemen of the Apocalypse* (Houndmills Hampshire, 2013). Luciano Pezzolo, "Bonds and Government Debt in Italian City States, 1250–1650" in *The Origin of Value: The Financial Innovations that Created Modern Capital Markets*, eds. William N. Goetzmann and K. Geert Rouwenhorst (Oxford 2005), 145–63.

[12] Malanima, in "La formazione di una regione economica," disagrees with Epstein's assessment of Florentine exploitation of its smaller peripheral cities, but Franceschi and Molà, in "Regional states and economic development," resolve the disagreement by agreeing with Epstein on wool but with Malanima on minor proto-industries. In support of Epstein's argument, once Florence finally shifted from a republic to a duchy in 1530, greater policy focus on the economic interests of the region, not just of the city, became manifest under Cosimo I.

[13] Petralia adds a very important background observation that puts Florence versus the Milan or Venice regional state structures into comparative context: "The catasto of 1427 illustrates, no less

The problem we have with Epstein's influential argument is that whether economic growth of the central city was attained through Epstein's preferred positive-sum "market integration" route of economic growth in the territory at large (Sicily and Milan), or through the zero-sum "exploitation" route of domination of peripheral cities (in Florence), territorial expansion should lead to economic growth for the central city. But we shall present evidence of economic decline, at least for the 1427–1458 period of our study, for the central city of Florence when war-induced taxation pressure was extreme.[14] Political expansion of Italian Renaissance states is not easily explained by "the economic interests of the dominant city." Indeed, "interests of the dominant city" are not straightforward to perceive, either by historians or by contemporaries.[15] In the conclusion to this article, we briefly shall survey the comparison cases of Venice and Milan, to show (with less complete data than for Florence) that their central-city economies also suffered from vigorous wars in pursuit of territorial expansion. Whether long-term economic benefits at the regional level exceeded short-term costs at the city level is an open question and is hard to operationalize. Arguably, expansionary wars in Italy were driven by reasons other than economics, even though "capital-intensive" merchants, not "coercive-intensive" warrior monarchs, were the heartbeat of most major Renaissance Italian cities.[16] At least in these Italian

from the structure of its fiscal income, the deformity of Florence's political body in the fifteenth century. The dominion possessed an extraordinarily large head in relation to its other members, with more than half of its inhabitants and more than three quarters of its wealth concentrated in the capital city and its own contado" in Giuseppe Petralia, "Fiscality, Politics and Dominion in Florentine Tuscany at the End of the Middle Ages," in *Florentine Tuscany*, eds. William J. Connell and Andrea Zorzi, 65–89, esp. 88. In any war between Florence and Milan or Venice, in other words, Florence was fighting above its weight class. Such interregional wars were closer to a city fighting a territorial state than one territorial state fighting another. Fiscal pressure on Florence's city economy, the topic of this article, was correspondingly intense.

[14] We do not preclude the possibility, however, of Florentine economic growth bouncing back once war-induced tax pressure was relieved.

[15] In Arthur Field, *The Intellectual Struggle for Florence: Humanists and the Beginnings of the Medici Regime, 1420–1440* (Oxford 2017), 26, Field counted 107 times between 1424 and 1427 that Florentine legislatures voted down repeated proposals by their leadership to institute the first 1427 catasto. While the Albizzi leadership eventually and doggedly prevailed, Florentine politicians of the time clearly did not perceive it as obvious what the Florentine collective interest in war and taxes really was. See also Conti, *L'imposta diretta*, for further discussion of the Florentine catasto debate.

[16] Paul D. McLean, "Patronage, Citizenship, and the Stalled Emergence of the Modern State in Renaissance Florence," *Comparative Study of Society and History* 47 (2005): 638–64, has been one of the most explicit in the literature of emphasizing the contextual multiplicity of politician roles, as opposed to an essentialism of imputed hierarchies of "core" interests. In Jonathan Schoots, Benjamin Rohr, Katalin Prajda, and John F. Padgett, "Conflict and Revolt in the Name of Unity: Florentine Factions in the *Consulte e Pratiche* on the Cusp of the Ciompi Revolt," *Poetics* 78 (2020): art. 101386, the authors have demonstrated empirically, in *Consulte e Pratiche* speeches, the fluidity of Florentines' self-reported interests depending upon institutional and circumstantial context.

cases, the pursuit of mercantile profit was not necessarily consistent with the pursuit of territorial expansion.[17]

Very recently, the current generation of economic historians in History departments has focused on "the new history of capitalism."[18] Dealing primarily with nineteenth-century America, this recent historiography is only tangentially related to Renaissance Italy. But to the extent that the spirit of this new historiography challenges the neoclassical economic orthodoxy of efficiency, our own emphasis on the particularistic social-network character of the Renaissance Florentine economy is in alliance with it.[19]

This article proceeds as follows: After describing the sources, including what made the Florentine *catasti* innovative, we first present our descriptive findings about business demography, by industry, in 1427, 1433, and 1458. The overall quantitative picture presented is one of economic decline, albeit with considerable variation by industry. Second, we quote interpretations by participants of the causes of their economic problems, as presented in contemporaneous *Consulte e Pratiche* political debates. Third, from these debates we extract four specific versions of the *strettezza di denari* (shortage of money) themes highlighted in those quotations, and then test those hypotheses against collateral evidence: namely, (a) shortage of species/gold due to exorbitant mercenary expenses, (b) collapse of government bond values, (c) flight abroad of liquid international capital, and (d) contagion of credit default among highly leveraged Florentine businesses who did repeat business with each other. The first two of these financial problems would apply to any Italian Renaissance state, in proportion to the tax magnitude of their war expense. The third and fourth of these mechanisms, if not unique

[17] David Stasavage, *States of Credit: Size, Power, and the Development of European Polities* (Princeton, NJ, 2011), has shown how republican Italian city-states were dominated politically by merchants. While true enough, this emphasis fails to explain why Florentine merchants, led by Rinaldo Albizzi, aggressively pursued an expansionist regional state policy so blatantly at odds with their own economic interests. The hybrid label "republican merchants" better highlights their dual, not always consistent, identities.

[18] Sven Beckert, "History of American Capitalism," in *American History Now*, edited by Eric Foner et al. (Philadelphia, 2011). Eric Hilt, "Economic History, Historical Analysis, and 'The New History of Capitalism,'" *The Journal of Economic History* 77 (2017): 511–36. Jonathan Levy, *Ages of American Capitalism: A History of the United States* (New York, 2021).

[19] See John F. Padgett and Paul D. McLean, "Economic Credit in Renaissance Florence," *Journal of Modern History* 83 (2011): 1–47. These authors measured and emphasized that dense commercial credit ties among Florentine businesses were social, embedded in, and generated by underlying "oligarchic" social and political relations among those companies' owners. These were not specialized businessmen, but rather multifunctional republican businessmen. For further statistical proof that Renaissance Florence was not a neo-classical market, see Paul D. McLean and John F. Padgett, "Was Florence a Perfectly Competitive Market? Transactional Evidence from the Renaissance," *Theory and Society* 26 (1997): 209–44.

to Florence, were at least exacerbated by the intense involvement of Florentine businesses in international and domestic banking and by the deep social embedding of the Florentine business-credit economy in its dense and mostly elite noneconomic social networks. The advanced stage of financial development of the Florentine economy was conducive both to rapid economic growth and to credit collapse.

The article will close by tracing an important political consequence of these economic events—namely, the rise of Cosimo de' Medici and the long-lasting Medici regime. The mechanism we highlight, previously undocumented, is the drastically increased domination of the Medici Bank within the organizational field of diversified partnership systems, an earlier organizational invention which we have studied previously.[20] This is a powerful example of unintended consequence of economics on politics.

The Florentine Catasto

Compared to Florence's previous tax system, the 1427 Florentine *catasto* was a major innovation both in assessment procedure and in geographical scope.[21,22] The innovation in assessment procedure was the inclusion of explicitly itemized business finances in the calculation of household wealth. The innovation in geography was the extension of the city's own taxation system to all of Florence's Tuscan regional territories.[23] Both of these

[20] See John F. Padgett and Paul D. McLean, "Organizational Invention and Elite Transformation: The Birth of Partnership Systems in Renaissance Florence," *American Journal of Sociology* 111 (2006): 1463–568.

[21] The word "catasto" in past and present Italian usage usually refers to land and real estate registries. For an early Trecento example, see Giovanni Cherubini, "La 'Tavola delle Possessioni' del commune di Siena." It was the inclusion of business wealth in the 1427, 1433, and 1459 Florentine *catasti* that made them innovative—and also more equitable and efficient in their measurement of total wealth, especially in economically advanced states like Florence. Extensive reliance on private account books made this city-wide self-reporting of business wealth possible (and auditable).

[22] Herlihy and Klapisch-Zuber, *Tuscans and Their Families*, 9–10, and Mueller, *The Venetian Money Market* (Baltimore, 1997), 492–501, discuss the extent to which the Venetian *Estimi* of 1403 and 1411 were precedents to the 1427 Florentine *catasto*. Certainly, Florentine politicians were aware of Venetian tax practices. Unfortunately, Venetian tax returns from these two *estimi* have not survived, to compare with Florence's rich records. Judging from Mueller's two surviving household examples, the legal categories were similar but with drastic differences in volume of credits and debits reported. This apparent difference in magnitude reflects not Venetian versus Florentine law but rather differences between the two economies themselves: According to Goldthwaite (personal communication), Florentine business relations with each other were intensive and repetitive, whereas business relations among Venetian international merchants were more episodic because their economy was "voyage" based.

[23] This second innovation provoked much hostility and resistance in peripheral territories, in part because it violated prior negotiated fiscal agreements between Florence and subject cities, but this is not the focus of our paper.

innovations were repealed in 1434, when Cosimo de' Medici came to power, but then were episodically reinstalled in 1458 and in 1469 only to be repealed again. The literature is not clear about why this revenue-effective Florentine *catasto* kept getting repealed,[24] but our paper provides one clear and straightforward answer—namely, the economic chaos that it provoked.

The Florentine tax system, both before and after *catasto* reform, had three components: (1) a direct tax, called *estimo*, was levied on rural properties (*contado*) outside of Florence itself;[25] (2) a system of indirect or sales taxes, called *gabelles*, was levied on a variety of commodities[26] throughout Florentine territories; and (3) a system of forced loans or involuntary government bonds, called *prestanze*, was levied on Florentine citizens themselves.[27] The forced loan or *prestanze* system funded the so-called Monte or government debt, in which Florentine citizens in exchange for their tax contributions received credits or bonds which paid regular interest, and promised (though hardly ever delivered) eventual repayment of principal.[28] Money to pay for *prestanze* interest payments came from revenues from *gabelles*. Hence, the combined *gabelles/prestanze* system represented a regressive net wealth transfer from Tuscan territories to Florence and from poorer to richer Florentines.[29]

The Florentine *estimo* tax on rural (and small town) properties has been coded and analyzed by Alfani and Ammannati, who coded and analyzed a

[24] Anthony Molho, in his "The State and Public Finance: A Hypothesis Based on the History of Late Medieval Florence," in Julius Kirshner (ed.), *The Origins of the State in Italy, 1300–1600* (Chicago, 1996), 97–135, raises the suspicion, seconded by Petralia, that the Albizzi regime was "modernising," whereas the Medici regime was clientelist in orientation. It was not as easy to manipulate tax assessments through favoritism in the *catasto* as it had been in the previous neighborhood-committee system. This indeed was one of the principle contemporary arguments for that reform.

[25] After 1315, Florentine citizens not only resisted but prohibited direct taxes like *estimi* on themselves, even though the topic was occasionally revisited and discussed (Brucker, *Florentine Politics*, 1962).

[26] In particular, salt, oil, wine, wheat, hogs, and, most importantly, gate customs.

[27] In addition, in subject cities in outlying territories (*distretto*), those cities' preexisting tax systems often were grandfathered in as "privileges" upon Florentine conquest, with negotiated revenue totals transferred to Florence. The standardized catasto violated those previous, heterogeneous "privileges," thereby provoking resentment and resistance in the subject cities. Volterra, in fact, briefly revolted over this issue.

[28] As discussed below, these bonds were transferrable on a secondary market, at fluctuating market rates (percentages of par). The Florentine Monte system was originally set up in 1343 (Marvin B. Becker, 1968. *Florence in Transition: Volume Two: Studies in the Rise of the Territorial State* (Baltimore, 1968)) in imitation of the earlier Monte government debt systems of Venice in 1262 and Genoa in 1274. See Luciano Pezzolo, "Bonds and Government Debt," 145–63.

[29] See Guido Alfani and Matteo DiTullo, *The Lion's Share: Inequality and the Rise of the Fiscal State in Preindustrial Europe* (Cambridge 2019) for a recent argument that premodern Italian wealth inequality was driven largely by regressive taxation systems, such as this one, and the Venetian case they studied.

sample of 14 Tuscan towns.[30] Alfani and Ammannati are the only researchers besides ourselves who have taken a comprehensive, quantitative, time-series approach to these Florentine tax sources.[31]

The *catasto* was itself a forced loan or *prestanze*, but with a revised wealth assessment procedure. Before the *catasto* and during its repeals, Florentine households' *prestanze* levies were determined by appointed committees of neighbors,[32] who based their guesstimates about their neighbors' relative household "wealth" mostly on publicly observable real estate and consumption patterns. This informal assessment of relative "wealth" opened the door to favoritism or discrimination among fractious neighbors—a source of constant complaint.

The *catasto* was designed to eliminate (or at least mitigate) such favoritism by requiring Florentine citizens explicitly to itemize and calculate all forms of their wealth, according to elaborate formal procedures and criteria established by the new *catasto* law.[33] In particular, the categories of reported wealth were required to include property and real estate, animals "of value," coined money, merchandise, credits, and shares in the public debt.[34] Business finances were reported in distinct company accounts or *bilanci* in the lead partner's declaration.

The main public argument used by Albizzi-regime political elites in favor of this reform was not higher taxes (needless to say) but rather fairness.[35] This was supposed to be, and for the most part was, "tax assessment by law, not by friends and enemies"—not that far removed, in fact, from our own income-tax (not wealth-tax) declarations.[36]

[30] Guido Alfani and Francesco Ammannati, "Long-term trends in economic inequality: the case of the Florentine state, c. 1300–1800," *The Economic History Review* 70 (2017): 1072–1102 used a long time-series sample to study these *estimi* levies on rural property and real estate.

[31] For a smaller-scale predecessor in this methodology, see Samuel K. Cohn, *Creating the Florentine State: Peasants and Rebellion, 1348–1434* (Cambridge, 1999). Alfani is in the process of ambitiously generalizing his *estimo* approach to many other premodern European cities in Italy, France, and the Low Countries in his ERC-funded SMITE program, "Social Mobility and Inequality across Italy and Europe, 1300–1800," www.dondena.unibocconi.eu/wps/wcm/connect/cdr/dondena/home/research+projects/smite. Methodologically, Guido Alfani's project is similar to ours.

[32] The procedure was complicated: "Within each ward, nine separate boards of assessors independently set an assessment for each household. To reach the final assessment, the three highest and the three lowest figures were excluded, and an average was taken of the middle three;" see Herlihy and Klapisch-Zuber, *Tuscans and Their Families*, 4.

[33] Published in Otto Karmin (ed.), *La Legge del Catasto Fiorentino del 1427* (Florence, 1906).

[34] For more details about catasto reporting procedures and criteria, see Herlihy and Klapisch-Zuber, *Tuscans and Their Families*.

[35] See footnote 25, plus Herlihy and Klapisch-Zuber, *Tuscans and Their Families*.

[36] While the word "modernity" is out of favor among historians, it is hard to avoid the use of this word in the Florentine *catasto*, which was a taxation system before its time. Of course, "modernity"

The precocious financial sophistication of these Florentine *catasto* submissions[37] presupposed widespread usage by Renaissance Florentines of private account books.[38] The financial information contained in these tax declarations was, for the most part, transcribed from taxpayers' private account books.[39] Indeed, the primary method that suspicious public officials used to check on the accuracy of these declarations was audit access to the account books from which declared financial information was copied. As such, the Florentine *catasti* represent extraordinary financial snapshots of all of the companies that were extant at the moment of *portate* (declaration).[40]

The social background of such account-book record-keeping was high literacy and numeracy, the education of which in the general working population was provided mostly by guild *abbacco* schools. Robert Black has estimated from his analyses of the handwriting of 1427 *portate* declarations that Florentine adult males had an astonishingly high literacy/numeracy rate of 69.3%.[41] That is, almost 70% of Florentine male heads of households filled out their own (complex) tax returns by themselves. Florentines simply could not do business with each other without account books, which had legal standing in courts. Unlike in other Italian cities, such as Genoa, account

does not imply that Florentines did not try to cheat in their tax returns, just like we do today. The important issue of attempted cheating, and the countervailing institutional efforts to combat it, will be addressed below.

[37] *Portate* were the original tax declarations submitted by Florentine citizens. *Campioni* were standardized transcriptions by Florentine tax officials of those citizens' *portate* declarations.

[38] See Richard A. Goldthwaite, "The Practice and Culture of Accounting in Renaissance Florence," *Enterprise and Society* 16 (2015): 611–47. Goldthwaite emphasized the "culture" of accounting, by which he meant widespread use of formal records for all sorts of household and real estate activities beyond (but certainly including) just business. The family-history version of these "account books" were called *ricordanze*, meaning "memories" or "diaries."

[39] Herlihy and Klapisch-Zuber, in *Tuscans and Their Families*, 16, mention that frequently taxpayers voluntarily appended copies of relevant sections of their account books, in order to reassure tax officials of the veracity of their declared information (and to preclude being called in for audit).

[40] See also Padgett and McLean, "Economic Credit." To measure just how extraordinary such comprehensive snapshots are: Both Francesco Bettarini and Spallanzani and Goldthwaite have published lists of those Florentine account books which still survive today; see Bettarini, Francesco, *A Census of Private Account Books in Florence, 1211–1499* (2020), https://phaidra.cab.unipd.it/detail/o:453620?mycoll=o:453426. Marco Spallanzani and Richard A. Goldthwaite, *Census of Private Account Books in Florence until 1600*. https://www.academia.edu/40196500/CENSIMENTO_di_libri_contabili_privati_fiorentini_fino_al_1600. (2020).

Bettarini's list includes (at least one book from) ten active major-industry companies that span 1427, three active major-industry companies that span 1433, and nine active major-industry companies that span 1458. These numbers translate into survival rates of major-industry companies with at least one surviving account book of 1.5%, 0.6%, and 2.0%, respectively. (Of course, survival rates of account books per se are much lower than this, because all companies maintained multiple, interrelated account books.) Low as these account-book survival rates are, they are high compared to any other city of the time period.

[41] Robert Black. *Education and Society in Florentine Tuscany: Teachers, Pupils and Schools, c. 1250–1500, volume I* (Leiden, 2007), 35.

books in Florence displaced notarial contracts as legally enforceable records in the realm of business.

Unlike the Florentine tax system as a whole, the *catasto* itself (isolated from other tax components) was a progressive, not a regressive tax. This was because, unlike in previous *prestanze* assessments, business wealth was explicitly included in the calculation of household wealth. This change, of course, had a huge effect on the taxation rate of the wealthy. In addition to the argument about "fairness," this progressive structure made the *catasto* a "popular" tax among the non-elite—at least before its unintended economic consequences became known. And, of course, this made it correspondingly unpopular with the wealthy themselves. It usually took a war (of which there were many) to swing elite Florentine public opinion toward reluctant support for heavily taxing themselves.

The magnitude of the progressivity of the tax structure of the Florentine catasto is documented in figure 8.1, which reveals for the case of the 1433 catasto that tax rates (that is, average catasto assessment/net wealth) increased linearly with percentile of reported net wealth. In particular, there was an increase of five times in the actually imposed (*catasto*)/(*sustanze*) assessment rate from the poorest decile (90–100%) of taxpayers in the city to the wealthiest (0–10%). It is no wonder that the catasto, which impacted business wealth, was unpopular with the rich. What is more surprising is that they levied this (or at least allowed this to be levied) upon themselves in the first place. Something more than (or at least in addition to) economic self-interest was driving these merchant-republicans.

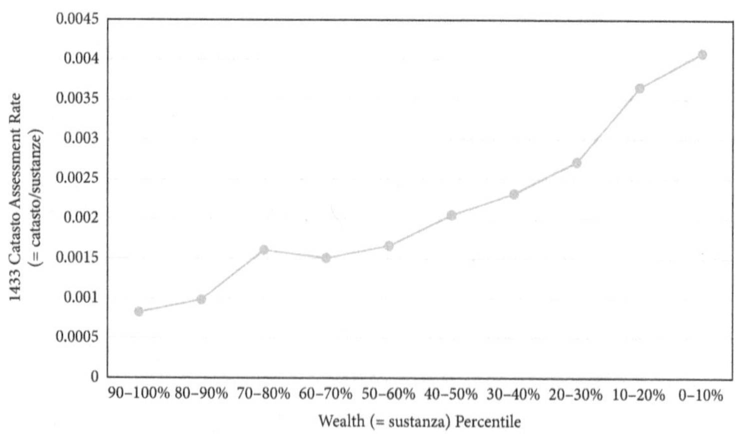

Figure 8.1 Progressive Tax Structure of Florentine Catasto

The Florentine Catasto as Source for Business Censuses

We can precisely study the macroeconomic history of Renaissance Florence because of business reports embedded in individual tax returns within the 1427, 1433, and 1458 Florentine tax registers or *catasti*. All of the 4,564 business reports contained therein have been coded by Francesco Bettarini.[42] These three sets of tax returns, among other things, constitute business censuses of every Florentine business at the time of filing because each Florentine head-of-household citizen was required to report legally itemized financial information on all of the businesses they owned. The ambitious public-finance innovation of the 1427 *catasto* was its attempt objectively[43] to measure overall net wealth—including moveable as well as immovable wealth. The complicated 1427 *catasto* wealth-assessment procedures were repeated in 1431, 1433, 1458, and 1469;[44] other than those years, Florentine tax assessment reverted to assessment of real estate only, which was simpler to observe and to measure—and which punished the wealthy less.

The first 1427 Florentine *catasto* was made famous in Florentine and in demography historiographies by the path-breaking research of David Herlihy and Christiane Klapisch-Zuber,[45] who analyzed the rich demographic and family-structure information contained therein. We refer readers to that book and also to Conti[46] for detailed background descriptions of the history, law, administration, and overall content of the Florentine *catasti*.

A few more technical features about the business accounts in these *catasti*, however, need to be mentioned here, in order to explain the structure of our dataset.

1. The Florentine *catasti* as a whole assessed households in all the Tuscan regions controlled by Florence, but we coded only registers for Florentine citizens. If Florentine citizens were residing abroad doing business, they would be included in these registers, in the volume of the neighborhood of those citizens' natal property. Conversely,

[42] Archival sources are as follows: (a) for the 1427 catasto, *Archivio di Stato di Firenze* (*A.S.F.*), *Catasto* 49, 64–81; (b) for the 1433 catasto, *A.S.F. Catasto* 429–484; (c) for the 1458 catasto, *A.S.F. Catasto* 785–833. Katalin Prajda also coded 1433. These volumes contain *campioni* (that is, scribally transcribed) versions of the original *portate* submissions by citizens. The *portate* version was consulted whenever the *campioni* version had missing data. Upon publication of this article, these data will be made publicly available on Padgett's website: https://home.uchicago.edu/jpadgett/

[43] That is, in contemporary sentiment "fairly by law," rather than unfairly by committees of neighbors, which was the previous assessment procedure.

[44] Conti, *L'imposta diretta.*

[45] Herlihy and Klapisch-Zuber, *Tuscans and Their Families.*

[46] Conti, *L'imposta diretta.*

non-Florentines doing business in Florence would not be included unless they had been admitted to citizenship.

2. The *catasti* were designed to calculate household net wealth, which in addition to business, included real estate, land, government bonds, credits and debts, cash, and even animals and slaves. The mobile wealth portion of this calculation was described in the same format throughout our three *catasti*, sometimes in random sequence:
   (a) Monte credits = shares of public debt;
   (b) partnership agreements and/or individual business descriptions;
   (c) balance sheets or *bilanci* of the business;
   (d) family credits (*creditori*), debts (*debitori*), and fixed costs (*incharichi*).[47]
3. Partnerships owned by more than one person would be reported in the tax return of the senior or managing partner, with cross-references in other partners' returns to that.
4. When businesses were owned exclusively by a single individual, such as an artisan, business and household expenses frequently were not as sharply segregated from each other as the above standardized format implies. In such cases, the operational features in the *catasti* that we used to identify an activity as a "business" were as follows:
   (a) Explicit mention of a business partnership (the easy case).
   (b) Description of warehouse stocks and work tools (*mercanzie* and *masserizie*) explicitly related to the business.
   (c) Credit statements (debtors and creditors), explicitly related to business activity.
   (d) Ownership or usufruct of a workshop (*bottegha*, *fondacho*, *descho*, *bancho*, *cella*, *forno*, etc.) explicitly related to business activity.
   (e) Ownership or usufruct of work tools (*telaio*, *filatoio*, *botte di vino* etc.) explicitly related to the business activity.

For practical purposes, these coding criteria constitute our precise definition of a "business.".

5. Many of the businesses reported in the *catasti* were no longer active. Reports on inactive businesses existed because unsettled credits and

[47] Paul McLean coded 15,317 credits and debts over 10 florins (both personal and company) for 1427. Katalin Prajda coded 12,495 person and company credits and debts over 10 florins for residents of the 1433 quarter of San Giovanni. The McLean dataset was analyzed in Padgett and McLean, "Economic Credit." The Prajda dataset has not yet been analyzed or published.

debts were still outstanding. Bettarini coded both active businesses and inactive businesses, with clear labeling of active/inactive status. The *catasti* are superb sources in providing hard-to-find opening and closing dates for partnerships. In our quantitative analyses, we focus on active businesses, currently in operation.

6. Further details about the *catasti* sources and our coding of them are provided in a twelve-page Appendix A by Bettarini, provided in online supplementary material to this article.

One particularly vexing issue in these tax-based business data affects our research strategy for analyzing them—namely, tax cheating. Both de Roover and Molho have shown that the Medici systematically underreported their *corpo* or starting capital by large percentages in 1458 and in 1451, respectively.[48] One should not exaggerate this problem, since Conti's comparison of a sample of "tens and tens" of 1427 business declarations to corresponding account books revealed little falsification. On the other hand, he concludes: "If the declaration of movable wealth in the catasto of 1427 maintains a certain degree of reliability, the subsequent ones of 1431 and 1433 must be taken with the benefit of the doubt, due to progressive reduction in revenue from those assessments."[49]

Systematic checks against tax fraud were built into the tax law—including, most importantly, official access to private account books, but in addition to that, administrative cross-checking of reported credits in one declaration with reported debits in other declarations, and an anonymous denunciation procedure (*tamburazione*) for unfriendly people to turn each other in for investigation.[50] Institutional checks notwithstanding, however, speakers in the *Consulte e Pratiche* complained incessantly about inequity between honest and dishonest tax declarers.[51]

[48] Raymond de Roover, *The Rise and the Decline of the Medici Bank, 1397–1494* (New York, 1966), 23, 73. Anthony Molho, *Florentine Public Finances in the Early Renaissance, 1400–1433* (Cambridge, MA, 1971), 95. William P. Caferro (2008, 180) also reports tax cheating by Tommaso Spinelli in 1447 in his "Warfare and Economy in Renaissance Italy, 1350–1450," *Journal of Interdisciplinary History* 39 (2008): 167–209.

[49] Conti, *L'imposta diretta*, 148, 149. An alternative explanation of this reduction, of course, is that businesses were not as profitable in 1431 and 1433 as they were in 1427. de Roover, *Medici Bank*, 230 reports exactly this for the Medici Florence bank in 1433. The research problem for us is that we cannot tell from fiscal declarations alone which of these two observationally equivalent hypotheses is true. We strongly suspect that both of them are true.

[50] With substantial financial rewards to denouncers whose denunciations were proven accurate—namely, one-quarter of undeclared assets and one-half of penalties collected (Herlihy and Klapisch, *Tuscans and Their Families*, 18).

[51] Conti, *L'imposta diretta*, 165–68.

Our research-strategy solution to this problem is two-fold: (1) we place greater emphasis on raw numbers of active companies in existence than we do on monetary values of self-reported financial declarations, and (2) we cross-check our business-census numbers with censuses from other sources, where that is possible.

The existence of an active business in Florence was public knowledge.[52] Florentine businesses operating in other cities were public knowledge among Florentine merchants operating there.[53] But the internal ledgers of those businesses were not and, hence, were easier to falsify. We still shall report summaries of financial self-reports in the *catasti*. We just shall treat these with a grain of salt, as Conti recommends, compared to the simpler but more reliable census numbers of active companies in various industries.

In the section after "**Business Census Results**," we also will cross-check our *catasti* business censuses with other business censuses from other sources and time periods, when that is possible, in order to situate them within longer time series. Triangulation possibilities are excellent for the wool, silk, and domestic banking industries. Other industries less so.

Business Census Results: Industrial Composition Over Time

The results of our three *catasti* business censuses are presented, by industry, in tables 8.1 and 8.2 for number of companies and for number of partners in those companies, respectively. Table 8.1 distinguishes between "active" companies, which were currently active at the time of reporting, and "inactive" companies, which were no longer in business, but whose leftover account books still had outstanding debts and credits to be cleared. Major industries are tabulated individually. Diverse minor-guild, artisanal industries are aggregated into "minor industries." Appendix B in the online supplementary materials details the artisanal composition of "minor industries."

The overall pattern is decline across the board from 1427 to 1433 to 1458, but with considerable variation by industry in the magnitude of that decline. The largest percentages of decline in numbers of active businesses,

[52] Herlihy and Klapisch, *Tuscans and Their Families*, 16.

[53] Fiscal authorities could get access to the public knowledge of merchants by consulting their lists of other merchants, reported as *creditori* and *debitori* in their declarations, exactly as Padgett and McLean, in "Economic Credit" did.

Table 8.1 Catasti Censuses of Businesses, by INDUSTRY

	1427		1433		1458	
	Active	Inactive	Active	Inactive	Active	Inactive
Merchant-banking, International	83	56	54	46	40	13
Merchant-banking, Florence-Pisa	32	23	27	26	19	6
Domestic Banking	39	25	27	14	16	6
Retail Cloth	29	19	23	24	10	6
Silk manufacturing	50	15	47	30	43	24
Wool manufacturing, San Martino	32	17	18	13	40	10
Wool manufacturing, Other	86	30	71	56	63	9
Dyeing	18	10	18	18	24	7
Subtotal: core industries [≈ major guilds]	370	195	286	227	254	81
All other industries [≈ minor guilds]	1297	95	815	82	769	91
Total # Businesses	1667	290	1101	309	1023	172

N.B.: *Accomandite* companies included in these tables (mostly relevant to 1427 MB, Intl.).

Table 8.2 Catasti Censuses of Partners, by Industry

	1427 Active	1433 Active	1458 Active
Merchant-banking, International	118	103	47
Merchant-banking, Florence-Pisa	55	56	42
Domestic Banking	83	49	33
Retail Cloth	67	51	23
Silk manufacturing	98	96	85
Wool manufacturing, San Martino	72	43	77
Wool manufacturing, Other	135	111	98
Dyeing	35	33	39
Subtotal: core industries [≈ major guilds]	663	542	444
Subtotal: other industries 1535 [≈ minor guilds]	1535	779	962
Total # Partners	2198	1321	1406

from 1427 to 1458, occurred in the industries Retail Cloth[54] (66% decline), Domestic Banking (60% decline), International Merchant-Banking (52% decline), Minor Industries (41% decline), and Florence/Pisa Merchant-Banking (34% decline). More modest rates of decline were experienced in Silk cloth manufacturing (16% decline) and in "Other Wool" [i.e., lower quality] cloth manufacturing (27% decline). Actual growth in numbers of companies was experienced in San Martino [high quality] Wool cloth manufacturing (25% growth) and in (cloth) Dyeing (21% growth). For sure, this is consistent with a Lopez-like portrait of "Hard Times," especially in the three banking industries, at least for this 30-year period.[55] With the help of Conti,[56] we shall demonstrate in the next section below that war-induced high taxes lie behind this decline.

These patterns are not substantially altered if one measures industry activity by numbers of active partners (Table 8.2), instead of by numbers of active companies (Table 8.1): From 1427 to 1458, Retail Cloth partners declined 66%, Domestic Banking partners declined 60%, International Merchant-Banking partners declined 60%, Florence/Pisa Merchant-Banking partners declined 24%, and Minor Industries partners declined 37%. Silk cloth manufacturing partners declined 13% and Other Wool cloth manufacturing 27%. Growth in numbers of partners was experienced in San Martino Wool cloth manufacturing by 7% and in (cloth) Dyeing by 11%.

As emphasized by Cipolla, however, to be statistically significant these industry-specific temporal trends need to be compared with the baseline population "universe" of how many households reported in each tax census.[57] The total numbers of such households were 9,780 for 1427, 8,888 for 1433, and 7,718 for 1458. In other words, from 1427 to 1433 there was a 9.1% decline in total number of fiscal households reporting to tax authorities. From 1427 to 1458 there was a 21.1% decline. Strikingly high as these baseline declines are, they are consistent with epidemic death rates measured through the Florentine Dowry Fund.[58]

[54] "Retail Cloth" merchants (*ritagliatori*) sold bolts of finished cloth, wool and silk, mostly to domestic customers, for them or their tailors to turn into clothing and the like.

[55] Roberto S. Lopez, "Hard Times and Investment in Culture," in *The Renaissance: A Symposium*. (New York, 1953), 19–32.

[56] Conti, *L'imposta diretta*.

[57] Carlo M. Cipolla, "Economic Depression of the Renaissance?" *The Economic History Review* 16 (1964): 519–24.

[58] "Based on our data, a mortality rate of 20 per 1,000 person-years seems to be a reasonable criterion to distinguish a year with a serious epidemic from other years. There were 17 years (1430, 1434, 1437–38, 1449–50, 1457–58, 1464, 1478–79, 1527–30, 1568, 1576) in which the rate was at

Because of this baseline decline in population, no industry-specific decline of 25% or less will be considered by us to indicate real per-capita decline in that industry. This per-capita restriction, however, still leaves Merchant Banking, Domestic Banking, Retail Cloth, and Minor Industries as registering significant per-capita declines during the three-decade period of our study.

A third method to measure industry activity is by company financial worth, measured in a variety of ways: (a) capital investment or *corpo*, (b) fiscal valuation or *valsente*,[59] and (c) total credits/debts. As explained above, we do not trust the accuracy of these self-reported financial data. For what it is worth, however, we nonetheless report industry averages of such self-reports in tables 8.3A, 8.3B, and 8.3C for the sample of cases on which we have such data. Despite Conti's and our skepticism of the reliability of such data, the pattern of decline in self-reported financial values of business is completely consistent with what we have reported in tables 8.1 and 8.2: The

Table 8.3 A Financial Sizes of Catasti Businesses (active companies only)

A. Corpo: investment capital (in florins)	**1427 Catasto**		**1433 Catasto**		**1458 Catasto**	
	number of companies	**average corpo**	**number of companies**	**average corpo**	**number of companies**	**average corpo**
M-B, International	83 (12)	3729	54 (7)	2487	40 (12)	2871
M-B, Florence-Pisa	6 (6)	8347	27 (9)	5908	19 (6)	4767
Domestic Banking	39 (11)	7814	27 (6)	5780	16 (8)	2176
Retail	29 (8)	3030	23 (1)	2688	10 (4)	1506
Silk	50 (17)	3030	47 (9)	3513	43 (22)	1873
Wool, San Martino	32 (14)	3643	18 (10)	3174	40 (17)	1547
Wool, Other	86 (25)	2027	71 (17)	1932	63 (15)	1038
Dyers	18 (7)	1213	18 (5)	1169	24 (4)	607

Note: The two columns of numbers under "number of companies" mean: (a) first column = all companies, and (b) second column = that subset of companies that have data on the variable in question. As can be seen, most company *bilanci* in the catasti have missing data on corpo. Therefore, these financial-size averages are based on samples only.

least that high," 531. Alan S. Morrison, Julius Kirshner, and Anthony Molho, "Epidemics in Renaissance Florence," *American Journal of Public Health* 75 (1985): 528–35. These numbers are striking especially because they do not include the more infamous plague years of 1348, 1363, and 1400.

[59] Fiscal valuation or *valsente* was the sum of investment capital (*corpo*), merchandise on hand, and total credits minus total debits.

Table 8.3 B Financial Sizes of Catasti Businesses (active companies only)

B. Valsente: fiscal valuation

	1427 Catasto		1433 Catasto		1458 Catasto	
(in florins)	number of companies	average Valsente	number of companies	average Valsente	number of companies	Average Valsente
M-B, International	83 (31)	2979	54 (14)	2209	40 (25)	2532
M-B, Florence-Pisa	32 (18)	5999	27 (22)	3466	19 (10)	3444
Domestic Banking	39 (33)	5760	27 (16)	3519	16 (11)	1792
Retail	29 (24)	2858	23 (17)	2039	10 (6)	1854
Silk	50 (36)	2586	47 (33)	1468	43 (35)	1607
Wool, San Martino	32 (26)	2952	18 (18)	3145	40 (32)	1649
Wool, Other	86 (65)	1713	71 (39)	1185	63 (51)	824
Dyers	18 (14)	878	18 (13)	549	24 (20)	488

Note: The two columns of numbers under "number of companies"mean: (a) all companies, and (b) that subset of companies that have data on the variable in question. The rest of the companies have missing data on that dimension. In other words, these financial-size data are samples only.

average financial sizes of Florentine firms shrunk along with their numbers. At minimum, these sample financial-worth figures demonstrate that the explanation for numerical declines in both companies and partners is not consolidation into fewer numbers of larger companies.

Comparison with Other Studies of Florentine Industries

Both for reasons of external validity[60] and because we are sensitive to the limited time frame of our study, in this section we compare our 1427–1458 findings, across all industries, with industry-specific censuses for other time periods that exist in the literature.[61] Wool and Silk cloth manufacturing have been the most heavily studied of Florentine industries, so we shall

[60] See John F. Padgett, "Triangulating on Causal Process," *American Politics Research* 39 (2011): 466–70 for a discussion of the methodological importance of "triangulating" across multiple sources in any historical or social science research.

[61] Other than Padgett and McLean, "Economic Credit," who also studied businesses in the 1427 *catasto*—albeit with a different counting method—no comprehensive cross-industry business censuses exist in the literature with which to compare ours. Because of its superior direct (*bilanci*), rather than indirect (debit and credit lists), method of counting, the 1427 data in table 8.1 in this paper supersede the table 8.1 data in Padgett and McLean, "Economic Credit," 7.

Table 8.3 C Financial Sizes of Catasti Businesses (active companies only)

C. Total Credits: business volume

(in florins)	1427 Catasto		1433 Catasto		1458 Catasto	
	number of companies	average total credits	number of companies	average total credits	number of companies	average total credits
M-B, International	83 (15)	17302 (xx)	54 (9)	1833 (?) (xx)	40 (9)	11,122 (xx)
M-B, Florence-Pisa	32 (11)	9656	27 (24)	11,578	19 (14)	12,899
Domestic Banking	39 (26)	23,756	27 (24)	17,247	16 (9)	11,013
Retail	29 (11)	7679	23 (9)	5673	10 (6)	1978
Silk	50 (29)	2127	47 (27)	3145	43 (22)	1900
Wool, San Martino	32 (19)	4014	18 (17)	3728	40 (22)	1570
Wool, Other	86 (46)	2467	71 (58)	1348	63 (39)	513
Dyers	18 (14)	1869	18 (17)	1020	24 (11)	916

Note 1: (?) refers to skewed sample: Medici companies, for example, did not report information on total credits and debts.
Note 2: The two columns of numbers under "number of companies" mean: (a) all companies, and (b) that subset of companies that have data on the variable in question. The rest of the companies have missing data on that dimension. In other words, these financial-size data are samples only.

begin there, before moving on to discuss Domestic Banking, International Merchant Banking, and finally Minor Industries. To our knowledge, no previous industry-level census for Florence/Pisa Merchant-Banking or for Retail Cloth exists to use for comparison.

Table 8.4 tabulates the findings of the many studies that have counted numbers of companies in the Wool and Silk cloth manufacturing industries, at various points in time. It is encouraging to find that the numbers of active companies in our study are remarkably consistent with the numbers of companies reported in the previous studies of others, despite differences in details of estimation methods.

Hoshino and Franceschi have already documented the sharp decline in Wool-cloth manufacturing (*lanaiuoli*) from 1382 until 1427, during the Albizzi regime shortly before our period.[62] With the exception of Wool,

[62] Hidetoshi Hoshino, *L'arte della Lana in Firenze nel Basso Medioevo* (Florence, 1980), 227, 229. Franco Franceschi, Franco, *Oltre il "Tumulto": I lavoratori fiorentini dell'Arte della Lana fra Tre e Quattrocento* (Florence, 1993). Padgett has verified Hoshino's count of 283 *lanaiuoli* firms in 1382, through coding *Archivio di Stato di Firenze, Arte della Lana* 46.

Table 8.4 Wool and Silk over Longue Durée: Comparison with other studies (active companies only)

Year	Author	Source	WOOL (lanaiouli)			SILK (setaiuoli)
			S. MARTINO	OTHER	TOTAL	(excl. 'aminuto')
1338	Giovanni Villani	Chronicle			"about 200"	
1382	Hoshino	Arte della Lana 46	92	191	283	
1393	Taviani	m-b account books				2
1427	Hoshino	Catasto	49	83	132	
1427	Padgett & McLean	Catasto creditori	41	82	123	46
1427	Bettarini & Padgett	Catasto bilanci	32	86	118	51
1427	Grossi	Catasto botteghe			127	51
1427	Edler de Roover	Catasto				33
1433	Bettarini & Padgett	Catasto bilanci	18	72	90	47
1446	Edler de Roover	?				42
1458	Bettarini & Padgett	Catasto bilanci	40	63	103	43
1458	Hoshino	Catasto	50	61	111	
1458	Edler de Roover	Catasto			110	48
1458	Dini	"L'industria serica"				39
1469	Hoshino	Catasto	47	75	122	
1472	Benedetto Dei	Chronicle				49
1480	Bianchi	Catasto botteghe			87(?)	44

San Martino in 1433, our numbers fit smoothly into that previous decline, which seems to have halted by 1427. What table 8.4 does not reveal (because of the absence of any business census for the later period) is the recovery in the production of lower quality wool-cloth (*garbo*)—"Wool, Other" in our terminology—after the fall of Constantinople in 1453, which eventually opened up that new market to the exportation of Florentine wool textiles.[63]

From 1427 to 1480, all studies, including ours, report the numbers of active Silk-cloth manufacturing companies of *setaiuoli*[64] to be fluctuating at around 40. Before that, during the Albizzi regime, there had been sharp and sudden growth from zero, starting in 1393.[65]

Whatever short-term tribulations were suffered during the 1427–58 period, in other words, no serious long-term damage was done to the Wool and Silk cloth manufacturing industries by the war-and-tax "hard times" of 1427–58.

Matters were quite different in the Domestic Banking industry. In figure 8.2, we supplement our 1427–58 *catasti* data with *Arte del Cambio* registrations of domestic banks, coded by Padgett.[66] These precious annual registrations by the banking guild of their members' active domestic banks cover the long time period of 1340–1502, with a 1400–1460 gap due to a lost archival volume. Despite radically different sources, these two estimates of numbers of Domestic Banks active in Florence are remarkably consistent with each other. The impressive consistency of both sources confirms the accuracy of each. In particular, our 1427–58 *catasti* data for that industry beautifully fills in the archival gap between the high plateau in *Arte del*

[63] Hoshino's report is inconsistent with the number of *lanaiuoli* shops in 1480 reported in Bianchi (2000), which is why we place a question mark next to that number.

[64] Specifically, *setaiuoli grossi*, who manufactured silk cloth. *Setaiuoli a minuti*, who produced ornaments and other small silk items, also existed in Florence but are not counted in our or in others' tabulations.

[65] In impressively original archival work, Carlo Taviani, "Taviani Report to JFP: Account Books," unpublished 2019, has discovered the first two *setaiuoli grossi* companies in Florence—namely, Domenico Corsi and Michele del Parente—from an examination of the surviving account books of Francesco Datini, of Lazzaro Bracci, and of 32 other international merchant-bankers during this period. These two silk companies both made their first appearances in the account books of Niccolò di Buono di Bese in 1393 and of Datini in 1394.

[66] From *Archivio di Stato di Firenze, Arte del Cambio* 11, 14, 15, 16. In order to be permitted to conduct domestic business in Florence with Florentine citizens, *cambio* banks had to register with the *Arte del Cambio* guild and pay an annual fee in order to avoid the legal charge of usury. Many of these "domestic" *cambio* banks, however, especially the larger ones, also conducted international business. "Domestic" meant to do banking with Florentine citizens in Florence, not to do business exclusively with Florentine citizens in Florence.

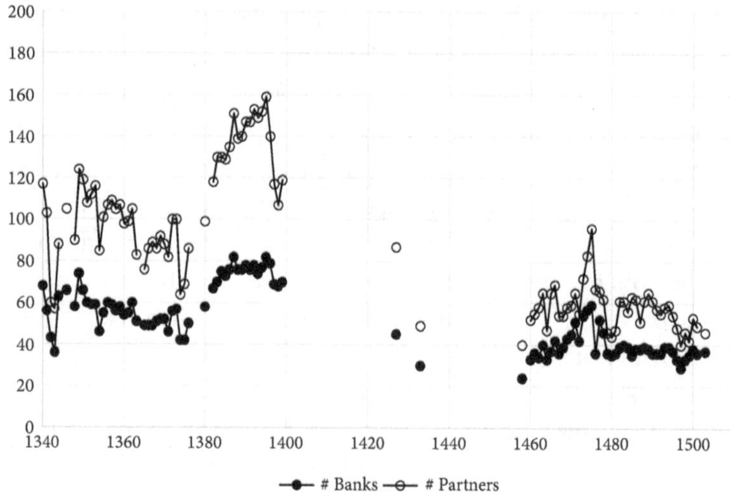

Figure 8.2 Domestic Banks in Arte del Cambio and Catasti Censuses

Sources: Archivio di Stato di Firenze, Arte del Cambio 11, 14, 15, 16. Intervening years 1427–1458 from our catasto dataset.

Cambio numbers of companies and partners during the late Trecento[67] and the low plateau in *Arte del Cambio* numbers during the late Quattrocento. The conclusion: Unlike the industries of Wool and Silk cloth production, which did not suffer, the 1427–58 decline in numbers of Domestic Banks was long-lasting, even after 1458.

The 1427–58 decline in International Merchant Banks is harder to cross-check because we lack time-relevant external lists of Florentine merchants in foreign cities, with which to verify our *catasti* findings.[68] To our knowledge, only one such list exists, for Roman customs duties on Florentine mercantile imports.[69] Scanty as this mere one comparison is, Esch itemized 16 Florentine businesses importing goods to Rome in 1458, compared to our own itemization of 14 Florentine businesses declaring themselves to be

[67] Actually, "high plateau in Trecento" does not accurately describe the time trend during that period, because there was a boom in Domestic Banking during the Albizzi years of 1380–1395 (until the war with Milan in 1395). This is an example of heterogeneity in industry dynamics: domestic and international banking were booming at the same time as wool cloth production was declining, exactly as Melis has claimed. Federigo Melis, *Aspetti della vita economica medievale* (Siena, 1962).

[68] On the other hand, "the great urban merchants were invariably involved in complex partnerships and companies, and this made their business affairs a matter of nearly public knowledge." Herlihy and Klapisch-Zuber, *Tuscans and Their Families*, 16.

[69] Arnold Esch, "Importe in das Rom der Frührenaissance: Ihr Volumen nach den römischen Zollregistern der Jahre 1452–62," Studi in Memoria di Federigo Melis, 3 (1978), 381–452.

actively operating in Rome in 1458. This agreement in number of companies is excellent. Unfortunately, only 6 companies are in common across these two lists. A combination of geographical fluidity of Florentine companies and the absence of pure bankers from Esch's list may account for this low overlap. At least there is no obvious evidence of *catasto* underreporting in this one city.

Obviously, it would be good to have more cities to cross-check.[70]

Even without many city lists available for cross-checking, however, we do report for inspection, in table 8.5, the distribution of active Florentine international merchant-bank businesses in various European cities. Two specific features of the decline described in table 8.2 seem readily explicable through this close-up look:

(a) The decline in numbers of 1458 Florentine companies in Venice and Spain was a consequence of the 1451 war of Florence against an alliance of Venice and Aragon, during which those enemies had expelled all Florentine merchants.[71] Even though the 1454 Peace of Lodi had repealed their war-time exile, our *catasto* data show that, by 1458, Florentine merchants still had not fully recovered their prewar numbers.

(b) *Accomandite* were limited-liability partnerships, formed by Florentines for short-term ventures, sometimes to explore the prospects for permanent branches.[72] This form of partnership, was used with some frequency in International Merchant-Banking in 1427 (n=19), but was largely abandoned in 1433 (n=6) and in 1458 (n=1). Indeed, abandonment of the *accomandite* form of partnership accounts for 43% of the 1427→1433 decline and 41% of the 1427→1458 decline in numbers of companies within that industry. This suggests to us,

[70] Maria Elisa Soldani, *Uomini d'affari mercanti Toscani nella Barcellona del Quattrocento*, Barcellona (2010), provides an excellent study of Florentines in Barcelona, but this relies heavily on the same *catasti* sources as we do. Therefore, it is not an independent check. Francesco Guidi Bruscoli, "Mercanti-banchieri fiorentini tra London e Bruges nel XV secolo," in *Uomini d'affari toscani in Europa e nel Mediterraneo tardomedievale* (Roma, 2012), 11–44 has provided another excellent study of Florentines in London and Bruges, but only one company in his list (13–14) was present in the *catasti* years of 1427, 1433, or 1458. Katalin Prajda, "Florentine merchant companies established in Buda at the beginning of the 15th century." *Mélanges de l'École française de Rome—Moyen Âge* (2013) studied Florentine companies in Buda but in a period earlier than ours.

[71] Reinhold Mueller, *The Venetian Money Market* (Baltimore, 1997), 284.

[72] For example, see Cosimo de' Medici's use of that legal form to explore the viability of a permanent branch in Geneva (de Roover, *Medici Bank*, 282).

Table 8.5 Distribution of Cities Among International Companies

open companies only:		1427 Catasto			1433 Catasto			1458 Catasto		
		m-b	other	total	m-b	other	total	m-b	other	total
ITALY:				**69**			**41**			**49**
Rome	(solo)	5	5	**10**	7	3	**10**	12	1	**43**
	(plus other cities)	1		**1**						
Venice	(solo)	10	3	**13**	11	**0**	**11**	5	1	**6**
	(plus other cities)		1	**1**						
Naples	(solo)	0	0	**0**	2	0	**2**	1	2	**3**
	(plus other cities)	1		**1**	1		**1**			
Genoa	(solo)	0	0	**0**	1	0	**1**	0	0	**0**
	(plus other cities)									
Milan	(solo)	0	0	**0**	1	0	**1**	0	0	**0**
	(plus other cities)									
Pisa	(solo)	10	3	**13**	4	2	**6**	8	3	**11**
	(plus other cities)	2		**2**	1		**1**	1		**1**
Other Tuscany	(solo)	5	4	**9**	0	2	**2**	5	2	7
	(plus other cities)									
Other Italy	(solo)	18	1	**19**	6	1	7	3	4	7
	(plus other cities)									
FRANCE:				**14**			**8**			5
Avignon	(solo)	10		**10**	**5**		5	3		3
	(plus other cities)	4		**4**	1		**1**			
Paris	(solo)	0		**0**	1		**1**	0		**0**
	(plus other cities)									

Geneva	(solo)	0	**0**	1	**1**	2	**2**
	(plus other cities)						
SPAIN:			**7**		**7**		**1**
Barcelona	(solo)	4	**4**	3	3	1	**1**
	(plus other cities)	1	**1**				
Valencia	(solo)	2	**2**	4	**4**	0	**0**
	(plus other cities)						
Other Spain	(solo)	0	**0**		**0**	0	**0**
	(plus other cities)						
BELGIUM/ENGLAND:			**8**		**7**		
Bruges	(solo)	1	**1**	**2**	**2**	**4**	**6**
	(plus other cities)	2	**2**	2	**2**	0	**4**
London	(solo)	5	**5**	3	**3**	2	**0**
	(plus other cities)						**2**
EASTERN EUROPE:			**7**		**0**		
Buda	(solo)	4	**4**	0	**0**	0	**0**
	(plus other cities)	1	**1**				**0**
Polonia		2	**2**				
LEVANT:			**1**		**0**		**0**
Constantinople	(solo)	0	**0**	0	**0**		**0**
	(plus other cities)	1	**1**			0	

N.B.: "plus other cities" means that company operated (and was named) in more than one city.
"m-b" stands for "merchant bank."

in the language of James G. March,[73] that internationally oriented Florentine companies might have been exploring new opportunities less and exploiting well-known routes of profit more during this uncertain and risky period.

A third potential explanation for decline in International Merchant Banking is harder to evaluate: *catasto* underreporting. It required work for fiscal authorities to verify the existence or nonexistence of companies when they were located outside of Florence itself.[74]

Of course, we are in an even less advantageous position to get direct leverage on this vexing issue than were the fiscal authorities. But we want to highlight one case in table 8.5 that strikes us as suspicious. The decline in "small cities in Italy" might be due to underreporting, since small cities had too few (and too unimportant) Florentine merchants to be organized into *nazioni* networks through which fiscal authorities could easily cross-check their existence.[75]

We must end our brief discussion of this important industry with the less-than-startling conclusion that the striking decline in International Merchant-Banking that we observe was due probably to some mixture of three reasons.

The final "industry" we shall discuss are artisans, aggregated by us into the composite category of "Minor Industries." (See Appendix B in the online supplementary materials.) Surprising, to us at least, was the sharp decline during our *catasti* period in the numbers of those artisanal businesses. We had assumed that internationally oriented industries would be volatile, but that purely local industries, like shoemaking, would not. Our *catasti* data,

[73] James G. March, "Exploration and Exploitation in Organizational Learning," *Organization Science* 2 (1991): 71–87.

[74] In larger cities, international Florentine businessmen resident in their places of work were organized into quasi-legal communities called *nazioni*. This gave fiscal authorities informational leverage, through merchant networks, on stable residents of those cities. A second, more administrative, method for fiscal authorities to discover unreported companies in other cities was in the lists of creditors and debtors provided by reporting companies (see Herlihy and Klapisch-Zuber, *Tuscans and Their Families* (New Haven, 1985), 16). This was the procedure used by Padgett and McLean, "Economic Credit," to construct their 1427 business census. That cross-checking method was as readily accessible to *catasto* officials as it was to us, if they wished to avail themselves of it.

[75] "The great merchants of Florence, keeping careful accounts, and involved in numerous partnerships, could not easily conceal movables. In the countryside, on the other hand, where the population was dispersed, the officials doubtless encountered much greater difficulties in uncovering hidden wealth" (Herlihy and Klapisch-Zuber, *Tuscans and Their Families*, 16).

however, reveal declines in numbers of active artisan businesses to have been just as severe as those of their banking social superiors. The working class was not immune to economic downturns.

Bianchi reports that in 1480, considerably after our period, the number of "Minor Industry" artisanal *botteghe* (shops), constrained to be the same list of occupations as ours, had recovered to 1256 (as compared with 1,213 Minor-Industry businesses in 1427, 786 in 1433, and 742 in 1458).[76] Hence artisanal businesses eventually did bounce back but after our time period.

To summarize, even after controlling for population baselines, per-capita industry declines in International Banking, Domestic Banking, Retail Cloth, and Minor Industries were serious in the *catasti* years of 1427–58, with considerable variation in the magnitudes of those declines. Wool and silk manufacturing, on the other hand, were not seriously damaged. Some of those declines appear ultimately to have been "transitory," even if 30 years is not such a "short term." In the notable case of the Domestic Banking industry, however, the decline in numbers of businesses and partners experienced in this period lasted throughout the Quattrocento.

Partnership Fluidity

To interpret industry decline, a methodological comment on the meaning of "business failure" in Renaissance Florence is in order at this point: Partnership contracts usually lasted only about three years. Founding contracts were renegotiable and renewable, so it was possible for partners to stay in continuous business together for longer than that. But ownership of Florentine businesses changed frequently, without necessarily implying any problem with the business. It was a normal part of a Florentine businessman's career to come and to go into business activity and to reshuffle and reinvest in different partnerships over time. Florentine businessmen were often "part-timers." In the *Arte del Cambio* data mentioned above, for example, Florentine domestic bankers were domestic bankers on average only for 8.3 years of their lives.[77] Especially at the elite level, politics was often

[76] M. L. Bianchi, "Le botteghe fiorentine nel catasto del 1480," *Ricerche Strache* 30 (2000): 119–70. In online Appendix B in the supplementary materials, we provide both the list of our own artisanal industries and the 1480 list of Bianchi for comparison.

[77] This datum was calculated on the basis of the longest continuous Trecento period of our *Arte del Cambio* archival records: 1340–1399. Banking companies in the end-point years of 1340 and

as time-consuming for these multifaceted Florentine merchant-republicans as was business.[78]

The magnitude of partner fluidity in our time period can be measured: Among all of our major industries pooled, only 26% of partners active in 1427 were still active in their industry in 1433. Eighteen percent transited from active companies in 1427 to inactive companies in 1433, implying that their original company had closed. But 56% of partners active in business in 1427 simply left their field of industry altogether.

These high dropout percentages were not unique to 1427/1433. No full-fledged *catasto* was levied in 1451, but in that year there was assessed a *Tassa dei Traffichi* on the investment capital (*corpo*) of enough businesses to provide a sample baseline for comparison with our 1458 *catasto*.[79] Again, among all of our major industries pooled, only 32% of partners active in 1451 were still active in their industry in 1458. Eleven percent transited from active companies in 1451 to inactive companies in 1458. But 57% of partners active in business in 1451 had simply left their industry in 1458. This does not mean, of course, that businessmen who had left their industries were destitute.

This fluidity of partners has implications for interpreting decline in number of businesses. On the one hand, it was not very costly for partnerships to go out of business. On the other hand, it was relatively easy to ride out temporary trouble on the sidelines and then return to business once the smoke had cleared. Even in hard times like 1427–58, rebound potential always existed in the "human capital" form of temporarily sidelined ex-businessmen, available to reenter their industries once times became more propitious. They had not necessarily lost their wealth in the interim. This is one of the flexibility mechanisms through which "Prosperity" and "Hard Times" could coexist.[80]

1399 were excluded from these calculations because of truncation issues—namely, we do not know the partnership histories of 1340 companies before that date, nor do we know the histories of 1399 companies after that date.

[78] Fluidity of occupation was also true at the artisan level; see William Caferro, *Petrarch's War: Florence and the Black Death in Context* (Cambridge UK, 2018), 165–68.

[79] Anthony Molho, "The Florentine '*Tassa dei Traffichi*' of 1451," *Studies in the Renaissance* 17 (1970): 73–118.

[80] Following Lopez (1953) and Brown (1989), the language of "Hard Times" versus "Prosperity" is provided in Caferro (2011). Robert Lopez, "Hard Times and Investment in Culture," *The Renaissance: A Symposium.* (New York, 1953), 19–32. Judith Brown, "Prosperity or Hard Times in Renaissance Italy?" *Renaissance Quarterly* 42 (1989): 761–780. William P. Caferro, *Contesting the Renaissance* (Malden, MA, 2011).

Contemporaneous Interpretations

The best place to start to find an explanation for the industry declines just documented is in the opinions of participants. In addition to his quantitative analysis of taxes, Conti has assembled a large number of quotations from contemporaneous discussions in the *Consulte e Pratiche*.[81] This advisory body was a set of handpicked elite councilors charged to give advice to city council about how to respond to vexing public-policy issues, including this one, which confronted the Florentine state.[82]

In order to set the stage and to give a preliminary hypothesis, we repeat on-the-ground private testimony reported by Molho about the scarcity of money:[83]

> Francesco Tornabuoni informed Averardo de'Medici in April 1431 that "business conditions were bad and that it was impossible to collect any debts from anyone. . ."
>
> Alamanno Salviati, writing to Averardo de'Medici in the fall of 1431, despaired of the seriousness of the situation, which was caused "by a greater scarcity of money than is necessary, and things get worse as time advances. Here everyone is predicting his own destruction, without an end or an improvement in sight, and with ruin overtaking all fairly rapidly."

Reinhold Mueller extended these observations to February 1449, through Matteo Strozzi's letter to his mother:[84]

> I warn you that there is a great famine of money in Florence, according to what I hear, that there are many men who, due to the famine in money, take away merchandise. . ., and with difficulty find half the money of what the merchandise they sell is worth.

As will be documented below, the first-order cause of this "scarcity of money" was the exorbitant cost (in gold) of mercenaries, but a secondary spillover was money fleeing the city, causing credit problems back home:[85]

[81] Conti, *L'imposta diretta.*

[82] For more details, see John F. Padgett, Katalin Prajda, Benjamin Rohr, and Jonathan Schoots, "Political Discussion and Debate in Narrative Time: The Florentine *Consulte e Pratiche*, 1376–78," *Poetics* 78 (2020): art. 101377.

[83] Molho, *Florentine Public Finances*, 154.

[84] Reinhold C. Mueller, *Venezia nel tardo medioevo /Late Medieval Venice* (Roma, 2021), 211.

[85] See also Francesco Bettarini, "I fiorentini all'esterno ed il catasto del 1427: frondi, elusioni, ipercorrettismi," *Annali di Storia di Firenze* 6 (2011): 37–64.

> Our city stands with merchandise: if you make the catasto, those who have cash will export it, and so the traffic will decrease.[86]

A *Consulte e Pratiche* quote confirms additional problems with merchant credit:[87]

> On July 5, 1431, a commission referred to the difficulty of drawing money on loan from the market, "due to the lack of credit that is in the merchants."[88]

This lack-of-credit comment recalls to mind the high leverage ratios of 1427 companies reported in Padgett and McLean.[89] Probably there had been a contagious credit contraction, based on the fact that affluent companies, used to growth, were overextended to begin with.[90]

A very specific reason for the decline in artisanal Minor Industries emerged in *Consulte e Pratiche* discussions:

> This [1433] law was motivated by the strong contraction that occurred in the renters' market, whenever the rumor of a new census was spread, because the amount of repeated taxation could easily exceed the income received.[91]
>
> The *catasto* has its use, I confess. But it destroys the city; the shops close and the money is hidden; and houses are not rented, so as not to pay the *catasto*.[92]
>
> Another drawback we find, that many shops and houses, which are registered in the second *catasto*, are found at present walled up, abandoned, and disposed of only in order not to give them to the *catasto*.[93]

[86] Conti, *L'imposta diretta*, 122–123.

[87] Molho's *Florentine Public Finances*, 155, translation of this quote is this: "Paolo di Vanni Rucellai deplored the 'lack of cash' (*mancamento del denaro*), while a commission appointed to investigate the general economic and fiscal situation in July 1431 reached the rather unoriginal but readily acceptable conclusion that the city's troubles stemmed from the *mancamento del credito che è ne' mercatanti*."

[88] Conti, *L'imposta diretta*, 157.

[89] Padgett and McLean, "Economic Credit," 8.

[90] Goldthwaite, *The Economics of Renaissance Florence*, 458–63, calls this general pattern of business credit "offsetting"—namely, the reciprocal settling of business debts not through cash but through buying from those to whom you had previously sold, registering it all in account books. Padgett and McLean, "Economic Credit," labeled this plus all repeated credits-without-immediate-payment "social exchange."

[91] Conti, *L'imposta diretta*, 170.

[92] Ibid., 176.

[93] Ibid., 176.

Decline in artisanal Minor Industries due to the rental market is explained by the fact that, under *catasto* law, property was assessed at a 7% rate of rental return. A tax-dodge implication of this for property owners was "No rental return, no taxable property value." To reduce their own taxes, property owners evicted artisan renters from the ground-floor shops or *botteghe* that they owned.

A summary of the variety of reasons for this dreary state of affairs was crisply provided at a later 1481 date when history repeated itself[94] with the 1480 "catasto," induced by the developing-but-averted war of the Pazzi conspiracy:

> The reasons for the unrest are obvious: the unbearable expenses of the war, for which all the revenue to the Monte were being used, except for interest and dowries; the diversity of currencies, because inflows to the Monte are for the most part in (silver) lire and outflows are in (gold) florins; the high interest paid; and finally not everyone paying their taxes.[95]

The reference to currencies stems from the fact that mercenaries demanded to be paid in gold florins, the currency of international trade, while taxpayers usually paid in silver lire and soldi, the currency of the domestic economy. Mercenaries' gold was a net drain of money out of Florence's economy,[96] albeit not necessarily out of Italy at large, even if some but not all of that was recycled.[97] This *strettezza* of gold in turn led to deflation in the value of normal people's silver coins.[98]

Causal Explanation: High Taxes?

Behind the specific business tribulations mentioned by contemporaries—namely, higher taxes than income, high interest, collapse of mercantile credit, flight of capital, rental market for shops, gold outflow to mercenaries,

[94] Tognetti gives an excellent account of this same state of affairs—in particular the contagious collapse of merchant credit—in the later but similar case of the failure of the Cambini bank in 1481: "Non era solo una questione di costo del denaro, ma di una temporanea perdita di fiducia del mercato." Sergio Tognetti, *Il Banco Cambini: Affari mercati di una compagnia mercantile-bancaria nella Firenze del XV secolo*. (Florence, 1999), 306–07.

[95] Conti, *L'imposta diretta*, 67.

[96] Giovanni Ciapelli, "Il cittadino fiorentino e il fisco alla fine del trecento e nel corso del quattrocento: Uno studio di due casi," *Società e Storia* 46 (1989): 828–90.

[97] William P. Caferro,"Warfare and Economy in Renaissance Italy, 1350–1450," *Journal of Interdisciplinary History* 39 (2008): 167–209, esp. 190, 193.

[98] Exchange rate data reported in Molho, *Florentine Public Finances*, 209–13.

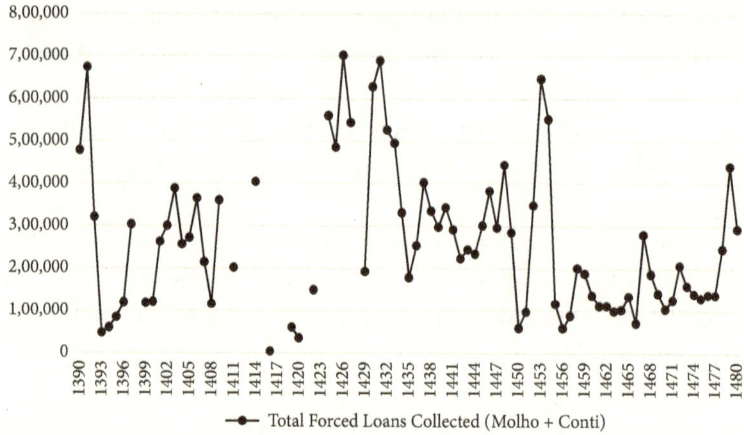

Figure 8.3 Annual Florentine Forced Loan Revenues Collected (in florins)

Sources: Anthony Molho, *Florentine Public Finances in the Early Renaissance, 1400–1433* (Cambridge, MA, 1971), 10, 62, and Elio Conti, *L'imposta diretta a Firenze nel Quattrocento, 1427–1494* (Roma, 1984), 81, 83.

devaluations of Monte bonds and of silver—lay a single ultimate cause: exorbitant taxes due to wars levied for too long. Figure 8.3 summarizes Molho's and Conti's reconstructions of Florentine forced-loan[99] revenues[100] during this period and beyond. These impressive archival reconstructions were not straightforward to achieve because "catasto" for an individual technically referred to that person's legal obligation for a single tax assessment, but *prestanze* and *catasti* tax assessments could be and were levied repeatedly, even within a single year, depending upon the republican government's decisions and perceived needs.[101] Taxes in Florence were not annual one-and-done affairs.

[99] "Forced loan" includes *prestanze* and *catasti*, since *catasti* levies technically were forced loans as well.

[100] These figures are not assessments but actually collected revenues. As reported by Molho, *Florentine Public Finances*, and by Conti, *L'imposta diretta*, for most years those figures were surprisingly close. The biggest discrepancies between city assessments and real revenues occurred in 1431 and 1432, when assessments shot up much higher than the war-time revenue figures shown in figure 8.3. To be specific, in 1431 and 1432, global city assessments were 46% above actually collected revenues. For the nearby years of 1429, 1430, and 1433, however, collected revenues were almost identical to city assessments. Incentives to cheat, in other words, while always present, were greatest in 1431 and 1432. See Molho, *Florentine Public Finances* (1971), 62, for data on revenues, and Conti, *L'imposta diretta* (1984), 81, for data on assessments.

[101] For example, Matteo Palmieri, whose account book (*ricordanze*) was published (1983) and studied by Conti (1984), received 64 1/3 *catasti* levies from July 1428 to June 1431. Elio Conti (ed.). *Matteo Palmieri: Ricordi Fiscali (1427–1474)* (Roma, 1983), 21. Similarly, *prestanze* were levied 57 times during 1423–25 (Molho, *Florentine Public Finances*, 89).

Not surprisingly, the peaks of Florentine forced-loan revenues were timed to wars: namely, the 1424–28 war with Milan, the 1429–33 war with Lucca, the 1451–54 war with Venice and Aragon, and after our period, the 1478–81 anticipated-but-averted Pazzi-conspiracy near-war with the pope.

One retrospective memory of this period was this:[102]

> In 1473 Giovanni di Pagolo Rucellai recalled that "our city had been at war and in serious spending for 30 years, that is, from 1423 to 1453"; this thirty-year period, which begins with the war against Filippo Maria Visconti and ends on the eve of the peace of Lodi, was followed by a twenty-year period of "peaceful peace," "that is, from 1453 to 1473, except for one year only."

To give a sense of the magnitude of these levies, the total of 1424–27 forced loans actually collected for the war with Milan totaled 2,294,216 florins,[103] as compared to the total taxable net wealth of the city calculated in the 1427 catasto of 7,610,824 florins.[104] This is a ratio of 30% of the city's wealth [not just its annual income] "expropriated" for that war. The total of 1429–33 forced loans actually collected for the war with Lucca totaled 2,535,575 florins,[105] as compared to the total city *sustanze* calculated in the 1433 catasto of 7,415,000 florins,[106] giving a ratio of 34% of total city wealth taken—on top of the 30% already taken. Then there was the 1431 *catasto*, which we have not studied.

In the face of tax rates such as these—on total patrimony, not on annual income no less—it is easy to understand the incentive for tax cheating through artificially lowering net wealth declarations, especially by wealthy businessmen.

If there were "hard times" in Renaissance Florence in 1427–1458, which we claim there were, there is no need to invoke structural weakness in the economy to explain that. The fiscal pressure on the city in this 30-year period was intense. All the collateral negative economic consequences for business, so salient to contemporaries, derived from that. Although we do not have

[102] Conti, *L'imposta diretta*, 83.

[103] Molho, *Florentine Public Finances*, 62. Molho, "Fisco ed economia a Firenze alla viglia del Consiglio," *Archivio Storico Italiano* 148 (1990): 807–44.

[104] The latter of these figures comes from summing TAXWEALTH in the Florence dataset of Herlihy and Klapisch.

[105] Conti, *L'imposta diretta*, 81.

[106] The latter of these figures comes from summing SUSTANZA_DECIMAL in the unpublished dataset of Prajda.

data to prove it (except for Bianchi's data on 1480 artisans), according to Giovanni di Pagolo Rucellai, much of the economy bounced back after that tax pressure was relieved.

Monte Government-Bond Price Collapse

In addition to the direct effect of tax extraction from the economy, a collateral money-supply problem was drastic devaluation of Monte government bonds on the secondary market of resales of such bonds. In principle, Florentine extraordinary war taxes were forced loans, which the government promised to pay back with interest. A large percentage of Florence's annual expenditures were devoted to such interest payments, left over from previous wars. This secondary market in Monte bonds functioned as a supplementary currency, which Florentines used to pay large debts, such as dowries, to each other.

Figure 8.4, however, shows a collapse in the resale value of Monte bonds, precisely at the time that the government was pressing citizens to pay more taxes, through the *catasti*.[107] The reason for this collapse was the inability of the fiscally overextended state to meet the interest payments that it had promised. At the very moment of their new tax bill coming due, in other words, Florentine citizens were deprived of paying their taxes through the most valuable and liquid resource that many of them had.[108] In fact, according to the 1427 *catasto* coded by Herlihy and Klapisch, 25% of the total reported net wealth of the city was comprised of Monte bonds.[109]

It requires more research to verify this hypothesis, but we believe that permanent collapse of the Monte secondary market, in which *cambio* banks had been important players,[110] was one factor in the inability of the Domestic Banking industry to recover.

[107] Sources for the data in this figure are Anthony Molho, *Florentine Public Finances*, 10, 62 and Elio Conti, *L'imposta diretta*, 81, 83.

[108] In this regard, see Molho, *Florentine Public Finances*, 157–160, for the poignant case of Palla di Nofri Strozzi.

[109] This figure calculated by sum(CRDPUB)/sum(TOTAL) in Klapisch's online version of the catasto: https://journals.openedition.org/acrh/4971, which is an extension of the original Herlihy online version: http://cds.library.brown.edu/projects/catasto/overview.html. [The Monte values reported in the 1427 catasto referred to 50% of face value, not to still lower secondary-market values. Herlihy and Klapisch-Zuber, *Tuscans and Their Families*, 16.]

[110] The centrality of *cambio* banks in this secondary market is very evident in the 1345 Monte that Bettarini and Padgett (unpublished) have coded.

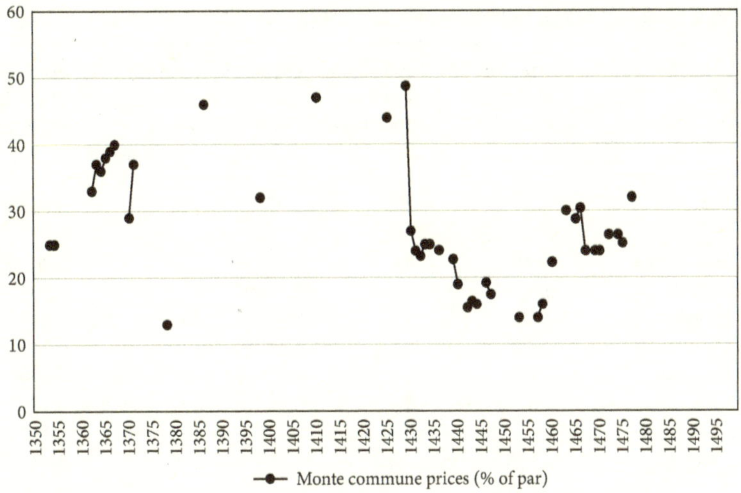

Figure 8.4 Monte Commune Prices

Sources: Elio Conti, *L'imposta diretta a Firenze nel Quattrocento, 1427–1494.* (Roma, 1984), and Giovanni Ciappelli, "Il mercato dei titoli del debtito pubblico a Firenze nel Tre-Quattrocento," 623–42 in Manuel Sanchez and Antoni Furio (eds.), *Actes: Colloqui Corona, Municipis i Fiscalitat a la Baixa Edat Mitjana* (Lleida, Spain, 1998).

Credit Default Contagion

In Table 8.6, we reproduce the leverage ratios calculated in Padgett and McLean, "Economic Credit," 8. In general, business "leverage" is total debts divided by total assets. High leverage implies low ability to cover one's debts if they all come due at once. Table 8.6 reports a variety of ways of calculating "assets," ranging from the narrow definition of start-up capital or *corpo* to a more expansive definition of "*corpo*+ profit + reinvested past profit (or *sopracorpo*) + merchandise inventory."

The main point of reproducing these numbers is to show the strong correlation between the industry decline rates demonstrated above and average leverage ratios in 1427, at the beginning of the crisis. Company numbers in industries declined more when the companies within those industries were, on average, highly leveraged.

In particular, companies in the International Merchant Banking (including Pisa), Domestic Banking, and Retail Cloth Sales industries had the high average leverage ratios in 1427 of 5.42, 4.93, and 2.20, respectively, as measured in the narrow *corpo* way. Their decline rates from 1427 to 1458 reflected this debt "overextension": −48.7%, −59.0%, and −65.5%,

Table 8.6 1427 Average Leverage = Σ_i (Total Debt) / Σ_i (Capital)

	% decline in # companies 1427–1458	n for avg. leverage Estimate	corpo1= Corpo Only	corpo2= corpo1 + profit + *sopraccorpo*	corpo3= corpo2 + inventory
Merchant Banks (Int'l. + Pisa)	−48.7%	12	5.42	4.98	3.62
Domestic Banks	−59%	14	4.93	3.29	3.20
Cloth Retail	−65.5%	14	2.2	1.66	1.15
Silk Manufacturing	−14%	19	0.94	0.86	0.66
Wool Manufacturing (San Martino)	25%	23	1.17	1.04	0.84
Wool Manufacturing (other)	−26.7%	16	0.54	0.48	0.41
Cloth Dyeing	+33.3%	7	2.27	2.03	1.44
All Other Industries (~minor guilds)	−40.7%				

Source: John F. Padgett and Paul D. McLean, "Economic Credit in Renaissance Florence," *Journal of Modern History* 83 (2011), 8.

respectively. In contrast to these, the Wool:San Martino, Wool:Other, and Silk industries had the low leverage ratios in 1427 of 1.17, 0.54, and 0.94, respectively, with correspondingly gentle declines of +25.0%, −26.7%, and −14.0%. The correlation is not perfect, but it is clear enough to give quantitative evidence for our (and contemporary Florentines') interpretation of a contagion in credit defaults. When debtor companies did not pay off their debts, that lowered the inflow of money to their creditors to pay off their debts, thereby generating concatenated chain reactions of credit default.

In that previous article, we also demonstrated that high business leverage, in turn, was rooted in the social embeddedness of Florentine businessmen in dense underlying social and political ties.[111] Hence, "credit bubbles" occurred even in personalistic early-modern economies, where social exchange and trust were high. The macroeconomic dynamics of premodern and early-modern economies are not studied as much as they should be.[112]

[111] Padgett and McLean, "Economic Credit." The "social exchange" documented in that article can be considered to be the "microeconomics" underlying the "macroeconomics" of this article.

[112] The economic-history literature on Venice contains the best studies of Italian economies over time: G. Luzzatto, *Storia economica di Venezia dall'XI al XVI secolo* (1961); Mueller, *The Venetian Money Market* (1997a); Pezzolo, "Bonds and Government Debt."

Political Corollary: Rise of Cosimo De' Medici

Finally, were there consequences of the economic slump reported here for Florentine politics? Molho, Kent, and Padgett and Ansell have already developed much of the story of the 1427–1434 rise of Cosimo de' Medici to take over the state. This shared story includes causal linkages to the Lucca war and its fiscal crises. For Molho, the key linkage was the enormous loans Cosimo gave to the Florentine state itself. For Kent, for Molho, and for Padgett and Ansell, the key linkage was the financial assistance Cosimo gave to his friends.[113] In this article, we provide a background for those analyses by documenting, for the first time, a more structural strand of causality—namely, the long-term impact of fiscal stress on increased economic concentration within partnership systems at the very peak of the Florentine economy. The Medici partnership system is what funded the various Cosimo clientage loans that Molho, Kent, and Padgett and Ansell were all talking about.

Partnership Systems

A partnership system is an assembly of legally independent[114] companies linked through part ownership by a single businessman or a holding company. Often these component companies were located in different industries; hence, diversified partnership systems spanned or cross-cut industries. In this sense, partnership systems are a higher-order form of "industrial structure"—namely, they were organizational networks linking industries. Large partnership systems, like that of the Medici "bank," were the organizational peak of the Florentine economy, bridging international and domestic industries through common organizational ownerships. Francesco Datini's *sistema di aziende*, studied by Melis,[115] is the most famous of these, but Padgett and McLean[116] have documented that this advanced business

[113] Anthony Molho, *Florentine Public Finances*. Anthony Molho, "Cosimo de' Medici: *Pater Patriae* or *Padrino*?" *Stanford Italian Review* 1 (1979): 5–33. Dale Kent, *The Rise of the Medici: Faction in Florence, 1426–1434* (Oxford, 1978). John F. Padgett and Christopher K. Ansell, "Robust Action and the Rise of the Medici, 1400–1434," *American Journal of Sociology* 98 (1993): 1259–319.

[114] That is, the individual component companies had different account books, different legal standing in court, and different partners (other than the one or two in common).

[115] Federigo Melis, *Aspetti della vita economica medievale* (Monte dei Paschi di Siena, 1962).

[116] John F. Padgett and Paul D. McLean, "Organizational Invention and Elite Transformation: The Birth of Partnership Systems in Renaissance Florence," *American Journal of Sociology* 111 (2006): 1463–568.

organizational form emerged suddenly in 1383 among five systems simultaneously, not just in its most famous Datini exemplar.[117] It was this innovative[118] organizational form that propelled the boom in merchant banking during the Albizzi regime. Padgett and McLean further showed that most early partnership systems (Datini excluded) grew out of their origins as Florentine domestic *cambio* banks to develop international branches. In addition, Padgett and McLean showed that this form of business was fertile organizational soil through which double-entry bookkeeping diffused rapidly throughout the Florentine economy at exactly the same time, with partnership systems as the lead adopters.[119] Between 1383 and 1400, the partnership system organizational form, which typically was centered in the domestic banking and the merchant-banking industries, spread to 39 other ownership-linked clusters of companies.[120]

Table 8.7 reports the fate of this innovative form of business organization during our subsequent 1427–1458 period of "hard times." It is not a happy story, except for the Medici themselves. The list of senior-partner leaders of the partnership systems reported in table 8.7 is provided in Appendix C in the online supplementary materials. More complete descriptions of these partnership systems—including business composition, all partner members, and fiscal valuations—are provided in Appendices D1and D2 in the online supplementary materials.

Because of differing sources, it is not clean to compare the ten-year 1390–1400 period of the Padgett and McLean study with the annual 1427, 1433, and 1458 data in our article. But the data in Padgett and McLean give the impression of robust presence of this innovative organizational form in that earlier Albizzi decade. Taking into consideration the different time spans of our sources, the first business census of 1427 seems to be a continuation of that earlier healthy organizational pattern.

The 1433 and 1458 *catasti*, on the other hand, unequivocally show decline in numbers of partnership systems compared to 1427. This parallels the

[117] The other four original partnership systems, all founded in 1383, were Vieri di Cambio de' Medici, Davanzato and Manetto di Giovanni Davanzati, Francesco di Neri Ardinghelli, and Ardingo di Corso Ricci & Gualtieri di Sandro Portinari, all of which began as domestic banks; see Padgett and McLean, "Organizational Invention and Elite Transformation," The partnership system of Francesco Datini of Prato (Melis 1962) is the most famous of these founding systems because it is the only one whose complete records have survived.

[118] Innovative because both are functionally flexible and operationally centralized. See Padgett and McLean, "Organizational Invention and Elite Transformation," 1476 for a more detailed list of organizational features.

[119] Ibid., 1540–41.

[120] Ibid., 1548–60.

Table 8.7 Comparative Tabulation of Partnership systems by Size (where "size" = # of component companies)

	1390–1400	1427	1433	1458
BANKING INDUSTRIES:				
n=2:	23 (11)	16 (7)	11 (1)	12 (4)
n=3:	13 (7)	6 (3)	3 (1)	2 (1)
n=4:	4 (2)	2 (1)	3 (1)	0
n=5:	3 (2)	2 (1)	1 (1)	0
n=6:	0	1 (1)	0	0
n=7:	1 (1)	0	0	0
n=8:	0	0	0	0
n=9:				
n=10:				
n=11:				
n=13:		0	0	1 (1)

N.B.: Figures in parentheses are numbers of partnership systems that include a Domestic Bank as a component company.

global declines of the banking industries in table 8.1. The numbers of smallest banking-centered partnership systems of only two companies went from 16 in 1427 to 11 in 1433 to 12 in 1458. The numbers of intermediate-sized partnership systems of 3–6 companies (excluding Cosimo de' Medici) went from ten in 1427 to six in 1433 to two in 1458. Only Cosimo de' Medici's own partnership system went ballistic in size from five companies in 1427 to five companies in 1433 to 13 companies in 1458. These numbers give the impression that Cosimo's (shall we say obese?) 1458 partnership system towered over the Florentine organizational world; it had moved into the space that other intermediate-sized partnership systems had recently evacuated. What had once been a business ecology of many businesses with the most advanced organizational form had shrunk to a business ecology dominated at the very top by only one.

This is not the place to investigate the details of Cosimo's business expansion policy. Raymond de Roover's magisterial study[121] presents branch-by-branch case studies—ranging from sluggish correspondents in Bruges to Sforza politics in Milan—but no single, unitary explanation of

[121] Raymond de Roover, *Medici Bank*. For Bruges, see especially p. 318; for Sforza politics in Milan see especially p. 261.

expansion emerges. Our contribution instead is to highlight not Cosimo's business brilliance but rather the decline in partnership-system competition to Cosimo.

In parentheses, table 8.7 also tabulates the numbers of partnership systems that included a Domestic Bank as one of its component companies. Padgett and McLean demonstrated that, Datini aside, almost all of the founding partnership systems emerged out of Domestic Banks, who developed international branches after the Ciompi Revolt. Large *cambio* domestic banks in most of these cases functioned as the Florentine "home branch" of a partnership system and, as such, engaged not only in local but also in international business.[122]

Table 8.7 demonstrates that in 1427 about half of all partnership systems were still anchored by Domestic Banks, just as they had been in 1383–1400. By 1433 and 1458, however, Domestic Banks had mostly disappeared from their centrally constitutive role. The drastic and long-term decline in the Domestic Banking industry, documented in figure 8.2, seems to have ripped the organizational glue out of most (but not all) of existing partnership systems, leaving the industry (and its *Arte del Cambio* guild) left mostly with the more ancient organizational form of "small fry" *cambiatori*, such as the Cerchi company, studied by Goldthwaite, which did only local business with local Florentines.[123]

Cosimo's Florentine Tavola, de Roover has shown, almost suffered the same fate. Among its other effects, Cosimo's bailing out of his Florentine Tavola in 1433 through Venice and Rome transfers preserved the home branch of his partnership system, thereby continuing his link of international economics with local economics and politics. Subsequent expansion by Cosimo probably also was facilitated by the post-1427 absorption of business from two other now defunct Medici partnership systems—namely that of Averardo de' Medici and that of Vieri di Nicola de' Medici.

The central point is that without thriving organizational seeds of Domestic Banks, upon which to build, it was harder (though not impossible[124])

[122] The Medici themselves had a holding company structure, centralized not only through Cosimo alone but also through Cosimo together with his brother Lorenzo. In contrast, most of the other partnership systems in our dataset were centralized more simply through one senior-partner businessman alone, whose names are reported in table 10 in the online appendix. See also de Roover, *Medici Bank*, and Sergio Tognetti, *Il Banco Cambini*.

[123] Richard A. Goldthwaite, "Local Banking in Renaissance Florence," *Journal of European Economic History* 14 (1985): 5–55.

[124] Besides Cosimo, the only 1458 partnership systems that still included Domestic Banks as components were Filippo and Luca Rinieri, Francesco and Carlo Cambini (Tognetti, *Il Banco Cambini*), Luigi di Giovanni Quaratesi, Rinaldo di ser Arrigo Portigiani, and Guglielmo di Cardinale Rucellai.

for new partnership systems to grow. Cosimo did not set out to destroy his economic competition, but he did benefit from their demise.

The dramatic expansion of the partnership system of Cosimo de'Medici had political consequences. With a partnership system so much larger than anyone else's, Cosimo could deal directly with foreign powers, not just through the state but also through the markets. No wonder that visiting foreign dignitaries went directly to the home of Cosimo to negotiate government policy, much to the consternation of bypassed Florentine republican officials. The shrinkage in the ecology of Florentine partnership systems set the organizational stage, on the economic front, for this centralization. Conversations about international diplomacy could be coupled to and coordinated with conversations about Florentine foreign exchange and investment, both to the benefit of Florentine state formation and to the benefit of Medici partnership system profit.[125]

Conclusion

This case study of the political economy of Renaissance Florence is consistent with case studies of other Italian Renaissance regional states of the same period. For Venice, Mueller has shown: "the existence of an acute crisis in the 1450s is reflected in almost all aspects of the city's economic life."[126] He attributes this Venetian economic crisis to the conjuncture of expensive *Terraferma* war against the alliance of Milan and Florence and a contemporaneous "second bullion famine."[127] A banking industry corollary of this general economic crisis in Venice, analogous to the collapse of domestic banking in Florence, was the bankruptcy at that time of two large Rialto banks, both owned by Benedetto and Giovanni Soranzo.[128] Mueller's analysis is confirmed by time-series graphs of the prices of Venetian

[125] Witness the close connection between Cosimo de' Medici and Francesco Sforza, transmitted through Pigello Portinari, manager of the Milan branch of the Medici Bank (de Roover, *Medici Bank*, 262) and through Nicodemo da Pontremoli, Sforza's confidential agent. See Garrett Mattingly, *Renaissance Diplomacy* (Boston, 1955).

[126] Reinhold C. Mueller, *Venezia nel tardo medioevo*, 203.

[127] For the latter, see also Day (1978, 26), who documented the low annual rate of Florentine mint production of florins (gold) and lire (silver) during our period. John Day, "The Great Bullion Famine of the Fifteenth Century," *Past and Present* 79 (1978): 3–54.

[128] Analyzed in detail in Reinhold C. Mueller, *The Venetian Money Market: Banks, Panics, and the Public Debt, 1200–1500* (Baltimore, 1997), 200–10.

government bonds, which show collapses in the secondary-market price of Venetian bonds similar to figure 8.3 about Florentine bonds.[129]

For a second comparative example, Caferro has documented for Siena an even more extreme fiscal crisis induced by mercenary wars, through mechanisms that sound eerily similar to the mechanisms observed in Florence:

> The payment of vast sums to the companies pumped money out of the city, touching off shortages of specie, damaging an already circumscribed economy. Meanwhile, the unprecedented reliance on loans and concomitant raises in gabelles weighed heavily on citizens and contadini, who found themselves taxed to the limit. . . Unfortunately, the same crises that necessitated the imposition of loans diminished the return from gabelles, the principal source of repayment. Thus, the city found itself in a vicious cycle. Loans begat more loans, and repayment was rendered all the more uncertain.[130]

Florence was inflicted with this same vicious cycle (among others), even though Florence ultimately had more "bounce back" resilience than did Siena, due to Florence's stronger economic base in wool and silk manufacturing.[131] Venice likewise, despite serious shock, had strong bounce-back potential due to its powerful position in international trade.[132]

Fiscal crisis due to war is also observed in Renaissance Milan in 1447, although seemingly not as severe or as long-lasting as in Renaissance Florence. This was as much a political as an economic crisis.[133] Perhaps the greater integration of Lombardy's polycentric regional markets, documented by Epstein, is responsible for this relatively modest economic response to war.

[129] Luciano Pezzolo, "Bonds and Government Debt," 154. Indeed, according to Pezzolo's graph, Venetian and Florentine Monte prices moved through time almost identically. If wars were behind it all, then it is not surprising that public finances were correlated across cities. Unfortunately, we do not have a similarly precise revenue time-series for Milan.

[130] William Caferro, *Mercenary Companies and the Decline of Siena* (Baltimore, 1998), 155.

[131] William Caferro, *Journal of Interdisciplinary History* 39 (2008): 167–209, esp. 155.

[132] Reinhold C. Mueller, "Effetti della guerra di Chioggia sulla vita economica e social di Venezia (1378–1381)", in his Venezia nel tardo medioevo 115–27.

[133] "Duke Filippo Maria's death, leaving no heirs, in 1447, the break-up of the state, the end of the republican experiment, the war and the conquest of Francesco Sforza, precipitated Milanese trade into a recession." (p. 128) Patrizia Maiono, "The Economy of Renaissance Milan," in *A Companion to Late Medieval and Early Modern Milan: The Distinctive Features of an Italian State*, ed. Andrea Gamberini (Brill, 2014), 118–41.

Our analyses of the underlying causes of fiscal crisis in Florence have emphasized not only the direct effect of tax extraction but also indirect spillovers of high tax extraction onto government *prestanze* bonds and onto credit contagion among highly interdependent companies. The fiscally innovative Florentine *catasti* strongly hit Florence's commercial credit networks, more so than did direct *estimo* taxes on property or *gabelle* sales taxes on commodities. Speaking generally, the political economies of warring Italian Renaissance states were affected not only directly by government economic and tax policies, but also indirectly by the underlying industrial composition and credit structures of those states' businesses, which determined how those economies responded to government economic and foreign policies.

This article adds to the growing historiography on the political economy of Italian Renaissance states both by emphasizing the nonlinearity of "economic growth" and by calling for greater specificity in social-science stereotypes of "strong versus weak states." "Political economy" puts the emphasis on interaction and feedback between politics and economics: on the one hand, politically motivated war and taxes impact economic growth; on the other hand, the structure of the economy channels the consequences of foreign policies, like those observed in political expansion in Italian Renaissance states. We strongly agree with this but emphasize unintended consequences in their interaction. The causal relationship between "strong states" and "strong markets" is not linear, as mostly argued in the literature, but depends on industrial composition and trading networks as intermediary catalysts. Intentional macroeconomic policy, because of this, can easily backfire, no matter how innovative and brilliant.

Acknowledgments

We are deeply grateful to Katalin Prajda and Claudia Tripodi, who were co-members of the archival research team out of which this project emerged. (See *Scientia.global* magazine September 5, 2018 for journalist report about and pictures of the team.) We also appreciate the useful comments and suggestions of Bill Caferro, Richard Goldthwaite, and the anonymous JMH referees.

9

Robust Action and the Rise of the Medici, 1400–1434

Introduction

Regardless of time or place, political centralization lies at the heart of state building. Less widely appreciated is the fact that the process of centralization is contradictory: its agents are forced to seek both reproduction and control. Centralization occurs, often abruptly, when founders emerge out of the soup of contending actors to establish (perhaps unintentionally) new rules for others' interaction. Reproduction ensues when rules induce roles, which induce interests, which induce strategic exchanges, which lock in patterns of collective action that depend on the rules.[1] Control is when others' locked-in interactions generate a flow of collective behavior that just happens to serve one's interests.

The contradiction, in state building or in any organization, is between judge and boss: founders cannot be both at once. Stable self-regulating maintenance of rules (i.e., legitimacy) hinges on the contending actors' conviction that judges and rules are not motivated by self-interest (Elster 1983; Padgett 1986; Douglas 1986). At the same time, the nightmare of all founders is that their organizational creation will walk away from them. As Weber recognized long ago, in crisis (sooner or later inevitable), direct intervention in or overt domination of locked-in interactions is a sure sign of control's absence, not of its presence. Tactical tinkering to maintain fleeting control sucks in founders to locked-in role frames, thereby inducing attributions of self-interest and undermining their judicial perch above the fray.

American Journal of Sociology 98 (May 1993): 1259–1319, with Christopher Ansell. Republished with permission.

[1] Feedback dependence is not necessarily of the form of everyone's obeying the rules. More common is when rules structure the patterned process of subverting themselves, thereby sustaining a mutual symbiosis between subversion and rules. See Padgett (1990a) for an example in the domain of courts.

Organizational Invention in Renaissance Florence. John F. Padgett, Oxford University Press.
© Oxford University Press (2026). DOI: 10.1093/oso/9780197789216.003.0009

This article analyzes one historical resolution of this state-building contradiction: the early fifteenth-century rise of Cosimo de' Medici in Renaissance Florence. We focus in particular on analyzing the structure and the sequential emergence of the marriage, economic, and patronage networks that constituted the Medicean political party and was used by Cosimo in 1434 to take over the budding Florentine Renaissance state.

The historical case is exemplary in numerous ways. From a state centralization perspective, the period marks the abrupt transition from the late medieval pattern of fluid urban factionalism to the birth of a regionally consolidated Renaissance state (Baron 1966).[2] Before the advent of the Medici, two centuries of late medieval Florentine politics could be characterized by a cyclic alternation between guild corporatism and warring urban feudal factions, as is implied by figure 9.1. Originally, the Medici partook of this ancient rhythm, which became puzzlingly muted thereby. After the rise of the Medici, the periodic explosion of the system, under the pressure of "new men" families surging from below, abruptly stopped, never to be renewed.[3]

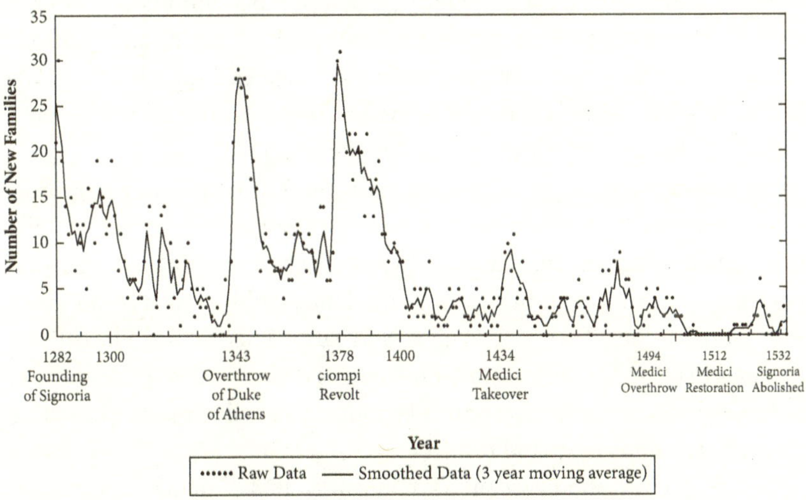

Figure 9.1 New Families Admitted to the Signoria, 1282–1532
Source: Najemy 1982, 320–22.

[2] The oligarchic regimes of Maso degli Albizzi/Niccolo da Uzzano (1382–1433) and Cosimo de' Medici (1434–1464) were significant in effecting this transition. The oligarchic regime spawned the formally democratic institutions that newly constituted "the consensual state" (Najemy 1982). Through political party networks, the Medicean regime learned how to use these institutions for purposes of control (Rubinstein 1966).

[3] "New men" *(novi cives)* refers to families only "recently" admitted to legal participation in the state. See figure 9.1.

The dynamic underlying Florentine state centralization, we shall show, was this: Unsuccessful class revolt (1378–82) and fiscal catastrophe due to wars (1424–33) were the ultimate causes, but these shocks were transmitted through the ratchet mechanism of elite network transformation. A citywide oligarchy, cemented through marriage, first emerged from a quasi-feudal federation of patrician neighborhood hierarchies. The very process of oligarchic consolidation, however, also produced the agent of its own destruction: the Medici party. The Medici party was a heterogeneous mixture of contradictory interests and cross-cutting networks. In stark contrast to this fact, contemporaries perceived the Medici categorically as "heroes of the new men." The Medici's contradictory agglomeration exhibited great cohesion and capacity for sustained collective action. But what the Medici stood for is unclear to this day.

On the surface, it seems obvious that Cosimo de' Medici (1389–1464) did it all. Cosimo de' Medici was multiply embedded in complicated and sprawling Florentine marriage, economic, and patronage elite networks. And he was riding herd on vast macropolitical and macroeconomic forces far beyond his control. Yet he founded a dynasty that dominated Florence for three centuries. He consolidated a Europe-wide banking network that helped induce both international trade and state making elsewhere (de Roover 1966). And he oversaw and sponsored the Florentine intellectual and artistic efflorescence that we now call "the Renaissance."

Contemporaries deeply appreciated Cosimo's power. Foreign princes after 1434 flocked to Cosimo's private palazzo to work out international relations, much to the consternation of bypassed Florentine officials. Cosimo was legally enshrined on his death as the father of his country—no mean recognition from citizens as cynical and suspicious as the Florentines. Machiavelli ([1525] 1988), almost a full century later, still held Cosimo and his family in awe—attributing both all good and all evil in recent Florentine history to Cosimo's deep and ruthless machinations.[4]

Yet the puzzle about Cosimo's control is this: Totally contrary to Machiavelli's portrait in *The Prince* of effective leaders as decisive and goal-oriented, eyewitness accounts describe Cosimo de' Medici as an indecipherable sphinx (Brown 1961, 186). "Cosimo was anxious to remain in

[4] This is not entirely surprising, since Niccolo Machiavelli enjoyed the freedom to write in the first place, because he had been outmaneuvered into exile by his boyhood friends, the Medici. Only their memory of his childhood saved Machiavelli from summary execution, a fact that probably focused his gaze.

the background, hiding his great influence, and acting, when need arose, through a deputy. As a result, very little is known of the measures for which he was directly responsible" (Gutkind 1938, 124). Despite almost complete domination of the state, Cosimo never assumed lasting public office.[5] And he hardly ever gave a public speech.[6] Lest one conclude that this implies only savvy back-room dealing, extant accounts of private meetings with Cosimo emphasize the same, odd passivity.[7] After passionate pleas by supplicants for action of some sort, Cosimo typically would terminate a meeting graciously but icily, with little more commitment than "Yes my son, I shall look into that" (cf. Vespasiano [ca. 1495] 1963, 223, 226).

Moreover, especially after 1434, all action by Cosimo (never explained or rationalized) appeared extraordinarily reactive in character. Everything was done in response to a flow of requests that, somehow or other, "just so happened" to serve Cosimo's extremely multiple interests.

We use the term "robust action" to refer to Cosimo's style of control. The key to understanding Cosimo's sphinxlike character, and the judge/boss contradiction thereby, we argue, is multivocality—the fact that single actions can be interpreted coherently from multiple perspectives simultaneously, the fact that single actions can be moves in many games at once, and the fact that public and private motivations cannot be parsed. Multivocal action leads to Rorschach blot identities, with all alters constructing their own distinctive attribution of the identity of ego. The "only" point of this, from

[5] The only state offices Cosimo ever held were short-term: three two-month terms as Gonfalonier of Justice (Gutkind 1938, 123), a one-year stint as one of the Ufficiali del Banco in 1428 (Molho 1971, 218), and a few martial and Monte commissions.

[6] We know of Cosimo's reticence because Florentine verbatim documentation of *Consulte e Pratiche* (an informal "inner elite" advisory body) and other speeches is very extensive. Two rare exceptions were a 1446 debate about potential electoral reforms (Rubinstein 1966, 24) and a vigorous public debate with Neri Capponi in 1450 about whether Florence should realign from Venice to Milan (Gutkind 1938, 110).

[7] Contemporaneous reports of Cosimo's personal style are as follows: "He acted privately with the greatest discretion in order to safeguard himself, and whenever he sought to attain an object he contrived to let it appear that the matter had been set in motion by someone other than himself... He replies were brief and sometimes obscure, so that they might be made to bear a double sense" (Vespasiano [ca. 1495] 1963, 223). "In 1432, just before his exile and triumphant return, a political opponent, Francesco Filefo, described in a letter how Cosimo, in contrast to his 'open and light-hearted' brother, Lorenzo, 'is, I notice, despite appearing devoted to me, the kind of man who feigns and dissembles everything. He is so taciturn that he can scarcely be understood even by his intimates and servants in his family circle'" (Brown 1992, 106). "Said Neri di Gino [Capponi] to Cosimo: I would like for you to say things clearly to me, so that I can understand you. He replied: 'Learn my language!'" (Poliziano [ca. 1478] 1985, 57). Cosimo's speech, when it occurred, was often Delphic in form. "As Gutkind has suggested, in this situation Cosimo's use of proverbs and fables served a useful political purpose—in delivering messages 'in such a way that no one noticed,' as Vespasiano put it" (Brown 1992, 106).

the perspective of ego, is flexible opportunism—maintaining discretionary options across unforeseeable futures in the face of hostile attempts by others to narrow those options.

Crucial for maintaining discretion is *not* to pursue any specific goals. For in nasty strategic games, like Florence or like chess, positional play is the maneuvering of opponents into the forced clarification of their (but not your) tactical lines of action.[8] Locked-in commitment to lines of action, and thence to goals, is the product not of individual choice but at least as much of others' successful "ecological control" over you (Padgett 1981). Victory, in Florence, in chess, or in *go* means locking in others, but not yourself, to goal-oriented sequences of strategic play that become predictable thereby.[9]

Robust action resolves the contradiction between judge and boss because, at the center, there are no unequivocal self-interests. Cosimo, after all, "merely" responded graciously to the flow of requests. Because requests had to flow to him, others, not Cosimo himself, struggled to infer and then to serve Cosimo's inscrutable interests. Control was diffused throughout the structure of others' self-fashionings.

Of course, robust action will not work for just anyone. For the flow of requests to be channeled, only some network structures will do. And for the resolution of judge and boss to be credible, coherent interests must remain opaque as far down as it is conceivable to peer.[10] Contra Machiavelli, even Cosimo himself did not set out with a grand design to take over the state: this assumption reads history backward. As this article will show, Cosimo's political party first emerged around him. Only later, during the Milan war, did Cosimo suddenly apprehend the political capacity of the social network

[8] Our original inspiration for the robust action idea was the research of Eric Leifer (1991; this is a revised version of his 1985 Harvard University dissertation), who studied chess. While skill, not identity, was Leifer's main focus, he did point out that experts' moves in chess and in dyadic roles often are directed toward maintaining multiple lines of play, especially in balanced situations. Of course, one difference between Florence and chess is that the multiple networks of Florence constituted an entire linked ecology of games, each game layered on top of another. One single action, therefore, might be a move in multiple games simultaneously.

[9] Harrison C. White (1992) argues along similar lines. John Holland was the one who informed us that locking in others, but not yourself, to clear lines of play is also the secret to victory in the Japanese game *go*.

[10] Of course, Cosimo had goals tied to specific roles—to make money as a banker, to increase family prestige through marriage, to maintain power as leader of Florence—but the points here are three: (1) goals are properties of roles, not of persons, (2) no overarching trade-off or utility function existed for Cosimo that could prioritize these possibly conflicting role-based goals, and (3) once he was in structural position, success in attaining these goals flowed to him without tactical intervention or even effort on his part. In Cosimo's special position, indeed, which role was in play at which time was not transparent. Therefore, whether Cosimo de' Medici was really a person, as conceived by modern liberalism, is undecidable by any means available to us, or to them (cf. Goffman 1975, 293–300; Foucault 1975).

machine that lay at his fingertips. The bulk of this article is an archaeological dig for the structural preconditions of that learning and of that success.

These arguments will be developed in the following stages: After a brief summary of data, we will analyze first the attributional composition and then the social network structure of the Medici party, during the period 1427–34, as compared with those of their opponents, the "oligarchs." After this cross-sectional anatomy, we will sketch the long-term historical dynamic—the emergence first of the marriage and second of the economic patronage halves of the Medici party as a function of ongoing transformations within the Florentine elite. At the end, we will show how contradictory networks induced both robust action in Cosimo and political legitimacy in the Medicean state.

Data Sources and Selection

This article is empirically possible because of the thorough and impressive work of many historians of Florence. In particular, we build on the work of Dale Kent, whose book, *The Rise of the Medici* (1978), in the tradition of Lewis Namier (1929), is an intimate prosopographical description of the network foundations both of the Medici party, or faction, and of the looser alliance system of their opponents.[11] From the detailed text of this account, we coded a core network dataset, which consists of information on the following nine types of relations among early fifteenth-century Florentine elite families: (*a*) one type of kinship relation—intermarriage ties,[12] (*b*) four types of economic relations—trading or business ties, joint ownerships or partnerships, bank employment, and real estate ties,[13] (*c*) two

[11] Some may question whether the term "party" is apt for such an early time period. If presentist definitions, which include reference to mass electorates, are insisted on, then of course the Medici did not organize a party. But the Medicean organization was mobilized, in part, in order to influence the outcomes of popular elections (called "scrutinies") for government office, albeit in a restricted electorate. This certainly fits dictionary meanings of the term.

[12] At the valuable suggestion of Ronald Breiger, we took care in the second round of our coding to distinguish the family that provided the marrying male from the family that provided the marrying female. Hence, unlike the data provided to Breiger and Pattison (1986), the interfamily marriage relations analyzed here are asymmetric. Only marriages occurring in the time period 1394–1434 were coded. The modern reader may need reminding that all of the elite marriages recorded here were arranged by patriarchs (or their equivalents) in the two families. Intraelite marriages were conceived of partially in political alliance terms. Hence, there is little doubt that, in this time and place, marriage relations were interfamily, not interpersonal, relations.

[13] Kent's sources for all these different types of economic relations (except bank employment) were the 1427 and 1433 *catasti*, which are registers of tax reports. Trading and partnership data were symmetric, by definition, since information on directionality of trade and magnitude of

types of "political" relations—patronage and personal loans,[14] and (*d*) two types of personal friendship relations—personal friends and *mallevadori*, or surety, ties.[15] Social network ties were constituents of, as well as backdrops to, Florentine political party formation.

These network data, coded from Kent, were supplemented with attributional data coded from a variety of sources: (*a*) economic wealth was obtained from the computer tape of the 1427 *catasto*, coded and generously made available for public access by the late David Herlihy and Christiane Klapisch-Zuber (1981);[16] (*b*) "date of first Prior," the Florentine measure of family social status, was obtained from Najemy (1982) and Kent (1975);[17] (*c*) neighborhood residence, at both the ward (*gonfalone*) and the quarter levels, was obtained from Herlihy and Klapisch-Zuber's tape (1981) and from Kent (1975); and (*d*) 1403 tax assessments, for the richest 600 households in the city, were obtained from Martines (1963). In addition, for interpretative purposes, systematic data over time on factional memberships, bank employment, city finances, and rates of neighborhood exogamy were obtained from Brucker (1962, 1977), de Roover (1966), Molho (1971), and Cohn (1980), respectively.

All in all, the unusual richness of these data, from such a distant time, bear witness to the impressive creativity and industry both of the original Florentine scribes and of the modern historians who labor in the Florentine field.

partnership investment was not provided by Kent. Kent's asymmetric bank employment data were coded mostly from de Roover (1966). Real estate ties were coded as symmetric when they referred to joint ownership of property, and as asymmetric when they referred to rental relations.

[14] "Political" is in quotations here because the motivations underlying these relations may be complicated: a mixture of political aid, economic exchange, personal friendship, and unspecified "building up of credits." Such mixtures of motives are typical of multifaceted patron–client relations.

[15] Personal friends were coded conservatively as such only when Kent seemed to indicate, on the basis of surviving letters, that the relationship had no political content. This coding rule keeps "friendship" from being confounded by our dependent variable, membership in political faction. *Mallevadori* are friends who put up surety, or bond, to guarantee the good behavior of an exile. "Citizens who helped relatives or friends accused of political crimes were motivated by a strong sense of obligation, for they were risking not only money, but their reputations and status" (Brucker 1977, 29).

[16] Household economic wealth was aggregated to the clan or "common last name" level of aggregation, to be consistent with other attributional data. Some small amount of error is inevitable in this procedure (Kent 1978, 119).

[17] The Priorate (or city council), first created in 1282, otherwise known as the Signoria, was Florence's governing body. This board was almost sacred in its ritual construction (Trexler 1980); membership, on a randomly rotating (within a select circle) two-month-term basis, was public confirmation of one's family's and one's own highest status and honor, in peers' eyes (Martines 1963). Hence, the date of first Prior measures how old and dignified one's family was. Consciousness of their family's date of entry into the elite, relative to other families' dates of entry, was acute among Florentines.

Two matters are important to clarify at the outset, in order to frame the universe of this study—the definition of "family" and the definition of "elite."

Operationally, "family" here means "people with a common last name." Hence, it is more equivalent to clan than to household.[18] This level of aggregation is forced on us by the nature of some of our data (particularly, date of first Prior and neighborhood).[19] However, F. W. Kent (1977) provides strong substantive justification for this coding. Relations between distant lineages in an elite clan were less solidary during the Renaissance than they had been in medieval *consorteria* times. But, contra Burckhardt ([1860] 1954) and Goldthwaite (1968), the Renaissance in Florence was not an era of individualism. Relations among households in a clan were typically, although not universally, very strong (see also Brucker 1977, 18–19). The turbulence of the times reinforced defensive cohesion (Brucker 1977, 19–21; Kent and Kent 1981). And communal citizenship and office-holding regulations during the early fifteenth century placed more emphasis on the unitary legal character of clans than before (Witt 1976, 262; Najemy 1982, chap. 8). In other words, while the clan level of data aggregation is indeed a data convenience it was also a Florentine social reality.

The definition of "elite" is more complicated. The Florentine political elite (called the *reggimento)* was in no way identical to the Florentine economic elite, in part because of volatility in international markets. In our definition, which emphasizes political practice, we follow the lead of Kent (1975), who in turn follows the practice of Brucker (1977).

For us, a Florentine family is politically elite if it satisfies any of the following criteria: (*a*) it had two or more members who spoke in the *Consulte e Pratiche* three or more times between January 1429 and December 1434, (*b*) it had three or more members who qualified in 1433 for scrutiny, or election to the leading public offices in Florence,[20] or (*c*) it was a magnate clan.[21]

[18] The median number of households in the 92 elite families studied here is nine. One household, in turn, may contain a number of politically active brothers, in addition to the patriarch father. See Herlihy and Klapisch-Zuber (1985) for more information on elite vs. nonelite household composition.

[19] But also Kent and Brucker, following the practice of Florentine chroniclers, frequently report alliances and ties by family name only.

[20] In particular, the so-called Tre Maggiori: the Signoria (or Priorate) and the Dodici and Sedici (auxiliary colleges to the Signoria).

[21] Magnate clans were old, previously powerful, and violent noble families that had misbehaved politically in the past. They and their offspring were punished by the victorious *popolani* in 1293, and occasionally thereafter, by being excluded legally from high public office (Becker 1965; Lansing 1991). They were politically defanged, however, only in this formal sense.

Information on the former two criteria is contained in Kent (1975); information on the last criterion (added because of the political importance of this legally excluded group) is contained in Becker (1965) and Lansing (1991). Since official Florentine political participation was comparatively broad, this liberal definition of the ruling elite contains more parvenu new men and upper middle classes than one might expect.

In all, 215 Florentine families (i.e., clans) satisfied one or more of these criteria. Attributes of these 215 families are analyzed in the following section. Kent's book (1978) contains information on at least one marriage or economic relation for 92 of these 215 families. These 92 families are the basis for the network analysis contained herein.

By intention, Kent's book is a comparative study of the Medici party and its oligarch opponents. Hence, the 92-family "sample" is skewed, relative to the 215-family elite "universe," toward active participation in factions and away from political neutrals.[22] We are not aware of any sample bias in Kent's selection of network data *among* partisans.[23]

Network Structure

Attributional Analyses of Florentine Partisanship

Let us begin our analysis in the traditional way: namely, let us ask, Who exactly were the Mediceans and their oligarch opponents? And what social interests did they represent? Four hypotheses (not necessarily mutually exclusive) have been presented in the literature, all built around a common assumption that politics fundamentally means a struggle between self-interested groups.

[22] This fact means that it is difficult, with these data, to study factional participation—only factional membership, given participation, can be studied. As will be seen in the attributional analyses below, however, "factional participation" included virtually all of the economically and socially important families in Florence. Nonparticipation was more an issue for the politically active, but not factional, middle classes. We are currently working to expand our network dataset with primary materials, in part in order to evaluate potential sample selection problems. Padgett has been coding original Carte dell'Ancisa marriage records in the Florentine archives, covering the *longue durée* period 1300–1500. Our colleague, Paul McLean, likewise has been coding original 1427 and 1433 *catasti* tax records in order to assemble a broader cross-section of economic relations in the Florentine elite. Analyses of these primary materials will be reported in future publications.

[23] In particular, residential distribution of marriage dyads (possibly relevant for bias in estimated exogamy rates, calculated below) is not seriously skewed. The slight overrepresentation of San Giovanni families, if anything, works against the Medici neighborhood exogamy finding reported below.

An older economic class hypothesis is that the oligarchs were rich, and the Mediceans were of the middling sort. Prominent recent exponents of the class perspective, albeit not explicitly applied to the Medici, include Martines (1963) and Cohn (1980). An important variant of the economic class hypothesis applies not to volume of wealth but to its change: The Mediceans were rising economic parvenus, while oligarchs were "old money," generally on the decline.[24]

Tables 9.1–9.4 present distributional data on these two economic class hypotheses for the entire 215-family universe of elite. Distributions of wealth and of change in wealth are tabulated for Medici partisan families, for oligarchic partisan families, and for neutral families. Party memberships were taken, here and throughout this paper, from the two lists published as appendices to Kent (1978).[25]

Table 9.1 *Reggimento* Family Distributions of Wealth in 1427

Gross Wealth (1000 florins)	No. of Oligarch Families	No. of Medicean Families	No. of Neutral Families	Total No. of Families	Proportion Partisan
More than 100	4	2	0	6	1.000
50–100	7	7	6	21	.714
10–50	16	23	44	86	.488
0–10	14	10	58	83	.301
Missing	0	0	18	19	.053
Total	41	42	126	215	.414

N.B.: Median gross wealth (in florins) was, for oligarch families, 21,053; for Medicean families, 20,874; for neutral families, 9,052; for total families, 12,414. The source for the data in this table is Herlihy and Klapisch-Zuber (1981). "Family" is operationally defined by common last name. Hence, the gross family wealth reported here is sums of the pre-deduction wealth of all households that shared last names in the 1427 *catasto*, according to Herlihy's computerized coding. Numbers do not add perfectly because of families whose partisan loyalties were split. When split families had a majority on one partisan side or the other, they were allocated to the majority side for purposes of the attributional analyses here. However, six families were tied, and excluded from all tabular breakdowns (but not from proportion partisan calculations).

[24] Logically, a third variant might be occupational in focus: the Mediceans were bankers, and the oligarchs rentiers. However, no one in the literature has, to our knowledge, seriously proffered this view, for the simple reason that Florentine economic elites are well-known to have been extremely multifaceted and nonspecialized in their money-making activities.

[25] Kent identified Medicean partisans primarily from private letters to and from the Medici. She identified oligarch partisans from lists of those exiled when the Medici took over.

Table 9.2 Kolmogorov-Smirnov Tests for Distributional Difference in Family Wealth

	Kolmogorov-Smirnov Statistic	One-tailed *P*
Mediceans vs. oligarchs	.1051	.632
Mediceans vs. neutrals	.3942	.000
Oligarchs vs. neutrals	.3202	.002

N.B.: Here and in tables 9.4 and 9.6, Kolmogorov-Smirnov statistics were calculated on the basis of underlying continuous distributions, not on the basis of the summary tables 9.1, 9.3, and 9.5, in which the data have been made ordinal through cut points. Stricter one-tailed tests which use the chi-square approximation, not the more usual two-tailed Kolmogorov-Smirnov tests, are applied in tables 9.2, 9.4, and 9.6 since the literature implies the following expectations: Mediceans were on average less wealthy, more recently wealthy, and newer (in terms of first Prior) than oligarchs. See Blalock (1972, 264) for this one-tailed chi-square approximation procedure, which makes it harder to reject the hypothesis that parties are different. (I thank Ed Laumann for this suggestion.)

Table 9.3 *Reggimento* Family Distributions of Relative Wealth Change, 1403–27

Estimated Change in Relative Wealth	No. of Oligarch Families	No. of Medicean Families	No. of Neutral Families	Total No. of Families	Proportion Partisan
More than 100%	2	7	7	17	.588
0% to 100%	15	11	19	46	.587
0% to −50%	8	7	17	34	.500
−50% to −100%	4	8	17	29	.414
Missing	12	9	66	89	.258
Total	41	42	126	215	.414

N.B.: Median tax in 1403 was 24 florins; median wealth in 1427 was 22, 500 florins. The sources for the data in this table are Herlihy and Klapisch-Zuber (1981) and Martines (1963). Since systematic data on wealth do not exist before the 1427 *catasto*, this table is based on the tax tables of 1403 *prestanza* (or forced loans) found in Martines (1963, 353–65). These tables report tax data only on the 150 wealthiest households in each of the four quarters—that is, 600 households in all. Thus, the 1403 *prestanza* information used here is a truncated dataset. *Prestanza* tax data of course are not comparable to gross wealth data, so both datasets were standardized by their medians before estimated change was calculated—that is, estimated change = [(1427 wealth/wealth median) – (1403 tax/tax median)]/(1403 tax/tax median). Because of this standardization, "estimated change" refers not to absolute change in florins, which is impossible to know, but rather to relative change in ranked comparison to peers. Data in the above table (and associated medians) include only those families with nonmissing data in both 1403 and 1427. Missing data is a serious problem here because of the truncated nature of Martines's 1403 "wealthiest" dataset.

Table 9.4 Kolmogorov-Smirnov Tests for Distributional Difference in (Estimated) Relative Wealth Change

	Kolmogorov-Smirnov Statistic	One-tailed *P*
Mediceans vs. oligarchs	.1735	.395
Mediceans vs. neutrals	.1606	.333
Oligarchs vs. neutrals	.2954	.033

N.B.: For an explanation of the statistics used, see table 9.2.

Both economic class hypotheses are false. While both the Mediceans and the oligarchs were significantly more wealthy than the neutrals, the two parties' wealth distributions were statistically identical to each other. Moreover, the elite was not split into partisan rich and neutral poor; both parties were extremely heterogeneous in their wealth composition. A similar story holds for change in wealth, as measured relative to a 1403 base. A Marxist class struggle this was not.

Correlated with but not identical to the economic class view is the social class (or prestige) argument: the oligarch party was recruited from older patricians, whereas the Mediceans were new men—defined not in terms of wealth but rather in terms of the political age of their families. Brucker (1962, 1977) and Becker (1962) are the most prominent exponents of the view that broad stretches of Florentine history should be analyzed primarily as a conflict between old and new family political cohorts. Bolstering this interpretation is the fact that numerous contemporaries, such as (alleged) Niccolo da Uzzano (Kent 1978, 212–14) and the chronicler Cavalcanti, forcefully analyzed the conflict in class terms, without always distinguishing between economic and social versions.

As presented in tables 9.5 and 9.6, evidence for the social class hypothesis is mixed. The oligarchs were indeed more skewed toward patricians than were the Mediceans, but this was due to the relative absence of new men from the oligarch party, not to the absence of patricians from the Medicean side. Mediceans were not "newer" men than the oligarchs; they simply were more socially heterogeneous. Relative to political neutrals as a control group, the Mediceans were distinctly old-guard patrician in cast.

Finally, both Dale Kent herself (1978; Kent and Kent 1982) and F. W. Kent (1977, 1987; Kent and Kent 1982), without directly disagreeing with

Table 9.5 *Reggimento* Family Distributions of Social Prestige

Date of First Prior	No. of Oligarch Families	No. of Medicean Families	No. of Neutral Families	Total No. of families	Proportion Partisan
1282–1299	24	19	26	72	.639
1300–1342	10	7	30	48	.375
1343–1377	5	9	31	45	.311
1378–1434	2	7	33	44	.250
Missing	0	0	6	6	.000
Total	41	42	126	215	.414

N.B.: Median date of first Prior is, for oligarch families, 1289; for Medicean families, 1318.5; for neutral families, 1349; for total families, 1327. The source for the data in this table is Najemy (1982, 323–27). Except for the arbitrary date of 1300, the intervals in dates reported here are defined by major revolutions in the history of Florence: 1282, 1343, and 1378. Since large waves of new families were admitted to eligibility in the priorate during these revolutions, the historical periodization in table 9.5 corresponds to discrete political cohorts. Old magnates either have no date of first Prior, by virtue of never being legally eligible for this office, or have a misleadingly recent date of first Prior, if they were reinstated as *popolani* somewhere along the line. Therefore, most magnates were coded as having a date of 1284, essentially the oldest possible. There are 21 magnate families in this dataset.

Table 9.6 Kolmogorov-Smirnov Tests of Distributional Difference in Social Prestige

	Kolmogorov-Smirnov Statistic	One-tailed P
Mediceans vs. oligarchs	.2968	.026
Mediceans vs. neutrals	.2619	.014
Oligarchs vs. neutrals	.4477	.000

N.B.: For an explanation of the statistics used, see table 9.2.

either class view, distinctively emphasize the importance of neighborhood: The Medici party was rooted in the San Giovanni quarter, particularly the Medici's home ward of Lion d'Oro, whereas their opponents were centered in the Santa Croce quarter.

Tables 9.7 and 9.8 show that there was no statistically significant difference between the two parties by neighborhood. This does not mean that geography was irrelevant: The two parties mirrored each other in geographical concentration, especially relative to neutrals. The Mediceans were indeed

Table 9.7 *Reggimento* Family Distributions of Neighborhood Residence

Quarter of City	No. of Oligarch Families	No. of Medicean Families	No. of Neutral Families	Total No. of Families	Proportion Partisan
Santo Spirito	7	8	36	52	.308
Santa Croce	14	6	33	55	.400
Santa Maria Novella	9	7	29	46	.370
San Giovanni	11	21	27	61	.557
Missing	0	0	1	1	.000
Total	41	42	126	215	.414

N.B.: The source for these data, both for the four quarters and for the 16 *gonfaloni* (or wards), is Kent (1975, 624–32).

Table 9.8 Chi-Square Tests of Distributional Difference in Residence

	Across Quarters (df = 3)		Across *Gonfaloni* (df = 15)	
	χ^2	P	χ^2	P
Mediceans vs. oligarchs	6.629	.084	17.806	.273
Mediceans vs. neutrals	12.554	.006	29.567	.014
Oligarchs vs. neutrals	2.683	.443	19.660	.185

overrepresented in San Giovanni but, then again, so were the oligarchs. San Giovanni was the most polarized of quarters; Santa Croce was a distant second.

The main theme that comes through these attributional analyses is similarity, not difference. With the important exception of the absence of new men from the oligarch side, the Mediceans and oligarchs were mirror images of each other. The elite as a whole appears to have fractured in two with no underlying social group basis.

A deep historical enigma remains. Contrary to these heterogeneous membership statistics, contemporaries had a perfectly clear, almost polemical, understanding of what was at stake. Virtually all recorded participants interpreted the partisan conflict in traditional economic and/or social class terms: The oligarchs were considered to be the conservative party of old, wealthy, and threatened patricians, and the Mediceans were considered to be the heroes of the economically rising new men (Brucker 1977; Kent 1978). This in spite of the fact that it does not objectively appear to be true.[26] A puzzling structural mismatch existed between clear cognitive typifications of social groups at the level of culture and extreme heterogeneity and overlap of social groups at the level of behavioral action.

This puzzle about mismatch between cognition and behavior remains to be solved but, even at this point, we can conclude that tables 9.1–9.8 provide prima facie evidence against classical group theories of parties, of either the pluralist or the neo-Marxist varieties. These theories assume that parties represent coalitions of groups. But political "groups" in the sense of sets of attributionally similar individuals who solve collective action problems in order to coordinate action on common (latent) interests simply did not exist in Renaissance Florence. Indeed, as we shall show below, the more homogeneous the attributes, the less coherent the collective action. We do not argue thereby that social attributes and groups are irrelevant to party formation, merely that their role needs to be understood within a deeper relational context. There is no simple mapping of groups or spatial dimensions onto parties; social attributes and group interests are "merely" *cognitive* categories, which party mobilization, networks, and action crosscut.

Social Structure: Blockmodel Analysis

We now look more directly at this mobilization through an analysis of our nine microstructural networks. Party organization was not reflective of any one of these networks, taken alone, but Kent has already demonstrated persuasively the fact that both parties were constructed from differing concatenations of preexisting social networks. We will return in subsequent sections to examine the consequences of these patterns of micromobilization for the aggregate social characteristics (or "interests") that they organized.

The essential step in this task is to derive an overall relational picture of Florence's social structure, within the 92-family ruling elite. For the purposes of this article, we define "social structure" to be marriage and economic

[26] Moreover, even if the difference were one of policy, not one of membership, figure 9.1 shows clearly that the Medici did not in fact represent the interests of the new men once they assumed office.

networks, which we take to be "strong ties" in Granovetter's (1973) sense.[27] Figure 9.2a presents, in graphical form, the result of our analyses: an aggregate blockmodel image of the marriage and economic networks, obtained by methods described in Appendix A. Figure 9.2b presents the parallel blockmodel image of "weak tie" political and friendship networks, based on the family clusters generated by the analysis of marriage and economic data. Appendix B (table 9.B1) lists the cluster memberships of those families that are contained in the various structural blocks graphed in figures 9.2a and 9.2b, along with those families' partisan affiliations and social attributes.

Methodological and goodness-of-fit issues are addressed in Appendix A. Suffice it to say here that the structuralist research style embedded in blockmodeling aggregates actors into structurally equivalent sets, or "blocks," in accordance with their common *external* ties with outsiders rather than in accordance with dense internal relations with each other (as in cliques). The sets of families observed in Appendix B, in other words, were clustered or "thrust together" by common third-party relations to outside families; the blocks need not (and usually do not) contain any ties within themselves.[28]

Three graphical points need to be borne in mind in order to interpret the figures: (1) Family labels in figures 9.2a and 9.2b do not indicate solo families; they encode the most prominent family in that structurally equivalent block of families (Appendix B gives details). (2) An image line or "bond" in this global portrait corresponds to at least two underlying ties between families in the linked blocks of the graphically indicated type. (3) The triangulated circle superimposed onto the blockmodel diagram contains the

[27] This distinction between "strong tie" marriage and economic networks and "weak tie" political and friendship networks was, to some extent, arrived at inductively. We were concerned from the beginning with excluding patronage and friendship networks from this particular analysis, because these might be too close to our dependent variable, political partisanship, to be considered legitimate independent predictors. Marriage and economic networks, on the other hand, are driven primarily by nonpartisan calculations. It goes against the whole thrust of our article to assert that these networks were independent of politics, but the first-order consideration in economic relations was making money, while the first-order consideration in marriage was hierarchical status. Furthermore, partisan politics operated on a higher-frequency temporal pulse than did the more glacially changing marriage and economic structures. Personal loans and *mallevadori* ties, however, were ambiguous in our minds. We ran the blockmodel analyses both including and excluding these networks and examined the robustness of the resulting partitions as well as the goodness of fit (see below). Including these two networks did not improve goodness of fit but did have the effect of breaking up the oligarch blocks into smaller "globules," an indicator of ties that cut across rather than reinforce the existing system. Figure 9.2b illustrates this graphically: Personal loans and *mallevadori* ties were sent not only to structural intimates but also to families far distant in the social structure. Perhaps these were the "bridges" to future structural change, as elite families attempted to reach to new partners, just as Granovetter's weak-tie image conveys.

[28] If they do, this is indicated in the figures by a circle around the block name.

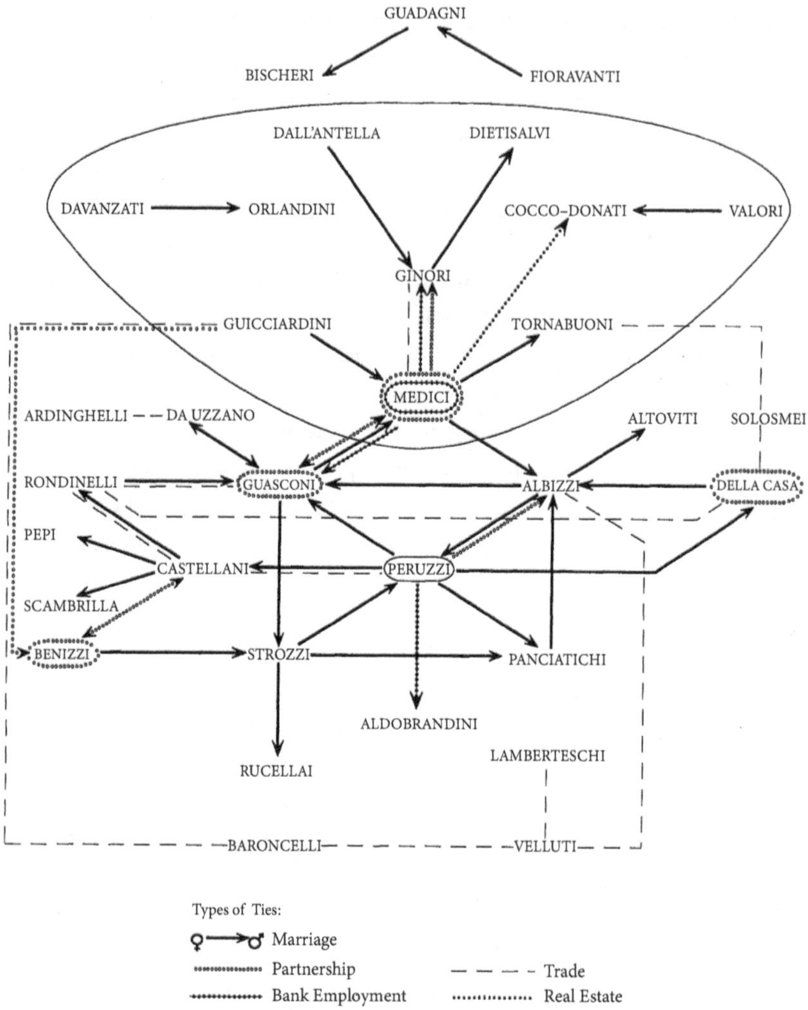

Figures 9.2a Marriage and Economic Blockmodel Structure (92 elite families)

dependent variable, Medici party membership. The bulk of oligarchic partisans are contained in the rectangular set of intermarrying blocks directly beneath the Medicean party.

The first thing to observe about figure 9.2a is that the capacity of marriage and economic blockmodels to predict political partisanship is remarkable, especially given the virtual attributional identity of the two parties. The partisanship of the Medici family itself is impossible to predict from social structure alone, since the Medici family was deeply tied to both sides. But given the Medici split from the lower set of blocks, prediction of Medicean

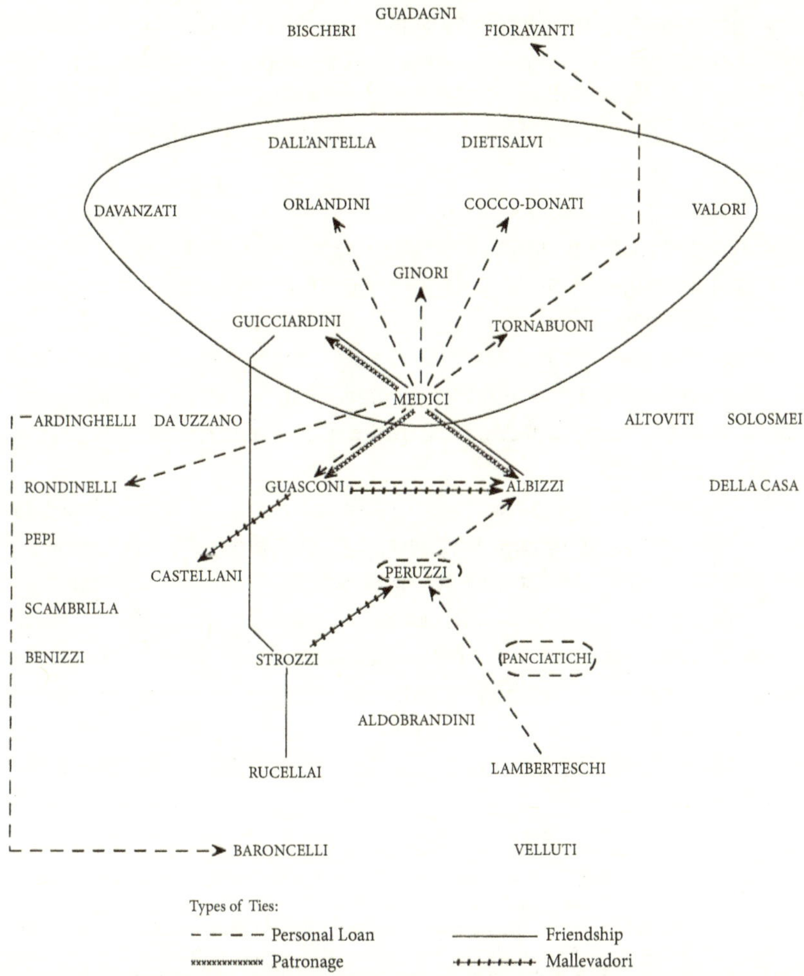

Figures 9.2b "Political" and Friendship Blockmodel Structure (92 elite families)

followers is obvious: The enclosed circle of blocks contains families that had systematic access to the rest of the elite only through the Medici.

More specifically, 93% of the families within the triangulated circle were mobilized actively into the Medici party. Fifty-nine percent of all other families, including neutrals, were organized actively into the oligarch party. Excluding neutrals, 82% of all other partisan families joined the oligarch side (see App. A and tables 9.Al and 9.A2, for details). Even errors in partisanship prediction here are a bit overstated: in fact, we would predict families in the cross-pressured Guasconi and Albizzi blocks to be split in their partisan loyalties, which for the most part they were. Truly, the microstructure of marriage and economics was central to the formation of parties in Florence.[29] Rather than parties being generated by social groups, we argue, both parties and social groups were induced conjointly by underlying networks.

We will return in a later section to a causal discussion of the exact temporal unfolding of this intimate connection between social networks and party membership. For now, we discuss only the consequences of this social structure for political control.

Contemporaries and historians have long known that the Medici party was far more cohesive and tightly centralized than was the looser and more cross-pressured oligarch faction. With the aid of figure 9.2a, it is easy to see why.

The Medici party was an extraordinarily centralized, a simple, "star" or "spoke" network system, with very few relations among Medici followers: the party consisted almost entirely of direct ties to the Medici family.[30] One important consequence for central control was that Medici partisans were connected to other Medici partisans almost solely through the Medici themselves. In addition, Medici partisans were connected to the rest of the oligarchic elite only through the intermediation of the Medici family. Medici partisans in general possessed remarkably few intraelite network ties; compared to oligarchs, they were structurally impoverished.[31]

[29] The lack of congruence between patronage (figure 9.2b) and the rest of the social structure (figure 9.2a) is worthy of note. A standard image is that patronage is the glue that binds parties together internally. Here, however, this is not particularly true. Elites did tax, job-hunting, court, and miscellaneous favors for other elites, almost regardless of partisanship, as much as they did favors for their client followers. Even though patronage was pervasive, in Renaissance Florence, party was far more deeply embedded in marriage and economic relations than it was in patronage relations.

[30] Graph centralization can be measured with the network betweenness statistic (C_B) of Freeman (1979, 230), usually interpreted as intensity of concentration of resource or information flows. Among Medicean families, marriage relations were concentrated at the level $C_B = .362$. Among oligarch partisans, marriage $C_B = .184$. On the economic front, $C_B = .429$ among Mediceans, compared to $C_B = .198$ among oligarchs. (Economic ties, including personal loans, were pooled for the latter calculations. Personal loans were included because otherwise the density of intra-Medicean ties was too low. All data were binarized and symmetrized for these calculations, as required by the Freeman measure.) We thank an *AJS* referee for the suggestion of calculating these statistics.

[31] Statistics on two-step ties—the number of families that families tied to the Medici were tied to (by marriage or economic relations)—demonstrate this clearly, especially for the case of marriage. Within this 92-family dataset, Medici marriage partners were married, on median, to only two other families. (According to blockmodel analysis, these two ties were structurally incoherent.) In contrast, the median number of marriage partners for two oligarch control groups (see below for description) were as follows: 6.5 for Santa Croce faction leader families and 4.5 for oligarchic superelite families. Data on "political" and friendship partners show the same pattern less dramatically: The median numbers of (marriage or economic) partners of Medici "political" or friendship partners were 2 and 3, respectively. This compares with the control groups' partners: 5.5 and 6.5 for the Santa Croce

In such an impoverished network context, it is easy to understand how a solo dependence on a powerful family would loom very large indeed (Emerson 1962).

Conversely, the oligarch side was densely interconnected, especially through marriage. Dense structural interconnection, however, did not lead to cohesive collective action. The oligarchs were composed of too many status equals, each with plausible network claims to leadership. In dense networks in times of crisis, cacophony ensued, as each family conspired privately with other families to which they were tied about the proper course of action. Simultaneous and contradictory conversations redounded through ambagious private network channels, generating cross-pressure on each family instead of collective convergence.

A concrete behavioral example, the final "military" showdown between the two sides, will illustrate this point. On the morning of September 26, 1433, Rinaldo Albizzi, titular leader of the oligarchs, passed the word to his supporters to assemble their troops at a certain piazza in order to forcibly seize the city hall and the government (Kent 1978, 332–34). At the appointed hour, only a portion of his supporters appeared. Each supporter looked around at, and no doubt consulted with, other supporters, and a stochastic threshold equilibrium ensued in which repeated efforts by Rinaldo to assemble more troops (especially from Palla Strozzi) were offset by other supporters' changing their mind and drifting away.

In contrast, while the oligarchs dithered, the Medici immediately and decisively mobilized their supporters to join the Priors in the embattled Palazzo Vecchio. The clarity of this coordinated response was astonishing, given the fact that Cosimo and Lorenzo de' Medici were in Venice at the time.[32] As a result of this Medicean mobilization, no military engagement actually ensued, since it became clear to Albizzi supporters, if not to Rinaldo himself, that they had no chance. At this point, popular opinion swung massively behind the Medici, Cosimo was recalled from Venice in triumph, and Cosimo's oligarchic enemies were exiled, this time for good.

Kent (1978, 228–34) also gives examples, less dramatic than this, of the greater cohesion of the Medici side during 1427–28 electoral maneuvering.

leaders, and 4 and 4 for the superelite. For economic partners, on the other hand, there was little difference: 3.5 for the Medici's partners versus 5 for Santa Croce partners, and only 3 for the partners of the superelite.

[32] Temporarily, the Medici brothers had been exiled. They were not, however, successfully cut off from secretly communicating with and issuing standing orders to their supporters.

Even granted this explanation of the greater cohesion of the Medici side, an equilibrium puzzle remains: How could such a centralized spoke system maintain itself? Florentine clientage systems historically had been notoriously fluid. And the oligarchs had a clear incentive to marry into or do business with Medici supporters, thereby inducing cross-pressure and sowing dissent. The Medici supporters would appear to have had an equally clear incentive to respond, in order to alleviate their extreme dependence. At the very least, one would assume Medicean supporters would want to interbreed among themselves, for defensive if no other purposes; for only then would they have the organizational capacity to resist Medici domination, should they ever choose to do so. Structural isolation among Medici partisans would seem to have been in the long-term self-interest only of the Medici.

This structural atomization puzzle is only deepened through closer inspection of figures 9.2a and 9.2b. Two large blocks of Medici supporters were connected to the Medici essentially through marriage alone. Other blocks of Medici supporters were connected to the Medici solely by economic or by personal loan relations. The Medici had strongly multiplex ties with the oligarch Guasconi block,[33] but, within their own party, the Medici did not marry those families with whom they engaged in economic relations, nor did they do business with those whom they married.[34]

This is in sharp contrast to the greater multiplexity of relations on the oligarch side: core oligarch families, the superelite and the Santa Croce faction leaders (see below), married into 40% and 38%, respectively, of the clans with whom they did business.

Most sociologists' Durkheimian presumptions are that the more overlapping ties one has with another, the more closely and holistically bound the other is to you. Obligations from one sphere spill over into another. The Medici, however, apparently believed the opposite: To control followers politically, segregate one's social relations with them. On the whole, multiplex ties (across marriage and economics) were discouraged. Thus, structural isolation operated in two ways: the marriage and economic isolation of partisans from all others (including other partisans), and the segregation of types of ties with the Medici themselves.

[33] The Medici bank was a primary source of these exceptional multiplex ties. Often such multiply tied exceptions did not politically support the Medici in the end—e.g., two prominent families in the Guasconi block, the Bardi and the Guasconi themselves.

[34] There was only one exception to this rule: the Tornabuoni.

Comparative Statics of Attributes with Networks

The beginnings of an understanding of stability can be gained from a reexamination of the social attributes listed in Appendix B. The large Guicciardini and Tornabuoni blocks, with whom the Medici were intermarried, were composed virtually entirely of patricians (i.e., date of first Prior before 1343) who also had substantial wealth. In sharp contrast, the Ginori, the Orlandini, and the Cocco-Donati blocks, to whom the Medici were connected through economic or personal loan ties, were composed almost entirely of new men (date of first Prior after 1343). The remaining Medicean blocks—the Davanzati, the dall'Antella, the Dietisalvi, and the Valori blocks—were for the most part patricians of only modest wealth. These blocks of families were connected to the Medici indirectly, via intermarriage with economically connected new men.

The hybrid social class character of the Mediceans, revealed in tables 9.5 and 9.6, has now been clarified: Actually, the Medici party was an agglomeration of structurally disjoint patrician and new men components. Different social class interests were embodied in the Medici party; (social) class contradiction was quite real. Not only that but, within the party, these elements were separately clustered by Medici ties and then kept rigidly segregated from each other, to be connected indirectly only through the Medici themselves.

Given this, there is no particular mystery about the low intermarriage rate among Mediceans: Patrician and new men supporters despised each other. Status-conscious patricians (Medici included) usually would not dream of sullying their own honor by marrying into new men families; such would be a downward-mobility admission of status equality. Part of the distinctive Medicean party organization, in other words, was simply leveraged off and sustained by the ordinary cognitive classifications and social marriage rules of Florentine elites.

A close reexamination of Appendix B also reveals a second striking attributional cleavage between these Medicean social class segments, this time on the dimension of neighborhood. Almost none of the patricians in the Guicciardini and Tornabuoni blocks came from the San Giovanni quarter, where the Medici resided. The Medici, in other words, did not marry those with whom they lived.[35] However, 10 of the 14 families in the other

[35] Weissman (1982) makes vivid the dense piazza-oriented street life of Renaissance Florence, in which one constantly mingled with (or at least ran into) one's neighbors.

Medici blocks—both new men and the indirectly tied patricians, married to new men—resided in San Giovanni. The Medici, in other words, did a great deal of business (plus personal loans) with those with whom they lived. In addition, they somehow induced local San Giovanni patrician supporters to marry into the families of their economic partners, rather than into their own.

Thus, the Medicean supporters were deeply cleaved on two attributional dimensions simultaneously: social class (i.e., prestige) and neighborhood. Not only did the various components despise each other, they did not run into each other much either. Only the Medici family itself linked the segments.

To give a more precise sense of the distinctiveness of this Medici agglomeration, we present table 9.9. The upper panels of the three parts tabulate prestige, wealth, and neighborhood endogamy rates for the Medici and for two comparable oligarch reference groups: a set of superelite families—the Peruzzi, the Strozzi, the Albizzi, and the Gianfigliazzi—and a set of Santa Croce faction leaders—the Peruzzi, the Ricasoli, and the Castellani families. The lower panels of the three parts give the partisanship consequences of the network mobilization ties tabulated in the upper panels.

We begin by discussing the first control group, the superelite. Table 9.9, part A, on prestige, shows that the Peruzzi, Strozzi, Albizzi, and Gianfigliazzi families were patrician to the core. It mattered not what the type of network relation was—marriage, economic, "political," or friendship—across the board, these families directed about 90% of their ties to fellow patricians. New men were snubbed in all spheres.

Table 9.9, part B, on wealth, tells a similar story, with one exception: the superelite did business with many less well-off families. But this was just another sign of their exclusivity on prestige. Even though many patricians had fallen on hard times, the superelite stuck with them in their economic relations rather than switch to wealthier new men.

Santa Croce factional leaders behaved little differently except, of course, that their degree of social exclusivity was slightly less than that of the superelite, since their own status was slightly lower.

Compared to these reference groups, the Medici's own network strategies were, as already argued, more differentiated. In marriage and friendship, the Medici were even more snobbish than the superelite, if that were possible. However, in the economic sphere, the Medici associated heavily with the new men, quite unlike their elite counterparts. "Political" ties (i.e., personal loans and patronage) were intermediate in social class endogamy; the Medici

Table 9.9 Social Attributes and Partisanship of Ties: Medici versus Superelite versus Santa Croce Faction Leaders

	Social Prestige: Date of First Prior								
	Medici			**Superelite**			**Santa Croce Faction Leaders**		
	Pre-1343	**Post-1343**	***n***	**Pre-1343**	**Post-1343**	***n***	**Pre-1343**	**Post-1343**	***n***
Allocation of types of ties:									
Marriage (M)	.93	.07	28	.93	.07	58	.87	.13	30
Friendship (F + M)	1.00	.00	9	.87	.13	31	.79	.21	14
"Political" (L + P)	.62	.38	45	.86	.14	21	.69	.31	16
Economic (T + P + B + R)	.44	.56	27	.88	.12	16	.86	.14	21
Total	.69	.31	109	.90	.10	126	.81	.19	81
Political support consequences of ties:*									
Marriage (M)	.71	1.0		.73	.31		.85	.37	
Friendship (F + M)	.76	. . .		.57	.00		.84	.00	
"Political" (L + P)	.58	.97		.42	.17		.82	.20	
Economic (T + P + B + R)	.55	.90		.81	. . .		.85	.50	
Total	.64	.94		.65	.25		.84	.27	

	Economic Class: Wealth (in 1000 Florins)								
	Medici			Superelite			Santa Croce Faction Leaders		
	More than 25	0–25	*n*	More than 25	0–25	*n*	More than 25	0–25	*n*
Allocation of types of ties:									
Marriage (M)	.82	.18	28	.79	.21	58	.83	.17	30
Friendship (F + M)	.89	.11	9	.81	.19	31	.86	.14	14
"Political" (L + P)	.51	.49	45	.71	.29	21	.94	.06	16
Economic (T + P + B + R)	.56	.44	27	.50	.50	16	.52	.48	21
Total	.63	.37	109	.75	.25	126	.78	.22	81

continued

Table 9.9 *continued*

	Social Prestige: Date of First Prior								
	Medici			Superelite			Santa Croce Faction Leaders		
	Pre-1343	Post-1343	*n*	Pre-1343	Post-1343	*n*	Pre-1343	Post-1343	*n*
Political support consequences of ties:*									
Marriage (M)	.72	.80		.72	.64		.74	1.0	
Friendship (F + M)	.73	. . .		.54	.33		.61	. . .	
"Political" (L + P)	.67	.74		.47	.17		.60	. . .	
Economic (T + P + B + R)	.61	.92		.79	.81		.76	.85	
Total	.68	.78		.63	.54		.69	.92	

	Neighborhood: City Quarter								
	Medici			Superelite			Santa Croce Faction Leaders		
	San Giovanni	Outside Quarter	*n*	In Quarter	Outside Quarter	*n*	Santa Croce	Outside Quarter	*n*
Allocation of types of ties:									
Marriage (M)	.14	.86	28	.36	.64	58	.33	.67	30
Friendship (F + M)	.33	.67	9	.29	.71	31	.36	.64	14
"Political" (L + P)	.40	.60	45	.48	.52	21	.50	.50	16
Economic (T + P + B + R)	.59	.41	27	.31	.69	16	.43	.57	21
Total	.38	.62	110	.36	.64	126	.39	.61	81
Political support consequences of ties:*									
Marriage (M)	.58	.76		.65	.73		.80	.77	
Friendship (F + M)	.78	.76		.33	.57		.70	.64	
"Political" (L + P)	.82	.62		.60	.18		.75	.50	
Economic (T + P + B + R)	.84	.60		.80	.80		.78	.82	
Total	.80	.68		.61	.62		.76	.72	

N.B.: superelite families are Peruzzi, Albizzi, Strozzi, and Gianfigliazzi. Santa Croce faction leaders of the oligarch side are Peruzzi, Ricasoli, and Castellani. Amount shown, except for *n*'s, are proportions.

* Political support consequences of ties = (no. of ties to fellow partisans)/(total no. of ties), with split families allocated proportionately. A tie to a neutral family is treated the same here as a tie to an enemy.

established such relations with both their economic and marriage partners. The Medici's distinctiveness within the elite, in other words, was not that they represented new men; their distinctiveness was that they associated with them at all.

The political responsiveness of those new men with whom the Medici chose to associate was breathtaking: 90% and 96% of those new men tied to the Medici through economic or "political" relations became active Medici partisans. This rate of response was so overwhelming, indeed, that the fact that the Medici did not associate with more new men shows that party building was not the only thing on their minds. New men not explicitly mobilized through Medici ties showed no great enthusiasm for the Medici cause (see tables 9.5 and 9.6).

Thus, we have an important insight into the reason for the strong contemporary image of the Medicean party affair as a social class struggle. It was not that the Medici did all that much actively to mobilize new men; rather it was that the oligarchs did so extraordinarily little. In as deeply elitist a context as Florence, a mere pittance thrown the new men's way, even by such an arch-patrician family as the Medici, could generate overwhelming response. Parvenu new men, anxious for inclusion but long barred from entry, were structurally available, awaiting mobilization, for reasons that had nothing to do with the Medici per se. The Medici opened the door just a crack, and for that they were polemically tarred by their enemies with the rhetorical brush of class traitor: The label "heroes of the new men" connoted contempt. *Cognitive classification of Medici group identity, both by contemporaries and by historians, was the product not of Medici action but of vitriolic oligarch polemics* (supported, no doubt, by wishful thinking among new men). Inscrutable Cosimo, of course, did nothing to deny it.

Table 9.9, part C, demonstrates statistically what we have already asserted about neighborhood. Both the superelite and the Santa Croce faction leaders were citywide in their networks, regardless of type of tie.[36] In contrast, the Medici's relations geographically were quite differentiated: only 14% of Medici marriages were within their home quarter, compared with 36% for the superelite. Yet 59% of Medici economic ties were within San Giovanni, compared with 31% for the superelite.

We now have a clear picture of the structure of the Medici party and of its roots in elite network strategies. The Medici party was an agglomeration

[36] Perhaps an exception could be argued for the cases of loans and patronage.

of doubly disarticulated parts: structurally isolated new men living within San Giovanni, whom the Medici mobilized directly through economic relations; and structurally isolated patricians residing outside San Giovanni, whom the Medici mobilized directly through marriage. Conscious residential segregation, as well as "natural" social class segregation, were keys to the inhibition both of independent ties among followers and of multiplex ties with the Medici themselves. The result was an awesomely centralized patrimonial machine, capable of great discipline and "top down" control because the Medici themselves were the only bridge holding this contradictory agglomeration together.[37]

The specific micromechanisms that translated this network structure into Medici control were as follows:

1. Spoke structure induced common dependence of partisans on the Medici for access to the rest of the elite, and it forced any sensitive intraparty communication that required tie-enforced trust to be channeled through the Medici (cf. Molho 1979, 19).
2. Double segregation of attributes inhibited defensive counter-alliance among mutually suspicious partisans: No "revolt of the colonels" was possible.[38]
3. Interactionally, marrying geographically distant patricians, whom the Medici only rarely met casually, kept affine relations socially proper and formal—thereby inhibiting unwanted presumptions of familiarity and status equality. In contrast, doing business with new men inside

[37] Our general position on the interrelation of social attributes and social networks can now be clarified. Obviously (contra some occasionally overstated polemics by network aficionados) we do not believe that social attributes are irrelevant: The particular way in which the Medici recombined social attributes through networks is the heart of the story here. What we object to is the arraying of attributes discretely as groups or spatially as grids—a procedure that presumes attributes to be behaviorally meaningful in a network vacuum. Of course, actors in the system, as well as researchers, do exactly these clustering procedures mentally when they analyze their own social structure; this is what "boundedly rational" cognitive classifications are all about. But there is a widely underappreciated gap between these macrocognitive (or "cultural") operations and microbehavioral "local actions" taken by concrete individuals in very particular, heterogeneous, and often cross-pressured circumstances. Simplifying social reality into homogeneous subsets "with common interests" rips individuals out of their (often contradictory) multiple network contexts and obscures the very heterogeneity and complexity of which organizations like the Medici party are constructed.

[38] A "revolt of the colonels" requires more than just comparing dissatisfactions. Colonels have to have confidence that other colonels are not just stabbing them in the back. There has to be an organizational infrastructure, independent of the boss, through which they can coordinate. And there has to be something they are offering to each other that is better than their current state. Crosscutting Medici networks inhibited each of these preconditions.

the neighborhood engendered motivationally useful friendliness. The status gap between Medici and new men was so enormous that the Medici did not need to fear any slackening of their abject deference.

4. The attributional heterogeneity of the party made the Medici party a swing vote, potent beyond its numbers, in Florentine legislative politics. The reason, explained below, was the bitter class polarization that was reviving in Florence.

Thus, attributional heterogeneity and contradiction of group interests were not a problem for Medici party control. Quite the contrary, they were the keys to Medici control. For this result to be generally true, however, surrounding cognitive group identities (and animosities) must be intense. Stable monopoly of broker position is leveraged off this, and practical political organization becomes cognitively invisible (or at least murky) to the outside world precisely when it cuts across strong identities.

Network Dynamics

The Dynamics of Party Formation: Patrician Marriage

We have insufficient space in this article to show how figure 9.2a emerged historically in detail, but in the next two sections we shall sketch the driving dynamic: Elite marriage and economic networks were reconfigured by working-class revolt and wartime fiscal crisis, respectively. Elite reconfiguration explains why oligarchs would not marry Medicean patricians.

Our core conclusion regarding party formation will be simple: Cosimo de' Medici did *not* design his centralized party, nor did he intend (until the very end) to take over the state. The network patterns of figure 9.2a were produced by oligarchs' earlier successful reassertions of their own control. The Medici party grew up around Cosimo and Lorenzo from raw network material unintentionally channeled to them by the oligarchs' previous smashing both of the wool workers known as *ciompi* (1378) and of the new men's challenge during the Milan and Lucca wars (1424–33). Only very late in the game, we shall argue, did the Medici adaptively learn of the political potential of the social network machine that lay at their fingertips. In almost Hegelian fashion, oligarchs crafted the networks of their own destruction.

Historical Trends in Neighborhood Exogamy

The first thing to appreciate in any dynamic analysis of Medicean marriage strategy is the fact, uncovered by Cohn (1980), that increasing rates of neighborhood exogamy were a historical trend in Florentine elite marriage behavior. The Medici were not tactical revolutionaries; they were simply the leading edge of an ongoing transformation in the network structure of the Florentine elite.

Table 9.10 presents a recalculated version of Cohn's neighborhood data, along with our own data for historical comparison. By coincidence, Cohn studied the mid-fourteenth- and late fifteenth-century periods, which bracket the early fifteenth-century focus of this study. Since Cohn's primary focus was on changing marriage patterns within the lower classes, the volume of elite marriages is lower than that which was extracted from Kent.[39] Cohn's listing of his late fifteenth-century data permitted a further breakdown into "state marriages" and others—a concept that has no real meaning

Table 9.10 Historical Trends in Elite Marriage

	No. within Parish	No. within Gonfalone	No. within Quarter	No. across Quarter	Total
I. Fourteenth-century elite marriages (1340–83)*					
	5	8.5	12	13	25
	(20)	(34)	(48)	(52)	
II. Early fifteenth-century elite marriages (1395–1434):†					
Patrician-patrician		16	37	92	129
		(12)	(29)	(71)	
Patrician-new man		8	17	13	30
		(27)	(57)	(43)	
New man-new man		1	1	1	2
Total		25	55	106	161
		(16)	(34)	(66)	

[39] For the lower classes, or *popolo minuto*, Cohn found a trend just the opposite of that of the elite: increasing rates of marriage *within* neighborhoods. Some portion, but not all, of this trend was due to growing immigrant ethnic enclaves, organized around the silk industry. Cohn argues forcefully that new administrative methods of lower-class control (containment within parishes) during the late fifteenth century inhibited cross-neighborhood contact and organization among workers. A recurrence of the Ciompi Revolt became well-nigh impossible (cf. Molho 1979).

	No. within Parish	No. within Gonfalone	No. within Quarter	No. across Quarter	Total
III. Late fifteenth-century elite marriages (1450–1530):‡					
State marriages:††					
Patrician-patrician		0	1	11	12
		(0)	(8)	(92)	
Patrician-new man		1	1	1	2
New man-new man		0	0	0	0
Total		1	2	12	14
		(7)	(14)	(86)	
Other elite marriages:					
Patrician-patrician		0	2	5	7
		(0)	(29)	(71)	
Patrician-new man		1	4	3	7
		(17)	(57)	(43)	
New man-new man		0	2	3	5
		(0)	(40)	(60)	
Total		1	8	11	19
		(5)	(42)	(58)	

N.B.: Numbers in parentheses are percentages.
* "Elite" is defined by family name plus a dowry of at least 400 florins. Data are from Cohn (1980, 52). To make the data comparable with others in this table, we report the number of marriages rather than Cohn's "number of marriage relations," which, for Cohn, equaled two times the number of marriages, i.e., one for each partner.
† "Elite" is defined by political participation (see text). Data are from this article. Except for "Total" in this category, entries refer to marriages between a patrician and a patrician within the political elite, to marriages between a patrician and a new man within the political elite, etc.
‡ "Elite" is defined by having passed scrutiny plus a dowry of at least 600 florins. Figures are from marriage data listed in Cohn (1980, 54–56.) Due to the passage of time, "new men" is defined here as post-Ciompi (post-1383), rather than post-1343 as in the rest of this paper.
†† These are marriages notarized by Lorenzo de' Medici's personal secretary (see Cohn 1980, 53).

for the period before the Medici changed the republic into a de facto principality.[40] It is reassuring, given different operational definitions of the elite, that neighborhood endogamy/exogamy estimates are perfectly consistent between our two studies.

[40] We label as "state marriages" those marriages registered by Lorenzo de' Medici's personal secretary. "The majority of these marriages were celebrated at the Medici palace and were witnessed by Lorenzo. In several instances Lorenzo even provided the dowry. We find the state, in effect, taking an active role in the structuring of marriage relations, which were at the same time political alliances" (Cohn 1980, p. 53).

These aggregate statistics demonstrate what has already been asserted: that rates of elite marriage outside neighborhood quarter increased progressively over the course of the fourteenth and fifteenth centuries. Cohn's elite marriage data are too scanty to disaggregate reliably by decade, but the combined data give the impression that the bulk of change occurred between 1383 and about 1420—namely, precisely at the time when the patrician elite reconsolidated its control after the disastrous (from their perspective) Ciompi revolution.

Cross-sectional estimates are also consistent: for both fifteenth-century periods, the higher the position in the elite hierarchy, the higher the rate of marriage outside neighborhood. Patricians married other patricians at higher exogamous rates than they married new men. And, most striking in spite of the low numbers, 92% of state marriages in the late fifteenth century were arranged across rather than within neighborhoods. In other words, what in the early fifteenth century was an innovative Medici strategy of partisan control, applicable only to their own marriages, later appears to have become official state policy, applicable to all their top supporters.

This trend is better interpreted from the perspective of its origin than from knowledge of its final result: patrician neighborhood clusters based on marriage gradually dissolved. The Peruzzi-Ricasoli-Castellani clique in Santa Croce, the Albizzi and Guadagni blocs in San Giovanni, and the Strozzi group in Santa Maria Novella indicate clearly that this process was hardly complete during our period (if indeed it ever was).[41] But this "neighborhood solidarity" mode of elite organization, which linked patricians of different stature, was a residue of the past.

In particular, this mode historically descended from feudalism. Florentine neighborhoods originally (in the 1200s) were settled by immigration from contiguous regions of the surrounding rural countryside. Urbanizing feudal lords brought their hierarchical retinues with them, thereby creating self-sufficient neighborhood pockets with stronger ties to the rural homeland than to other parts of Florence (Weissman 1982, 7–9). By the fifteenth century, "feudalism" is hardly an apt description of Florentine neighborhoods, but hierarchical intra-neighborhood marriage among patricians persisted.

[41] Given the vigor of F. W. Kent's recent defense (1987) of the continuing importance of neighborhood in quattrocento Florence, a clarification is in order. We are not arguing that the importance of neighborhood for patricians declined, in some totalistic sense. In fact, we agree with Kent's emphasis on neighborhood patronage (and, we would add, neighborhood economics). However, marriage was no longer the primary basis of elite consolidation within quarter.

As neighborhood marriage solidarity disintegrated roughly around the turn of the century, however, patricians may have been almost forced to reach outside the comfortable (and essentially defensive) shells of their own wards, parishes, and piazzas. Later, such marriage outreach would provide the organizational infrastructure to undergird the emergence of a self-consciously "city" elite, psychologically (though not materially) decoupled from its original neighborhood base.[42]

The question therefore arises: What forces led to this widespread corrosion of elite neighborhood solidarity and to its replacement by elite neighborhood exogamy? The answer to this question will take us far toward understanding the historical roots of the Medici's own innovative marriage strategy.

Political Vulnerability Among Medicean Patricians

The mid-fourteenth-century, pre-Ciompi story is best told by Brucker (1962). Progressive waves of new men were economically thrust up by the internationalization of trade and finance. Without aristocratic sponsorship, such mercantile new men (hardly radicals in any event) were doomed to political ostracism and frustration. However, this upward thrust often coincided with intraelite factional cleavage. The Albizzi-Ricci factions were the most important such split in the mid-fourteenth century, with the Ricci garnering more new men's support. Intense politics ensued from 1343 to 1378 about who was to be eligible for election to the Signoria. The new men (with artisan support) took the tack of trying to label their opponents officially as lawless magnates, and the old guard countered by trying to get their opponents designated as traitorous antipapal Ghibellines.

Eventually, such aristocratic-mercantile feuding got out of hand, and the Ciompi rose up in alliance with the artisans to take over the state for two months in 1378. Through their major guilds, the merchants quickly realigned with artisans in minor guilds to reestablish control, but in 1382 this alliance in turn was overthrown by an embittered patrician elite (which

[42] This extrapolation into psychology is not fanciful. Without much commentary, Cohn reports (1980, p. 37) that he had much trouble reconstructing the neighborhood residences of his late fifteenth-century families, because notaries of the time, who registered the marriage deeds, recorded these families only as *cives Florentinis* (citizens of Florence). In contrast, in the fourteenth century, residence down to the level of parish was routinely recorded, irrespective of status.

included earlier cohorts of now old "new men" merchants). These "oligarchs" excluded the artisans and ruled Florence until the Medici took over in 1434.[43]

For us, the clue in this account is to understand how first the Albizzi-Ricci factional feuds and then the searing revolt of the Ciompi placed strain on neighborhood solidarities. Could it be that intraelite factional struggles of the fourteenth century were so intense that, first following medieval patterns, they polarized each neighborhood into competing patrician clusters (cf. Barth 1959), but then, because of Ciompi escalation, they pulverized the losing patrician side into structural isolates, which the Medici much later exploited? If so, this would account in part for the increasing rate of neighborhood exogamy, as the winners and, even more, the losers had fewer compatible intra-neighborhood marriage options to choose from. Assuming social class endogamy, Florentine patrician marriages would be forced outward because of neighborhood blockage, or structural "holes," within.

We will test the plausibility of this account in pieces. One observable corollary of the hypothesis is that Medicean patrician support derived disproportionately from losers of earlier factional struggles. We have gathered evidence from secondary sources (*a*) about patrician family membership in the mid-fourteenth century Albizzi and Ricci factions and (*b*) about patrician support for the 1378–82 Ciompi/artisan regime. We also have very limited information about the Alberti faction (a transformed descendant of the Ricci) of 1385–1400.

From the detailed text of Brucker (1962), we could identify 39 fourteenth-century families from the Albizzi or Ricci factions that also appeared in Dale Kent's (1978) list of 1434 partisans. The relationship between these two lists of partisans is shown in table 9.11. The evidence is much stronger for the historical continuity of the winning oligarchic side than it is for the losing "liberal" Ricci. The Medici did indeed gain some support from families of the old fourteenth-century Ricci faction, but this support is not a major factor in Medicean mobilization.[44]

[43] In the field of Florentine studies, Brucker represents the highest quality of history written with groups as the primary agents. While I disagree with his group-based approach, I have nothing but the highest respect for his pathbreaking research.

[44] In hindsight, perhaps we should not have expected much from such a lengthy time-lagged effect. Not only did much transpire between the Ricci and the Medici, but the leaders of the Ricci and Alberti factions were not just ostracized; their participation, and even life, in the regime was completely obliterated.

Table 9.11 Legacy of Mid-Fourteenth Century Partisanship

1360 Partisan Families*	1434 Partisan Families†		
	Medici	Split	Oligarch
Albizzi faction	4	3	12
Split loyalties	4	4	2
Ricci faction	5	2	3
Not mentioned in Brucker	44	3	34

* Brucker (1962).
† Kent (1978).

More convincing evidence of historical continuity dates from the 1378–82 period. Najemy (1982, 260) has published a list of families from "traditional inner elite" families that were members of the governing Signoria during the 1378–82 corporatist guild regime. This list of 15 "collaborator" patrician families is as follows: Alberti, Aldobrandini, Ardinghelli, del Bene, Corbinelli, Corsini, Davanzati, Medici, Pitti, Rinuccini, Salimbeni, Salviati, Scali, Strozzi, and Vecchietti.

Six of these families were unequivocal Medici supporters in 1434. Moreover, the split Salviati family leaned strongly to the Medici side (Kent 1978, 55), and the technically neutral Corsini were in the process of joining the Medici when 1434 arrived (Kent 1978, 53). Only three collaborator families supported the oligarchs in 1434.[45]

The Alberti faction of 1385–1400 was the last barrier of opposition to the revived patrician oligarchy (Brucker 1977, 75–102). However, apart from descriptions of the extremely wealthy Alberti themselves, who were papal bankers before the Medici replaced them as a result of the Alberti's 1393 exile (Holmes 1968; Foster 1985), almost no published information exists on the composition of this faction. We do know, however, that Acciaiuoli support for the Medici dated from the exile of Alberti supporter Donato Acciaiuoli (Brucker 1977, 97; Kent 1978, 59).[46] In addition, the close friends of Acciaiuoli who put up 20,000 florins as security for his exile included

[45] The Rinuccini and Salimbeni, along with the exiled del Bene and Scali, no longer figured prominently in Florentine politics.

[46] A close relationship between the Acciaiuoli and the Medici families, however, predated this period. In the mid- to late fourteenth century, an important client of the banker Vieri di Cambio de' Medici was Bishop Angelo Acciaiuoli, who played a major role in Florentine politics while occupying the city's episcopal; see Brucker (1977, 10). A marriage around 1405 consolidated this family relationship.

three Cavalcanti, Luigi Guicciardini, and Nicola di Vieri de' Medici (Brucker 1977, 29)—all later patrician supporters of the Medici.

In sum, while the evidence that historical continuity among Medicean patricians went back as far as the mid-fourteenth century is very weak, the evidence for grounding our understanding of patrician support for the Medici in the events of the Ciompi revolution and its immediate aftermath is quite strong (although, still only suggestive). Our data on neighborhood exogamy, merged with Cohn's, support the view that elite neighborhood solidarity dissolved in the decades following the Ciompi revolution; the data on patrician factional continuity support the further view that structural isolation among Medicean patricians dates from this period as well.

Oligarchic Elite Closure

Establishing the existence of historical continuity, however important, is not the same thing as establishing the mechanism through which such continuity was created. A priori, there is no obvious reason that factional wounds could not have been gradually healed (perhaps under the goad of a massive external threat, like the Milanese war), that disaffected elites could not have been reabsorbed (under careful controls), or that the political system could not therefore have returned to its routinely tumultuous stochastic equilibrium. In reality, however, an irreversible "ratchet effect" appears to have occurred, which we need to explain.

In particular, we argue, elite marriage networks shifted permanently during the period from 1385 to about 1420 from a quasi-feudal pattern of parallel, intra-neighborhood marriage hierarchies, which had incorporated most patrician families, toward a citywide elitist pattern of cross-neighborhood marriage cycles, which co-opted "politically correct" patrician families while structurally isolating patrician "class traitors" who had collaborated with the Ciompi and artisan guilds. The folding of a dense oligarchic core into itself (the rectangular set of blocks in figure 9.2a) and the segregation of patrician Medici supporters from this core (the Guicciardini and Tornabuoni blocks in figure 9.2a), in other words, were two sides of the same elite reconsolidation process.[47] The effect of this marriage transformation was to keep

[47] The shift from neighborhood to city wide patrician elites is exemplified in figure 9.2a by the contrast between, on the one hand, the old Santa Croce hierarchical organization of Peruzzi→Castellani→Pepi and, on the other hand, the newer self-encapsulating organization of Guasconi→Strozzi→Panciatichi→Albizzi→Guasconi (and similar cycles).

Ciompi-type challenges from ever arising again; no longer were there fluid elite factions to play off one another.

The process is illustrated graphically in figure 9.3. The solid lines give a stylized portrait of the quasi-feudal pattern of parallel neighborhood hierarchies before the Ciompi.[48] As mentioned above, this marriage pattern originally derived, centuries before, from rural lord-retinue hierarchies transplanted to local city neighborhoods. During the late medieval interim, however, neighborhood hierarchies were sustained by a logic of status: enshrouded within overtly symmetric political alliance marriages, arranged by Florentine patriarchs,[49] was an implicit claim on the part of the family giving the dowried wife to be superior in status to the family receiving the dowried wife.[50] The reasons for this were two: (*a*) culturally, in all ceremonial exchange or gift-giving systems, prestige accrues to the more (competitively) generous (Mauss [1925] 1967);[51] (*b*) structurally, son-in-law relations often were the raw material for constructing political lieutenants (Kent 1978, 55).[52]

Because of intense status competition, wife-giving families could not take back daughters from their wife-receiving affines without thereby relinquishing their claim to superiority. *Gonfaloni* neighborhoods in particular were strongly bounded hothouses, in which frequencies of both interaction and status rivalry were high (Weissman 1982; Kent 1977). Add asymmetric marriage to bounded neighborhoods and the result is the network pattern drawn in figure 9.3: hierarchical linear trees or "pecking orders."[53]

[48] This portrait may conflate prematurely the Albizzi-Ricci factional underpinnings with earlier Guelf-Ghibelline and Black-White Guelf marriage structures, but no data exist at present to trace medieval stages of transformation, if any. With the new Carte dell'Ancisa marriage information currently being processed, we will be able to investigate this further.

[49] Needless to say, modern conceptions of romance are anachronistic in this deeply sexist context. Patrician fathers arranged marriages between sons around 35 years old and daughters in their teens (Herlihy and Klapisch-Zuber 1985).

[50] This combination of implicit domination enshrouded in a cultural veneer of friendship is typical of patron–client relations.

[51] This also fits with the Catholic principle of plenitude, or grace—the ideological foundation for European nobility (Lovejoy 1936; Duby 1980).

[52] This potential could be actualized most easily in two circumstances: (*a*) when the son-in-law came from a small, disorganized clan, in which therefore the potentially countervailing father of the son was weak, or (*b*) when the son-in-law was a "black sheep" for whatever reason. Examples of both cases can easily be found in the Medici party.

[53] Of course, top-level lords also had to get wives from somewhere. Inability to accept daughters from below, within their neighborhood, forced them to trade among themselves, across neighborhoods, but only at the very top. Some neighborhood bosses were prestigious enough to obtain wives from outside the city.

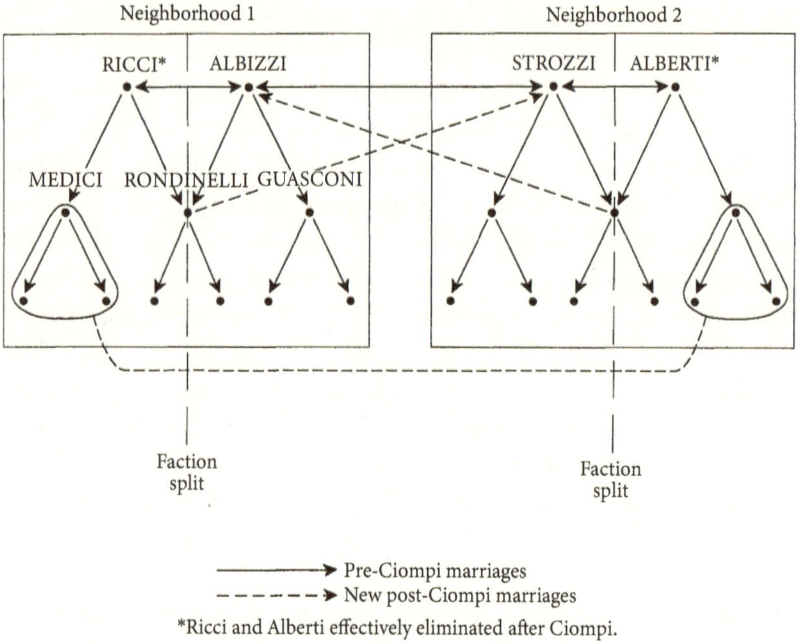

Figure 9.3 Mechanics of Elite Closure (1380–1420)

Medieval factions were driven by local neighborhood antagonisms at their root, even when they aggregated under broader pope-versus-emperor banners (Waley 1969, 203). This is shown in figure 9.3 by factional splits between rival lords within each neighborhood. The factions link up, in geographical checkerboard fashion, across neighborhoods (cf. Barth 1959).[54] The medieval dynamic at this point was that things eventually would explode, with top leaders of the losing side suffering exile, expropriation of wealth, and burning of homes. After a rocky period of probation, however, losing lieutenants and those lower down slowly would be reabsorbed back into the system through asymmetric marriage (since new local challengers in the old winning faction reached to them for support).

The Albizzi-Ricci feuds of the mid-fourteenth century, we argue, were just this sort of traditional medieval factional affair, except for one catastrophic complication: The working-class Ciompi Revolt threatened the elite in toto,

[54] That is, each local faction was surrounded by its enemies. The aggregation logic here is balance theory: "[neighboring] enemies of my [neighboring] enemies are my friends."

which suddenly was confronted with mass exile. Ricci partisans and, even more, patrician sympathizers with the Ciompi (like the Medici) now were not just normal elite from a losing faction; they were class traitors in a very direct and deep sense. Resurgent oligarch consciousness was seared by the Ciompi event to a degree that it structured both polemics and virtually every domestic institutional reform for decades (Brucker 1977; Najemy 1982).

After the oligarchs' return to power in 1382, the reverberating consequences for intraelite marriage networks were profound.

1. Class traitor patrician sympathizers with the Ciompi were shunned in marriage by victorious oligarch families. This is the source of the structural barrier to marriage between the oligarchs and the Guicciardini and Tornabuoni Medicean blocks, observed in figure 9.2a. To see the dynamic of how this came to be, refer again to figure 9.3: (*a*) Ricci and Alberti families were effectively expunged from the diagram, the normal consequence of being leaders of losing medieval factions. (*b*) This left losing and now leaderless lieutenant families, such as the Medici, structurally isolated and cut off from their victorious neighbors. (*c*) Cross-pressured "swing-vote" families, such as the Rondinelli, who might be potential bridges for reintegrating the losers, were temporarily left hanging. But (*d*) marriage ostracism of patrician losers by victorious oligarchs was exceedingly intense and vengeful.

This last assertion is not mere hypothesis. When the Alberti males were finally banished in 1397, virtually no one would marry them (Foster 1985, 321). Before that, in 1394, the very prestigious moderate, Filippo Bastari, was sentenced to perpetual exile merely for trying to talk Rinaldo Gianfigliazzi into changing his mind about withdrawing from a marriage agreement with the Alberti. Gianfigliazzi had withdrawn from the Alberti agreement in the first place because of pressure he had received from Maso degli Albizzi (Brucker 1977, 95–96).[55] This prominent example apparently was taken to heart, and routinized into marriage maxims, by the patrician rank and file desirous of advancement within the new regime.[56]

[55] Such cross-family consultations about politically significant marriages involving only one of them may have been common. Kent (1978, 130) cites a much later 1431 case of Alamanno Salviati's consulting Averardo de' Medici, his father-in-law, about the proposed marriage of Salviati's daughter to a Frescobaldi. (Averardo apparently okayed the deal.)

[56] In the early fifteenth century, Giovanni Morelli wrote as follows in his memoirs, intended as posthumous instruction for his sons: "[When you decide to marry] think of this first of all: don't

2. Not only were Ciompi sympathizers shunned, however, but oligarchs themselves were restructured by their vengeful ostracism: cross-neighborhood marriage cycles began to form.[57] A dense, citywide elite was created thereby, which transcended its earlier neighborhood base.[58]

The short-term motivation for cross-neighborhood marriage cycles, we argue, was co-optation, especially of potentially bridging swing-vote families, such as the Rondinelli in figure 9.3. Oligarchs wanted the doors completely slammed in traitors' faces, without leaving open the traditional route for rehabilitation. And they certainly did not want to give patrician outcasts any network room to pluck away wavering supporters from themselves.

The complication was the status implications of intermarriage, mentioned above. "Big cheese" families could not reach down to, and accept daughters from, middling swing-vote patricians in the same neighborhood, without at the same time jeopardizing their own status positions in the local pecking order. But other prominent oligarch families, outside the neighborhood, could do so without disrupting either local neighborhood order. Given the decline in neighborhood intermarriage because of the ostracism, moreover, there was a demographic push to do just that. Cross-neighborhood co-optative daughter flows are illustrated as dotted lines in figure 9.3. Marriage cycles are the straightforward, even if unintended, result.

Since this co-optation process was occurring in all neighborhoods simultaneously (the consequence of the checkerboard pattern), the oligarchic elite as a whole closed in on itself: Given the unexpected windfall of exogamous marriage into the truly elite, patricians of moderate position had fewer

demean yourself with an inferior person; try instead to improve your condition, though not to such an extent that she would want to be the husband and make you the wife. . . . Aside from being of old stock in the city, they should also be Guelfs who are honored by the Commune and who are free of all stains, such as those associated with treason. . . . In marriage, connect yourself with a Guelf family in government; it ought to be a powerful and trusted family, free of all scandal" (cited in Martines 1963, 58–59). According to Martines, Morelli was particularly sensitive about this subject because he himself had made the mistake of marrying into the Alberti. "According to Morelli's testimony, this marriage hurt his career in public life, undermined his contacts, and left him exposed, during a period of twenty years, to tax rates aimed at his ruin" (Martines 1963, 59; we thank Samuel Cohn for suggesting the relevance of Morelli's memoirs).

[57] From a network perspective, triadic cycles cause networks to fold into themselves, thereby creating clear "group" boundaries. Understanding how cyclic marriage triads formed, therefore, is the microbehavioral essence of understanding how the reconstituted patrician elite congealed.

[58] Civic humanism, a 1400–1430 ideology of citywide elites, arguably was built on top of this new elite marriage network foundation, even as it was catalyzed more proximately by 1390–1402 wars with Milan (Baron 1966).

daughters available to send down. But this new cross-neighborhood elite was far more expansive and inclusive in status than had been the earlier medieval pattern of a federated alliance of neighborhood bosses: because of co-optation, the truly elite had fewer sons available to trade among themselves. The net result was the rectangular clique of oligarch blocks in figure 9.2a.

3. A final consequence was cross-neighborhood intermarriage among structurally isolated class traitor patricians. Given successful co-optation of swing votes into the reconsolidated elite and their own geographical scatter, outcast patricians were left with very few status-appropriate marriage options in their own neighborhoods. (We have argued, of course, that that was precisely the point.)

This left such patricians with two marriage options. (*a*) They could start to accept daughters from lower social groups. But this moved patricians down to the new men's status level in other patricians' eyes.[59] (*b*) Alternatively, they could start to marry fellow isolates outside the neighborhood. This at least preserved their claim to status, even if it did nothing to restore power. For outcasts who wanted to remain patricians, this extra-neighborhood marriage game was the only game in town. Hence, even though exogamy rates were increasing for all, intra-patrician exogamy rates were higher among outcasts than among oligarchs: Oligarchs married both outside and inside the neighborhood.

In short, this is how we claim the outcast Medici discovered their "leading edge" and highly consequential marriage strategy. Near exclusive intermarriage with patricians outside their own neighborhood was a network strategy forced on the Medici by the resurgent oligarchs' successful blockage of Medici marriage with their San Giovanni patrician neighbors. The half of the Medici party that was based on marriage was "chosen" by the Medici family only in the sense of positional chess: Oligarchs structurally induced their choice.

Thus, the oligarchic clique and the Medicean spoke marriage networks were not two separate party organizations, later to butt heads as

[59] This is not to say that patricians never would do this—say, for money. But wealthy dowries from new men daughters were always implicitly purchased at the cost of lowered prestige. The dowry money was tainted, a sign of patricians on hard times.

autonomous units. They emerged in tandem, as a single network, each reflexively and asymmetrically structuring the other.[60]

Data on Change in Elite Marriage Strategy Over Time

We still have not shown how the Medici themselves, alone among patrician outcasts, eventually came to marry into the oligarchy. But before we solve this final puzzle, let us present evidence in support of the above account.

We have attempted to date the 162 marriages in our dataset, which span the period from about 1395 to 1434. Fifty-three of these marriages are precisely dated by Kent (1978) in her book. For 84 of the remaining 109 marriages, we have been able to estimate the decade of the marriage, usually through triangulating the known dates of relatives with genealogical information contained in Florentine names.[61] Because of this estimation procedure, table 9.12 contains a measurement error, which will be reduced through ongoing archival work. For our purposes,

Table 9.12 Elite Marriages over Time

Neighborhood by Estimated Date of Marriage	Overall	1395–1410	1411–20	1421–29	1430–34	No Date
Medici marriage strategies:						
San Giovanni	4 (.143)	0	0	3	0	1
Santo Spirito	10 (.357)	1	2	3	4	0
Santa Maria Novella	9 (.321)	2	4	2	0	1
Santa Croce	5 (.179)	2	1	2	0	0
Total	28					
Peruzzi + Ricasoli + Castellani marriage strategies:						
San Giovanni	10 (.345)	2	3	1	3	1
Santo Spirito	5 (.172)	0	1	0	4	0
Santa Maria Novella	6 (.207)	3	1	1	1	0

[60] Padgett (1990a, 450) develops a similar "reflexive structuring through mutual contestation" argument in a totally different empirical context, that of professionalism and plea bargaining in U.S. criminal courts.

[61] Florentine names usually include the father, and frequently the grandfather, in them—e.g., Cosimo di Giovanni di Bicci de' Medici. This is yet another indicator of the Florentine concern with patrilineage.

Neighborhood by Estimated Date of Marriage	Overall	1395–1410	1411–20	1421–29	1430–34	No Date
Santa Croce	8 (.276)	4	0	1	3	0
Total	29					
Strozzi + Gianfigliazzi marriage strategies:						
San Giovanni	11 (.344)	4	2	1	2	2
Santo Spirito	6 (.188)	2	0	0	3	1
Santa Maria Novella	9 (.281)	4	2	1	1	1
Santa Croce	6 (.188)	3	1	0	2	0
Total	32					
Albizzi + Guadagni marriage strategies:						
San Giovanni	13 (.591)	2	5	5	0	1
Santo Spirito	4 (.182)	2	0	1	1	0
Santa Maria Novella	3 (.136)	3	0	0	0	0
Santa Croce	2 (.091)	0	1	0	0	1
Total	22					

N.B.: values in parentheses are percentages of total.

however, these best estimates are sufficient to reveal broad trends in strategic behavior of the elite.

Table 9.12 presents, for the leading elite families in various quarters, the number of their marriages into families in all other quarters (including their own), broken down by decade. The Medici lived in the western portion of San Giovanni; the rival but intimately connected Albizzi and Guadagni lived in the eastern half. The Peruzzi, Ricasoli, and Castellani were leaders of Santa Croce, as already mentioned. And the Strozzi and Gianfigliazzi were the most prominent families in Santa Maria Novella. No family in Santo Spirito had a volume of marriages high enough to warrant inclusion in this table.

If one looks first at the overall figures, what is most striking about these data is the fact that all of the most prestigious oligarch families intermarried at the highest rate with patrician families in San Giovanni—the Medici's own homeland. We have already established that the Medici themselves married at very low rates into their own neighborhood. We now have a better sense of why: They were surrounded by patrician enemies (Kent 1978,170) whom the oligarchs already had successfully wired into themselves. The more detailed timing data also support this conclusion: the oligarchs were active in the 1395–1420 period in establishing marriage links with San Giovanni, during which time the Medici made not a single marriage (in our dataset, at least). Apparently, the oligarchs were quite aware of the potential for trouble from this quarter (also home to the Ricci) and took active steps to contain it at its source.

The case of the Rondinelli, mentioned above as a swing vote, illustrates the oligarchs' strategy more precisely. In the 1340s the Medici, the Rondinelli, and the della Stufa had formed a San Giovanni clique, apparently of the traditional sort (Kent 1978, 65). As late as the 1370s, the Rondinelli were active, along with a portion of the Medici, in the Ricci's San Giovanni faction (Brucker 1977, 34, 125). Hence, the Rondinelli were prime candidates for neighborhood intermarriage with the Medici and for pariah status. However, an early wife-giving marriage with the Strozzi (themselves split between Albizzi and Ricci factions), followed by both types of marriage with the Guasconi (who themselves furnished an early wife to the Strozzi) apparently saved them from ostracism and turned them into avid oligarchs. In this manner, the Strozzi dissolved the Medici's local patrician clique.

In addition to such innovative cross-neighborhood raiding into the Medici's base by the Santa Maria Novella and the Santa Croce elites, the data reveal that the Medici's San Giovanni heartland was being squeezed in a traditional way. For reasons we do not know, from 1410 on, the old-line Albizzi and Guadagni retreated to an old-fashioned but successful neighborhood consolidation strategy. This retreat made them less integrated into the elite than one might suspect from their stature (cf. Kent 1978, 177). But it also made it harder for the Medici to rebuild their own local patrician base.

So far, the data are consistent with our expectations. In addition to this (although loose) confirmation, however, the data contain a surprise. The oligarchy worked so hard on controlling San Giovanni that they apparently overlooked the "older suburb" quarter of Santo Spirito (that is, until the 1430s). Perhaps this was a simple and traditional oversight on their part, based on the slightly less prestigious character of this district; but we suspect that the overemphasis on San Giovanni, relative to Santo Spirito, was at least partly a conscious allocation of scarce marriage resources.[62]

[62] Santo Spirito, located across the Arno river (on the "other side of the tracks"), originally was more like an old suburb than a part of the city's geographical core (Weissman 1982, 6). It was the heart of the Ciompi wool workers' district. This hardly implied that the quarter contained nothing but workers and new men—after all, many old magnate families resided there. But it does imply that

In any event, this oversight represented a clear "structural hole" within the oligarchic marriage network, which the data reveal the Medici to have exploited—at first gradually, but then with a vengeance, as they incrementally but clearly learned about the political potential in Santo Spirito: By the early 1430s, 100% of the Medici's own marriages were directed to this quarter. Three of every four of these late Medici marriages were wife-receiving rather than wife-giving—an indication that the Medici by this point were not particularly picky about relative status claims. One of these wife-receiving marriages was with the Guicciardini, a family fairly well integrated into the elite, in order to reinforce an old marriage alliance under siege.[63] But all the others (with the Corbinelli, the Corsini, and the Ridolfi) fit the classic Medicean pattern of marriage to patrician structural isolates.

The oligarch families apparently were not fools, and so moved quite late to repair this breach in their own defenses. As was the oligarchs' wont, all of these Santo Spirito marriages in the 1430s were to old-line families, already well integrated into the Florentine marriage network, although not at the highest levels. Thus, the late but intense mobilization of Santo Spirito patricians, by both sides, followed in microcosm the same pattern as that found in the global blockmodel—successful Medicean mobilization of structurally isolated patricians, and successful oligarchic co-optation of fairly well integrated patricians.

It may be of more general interest to pause here for an observation about the apparent microbehavioral decision processes revealed in these data. This sequence of structural holes, created in the first place by active elite attention focused elsewhere and then exploited gradually but surely by opponents, suggests more than anything that elite tactics evolve not as part of interacting sets of omniscient "grand strategies," à la game theory, but rather as a mutually adaptive learning process (Lave and March 1975).

Florentine families were extremely shrewd and opportunistic, but nonetheless they were always engaged in boundedly rational local action dictated by their own deep embedding through networks in localistic and highly idiosyncratic circumstances. Any complicated and endogenous

the elite of this quarter were somewhat less densely integrated by marriage (though not economics) into themselves and into other neighborhood elites.

[63] The Peruzzi also arranged a marriage with the Guicciardini, in 1434, in an apparent effort to induce the Guicciardini to switch sides. The net effect of these offsetting moves was a Guicciardini family split in its partisan loyalties.

marriage system presents each actor with narrow and changing opportunities, derived like vacancy chains (White 1970) from the actions and inactions of others in other arenas. Yet no one, not even Cosimo de' Medici, possessed the clear global overview of figure 9.2a. Everyone looked out at elite structure egocentrically from the vantage point of his or her own network location. This conclusion is not to doubt that families learned, and often shrewdly so, but to question the plausibility of historical explanations that place much weight on Machiavellian foresight and planning, especially in tumultuous times (cf. Skocpol 1979, 14–18).

The Medici's Own Structurally Anomalous Position

Finally, we need to explain: Given a global predisposition to form parties, why the Medici in particular as leaders of that party? After all, given the success of their opponents' control strategy against them, and especially given the depth of their involvement in previous discredited regimes,[64] the Medici emergence to take over the state in 1434 would seem, from the perspective of 1400, to be little short of miraculous.

One possible explanation might be the Medici bank, founded on ties with the pope. But this is not convincing. As a "cash cow" generator of personal wealth, which the Medici used both for personal patronage (Molho 1979) and for city loans (Molho 1971,168), the role of the bank is clear. However, an identical economic position did not save the Alberti, who were the pope's primary bankers before their exile. And the Medici bank as an institution (not just as a generator of wealth) was useless for political mobilization: apart from the fact that not many families were involved, the bank was heavily infiltrated with oligarchic partners and employees (particularly the Bardi, but also the Guasconi and della Casa), later purged (de Roover 1966, 56).

A better answer, we believe, has to do with the Medici's own anomalous or structurally contradictory position in the patrician networks. They were the

[64] Salvestro di Alamanno de' Medici was the forceful, and somewhat demagogic, leader of the campaign against the Parte Guelfa that triggered the Ciompi Revolt (Brucker 1962, chap. 8). For this role, and his subsequent leadership, he was the Ciompi's hero. On the very day of their street triumph, as patrician houses burned, the Ciompi "mob" knighted Salvestro for his services to the *popolo*. Other Medici followed in Salvestro's footsteps, through their heavy involvement with the Alberti faction. In 1397, shortly after the 1393 downfall of the Alberti, Bastardino de' Medici (along with Maso de' Ricci) was executed for attempting to assassinate Maso degli Albizzi and Rinaldo Gianfigliazzi and, thereby, overthrow the regime (Brucker 1977, 100). In 1400, the Medici were involved in another such conspiracy and assassination attempt, with the result that the entire Medici family (along with the Alberti and Ricci) were excluded from holding public office for 20 years. Actions more anathema to the oligarch regime can hardly be imagined.

only major Florentine family to span the structural chasm created by elite closure and to participate simultaneously in the two disarticulated patrician worlds. (Refer to Medici links to the Guasconi and Albizzi blocks in figure 9.2a.) To understand this oddity, we need more information on the Medici's own, rather peculiar, family history.

Brucker's article (1957) on the fourteenth-century Medici makes it clear that the Medici were hardly a mercantile banking family throughout most of their history. On the whole, they were a rather violent and lawless bunch—*popolani* imitating magnates. Only Vieri di Cambio engaged in banking, and even then the Medici economic fortunes did not really begin to rise until Giovanni de' Medici used the remnants of Vieri's firm to capture the pope's business from the discredited Alberti (Holmes 1968). Perhaps in part because of his relative Salvestro's Ciompi exploits (see n. 65), Giovanni himself assiduously avoided politics throughout his lifetime (1360–1429) and tried to talk his sons, Cosimo and Lorenzo, into the same course (Machiavelli [1525] 1988, 161).

More particularly, Machiavelli describes (on the basis of earlier chronicles) two incidents that may account for how the Medici avoided utter, rather than just heavy, ostracism after 1382.

In 1393, immediately after the Alberti were finally banished by the Albizzi oligarchs, a crowd of guildsmen and *popolo minuto* ran to the house of Vieri di Cambio, who was left head of the Medici clan after the death of Salvestro in exile in 1388. According to Machiavelli ([1525] 1988, 139–140), this crowd implored Vieri in the name of Salvestro to lead a pro-Alberti revolt to topple the oligarchic regime. Vieri's kinsman Antonio also urged Vieri to commit the Medici to immediate revolt. However,

> Going among them in the piazza and from there into the palace, he said before the Signoria that he could not in any mode regret having lived in such a manner that the people of Florence loved him, but that he regretted very much the judgment that had been made of him, which his past life did not deserve. . . . He therefore begged the Signoria that the ignorance of the multitude not be imputed to his sin because, as far as he was concerned, as soon as he could he had put himself in [the Signoria's] power. . . . After these words, Messer Veri returned to the piazza and joined his followers with those who had been led by Messer Rinaldo [Gianfigliazzi] and Messer Donato [Acciaiuoli]. . . . He begged [the mob] to put down their arms and obey the Signoria [which they did]. (Machiavelli 1988, 140)

Much later, in 1426, Giovanni de' Medici behaved in much the same way, although a change in who initiated the action reveals how far roles had altered in the interval. Rinaldo Albizzi came to Giovanni to ask him to join his faction of oligarchs in their efforts to disenfranchise new men (about which we discuss below). He refused, saying that he opposed factions of any sort.

> These things, so dealt with, were learned of outside and brought more reputation to Giovanni and hatred to the other citizens. But Giovanni sought to detach himself from this so as to give less spirit to those who might plan new things under the cover of his favor.... Many of those who followed his part were malcontent at this because they would have liked him to show himself more active in things. Among these was Alamanno de' Medici [son of Salvestro], who was fierce by nature and did not cease inciting him for his coldness and for his mode of proceeding slowly, which, he said, was the cause of his enemies' dealing against him without respect.... Inspiring him also in the same way was his son Cosimo. Nonetheless, Giovanni ... did not budge from his position. (Machiavelli 1988, 156)

In other words, throughout the decades following the Ciompi Revolt, the leaders of the Medici clan tried hard to distance themselves from their more fractious relatives and to reestablish their family within the conservative oligarchic regime. Not only that, they went out of their way to keep the lid on trouble. As the Machiavelli accounts make clear (see also Martines 1963, 55), this docile political behavior did not expunge the pro-new-men image that the Medici name had in the popular mind. But, for their role in squelching discontent, the oligarchs apparently were begrudgingly grateful.

Even so, it was not until the 1420s that the oligarchs relented and began to co-opt the Medici through marriage cycles. Except for marriages with the Bardi, all of the marriages between the Medici and the oligarch blocks in figure 9.2a were recent.[65] This readmission of the Medici into elite circles was just what the cautious Giovanni had struggled for all his life. But what would have worked splendidly with the older generation of Vieri and Giovanni was too late for the fractious Young Turks Cosimo and Lorenzo di Giovanni and

[65] The early 1420s period of this co-optative marriage behavior is quite narrow, so the volume of evidence is not overwhelming. But what we have in mind here are the 1420s wife-giving marriages with Luca di Maso Albizzi (after the death of his father), with the Gianfigliazzi, and with the Barbadori—in other words, with the Albizzi block of figure 9.2a. In addition, there was a wife-receiving marriage with the Guasconi.

their cousin Averardo di Francesco. Events sketched in the next section led the die to be cast.

Thus, we lay at Vieri di Cambio's doorstep the explanation of the structurally anomalous position that the Medici house held in fifteenth-century patrician marriage networks. Giovanni followed up Vieri's abject plea with exemplary circumspection, but it was the defusion of popular rebellion by Vieri di Cambio, we argue, that saved the Medici name in oligarchs' eyes.[66]

Even so, oligarchic acceptance of Giovanni de' Medici, however delimited, suspicious, and constrained, did not occur without a debate. "Niccolo da Uzzano did not fail to alert the other citizens—about the political inclusion of Giovanni di Bicci—by pointing out how dangerous it was to foster one who had such a reputation in the generality of people, and how easy it was to oppose disorders in their beginnings, but how difficult it was to remedy them when they were left alone to increase; and he recognized in Giovanni many parts superior to those of Messer Salvestro. Niccolo was not heeded by his peers because they were envious of his reputation and desired to have partners in defeating him" (Machiavelli 1988, 148).

The Dynamics of Party Formation: New Men Economic Ties

We shall now sketch, in exceedingly brief compass because of space limitations, the 1420s and 1430s Medici mobilization, through economic ties, of the second half of their party—the San Giovanni new men. In this reconstruction, we rely heavily on hard-earned data and interpretation in Molho (1971), Brucker (1977), and Kent (1978). The Milan and Lucca wars of 1424–33, we shall argue, were the short-term catalysts that galvanized San Giovanni new men into support and triggered, thereby, self-consciousness of the Medici as party. The argument in brief is as follows:[67]

The Milan and Lucca wars triggered tax extraction of such magnitude that entire family patrimonies, both of patricians and of new men, were being destroyed. This set off a frantic scramble, among everyone, to escape ruinous tax assessment.

[66] Further evidence of this is the fact that only the descendants of Vieri were exempted from the oligarchs' blanket proscription of the Medici clan in 1433 (Kent 1978, 295).

[67] Readers interested in documentation of the claims herein can write the authors for an earlier draft of this paper. We have chosen to respond to page limitations by drastically shortening this section on new men, because the argument in this section is primarily a synthesis of secondary sources.

Taxes were levied administratively by neighborhood; thus, fiscal crisis revived the politics of neighborhood. Neighbors looked to neighbors to gain leverage on other neighbors who allocated assessments through rotating offices.

Administrative assessment procedures could more easily uncover fixed assets, like real estate, than liquid assets, like cash and business investments. Patricians went on the legislative offensive to squeeze more offices and taxes out of mercantile new men.

New men responded initially by banding together in parish-based secret societies: the religious confraternities. While not class homogeneous, this corporate form was a first step toward organized class solidarity and resistance.

Oligarchs responded with vicious and successful repression. Abolition of confraternities left new men bereft of coordinated local neighborhood support from each other.

New men responded in the only way left: supplication of local neighborhood patrician patrons for help. But successful mobilization of patricians for class repression had locked in most oligarchs against responding to appeals from below. The enforcement mechanism behind this coordinated class rejection of new men was the dense marriage network analyzed above.

The Medici were the only exception: their structurally contradictory position within elite marriage networks gave Giovanni and Cosimo the truly discretionary choice of responding or not to pleas from San Giovanni new men. Giovanni de' Medici, late in his life, responded to Rinaldo Albizzi's explicit request to join him in repression in the manner described in the quotation from Machiavelli above. In the sharply polarized context of the time, the hotheaded Rinaldo probably took Giovanni's equivocal response as throwing down the Ciompi (or at least new men) gauntlet. Henceforth (after 1426), the Medici family was severed from budding oligarchic co-optation and was now afloat as a distinct political faction.

San Giovanni new men received patronage, through economic ties, from their neighbors the Medici, but other new men did not—from the Medici or any other source.[68]

Therefore, we believe that the surge of supplication from San Giovanni new men during the Milan war is what triggered Medici self-consciousness

[68] Hence, the 1434 peak of newly admitted families is only one-fourth as large as the historical average. See figure 9.1.

of themselves as a political party (as opposed to just an outcast family struggling desperately to regain admittance to the club). Oligarchs funneled new men's support to them and then cut off any possibility of equivocating response. Certainly, the first evidence of intentional and coordinated Medici manipulation of elections dates from 1427, right after this period.

Network Identities

Robust Action

With these analyses of Medicean party dynamics in hand, we are now in position to understand the structural preconditions for robust action. We can only assume that Cosimo learned his sphinxlike behavior at his father Giovanni's knee and then adapted that to revolutionary circumstances. The strategy certainly was not unknown in Florence (Weissman 1989). But robust action is not just a matter of behaving ambiguously. Others are too shrewd not to see through behavioral facades down to presumed self-interested motivations. To act credibly in a multivocal fashion, one's attributed interests must themselves be multivocal.

Within the Medici party itself, the structural underpinnings for contradictory attributions of "Medici self-interest" are clear. The Medici were heroes of the new men not just because they inherited the historical legacy of Salvestro d'Alamanno. They did sponsor a few San Giovanni families of new men, quite unlike their oligarch opponents. And, after Giovanni spurned Rinaldo Albizzi's class alliance request, oligarchs heaped the scornful opprobrium of that label on Medici heads in a polemical effort to whip up patrician fury. At the same time, the Medici's deep patrician roots were clear enough to those whom they married. One can easily imagine Medicean patrician supporters knowingly winking at each other on hearing the public charges of favoring the new men that swirled around their in-laws. Such patricians' hatred of the oligarchs ran deep, and "everyone knows that tactical alliances are sometimes necessary to reestablish an old regime." After all, it would not be the first or last time in Florentine history that the new men had been sold down the river.

Which attribution was true? Plausible evidence could be assembled for either view, but new men and patrician supporters of the Medici hardly ever had the opportunity to get together privately to compare contradictory notes. Even if they had, trust between them was so low that neither should have believed a word of the other. Robust action by the Medici was credible precisely because of the contradictory character of their base of support.

Descending to more micro levels does not help to clarify attributions. Everyone knew that the Medici wanted, as bankers, to make money; as families, to increase prestige; as neighborhood patrons, to amass power. But which of the goals (which really are roles) was in play when? Given fixed role frames, self-interests (and attributions) are clear; but in complicated chaos, like the Milan and Lucca wars, the games themselves are all up for grabs. Rational choice requires a common metric of utility for footing, but revealed preferences (the basis for inferring trade-offs across goals/roles) only exist post hoc.

A Medicean goal of taking over the state can be inferred from the historical record, but only after their choice already had been narrowed to that or exile. Before that, the Medici appear to have been traditional incrementalists, trying only to worm their way back into oligarchs' good graces. Yet, at the level of sphinxlike style, it is not at all clear that Cosimo and Giovanni were any different. Both were shrewd and multivocal opportunists, pursuing openings whenever they presented themselves. Clear goals of self-interest, we conclude, are not really features of people; they are Florentine (and our) interpretations of varying structures of games.

Legitimacy

Besides multivocal placement in contemporary conflict, however, there was a second dimension to Medicean robust action. Not only has Cosimo been remembered in history as a Machiavellian deep thinker, but also at his death he was legally enshrined as *pater patriae*, father of his country, by his contemporaries (cf. Schwartz 1983). The very ambiguity of his placement in self-interest somehow became elevated, in the public mind, into the essence of public interest.

This transposition from hero of the new men to Solomonic sage, we believe, can be understood by returning to those Florentines who have remained on the margins of our account so far—the political neutrals.

Cosimo never beat the oligarchs in pitched battle; he was recalled from Venetian exile in public triumph, as savior of the republic.[69]

The key is the cognitive category "oligarch." After all, when the oligarchs were firmly in control, they were not labeled "oligarchs"; they were republican "public citizens of the state." Loss of legitimacy and Medici victory are what got them their pejorative tag. No longer public-spirited and selfless in attribution, they came to epitomize class self-interest in Florentine eyes.

How did this delegitimizing change in attribution come to pass? Our answer, basically, is positional chess. The Medici themselves never slung "oligarch" mud back into oligarch eyes. As mentioned in the introduction, Cosimo never said a clear word in his life. Instead, others—new men and eventually political neutrals—were the agents of active tactical slashing.

The sequence went like this: As already described, the fiscal crisis of the wars repolarized social classes and tempted oligarchs into a successful (in the short run) repression campaign. This campaign earned them their label in new men's eyes. However, as Kent (1978) makes clear, the oligarchs' attack was not just a rash tilt at windmills, based on lack of sophisticated foresight. Oligarchs' ability to control the legislative process (especially the colleges), and therefore to attain their goals peacefully, had been hindered recently by the network tentacles of the duplicitous Medici faction. Medicean latent appeal to new men and heterogenous control of some offices gave them swing-vote influence out of proportion to their numbers—even though, legislatively, all they did was to block. In the context of vanishing patrician patrimonies, however, mere blockage was sufficient to force oligarchs onto the offensive. Either they purged the opposition or else all their wealth would be gone.

Cosimo, in contrast, behaved in his typically reactive fashion of only responding to requests. He funneled a sizable portion of the assets of his bank into funding the state's short-term debt, for which he was rewarded with brief public office—member of the Ufficiali del Banco, from November 1427 to December 1428.[70] The monetary catch was this: as incentive to grant such emergency loans, the state offered above-average short-term returns. Thus, while his opponents faced financial catastrophe, Cosimo actually may

[69] The irony, of course, is that most historians regard Cosimo as the destroyer of republicanism (Rubinstein 1966).

[70] Even after Cosimo left this post, his supporters continued to dominate this financial nerve center (Molho 1971).

have made money.[71] More to the point here, once Florence survived, Cosimo de' Medici took on the appearance of financial savior of the city (Molho 1971).

Knowing this, once the Lucca war had ended, the oligarchs moved quickly to send Cosimo, Lorenzo, and other Medici and lieutenants into exile in Venice (and elsewhere). In anticipation of this very move, Cosimo had shifted much of his wealth out of the city, away from potential expropriation, and used it to cultivate Venetian support (de Roover 1966, 54; Kent 1978, 304–08). Oligarchic legitimacy was now in deep trouble. They still did not have enough control to purge sufficiently the Signoria electoral bags,[72] so, when the lottery randomly produced too many Medicean officeholders (Kent 1978, 328), the oligarchy was forced to take desperate action. Rinaldo Albizzi sent out the word to assemble the troops in order to forcibly seize the Signoria, with the stochastic turnout consequences described above. Political neutrals joined the cry for Medici return, and Cosimo became, in public acclamation, the political as well as financial savior of Florence.

War of course was the sine qua non, but note that at each step of the way Cosimo's careful positional maneuvering forced or enticed oligarchs into offensive lines of action, which connoted private self-interest. These were clear, irrevocable, and hence foreseeable. The reactive character of his robust and multivocal actions gained for Cosimo, the revolutionary, the legitimizing aureole of protector of the status quo. Party transmuted into state.

Conclusion

We shall not summarize the arguments in this paper, except for this: State centralization and the Renaissance emerged from the grinding of tumultuous historical events, as these were filtered through elite transformation. Cosimo did not create the Medici party, but he did shrewdly learn the rules of the networks around him. Rather than dissipate this power through forceful command, Cosimo retreated behind a shroud of multiple identities,

[71] A number of oligarchs possessed as much, or almost as much, raw wealth as did Cosimo, but theirs often was not as liquid as his—a consequence of Cosimo's special ties to the pope.

[72] The Florentines had an elaborate electoral system that involved electing candidates to bags, one bag for every class of offices. Offices were filled every two months by randomly drawing names from the bags and checking these against various legal restrictions. The whole republican purpose of the system was to make it hard for any one faction to consolidate control. See Najemy (1982).

impenetrable to this day. These credibly imparted multivocal meanings to all his reactive actions. Robust discretion, in the face of unpredictably hostile futures, and Solomonic legitimacy above the self-interested fray, were the intended or unintended (who knows?) consequences.

We close on this methodological note: To understand state building, we have argued, one needs to penetrate beneath the veneer of formal institutions and apparently clear goals, down to the relational substratum of people's actual lives. Studying "social embeddedness," we claim, means not the denial of agency, or even groups, but rather an appreciation for the localized, ambiguous, and contradictory character of these lives. Heterogeneity of localized actions, networks, and identities explains both why aggregation is predictable only in hindsight and how political power is born.

Appendix A Blockmodeling Methods

We adopt correlation as our operational measure of structural equivalence, just as in CONCOR (White, Boorman, and Breiger 1976). A frequently used alternative measure, Euclidean distance (Burt 1976), gives weight to volume of ties as well as to pattern of ties (Faust and Romney 1985). In the current context, in which parties and class crosscut, this weighting unhelpfully differentiates elite from nonelite rather than one party from another. Unlike CONCOR, however, we prefer agglomerative to divisive clustering.[73]

Thus, our method is to correlate columns of "stacked" matrices (and transposes), across all strong tie networks, and then to input the resulting correlation matrix into the standard Johnson's complete-link clustering algorithm.[74] This produced the partition of families given in Appendix B. To get the structural portraits of figures 9.2a and 9.2b, blockmodel images of social bonds among clusters were generated by (*a*) aggregating each raw

[73] The reason is the two procedures' differing treatments of structural isolates. We prefer to inhibit these "irrelevant" actors from contaminating our structural picture of relations within the core. (This does not mean that information on ties between central and isolated families is ignored in the discovery of the core. Such information already has been incorporated into the original correlation measure.)

[74] In addition to this computer output, we did one manual correction: We merged the Capponi/Busini block with the Strozzi solo block. This merger improved (marginally) goodness-of-fit. More important, Kent (1978, 184) makes a strong case for the structural equivalence of Strozzi and Capponi. In addition, it was clear from comparing D. Kent [1978] to F. W. Kent [1977] that we possessed only limited marriage and economic data on Capponi.

network matrix according to Appendix B's clustering of families and then (*b*) defining and drawing a social "bond" whenever the number of raw network ties between clusters equaled or exceeded two.[75]

Tables 9.A1 and 9.A2 address goodness-of-fit issues. There are two such issues: How well do the simplified blockmodels represent the more complex actual network data? How well does the blockmodel partition predict actual party memberships, as recorded in Kent (1978)? The first issue is assessed in table 9.A1 in two ways: (*a*) by the percentage of actual ties among families represented in figure 9.2's image bonds among blocks and (*b*) by correlations between raw data matrices and block mean densities, based on the partitions in Appendix B (Noma and Smith 1985).

Table 9.A1 Goodness of Fit of Blockmodel Image to Raw Network Data

	Overall			Medici	
Type of Relation	**No. of Ties**	**Proportion of Ties in Image**	**Correlation with Block Means**	**No. of Ties**	**Proportion of Ties in Image**
Marriage	161	.646	.492	28	.964
Trade	92	.674	.561	10	.800
Partnership	45	.556	.513	13	.846
Bank	13	.769	.415	10	.800
Real estate	22	.091	.378	5	.400
Subtotal*	333	.610		66	.848
Mallevadori	31	.194	.338	3	.000
Friendship	50	.360	.381	14	.714
Personal loan	89	.404	.408	25	.840
Patronage	36	.222	.389	21	.381
Subtotal*	206	.330		63	.619
Total	539	.503		129	.736

* The blockmodel partitions were derived from data on the first five of these relations only. Goodness-of-fit measures for the last four relations derive from the superposition of best-fitting partitions from the first five relations. All correlations are significant at the $P < .001$ level, according to the nonparametric QAP procedure (Baker and Hubert 1981), implemented in UCINET.

[75] Often, density percentages are used as cutoff criteria, instead of raw number of ties, as is the case here. The reason for our approach is that, with small block sizes, percentages are not robust: A single actual tie can mean as much as a 50% density.

Table 9.A2 Goodness of Fit of Blockmodel Partitions to Party Membership

No. of Families	Medici Blocks	All Other Blocks	Elite Blocks	Nonelite Blocks
Mediceans	26	4	2	2
Split loyalty	2	10	6	4
Oligarchs	0	31	8	23
Neutrals	1	18	2	16
Proportion mobilized*	966	.714	.889	.644
Proportion own party†	958	.823	.737	.871

* % Mobilized measures relative recruitment of blocked families into any party; i.e., proportion mobilized = (no. of families − no. of neutral families)/(no. of families).
† % Own party measures relative partisanship of activists; i.e., proportion own party = (no. of families in own party)/(no. of families − no. of neutral families), with split families allocated proportionately.

All correlations in tables 9.A1 and 9.A2 are significant at the $P < .001$ level, according to the QAP procedure of Baker and Hubert (1981).[76] Moreover, 50% of the total volume of ties,[77] 61% of marriage and economic ties (figure 9.2a), and 33% of "political" and friendship ties (figure 9.2b) are captured by the central tendencies in the blockmodel. Given that the blockmodel was derived from the strong tie marriage and economic relations alone, we were pleasantly surprised by the weak tie performance.

More particularly, it is clear that marriage and trading relationships are the primary driving forces behind this blockmodel portrait of the Florentine elite. In part, this is because of their high rates of inclusive success, but it is also due to the higher volume of data. Partnerships and especially bank employment relations were very important when they appeared, but they do not span much of the elite. Real estate relations essentially were irrelevant.

[76] In the nonparametric QAP procedure (Baker and Hubert 1981), an empirical distribution of random correlations is generated by repeatedly permuting rows and columns of the raw data matrix and then correlating this with the fixed image matrix. In no case, out of about 1,000 trials, did any of our own simulated random correlations exceed .10. More formal parametric significance tests are rarely possible with network data, since the data grossly violate the "independent observations" assumptions of traditional tests.

[77] Considering that this blockmodel has been disaggregated to an average of 2.7 families per block, and considering that the average overall density of the nine historical networks here is an extremely sparse 0.7%, this is excellent performance.

On the weak tie side, personal friendships and personal loans operated in large part within the framework of marriage and economic relations. *Mallevadori* and patronage relations, however, were not well predicted by marriage and economic ties.

The success with which the blockmodel predicts political partisanship, in the table 9.A2, speaks for itself. Ninety-three percent of the families in the Medicean blocks were mobilized into the Medici party. Fifty-nine percent of the families in the non-Medicean blocks were mobilized into the oligarch party.

Appendix B

Table 9.B1 Block Memberships: Clustering of Correlations of Marriage, Trade, Partnership, Bank, and Real Estate Relations

Reggimento Family	Party*	Gross Wealth (Florins)	Date of First Prior	Neighborhood (*Gonfalone*)†
Medicean blocks:				
MEDICI:				
Medici	Medici (5)	199,672	1291	41
Carnesecchi	Medici	42,316	1297	42
Berlinghieri	Medici	6117	1365	22
TORNABUONI:				
Tornabuoni/ Tornaquinci	Medici	121,310	Magnate	34
Salviati	Split loyalties (1/1)	29,964	1297	24
Serristori	Medici	56,675	1392	23
Giugni	Medici (3)	41,086	1291	24
Pecori	Medici	17,244	1284	42
Corsini		16,387	1290	13
Vecchietti	Medici	17,212	Magnate	34
GUICCIARDINI:				
Acciaiuoli	Medici	28,200	1282	31
Guicciardini	Medici	60,060	1302	12

Reggimento Family	Party*	Gross Wealth (Florins)	Date of First Prior	Neighborhood (*Gonfalone*)†
Ridolfi	Medici	46,196	1290	13
Pitti	Medici (2)	9676	1283	12
Corbinelli	Medici	58,955	1286	12
GINORI:				
Ginori	Medici (3)	34,831	1344	41
Martelli	Medici (8)	7502	1343	41
DIETISALVI:				
Dietisalvi	Medici (2)	3943	1291	41
Ciai	Medici	22,331	1389	41
DALL'ANTELLA:				
dall'Antella	Split loyalties (1/2)	18,437	1282	21
Bartolini	Medici	19,477	1299	42
ORLANDINI:				
Orlandini	Medici	11,012	1420	42
Lapi	Medici	5303	1394	44
DAVANZATI:				
Davanzati	Medici (2)	19,887	1320	32
COCCO-DONATI:				
Cocco-Donati	Medici (2)	2580	1376	22
Arnolfi	Medici	4160	1318	42
Pandolfini	Medici	30,520	1381	43
VALORI:				
Valori	Medici	15,213	1322	43
del Benino	Medici	22,629	1345	13
Non-Medicean blocks:				
ARDINGHELLI:				
Ardinghelli	Oligarch	57,596	1282	32
da Panzano	Split loyalties (1/1)	...	1312	22
DA UZZANO:				
da lizzano		75,737	1363	11
Bucelli	Oligarch	20,394	1284	22

continued

Table 9.B1 *continued*

Reggimento **Family**	**Party***	**Gross Wealth (Florins)**	**Date of First Prior**	**Neighborhood (*Gonfalone*)†**
GUASCONI:				
Guasconi	Oligarch (3)	29,074	1314	41
Bardi	Split loyalties (3/5)	189,452	Magnate	11
Cavalcanti	Split loyalties (1/1)	50,122	Magnate	31
Pazzi	Medici	72,550	Magnate	43
RONDINELLI:				
Rondinelli	Oligarch	21,053	1296	41
Brancacci	Oligarch (4)	15,697	1317	14
Mancini		6838	1284	22
ALDOBRANDINI:				
Aldobrandini	Oligarch	7171	1307	34
Raugi	Oligarch	3634	1304	21
PERUZZI:				
Peruzzi	Oligarch (8)	104,795	1283	23
Ricasoli	Oligarch (2)	36,178	Magnate	21
degli Agli		9402	Magnate	42
CASTELLANI:				
Castellani	Oligarch (5)	61,696	1326	21
Spini	Oligarch	39,553	Magnate	32
Fagni		10,106	1295	23
PEPI:				
Pepi	Oligarch	2865	1301	23
Doffi	Oligarch	12,700	1393	22
Morelli		27,535	1387	23
SCAMBRILLA:				
Scambrilla	Oligarch (2)	148	1387	21
Sertini		...	1376	34
BENIZZI:				
Benizzi	Oligarch (2)	9672	1301	12
Manelli		16,421	Magnate	12
STROZZI:				
Strozzi	Oligarch (4)	296,250	1283	33

Reggimento Family	Party*	Gross Wealth (Florins)	Date of First Prior	Neighborhood (*Gonfalone*)†
Capponi	Medici	54,027	1287	12
Busini		57,019	1345	23
RUCELLAI:				
Rucellai		54,968	1302	33
Baldovinetti	Oligarch (2)	9831	1287	31
Sacchetti		29,092	1335	22
PANCIATICHI:				
Frescobaldi	Oligarch	28,898	Magnate	12
Panciatichi	Oligarch	151,542	Consular	42
Manovelli	Oligarch	13,438	1283	42
ALBIZZI:				
Albizzi	Split loyalties (1/2)	92,599	1282	43
Gianfigliazzi	Split loyalties (1/5)	47,853	Magnate	32
Barbadori	Split loyalties (1/2)	98,663	1295	12
Belfradelli	Oligarch (2)	9014	1321	12
Bencivenni	Split loyalties (1/1)	1811	1389	43
ALTOVITI:				
Altoviti	Oligarch (2)	42,357	1282	31
del Palagio		8676	1328	43
Corsi	Split loyalties (1/3)	26,588	1354	23
DELLA CASA:				
della Casa	Split loyalties (1/1)	31,069	1393	42
Adimari		45,689	Magnate	44
Serragli		63,866	1325	14
SOLOSMEI:				
Solosmei	Oligarch (2)	5757	1364	41
LAMBERTESCHI:				
Lamberteschi	Oligarch (2)	52,524	Consular	21
Baronci	Oligarch	12,251	1330	42

continued

Table 9.B1 *continued*

Reggimento Family	Party*	Gross Wealth (Florins)	Date of First Prior	Neighborhood (*Gonfalone*)†
VELLUTI:				
Velluti	Split loyalties (1/1)	22,372	1283	12
Arrigucci	Oligarch	5736	Magnate	42
BARONCELLI:				
Baroncelli		67,966	1287	21
Rossi	Oligarch	24,649	Magnate	44
GUADAGNI:				
Guadagni	Oligarch (5)	25,179	1289	43
BISCHERI:				
Bischeri	Oligarch	55,230	1309	44
Arrighi		23,499	1373	43
FIORAVANTI:				
Donati		26,099	Magnate	43
Scolari		12,074	Magnate	43
Fioravanti	Medici	19,501	1344	43
Miscellaneous (unblocked):				
Carducci	Medici (2)	28,909	1380	31
Fortini		30,645	1386	43
del Forese	Oligarch	4220	1296	24
Bartoli	Oligarch	54,956	1345	32

* For Medici and oligarch parties, numbers in parentheses are numbers active, if more than one. For split loyalties, numbers in parentheses are, first, number of Mediceans and, second, number of oligarchs. Blank spaces indicate that there were no active partisans.

† For Santo Spirito quarter, 11 = Scala *gonfalone*, 12 = Nicchio *gonfalone*, 13 = Ferza *gonfalone*, 14 = Drago Verde *gonfalone*. For Santa Croce quarter, 21 = Carro *gonfalone*, 22 = Bue *gonfalone*, 23 = Lion Nero *gonfalone*, 24 = Ruote *gonfalone*. For Santa Maria Novella quarter, 31 = Vipera *gonfalone*, 32 = Unicorno *gonfalone*, 33 = Lion Rosso *gonfalone*, 34 = Lion Bianco *gonfalone*. For San Giovanni quarter, 41 = Lion d'oro *gonfalone*, 42 = Drago San Giovanni *gonfalone*, 43 = Chiavi *gonfalone*, 44 = Vaio *gonfalone*.

Appendix

Data Sources and Bibliography

Archival Primary Sources

Archivio di Stato di Firenze [A.S.F.], *Arte del Cambio* 11, 14, 15, 16: Annual guild censuses of banks doing business in Florence, covering periods 1340–1399 and 1460–1520. (Books for intervening period 1400–1459 unfortunately are lost.)

A.S.F., *Arte del Cambio* 12: Matriculants (1330–1500) and consuls (1280–1500) of the banking guild.

A.S.F., *Arte della Lana* 18–20: Matriculants (1304–1406) into the wool guild.

A.S.F., *Arte della Lana* 20: 1353 census of active wool manufacturers.

A.S.F., *Arte della Lana* 46: 1382 census of wool manufacturing firms by the wool guild (pp. 114–17); 1384 *balìa* membership and decisions (pp. 154–66).

A.S.F., *Atti di Esecutore degli Ordinamenti della Giustizia* 791, 800: 1377–78 *ammonizione* denunciations.

A.S.F., *Balìe* 16: 1378 *balìa.*

A.S.F., *Balìe* 17: 1382 *balìa* membership (pp. 22; see also Stefani pp. 394–96); 1393 *balìa* membership (pp. 80–86, 105–07).

A.S.F., *Carte Strozziane, serie II*, 7: *ricordi* of Paliano di Falco, 1382–1404.

A.S.F., *Carte Strozziane, serie V*, 22: account books of Filippo di Matteo Strozzi.

A.S.F., *Catasto* 15–63 (*Portate dei Cittadini*): Original 1427 tax submissions of Florentine citizens.

A.S.F., *Catasto* 64–85 (*Campioni dei Cittadini*): Scribal summaries of citizens' 1427 tax submissions. [Thanks to the labors of David Herlihy and Christianne Klapisch-Zuber, a computerized subset of this information, not including the *debitori* and *creditori* analyzed here, is available online at https://cds.library.brown.edu/projects/catasto.overview.html. These researchers also deposited a microfilm copy of the *campioni* documents themselves at the Center for Research Libraries at the University of Chicago.]

A.S.F. *Catasto* 487–500 (*Campioni dei Cittadini*): Scribal summaries of citizens' 1433 tax submissions.

A.S.F., *Consulte e Pratiche* 14, 15: textual summaries of elite debates on foreign policy.

A.S.F., *Estimo* 268: 1379 *estimo* tax assessments for Santo Spirito residents.

A.S.F., *Estimo* 306: 1352 tax assessments of Florentine residents. [Microfilm copy generously donated to Padgett by Samuel Cohn.]

A.S.F., *Manoscritto* 496: copy of 1325 Prestanze for sesto of San Piero Scheraggio.

A.S.F., *Manoscritto* 540–41: *Arte della Lana* matriculation (1406–1500) into wool guild.

A.S.F., *Manoscritto* 543: *Arte della Por Santa Maria* matriculation (1328–1500) into silk guild.

A.S.F., *Manoscritto* 545: *Arte della Calimala* matriculation (1235–1500) into international merchant guild.

A.S.F., *Manoscritto* 548: scrutiny votes in 1382 for elections to Priorate. (See also Ildefonso di San Luigi.)

A.S.F., *Manoscritti Carte dell'Ancisa* 348–361: Fourteen volumes of hand-transcribed marriage information from Renaissance Florentine dowry contracts, originals mostly now lost, produced in the 17th century by Pierantonio dell'Ancisa. (Listed in A.S.F. inventory N/187, p. 153.)

A.S.F., *Manoscritti Carte dei Mariani-Dei* 519: early attempts, often disorganized and incomplete, to reconstruct genealogical descent within Florentine families.

A.S.F., *Mercanzia* 129: List of members (1310–1500) of the commercial court.

A.S.F., *Prestanze* 367–369: 1379 *estimo* tax assessments of Florentine residents, Santa Croce, Santa Maria Novella, and San Giovanni residents. [Microfilm copy generously given to Padgett by Samuel Cohn.]

A.S.F., *Prestanze* 1989–2020: 1403 forced-loan tax assessments of Florentine residents.

A.S.F., *Prestanze* 834–837: 1458 *catasto* tax assessments of Florentine residents.

A.S.F., *Tratte* 355: 1382 scrutiny.

A.S.F., *Tratte* 357: 7–20: 1393 electoral results, winners being *reggimento*.)

A.S.F., *Tratte* 359: scrutiny votes in 1411 and in 1433 for elections to Priorate.

A.S.F., *Tratte Libri d'età* 77, 79: birthdates of Florentine citizens from 1378 to 1456.

Archivio di Stato di Lucca, *Corte dei Mercanti*, n. 82–86: *Libri dei mercanti, 1371, 1372, 1381, 1407 e 1488.* Along with Lazzareschi (1947), these are censuses of Lucca companies.

Archivio di Stato di Prato, *Datini* 1, 4–6, 16–22, 357–360, 365, 555, 723–725, 799: various account books of Francesco Datini, consulted in order to identify dates of adoption of bilateral or *contrapposto* bookkeeping format.

Newberry Library, Chicago. *Priorista descritto a Tratte riscontro con quello delle riformagioni e con alter scritture publiche*: An eighteenth-century hand copy of the official list of elected Priors, the *Priorista Mariani* original of which is A.S.F., *Manoscritti* 248–252. [Thanks to the labors of the late David Herlihy and Burr Litchfield, this information can now be obtained online at www.cds.library.brown.edu/projects/tratte.]

Published Primary Sources

Aiazza, Giuseppe (ed.). 1840. *Ricordi storici di Filippo di Cino Rinuccini dal 1280 al 1460.* Firenze.

Alberti, Leon Battista. [1433] 1971. *The Albertis of Florence: Leon Battista Alberti's Della Famiglia*, edited by Guido Guarino. Lewisburg, PA: Bucknell University Press.

Alberti, Leon Battista. [1435] 1991. *On Painting.* London: Penguin Books.

Bond, Edward Augustus (ed.). 1840. *Extracts from the Liberate Rolls, Relative to Loans Supplied by Italian Merchants to the Kings of England in the Thirteenth and Fourteenth centuries.* London: J. B. Nichols and Son.

Branca, Vittore (ed.). 1986. *Mercanti scrittori: Riccordi nella Firenze tra Medioevo e Rinascimento.* Milano: Rusconi.

Brucker, Gene A. (ed.). 1968. *Two Memoirs of Renaissance Florence: The Diaries of Buonaccorso Pitti and Gregorio Dati.* New York: Harper Torchbooks.

Compagni, Dino. [1311] 1986. *Dino Compagni's Chronicle of Florence*, edited by Daniel Bornstein. Philadelphia: University of Pennsylvania Press.

Davanzati, Bernardo. 1923. *Le opera di Bernardo Davanzati.* Firenze.

Dei, Benedetto. 1984. *La cronica dall'anno 1400 all'anno 1500.* Firenze. [original c.1480]

Frangioni, Luciana (ed.). 1994. *Milano fine trecento: Il carteggio Milanese dell'Archivio Datini di Prato.* Firenze: Opus libri.

Gherardi, Alessandro (ed.). [1389] 1876. "Diario d'Anonimo Fiorentino dall'anno 1358 al 1389." In *Documenti di storia italiana*, edited by Deputazione sugli studi di storia patria. Firenze: M. Cellini, 207–481.

Gherardi, Alessandro. [1280–98] 1896. *Le Consulte della Repubblica Fiorentina.* Firenze: G. C. Sansoni, editore.

Goldthwaite, Richard A., Enzo Settesoldi, and Marco Spallanzani (eds.). 1995. *Due libri mastri degli Alberti: una grande compagnia di Calimala, 1348–1358.* Firenze: Cassa di Risparmio di Firenze.

Gregory, Heather (ed.). 1997. *Selected Letters of Alessandra Strozzi.* Berkeley: University of California Press.

Guicciardini, Francesco. [1512] 1994. *Dialogue on the Government of Florence.* Cambridge: Cambridge University Press.

Herlihy, David, and Christiane Klapisch-Zuber. 1981. *Census and Property Survey of Florentine Domains in the Province of Tuscany, 1427–1480.* Madison, WI: Data and Program Library Service, University of Wisconsin.

Ildefonso di San Luigi (ed.). 1770–89. *Delizie degli eruditi toscani, XVI.* Firenze: Gaetano Cambiagi editore.

Lazzareschi, Eugenio. 1947. *Il libro della communità dei mercanti lucchesi in Bruges.* Milan: Rodolfo Malfesi.

Les Registres d'Innocent IV, vol. 1, par Élie Berger. Paris: Ernest Thorin éditeur, 1884.

Les Registres d'Innocent IV, vol. 2, par Élie Berger. Paris: Ernest Thorin éditeur, 1887.

Les Registres d'Innocent IV, vol. 3, par Élie Berger. Paris: Albert Fontemoing éditeur, 1897.

Les Registres d'Alexandre IV, vol 1, edited by C. Bourel de la Roncière. Paris: Albert Fontemoing, éditeur, 1902.

Les Registres d'Alexandre IV, vol 2, edited by Joseph de Loye, Pierre de Cenival. Paris: Fontemoing & cie., éditeurs, 1917.

Les Registres d'Alexandre IV, vol 3, edited by Auguste Coulon. Paris: Fontemoing & cie., éditeurs, 1953.

Les Registres d'Urban IV, vol 1, edited by M. Jean Guiraud. Paris: Albert Fontemoing, éditeur, 1901.

Les Registres d'Urban IV, vol 2, edited by M. Jean Guiraud. Paris: Albert Fontemoing, éditeur, 1901.

Les Registres d'Urban IV, vol 3, edited by M. Jean Guiraud. Paris: Albert Fontemoing, éditeur, 1904.

Les Registres de Clément IV, (1265–1268), only 1 vol., par M. Édouard Jordan. Paris: Albert Fontemoing, éditeur, 1893.

Litta, Pompeo, conte, Luigi Passerini, and Federico Odorici. 1819–1907. *Famiglie celebri italiane*. Milano: Giulio Ferrari editore. (multiple volumes).

Machiavelli, Niccolo. (1525) 1988. *Florentine Histories*, translated by Laura F. Banfield and Harvey Mansfield, Jr. Princeton, NJ: Princeton University Press.

Machiavelli, Niccolò. [1531] 1996. *Discourses on Livy*, translated by Harvey C. Mansfield and Nathan Tarcov. Chicago: University of Chicago Press.

Melis, Federigo. 1962. *Aspetti della vita economica medievale: Studi nell'Archivio Datini di Prato*. Siena: Leo S. Olschki editore.

Molho, Anthony. 1970. "The Florentine 'Tassa dei Traffichi' of 1451." *Studies in the Renaissance* 17: 73–118.

Morlacchi, Pierangela. 2005. "List of Florentine Account Books, Coded for Bilateral Format." home.uchicago.edu/~jpadgett.

Padgett, John F. 2009a. "Extracts from Papal Registers Involving Italian Bankers." Unpublished, home.uchicago.edu/~jpadgett.

Passerini, Luigi. 1869. *Gli Alberti di Firenze: Genealogia, storia e documenti*. Firenze: M. Cellini.

Passerini, Luigi. 1871. *Genealogia e storia della famiglia Altoviti*. Firenze: M. Cellini.

Passerini, Luigi. 1858. *Genealogia e storia della famiglia Corsini*. Firenze: M. Cellini.

Passerini, Luigi. 1876. *Genealogia e storia della famiglia Ginori*. Firenze: M. Cellini.

Passerini, Luigi. 1873. *Genealogia e storia della famiglia Guadagni*. Firenze: M. Cellini.

Passerini, Luigi. 1870. *Genealogia e storia della famiglia Niccolini*. Firenze: M. Cellini.

Passerini, Luigi. 1858. *Genealogia e storia della famiglia Panciatichi*. Firenze: M. Cellini.

Passerini, Luigi. 1861. *Genealogia e storia della famiglia Ricasoli*. Firenze: M. Cellini.

Passerini, Luigi. 1861. *Genealogia e storia della famiglia Rucellai*. Firenze: M. Cellini.

Poliziano, Angelo. [ca. 1478] 1985. *I detti piacevoli*, edited by Mariano Fresta. Siena: Editori del Grifo.

Sapori, Armando. 1934. *I libri di commercio dei Peruzzi*. Milano: Fratelli Treves.

Sapori, Armando con uno studio da Giulio Mandich. 1970. *Libro giallo della compagnia dei Covoni*. Milano: Istituto editoriale Cisalpino.

Silva, P. 1908. "L'ultimo trattato commerciale tra Pisa e Firenze." *Studi storici diretti da F. Crivellucci* 27: 679–83.

Stefani, Marchionne di Coppo. [1385] 1903. *Cronica Fiorentina di Marchionne di Coppo Stefani*, edited by Niccolò Rodolico. Città di Castello: S. Lapi editore.

Strozzi, Alessandra Macinghi. 1997. *Selected Letters of Alessandra Strozzi*. Edited and translated by Heather Gregory. Berkeley: University of California Press.

Vaughan, Richard (ed.). [1247–1250] 1986. *Chronicles of Matthew Paris: Monastic Life in the Thirteenth Century*. New York: St. Martin's Press.

Velluti, Donato. [original c. 1367-70] 1914. *La Cronica Domestica di messer Donato Velluti*. Firenze: G. C. Sansone.

Vespasiano da Bisticci. [ca. 1495] 1963. *Renaissance Princes, Popes, and Prelates: The Vespasiano Memoirs*, edited by Myron P. Gilmore. New York: Harper & Row.

Villain-Gandossi, Christiane (ed.). 1969. *Comptes du sel (Libro di ragione e conto di sale) de Francesco di Marco Datini pour sa compagnie d'Avignon, 1376–1379*. Paris: Bibliothèque nationale.

Consolidated Bibliography of Secondary Sources

Abu-Lughod, Janet. 1989. *Before European Hegemony: The World System A.D. 1250–1350*. Oxford: Oxford University Press.

Adams, Julia. 2005. *The Familial State: Ruling Families and Merchant Capitalism in Early-Modern Europe*. Ithaca, NY: Cornell University Press.

Ammirato, Scipione. [1615] 1969. *Delle Famiglie Nobili Fiorentine*. Bologna.

Arias, Gino. 1902. *Studi e documenti di storia del diritto*. Firenze: Successori le Monnier.

Astorri, Antonella. 1998. *La Mercanzia a Firenze nella prima meta del Trecento*. Firenze: Leo S. Olschki editore.

Baker, Frank B., and J. Lawrence Hubert. 1981. "The Analysis of Social Interaction Data: A Nonparametric Technique." *Sociological Methods and Research* 9: 339–61.

Baker, Nicholas. 2014. "Discursive Republicanism in Renaissance Florence: Deliberation and Representation in the Early Sixteenth Century." *Past and Present* 225: 47–77.

Barbadoro, Bernardino. 1933. "Finanza e demografia nei ruoli fiorentini d'imposta del 1352–1355." Atti del Congresso internazionale per lo studio dei problemi della popolazione 9: 615–29.

Barbagli, Marzio. 1984. *Sotto lo stesso tetto: Mutamenti della famiglia in Italia dal XV al XX secolo*. Bologna: Il Mulino.

Barley, Stephen R. "The Alignment of Technology and Structure through Roles and Networks." *Administrative Science Quarterly* 35 (1990): 61–103.

Baron, Hans. 1966. *The Crisis of the Early Italian Renaissance: Civic Humanism and Republican Liberty in an Age of Classicism and Tyranny*. Princeton, NJ: Princeton University Press.

Barth, Fredrik. 1959. *Political Leadership among Swat Pathans*. London: Athlone.

Baxendale, Susannah Foster. 1991. "Exile in Practice: The Alberti Family in and out of Florence 1401–1428." *Renaissance Quarterly* 44: 720–56.

Baxandall, Michael. [1972] 1988. *Painting and Experience in Fifteenth Century Italy*. Oxford: Oxford University Press.

Bearman, Peter. 1993. *Relations into Rhetorics: Local Elite Social Structure in Norfolk, England, 1540–1640*. New Brunswick, NJ: Rutgers University Press.

Bechtel, William, and Adele Abrahamsen. 1991. *Connectionism and the Mind*. Cambridge, MA: Basil Blackwell.

Becker, Marvin B. 1962. "An Essay on the 'Novi Cives' and Florentine Politics, 1343–1382." *Medieval Studies* 24: 35–82.

Becker, Marvin B. 1965. "A Study in Political Failure: The Florentine Magnates, 1280–1343." *Medieval Studies* 27: 246–308.

Becker, Marvin B. 1967. *Florence in Transition. Volume One: The Decline of the Commune.* Baltimore: The Johns Hopkins Press.

Becker, Marvin B., and Gene A. Brucker. 1956. "The *Arti Minori* in Florentine Politics, 1342–1378." *Medieval Studies* 18: 93–104.

Bensa, Enrico. 1928. *Francesco di Marco da Prato.* Milano: Fratelli Treves editori.

Berlow, Rosalind Kent. 1971. "The Development of Business Techniques Used at the Fairs of Champagne from the End of the Twelfth Century to the Middle of the Thirteenth Century." *Studies in Medieval and Renaissance History* 8: 3–32.

Bizzocchi, Roberto. 1982. "La dissoluzione di un clan familiare: i Buondelmonti di Firenze nei secoli XV e XVI." *Archivio storico italiano* 140: 3–46.

Black, Robert. 2007. *Education and Society in Florentine Tuscany: Teachers, Pupils and Schools, c. 1250-1500.* Leiden: Brill.

Blalock, Hubert. 1972. *Social Statistics.* New York: McGraw-Hill.

Blomquist, Thomas W. 1971. "Commercial Association in Thirteenth-Century Lucca." *Business History Review* 45: 157–178. [reprinted posthumously in his *Merchant Families, Banking and Money in Medieval Lucca.*]

Blomquist, Thomas W. 1980. "Lineage, Land and Business in the Thirteenth Century: The Guidiccioni Family of Lucca." *Actum Luce* 9: 7–29. [reprinted in his *Merchant Families, Banking and Money in Medieval Lucca.*]

Blomquist, Thomas W. 1982. "Lineage, Land and Business in the Thirteenth Century: The Guidiccioni Family of Lucca." *Actum Luce* 11: 7–34. [reprinted in his *Merchant Families, Banking and Money in Medieval Lucca.*]

Blomquist, Thomas W. 2005. *Merchant Families, Banking and Money in Medieval Lucca.* Burlington, VT: Ashgate Publishing.

Boorman, Scott A., and Harrison C. White. 1976. "Social Structure from Multiple Networks. II. Role Structures." *American Journal of Sociology* 81: 1384–446.

Borsari, Silvano. 1994. *Una compagnia di Calimala: gli Scali (secc. XIII–XIV).* Macerata: Università degli studi di Mercerata.

Botticini, Maristella. 1999. "A Loveless Economy? Intergenerational Altruism and the Marriage Market in a Tuscan Town, 1415–1436." *Journal of Economic History* 59: 104–21.

Botticini, Maristella. 2000. "A Tale of 'Benevolent' Governments: Private Credit Markets, Public Finance, and the Role of Jewish Lenders in Medieval and Renaissance Italy." *Journal of Economic History* 60: 164–89.

Botticini, Maristella, and Aloysius Siow. 2003. "Why Dowries?" *American Economic Review* 93: 1385–98.

Bourdieu, Pierre. 1984. *Distinction: a social critique of the judgement of taste.* Cambridge, MA: Harvard University Press.

Braudel, Fernand. [1949] 1972. *The Mediterranean and the Mediterranean World in the Age of Philip II.* New York: Harper Colophon Books.

Breiger, Ronald L. 1974. "The Duality of Persons and Groups," *Social Forces* 53: 181–90.

Breiger, Ronald L., and Philippa E. Pattison. 1986. "Cumulated Social Roles: The Duality of Persons and Their Algebras." *Social Networks* 8: 215–56.

Brown, Allison M. 1961. "The Humanist Portrait of Cosomo de' Medici, Pater Patriae." *Journal of the Warburg and Courtauld Institutes* 26: 186–221.

Brown, Allison M. 1992. "Cosimo de' Medici's Wit and Wisdom." In *Cosimo 'il Vecchio' de' Medici, 1389–1464*, edited by Francis Ames-Lewis, 95–113. Oxford: Clarendon Press.

Brucker, Gene A. 1957. "The Medici in the Fourteenth Century." *Speculum* 32: 1–26.

Brucker, Gene A. 1962. *Florentine Politics and Society, 1343–1378.* Princeton, NJ: Princeton University Press.

Brucker, Gene A. 1968. "The Ciompi Revolution." In *Florentine Studies: Politics and Society in Renaissance Florence*, edited by Nicolai Rubinstein, 314–56. London: Faber.

Brucker, Gene A. 1969. *Renaissance Florence.* Berkeley, CA: The University of California Press.

Brucker, Gene A. 1977. *The Civic World of Early Renaissance Florence.* Princeton, NJ: Princeton University Press.

Bruscoli, Francesco Guidi. 1997. "Politica matrimoniale e matrimoni politici nella Firenze di Lorenzo de' Medici." *Archivio storico italiano* 155: 347–98.

Burckhardt, Jacob. [1860] 1954. *The Civilization of the Renaissance in Italy.* Translated by S. G. C. Middlemore. London: Phaidon.

Burckhardt, Jacob. [1878] 1990. *The Civilization of the Renaissance in Italy.* New York: Penguin.

Burt, Ronald. 1976. "Positions in Networks." *Social Forces* 55: 93–122.

Burt, Ronald S. 2004. "Structural Holes and Good Ideas." *American Journal of Sociology* 110: 349–99.

Carruthers, Bruce G. 1996. *City of Capital: Politics and Markets in the English Financial Revolution.* Princeton, NJ: Princeton University Press.

Carus-Wilson, E. M. 1967. "Trends in the Export of English Woolens in the Fourteenth Century." In *Medieval Merchant Venturers: Collected Studies*, E. M. Carus-Wilson, 239–64. London: Methuen.

Carus-Wilson, E.M., and Olive Coleman. 1963. *England's Export Trade, 1275–1547.* Oxford: Clarendon Press.

Ceccherelli, Alberto. 1913. *I libri di mercatura della Banca Medici, e l'applicazio Della partita doppia a Firenze nel secolo XIV.* Firenze: R. Bemporad & figlio.

Cellati, Antonio. 1790. *Compendio storico-genealogico dell'origine, accidenti, progressi e diramazioni dell'antichissima e nobilissima famiglia degli Anselmi.* Parma.

Chabod, Isabelle. 1995. *La dette des familles: Femmes, lignages et patrimonies àFlorence aux XIVe ey XVe siècles.* PhD diss., Department of History, European University Institute.

Chandler, Alfred D. 1962. *Strategy and Structure: Chapters in the History of the American Industrial Enterprise.* Cambridge: Massachusetts Insititute of Technology Press.

Chandler, Alfred D. 1977. *The Visible Hand: The Managerial Revolution in American Business.* Cambridge, MA: Harvard University Press.

Chiaudano, Mario. 1930. "Note e documenti sulla compagni dei Bonsignori." In his *Studi e documenti per la storia del diritto commerciale italiano nel sec. XIII*, 114–142. Torino: Istituto Giuridico della R Università.

Chiaudano, Mario. 1935. "I Rothschild del Dugento: La Gran Tavola di Orlando Bonsignori." *Bullettino Senese di storia patria*, Anno VI: 103–42.

Ciappelli, Giovanni. 1995. *Una famiglia e le ricordanze: i Castellani di Firenze nel Tre-Quattrocento.* Firenze: L.S. Olschki.

Clark, Gregory. 2007. *A Farewell to Alms.* Princeton. NJ: Princeton University Press.

Cohn, Samuel K. 1988. *Death and Property in Siena, 1205–1800.* Baltimore: Johns Hopkins University Press.

Cohn, Samuel K. 1992. *The Cult of Remembrance and the Black Death.* Baltimore: Johns Hopkins University Press.

Cohn, Samuel K. 1996. *Women in the Streets.* Baltimore: Johns Hopkins University Press.

Cohn, Samuel K. 1998. "Marriage in the Mountains: The Florentine Territorial State, 1348–1500." In *Marriage in Italy, 1300–1650*, edited by Trevor Dean and K. J. P. Lowe, 174–96. Cambridge: Cambridge University Press.

Cohn, Samuel K. 1999. *Creating the Florentine State: Peasants and Rebellion, 1348–1434.* Cambridge: Cambridge University Press.

Cohn, Samuel K. 2002. *The Black Death Transformed: Disease and Culture in Early Renaissance Europe.* New York: Oxford University Press.

Cohn, Samuel Kline. 1980. *The Laboring Classes in Renaissance Florence.* New York: Academic Press.

Conti, Elio. 1984. *L'imposta diretta a Firenze nel Quattrocento (1427–1494).* Roma: Nella sede dell'Istituto.

Corbinelli, Jean de. 1705. *Histoire genealogique de la maison de Gondi.* Paris: Chez Jean-Baptiste Coignard.

Crabb, Ann. 2000. *The Strozzi of Florence: Widowhood and Family Solidarity in the Renaissance.* Ann Arbor: University of Michigan Press.

Cyert, Richard M., and James G. March. 1963. *A Behavioral Theory of the Firm.* Englewood Cliffs, NJ: Prentice-Hall.

de la Roncière, Charles M. 1973. *Un changeur florentin du Trecento: Lippo di Fede del Sega (1285 env. - 1363 env.).* Paris: Ècole pratique des hautes ètudes.

Del Punta, Ignazio. 2004. *Mercanti e banchieri lucchesi nel Dugento.* Pisa: Pisa University Press.

de Roover, Raymond. 1944. "Early Accounting Problems of Foreign Exchange," *The Accounting Review* 19: 381–407.

de Roover, Raymond. 1949. "La communauté des marchands Lucquois à Bruges de 1377 à 1404." *Annales, Société d'émulation de Bruges* 86: 23–89.

de Roover, Raymond. 1963. "The Organization of Trade". In *The Cambridge Economic History of Europe, volume III: Economic Organization and Policies in the Middle Ages*, edited by M.M. Postan, E.E. Rich, and Edward Miller, 42–118. Cambridge: Cambridge University Press.

de Roover, Raymond. 1966. *The Rise and Decline of the Medici Bank, 1397–1494.* New York: Norton.

de Roover, Raymond. [1956] 1974a. "The Development of Accounting Prior to Luca Pacioli According to the Account Books of Medieval Merchants." In *Business, Banking, and Economic Thought in Late Medieval and Early Modern Europe*, edited by Julius Kirshner, 119–79. Chicago: The University of Chicago Press.

de Roover, Raymond. [1965] 1974b. "The Antecedents of the Medici Bank: The Banking House of Messer Vieri di Cambio de' Medici." In *Business, Banking, and Economic Thought in Late Medieval and Early Modern Europe* by Raymond de Roover, edited by Julius Kirshner, 260–272. Chicago: University of Chicago Press.

Dini, Bruno. 2001. "Le forme e le tecniche del prestito nel tardo Medioevo." In *Manifattura, commercio e banca nella Firenze medievale*. Firenze: Nardini editore, 83–102.

Dix, Gregory. 1946. "The Ministry in the Early Church." In *The Apostolic Ministry*, edited by Kenneth E. Kirk, 183–303. New York: Morehouse-Gorham.

Douglas, Mary. 1966. *Purity and Danger: An Analysis of Concepts of Pollution and Taboo*. London: Routledge & Kegan Paul.

Douglas, Mary. 1986. *How Institutions Think*. Syracuse, NY: Syracuse University Press.

Duby, Georges. 1980. *The Three Orders: Feudal Society Imagined*. Chicago: University of Chicago Press.

Dumont, Louis. 1970. *Homo Hierarchicus: The Caste System and Its Implications*. Chicago: University of Chicago Press.

Elster, Jon. 1983. *Sour Grapes: Studies in the Subversion of Rationality*. Cambridge: Cambridge University Press.

Emerson, Richard M. 1962. "Power-Dependence Relations." *American Sociological Review* 27: 31–40.

Emigh, Rebecca Jean. 1997a. "Land Tenure, Household Structure, and Age at Marriage in Fifteenth-Century Tuscany." *Journal of Interdisciplinary History* 27: 613–635.

Emigh, Rebecca Jean. 1997b. "Land Tenure, Household Structure, and Fertility: Aggregate Analyses of Fifteenth-century Rural Tuscan Communities." *The International Journal of Sociology and Social Policy* 17: 220–254.

Emigh, Rebecca Jean. 2000. "Forms of Property Rights or Class Capacities: The Example of Tuscan Sharecropping." *Archives Europeennes de Sociologie* 41: 22–52.

Emigh, Rebecca Jean. 2003. "Property Devolution in Tuscany." *Journal of Interdisciplinary History* 33: 385–420.

Emirbayer, Mustafa and Jeff Goodwin. 1994. "Network Analysis, Culture and the Problem of Agency." *American Journal of Sociology* 99: 1411–54.

English, Edward D. 1988. *Enterprise and Liability in Sienese Banking, 1230–1350*. Cambridge, MA: The Medieval Academy of America.

Epstein, Steven. 1996. *Genoa and the Genoese, 958–1528*. Chapel Hill, NC: University of North Carolina Press.

Esch, Arnold. 1966. "Bankiers der Kirche im grossen Schisma," *Quellen und Forschungen aus italienischen Archiven und Bibliotheken* 46: 277–398.

Fabbri, Lorenzo. 1991. *Alleanza matrimoniale e patriziato nella Firenze del' 400. Studio sulla famiglia Strozzi*. Firenze: Leo S. Olschki editore.

Face, Richard D. 1958. "Techniques of Business in the Trade between the Fairs of Champagne and the South of Europe in the Twelfth and Thirteenth Centuries." *Economic History Review* 10: 427–438.

Face, Richard D. 1969. "Symon de Gualterio: A Brief Portrait of a Thirteenth-Century Man of Affairs." In *Economy, Society, and Government in Medieval Italy: Essays in Memory of Robert L. Reynolds*, edited by David Herlihy, Robert S. Lopez, and Vsevolod Slessarev, 75–94. Kent, OH: Kent State University Press.

Faust, Katherine, and A. Kimball Romney. 1985. "Does STRUCTURE find Structure?: A Critique of Burt's Use of Distance as a Measure of Structural Equivalence." *Social Networks* 7: 77–103.

Fell, David. 1997. *Understanding the Control of Metabolism*. London: Portland Press.

Fleming, Lee. "Finding the Sources of Technological Breakthroughs: The Story of Hewlett-Packard's Thermal Ink-Jet." 2002. *Industrial and Corporate Change* 11: 1059–84.

Fligstein, Neil. 1990. *The Transformation of Corporate Control*. Cambridge, MA: Harvard University Press.

Fontana, Walter, and Leo Buss. 1994. "The Arrival of the Fittest: Toward a Theory of Biological Organization." *Bulletin of Mathemaical Biology* 56: 1–64.

Foster, Susannah. 1985. "The Ties that Bind: Kinship Association and Marriage in the Alberti Family, 1378–1428." PhD diss. Department of History, Cornell University, Ithaca, NY.

Foucault, Michel. 1975. "What Is an Author?" *Partisan Review* 42: 603–14.

Franceschi, Franco. 1993a. *Oltre il "Tumulto": I lavoratori fiorentini dell'Arte della Lana fra Tre e Quattrocento*. Firenze: Leo S. Olschki Editore.

Franceschi, Franco. 1993b. "Intervento del potere centrale e ruolo delle Arti nel governo dell'economia fiorentina del Trecento e del primo Quattrocento. Linee generali." *Archivio Storico Italiano* 151: 863–909.

Franceschi, Franco. 1994. "Istituzioni e attivita economica a Firenze: considerazioni sul governo del settore industriale (1350–1450)." In *Istituzioni e societa in Toscan nell'eta moderna*, edited by C. Lamioni. Firenze: Edifir, 76–117.

Freeman, Linton C. 1979. "Centrality in Social Networks: Conceptual Clarification." *Social Networks* 1: 215–39.

Galison, Peter. 1997. *Image and Logic: A material culture of microphysics*. Chicago: University of Chicago Press.

Galison, Peter. 2003. *Einstein's Clocks, Poincaré's Maps: Empires of Time*. New York: Norton.

Gamurrini, Eugenio. *Istoria genealogia delle famiglie nobil toscane et vmbre*. Fiorenza, 1668, 1671, 1673, 1679, 1685.

Gasquet, Abbot Francis A. 1905. *Henry the Third and the Church*. London: George Bell.

Gensicke, Hellmulth. 1965. "Der Adel im Mittelrheingebiet." In *Deutscher Adel, 1430–1555*, edited by Hellmuth Rossler, 127–152. Darmstadt: Wissenschaftliche Buchgesellschaft.

Gibson, David. 2012. *Talk at the Brink: Deliberation and Decision during the Cuban Missile Crisis*. Princeton, NJ: Princeton University Press.

Goffman, Erving. 1975. *Frame Analysis*. Boston: Northeastern University Press.

Goldthwaite, Richard A. 1968. *Private Wealth in Renaissance Florence: A Study of Four Families*. Princeton, NJ: Princeton University Press.

Goldthwaite, Richard A. 1972. "The Florence Palace as Domestic Architecture." *American Historical Review* 77: 977–1012.

Goldthwaite, Richard A. 1983. "Organizzazione economica e struttura famigliare." In *I ceti dirigenti nella Toscana tardo comunale*, edited by Donatella Rugiadini, 1–14. Firenze: Francesco Papafava editore.

Goldthwaite, Richard A. 1985. "Local Banking in Renaissance Florence." *The Journal of European Economic History* 14: 5–55.

Goldthwaite, Richard A. 1987. "The Medici Bank and the World of Florentine Capitalism." *Past and Present* 114: 3–31.

Goldthwaite, Richard A. 1993. *Wealth and the Demand for Art in Italy*. Baltimore: Johns Hopkins University Press.

Goldthwaite, Richard A. 2009. *The Economy of Renaissance Florence*. Baltimore: Johns Hopkins University Press.

Goldthwaite, Richard A. 2015. "The Practice and Culture of Accounting in Renaissance Florence." *Enterprise and Society* 16: 611–47.

Goldthwaite, Richard A., Enzo Settesoldi, and Marco Spallanzani, eds. 1995. *Due libri mastri degli Alberti: una grande compagnia di Calimala, 1348–1358*. Firenze: Cassa di Risparmio di Firenze.

Gompers, Paul, and Josh Lerner. 1999. *The Venture Capital Cycle*. Cambridge, MA: Massachusetts Institute of Technology Press.

Granovetter, Mark S. 1973. "The Strength of Weak Ties." *American Journal of Sociology* 78: 1360–80.

Granovetter, Mark. 1985. "Economic Action and Social Structure: The Problem of Embeddedness." *American Journal of Sociology* 91: 481–510.

Grant, Alexander. 1985. "Extinction of Direct Male Lines among Scottish Noble Families in the Fourteenth and Fifteenth Centuries." In *Essays on the Nobility of Medieval Scotland*, edited by K. J. Stringer, 210–231. Edinburgh: J. Donald Publishers.

Gras, Norman S. B. 1939. *Business and Capitalism: An Introduction to Business History*. New York: F. S. Crofts.

Greif, Avner. 1994. "Cultural Beliefs and the Organization of Society: A Historical and Theoretical Reflection on Collectivist and Individualist Societies," *Journal of Political Economy* 102: 912–950.

Greif, Avner. 2006. *Institutions and the Path to the Modern Economy*. Cambridge: Cambridge University Press.

Grimmer, Justin, and Brandon M. Stewart. 2013. "Text as Data: The Promise and Pitfalls of Automatic Content Analysis Methods for Political Texts." *Political Analysis* 21: 267–97.

Grossman, Ronald P. 1965. *The Financing of the Crusades*. Ph.D. dissertation, Department of History, University of Chicago.

Gutkind, Curt S. 1938. *Cosimo de' Medici: Pater Patriae, 1389–1464*. Oxford: Oxford University Press.

Hankins, James. 1995. "The Baron Thesis after Forty Years." *Journal of the History of Ideas* 56: 309–38.

Hankins, James (ed.). 2000. *Renaissance Civic Humanism*. Cambridge: Cambridge University Press.

Hedstrom, Peter. 2005. *Dissecting the Social: On the Principles of Analytic Sociology*. Cambridge: Cambridge University Press.

Heers, Jacques. 1983. *Genova nel '400: Civiltà mediterranea, grande capitalismo e capitalismo popolare*. Milano: Jaca book. [Italian translation of French original]

Herlihy, David. 1973. "Three Patterns of Social Mobility in Medieval History." *Journal of Interdisciplinary History* 4: 623–47.

Herlihy, David. 1985a. "Did Women Have a Renaissance? A Reconsideration." *Medievalia et Humanistica* 13: 1–22.

Herlihy, David. 1985b. *Medieval Households*. Cambridge, MA: Harvard University Press.

Herlihy, David, and Christiane Klapisch-Zuber. 1978. *Les Toscans et leurs familles. Un etude du catasto florentin de 1427*. Paris: Ecole des hautes etudesen sciences sociales.

Herlihy, David, and Christiane Klapisch-Zuber. 1981. *Census and Property Survey of Florentine Domains in the Province of Tuscany, 1427–1480*. Madison: University of Wisconsin, Data and Program Library Service.

Herlihy, David, and Christiane Klapisch-Zuber. 1985. *Tuscans and Their Families: A Study of the Florentine Catasto of 1427*. New Haven, CT: Yale University Press.

Hoffman, Philip T., Gilles Postel-Vinay, and Jean-Laurent Rosenthal. 2000. *Priceless Markets: The Political Economy of Credit in Paris, 1660–1870*. Chicago: The University of Chicago Press.

Holmes, George. 1968. "How the Medici Became the Pope's Bankers." In *Florentine Studies*, edited by Nicolai Rubinstein, 357–80. Evanston, IL: Northwestern University Press.

Horwitz, Morton J. 1977. *The Transformation of American Law, 1780–1860*. Cambridge, MA: Harvard University Press.

Hoshino, Hidetoshi. 1966. "Francesco di Jacopo del Bene, cittadino fiorentino del Trecento." *Annuario, Istituto Giapponese di Cultura in Roma* 4: 29–119.

Hoshino, Hidetoshi. 1980. *L'Arte della Lana in Firenze nel basso medioevo*. Florence: Leo S. Olschki editore.

Housley, Norman. 1982. *The Italian Crusades: The Papal-Angevin alliance and the Crusades against Christian lay powers, 1254–1343*. Oxford: Clarendon Press.

Hughes, Diane Owens. 1975a. "Urban Growth and Family Structure in Medieval Genoa." *Past and Present* 66: 3–28.

Hughes, Diane Owens. 1975b. "Domestic Ideals and Social Behavior: Evidence from Medieval Genoa." In *The Family in History*, edited by Charles Rosenberg, 115–43. Philadelphia: University of Pennsylvania Press.

Hughes, Diane Owens. 1977. "Kinsmen and Neighbors in Medieval Genoa." In *The Medieval City*, edited by Harry Miskimin and David Herlihy, 95–111. New Haven, CT: Yale University Press.

Hughes, Diane Owens. 1978. "From Brideprice to Dowry in Mediterranean Europe," *Journal of Family History* 3: 262–96.

Hunt, Edwin S. 1994. *The Medieval Super-companies: A Study of the Peruzzi Company of Florence*. Cambridge: Cambridge University Press.

Hurtubise, Pierre. 1985. *Une famille-témoin, Les Salviati*. Città del Vaticano.

Hutchins, Edwin. *Cognition in the Wild*. Cambridge: Massachussets Institute of Technology Press, 1995.

Istituto nazionale di studi sul Rinascimento (editors). 1981. *Il tumulto dei Ciompi: Un momento di storia fiorentino ed europa*. Firenze: Leo. S. Olschke editore.

Jacks, Philip, and William Caferro. 2001. *The Spinelli of Florence: Fortunes of a Renaissance Merchant Family*. University Park, PA: Penn State University Press.

Jones, Philip. 1997. *The Italian City-State: From Commune to Signoria*. Oxford: Clarendon Press.

Jordan, E. J. 1902. "La fallite des Buonsignori." In *Mélanges Paul Fabre: Études d'histoire du Moyen Age*, 116–35. Paris: Alphonse Picard et fils.

Jordan, E. J. 1909. *De Mercatoribus Camerae Apostolocae, saeculo XIII*. Paris: Condate Rhedonum, Apud Oberthur typographum.

Kaeuper, Richard W. 1973. *Bankers to the Crown: The Riccardi of Lucca and Edward I*. Princeton, NJ: Princeton University Press.

Kantorowicz, Ernst H. 1957. *The King's Two Bodies: A Study in Medieval Political Theology*. Princeton, NJ: Princeton University Press.

Kauffman, Stuart A. 1993. *The Origins of Order: Self-organization and Selection in Evolution*. New York: Oxford University Press.

Kay, Richard. 1970. "Rucco di Cambio de' Mozzi in France and England." *Studi Danteschi* 47: 49–53.

Kelly-Gadol, Joan. 1977. "Did Women have a Renaissance?" In *Becoming Visible: Women in European History*, 175–201, edited by Renate Bridenthal and Claudia Koonz. Boston: Houghton Mifflin.

Kent, D. V., and F. W. Kent. 1981. "A Self-disciplining Pact Made by the Peruzzi Family of Florence (June 1433)." *Renaissance Quarterly* 34: 337–55.

Kent, D. V., and F. W. Kent. 1982. *Neighbours and Neighbourhood in Renaissance Florence: The District of the Red Lion in the Fifteenth Century*. Locust Valley, NY: J. J. Augustin.

Kent, Dale. 1975. "The Florentine *Reggimento* in the Fifteenth Century." *Renaissance Quarterly* 28: 575–638.

Kent, Dale. 1978. *The Rise of the Medici: Faction in Florence, 1426–1434*. Oxford: Oxford University Press.

Kent, Dale. 2000. *Cosimo de' Medici and the Florentine Renaissance*. New Haven, CT: Yale University Press.

Kent, F. W. 1991. *Bartolomeo Cederni and His Friends: Letters to an Obscure Florentine*. Firenze: Leo S. Olschki editore.

Kent, Francis William. 1977. *Household and Lineage in Renaissance Florence: The Family Life of the Capponi, Ginori, and Rucellai*. Princeton, NJ: Princeton University Press.

Kent, Francis William. 1987. "Ties of Neighborhood and Patronage in Quattrocento Florence." In *Patronage, Art, and Society in Renaissance Italy*, edited by F. W. Kent and Patricia Simons, 79–98. Oxford: Clarendon Press.

Kessler, Jason S. 2017. "Scattertext: a Browser-Based Tool for Visualizing how Corpora Differ." *arXiv preprint*: 1703.00565.

Klapisch-Zuber, Christiane. 1985. *Women, Family, and Ritual in Renaissance Italy.* Chicago: The University of Chicago Press.

Klapisch-Zuber, Christiane. 1988. "Ruptures de parente et changements d'identite chez les magnats florentins du XIV siecle." *Annales ESC* 5: 1205–1240.

Klapisch-Zuber, Christiane. 2000. *L'ombre des ancetres: essai sur l'imaginaire medieval de la parente.* Paris: Fayard.

Klapisch-Zuber, Christianne. 2006. *Retour à la cité: Les magnats de Florence, 1340–1440.* Paris: Ecole des hautes études en sciences sociales.

Kuehn, Thomas. 1991. *Law, Family, and Women: Toward a Legal Anthropology of Renaissance Italy.* Chicago: University of Chicago Press.

Kuehn, Thomas. 2002. "Inheritance and Identity in Early Renaissance Florence: The Estate of Paliano di Falco," In *Society and Individual in Renaissance Florence*, ed. William J. Connell, 137–54. Berkeley: University of California Press.

Lachmann, Richard. 2000. *Capitalists in Spite of Themselves: Elite Conflict and Economic Transitions in Early Modern Europe.* New York: Oxford University Press.

Lane, Frederic C. 1967. *Andrea Barbarigo, Merchant of Venice 1418–1449.* New York: Octagon Books.

Lane, Frederic C. 1973. *Venice: A Maritime Republic.* Baltimore: Johns Hopkins University Press.

Lansing, Carol. 1991. *The Florentine Magnates: Lineage and Faction in a Medieval Commune.* Princeton, NJ: Princeton University Press.

Laslett, Peter. 1965. *The World We Have Lost: England before the Industrial Age.* New York: Scribner.

Laslett, Peter (ed.). 1972. *Household and Family in Past Time.* Cambridge: Cambridge University Press.

LaSoursa, Saverio. 1904. *L'organizzazioni dei cambiatori fiorentini nel medio evo.* Cerignola: Tip. edit. dello scienza e diletto.

Latour, Bruno. 1988. *The Pasteurization of France.* Cambridge, MA: Harvard University Press.

Lave, Charles A., and James G. March. 1975. *An Introduction to Models in the Social Sciences.* New York: Harper & Row.

Leifer, Eric. 1988. "Interaction Preludes to Role Setting: Exploratory Local Action." *American Sociological Review* 53: 865–78.

Leifer, Eric. 1991. *Actors as Observers: A Theory of Skill in Social Relationships.* New York: Garland.

Litchfield, R. Burr. 1986. *Emergence of a Bureaucracy: The Florentine Patricians, 1530–1790.* Princeton, NJ: Princeton University Press.

Long, J. S. 1997. *Regression Models for Categorical and Limited Dependent Variables.* Thousand Oaks, CA: Sage Publications.

Lopez, Robert S. 1952. "The Trade of Medieval Europe: The South." In *Cambridge Economic History of Europe*, edited by M. Postan and E. E. Rich, 257–354. Cambridge: Cambridge University Press.

Lopez, Robert S. 1976. *The Commercial Revolution of the Middle Ages, 950–1350.* Cambridge: Cambridge University Press.

Lopez, Robert S., and Irving W. Raymond. 1955. *Medieval Trade in the Mediterranean World.* New York: Columbia University Press.

Lopez, Robert S., and Irving W. Raymond. 1990. *Medieval Trade in the Mediterranean World: Illustrative Documents.* New York: Columbia University Press.

Lovejoy, Arthur O. 1936. *The Great Chain of Being.* Cambridge, MA: Harvard University Press.

Luhmann, Niklas 1995. *Social Systems.* Stanford, CA: Stanford University Press.

Lunt, William E. 1934. *Papal Revenues in the Middle Ages.* New York: Columbia University Press.

Lunt, William E. 1939. *Financial Relations of the Papacy with England to 1327.* Cambridge, MA: The Medieval Academy of America.

Machiavelli, Niccolo. [1525] 1988. *Florentine Histories*, translated by Laura F. Banfield and Harvey Mansfield, Jr. Princeton, NJ: Princeton University Press.

Maitland, F. W. 1900. "Translator's Introduction." In *Political Theories of the Middle Age*, edited by Otto Gierke, vii–xiv. Cambridge: Cambridge University Press.

Mandich, Giulio. 1984. "Una compagnia fiorentina a Venezia nel quarto decennio del secolo XIV (Un libro di conti)," *Rivista storica italiana.* XCVI: 129–49.

Mansfield, Mildred. 1922. *A Family of Decent Folk, 1200–1741: A Study in the Centuries Growth of the Lanfredini.* Firenze.

March, James G. 1991. "Exploration and Exploitation in Organizational Learning." *Organization Science* 2: 71–87.

March, James G. 1999. *The Pursuit of Organizational Intelligence.* Malden, MA: Blackwell Publishers.

March, James G. 2008. *Heroes and History.* Schechter films. http://www.gsb.stanford.edu/news/bmag/sbsm0305/leadership2.shtml.

Markoff, John. 1996. *The Abolition of Feudalism.* University Park, PA: Penn State University Press.

Martines, Lauro. 1963. *The Social World of the Florentine Humanists, 1390–1460.* Princeton, NJ: Princeton University Press.

Martines, Lauro. 1979. *Power and Imagination: City-States in Renaissance Florence.* New York: Vintage Books.

Maturana, Humberto, and Francisco Varela. 1980. *Autopoesis and Cognition: The Realization of the Living.* Boston: Reidel Publishing.

Mauss, Marcel. [1925] 1967. *The Gift: Forms and Functions of Exchange in Archaic Societies.* New York: Norton.

Maxon, Brian. 2014. *The Humanist World of Renaissance Florence.* Cambridge: Cambridge University Press.

McCarthy, Cormac. 2006. *The Road.* New York: Alfred A. Knopf.

McFarlane, K. B. 1973. *The Nobility of Later Medieval England.* Oxford: Clarendon Press.

McLean, Paul D. 1996. *Patronage and Political Culture: Strategies of Self-Presentation.* PhD diss., Department of Political Science, University of Chicago.

McLean, Paul D. 1998. "A Frame Analysis of Favor Seeking in the Renaissance: Agency, Networks, and Political Culture." *American Journal of Sociology* 104: 51–91.

McLean, Paul D. 2007. *The Art of the Network: Strategic Interaction and Patronage in Renaissance Florence.* Durham, NC: Duke University Press.

McLean, Paul D., and John F. Padgett. 1997. "Was Florence a perfectly competitive market? Transactional evidence from the Renaissance," *Theory and Society* 26: 209–44.

McMahan, Peter. 2007. "Structurally Cohesive Blocking Algorithm and Utilities." http://home.uchicago.edu/~jpadgett.

Melis, Federigo. 1956. "Malaga sul sentiero economic del XIV e XV secolo," *Economiae storia* 3: 19–59.

Melis, Federigo. 1962. *Aspetti della vita economica medievale: Studi nell'ArchivioDatini di Prato.* Siena: Leo S. Olschki editore.

Melis, Federigo. [1955] 1987. *La banca Pisana e le origini della banca moderna.* Prato: Istituto internazionale di storia economia 'F. Datini.'

Melis, Federigo. [1972] 1987. "La grande conquista trecentesca del 'credito di esercizio'e la tipologia dei suoi strumenti sino al XVI secolo." In *La Banca pisana e le origini della banca moderna*, edited by M. Spallanzi, 307–324. Firenze: Le Monnier.

Melis, Federigo. [1946–1977] 1991. *L'azienda nel medioevo.* Firenze: Le Monnier.

Merton, Robert K. 1968. "Manifest and Latent Functions." In *Social Theory and Social Structure*, edited by Robert K. Merton, 73–138. New York: The Free Press.

Mirot, Léon. 1928. "La société des Raponde," *Bibliothèque de l'école des Chartes revue d'érudition* 88: 50–86, 275–314.

Molho, Anthony. 1968a. "The Florentine Oligarchy and the *Balìe* of the late Trecento." *Speculum* 43: 23–51.

Molho, Anthony. 1968b. "Politics and the Ruling Class in early Renaissance Florence." *Nuova Rivista Storica* 52: 401–20.

Molho, Anthony. 1971. *Florentine Public Finances in the Early Renaissance, 1400–1433.* Cambridge, MA: Harvard University Press.

Molho, Anthony. 1979. "Cosimo de' Medici: Pater Patriae or Padrino?" *Stanford Italian Review* 1: 5–33.

Molho, Anthony. 1994. *Marriage Alliance in Late Medieval Florence.* Cambridge, MA: Harvard University Press.

Molho, Anthony. 2000. "Names, Memory, Public Identity in Late Medieval Florence." In *Art, Memory, and Family in Renaissance Florence*, edited by Giovanni Ciappelli and Patricia Lee Rubin, 237–52. Cambridge: Cambridge University Press.

Monroe, Burt L., Michael P. Colaresi, and Kevin M. Quinn. 2008. "Fightin' Words: Lexical Feature Selection and Evaluation for Identifying the Content of Political Conflict." *Political Analysis* 16: 372–403.

Moody, James, and Douglas R. White. 2003. "Structural Cohesion and Embeddedness: A Hierarchical Concept of Social Groups." *American Sociological Review* 68: 103–27.

Morrison, Alan S., Julius Kirshner, and Anthony Molho. 1985. "Epidemics in Renaissance Florence." *American Journal of Public Health* 75: 528–35. Litchfield

Mucciarelli, Roberta. 1995. *I Tolomei banchieri di Siena: La parabola di un casato nel XIII e XIV secolo.* Siena: Protagon.

Mueller, Reinhold C. 1997a. *The Venetian Money Market: Banks, Panics, and the Public Debt, 1200–1500.* Baltimore: The Johns Hopkins University Press.

Mueller, Reinhold C. 1997b. "Boccaccino, Giovanni Boccaccio, and Venice." Studi sul *Boccaccio* 25: 133–42.

Najemy, John M. 1972. *The Guilds in Florentine Politics, 1292–1394.* PhD diss., Department of History, Harvard University.

Najemy, John M. 1981. "Audiant Omnes Artes: Corporate Origins of the Ciompi Revolution." In *Il Tumulto dei Ciompi: Un Momento si Storia Fiorentina ed Europea*, 59–93. Florence: Leo S. Olschki editore.

Najemy, John M. 1982. *Corporatism and Consensus in Florentine Electoral Politics, 1280–1400.* Chapel Hill, NC: University of North Carolina Press.

Najemy, John M. 1991. "The Dialogue of Power in Florentine Politics." In *City-States in Classical Antiquity and Medieval Italy*, edited by Anthony Molho, Kurt Raaflaub, and Julia Emlen, 269–88. Ann Arbor: University of Michigan Press.

Najemy, John M. 1995. "The Republic's Two Bodies: Body Metaphors in Italian Renaissance Political Thought." In *Language and Images of Renaissance Italy*, edited by Alison Brown, 237–62. Oxford: Clarendon Press.

Najemy, John M. 2000. "Civic Humanism and Florentine Politics." In *Renaissance Civic Humanism*, edited by James Hankins, 75–104. Cambridge: Cambridge University Press.

Najemy, John M. 2006. *A History of Florence, 1200–1575.* Malden, MA: Blackwell.

Namier, Lewis. 1929. *The Structure of Politics at the Accession of George III.* New York: Macmillan.

Nicolis, Grégoire and Ilya Prigogine. 1989. *Exploring Complexity.* New York: Freeman.

Noma, Elliot, and D. Randall Smith. 1985. "Benchmark for the Blocking of Sociometric Data." *Psychological Bulletin* 97: 583–91.

Obert, Jonathan, and John F. Padgett. 2012. "Conflict Displacement and Dual Inclusion in the Construction of Germany." In *The Emergence of Organizations and Markets*, edited by John F. Padgett and Walter W. Powell, 235–66. Princeton: Princeton University Press.

Olsen, Glenn. 1969."Italian Merchants and the performance of Papal Banking functions in the early thirteenth century." In *Economy, Society, and Government in Medieval Italy: Essays in memory of Robert L. Reynolds*, edited by David Herlihy, Robert S. Lopez, and Vsevolod Slessarev, 43–63. Kent, OH: Kent State University Press.

Origo, Iris. [1957] 1992. *The Merchant of Prato: Francesco di Marco Datini.* New York: Penguin Books.

Ottokar, Nicola. 1962. *Il Comune di Firenze alla fine del Dugento.* Torino: Giulio Einaudi.

Padgett, John F. 1981. "Hierarchy and Ecological Control in Federal Budgetary Decision Making." *American Journal of Sociology* 87: 75–129.

Padgett, John F. 1986. "Rationally Inaccessible Rationality." *Contemporary Sociology* 15: 26–28.

Padgett, John F. 1990a. "Mobility as Control: Congressmen through Committees." In *Social Mobility and Social Structure*, edited by R. L. Breiger, 27–58. New York:Cambridge University Press.

Padgett, John F. 1990b. "Plea Bargaining and Prohibition in the Federal Courts, 1908–1934." *Law and Society Review* 24: 413–50.

Padgett, John F. 1994. "Marriage and Elite Structure in Renaissance Florence, 1282–1500," unpublished paper presented to the Social Science History Association. http://home.uchicago.edu/~jpadgett

Padgett, John F. 1997. "The Emergence of Simple Ecologies of Skill: A Hypercycle Approach to Economic Organization." In *The Economy as an Evolving Complex System II*, edited by Brian Arthur, Steven Durlauf, and David Lane, 199–222. Reading, MA: Addison-Wesley.

Padgett, John F. 2001. "Organizational Genesis, Identity, and Control: The Transformation of Banking in Renaissance Florence." In *Networks and Markets*, edited by James E. Rauch and Alessandra Casella, 211–57. New York: Russell Sage Foundation.

Padgett, John F. 2005a. "Early Florentine Companies, 1300–1378." home.uchicago.edu/~jpadgett.

Padgett, John F. 2005b. "Business census from 1427 *catasto*." http://home.uchicago.edu/~jpadgett.

Padgett, John F. 2006. "Organizational Genesis in Florentine History: Four multiple-network mechanisms." Unpublished, home.uchicago.edu/~jpadgett.

Padgett, John F. 2009b. "Extracts from Secondary Literature about Dugento Italian merchant-bankers." Unpublished, home.uchicago.edu/~jpadgett.

Padgett, John F. 2010. "Open Elite? Social Mobility, Marriage and Family in Florence, 1282–1494." *Renaissance Quarterly* 63: 357–411.

Padgett, John F. 2018a. "Faulkner's Assembly of Memories into History: Narrative Networks in Multiple Times." *American Journal of Sociology* 124: 406–79.

Padgett, John F. 2018b. "The Social Context of Innovation," *Scientia* (September 5, 2018)

Padgett, John F. 2021. "A Dynamic Framework for Studying the Emergence of Organizational Forms." *Scientia* (April 14, 2021).

Padgett, John F., and Christopher K. Ansell. 1993. "Robust Action and the Rise of the Medici, 1400–1434." *American Journal of Sociology* 98: 1259–319.

Padgett, John F., and Paul D. McLean. 2002. "Economic and Social Exchange in Renaissance Florence," Santa Fe Institute working paper 02-07-032.

Padgett, John F., and Paul D. McLean. 2004. "Economic Transformation and Economic Credit in Renaissance Florence." Unpublished manuscript.

Padgett, John F., and Paul D. McLean. 2006. "Organizational Invention and Elite Transformation: The Birth of the Partnership System in Renaissance Florence." *American Journal of Sociology* 111: 1463–1568.

Padgett, John F., and Paul D. McLean. 2011. "Economic Credit in Renaissance Florence." *Journal of Modern History* 83: 1–47.

Padgett, John F., Doowan Lee, and Nick Collier. 2003. "Economic Production as Chemistry." *Industrial and Corporate Change* 12: 843–77.

Padgett, John F., and Walter W. Powell. *The Emergence of Organizations and Markets*. Princeton, NJ: Princeton University Press, 2012.

Padgett, John F., and Katalin Prajda. 2015. "The Evolution of Public Discussion in Renaissance Florence: Trends in *Consulte e Pratiche*." Talk at annual conference of Renaissance Society of America, Berlin.

Padgett, John F., Katalin Prajda, Benjamin Rohr, and Jonathan Schoots. 2020. "Political Discussion and Debate in Narrative Time: The Florentine *Consulte e Pratiche*, 1376–78." *Poetics* 78: art. 101377.

Pampaloni, G. 1964. "Il giuramento pubblico in Palazzo Vecchio a Firenze e un patto giurato degli anti-medicei, maggio 1466." *Bollettino Senese di storia patria* 71: 212–38.

Parel, Anthony J. 1992. *The Machiavellian Cosmos*. New Haven, CT: Yale University Press.

Pattison, Philippa. 1993. *Algebraic Models for Social Networks*. New York: Cambridge University Press.

Perroy, Edouard. 1962. "Social Mobility among the French Noblesse in the Later Middle Ages." *Past and Present* 21: 25–38.

Peruzzi, Simone Luigi. 1868. *Storia del commercio e dei banchieri di Firenze in tutto Mondo conosciuto dal 1200 al 1345*. Firenze: M. Cellini.

Phillips, Mark. 1987. *The Memoir of Marco Parenti: A Life in Medici Florence*. Princeton, NJ: Princeton University Press.

Plebani, Eleonora. 2002. *I Tornabuoni: Una famiglia fiorentina alla fine del Medioevo*. Milano: F. Angeli.

Pocock, J. G. A. 1975. *The Machiavellian Moment: Florentine Political Thought and the Atlantic Republican Tradition*. Princeton, NJ: Princeton University Press.

Polanyi, Karl. 1957. "The Economy as an Instituted Process." In *Trade and Markets in the Early Empires*, edited by Karl Polanyi, Conrad M. Arensberg, and Harry W. Pearson, 243–69. Glencoe, IL.: Free Press.

Poliziano, Angelo. [ca.1478]. 1985. *1 detti piacevoli*, edited by Mariano Fresta. Siena: Editori del Grifo.

Post, Gaines. 1934. "Parisian Masters as a Corporation, 1200–1246." *Speculum* 9: 421–45.

Powell, Walter W. 1990. "Neither Market nor Hierarchy: Network Forms of Organization." In *Research in Organizational Behavior*, edited by B. Straw and L. L. Cummings, 295–336. Greenwitch, CT: JAI Press.

Powell, Walter W., Kenneth W. Koput, and Laurel Smith-Doerr. 1996. "Interorganizational Collaboration and the Locus of Innovation: Networks of Learning in Biotechnology." *Administrative Science Quarterly* 41: 116–45.

Rabil, Albert, Jr. 1991. *Knowledge, Goodness and Power: The Debate over Nobility among Quattrocento Italian Humanists*. Binghamton, NY: Medieval and Renaissance Texts & Studies.

Raveggi, Sergio, Massimo Tarassi, Daniela Medici, and Patrizia Parenti. 1978. *Ghibellini, guelfi e popolo grasso: i detentori del potere politico a Firenze nella seconda metà del Duecento*. Firenze: La Nuova Italia.

Re, Emilo. "La compagnia dei Riccardi in Inghilterra." *Archivio della società Romana di storia patria* 37 (1914): 87–138.

Renouard, Yves. 1938. "Le compagnie commerciali fiorentine del Trecento," *Archivio storico italiano* 96: 41–68, 163–79.

Renouard, Yves. 1941. *Les Relations des Papes d'Avignon et des Compagnies Commerciales et Bancaires de 1316 a 1378*. Paris: E. de Boccard.

Reynolds, Robert L. 1952. "Origins of Modern Business Enterprise." *Journal of Economic History* 12: 350–65.

Rhodes, Walter E. 1907. "The Italian Bankers in England and their Loans to Edward I and Edward II." In *Historical Essays in Commemoration of the Jubilee of the Owens College*, edited by T. F. Tout and James Tait, 137–68. Manchester: Manchester at the University Press.

Rodolico, Niccolò. 1905. *La democrazia fiorentina nel suo tramonto 1378–1382.* Bologna: N. Zanichelli editore.

Rubinstein, Nicolai. 1966. *The Government of Florence Under the Medici (1434 to 1494).* Oxford: Oxford University Press.

Runciman, Steven. 1958. *The Sicilian Vespers.* Cambridge: Cambridge University Press.

Ruttan, Vernon W., 1959. "Usher and Schumpeter on Invention, Innovation, and Technological Change." *The Quarterly Journal of Economics* 73:596–606.

Santini, P. 1887. "Società delle Torre in Firenze," *Archivio storico italiano* 20: 25–58, 178–204.

Sapori, Armando. 1926. *La crisi delle compagnie mercantili dei Bardi e dei Peruzzi.* Firenze: Leo S. Olschki.

Sapori, Armando. 1947. *La compagnia dei Frescobaldi in Inghilterra.* Firenze: Leo S. Olschki.

Sapori, Armando. 1955a. "Cosimo Medici e un 'patto giurato' a Firenze nel 1449." In *Studi di storia economica*, vol. 1, 407–26. Firenze: G. C. Sansoni.

Sapori, Armando. [1939a] 1955b. "Il personale delle compagnie mercantili del Medioevo." In his *Studi di storica economica (secoli XIII–XIV–XV), volume secondo*, 695–763. Firenze: G. C. Sansoni.

Sapori, Armando. [1939b] 1955c. "Le compagnie mercantili Toscane del Dugento e dei primi del Trecento: La responsibilià dei compagni verso i terzi." In *Studi di storica economica (secoli XIII–XIV–XV), volume secondo*, edited by Armando Sapori, 765–808. Firenze: G. C. Sansoni.

Sapori, Armando. 1955d. *Studi de storia economica (secoli XII–XIV–XV).* Firenze: G.C.Sansoni.

Sapori, Armando. 1970. *The Italian Merchant in the Middle Ages.* New York: Norton.

Sayous, André-E. 1931. "Les mandats de Saint Louis sur son trésor et le movement international des capitaux pendent la septième croisade (1248–1254)." *Revue Historique* 56: 254–304.

Sayous, André-E. 1932. "Les opérations des banquiers Italiens en Italie et aux foires de Champagne pendent le XIIIe siècle," *Revue Historique* 57: 1–31.

Schaube, Adolf. 1908. "Die Wollausfuhr Englands vom Jahre 1273," *Vierteljahrschrift fur Social- und Wirtschaftsgeschichte* 6.

Schevill, Ferdinand. [1936] 1963. *Medieval and Renaissance Florence.* New York: Harper Torchbooks.

Schumpeter, Joseph A., 1939. *Business Cycles: A Theoretical, Historical, and Statistical Analysis of the Capitalist Process.* New York: McGraw-Hill Book Company.

Schwartz, Barry. 1983. "George Washington and the Whig Conception of Heroic Leadership." *American Sociological Review* 48: 18–33.

Sewell, William H. Jr. 1985. *Structure and Mobility: The Men and Women of Marseille, 1820–1870*. Cambridge: Cambridge University Press.

Sewell, William H. Jr. 2005. *Logics of History: Social Theory and Social Transformation*. Chicago: University of Chicago Press.

Shaw, Christine. 2000. *The Politics of Exile in Renaissance Italy*. Cambridge: Cambridge University Press.

Silge, J., and Robinson, D. 2016. "tidytext: Text mining and analysis using tidy data principles in R." *Journal of Open Source Software* 1: 37.

Skocpol, Theda. 1979. *States and Social Revolutions*. Cambridge: Cambridge University Press.

Slapin, Jonathan, and Sven-Oliver Proksch. 2008. "A Scaling Model for Estimating Time-Series Party Positions from Texts." *American Journal of Political Science* 52: 705–22.

Spufford, Peter. 1988. *Money and Its Use in Medieval Europe*. Cambridge: Cambridge University Press.

Stella, Alessandro. 1993. *La revolte des Ciompi: les hommes, les lieux, le travail*. Paris: Editions de l'Ecole des haute etudes en sciences socials.

Stinchcombe, Arthur L. 1965. "Social Structure and Organization." In *Handbook of Organizations*, edited by J. G. March, 142–93. Chicago: Rand-McNally.

Stone, Lawrence. 1965. *The Crisis of the Aristocracy, 1558–1641*. Oxford: Clarendon Press.

Stone, Lawrence, and Jeanne C. Fawtier-Stone. 1984. *An Open Elite? England 1540–1880*. Oxford: Oxford University Press.

Strayer, Joseph R. "Italian bankers and Philip the Fair." In *Economy, Society, and Government in Medieval Italy: Essays in memory of Robert L. Reynolds*, edited by David Herlihy, Robert S. Lopez, and Vsevolod Slessarev, 113–21. Kent, OH: Kent State University Press, 1969.

Swidler, Ann. 1986. "Culture in Action: Symbols and Strategies." *American Sociological Review* 51: 273–286.

Teja, Antonio. 1936. *Aspetti della vita economia di Zara dal 1289 al 1409. Part I: La pratica bancaria*. Zara: tip. edit. sp. artale

Tilly, Charles. 1964. *The Vendée*. Cambridge, MA: Harvard University Press.

Tilly, Charles. 1975. *The Formation of National States in Western Europe*. Princeton, NJ: Princeton University Press.

Tilly, Charles. 1992. *Coercion, Capital, and European States, AD 990–1992*. Oxford: Blackwell.

Tilly, Charles. 1995. *Popular Contention in Great Britain, 1758–1834*. Cambridge, MA: Harvard University Press.

Tolstoy, Leo. [1869] 1978. *War and Peace*. London: Penguin Books.

Trexler, Richard C. 1974. *The Spiritual Power: Republican Florence under Interdict*. Leiden, Netherlands: E. J. Brill.

Trexler, Richard C. 1980. *Public Life in Renaissance Florence*. New York: Academic Press.

Trexler, Richard C. 1998. *The Workers of Renaissance Florence*. Asheville, NC: Pegasus Press.

Usher, Abbott Payson. 1943. *The Early History of Deposit Banking in Mediterranean Europe*. Cambridge, MA: Harvard University Press.

Van Nierop, H. K. F. 1993. *The Nobility of Holland: From Knights to Regents, 1500–1650.* Cambridge: Cambridge University Press.

Vasari, Georgio ([1550] 1991). *The Lives of the Artists.* New York: Oxford University Press.

Verlinden, O. 1963. "Markets and Fairs." In *The Cambridge Economic History of Europe, volume III: Economic Organization and Policies in the Middle Ages*, edited by M. M. Postan, E. E. Rich, and Edward Miller, 42–118. Cambridge: Cambridge University Press.

Vespasiano da Bisticci. [ca. 1495] 1963. *Renaissance Princes, Popes, and Prelates: The Vespasiano Memoirs*, edited by Myron P. Gilmore. New York: Harper & Row.

Wagner, Gunter, and Lee Altenberg. 1996. "Complex Adaptations and the Evolution of Evolvability." *Evolution* 50: 967–76.

Waley, Daniel. 1961. *The Papal State in the Thirteenth Century.* London: MacMillan.

Waley, Daniel. 1969. *The Italian City-Republics.* New York: World University Library.

Weber, Max. [1917–19] 1952. *Ancient Judaism.* New York: The Free Press.

Weber, Max. 2003. *The History of Commercial Partnerships in the Middle Ages.* Lanham, MD: Rowman & Littlefield.

Weissman, Ronald F. E. 1982. *Ritual Brotherhood in Renaissance Florence.* New York: Academic Press.

Weissman, Ronald F. E. 1989. "The Importance of Being Ambiguous: Social Relations, Individualism, and Identity in Renaissance Florence." In *Urban Life in the Renaissance*, edited by Susan Zimmerman and Ronald Weissman, 269–80. Dover: University of Delaware Press.

White, Harrison C. 1970. *Chains of Opportunity.* Cambridge, MA: Harvard University Press.

White, Harrison C. 1992. *Identity and Control: A Structural Theory of Social Action.* Princeton, NJ: Princeton University Press.

White, Harrison C., Scott A. Boorman, and Ronald L. Breiger. 1976. "Social Structure from Multiple Networks. I. Blockmodels of Roles and Positions." *American Journal of Sociology* 81: 730–50.

Whitwell, Robert Jowitt. 1904. "English Monasteries and the Wool Trade in the 13th Century." *Vierteljahrschrift fur Social-und Wirtschaftsgeschichte* 2: 1–33.

Whitwell, Robert Jowitt. 1903. "Italian Bankers and the English Crown." *Transactions of the Royal Historical Society* 17: 175–233.

Witt, Ronald G. 1976. "Florentine Politics and the Ruling Class, 1382–1407." *Journal of Medieval and Renaissance Studies* 6: 243–67.

Witt, Ronald G. 1983. *Hercules at the Crossroads: The Life, Works, and Thought of Coluccio Salutati.* Durham, NC: Duke University Press.

Witt, Ronald G. 2003. *In the Footsteps of the Ancients: The Origins of Humanism from Lovato to Bruni.* Boston: Brill.

Wood, James B. 1977. "Demographic Pressure and Social Mobility among the Nobility of Early Modern France." *The Sixteenth Century Journal* 8: 3–16.

Zervas, Diane Finiello. 1987. *The Parte Guelfa, Brunelleschi & Donatello.* Locust Valley, NY: J. J. Augustin.

Index

For the benefit of digital users, indexed terms that span two pages (e.g., 52–53) may, on occasion, appear on only one of those pages.

Note: Tables and figures are indicated by an italic *t* or *f*.

www.ingramcontent.com/pod-product-compliance
Lightning Source LLC
LaVergne TN
LVHW102010210926
848483LV00010B/241